CLASSIC
FOLK·TALES
FROM AROUND
THE WORLD

CLASSIC FOLK·TALES FROM AROUND THE WORLD

INTRODUCTION BY
ROBERT NYE

BRACKEN BOOKS
LONDON

Classic Folktales From Around the World

This edition published in 1994 by Bracken Books, an imprint
of Studio Editions Ltd, Princess House, 50 Eastcastle Street,
London W1N 7AP, England

ISBN 1 85891 149 4

Printed at Thomson Press (India) Ltd.

CONTENTS

CONTENTS

INTRODUCTION

In this book you will find some of the world's best-known and best-loved stories. All of them are what we now call folktales, a name of more recent origin than may be commonly supposed. The usage of it recorded by the *Oxford English Dictionary* dates from 1891, nearly half a century after W. J. Thoms invented the good Anglo-Saxon compound folk-lore to describe those legends, customs, and beliefs of any nation which previously had been referred to in English as 'Popular Antiquities'.

Folktales are of course very much older than their name or study. A folktale is a story which has been transmitted orally, coming down to us from the lips of the 'folk' – that is to say, the common people of any land. The true folktale is by definition anonymous – it has, in other words, no known original author, whoever may have chosen to write it down later. It is also usually a widespread tale, a tale which appears in different forms in different countries, where in each case the local setting gives a particular flavour to the tale.

Folktales are in fact the earliest form of traditional imaginative literature which we have. They comprise the unwritten fiction of early man and of unsophisticated people in all parts of the world. They give us the human imagination in its childhood; the attempts of our ancestors to dress their understanding of the world, their ideas and their beliefs, their customs and manner of living, in the garb of memorable narrative. Though other causes have led to their origin or have moulded their form once they originated, folktales owe their birth in great part to the universal human desire to listen to stories. 'Tell me a story,' cries the child, and in the childhood of every society there must have been heard the same cry, followed by an inspired response from those in whom imagination and the faculty of story-making were most active.

How powerful and pervasive this desire has been is proved by the widely various provenance of the tales in this book, gathered from all parts of the world. Yet it does not surprise me that there are stories here from China and Africa and South America which I heard first from my grandmother who told me versions which she thought were English. Jacob and Wilheim Grimm, having collected and published the tales current among the German peasantry at the end of the eigh-teenth and the beginning of the nineteenth centuries, came to the conclusion that there was a common mythopoeic impulse at work in them, making the figures of the folktale the lineal representatives of ancient gods, as the folktales themselves were of the myths. Later folklorists have questioned this philological view, which interprets myths and their supposed descendants, folktales, as relating to the sun, the moon, the dark, the dawn, and so on. All the same, it cannot be denied that similar themes and motifs crop up in the folktales of different countries, and what the Brothers Grimm called 'the mythopoeic impulse' has been given new credit by the psychologist Carl Jung's writings on the subject of archetypes and the collective unconscious.

None of which should be allowed to spoil the pleasure still to be had from a first, a second, or even a seventy-seventh encounter with stories as good as *Cinderella* and *Little Red Riding Hood* and *The Story of Ra and Isis*. Here are tales which teach us that the world is miraculous, and that men and women belong in it in love. The matter of some of these stories is so ancient as to seem prehistoric. Yet elements of them appear in the most sophisticated literature. In Shakespeare's *King Lear*, for instance, Lear's testing of his daughters, and the fact that only one of the three tells him the truth, is a typical folktale situation, echoed in several stories in this book.

Here are tales that express in simple form the essential imaginings of us all, all of them told with an insistence on virtue which seldom cloys because it is so clean and honest. Folktales are not to be confused with popular romantic fantasies of wish-fulfilment. The best of them bring news of heaven and hell, as well as earth. Here the good and the true achieve happiness not by craft or luck or magic, but by love. Living happily ever after, it will be noticed, is not a fate promised or awarded indiscriminately to all. Not only does evil never triumph in the end; the wicked dance to death in their red-hot shoes.

The tales in this volume comprise a kind of primer of fundamental human story-telling, drawn from many sources, spanning a period from prehistory to the day before yesterday. Here is a treasure-chest of stories that are older than alphabets, yet fresh as dew with each new telling of them; stories that are wise and innocent in the same breath; stories that make you feel that the present does not exist even as they make you feel the more alive in the living moment.

The poet William Blake once said that the making of a flower was the labour of ages. The making of a folktale is a similar matter. That is why the stories in this book took so long to be written down, and how no one came to write them in the first place. The true folktale is like a dream, it speaks straight from the unconscious. Here are stories that read like dreams which we all have dreamt.

Robert Nye

AFRICA

I. NORTHERN NIGERIA

IN Northern Nigeria, and also near the Gold Coast, are found the Hausas. They are, however, great traders and travellers and hence are met with all over the Sudan. Whether they are indigenous or whether they came originally from the east or north-east is uncertain. Be that as it may, they are extremely fond of tales, and when telling them will sit cross-legged on the ground and scarcely move anything save their eyes and lips. Almost every well-known animal and nearly every trade or profession is represented in the folk-lore of the people. According to the Hausas all the animals lived together at one time as members of a single community in a kind of Garden of Eden, but the sins of one of their number—usually the tricks of the spider or the thefts of the hyena-broke up the happy family. The great hero is the spider, who is the king of cunning. He bears a charmed life and overcomes all intrigues. Some writers consider that the spider stands for a legendary hero who conquered the indigenous inhabitants; others judge that it represents the supreme power of the sun.

THE SPIDER, THE GUINEA-FOWL, AND THE FRANCOLIN

THE Francolin said to the Guinea-Fowl, "Will you go with me on a journey?" But just then the Spider arrived, and said, "Come with me, I am going to visit my Mother-in-Law." Then the Guinea Fowl said, "Your journey is the more important, let us go together, you and I." So they started to go to the town where the Spider's parents lived.

While on the road, the Spider said to the Guinea-Fowl, "See this grass, if when we have arrived at the town, they bring me some ground-nuts, you come back here and get some of this grass so that we can roast them." "Very well," said the Guinea-Fowl.

They went on, and as they were travelling, the Spider said, "There is a spoon,[1] if when we have arrived at the town they bring me porridge, you come back here and get the spoon so that we can eat it."[2]

Soon they arrived at the house, and porridge was made and brought to them, so the Spider said to the Guinea-Fowl, "Go, get the spoon and bring it." As soon

---

[1] Probably a gourd from which spoons are made.
[2] This is really affectation on the Spider's part for most of the people use their fingers

1

as she had gone to bring the spoon, the Spider ate up all the porridge except for a little bit, and when she returned, he said, "Oh, you Sluggard, you have been a long time going, the People have since come and taken away their porridge."

Then he said, "But see, they have brought ground-nuts, get that grass and bring it here so that we may roast them." So she went off to get the grass, and when she returned she found that the Spider had eaten up all the ground-nuts. He said, "You have been so long that the People took away their ground-nuts."

Next morning they said, "Now, we must go home." So the Spider's load was tied up, and that of the Guinea-Fowl also, and they started off on the road. Soon they came to the bank of a big river, and the Spider lighted a fire, and said, "Stop here, I am going over there, if you hear me fall into the water, you throw yourself into the fire."[3] So he went on, and took a stone and threw it into the water so that it made a sound like *pinjim*. When the Guinea-Fowl heard this, she said, "The Spider is dead," so she threw herself into the fire so that she also might die. Then the Spider came and pulled the dead Guinea-Fowl out of the fire, and plucked her feathers out of her body, and ate it. Then he took the Guinea-Fowl's load, tied it on to his own, and went off home.

Some time afterward he went to see the Francolin, and said, "Oh, Francolin, will you not also accompany me on a journey?" And when she had agreed, off they went. As they were travelling they came to the grass, and the Spider said, "See this grass, if when we have arrived at the town they bring us ground-nuts,' you come back here and get this grass so that we can roast them." But the Francolin picked some grass on the sly and hid it.

Then the Spider said, "There is a spoon, if when we have arrived at the town they give us porridge, you come back here and get the spoon." "Very well," said the Francolin, but she took it then, and hid it.

Soon they arrived at the town, and porridge was brought, so the Spider said, "Go and get that spoon." The Francolin said, "Oh, you said to bring it, here it is." Then the Spider was very angry, and said, "Very well, take the porridge yourself and eat it." So the Francolin took and ate all but a little bit which she gave to the Spider to eat.

Then ground-nuts were brought to them, and the Spider said, "Go and get some grass that we may roast them." But she replied, "Oh, here it is, I got it long ago." Then the Spider was furious, and he said, "Take the ground-nuts and eat them." But when the Francolin had roasted them, and had eaten all but a few, the Spider snatched them away and ate them.

Next morning they said, "Well, we must go home," so the Spider's load was bound up for him, and the Francolin's for her, and they took them and started off.

---

[3] As an obligation.

Soon they arrived at the bank of the river, and the Spider lighted a fire, and said, "Stay here, I am going over there, if you hear me fall into the water, you throw yourself into the fire." "Very well," said she. So he went and took a stone and threw it into the water, and it made a sound like *pinjim*. Then the Francolin went and got one of the Spider's long boots and put it on the fire, while she herself crawled inside the Spider's load, and hid. Soon the Spider came and searched in the fire, and took out the boot and ate it. "Well," said he, "the Guinea-Fowl was certainly more juicy than this Francolin." So he took the Francolin's load and tied it on to his own, and started off home.

Then the Francolin, who was inside, said, "The Spider is a fool, he has eaten his boot," and when the Spider heard this he was so frightened that he ran away, he thought that he heard the Francolins' war-drums beating.[4]

When he returned home, he untied the load, and he had begun putting the contents into a calabash, when the Francolin flew out and settled on the Spider's Wife's head. Then the Spider said to his Wife, "Stand still, do not move," and he picked up the wooden pestle to strike the Francolin, while on the Female Spider's head, but the Francolin flew off, and the Spider missed him, but killed his Wife. Then the Francolin settled on his Son's head, and the Spider struck at him but killed his own Son. Then the Francolin settled on the head of the Spider's Baby, and the Spider took the pestle and missed, and killed his Baby in the same way. Then the Francolin settled on the head of the Spider himself. The Spider ran outside and climbed up and up a tree until he had come to the top, and then he bobbed his head so that he might throw the Francolin down and kill her, but she saved herself with her wings, and the Spider fell down and was killed.

Then the Francolin went and seized all the Spider's possessions, and went away.

ONE CANNOT HELP AN UNLUCKY MAN

THERE was a certain Man, a Pauper, who had nothing but husks for himself and his Wife to eat. There was another Man who had many Wives and Slaves and Children, and the two Men had farms close together. One day a Very-Rich-Man who was richer than either came, and was going to pass by on the road. He had put on a ragged coat and torn trousers, and a holey cap, and the People did not know that he was rich, they thought that he was a beggar. Now when he had come up close, he said to the Rich-Man, "Hail to you in your work," but when he had said, "Hail," the Rich-Man said, "What do you mean by speaking to me, you may be a

---

[4] A signal of alarm meaning that he was to be pursued for having killed one of their number.

Leper for all we know!" So he went on, and came to the Poor-Man's farm, and said, "Hail to you in your work." And the Poor Man replied, "Um hum," and said to his Wife, "Quick, mix some husks and water, and give him to drink." So she took it to him, and knelt, and said, "See, here is some of that which we have to drink." So he said, "Good, thanks be to God," and he put out his lips as if he were going to drink, but he did not really do so, he gave it back to her, and said, "I thank you."

So he went home and said, "Now, that Man who was kind to me I must reward." So he had a calabash washed well with white earth,[1] and filled up to the top with dollars, and a new mat[2] was brought to close it. Then the Very-Rich-Man sent his Daughter, who carried the Calabash, in front, and when they had arrived at the edge of the bush he said, "Do you see that crowd of People over there working?" And she replied, "Yes, I see them." He said, "Good, now do you see one Man over there working with his Wife?" And she replied, "Yes." "Good," he said, "to him must you take this calabash." Then she said, "Very well," and she passed on, and came to where the Poor-Man was, and said, "Hail," and continued, "I have been sent to you, see this calabash, I was told to bring it to you."

Now the Poor-Man did not open it to see what was inside, his poverty prevented him,[3] but he said, "Take it to Malam Abba, and tell him to take as much flour as he wants from it, and to give us the rest." But when it had been taken to Malam Abba, he saw the dollars inside, and he put them into his pockets, and brought guinea-corn flour and pressed it down in the calabash, and said, "Carry it to him, I have taken some." And the Poor-Man (when he saw that there was some flour left) said, "Good, thanks be to God, pour it into our calabash, and depart. I thank you." Now the Very-Rich-Man had been watching from a distance, and (when he saw what had happened) he was overcome with rage, and said, "Truly if you put an unlucky Man into a jar of oil he would emerge quite dry. I wanted him to have some luck, but God has made him thus."

HOW THE SPIDER ATE THE HYENA-CUBS' FOOD

ONE day the Spider went to the Hyena's house when he knew that she was out for a walk, and began talking to the Cubs. He asked one what his name was, and the Cub answered, "Mohammadu." Then he said to another, "And what is your name?" and he replied, "Isa." Then the Spider asked a third Cub his name

---

[1] This can be used like whitewash, and the calabashes are coated outside, a decoration used at wedding feasts or to show special honour to a guest.

[2] Little round grass mats which act as covers or lids.

[3] He was so hungry that he would have been unable to resist eating the whole, for he thought it contained food.

and he said, "It is Na-taala." When he had asked them all, he said, "Now, look here, your Mother-Hyena asked me to come here and live with you, so you must know my name, it is For-you-all."

Now whenever the Hyena brought food she used to say, "It is for you all, and so after that the Spider would at once exclaim, "You see, it is all for me only, you heard what our Mother has said." So the Spider would eat up all the food.

This went on for about a month, and as the Spider had always taken the whole food, the Cubs by this time had wasted away. Then one day the Hyena said, "Come out of the den, My Children, and let me see you." Now when they appeared, she saw that they had become very thin, and she said, "Whatever has happened to you, O My Children, to make you so thin?" "Ah," replied they, "you have brought us no food." "What!" she exclaimed. "What about all that which I have been bringing for you all?" "Oh," they replied, "For-you-all has eaten it, he is in there." "Where is For-you-all?" she said. "Let him come out and show himself." Then the Spider pushed forward his ears until they were sticking out of the hole, and said, "Catch hold of my boots first, then I will come out and you can see me." Immediately the Hyena seized hold of the ears, and angrily threw them behind her, and the Spider (for his whole body had been pulled out) got up, and ran away. Then she said, "Where is For-you-all?" And her Cubs said, "It was he whom you threw over there behind you."

Now the Spider ran on to the house of the Dog, where he was weaving, and he sat down. But soon the Hyena approached, looking for the Spider, and she came upon the Dog and the Spider sitting there by the loom. Then she said, "Of you two, whom was I chasing?" And the cunning Spider at once replied, "Look at the Dog's mouth, he is panting tremendously, that is proof that it was he who has been running away."

Immediately the Hyena sprang toward the Dog, but the Dog got away in time, and the Spider also ran away, so both escaped from the Hyena.

THE SPIDER WHICH BOUGHT A DOG
AS A SLAVE

ONE day the Spider went to the market and saw some Dogs for sale, so he went home and thrashed his guinea-corn, and said that he was going to buy a Slave with it. So he did so, and brought the Dog home. Then he went and bought a hoe, and gave it to the Dog, and told him to go and work on the farm but the Dog only lay still and took no notice. So the Spider seized the hoe and they went off to the forest, but when he told the Dog to get up and work the Dog only lay still, and said nothing. Then the Spider pointed out the limits of the day's work, and said that when they had done so much they would return, but the Dog only lay still and said nothing. So the Spider himself began digging, and said that as the Dog was panting so hard he must be tired, so he could lie down.

Now as the Dog was lying there, a Hare passed by, and immediately the Dog arose, ran off, and caught the Hare. And then the Spider said, "Well I never, so my Slave is a Hunter, he who can kill with his teeth," he continued, "will do better with an arrow." So he took the Dog's hoe, and brought it to the Monkey, the Smith, and told him to make arrowheads out of it, so that he could give them to the Dog. And he and the Dog returned home.

Now the Spider was always going to the Monkey's forge, and asking if the arrow-heads would be finished that day, and one day the Monkey said to the Spider, "Have you obtained a Slave !" And he replied, "Yes, it is for him that I want the arrow-heads, so that he may enjoy the chase." Then the Spider said that he would bring the Dog, but the Monkey asked him not to do so. The Spider was always going to the Monkey and complaining that the arrow-heads were not being done quickly, until at last he became angry, and brought the Dog, and the Dog, when he saw the Monkey, began stalking him, and when they had come close the Monkey ran away, and the Dog ran after him and caught him. As he was bringing the Monkey back, the Spider said, "Let him go, it is the Smith, do not seize him," and then (being afraid that he too would be seized) he fled, and he ran on past his house, not stopping to go inside, and called out to his Wife, "Get up, and run away, see, the Dog is seizing people, and eating them."

Now, as they had run away, they had left the house with no one to claim it except the Dog, so he took it for his own, and the Spider and his Wife disappeared into the forest.

II. SOUTHERN NIGERIA

FROM the earliest time there has grown up a stock of traditions about animals—the Beast Epic—which is full of the liveliest traits of nature. It arose out of a close observation of the habits of animals, a study most possible in an early and simple stage of society.

In these folk-stories of Southern Nigeria one is struck by the deference paid to Ju-Jus (whether ghosts or fiends). Sacrifices are offered to them to propitiate their anger. God, though recognized as creator, receives no sacrifices, for to the native mind he is "too high and too far."

THE KING AND THE JU-JU TREE

U DO UBOK UDOM was a famous king who lived at Ham, which is an inland town, and does not possess a river. The King and his wife therefore used to wash at the spring just behind their house.

King Udo had a daughter of whom he was very fond, and looked after her most carefully, and she grew up into a beautiful woman. For some time the King had been absent from his house, and had not been to the spring for two years. When he went to his old place to wash, he found that the Idem Ju-Ju tree had grown up all round the place, and it was impossible for him to use the spring as he had done formerly. He therefore called fifty of his young men to bring their marchets [1] and cut down the tree. They started cutting the tree, but it had no effect, as, directly they made a cut in the tree, it closed up again; so, after working all day, they found they had made no impression on it.

When they returned at night, they told the King that they had been unable to destroy the tree. He was very angry when he heard this, and went to the spring the following morning, taking his own matchet with him. When the Ju-Ju saw that the King had come himself and was starting to try to cut his branches, he caused a small splinter of wood to go into the King's eye. This gave the King great pain, so he threw down his marcher and went back to his house. The pain, however, got worse, and he could not eat or sleep for three days.

He therefore sent for his witch men, and told them to cast lots to find out why he was in such pain. When they had cast lots, they decided that the reason was that the Ju-Ju tree was angry with the King, because he wanted to wash at the spring and had tried to destroy the tree.

They then told the King that he must take seven baskets of flies, a white goat, a white chicken, and a piece of white cloth, and make a sacrifice of them in order to satisfy the Ju-Ju.

The King did this, and the witch men tried their lotions on the King's eye, but it got worse and worse.

He then dismissed these witches and got another lot. When they arrived they told the King that, although they could do nothing themselves to relieve his pain, they knew one man who lived in the spirit land who could cure him; so the King told them to send for him at once, and he arrived the next day.

Then the spirit man said, "Before I do anything to your eye, what will you give me?" So King Udo said, "I will give you half my town with the people in it, also seven cows and some money." But the spirit man refused to accept the King's offer. As the King was in such pain, he said, "Name your own price, and I will pay

_____
[1] A long sharp knife.

you." So the spirit man said the only thing he was willing to accept as payment was the King's daughter. At this the King cried very much, and told the man to go away, as he would rather die than let him have his daughter.

That night the pain was worse than ever, and some of his subjects pleaded with the King to send for the spirit man again and give him his daughter, and told him that when he got well he could no doubt have another daughter, but that if he died now he would lose everything.

The King then sent for the spirit man again, who came very quickly, .and in great grief the King handed his daughter to the spirit.

The spirit man then went out into the bush, and collected some leaves, which he soaked in water and beat up. The juice he poured into the King's eye, and told him that when he washed his face in the morning he would be able to see what was troubling him in the eye.

The King tried to persuade him to stay the night, but the spirit man refused, and departed that same night for the spirit land, taking the King's daughter with him.

Before it was light the King rose up and washed his face, and found that the small splinter from the Ju-Ju tree, which had been troubling him so much, dropped out of his eye, the pain disappeared, and he was quite well again. When he came to his proper senses he realized that he had sacrificed his daughter for one of his eyes, so he made an order that there should be general mourning throughout his kingdom for three years. For the first two years of the mourning the King's daughter was put in the fatting house by the spirit man, and was given food; but a skull, who was in the house, told her not to eat, as they were fatting her up, not for marriage, but so that they could eat her. She therefore gave all the food which was brought to her to the skull, and lived on chalk herself.

Toward the end of the third year the spirit man brought some of his friends to see the King's daughter, and told them he would kill her the next day, and they would have a good feast off her. When she woke up in the morning the spirit man brought her food as usual; but the skull, who wanted to preserve her life, and who had heard what the spirit man had said, called her into the room and told her what was going to happen later in the day. She handed the food to the skull, and he said: "When the spirit man goes to the wood with his friends to prepare for the feast, you must run back to your father."

He then gave her some medicine which would make her strong for the journey, and also gave her directions as to the road, telling her that there were two roads but that when she came to the parting of the ways she was to drop some of the medicine on the ground and the two roads would become one.

He then told her to leave by the back door, and go through the wood until she came to the end of the town; she would then find the road. if she met people on the road she was to pass them in silence, as if she saluted them they would know that she was a stranger in the spirit land, and might kill her. She was also not to turn round if anyone called to her, but was to go straight on until she reached her father's house.

Having thanked the skull for his kind advice, the King's daughter started off, but when she reached the end of the town and found the road, she ran for three hours, and at last arrived at the branch roads. There she dropped the medicine as she had been instructed, and the two roads immediately became one; so she went straight on and never saluted anyone or turned back, although several people called to her.

About this time the spirit man returned from the wood, and went to the house, only to find the King's daughter was absent. He asked the skull where she was, and he replied that she had gone out by the back door, but he did not know where she had gone to. Being a spirit, however, he very soon guessed that she had gone home; so he followed as quickly as possible, shouting out all the time.

When the girl heard his voice she ran as fast as she could, and at last arrived at her father's house, and told him to take at once a cow, a pig, a sheep, a goat, a dog, a chicken, and seven eggs, and cut them into seven parts as a sacrifice, and leave them on the road, so that when the spirit man saw these things he would stop and not enter the town. This the King did immediately, and made the sacrifice as his daughter had told him.

When the spirit man saw the sacrifice on the road, he sat down and at once began to eat. When he had satisfied his appetite, he packed up the remainder and returned to the spirit land, not troubling any more about the King's daughter.

When the King saw that the danger was over, he beat his drum, and declared that for the future, when people died and went to the spirit land, they should not come to earth again as spirits to cure sick people.

HOW THE TORTOISE OVERCAME THE ELEPHANT AND THE HIPPOPOTAMUS

THE elephant and the hippopotamus always used to feed together, and were good friends.

One day, when they were both dining together, the tortoise appeared and said that although they were both big and strong, neither of them could pull him out of the water with a strong piece of tie-tie, and he offered the elephant ten thousand rods if he could draw him out of the water the next day. The elephant, seeing that the tortoise was very small, said, "If I cannot draw you out of the water I will give you twenty thousand rods."

So on the following morning the tortoise got some very strong tie-tie and made it fast to his leg, and went down to the river. When he got there, as he knew the place well, he made the tie-tie fast round a big rock, and left the other end on the shore for the elephant to pull by, and then went down to the bottom of the river and hid himself. The elephant then came down and started pulling, and after a time he smashed the rope.

Directly this happened, the tortoise undid the rope from the rock and came to the land, showing all the people that the rope was still fast to his leg, but that the elephant had failed to pull him out. The elephant was thus forced to admit that the tortoise was the winner, and paid to him the twenty thousand rods, as agreed. The tortoise then took the rods home to his wife, and they lived together very happily.

After three months had passed, the tortoise, seeing that the money was greatly reduced, thought he would make some more by the same trick, so he went to the hippopotamus and made the same bet with him. The hippopotamus said, "I will make the bet, but I shall take the water and you shall take the land; I will then pull you into the water." To this the tortoise agreed, so they went down to the river as before, and having got some strong tie-tie, the tortoise made it fast to the hippopotamus' hind leg, and told him to go into the water. Directly the hippo had turned his back and disappeared, the tortoise took the rope twice round a strong palm-tree which was growing near, and then hid himself at the foot of the tree.

When the hippo was tired of pulling, he came up puffing and blowing water into the air from his nostrils. Directly the tortoise saw him coming up, he unwound the rope, and walked down toward the hippopotamus, showing him the tie-tie round his leg. The hippo had to acknowledge that the tortoise was too strong for him, and reluctantly handed over the twenty thousand rods.

The elephant and the hippo then agreed that they would take the tortoise as their friend, as he was so very strong; but he was not really so strong as they thought, and had won because he was so cunning.

He then told them that he would like to live with both of them, but that, as he could not be in two places at the same time, he said that he would leave his son to live with the elephant on the land, and that he himself would live with the hippopotamus in the water.

This explains why there are both tortoises on the land and tortoises who live in the water. The water tortoise is always much the bigger of the two, as there is plenty of fish for him to eat, whereas the land tortoise is often very short of food.

THE BUSH COW AND THE ELEPHANT

THE bush cow and the elephant were always bad friends, and as they could not settle their disputes between themselves, they agreed to let the head chief decide. The cause of their unfriendliness was that the elephant was always boasting about his strength to all his friends, which made the bush cow ashamed of himself, as he was always a good fighter and feared no man or animal. When the matter was referred to the head chief, he decided that the best way to settle the dispute was for the elephant and bush cow to meet and fight one another in a large open space. He decided that the fight should take place in the market-place on the next market-day, when all the country people could witness the battle.

When the market-day arrived, the bush cow went out early in the morning and took up his position some distance from the town on the main road to the market, and started bellowing and tearing up the ground. As the people passed he asked them whether they had seen anything of the "Big, Big One," which was the name of the elephant. A bush buck, who happened to be passing, replied, "I am only a small antelope, and am on my way to the market. How should I know anything of the movements of the 'Big, Big One'?" The bush cow then allowed him to pass.

After a little time the bush cow heard the elephant trumpeting, and could hear him as he came nearer, breaking down trees and trampling down the smallbush.

When the elephant came near the bush cow, they both charged one another, and a tremendous fight commenced, in which a lot of damage was done to the surrounding farms, and many of the people were frightened to go to the market, and returned to their houses.

At last the monkey, who had been watching the fight from a distance whilst he was jumping from branch to branch high up in the trees, thought he would report what he had seen to the head chief. Although he forgot several times what it was he wanted to do, which is a little way monkeys have, he eventually reached the chief's house, and jumped upon the roof, where he caught and ate a spider. He then climbed to the ground again, and commenced playing with a small stick. But he very soon got tired of this, and then, picking up a stone, he rubbed it backward and forward on the ground in an aimless sort of way, whilst looking in the opposite direction. This did not last long, and very soon he was busily engaged in a minute personal inspection. His attention was then attracted by a large praying mantis, which had fluttered into the house, making much clatter with its wings. When it settled, it immediately assumed its usual prayerful attitude.

The monkey, after a careful stalk, seized the mantis, and having deliberately pulled the legs off one after the other, he ate the body, and sat down with his head on one side, looking very wise, but in reality thinking of nothing.

Just then the chief caught sight of him while he was scratching himself, and shouted out in a loud voice, "Ha, monkey, is that you? What do you want here?"

At the chief's voice the monkey gave a jump, and started chattering like anything. After a time he replied very nervously, "Oh, yes, of course! Yes, I came to see you." Then he said to himself, "I wonder what on earth it was I came to tell the chief?" but it was no use, everything had gone out of his head.

Then the chief told the monkey he might take one of the ripe plantains hanging up in the verandah. The monkey did not want telling twice, as he was very fond of plantains. He soon tore off its skin, and holding the plantain in both hands, took bite after bite from the end of it, looking at it carefully after each bite.

Then the chief remarked that the elephant and the bush cow ought to have arrived by that time, as they were going to have a great fight. Directly the monkey heard this he remembered what it was he wanted to tell the chief; so, having swallowed the piece of plantain he had placed in the side of his cheek, he said, ".Ah! that reminds me," and then, after much chattering and making all sorts of funny grimaces, finally made the chief understand that the elephant and bush cow, instead of fighting where they had been told, were having it out in the bush on the main road leading to the market, and had thus stopped most of the people coming in.

When the chief heard this he was very angry and called for his bow and poisoned arrows, and went to the scene of the combat. He then shot both the elephant and the bush cow, and throwing his bow and arrows away, ran and hid himself in the bush. About six hours afterward both the elephant and bush cow died in great pain.

Ever since, when wild animals want to fight between themselves, they always fight in the big bush and not on the public roads; but as the fight was never definitely decided between the elephant and the bush cow, wherever they meet one another in the forest, even to the present time, they always fight.

III. WEST AFRICA

THE general economic development of the Gold Coast Colony and the fact that serious study of the folk-lore of these people is of comparatively recent date make it difficult to obtain native stories unaffected by outside influences. These very interesting West African folk-tales can be compared with those of the Hausa tribe in that the Spider is dominant. Its power can be gauged by the following extracts from stories:

The wisdom of the spider is greater than that of all the world together.
Woe to one who would put his trust in Anansi—a sly, selfish, and greedy person.

OHIA AND THE THIEVING DEER

THERE once lived upon the earth a poor man called Ohia, whose wife was named Awirehu. This unfortunate couple had suffered one trouble after another. No matter what they took in hand misfortune seemed to lie in wait for them. Nothing they did met with success. They became so poor that at last they could scarcely obtain a cloth with which to cover themselves.

Finally, Ohia thought of a plan which many of his neighbours had tried and found successful. He went to a wealthy farmer who lived near, and offered to hew down several of his palm-trees. He would then collect their sap to make palm wine. When this should be ready for the market, his wife would carry it there and sell it. The proceeds would then be divided equally between the farmer, Ohia, and Awirehu.

This proposal having been laid before the farmer, he proved quite willing to agree to it. Not only so, but he granted Ohia a supply of earthen pots in which to collect sap, as the miserable man was far too poor to buy any.

In great delight Ohia and his wife set to work. They cut down the trees and prepared them—setting the pots underneath to catch the sap. Before cock-crow on market-day, Ohia set off, with a lighted torch, to collect the wine and prepare it for his wife to take into the town. She was almost ready to follow.

To his great distress, on arriving at the first tree, instead of finding his earthen pot filled with the sweet sap, he saw it lying in pieces on the ground—the wine all gone. He went on to the second and third trees—but there, and at all the others, too, the same thing had happened.

His wife, in high spirits and ready for market, joined him at this moment. She saw at once by his face that some misfortune had again befallen them. Sorrowfully, they examined the mischief, and agreed that some wicked person had stolen the wine and then broken the pots to hide the theft. Awirehu returned home in despair, but Ohia set to work once more. He fetched a second supply of pots and placed them all ready to catch the sap.

On his return next morning, he found that the same behaviour had been repeated. All his wine was again stolen and his pots in fragments. He had no resource but to go to the farmer and tell him of these fresh misfortunes. The farmer proved to be very kind and generous and gave orders that Ohia might have as many pots as he should require. Once more the poor fellow returned to the palm-trees, and set his pots ready. This third attempt, however, met with no better result than the two previous. Ohia went home in despair. His wife was of the opinion that they should give up trying to overcome their evil fortunes. It was quite evident that they could never attain success. The husband, however, determined that, at least, he would find and punish the culprit if that were possible.

Accordingly, he bravely set his pots in order for the last time. When night came, he remained on guard among the trees. Midnight passed and nothing happened, but toward two o'clock in the morning a dark form glided past him to the nearest palm-tree. A moment after he heard the sound of a breaking pot. He stole up to the form. On approaching it he found that the thief was a bush-deer, carrying on its head a large jar, into which it was pouring the wine from Ohia's pots. As it emptied them it threw them carelessly on the ground, breaking them in pieces.

Ohia ventured a little nearer, intending to seize the culprit. The latter, however, was too quick for him and escaped, dropping his great pot on the ground as he ran. The deer was very fleet, but Ohia had fully determined to catch him—so followed. The chase continued over many miles until midday arrived, at which time they had reached the bottom of a high hill. The deer immediately began to climb, and Ohia—though almost tired out—still followed. Finally, the summit of the hill was reached, and there Ohia found himself in the midst of a great gathering of quadrupeds. The deer, panting, threw himself on the ground before King Tiger.[1] His Majesty commanded that Ohia should be brought before him to be punished for this intrusion into such a serious meeting.

Ohia begged for a hearing before they condemned him. He wished to explain fully his presence there. King Tiger, after consulting with some of the other animals, agreed to listen to his tale. Thereupon Ohia began the story of his unfortunate life. He told how one trial after another had failed, and how, finally, he had thought of the palm wine. He described his feelings on discovering the first theft—after all his labour. He related his second, third, and fourth attempts, with the result of each. He then went on to tell of his chase after the thief, and thus explained his presence at their conference. The quadrupeds listened very attentively to the recital of Ohia's troubles. At the conclusion they unanimously agreed that the deer was the culprit and the man blameless. The former was accordingly sentenced to punishment, while the latter received an apology in the name of the entire conference. King Tiger, it appeared, had each morning given Deer a large sum of money wherewith to purchase palm wine for the whole assembly. The deer had stolen the wine and kept the money.

To make up to Ohia for his losses, King Tiger offered him, as a gift, the power of understanding the conversation of all animals. This, said he, would speedily make Ohia a rich man. But he attached one condition to the gift. Ohia must never— on pain of instant death—tell any one about his wonderful power.

The poor man, much delighted, set off for home. When it was reached, he lost no time in setting to work at his palm-trees again. From that day his troubles seemed over. His wine was never interfered with, and he and Awirehu became more and more prosperous and happy.

One morning, while he was bathing in a pool quite close to his house, he heard

---

[1] "Tiger" in West African stories is a leopard.

a hen and her chickens talking together in his garden. He listened, and distinctly heard a chicken tell Mother Hen about three jars of gold buried in Ohia's garden. The hen bade the chicken to be careful, lest her master should see her scraping near the gold, and so discover it.

Ohia pretended to take no notice of what they were saying, and went away. Presently, when Mother Hen and her brood had gone, he came back and commenced digging in that part of the garden. To his great joy, he soon found three large jars of gold. They contained enough money to keep him in comfort all his life. He was careful, however, not to mention his treasure to anyone but his wife. He hid it safely inside his house.

Soon he and Awirehu had become one of the richest couples in the neighbourhood, and owned quite a large amount of property. Ohia thought he could afford now to keep a second wife, so he married again. Unfortunately, the new wife did not at all resemble Awirehu. The latter had always been a good, kind, honest woman. The new wife was of a very jealous and selfish disposition. In addition to this she was lame, and continually imagined that people were making fun of her defect. She took the idea into her head that Ohia and Awirehu—when together—were in the habit of laughing at her. Nothing was further from their thoughts, but she refused to believe so. Whenever she saw them together she would stand and listen outside the door to hear what they were saying. Of course, she never succeeded in hearing anything about herself. At last, one evening, Ohia and Awirehu had gone to bed. The latter was fast asleep when Ohia heard a conversation which amused him very much. A couple of mice in one corner of the room were arranging to go to the larder to get some food, as soon as their master—who was watching them—was asleep. Ohia, thinking this was a good joke, laughed outright. His lame wife heard him, and rushed into the room. She thereupon accused him of making fun of her again to Awirehu. The astonished husband, of course, denied this, but to no purpose. The jealous woman insisted that, if he were laughing at an innocent joke, he would at once tell it to her.

This Ohia could not do, without breaking his promise to King Tiger. His refusal fully confirmed the lame woman's suspicions, and she did not rest till she had laid the whole matter before the chief. He, being an intimate friend of Ohia, tried to persuade him to reveal the joke and set the matter at rest. Ohia naturally was most unwilling to do anything of the sort. The persistent woman gave the chief no peace till he summoned her husband to answer her charge before the Assembly.

Finding no way of escape from the difficulty, Ohia prepared for death. He first called all his friends and relatives to a great feast, and bade them farewell. Then he put his affairs in order—bequeathed all his gold to the faithful Awirehu, and his property to his son and servants. When he had finished, he went to the Assembly Place where the people of the neighbourhood were gathered together.

He first took leave of the chief, and then commenced his tale. He related the story of his many misfortunes—of his adventure with the deer, and of his promise to King Tiger. Finally, he explained the cause of his laughter which had annoyed his wife. In so speaking he fell dead, as the Tiger had warned him.

He was buried amid great mourning, for every one had liked and respected him. The jealous woman who had caused her husband's death was seized and burnt as a witch. Her ashes were then scattered to the four winds of heaven, and it is owing to this unfortunate fact that jealousy and selfishness are so widespread through the world, where before they scarcely existed.

WHY WE SEE ANTS CARRYING BUNDLES AS BIG AS THEMSELVES

KWEKU Anansi and Kweku Tsin—his son—were both very clever farmers. Generally they succeeded in getting fine harvests from each of their farms. One year, however, they were very unfortunate. They had sown their seed as usual, but no rain had fallen for more than a month after and it looked as if the seeds would be unable to sprout.

Kweku Tsin was walking sadly through his fields one day looking at the bare, dry ground, and wondering what he and his family would do for food, if they were unable to get any harvest. To his surprise he saw a tiny dwarf seated by the roadside. The little hunchback asked the reason of his sadness, and Kweku Tsin told him. The dwarf promised to help him by bringing rain on the farm. He bade Kweku fetch two small sticks and tap him lightly on the hump, while he sang:

> "O water, go up, O water, go up
> And let rain fall, and let rain fall."

To Kweku's great joy rain immediately began to fall, and continued till the ground was thoroughly well soaked. In the days following the seeds germinated, and the crops began to promise well.

Anansi soon heard how well Kweku's crops were growing—whilst his own were still bare and hard. He went straightway to his son and demanded to know the reason. Kweku Tsin, being an honest fellow, at once told him what had happened.

Anansi quickly made up his mind to get his farm watered in the same way, and accordingly set out toward it. As he went, he cut two big, strong sticks, thinking, "My son made the dwarf work with little sticks. I will make him do twice as much with my big ones." He carefully hid the big sticks, however, when he saw the dwarf coming toward him. As before, the hunchback asked what the trouble was, and Anansi told him. "Take two small sticks, and beat me lightly on the hump," said the dwarf. "I will get rain for you."

But Anansi took his big sticks and beat so hard that the dwarf fell down dead. The greedy fellow was now thoroughly frightened, for he knew that the dwarf was jester to the King of the country, and a very great favourite of his. He wondered how he could fix the blame on some one else. He picked up the dwarf's dead body and carried it to a kola-tree. There he laid it on one of the top branches and sat down under the tree to watch.

By and by Kweku Tsin came along to see if his father had succeeded in getting rain for his crops. "Did you not see the dwarf, Father?" he asked, as he saw the old man sitting alone. "Oh, yes!" replied Anansi; "but he has climbed this tree to pick kola. I am now waiting for him." "I will go up and fetch him," said the young man—and immediately began to climb. As soon as his head touched the body the latter, of course, fell to the ground. "Oh! what have you done, you wicked fellow?" cried his father. "You have killed the King's jester!" "That is all right," quietly replied the son (who saw that this was one of Anansi's tricks). "The King is very angry with him, and has promised a bag of money to anyone who would kill him. I will now go and get the reward." "No! No! No!" shouted Anansi. "The reward is mine. I killed him with two big sticks. *I* will take him to the King." "Very well!" was the son's reply. "As you killed him, you may take him."

Off set Anansi, quite pleased with the prospect of getting a reward. He reached the King's court, only to find the King very angry at the death of his favourite. The body of the jester was shut up in a great box and Anansi was condemned—as a punishment—to carry it on his head for ever. The King enchanted the box so that it could never be set down on the ground. The only way in which Anansi could ever get rid of it was by getting some other man to put it on his head. This, of course, no one was willing to do.

At last, one day, when Anansi was almost worn out with his heavy burden, he met the Ant. "Will you hold this box for me while I go to market and buy some things I need badly?" said Anansi to Mr. Ant. "I know your tricks, Anansi," replied the Ant. "You want to be rid of it." "Oh, no, indeed, Mr. Ant," protested Anansi. "Indeed I will come back for it, I promise."

Mr. Ant, who was an honest fellow, and always kept his own promises, believed him. He took the box on his head, and Anansi hurried off. Needless to say, the sly fellow had not the least intention of keeping his word. Mr. Ant waited in vain for his return—and was obliged to wander all the rest of his life with the box on his head. That is the reason we so often see ants carrying great bundles as they hurry along.

ANANSI AND NOTHING

NEAR Anansi's miserable little hut there was a fine palace where lived a very rich man called. Nothing. Nothing and Anansi proposed, one day, to go to the neighbouring town to get some wives. Accordingly, they set off together. Nothing, being a rich man, wore a very fine velvet cloth, while Anansi had a ragged cotton one. While they were on their way Anansi persuaded Nothing to change clothes for a little while, promising to give back the fine velvet before they reached the town. He delayed doing this, however, first on one pretext, then on another—till they arrived at their destination.

Anansi, being dressed in such a fine garment, found no difficulty in getting as many wives as he wished. Poor Nothing, with his ragged and miserable cloth, was treated with great contempt. At first he could not get even one wife. At last, however, a woman took pity on him and gave him her daughter.

The poor girl was laughed at very heartily by Anansi's wives for choosing such a beggar as Nothing appeared to be. She wisely took no notice of their scorn.

The party set off for home. When they reached the cross-roads leading to their respective houses the women were astonished. The road leading to Anansi's house was only half cleared. The one which led to Nothing's palace was, of course, wide and well made. Not only so, but his servants had strewn it with beautiful skins and carpets, in preparation for his return.

Servants were there, awaiting him, with fine clothes for himself and his wife. No one was waiting for Anansi.

Nothing's wife was queen over the whole district and had everything her heart could desire. Anansi's wives could not even get proper food; they had to live on unripe bananas with peppers. The wife of Nothing heard of her friends' miserable state and invited them to a great feast in her palace. They came and were so pleased with all they saw that they agreed to stay there. Accordingly, they refused to come back to Anansi's hut.

He was very angry, and tried in many ways to kill Nothing, but without success. Finally, however, he persuaded some rat friends to dig a deep tunnel in front of Nothing's door. When the hole was finished Anansi lined it with knives and broken bottles. He then smeared the steps of the palace with *okro* to make them very slippery, and withdrew to a little distance.

When he thought Nothing's household was safely in bed and asleep, he called Nothing to come out to the courtyard and see something. Nothing's wife, however, dissuaded him from going. Anansi tried again and again, and each time she bade her husband not to listen. At last Nothing determined to go and see this thing. As he placed his foot on the first step, of course he slipped, and down he fell into the hole. The noise alarmed the household. Lights were fetched and Nothing was found in the ditch, so much wounded by the knives that he soon died.

His wife was terribly grieved at his untimely death. She boiled many yams, mashed them, and took a great dishful of them round the district. To every child she met she gave some, so that the child might help her to cry for her husband. This is why, if you find a child crying and ask the cause, you will often be told he is "crying for nothing."

THE CONCEITED SPIDER

IN the olden days all the stories which men told were stories of Nyankupon, the chief of the Gods. Spider, who was very conceited, wanted the stories to be told about him.

Accordingly, one day he went to Nyankupon and asked that, in future, all tales told by men might be Anansi stories, instead of Nyankupon stories. Nyankupon agreed, on one condition. He told Spider (or Anansi) that he must bring him three things: the first was a jar full of live bees, the second was a boa-constrictor, and the third a tiger. Spider gave his promise.

He took an earthen vessel and set out for a place where he knew were numbers of bees. When he came in sight of the bees he began saying to himself, "They will not be able to fill this jar."—"Yes, they will be able."—"No, they will not be able," until the bees came up to him and said, "What are you talking about, Mr. Anansi?" He thereupon explained to them that Nyankupon and he had had a great dispute. Nyankupon had said the bees could not fly into the jar—Anansi had said they could. The bees immediately declared that of course they could fly into the jar—which they at once did. As soon as they were safely inside, Anansi sealed up the jar and sent it off to Nyankupon.

Next day he took a long stick and set out in search of a boa-constrictor. When he arrived at the place where one lived he began speaking to himself again. "He will be just as long as this stick."—"No, he will not be so long as this."—"Yes, he will be as long as this."

These words he repeated several times, till the boa came out and asked him what was the matter. "Oh, we have been having a dispute in Nyankupon's town about you. Nyankupon's people say you are not as long as this stick. I say you are. Please let me measure you by it." The boa innocently laid himself out straight, and Spider lost no time in tying him on to the stick from end to end. He then sent him to Nyankupon.

The third day he took a needle and thread and sewed up his eye. He then set out for a den where he knew a tiger lived. As he approached the place he began to shout and sing so loudly that the tiger came out to see what was the matter. "Can you not see?" said Spider. "My eye is sewn up and now I can see such wonderful things that I must sing about them." "Sew up my eyes," said the tiger, "then I too can see these surprising sights." Spider immediately did so. Having thus made the tiger helpless, he led him straight to Nyankupon's house. Nyankupon was amazed at Spider's cleverness in fulfilling the three conditions. He immediately gave him permission for the future to call all the old tales Anansi tales.

IV. KAFFIR TALES

THESE stories are current among the people living on the eastern border of the Cape Colony. They have been gathered chiefly from ancient dames. They are the best narrators, and they will tell their stories only in the evening, when the belief in the supernatural is stronger than by day. The tales are already becoming modified by recent story-tellers, because of the influx of modern ideas. Often parts of one story are used in varied combinations with others—just as the same blocks in a box of bricks may be used to form different pictures—and thus a new story is produced.

THE STORY OF FIVE HEADS

THERE was once a man living in a certain place, who had two daughters big enough to be married. One day the man went over the river to another village, which was the residence of a great chief. The people asked him to tell them the news. He replied that there was no news in the place he came from. Then the man inquired about the news of their place. They said the news of their place was that the chief wanted a wife.

The man went home and said to his two daughters, "Which of you wishes to be the wife of a chief?"

The eldest replied: "I wish to be the wife of a chief, my father." The name of that girl was Mpunzikazi.

The man said: "At that village which I visited, the chief wishes for a wife; you, my daughter, shall go."

The man called all his friends, and assembled a large company to go with his daughter to the village of the chief. But the girl would not consent that those people should go with her. She said: "I will go alone to be the wife of the chief."

Her father replied: "How can you, my daughter, say such a thing? Is it not so that when a girl goes to present herself to her husband she should be accompanied by others? Be not foolish, my daughter."

The girl still said, "I will go alone to be the wife of the chief."

Then the man allowed his daughter to do as she chose. She went alone, no bridal party accompanying her, to present herself at the village of the chief who wanted a wife.

As Mpunzikazi was in the path she met a mouse. The mouse said, "Shall I show you the way?"

The girl replied: "Just get away from before my eyes."

The mouse answered: "If you do like this, you will not succeed."

Then she met a frog.

The frog said: "Shall I show you the way?"

Mpunzikazi replied: "You are not worthy to speak to me, as I am to be the wife of a chief."

The frog said: "Go on, then; you will see afterward what will happen."

When the girl got tired, she sat down under a tree to rest. A boy who was herding goats in that place came to her, he being very hungry. The boy said: "Where are you going to, my eldest sister?"

Mpunzikazi replied in an angry voice: "Who are you that you should speak to me? Just get away from before me."

The boy said: "I am very hungry; will you not give me of your food?"

She answered: "Get away quickly."

The boy said:"You will not return if you do this."

She went on her way again, and met with an old woman sitting by a big stone.

The old woman said: "I will give you advice. You will meet with trees that will laugh at you: you must not laugh in return. You will see a bag of thick milk: you must not eat of it. You will meet a man whose head is under his arm: you must not take water from him."

Mpunzikazi answered: "You ugly thing! Who are you that you should advise me?"

The old woman continued in saying these words. The girl went on. She came to a place where were many trees. The trees laughed at her, and she laughed at them in return. She saw a bag of thick milk, and she ate of it. She met a man carrying his head under his arm, and she took water to drink from him.

She came to the river of the village of the chief. She saw a girl there dipping water from the river. The girl said: "Where are you going to, my sister?"

Mpunzikazi replied: "Who are you that you should call me sister? I am going to be the wife of a chief."

The girl drawing water was the sister of the chief. She said: "Wait, I will give you advice. Do not enter the village by this side."

Mpunzikazi did not stay to listen but just went on. She reached the village of the chief. The people asked her where she came from and what she wanted.

She answered, "I have come to be the wife of the chief."

They said: "Who ever saw a girl go without a retinue to be a bride?"

They also said, "The chief is not at home; you must prepare food for him, that when he comes in the evening, he may eat."

They gave her millet to grind. She ground it very coarse, and made bread that was not nice to eat. In the evening she heard the sound of a great wind. That wind was the coming of the chief. He was a big snake with five heads and large eyes. Mpunzikazi was very much frightened when she saw him. He sat down before the door and told her to bring his food. She brought the bread which she had made. Makanda Mahlanu (Five Heads) was not satisfied with that bread. He said: "You shall not be my wife," and he struck her with his tail and killed her.

Afterward the sister of Mpunzikazi said to her father: "I also wish to be the wife of a chief." Her father replied: "It is well, my daughter; it is right that you should wish to be a bride."

The man called all his friends, and a great retinue prepared to accompany the bride. The name of the girl was Mpunzanyana.

In the way they met a mouse.

The mouse said: "Shall I show you the road?"

Mpunzanyana replied: "If you will show me the way I shall be glad." Then the mouse pointed out the way. She came into a valley, where she saw an old woman standing by a tree.

The old woman said to her: "You will come to a place where two paths branch off. You must take the little one, because if you take the big one you will not be fortunate."

Mpunzanyana replied: "I will take the little path, my mother." She went on. Afterward she met a cony.

The cony said: "The village of the chief is close by. You will meet a girl by the river: you must speak nicely to her. They will give you millet to grind: you must grind it well. When you see your husband, you must not be afraid."

She said: "I will do as you say, Cony."

In the river she met the chief's sister carrying water. The chief's sister said: "Where are you going to?"

Mpunzanyana replied: "This is the end of my journey."

The chief's sister said: "What is the object of your coming to this place ?"

Mpunzanyana replied: "I am with a bridal party."

The chief's sister said: "That is right, but will you not be afraid when you see your husband?"

Mpunzanyana answered: "I will not be afraid."

The chief's sister pointed out the hut in which she should stay. Food was given to the bridal party. The mother of the chief took millet and gave to the bride, saying: "You must prepare food for your husband. He is not here now, but he will come in the evening."

In the evening she heard a very strong wind, which made the hut shake. The poles fell, but she did not run out. Then she saw the chief Makanda Mahlanu coming. He asked for food. Mpunzanyana took the bread which she had made, and gave it to him. He was very much pleased with that food, and said:

"You shall be my wife." He gave her very many ornaments.

Afterward Makanda Mahlanu became a man, and Mpunzanyana continued to be the wife he loved best.

THE GREAT CHIEF OF THE ANIMALS

THERE was once a woman who had occasion to leave her home for a short time, and who left her children in charge of a hare. The place where they lived was close to a path, along which droves of wild animals were accustomed to pass.

Soon after the woman left, the animals appeared, and the hare at sight of them became frightened. So she ran away to a distance, and stood to watch. Among the animals was one terrible monster, which called to the hare, and demanded to know what children those were. The hare told their names, upon which the animal swallowed them entire.

When the woman returned, the hare told her what had happened. Then the woman gathered some dry wood, and sharpened two pieces of iron, which she took with her and went along the path.

Now this was the chief of the animals; therefore, when she came on a hill over against him, the woman began to call out that she was looking for her children. The animal replied: "Come nearer, I cannot hear you."

When she went, he swallowed her also. The woman found her children alive, and also many other people, and oxen, and dogs. The children were hungry, so the woman with her pieces of iron cut some pieces of flesh from the animal's ribs. She then made a fire, cooked the meat, and the children ate.

The other people said: "We also are hungry, give us to eat."

Then she cut and cooked for them also. The animal felt uncomfortable under this treatment, and called his counsellors together for advice, but they could suggest no remedy. He lay down and rolled in the mud, but that did not help him, and at last he went and put his head in the kraal fence and died.

His counsellors were standing at a distance, afraid to approach him, so they sent a monkey to see how he was. The monkey returned and said: "Those whose home is on the mountains must hasten to the mountains; those whose home is on the plains must hasten to the plains; as for me, I go to the rocks."

Then the animals all dispersed.

By this time the woman had succeeded in cutting a hole through the chief's side, and came forth, followed by her children.

Then an ox came out, and said: "Bo! bo! who helped me?"

Then a dog, who said: "Ho! ho! who helped me?"

Then a man, who said: "Zo! zo! who helped me?"

Afterward all the people and cattle came out. They agreed that the woman who helped them should be their chief.

When her children became men, they were out hunting one day, and saw a monstrous cannibal, who was sticking fast in a mud hole. They killed him, and then returned to tell the men of their tribe what they had done. The men went and skinned the cannibal, when a great number of people came from him also. These joined their deliverers, and so that people became a great nation.

THE WONDERFUL HORNS

THERE was once a boy whose mother that bore him was dead, and who was ill-treated by his other mothers. On this account he determined to go away from his father's place. One morning he went, riding on an ox which was given to him by his father. As he was travelling, he came to a herd of cattle with a bull.

His ox said: "I will fight and overcome that bull."

The boy then dismounted. The fight took place, and the bull was defeated. The boy mounted again.

About midday, feeling hungry, he struck the right horn of his ox, and food came out. After satisfying his hunger, he struck the left horn, and the rest of the food went in again.

The boy saw another herd of dun-coloured cattle.

His ox said: "I will fight and die there. You must break off my horns and take them with you. When you are hungry, speak to them, and they will supply you with food."

In the fight the ox was killed, as was said. The boy took his horns, and went on walking till he came to a village where he found the people cooking a weed (called *tyutu*), having no other food to eat.

He entered one of the houses. He spoke to his horn, and food came out, sufficient to supply the owner of the house and himself. After they had eaten they both fell asleep. The owner of the house got up and took away the horns. He concealed them, and put two others in their place.

The boy started next morning with the horns, taking them to be the right ones. When he felt hungry, he spoke to the horns, but nothing came out. He therefore went back to the same place where he slept the previous night. As he drew near, he heard the owner of the place speaking to the horns, but without any avail. The boy took his horns from the thief, and went on his way. He came to a house, and asked to be entertained. The owner refused, and sent him away, on account of his garment being in shreds and his body soiled with travel.

After that he came to a river and sat down on the bank. He spoke to his horns and a new mantle and handsome ornaments came out. He dressed himself, and went on. He came to a house where there was a very beautiful girl. He was received by the girl's father and stayed there. His horns provided food and clothing for all.

After a time he married the girl. He then returned home with his wife, and was welcomed by his father. He spoke to his horns, and a fine house came out, in which he lived with his wife.

THE STORY OF LION AND LITTLE JACKAL

LITTLE Jackal one day went out hunting, when he met Lion. Lion proposed that they should hunt together, on condition that if a small antelope was killed it was to be Little Jackal's, and if a large one was killed it was to be Lion's. Little Jackal agreed to this.

The first animal killed was a large eland. Lion was very glad, and said to Little Jackal: "I will continue hunting while you go to my house and call my children to carry the meat home."

Little Jackal replied: "Yes, I agree to that."

Lion went away to hunt. When he had gone, Little Jackal went to his own house and called his own children to carry away the meat. He said: "Lion takes me for a fool if he thinks I will call his children while my own are dying with hunger."

So Little Jackal's children carried the meat to their home on the top of a high rock. The only way to get to their house was by means of a rope. Lion caught nothing more, and after a time he went home and asked his wife where the meat was. She told him there was no meat. He said: "Did not Little Jackal bring a message to my children to carry meat ?"

His wife replied: "No; he was not here. We are still dying with hunger."

Lion then went to Little Jackal's house, but he could not get up the rock to it. So he sat down by the water, waiting. After a time Little Jackal went to get some water. He was close to the water when he saw Lion. He at once ran away, and the Lion ran after him. He ran into a hole under a tree, but Lion caught his tail before he got far in. He said to him: "That is not my tail you have hold of; it is a root of the tree. If you do not believe me, take a stone and strike it, and see if any blood comes."

Lion let go the tail, and went for a stone to prove what it was. While he was gone for the stone, Little Jackal went far into the hole. When Lion returned, he could not be found. Lion lay down by the hole and waited. After a long time Little Jackal wanted to come out. He went to the entrance and looked round, but he could not see Lion. To make sure, he said: "Ho, I see you, my master, although you are in hiding."

Lion did not move from the place where he lay concealed. Then Little Jackal went out, and Lion pursued him, but he got away.

Lion watched for him, and one day, when Little Jackal was out hunting, he came upon him in a place where he could not escape. Lion was just about to spring upon him, when Little Jackal said softly: "Be still. do you not see that bush buck on the other side of the rock? I am glad you have come to help me. Just remain here while I run round and drive him toward you."

Lion did so, and Little Jackal made his escape.

At another time there was a meeting of the animals, and Lion was the chief at the meeting. Little Jackal wanted to attend, but there was a law made that no one should be present unless he had horns. So Little Jackal took wax out of a nest of bees, and made horns for himself with it. He fastened the horns on his head, and went to the meeting. Lion did not know him on account of the horns. But he sat near the fire and went to sleep, when the horns melted.

Lion looked at him and saw who it was. He immediately tried to catch him, but Little Jackal was quick in springing away. He ran under an overhanging rock and sang out: "Help! help! This rock is falling upon me!" Lion went for a pole to prop up the rock that he might get at Little Jackal. While he was away, Little Jackal escaped.

After that they became companions again, and went hunting another time. They killed an ox. Lion said: "I will watch it while you carry the pieces away."

Lion gave him the breast, and said: "Take this to my wife."

Little Jackal took it to his own wife. When he returned, Lion gave him a shin, and said: "Take this to your wife."

Little Jackal took the shin to Lion's house. Lion's wife said: "I cannot take this, because it should not come here."

Little Jackal thereupon struck Lion's wife in the face, and went back to the place where the ox was killed. Lion gave him a large piece of meat, and said: "Take this to my wife."

Little Jackal took it to his own wife. This continued till the ox was finished. Then they both went home. When Lion arrived at his house he found there was weeping in his family. His wife said: "is it you who sent Little Jackal to beat me and my children, and is it you who sent this shin? Did I ever eat a shin?"

When Lion heard this he was very angry and at once went to Little Jackal's house. When he reached the rock, Little Jackal looked down and said: "Who are you, and what is your name, and whose son are you, and where are you from, and where are you going to, and whom do you want, and what do you want him for?"

Lion replied: "I have merely come to see you. I wish you to let down the rope."

Little Jackal let down a rope made of mouse skins, and when Lion climbed a little way up, the rope broke, and he fell and was hurt. He then went home.

V. HOTTENTOT TALES

IN *Reynard the Fox* one finds stories, which may almost be considered as fables. The Hottentots are very different from the ordinary blacks of South Africa and may be of North-African origin. They are very low in the scale of intellect, and their stories cannot be said to be very numerous or of a high order.

THE JACKAL'S BRIDE

THE Jackal, it is said, married the Hyena, and carried off a cow belonging to ants, to slaughter her for the wedding; and when he had slaughtered her, he put the cow-skin over his bride; and when he had fixed a pole (on which to hang the flesh), he placed on the top of the pole (which was forked) the hearth for cooking, in order to cook upon it all sorts of delicious food. There came also the Lion to the spot, and wished to go up. The Jackal, therefore, asked his little daughter for a thong with which he could pull the Lion up, and he began to pull him up; and when his face came near to the cooking-pot, he cut the thong in two, so that the Lion tumbled down. Then the Jackal upbraided his little daughter with these words: "Why do you give me such an old thong?" And he added, "Give me a fresh thong." She gave him a new thong, and he pulled the Lion up again, and when his face came near the pot, which stood on the fire, he said, "Open your mouth." Then he put into his mouth a hot piece of quartz which had been boiled together with the fat, and the stone went down, burning his throat. Thus died the Lion.

There came also the ants running after the cow, and when the Jackal saw them he fled. Then they beat the bride in her brookaross dress. The Hyena, believing that it was the Jackal, said:

"You tawny rogue! have you not played at beating long enough? Have you no more loving game than this?"

But when she had bitten a hole through the cow-skin, she saw that they were other people; then she fled, falling here and there, yet she made her escape.

THE WHITE MAN AND THE SNAKE

A DUTCHMAN was walking by himself, and saw a Snake lying under a large stone. The Snake implored his help; but when she had become free, she said, "Now I shall eat you."

The Man answered, "That is not right. Let us first go to the Hare."

When the Hare had heard the affair, he said, "it is right." "No," said the Man, "let us ask the Hyena."

The Hyena declared the same, saying, "It is right."

"Now let us at last ask the Jackal," said the Man in his despair.

The Jackal answered very slowly and considerately, doubting the whole affair, and demanding to see first the place, and whether the Man was able to lift the stone. The Snake lay down, and the Man, to prove the truth of his account, put the stone again over her.

When she was fast, the Jackal said, "Now let her lie there."

THE DOVE AND THE HERON

THE Jackal, it is said, came once to the Dove, who lived on the top of a rock, and said, "Give me one of your little children." The Dove answered, "I shall not do anything of the kind." The Jackal said, "Give it me at once! Otherwise, I shall fly up to you." Then she threw one down to him.

He came back another day, and demanded another little child, and she gave it to him. After the Jackal had gone, the Heron came, and asked, "Dove, why do you cry?" The Dove answered him: "The Jackal has taken away my little children; it is for this that I cry." He asked her, "In what manner can he take them?" She answered him: he asked me I refused him; but when he said, 'I shall at once fly up, therefore give it me,' I threw it down to him."

The Heron said, "Are you such a fool as to give your children to the Jackals, who cannot fly?" Then, with the admonition to give no more, he went away.

The Jackal came again, and said, "Dove, give me a little child." The Dove refused, and told him that the Heron had told her that he could not fly up. The Jackal said, "I shall catch him."

So when the Heron came to the banks of the water, the Jackal asked him: "Brother Heron, when the wind comes from this side, how will you stand?" He turned his neck toward him and said, "I stand thus, bending my neck on one side." The Jackal asked him again, "When a storm comes and when it rains, how do you stand?" He said to him: "I stand thus, indeed, bending my neck down." Then the Jackal beat him on his neck, and broke his neck in the middle.

Since that day the Heron's neck is bent.

VI. THE CONGO

THESE stories from the Congo have a delightful freshness and humour. They were told by the Alo Man (the wandering story teller of these African villages). No one could make the people see pictures in their minds as he could. No one had seen so many wonderful and interesting things among the people of so many different tribes. As he told these tales his white teeth would flash and his eyes shine, while all his hearers sat spellbound.

THE CAT AND THE RAT

I OFTEN think [said the Alo Man] of the time, very long ago, when the Cat and the Rat were friends and lived together on an island. It was so long ago that they have both forgotten it, but they led a very happy life. There were birds in the trees for the Cat to eat, and there were nuts and manioc roots for the Rat to eat.

But nobody was ever so happy as not to want something more. One day the Rat said, "I am tired of living on this island. Let us go and find a village to live in. There you can have food without catching birds, and I can have food without digging in the ground."

"That will be delightful," said the Cat. "But how are we to cross this great water?"

"Nothing is more easy," said the Rat, "We will carve a boat from the root of a manioc."

Then the Cat and the Rat dug up a large manioc root and began making it into a boat.

The Rat gnawed and gnawed and gnawed with his sharp teeth, until he had made a hollow large enough to hold the two friends. While he was busy at this, the Cat scratched and scratched and scratched, to make the outside of the boat smooth and to scrape off all the earth that clung to the great root.

Then the Cat and the Rat made two little paddles and started out in their boat.

It was much farther across the great water than it had looked from their island. Also they had forgotten to put any food into the boat. Presently the cat began to say "Caungu! Caungu!" which means "I am hungry! I am hungry!"

And the Rat said "Quee! Quee!" which means in his language, "I am hungry! I am hungry!"

But that did not do any good. They grew hungrier and hungrier. At last the Cat said "Caungu! Caungu!" very faintly, and curled her self up to sleep. And the Rat said "Quee! Quee!" very faintly, and curled himself up also, at the other end of the boat.

But while the Cat slept, the Rat stayed awake and thought. Suddenly he remembered that the boat itself was made of manioc. He had eaten so much while he was gnawing out the hollow that he had not wanted any more for some time, but now he said, "Good! I will eat a little more and make the hollow deeper."

So he began—nibble, nibble, nibble!

"What is that noise?" exclaimed the Cat, waking at the sound.

But the Rat had shut his eyes and made himself as if he were fast asleep.

"I must have been dreaming," said the Cat, and she laid her head down on her paws and went to sleep again.

The Rat began again—nibble, nibble, nibble!

"What is that noise?" cried the Cat, waking up.

But the Rat made himself seem to be fast asleep.

"What strange dreams I have," said the Cat, as she curled herself up and went to sleep again.

Once more the Rat began to nibble very fast, and the noise awoke the Cat.

"What is that noise?" asked the Cat.

But the Rat made believe to be sound asleep.

"My dreams are certainly very troublesome," said the Cat, as she curled herself up and went to sleep once more with her paw folded over her eyes.

Then the Rat began nibbling again, and this time he gnawed a hole right through the bottom of the boat, and the water began to come in.

"What is this?" cried the Cat, jumping up quickly.

"Quee, quee, quee!" squealed the Rat, perching on one end of the boat.

"Caungu! Caungu!" miaued the Cat, climbing up on the other end, for she did not like the water at all. "Quee, quee !"

"Caungu! Ca-ungu-u-u!"

"Quee, quee!"

"You did this, you wicked creature!" squalled the Cat.

"I was so hungry!" squeaked the Rat, and then the boat began to sink, and there was no time for any more talk. They had to swim for their lives.

"I am going to eat you," said the Cat, glaring at the Rat as they swam.

"I deserve it," squeaked the Rat; "but don't eat me now or you will be choked by the water. Wait until we reach the shore."

"I will wait," said the Cat, "but when we reach the shore I will certainly eat you."

At last they reached the dry land.

"Now," said the Cat, "I will eat you."

"I deserve it," said the Rat, "but I am too wet to be good eating now. Let me dry myself, while you dry your own beautiful coat. I shall be ready when you are."

They sat down and began to dry their coats. And the Cat was so interested in making her beautiful coat quite smooth and glossy that she did not see that the Rat was busily digging a hole in the earth behind her.

"Are you ready?" asked the Cat at last, when every part of her coat was dry and glossy and smooth.

"Certainly," said the Rat, and he disappeared into the hole.

"You rascal!" cried the Cat, for the hole was only just big enough for the Rat to dive into it.

"Quee, quee!" said the Rat from the bottom of the hole.

"You will never get out of that hole alive," said the Cat. "I will stay here and wait for you, and when you come out I will eat you."

"What if I never come out?" said the Rat. "Quee, quee!"

"Then you can stay in that hole and starve," said the Cat, and she settled down in front of the hole with her nose on her paws and all four feet under her, watching for the Rat to come out.

"Quee, quee!" said the Rat, in the hole, and he began to dig himself in deeper.

All day long the Rat went on digging.

All day long the Cat watched beside the hole.

When night came, the Rat had dug down under a tree root and had come up on the other side of the tree, and he crept out of the other end of his tunnel and went on to the village, while the Cat still watched at her end.

From that day to this the Cat is never so fast asleep that she does not hear the gnawing of a Rat, and she is never tired of watching for the Rat to come out of a hole. And from that day to this the Rat knows that if there is a Cat in the village where he goes to steal grain, he will find the Cat waiting for him at one end or the other of his hole in the ground.

THE JACKAL AND THE DROUGHT

THERE was once a very dry time in the land when many animals died of thirst. It was in the days when the animals lived in villages and talked one with another, and when the drought was over the Lion called the animals together and said that some plan must be found to keep this from ever happening again.

The Ape said that they might go to some country where there were no droughts, but the Tortoise said that he would never live to complete such a long journey.

"Let us sleep through the next dry season," said the Snake.

"That would never suit me," said the Hare.

At last, after a great deal of discussion, the Jackal and the Hyena suggested that they might all join in digging a great pool to hold water through the next dry season.

This seemed a wise plan, and on the very next day the animals came to dig the hole.

They agreed to take turns. It was settled that as the Hyena and the Jackal had made the plan, the Hyena should be first and the Jackal last; but when the Jackal's turn came he was nowhere to be found. The pool was almost finished, and the others decided to go on and get it done without him. Soon the rain began to fall, and filled it full of pure, sweet water. Then a rule was made that no one except those who had helped to dig the pool should be allowed to drink there.

The Jackal was hiding in the bushes and heard all that was said, and he came very early the next morning and drank all that he wanted. Every morning, before anyone else was about he did this, and after a while he grew bolder and took a swim in the pool, so that the water was muddy when the others came to drink.

"Who did this?" asked the Lion.

"Who did this?" asked the Leopard.

"Who did this?" asked all the other animals when they came to drink.

But no one knew.

"I will tell you what we can do," said the Tortoise. "Cover my shell with beeswax to make it sticky, and I will watch all night by the pool and catch the rascal."

So the shell of the Tortoise was covered with a thick coat of sticky wax, and he took his place beside the pool to watch for trespassers. He drew his head and his tail and his feet inside his shell, so that he looked like a flat brown stone. From time to time he would stick his head out cautiously to see if anyone was coming. After waiting all night long, he heard a noise in the bushes. He crept down to the very edge of the water, drew his head and feet into his shell, and kept as still as a stone.

Then the Jackal came sneaking down to the pool, looking from side to side to make sure that no one was set to guard it.

"What a very convenient stepping-stone," he said, and he placed his two fore feet upon the Tortoise's shell and bent down to drink. No sooner had he done this than he discovered, to his great surprise and terror, that his feet were stuck fast.

"Ow! Ow! Let me go! This is a mean trick!" howled the Jackal.

"You are not the only one who knows how to play tricks," said the Tortoise, and he began to move away.

"Yah! Yah! Let me go!" yelled the Jackal. "if you don't let me go, I will kick your shell to pieces with my hind feet."

"You may do just as you please about that," said the Tortoise, moving on away from the pool.

The Jackal kicked as hard as he could at the Tortoise with his hind feet, and first one and then the other stuck fast to the shell.

"Wow! Wow! Let me go!" squalled the Jackal. "if you don't let me go, I will bite you in two!"

"Try it and see what happens," said the Tortoise quietly, moving on along the path.

The Jackal bit the shell as hard as he could, and his jaws stuck to it fast. He was dragged along, until, after some time, the Tortoise arrived at the Lion's house and told how he had caught the thieving Jackal.

All the animals, when they heard the news, gathered to see the Jackal in his miserable captivity, but not one of them had any pity for him. Every one said that he ought to die for his dishonesty and his mischief making.

"You may live until to-morrow," said the Lion, "and we will allow you this favour: you may choose the way you will die."

"Thank you," said the Jackal, meekly. Then he began to think whether there was not some plan by which he might escape even now.

All the animals came to see the Jackal executed, and the Hyena was made the executioner.

"Have you made up your mind in what way you wish to be killed?" asked the Lion.

"I once saw a monkey kill a rat," said the Jackal, "by swinging it around by the tail and dashing it against a tree. I think I should prefer to be killed in that way."

"Very well," said the Lion, "the Hyena will take you by the tail and swing you round and round and dash you against a tree,"

"Thank you," said the Jackal, meekly. "If I might be so free as to make a suggestion, permit me to say that the other animals might be safer if they sat as far away as possible. Otherwise, when the Hyena lets go of me, I might hit one of them instead of the tree, and that would be very unfortunate."

The animals thought that this was a good suggestion, and went as far away as they could go without being out of sight of the execution.

Now the Jackal had saved some fat from the meat they gave him for his dinner, and he had greased his tail all the way to the tip, so that it was as slippery as a lump of butter.

The Hyena grasped the Jackal firmly by the tail and began to swing him round his head with all his might, but the harder he swung the more quickly the tail slipped out of his hand. In spite of all he could do, the Hyena could not keep hold of the slippery tail, and before he knew what had happened, the Jackal had landed on the ground and was running away through the forest for dear life. As for the Hyena, he lost his grip so suddenly that he was upset entirely, and sat down hard against. a tree. And as for the other animals, they were so surprised that not one of them started to run after the Jackal until he was out of sight.

The Jackal never came back to disturb the waters of the pool. A long time after every one who had helped to build it was dead, it was still known to all the animals of the forest, and it never was dry even in the hottest weather. But the Tortoises never forgot how the Jackal came to steal the water from the pool, and if you were to go there now you would probably find one of them on the bank, watching to see that no one troubles the waters.

THE RABBIT AND THE CROCODILE

LONG and long ago the creatures lived in towns like people, and had their own farms.

The Crocodile had a farm by the river, and he used to come up on land when he liked. One day, as he lay sunning himself on his farm, the Rabbit saw him.

"How do you do, Uncle?" said the Rabbit, edging up toward him. "You seem to be taking life easy. All you have to do is to sleep, and eat, and bathe, and enjoy yourself."

"Let me alone," grunted the Crocodile, who was sleepy. And he shut his eyes.

Close to the Crocodile's nose there grew a nice juicy bunch of young plantains.

"How good those leaves do look!" thought the Rabbit. "And there they grow and flourish under the very nose of a creature who never eats them. I wonder if I could not get just one good bite, and then run?"

The Rabbit crept up closer and closer, but just as he was going to nibble at the leaves, the Crocodile woke up and yelled at him.

"Get away from here, you little thief!" he roared, and he snapped so savagely with his sharp, white, pointed teeth that the Rabbit ran faster than he had ever thought he possibly could run, and never stopped until he reached home.

He told his wife and children about the selfish old Crocodile, who was so full of dinner that he could not keep awake and who would not let a hungry little Rabbit nibble the leaves that he did not want himself. When the little Rabbits heard why they had no supper that night, they had a great deal to say about the Crocodile.

"That is all very well," said the Rabbit, "but when a chicken is the judge, the cockroach gets no justice. We cannot depend on anyone else to punish the Crocodile; we must do it ourselves. Come, all of you, and get dry grass and leaves, and we will go and lay them in a circle around the Crocodile while he is asleep, and then we will set them on fire. We'll give him a fine scare."

Then all the Rabbits wriggled with joy and kicked up their heels at the thought of what was going to happen, and they gathered many armfuls of grass and leaves and laid them in a circle round the Crocodile. The fire was kindled, and it began to blaze up and smoke. The Rabbits hid themselves in the bushes and kept as still as stones.

Crackle—crackle—snap-snap-snap! went the fire, but the Crocodile did not wake up.

Snap! snap! snap! went the burning twigs, but the Crocodile did not wake up.

The smoke began to get thicker and blacker, until at last they could not see the Crocodile, but they heard him cough in his sleep. Then he turned over, and coughed again.

"Haugh! Haugh! What's the matter here? I can't breathe!" grunted the Crocodile.

Then he choked, and coughed, and opened his mouth so wide that a live coal flew into it. At that he woke up completely. He made a rush to get away from the fire, but found it in front of him. He turned round, and saw it still in front of him, while at the same time it was behind him scorching the end of his tail. Then he made one big jump and got out of the circle of fire, and his hide was so thick that he was hardly burned at all, but he was badly scared and very angry. When he heard all the squealing and laughter of the Rabbits in the bushes, he was so angry he could hardly speak.

"Don't you ever dare to come near the river again!" he shouted, and off he waddled as fast as he could go, to get into the cool water and put mud on his burned places.

"Don't you ever dare to come up here on the land again!" squealed the Rabbits, and they set about gathering the plantains and other vegetables on the Crocodile's farm where the fire had not come.

And from that day to this the Rabbits never go near the river if they can help it, and the Crocodile never goes far from the river if he can help it. He does not like to be reminded of the time when he was caught in the fire by a trick and the Rabbits laughed at him, for the news went from one tongue to another, and the Crocodile has never heard the last of it.

VII. THE MASAI

THE Masai tribe, formerly a bloodthirsty nomadic people of British and German East Africa, are now becoming colonized by the white races. Their stories are quaint and contrast strongly with the humour of the Alo Man.

THE WARRIORS AND THE MONKEYS

SOME warriors once wished to go and raid, so they consulted a medicine-man before starting, and were told that if they killed any monkeys on the road, the expedition would prove a failure.

One of the warriors was a coward, and when he heard what had been predicted, he made up his mind if a chance presented itself to kill a monkey.

On the road the warriors saw two monkeys and called one another's attention to them. The coward also saw them, and stayed behind on the pretext of having broken his sandal. He waited until his companions had passed on, and then killed one of the monkeys which, being ill, was unable to run away. He afterward rejoined the other warriors, and they continued their journey.

In the meantime the monkey which had escaped returned to its dead comrade and lamented its loss. "O! my brother," it said, "I tried to persuade you to run away, and you said you were not able. Then the cursed one came and killed you. O! my brother."

When the warriors reached the country they intended to attack, they saw one of the inhabitants sitting under a stone trapping rock-rabbits. They crept up to him and threw a club at him. Although the club hit the mark, the man only complained of the flies that bit him. Another club was thrown with a like result. The man then turned round and, seeing the warriors, sprang at them, and although unarmed put them to flight.

The warriors at once knew that the coward had killed the monkey contrary to the medicine-man's advice, and they put him to death on the spot.

THE WOMEN AND THE CHILDREN
OF THE SYCAMORE TREE

THERE was once a woman who had no husband, and she lived for many days in trouble. One day she said to herself: "Why do I always feel so troubled? It is because I have neither children nor husband. I will go to the medicine-man and get some children."

She went to the medicine-man and told him she was unhappy owing to the fact that although she had now grown old she had neither husband nor children. The medicine-man asked her which she wanted, husband or children; and she told him she wanted children.

She was instructed to take some cooking-pots—three or as many as she could carry—and to search for a fruit-bearing sycamore, to fill the pots with the fruit, to put them in her hut, and to go for a walk.

The woman followed out these instructions implicitly. She gathered the fruit, filled the pots, placed them in her hut, and went for a walk till the evening.

On arriving near the kraal, she heard the sound of voices and asked herself: "Why does one hear the voices of children in the kraal?" She approached nearer, and found her hut filled with children, all her work finished, the boys herding the cattle, the hut swept clean by the girls, the warriors singing and dancing on the common, and the little children waiting to greet her. She thus became a rich woman, and lived happily with her children for many days. One day, however, she scolded the children, and reproached them with being children of the tree. They remained silent and did not speak to her; then, when she went to see her friends in the other kraals, they returned to the sycamore tree, and became fruit again. On her return to her own kraal, the woman wept bitterly when she found it empty, and paid another visit to the medicine man, whom she taxed with having spirited away her children. The medicine-man told her that he did not know what she should do now, and when she proposed to go and look at the sycamore tree, he recommended her to try.

She took her cooking-pots to the tree and climbed up into it. But when she reached the fruit they all put forth eyes and stared at her. This so startled her that she was unable to descend, and her friends had to come and help her down.

She did not go to the tree again to search for children.

THE OSTRICH CHICKS

THERE was once upon a time an ostrich, which, having laid some eggs, hatched them, and reared the chicks.

One day a lion came, and took the chicks away and hid them. The mother bird followed the thief and demanded her young ones; but the lion refused to give them up and drove her away. She appealed to the counsellors, but they were afraid of the lion, and decided that the chicks were his. The ostrich then went to call a meeting of all the animals. When she arrived at the place where the mongoose lived, he told her to go and dig a hole under an ant-hill with two exits. This she did, and then collected all the animals at this spot. Like the counsellors, however, they feared the lion, and said the chicks were his. When it came to the mongoose's turn to be asked, he cried out: "We have never seen hairs beget feathers. Think what you are saying. The chicks are the ostrich's." And having said that, he jumped down the hole under the ant-hill, and escaped at the other end. The lion jumped after him, and not knowing of the second exit, waited for him to come out of the hole by which he had entered. As time wore on, the lion became hungry, but he still kept watch, for he thought that if he went to search for food the mongoose would get away. At length he died, and the ostrich recovered her chicks.

AMERICA

I. ESKIMO TALES

THESE stories reflect the struggles of the people for a livelihood. There is a great charm about the incident of the Crow and the Day light, which cannot fail to impress the hearer. In the story entitled "The Running Stick" it will be noticed that the ice and the frost, usually great adverse forces, are instrumental in helping the poor man. In this northern land the bear is appropriately the king of beasts. Indeed the Lapps consider him as being akin to man rather than as a beast. They say that he has the strength of ten men and the wit of twelve. Yet he was overcome by the little Robin Redbreast.

THE CROW AND THE DAYLIGHT

LONG, long ago, when the world was new, there was no daylight in Alaska. It was dark all the time, and the people in Alaska were living in the dark, just doing the best they could. They used to quarrel about whether it was day or night. Half the people slept while the other half worked; in fact, no one really knew when it was time to go to bed, or if in bed when to get up, because it was dark all the time.

In one village lived a crow. The people liked this crow because they thought him very wise; in fact, he told them so himself; so they let him live in their *kasga*.

The crow used to talk a lot, too, and tell of all the wonderful things he had seen and done, when he had spread his wings and flown away on his long journeys to distant lands. The people of Alaska had no light but the flame of their seal-oil lamps.

One evening the crow seemed very sad and did not speak at all. The people wondered what was the matter, and felt sad too, because they missed their lively crow, so they asked him: "Crow, what makes you so sad?"

"I am sorry for the people of Alaska," said the crow, "because they have no daylight."

"What is daylight?" said they. "What is it like? We have never heard of daylight."

"Well," said the crow, "if you had daylight in Alaska you could go everywhere and see everything, even animals from far away."

This seemed very wonderful to them all, and they asked the crow if he would try to get them that "daylight." At first the crow refused all their entreaties. "I know where it is," said he, "but it would be too hard for me to get it here."

Then they all crowded round and begged him to go to the place where daylight was and bring them some. Still the crow refused, and said he could not possibly get that light; but they coaxed him nicely, and the chief said, "Oh, Crow, you are so clever and so brave, we know you can do that."

At last the crow said, "Very well, I will go."

The next day he started on his journey. Of course, it was dark, but it was not stormy, and when he had said good-bye to all the people he spread his wings and flew away toward the East, for the sun comes from the East. He flew on and on in the dark, until his wings ached and he was very tired, but he never stopped. After many days he began to see a little bit, dimly at first, then more and more, until the sky was flooded with light.

Perching on the branch of a tree to rest, he looked about him to see if he could find where the light came from. At last he saw that it was shining from a big snow-house in a village near by.

Now in that snow-house lived the chief of the village, and that chief had a daughter who was very beautiful. This daughter came out of the house every day to fetch water from the ice-hole in the river; which is the only way the Eskimos can get fresh water in winter. After she had come out the crow slipped off his skin and hid it in the entrance of the house; then he covered himself with dust, and said some magic words, which sounded something like this:

> "Ya-ka-ty, ta-ka-ty, na-ka-ty-o.
> Make me little that I won't show.
> Only a tiny speck of dust,
> No one will notice me, I trust."

Then he hid on a sunbeam in a crack near the door, and waited for the chief's daughter. When she had filled her seal-skin water-bag she came back from the river, and the crow, who looked like nothing but a speck of dust floating on the sunbeam, lighted on her dress and passed with her through the door into the house where the daylight came from.

Inside, the place was very bright and sunny, and there was a dear little dark-eyed baby playing on the floor, on the skin of a polar bear which had recently been killed.

That baby had a lot of little toys, carved out of walrus ivory. There were tiny dogs and foxes, and little walrus heads, and *kayaks*. He kept putting the toys into an ivory box with a cover, then spilling them out again.

The chief was watching the baby very proudly, but the little one did not seem satisfied with his toys.

When the chief's daughter came in she stooped to pick the baby from the floor, and a little speck of dust drifted from her dress to the baby's ear. The dust was the crow, of course.

The baby began to cry and fuss, and the chief said, "What do you want?" and the crow whispered into the child's ear, "Ask for the daylight to play with." The baby asked for the daylight, and the chief told his daughter to give the baby a small, round daylight to play with.

The woman unwound the raw-hide string from his hunting bag and took out a small wooden chest covered with pictures, which told the story of the brave things the chief had done. From the chest she took a shining ball, and gave it to the child.

The baby liked the shining ball, and played with it a long time; but the crow wanted to get that daylight, so he whispered in the little one's ear to ask for a string to tie to his ball. They gave the baby a string, and tied the daylight to it for him; then the chief and his daughter went out, leaving the door open behind them, much to the delight of the crow, who was waiting for just that chance.

When the little boy got near the door in his play the crow whispered again in his ear, and told him to creep out into the entrance with his daylight.

The baby did as the crow told him, and as he passed the spot where the crow's skin was hidden the speck of dust slipped out of the child's ear back into the crow's skin, and the crow was himself again. Seizing the end of the string in his beak, away flew Mr. Crow, leaving the howling baby on the ground.

The child's cries brought the chief and his daughter and all the people of the village rushing to the spot; and they saw the crow flying away with their precious daylight. In vain they tried to reach him with their arrows, but he was too quickly out of sight.

When the crow came near the land of Alaska he thought he would try the daylight to see how it worked, so when he passed over the first dark village he scratched a little bit of the brightness off, and it fell on the village and lighted it up beautifully. Then at every village he came to he did the same thing, until at last he reached his home village, where he had started from. Hovering over it, he shattered the daylight into little bits, and scattered them far and wide.

The people greeted him with shouts of delight. They were so happy that they danced and sang, and prepared a great feast in his honour. They were so grateful to him that they couldn't thank him enough for bringing that daylight.

The crow told them that if he had taken the big daylight it would never be dark in Alaska, even in winter, but he said that the big daylight would have been too heavy for him to carry.

The people have always been thankful to the crow since then, and never try to kill him.

THE RUNNING STICK

LONG ago, in the village of Na-ki-a-ki-a-mute, there lived a strong man, or chief with his wife, to whom he was very devoted. They had no children, but among their neighbours was a little girl who lived in a tiny house with her grandmother. These two were very poor, but the chief was rich, and the chief's wife loved the little girl and had her often with her. Indeed, the child used to come every day to fetch water for the chief's wife, from the water-hole through the ice in the river near by.

One day the man went off hunting, and when he came back with a fine fat seal for their food his wife was gone. He called and called her, but she did not answer. Then he went to all his neighbours seeking her, but no one had seen her, and no trace of her could he find anywhere. There was not even a footprint to show in which direction she had gone. The poor man was nearly crazy with grief and anger, for he felt sure someone must have taken his wife away from him. He became fierce and sullen, brooding over his troubles and loneliness, and would speak to no one. In fact, no one dared to come near him for fear of being killed.

All day long he would sit out in front of his house with his big bow and quiver full of arrows, watching; and at night he did not sleep, nor could he eat.

One day the old grandmother said to the little girl, "I am sorry for that poor man; he is so unhappy. You go to him and ask him to come and eat with us. His wife loved you. He will not hurt you. Try to bring him back with you."

Very timidly the little girl obeyed, for in her heart she was afraid to go. When she got near the chief's house she stopped and felt like turning back, for he sat there looking so fierce and gloomy that she was frightened; but when he saw the child standing there he motioned to her to come. Then she felt no longer afraid, but went and sat beside him, and told him what her grandmother had said. The chief answered nothing, but when she slipped her little hand into his he got up and went with her to her home, where the old woman had already cooked him a fine supper of reindeer meat.

The poor man had not eaten for so long that he was starving, and, when he had finished all the meat the old woman had, he sent the little girl to his own house to get some more.

As soon as the little one had gone out of the room the grandmother said to him, "I sent for you because you have been kind to us, and I believe I can help you to find your wife. You must make a good strong staff of driftwood, then take this bunch of charms, and tie it firmly to the stick," and she gave him a little bunch of charms. These charms were ivory animals and faces and some tufts of feathers from sea-birds.

Next she said that he must set the stick upright in the ground, in front of his house, very firmly, so that the wind could not blow it over. When he had done this he should go to bed and sleep. In the morning he must examine the stick carefully, and go in the direction in which the stick leaned. Wherever he stopped for the night he must set the stick up in the same way, and in the morning the stick would point in the direction he must follow to find his wife.

"If you obey my instructions," said she, "the stick will lead you straight to your wife."

Then the little girl came in with some more reindeer meat, and the man ate until he was satisfied, and went home.

As soon as he reached his house he made a fine staff, tied the charms to it, and planted it firmly in the ground before the door. Then he went in, and rolling himself up in a big bear-skin, fell asleep.

He woke up in the morning feeling well rested, and more like himself than at any time since his wife's disappearance. It was late, and the sun had already risen. He hurried out anxiously to look at his stick. It was bent directly toward the north, so he pulled it up and started on his journey, with the staff moving along before him.

For two days and two nights he travelled without rest, having a hard time to keep up with that stick, which hopped along in front of him. Then, being tired, he stuck the staff into the ground and went to sleep.

When he awoke the stick was again pointing north. This time it leaned over more than before. For three days and nights he travelled, then he slept, and in the morning his faithful staff was bending right over, still toward the north. "Now my wife cannot be very far away," he thought.

That night he slept again, and when he awoke, the staff had leaned so far over that the tip almost touched the ground; so he felt sure he must be near his journey's end.

About noon, when the sun hung very round and very red, low down in the sky, he came to a huge snow-house, the biggest house he had ever seen. Right by the house stood four posts close together, and on these posts was hung the skin of an enormous bird.

Hiding himself among some willow-bushes, he watched to see what would happen.

Pretty soon a very tall man came out of the house and went to the posts. Climbing up on them, he took the skin, put it on, and flew away over the sea.

When the bird-man was out of sight our friend took his faithful staff and went into the house. There he found his wife, who was very happy to see him. "I knew you would come and find me," she said. "That terrible big bird carried me away in his claws; that is why you could not find my footprints in the snow."

Her husband wanted her to come home with him at once, but she told him that it would be better if she could first see the bird-man, who would soon come back again. Her plan was to send the bird-man on some far distant flight, so that they might get away during his absence. She gave her husband some food, and he went back to his hiding-place to wait for the bird-man to come and go.

After a short time the bird came back with a walrus in one claw and a seal in the other. Flying to the rack, he took off the bird-skin, hung it up, and went into the house. When he came in he found the woman crying. "What do you want?" said he. "I want a white whale and a hump-back whale. I didn't want any seal. I am tired of seal and walrus meat. Boo-hoo!" and she howled and wailed dismally.

"Only be quiet," said the bird-man, "and I will get you what you want." And he came out again and, putting on his bird-skin, once more flew out over the sea.

When the bird was out of sight the woman ran from the house to her husband, who put her on his back, and started for home as fast as he could go. He was the swiftest runner in his village, and covered the ground pretty fast; but, after all, legs are not wings. It was not long before they met the bird-man coming back with a whale in each of his talons. When he saw the man carrying the 'woman away on his back the bird was very angry, and, circling about in the air over their heads, called out to them, "I shall kill you. First, however, I am going to take these two whales home; then I shall come back and kill you." And away he flew.

The man ran as fast as he could, but just as they reached the banks of a big river the bird came in sight.

The man and his wife dug a cave in the river bank, and hid in it while the bird flew by looking for them. Nowhere could the big bird find those two people, although he was sure they must be hiding somewhere near by. Suddenly he circled about, and flew down to the water. "I shall set my great wing across the river like a dam, and the water will rise and drown them," cried he; so he stretched his great wing across the river and the water rose over the wing, and crept nearer and nearer to where the man and his wife were hidden.

The two poor people were in despair. They thought that surely they would be drowned, when suddenly the man remembered his father, who was a witch-doctor, and some magic words came to his mind:

> "Kluk-a-luk.
> Muk-a-luk.
> Puk-a-luk.
> Freeze up hard,
> Or you must run dry."

He said these words over three times aloud. At that moment the water of the river began to freeze. It was the month called *Naz-ze-rak-sek* by the Eskimos, which means October.

At last the river froze so hard and solid that the bird's wing was frozen fast into the ice, and he could not pull it out. Then the husband killed the wicked bird, and, plucking one of the long feathers from its wing for a charm, took his wife safely home without any further trouble.

They brought the old grandmother and the little girl to live with them, and they were all happy the whole winter long with the meat of the big bird for food.

II. THE NORTH-AMERICAN INDIANS

THE presence of many tribes among these Indians makes it difficult to generalize on the subject of their folk-tales. Some tribes are war like, others live by the chase, some depend on agriculture for sustaining life. The Indian is usually proud and reserved, serious, courageous, and dignified. Often gloomy in his views of life, he is comparatively indifferent to wit or pleasantry. He is extremely cautious, kind, and hospitable to strangers, yet revengeful and cruel to enemies. These characteristics can be traced clearly in his folk-tales. These stories have been told by many a squaw to her children as they crouched inside their wigwams or sat round the camp fire.

THE WONDERFUL KETTLE

TWO brothers lived in the wilderness far from all human habitation. The elder brother went into the forest to hunt game, while the younger stayed at home and tended the hut, cooked the food, and gathered firewood.

One evening the tired hunter returned from the chase, and the younger brother took the game from him as usual and dressed it for supper. "I will smoke awhile before I eat," said the hunter, and he smoked in silence for a time. When he was tired of smoking he lay down and went to sleep.

"Strange," said the boy; "I should have thought he would want to eat first."

When the hunter awoke he found that his brother had prepared the supper and was waiting for him. "Go to bed," said he; "I wish to be alone."

Wondering much, the boy did as he was bidden, but he could not help asking himself how his brother could possibly live if he did not eat. In the morning he observed that the hunter went away without tasting any food, and on many succeeding mornings and evenings the same thing happened.

"I must watch him at night," said the boy to himself, "for he must eat at night, since he eats at no other time."

That same evening, when the lad was told as usual to go to bed, he lay down and pretended to be sound asleep, but all the time one of his eyes was open. In this cautious fashion he watched his brother, and saw him rise from his couch and pass through a trap-door in the floor, from which he shortly emerged bearing a rusty kettle, the bottom of which he scraped industriously. Filling it with water, he set it on the blazing fire. As he did so, he struck it with a whip, saying at every blow: "Grow larger, my kettle!"

The obedient kettle became of gigantic proportions, and after setting it aside to cool the man ate its contents with evident relish.

His watchful younger brother, well content with the result of his observation, turned over and went to sleep.

When the elder had set off next morning, the boy, filled with curiosity, opened the trap-door and discovered the kettle. "I wonder what he eats," he said, and there within the vessel was half a chestnut! He was rather surprised at this discovery, but he thought to himself how pleased his brother would be if on his return he found a meal to his taste awaiting him. When evening drew near he put the kettle on the fire, took a Whip, and, hitting it repeatedly, exclaimed: "Grow larger, my kettle!"

The kettle grew larger, but to the boy's alarm it kept on growing until it filled the room, and he was obliged to get on the roof and stir it through the chimney.

"What are you doing up there?" shouted the hunter, when he came within hail.

"I took your kettle to get your supper ready," answered the boy.

"Alas!" cried the other, "now I must die!"

He quickly reduced the kettle to its original size and put it in its place. But he still wore such a sad and serious air that his brother was filled with dismay, and prayed that he might be permitted to undo the mischief he had wrought.

When the days went past and he found that his brother no longer went out to hunt or displayed any interest in life, but grew gradually thinner and more melancholy, his distress knew no bounds.

"Let me fetch you some chestnuts," he begged earnestly. "Tell me where they may be found."

"You must travel a full day's journey," said the hunter in response to his entreaties. "You will then reach a river which is most difficult to ford. On the opposite bank there stands a lodge, and near by a chestnut tree. Even then your difficulties will only be begun. The tree is guarded by a white heron, which never loses sight of it for a moment. He is employed for that purpose by the six women who live in the lodge, and with their war-clubs they slay anyone who has the temerity to approach. I beg of you, do not think of going on such a hopeless errand." But the boy felt that were the chances of success even more slender he must make the attempt for the sake of his brother, whom his thoughtlessness had brought low.

He made a little canoe about three inches long, and set off on his journey, in the direction indicated by his brother. At the end of a day he came to the river, whose size had not been underestimated. Taking his little canoe from his pocket, he drew it out till it was of a suitable length, and launched it in the great stream. A few minutes sufficed to carry him to the opposite bank, and there he beheld the lodge and the chestnut tree. On his way he had managed to procure some seeds of a sort greatly liked by herons, and these he scattered before the beautiful white bird strutting round the tree. While the heron was busily engaged in picking them up the young man seized his opportunity and gathered quantities of the chestnuts, which were lying thickly on the ground. Ere his task was finished, however, the heron perceived the intruder, and called a loud warning to the women in the lodge, who were not slow to respond. They rushed out with their fishing lines in their hands, and gave chase to the thief. But fear, for his brother as well as himself, lent the youth wings, and he was well out on the river in his canoe when the shrieking women reached the bank. The eldest threw her line and caught him, but with a sharp pull he broke it. Another line met with the same fate, and so on, until all the women had thrown their lines. They could do nothing further, and were obliged to watch the retreating canoe in impotent rage.

At length the youth, having come safely through the perils of the journey, arrived home with his precious burden of chestnuts. He found his brother still alive, but so weak that he could hardly speak. A meal of the chestnuts, however, helped to revive him, and he quickly recovered.

THE HEALING WATERS

IT was winter, the snow lay thickly on the ground, and there was sorrow in the encampment, for with the cold weather a dreadful plague had visited the people. There was not one but had lost some relative, and in .some cases whole families had been swept away. Among those who had been most sorely bereaved was Nekumonta, a handsome young brave, whose parents, brothers, sisters and children had died one by one before his eyes, the while he was powerless to help them. And now his wife, the beautiful Shanewis, was weak and ill. The dreaded disease had laid its awful finger on her brow, and she knew that she must shortly bid her husband farewell and take her departure for the place of the dead. Already she saw her dead friends beckoning to her and inviting her to join them, but it grieved her terribly to think that she must leave her young husband in sorrow and loneliness. His despair was piteous to behold when she broke the sad news to him, but after the first outburst of grief he bore up bravely, and determined to fight the plague with all his strength.

"I must find the healing herbs which the Great Manitou has planted," said he. "Wherever they may be, I must find them."

So he made his wife comfortable on her couch, covering her with warm furs, and then, embracing her gently, he set out on his difficult mission. All day he sought eagerly in the forest for the healing herbs, but every where the snow lay deep, and not so much as a blade of grass was visible. When night came he crept along the frozen ground, thinking that his sense of smell might aid him in his search. Thus for three days and nights he wandered through the forest, over hills and across rivers, in a vain attempt to discover the means of curing the malady of Shanewis.

When he met a little scurrying rabbit in the path he cried eagerly: "Tell me, where shall I find the herbs which Manitou has planted?"

But the rabbit hurried away without reply, for he knew that the herbs had not yet risen above the ground, and he was very sorry for the brave.

Nekumonta came by and by to the den of a big bear, and of this animal also he asked the same question. But the bear could give him no reply, and he was obliged to resume his weary journey. He consulted all the beasts of the forest in turn, but from none could he get any help. How could they tell him, indeed, that his search was hopeless?

On the third night he was very weak and ill, for he had tasted no food since he had first set out, and he was numbed with cold and despair. He stumbled over a withered branch hidden under the snow, and so tired was he that he lay where he fell, and immediately went to sleep. All the birds and the beasts, all the multitude of creatures that inhabit the forest, came to watch over his slumbers. They remembered his kindness to them in former days, how he had never slain an animal unless he really needed it for food or clothing, how he had loved and protected the trees and the flowers. Their hearts were touched by his courageous fight for Shanewis, and they pitied his misfortune. All that they could do to aid him they did. They cried to the Great Manitou to save his wife from the plague which held her, and the Great Spirit heard the manifold whispering and, responded to their prayers.

While Nekumonta lay asleep there came to him the messenger of Manitou, and he dreamed. In his dream he saw his beautiful Shanewis, pale and thin, but as lovely as ever, and as he looked she smiled at him, and sang a strange, sweet song, like the murmuring of a distant waterfall. Then the scene changed, and it really was a waterfall he heard. In musical language it called him by name, saying: "Seek us, O Nekumonta, and when you find us Shanewis shall live. We are the Healing Waters of the Great Manitou."

Nekumonta awoke with the words of the song still ringing in his ears. Starting to his feet, he looked in every direction; but there was no water to be seen, though the murmuring sound of a waterfall was distinctly audible. He fancied he could even distinguish words in it.

"Release us!" it seemed to say. "Set us free, and Shanewis shall be saved!"

Nekumonta searched in vain for the waters. Then it suddenly occurred to him that they must be underground, directly under his feet. Seizing branches, stones, flints, he dug feverishly into the earth. So hard was the task that before it was finished he was completely exhausted. But at last the hidden spring was disclosed, and the waters were rippling merrily down the vale, carrying life and happiness wherever they went. The young man bathed his aching limbs in the healing stream, and in a moment he was well and strong. Raising his hands, he gave thanks to Manitou. With eager fingers he made a jar of clay, and baked it in the fire, so that he might carry life to Shanewis. As he pursued his way homeward with his treasure his despair was changed to rejoicing and he sped like the wind.

When he reached his village his companions ran to greet him. Their faces were sad and hopeless, for the plague still raged. However, Nekumonta directed them to the Healing Waters and inspired them with new hope. Shanewis he found on the verge of the Shadow-land, and scarcely able to murmur a farewell to her husband. But Nekumonta did not listen to her broken adieux. He forced some of the Healing Water between her parched lips, and bathed her hands and her brow till she fell into a gentle slumber. When she awoke the fever had left her, she was serene and smiling, and Nekumonta's heart was filled with a great happiness.

The tribe was forever rid of the dreaded plague, and the people gave to Nekumonta the title of "Chief of the Healing Waters," so that all might know that it was he who had brought them the gift of Manitou.

THE BOY MAGICIAN

IN the heart of the wilderness there lived an old woman and her little grandson. The two found no lack of occupation from day to day, the woman busying herself with cooking and cleaning, and the boy with shooting and hunting. The grandmother frequently spoke of the time when the child would grow up and go out into the world.

"Always go to the east," she would say. "Never go to the west, for there lies danger."

But what the danger was she would not tell him, in spite of his importunate questioning. Other boys went west, he thought to himself, and why should not he? Nevertheless, his grandmother made him promise that he would not go west.

Years passed by, and the child grew to be a man, though he still retained the curiosity and high spirits of his boyhood. His persistent inquiries drew from the old grandmother a reluctant explanation of her warning.

"In the west," said she, "there dwells a being who is anxious to do us harm. If he sees you it will mean death for both of us."

This statement, instead of frightening the young Indian, only strengthened in him a secret resolution he had formed to go west on the first opportunity. Not that he wished to bring any misfortune on his poor old grandmother, any more than on himself, but he trusted to his strong arm and clear head to deliver them from their enemy. So with a laugh on his lips he set off to the west.

Toward evening he came to a lake, where he rested. He had not been there long when he heard a voice saying: "Aha, my fine fellow, I see you!"

The youth looked all round him, and up into the sky above, but he saw no one.

"I am going to send a hurricane," the mysterious voice continued, "to break your grandmother's hut to pieces. How will you like that?"

"Oh, very well," answered the young man gaily. "We are always in need of firewood, and now we shall have plenty."

"Go home and see," the voice said mockingly. "I daresay you will not like it so well."

Nothing daunted, the young adventurer retraced his steps. As he neared home a great wind sprang up, seeming to tear the very trees out by the roots.

"Make haste!" cried the grandmother from the doorway. "We shall both be killed !"

When she had drawn him inside and shut the door she scolded him heartily for his disobedience, and bewailed the fate before them. The young man soothed her fears, saying: "Don't cry, grandmother. We shall turn the lodge into a rock, and so we shall be saved."

Having some skill in magic, he did as he had said, and the hurricane passed harmlessly over their heads. When it had ceased they emerged from their retreat, and found an abundance of firewood all round there.

Next day the youth was on the point of setting off toward the west once more, but the urgent entreaties of his grandmother moved him to proceed eastward— for a time. Directly he was out of sight of the lodge he turned his face once more to the west. Arrived at the lake, he heard the voice once more, though its owner was still invisible.

"I am going to send a great hailstorm on your grandmother's hut," it said. "What do you think of that?"

"Oh," was the response, "I think I should like it. I have always wanted a bundle of spears."

"Go home and see," said the voice.

Away the youth went through the woods. The sky became darker and darker as he neared his home, and just as he was within a bow-shot of the little hut a fierce hailstorm broke, and he thought he would be killed before he reached shelter.

"Alas!" cried the old woman when he was safely indoors, "we shall be destroyed this time. How can we save ourselves?"

Again the young man exercised his magic powers, and transformed the frail hut into a hollow rock, upon which the shafts of the hailstorm spent themselves in vain. At last the sky cleared, the lodge resumed its former shape, and the young man saw a multitude of sharp, beautiful spear-heads on the ground.

"I will get poles," said he, "to fit to them for fishing."

When he returned in a few minutes with the poles he found that the spears had vanished.

"Where are my beautiful spears?" he asked his grandmother.

"They were only ice-spears," she replied. "They have all melted away."

The young Indian was greatly disappointed, and wondered how he could avenge himself on the being who had played him this malicious trick.

"Be warned in time," said the aged grandmother, shaking her head at him. "Take my advice and leave him alone."

But the youth's adventurous spirit impelled him to see the end of the matter, so he took a stone and tied it round his neck for a charm, and sought the lake once again. Carefully observing the direction from which the voice proceeded, he saw in the middle of the lake a huge head with a face on every side of it.

"Aha! uncle," he exclaimed, "I see you! How would you like it if the lake dried up?"

"Nonsense !" said the voice angrily, "that will never happen."

"Go home and see," shouted the youth, mimicking the mocking tone the other had adopted on the previous occasions. As he spoke he swung his charmed stone round his head and threw it into the air. As it descended it grew larger and larger, and the moment it entered the lake the water began to boil.

The lad returned home and told his grandmother what he had done.

"It is of no use," said she. "Many have tried to slay him, but all have perished in the attempt."

Next morning our hero went westward again, and found the lake quite dry, and the animals in it dead, with the exception of a large green frog, who was in reality the malicious being who had tormented the Indian and his grandmother. A quick blow with a stick put an end to the creature, and the triumphant youth bore the good news to his old grandmother, who from that time was left in peace and quietness.

THE SNAKE OGRE

ONE day a young brave, feeling at variance with the world in general, and wishing to rid himself of the mood, left the lodges of his people and journeyed into the forest. By and by he came to an open space, in the centre of which was a high hill. Thinking he would climb to the top and reconnoitre, he directed his footsteps thither, and as he went he observed a man coming in the opposite direction and making for the same spot. The two met on the summit, and stood for a few moments silently regarding each other.

The stranger was the first to speak, gravely inviting the young brave to accompany him to his lodge and sup with him. The other accepted the invitation, and they proceeded in the direction the stranger indicated.

On approaching the lodge the youth saw with some surprise that there was a large heap of bones in front of the door. Within sat a very old woman tending a pot. When the young man learned that the feast was to be a cannibal one, however, he declined to partake of it. The woman thereupon boiled some corn for him, and while doing so told him that his host was nothing more nor less than a snake-man, a sort of ogre who killed and ate human beings. Because the brave was young and very handsome the old woman took pity on him, bemoaning the fate that would surely befall him unless he could escape from the wiles of the snake-man.

"Listen," said she: "I will tell you what to do. Here are some moccasins. When the morning comes, put them on your feet, take one step, and you will find yourself on that headland you see in the distance. Give this paper to the man you will meet there, and he will direct you further. But remember that however far you may go, in the evening the Snake will overtake you. When you have finished with the moccasins take them off, place them on the ground facing this way, and they will return."

"Is that all?" said the youth,

"No," she replied. "Before you go you must kill me and put a robe over my bones."

The young brave forthwith proceeded to carry these instructions into effect. First of all he killed the old woman, and disposed of her remains in accordance with her bidding. In the morning he put on the magic moccasins which she had provided for him, and with one great step he reached the distant headland. Here he met an old man, who received the paper from him, and then, giving him another pair of moccasins, directed him to a far-off point where he was to deliver another piece of paper to a man who would await him there. Turning the first moccasins homeward, the young brave put the second pair to use, and took another gigantic step. Arrived at the second stage of his journey from the Snake's lodge, he found it a repetition of the first. He was then directed to another distant spot, and from that to yet another. But when he delivered his message for the fourth time he was treated somewhat differently.

"Down there in the hollow," said the recipient of the paper, "there is a stream. Go toward it, and walk straight on, but do not look at the water."

The youth did as he was bidden, and shortly found himself on the opposite bank of the stream. He journeyed up the creek, and as evening fell he came upon a place where the river widened to a lake. Skirting its shores, he suddenly found himself face to face with the Snake. Only then did he remember the words of the old woman, who had warned him that in the evening the Snake would overtake him. So he turned himself into a little fish with red fins, lazily moving in the lake.

The Snake, high up on the bank, saw the little creature, and cried: "Little Fish! have you seen the person I am looking for? If a bird had flown over the lake you must have seen it, the water is so still, and surely you have seen the man I am seeking?"

"Not so," replied the Little Fish, "I have seen no one. But if he passes this way I will tell you." So the Snake continued downstream, and as he went there was a little grey toad right in his path.

"Little Toad," said he, "have you seen him for whom I am seeking? Even if only a shadow were here you must have seen it."

"Yes," said the Little Toad, "I have seen him, but I cannot tell you which way he has gone."

The Snake doubled and came back on his trail. Seeing a very large fish in the shallow water, he said: "Have you seen the man I am looking for?"

"That is he with whom you have just been talking," said the Fish, and the Snake turned homeward. Meeting a musk-rat, he stopped.

"Have you seen the person I am looking for?" he said. Then, having his suspicions aroused, he added craftily: "I think that you are he." But the Musk-rat began a bitter complaint.

"Just now," said he, "the person you seek passed over my lodge and broke it." So the Snake passed on, and encountered a red-breasted turtle.

He repeated his query, and the Turtle told him that the object of his search was to be met with farther on.

"But beware," he added, "for if you do not recognize him he will kill you."

Following the stream, the Snake came upon a large green frog floating in shallow water.

"I have been seeking a person since morning," he said. "I think that you are he." The Frog allayed his suspicions, saying: "You will meet him farther down the stream."

The Snake next found a large turtle floating among the green scum on a lake.

Getting on the Turtle's back, he said: "You must be the person I seek," and his head rose higher and higher as he prepared to strike.

"I am not," replied the Turtle. "The next person you meet will be he. But beware, for if you do not recognize him he will kill you."

When he had gone a little farther down the Snake attempted to cross the stream. In the middle was an eddy. Crafty as he was, the Snake failed to recognize his enemy, and the eddy drew him down into the water and drowned him. So the youth succeeded in slaying the Snake who had sought throughout the day to kill him.

THE ORIGIN OF FIRE

THE Karok had plenty of food, but there was no fire to cook it with. Far away toward the rising sun, somewhere in a land which no Karok had ever seen, Kareya had made fire and hidden it in a casket, which he gave to two old hags to keep, lest some Karok should steal it. So now the coyote befriended the Karok, and promised to bring them some fire.

He went out and got together a great company of animals of every kind, from the lion down to the frog. These he stationed in a line all along the road from the home of' the Karok to the far-distant land where the fire was, the weakest animal nearest home and the strongest near the fire. Then he took an Indian with him and hid him under a hill, and went to the cabin of the hags who kept the casket, and rapped on the door. One of them came out, and he said, "Good evening," and they replied, "Good evening." Then he said, "it's a pretty cold night; can you let me sit by your fire?" And they said, "Yes, come in." So he went in and stretched himself out before the fire, and reached his snout out toward the blaze, and sniffed the heat and felt very snug and comfortable. Finally he stretched his nose out along his fore paws, and pretended to go to sleep, though he kept the corner of one eye open watching the old hags. But they never slept day or night, and he spent the whole night watching and thinking to no purpose. So next morning he went out and told the Indian, whom he had hidden under the hill, that he must make an attack on the hags' cabin, as if he were about to steal some fire, while he (the coyote) was in it. He then went back and asked the hags to let him in again, which they did, as they did not think a coyote would steal any fire. He stood close by the casket of fire, and when the Indian made a rush on the cabin, and the hags dashed out after him at one door, the coyote seized a brand in his teeth and ran out at the other door. He almost flew over the ground; but the hags saw the sparks flying and gave chase, and gained on him fast. But by the time he was out of breath he reached the lion, who took the brand and ran with it to the next animal, and so on, each animal barely having time to give it to the next before the hags came up.

The next to the last in the line was the ground squirrel. He took the brand and ran so fast with it that his tail got afire, and he curled it up over his back, and so burned the black spot we see to this day just behind his fore-shoulders. Last of all was the frog, but he, poor brute! couldn't run at all, so he opened his mouth wide and the squirrel chucked the fire into it, and he swallowed it down with a gulp. Then he turned and gave a great jump, but the hags were so close in pursuit that one of them seized him by the tail (he was a tad-pole then) and tweaked it off, and that is the reason why frogs have no tails to this day. He swam under water a long distance, as long as he could hold his breath, then came up and spit out the fire into a log of driftwood, and there it has stayed safe ever since, so that when an Indian rubs two pieces of wood together the fire comes forth.

THE CREATION OF MAN

AFTER the coyote had finished all the work of the world and the inferior creatures, he called a council of them to deliberate on the creation of man. They sat down in an open space in the forest all in a circle, with the lion at the head. On his right sat the grizzly bear, next the cinnamon bear, and so on around according to rank, ending with the little mouse, which sat at the lion's left. The lion was the first to speak, and he declared he should like to see man created with a mighty voice like himself, wherewith he could frighten all animals. For the rest he would have him well covered with hair, terrible fangs in his claws, strong talons, etc.

The grizzly bear said it was ridiculous to have such a voice as his neighbour, for he was always roaring with it, and scared away the very prey he wished to capture. He said the man ought to have prodigious strength, and move about silently, but very swiftly if necessary, and be able to grip his prey without making a noise.

The buck said the man would, in his way of thinking, look very foolish unless he had a magnificent pair of antlers on his head to fight with. He also thought it very absurd to roar so loudly, and he would pay less attention to a man's throat than he would to his ears and his eyes, for he would have the first like a spider's web, and the second like fire.

The mountain sheep protested he never could see what sense there was in such antlers branching every way only to be caught in the thickets. If the man had horns, mostly rolled up, they would be like a stone on each side of his head, giving it weight and enabling him to butt a great deal harder.

When it came to the coyote's turn to speak, he declared all these were the stupidest speeches he had ever heard, and that he could hardly keep awake while listening to such a pack of noodles and nincompoops. Every one of them wanted to make the man like himself. They might just as well take one of their own cubs and call it a man. As for himself, he knew he was not the best animal that could be made, and he could make one better than himself or any other. Of course the man would have to be like himself in having four legs, five fingers, etc. It was well enough to have a voice like the lion, only the man need not roar all the while with it. The grizzly bear had some good points, one of which was the shape of his feet, which enabled him easily to stand erect; and he was in favour, therefore, of making the man's feet nearly like the grizzly's. The grizzly, also, was happy in having no tail, for he had learned from his own experience that that organ was only a harbour for fleas. The buck's eyes and ears were pretty good, perhaps better than his own. Then there was the fish, which was naked, and which he envied, because hair was a burden most of the year; and he, therefore, favoured a man without hair. His claws ought to be as long as the eagle's, so that he could hold things in them. But after all, with all their separate gifts, they must acknowledge that there was no animal besides himself that had wit enough to supply the man, and he should be obliged, therefore, to make him like himself, in that respect also-cunning and crafty.

After the coyote had made an end, the beaver said he never heard such nonsense and twaddle in his life. No tail, indeed! He would make a man with a broad flat tail, so he could haul mud and sand on it.

The owl said all the animals seemed to have lost their senses, none of them wanted to give the man wings. For himself, he could not see of what use anything on earth could be to himself without wings.

The mole said it was perfect folly to talk about wings, for with them the man would be certain to bump his head against the sky. Besides that, if he had wings and eyes both, he would get his eyes burnt out by flying too near the sun; but without eyes he could burrow in the cool, soft earth and be happy.

Last of all, the little mouse squeaked out that he would make a man with eyes, of course, so that he could see what he was eating; and as for burrowing in the ground, that was absurd.

So the animals disagreed among themselves, and the council broke up in a row. The coyote flew at the beaver and nipped a piece out of his cheek; the owl jumped on top of the coyote's head and commenced lifting his scalp, and there was a high time. Every animal set to work to make a man according to his own ideas, and taking a lump of earth each one commenced moulding it like himself, but the coyote began to make one like he had described in the council. It was so late before they fell to work that nightfall came on before anyone had finished his model, and they all lay down and fell asleep. But the cunning coyote stayed awake and worked hard on his model all night. When all the other animals were sound asleep, he went around and poured water on their models, and so spoiled them. In the morning early he finished his model, and gave it life, long before the others could make new models; and thus it was that man was made by the coyote.

FABLE OF THE ANIMALS

A GREAT many hundred snows ago, Kareya, sitting on the Sacred Stool, created the world. First he made the fishes in the big water, then the animals on the green land, and last of all The Man. But the animals were all alike in power, and it was not yet ordained which should be for food to others, and which should be food for The Man. Then Kareya bade them all assemble together in a certain place, that The Man might give each his power and his rank. So the animals all met together, a great many hundred snows ago, on an evening when the sun was set, that they might wait over night for the coming of The Man on the morrow. Now Kareya commanded The Man to make bows and arrows, as many as there were animals, and to give the longest to the one that should have the most power, and the shortest to the one that should have the least. So he did, and after nine sleeps his work was ended, and the bows and arrows which he made were very many. Now the animals being gathered together in one place, went to sleep, that they might rise on the morrow and go forth to meet The Man. But the coyote was exceedingly cunning, above all the beasts that were, he was so cunning. So he considered within himself how he might get the longest bow, and so have the greatest power, and have all animals for his meat. He determined to stay awake all night, while the others slept, and so go forth first in the morning and get the longest bow. This he devised within his cunning mind, and then he laughed to himself and stretched out his snout on his forepaws, and pretended to sleep like the others. But about midnight he began to get sleepy, and he had to walk around camp and scratch his eyes a considerable time to keep them open. But still he grew more sleepy, and he had to skip and jump about like a good one to keep awake. He made so much noise this way that he woke up some of the other animals, and he had to think of another plan. About the time the morning star came up he was so sleepy that he couldn't keep his eyes open any longer. Then he took two little sticks, and sharpened them at the ends, and propped open his eyelids, whereupon he thought he was safe, and he concluded he would just take a little nap with his eyes open, watching the morning star. But in a few minutes he was sound asleep, and the sharp sticks pierced through his eyelids, and pinned them fast together.

So the morning star mounted up very swiftly, and then there came a peep of daybreak, and the birds began to sing, and the animals began to wake and rise, and stretch themselves, but still the coyote lay fast asleep. At last it was broad daylight, and then the sun rose, and all the animals went forth to meet The Man. He gave the longest bow to the cougar, so he had the greatest power of all; and the second longest to the bear; and so on, giving the next to the last to the poor frog. But he still had the shortest one left, and he cried out, "What animal have I missed?" Then the animals began to look about, and they soon spied the coyote lying fast asleep, with the sharp sticks pinning his eyelids together. Upon that all the animals set up a great laugh, and they jumped on the coyote and danced upon him. Then they led him to The Man—for he could see nothing because of the sticks—and The Man pulled out the sticks, and gave him the shortest bow of all, which would hardly shoot an arrow more than a foot. And all the animals laughed very much.

But The Man took pity on the coyote, because he was now the weakest of all animals, even than the frog, and he prayed to Kareya for him, and Kareya gave him cunning, ten times more than before, so that he was cunning above all the animals of the wood. So the coyote was a friend to The Man and to his children after him, and helped him, and did many things for him.

PUCK WUDJ ININEE
OR
HE OF THE LITTLE SHELL

ONCE upon a time all the inhabitants of the earth had died, excepting two helpless children, a baby boy and a little girl. When their parents died, these children were asleep. The little girl, who was the elder, was the first to awake. She looked around her, but seeing nobody but her little brother, who lay asleep, she quietly resumed her bed.

At the end of ten days her brother moved, without opening his eyes.

At the end of ten days more he changed his position, lying on the other side.

The girl soon grew up to woman's estate, but the boy increased in stature very slowly. It was a long time before he could even creep. When he was able to walk, his sister made him a little bow and arrows, and suspended around his neck a small shell, saying:

"You shall be called Wa-Dais-Ais-Imid or He of the Little Shell." Every day he would go out with his little bow, shooting at the small birds. The first bird he killed was a tom-tit. His sister was highly pleased when he took it to her. She carefully skinned and stuffed it, and put it away for him.

The next day he killed a red squirrel. His sister preserved this too. The third day he killed a partridge which she stuffed and set up. After this he acquired more courage and would venture some distance from home. His skill and success as a hunter daily increased, and he killed the deer, bear, moose, and other large animals inhabiting the forest. In time, he became a great hunter. He had now arrived to maturity of years but remained a perfect infant in stature. One day, walking about, he came to a small lake.

It was in the winter season. He saw a man on the ice killing beavers. He appeared to be a giant. Comparing himself to this great man, he appeared no bigger than an insect. He seated himself on the shore and watched his movements.

When the large man had killed many beavers, he put them on a hand-sled which he had, and pursued his way home. When he saw him retire, he followed him, and, wielding his magic shell, cut off the tail of one of the beavers and ran home with the trophy.

When the tall stranger reached his lodge with his sled-load of beavers, he was surprised to find the tail of one of them gone, for he had not observed the movements of the little hero of the shell.

The next day WA-DAIS-AIS-IMID went to the same lake. The man had already fixed his load of beavers on his sled and commenced his return. But he nimbly ran forward, and overtaking him, succeeded, by the same means, in securing another of the beavers' tails.

When the man saw that he had lost another of this most esteemed part of the animal, he was very angry. "I wonder," said he, "what dog it is, that has thus cheated me. Could I meet him, I would make his flesh quiver at the point of my lance."

Next day he pursued his hunting at the beaver-dam near the lake, and was followed again by the little man of the shell. On this occasion the hunter had used so much expedition, that he had accomplished his object and nearly reached his home before our tiny hero could overtake him. He nimbly drew his shell and cut off another beaver's tail.

In all these pranks he availed himself of his power of invisibility and thus escaped observation. When the man saw that the trick had been so often repeated, his anger was greater than ever. He gave vent to his feelings in words. He looked carefully around to see whether he could discover any tracks. But he could find none. His unknown visitor had stepped so lightly as to leave no track.

Next day the giant resolved to disappoint him, by going to his beaver pond very early. When WA-DAIS-AIS-ÍMID reached the place, he found the fresh traces of his work, but he had already returned. He followed his tracks, but failed to overtake him. When he came in sight of the lodge, the stranger was in front of it, employed in skinning his beavers.

As he stood looking at him, he thought: "I will let him see me."

Presently the man, who proved to be no less a personage than Manabozho, looked up and saw him. After regarding him with attention Manabozho said: "Who are you, little man? I have a mind to kill you."

The little hero of the shell replied:

"If you were to try to kill me you could not do it."

At this Manabozho tried to capture him, but Little Shell vanished each time.

When he returned home he told his sister that they must separate. "I must go away," said he, "it is my fate. You too," he added, "must go away soon. Tell me where you would wish to dwell." She said, "I would like to go to the place of the breaking of daylight. I have always loved the East. The earliest glimpses of light are from that quarter, and it is to my mind the most beautiful part of the heavens. After I get there, my brother, whenever you see the clouds, in that direction, of various colours, you may think that your sister is painting her face."

"And I," said he, "my sister, shall live on the mountains and rocks. There I can see you at the earliest hour and there the streams of water are clear and the air is pure. And I shall ever be called 'Puck Wudj Ininee,' or the 'Little Wild Man of the Mountains.' But," he resumed, "before we part forever, I must go and try to find some Manitoes."

He left her and travelled over the surface of the globe, and then went far down into the earth. He had been treated well wherever he went. At last he found a giant Manito, who had a large kettle, which was forever boiling. The giant regarded him with a stern look, and then took him up in his hand and threw him unceremoniously into the kettle. But by the protection of his personal spirit, he was shielded from harm, and with much ado got out of it and escaped.

He returned to his sister and related his rovings and misadventures. He finished his story by addressing her thus:

"My sister, there is a Manito at each of the four corners of the earth. There is also one above them, far in the sky, and last," continued he, "there is another and wicked one, who lives deep down in the earth. We must now separate. When the winds blow from the four corners of the earth, you must then go. They will carry you to the place you wish. I go to the rocks and mountains, where my kindred will ever delight to dwell."

He then took his bull-stick and commenced running up a high mountain, whooping as he went.

Presently the winds blew and as he predicted, his sister was borne by them to the eastern sky, where she has ever since been and her name is the Morning Star.

Blow, winds, blow! my sister lingers
For her dwelling in the sky,
Where the morn, with rosy fingers,
Shall her cheeks with vermil dye.

There my earliest views directed,
Shall from her their colour take,
And her smiles, through clouds reflected,
Guide me on by wood or lake.

While I range the highest mountain,
Sport in valleys green and low,
Or, beside our Indian fountains,
Raise my tiny hip-hallo.

AGGO DAH GAUDA
OR
THE MAN WITH HIS LEG TIED UP

OGGO DAH GAUDA had one leg looped up to his thigh, so that he was obliged to get along by hopping. He had a beautiful daughter, and his chief care was to secure her from being carried off by the king of the buffaloes. He differed from other Indians in that he lived in a log house and he advised his daughter to keep within door, and never go out into the neighbourhood for fear of being stolen away.

One sunshiny morning Aggo Dah Gauda prepared to go out a-fishing; but before he left the lodge he reminded his daughter of her strange and persecuting lover, whom she had never seen. "My daughter," said he, "I am going out to fish, and as the day will be a pleasant one you must recollect that we have an enemy near, who is constantly going about and do not expose yourself out of the lodge." When he had reached the fishing-ground, he heard a voice singing at a distance the following song, mocking him:

"Man with the leg tied up,
Man with the leg tied up,
Broken hip- hip-
Hipped.

"Man with the leg tied up,
Man with the leg tied up,
Broken leg- leg-
Legged."

He saw no one, but suspecting it to come from his enemies the buffaloes, he hastened home.

Meantime, the daughter had no sooner been left alone in the lodge than she thought in her mind, "It is hard to be thus forever kept indoors. The spring is now coming on, and the days are so sunny and warm that it would be very pleasant to sit out of doors. But my father says it would be dangerous. I know what I will do. I will get on the top of the house, and there I can comb and dress my hair, and no one can harm me." She accordingly got up on the roof of the small house and busied herself in untying and combing her beautiful hair, for her hair was not only of a fine, glossy quality, but was so very long that it reached down on the ground, over the eaves of the house, as she sat dressing it.

She was so intent upon this that she forgot all ideas of danger, till it was too late to escape. For all of a sudden the king of the buffaloes came dashing on with his herd of followers, and taking her between his horns, away he cantered over the plains, plunged into a river that bounded his land, and bore her safely to his lodge on the other side.

Here he paid every attention to gain her affections, but all to no purpose, for she sat pensive and disconsolate in the lodge among the other women. She scarcely ever spoke, and took no part in the affairs of the king's household. He, on the contrary, did everything he could think of to please her and win her affections.

The king told the others in his lodge to give to Aggo's daughter everything that she wanted, and to be careful not to displease her. They set before her the choicest food. They gave her the seat of honour in the lodge. The king himself went out hunting to obtain the most dainty bits of meats both of animals and wild fowl. And not content with these proofs of his attachment, the king would sometimes fast from all food, and he would often take his Indian flute, sit near the lodge, and repeat in pensive notes:

> "My sweetheart,
> My sweetheart,
> Ah me!
> When I think of you,
> When I think of you,
> Ah me!

> "How I love you,
> How I love you,
> Ah me!
> Do not hate me,
> Do not hate me,
> Ah me!"

In the meantime Aggo Dah Gauda came home, and finding that his daughter had been stolen, determined to get her back. For this purpose he immediately set out. He could easily track the buffalo-king until he came to the banks of the river, where he saw that he had plunged in and swum over. But there had been a frosty night or two since, and the water was so covered with thin ice that he could not walk on it. He determined to encamp hard by till it became more solid, and then crossed over and pursued the trail.

As he went along he saw branches broken off and strewed behind, for these had been purposely cast along by the daughter that the way might be found. And the manner in which she had accomplished it was this. Her hair was all untied when she was caught up, and being very long, it caught on the branches as they darted along, and it was these twigs that she broke off for signs to her father.

When he came to the king's lodge it was evening. Carefully approaching it, he peeped through the sides, and saw his daughter sitting disconsolately. She immediately caught his eye, and knowing that it was her father come for her, she all at once appeared to relent in her heart, and asking for the royal dipper, said to the king: "I will go and get you a drink of water." This token of submission delighted him, and he waited with impatience for her return. At last he went out with his followers, but nothing could be seen or heard of the captive daughter. They sallied out in the plains, but had not gone far, by the light of the moon, when a party of hunters, headed by the father-in-law of Aggo Dah Gauda, set up their yells in their rear, and a shower of arrows was poured in upon them.

Many of their numbers fell, but the king being stronger and swifter than the rest, fled toward the west, and never again appeared in that part of the country.

While all this was passing Aggo Dab Gauda, who had met his daughter the moment she came out of the lodge, and being helped by his guardian spirit, took her on his shoulders and hopped off, a hundred steps in one, till he reached the stream, crossed it and brought back his daughter in triumph to his lodge.

III. LOUISIANA

LOUISIANA is now one of the Gulf States of the American Union and includes the lower course of the Mississippi River. In 1682 La Salle sailed down the river and claimed the country for France, naming it Louisiana in honour of Louis XIV. Since then its career has been a troublous one. It was ceded to Spain, then returned to France, and sold to the United States by Napoleon in 1765. The population is very mixed, more than half in the country districts being of negro origin.

These tales are genuine folk-tales—no personal touches have been added by the collector. Many of the animal stories are of African origin while the fairy tales, or *Märchen,* are attributed to Indian influences. These tales were told to children by child-like people—this accounts for their *naïveté.* It is interesting to notice that here Compair Lapin (the "Brer Rabbit" of negro fame) also gains the victory by his cunning ways.

COMPAIR LAPIN AND THE EARTHWORM

IT was a day in spring, the little birds were singing, the butterflies were flying about from one flower to another. It seemed as if all animals were rendering thanks to God for his kindness to them. A little earthworm was the only one which was crying and complaining. He said he was so small, he had neither feet, nor hands, nor wings, and was obliged to remain in his hole. The little birds, the lizards, and even the ants were troubling him and eating his little ones. If God would make him big and strong, like other animals, then he would be contented, because he would be able to defend himself, while now he was helpless in his hole. He cried and cried and said he would be glad if he belonged to the Devil. Hardly had he spoken when he saw the Devil at his side.

"Well, I heard all you said; tell me what you want; I shall grant it to you, and you will belong to me when you die."

"What I want?—Yes.—I want strength, I want to become big, big, and beat everybody who will come to trouble and bother me. Give me only that and I shall be satisfied."

"That is all right," said the Devil; "let me go, in a short while you will be contented."

As soon as the Devil had gone, the worm found himself strong and big. The change had come suddenly, and his hole had become large and as deep as a well. The worm was so glad that he began to laugh and to sing. At that very moment Lapin passed, and he was terribly frightened. He ran until he was unable to go any farther, and, when he stopped, he whistled, "fouif." "Never," said he, "was I more frightened. I shall never sleep again as long as that big earthworm will remain in this country. If I had not been so foolish as to boast that I could beat the elephant, I should go to him. It is Bouki who told on me; but perhaps if I speak to him I shall be able to fix up matters. I must try to make them meet and fight, and perhaps I shall get rid of both at the same time. It would be a pretty fight. Let me go and see the elephant, or I won't be able to sleep to-night. Besides, the earthworm said that he would fix me. I can't live that way. Good gracious! what am I to do? Let me arrange in my head what I am going to tell the elephant in order to please him."

He went on until he met the elephant. He bowed very politely, and the elephant did likewise, and asked him how he was.

"Oh! I am very sick," said Compair Lapin; "another time I shall come to try my strength with you; I think I can beat you."

"You are a fool," said the elephant. "Go away, I don't want to harm you; I take pity on you."

"I bet you," said Compair Lapin, "that I can beat you." "All right, whenever you want."

"A little later; but as I know you are good, I had come to ask you a favour." "What is it?"

"It is to help me, to give me a hand to carry lumber to build my cabin."

"Let us go right off, if you want."

Compair Lapin, who had carried his axe with him, cut down a big tree, and said to the elephant: "Take it by the big end. I shall raise the branches, and we shall carry the tree to the place where I wish to build my cabin."

The elephant put the tree on his shoulder without looking behind him, and Compair Lapin climbed into the branches, and let the elephant do all the work. When the latter was tired he would stop to rest a little, and Compair Lapin would jump down and run up to the elephant to encourage him. "How is that, Compair, you are already tired; but that is nothing. Look at me, who have been working as much as you. I don't feel tired."

"What! That is mightily heavy," said the elephant.

"Let us go," said Lapin; "we have not far to go."

The big animal put the load again on his back and Compair Lapin appeared to be lifting the branches. Whenever the elephant would not be looking Lapin would sit on a branch and say: "A little farther; go to the right, go to the left."

At last they came to the hole of the earthworm, and Lapin told the elephant to put down the tree. He let it fall right upon the worm, who was sleeping. The latter pushed out the tree as if it were a piece of straw, and coming out he began to insult the elephant. Compair Lapin went to hide in a place where he could see and hear all. The elephant lost patience and struck the worm with his trunk.

The worm then climbed up the back of the elephant, and there was a terrible fight for more than two hours, until they were nearly dead. The worm finally hid in his hole, and the elephant lay down dying. Compair Lapin mounted upon him, pulled his ears, and beat him, and said to him: "Didn't I tell you I would beat you?"

"Oh! yes, Compair Lapin; I have enough; I am dying."

Lapin then left him, and, going into the worm's hole, he broke his head with a stick. "Now," said he, "I am rid of both of them."

A little later Compair Lapin met Compair Bouki and told him how he had made the elephant and the earthworm fight until they had killed one another. "You see, my friend, when two fellows are in your way, you must make them fight, then you will always save your skin."

COMPAIR LAPIN AND COMPAIR L'OURS

ONE day Compair l'Ours invited Compair Lapin and Compair Bouki to dine with him. He told them he had bought butter, cheese, and biscuits, but he said: "Before dinner you must come to help me break some corn for my horse."

Compair Lapin and Compair Bouki accepted the invitation of Compair l'Ours, and all three went into the field before daybreak.

At nine o'clock they saw Compair Lapin prick up his ears. "What is the matter?" said Compair l'Ours.

"I never saw anything so annoying as the people at my house. They are calling me and disturbing me in my work."

"I don't hear anything," said Compair l'Ours.

"It is because you and Compair Bouki have such small ears that you can't hear. My ears are so long that I hear miles away."

He went away and came back a moment later, saying it was for his wife who was beginning to be sick. He did the same thing three times during the day. At noon he said his wife was in the middle of her sickness, at three o'clock he came back very sad, and said merely: "All is finished."

Compair l'Ours and Compair Bouki pitied him very much because they thought it was his wife who was dead. Instead of that, each time Compair Lapin had said he was going to his wife's house he went to the house of Compair l'Ours and ate a little of his provisions, and when he said: "It is finished," he had finished eating all. At five o'clock the three friends left their work and went to the house of Compair l'Ours. You may imagine how Compair l'Ours was angry when he saw that all his provisions had disappeared. Immediately he accused Compair Lapin, but he swore it was not he.

"I shall know right off all three of us will go and lie down on that plank which is in the water in the sun, and the thief will surely be sick." Compair Lapin, who was very impudent, said yes, because he expected to lie down in the shade by the side of Compair l'Ours, who was much larger than he. Compair Bouki said yes also.

They went to the plank, and Compair Lapin was not pleased when he saw that it was the stage of a boat, and he would not be able to stick to Compair l'Ours to be in the shade. They lay down on the plank, at a distance from one another, and no sooner were they there when Compair Lapin felt very sick on account of the water and the sun, and he began to throw up all that he had eaten.

"Ah! I have caught you, comrade," said Compair l'Ours. "You will pay for that, and I'm going to hang you."

"Hang me if you wish, I don't care," said Compair Lapin, "but if you want I shall give you a good way. Make a hole in the wall, pass the rope through it, you and Compair Bouki will not be in the sun to pull the rope to hang me. While you will be hanging me I shall cry, and when I shall not cry it will be a sign I have no voice left and I shall be dead."

Compair l'Ours did what Compair Lapin had said and tied him, but when Compair l'Ours and Compair Bouki were in the house, he untied himself and hung by his feet. Compair l'Ours pulled on the rope, Compair Lapin cried loud, then so low that Compair l'Ours and Compair Bouki thought he was dead, and they went to see on the other side of the wall. They only saw the dust Compair Lapin was making, and they heard his voice saying: "You see I am smarter than you, and I thank you for the good dinner I had at your house."

COMPAIR BOUKI AND THE MONKEYS

COMPAIR BOUKI put fire under his kettle, and when the water was very hot he began to beat his drum and cry out:

"Sam-bombel! Sam-bombel tam!
Sam-bombel! Sam-bombel tam!"

The monkeys heard and said: "What? Bouki has something good to eat, let us go," and they ran up to Bouki and sang: "Molése cherguinet, chouvan! Chéguillé, chouvan!" Compair Bouki then said to the monkeys: "I shall enter into the kettle, and when I say, `I am cooked,' you must take me out." He jumped into the kettle, and the monkeys pulled him out as soon as he said, "I am cooked."

The monkeys, in their turn, jumped into the kettle, and cried out, immediately on touching the water, "We are cooked." Bouki, however, took his big blanket, and covering the kettle, said: "if you were cooked you could not say so." One little monkey alone escaped, and Bouki ate all the others. Some time after this Compair Bouki was hungry again, and he called the monkeys:

"Sam-bombel! Sam-bombel tam!
Sam-bombel ! Sam-bombel tam!"

When the monkeys came, he jumped into the kettle again and said, "I am cooked, I am cooked."

The monkeys, however, who had been warned by the little monkey which had escaped the first time, did not pull Bouki out, but said: "if you were cooked you could not say so."

MR. MONKEY THE BRIDEGROOM

THERE was a monkey which fell in love with a beautiful young girl. He dressed as a man and went to call on her. He was so well received that one day he took his best friend with him to see his lady-love. The young girl's father asked Mr. Monkey's friend some questions about his daughter's lover. The friend said that Mr. Monkey was good and rich, but there was a secret about him. The father wanted to know the secret, but the friend said he would tell him another day. Mr. Monkey was finally engaged to the young lady, and the night of the wedding he invited his friend to the supper. The latter was jealous of Mr. Monkey, and at the end of the supper he began to sing. This was a song that made all monkeys dance, whether they wished to or not, so Mr. Monkey looked at his friend and beckoned him to stop singing. He continued, however, to sing, and all at once Mr. Monkey got up and began to dance. He jumped about so wildly that his tail came out of his clothes, and everyone saw that he was a monkey. The father under stood the secret, and beat him dreadfully. His friend, however, ran off dancing and singing.

THE TORTOISE

A GENTLEMAN who was living on the banks of a bayou caught a large tortoise, and went immediately to invite some friends to take dinner with him. His little boy, in his absence, went to the cage where was the tortoise, and the latter began to whistle. "How well you whistle!" said the child. "Oh! that is nothing; open the cage, and you will see." The boy opened the cage, and the tortoise whistled better than ever. The boy was delighted. "Put me down on the floor and you will see," said the tortoise. The boy did so, and the tortoise danced and sang. "Oh! how well you dance and sing!" said the boy. "Put me on the bank of the bayou, and you will see," said the tortoise. The boy took her to the bayou, and the tortoise danced and sang. All at once she disappeared in the water, and the boy began to cry. The tortoise rose in the middle of the bayou and said: "Learn not to trust, hereafter, people whom you do not know."

The boy was afraid of his father, and put a large flat stone into the cage. The cook, thinking it was the tortoise, put the stone into the kettle. She was astonished to see it remain hard so long, and she called the master's attention to it. He ordered the tortoise to be put upon the table, and he took his table knife to cut it. It was in vain. He took the carving-knife, in vain. He took the hatchet, in vain. He took the axe, he broke the dishes, the table, but the tortoise remained intact. He then saw it was a stone, and to this day he has not understood how his tortoise was changed to a stone.

COMPAIR BOUKI, COMPAIR LAPIN, AND THE BIRDS' EGGS

COMPAIR BOUKI and Compair Lapin were neighbours. One day Compair Bouki said to himself that he wished to see what Compair Lapin was cooking every evening in his cabin. He went to Compair Lapin's cabin and saw a big kettle on the fire. "Oh! what a toothache I have! Compair Lapin, what do you have in that kettle?"

"It is not your business, Compair Bouki."

"What smells so good in that kettle, Compair Lapin? Oh! what a toothache I have!"

"It is birds' eggs, Compair Bouki; don't bother me."

"Oh! what a toothache I have! Let me taste what you have here. It will cure me."

Compair Lapin gave him a few eggs, and Compair Bouki found them so good that he wished to know where they were to be found. Compair Lapin told him he would take him with him the next day.

Compair Bouki went home and told his mother that he had a splendid supper at Compair Lapin's. His mother told him to open his mouth that she might smell what it was that he had eaten. She then took a small piece of wood and scraped off the teeth of Compair Bouki the small pieces of egg that remained there.

"Oh! how good it is," she said; "you must get me some."

Compair Bouki went early the next morning with Compair Lapin, who showed him where the eggs were and told him not to take more than one from each nest, because the birds would perceive it. Compair Bouki, however, as soon as Lapin was gone, took all the eggs from every nest. When the birds returned and saw that all the eggs had been stolen, they were furious, and formed a plan to avenge themselves. There was in the wood a bayou which was the only place where the animals could drink. The birds placed themselves around the bayou and saw an ox coming.

"Compair Bef, was it you who ate our eggs?"

"No, my friends, I eat nothing but grass."

The horse said he ate nothing but hay. Compair Lapin said that he ate nothing but carrots and lettuce; but when they questioned Compair Bouki, he replied boastfully and foolishly:

"Yes, it is I who ate your eggs."

No sooner had he spoken when the birds fell upon him; they put out his eyes and nearly tore him to pieces.

IV. MEXICO AND PERU

AMERICA is sometimes spoken of as "a continent without a history," but this is not true concerning the Maya race in Central America. These people possessed arts and industries of their own invention, and bore the stamp of an origin of considerable antiquity. They were the supreme intellectual race of America. Our knowledge of the mythology of the Maya is derived from a book called the *Popol Vuh,* or "The Collection of Written Leaves." It is of native compilation, the only native American work of this part which has come down to us from pre-Columbian times. This seventeenth-century book was lost for a long time and then was found in 1854 in the University of San Carlos in Guatemala.

In comparing these myths with those of other races, one is struck by the sense of strangeness and remoteness pervading the American stories. The Maya story of the creation is perhaps unique. Hurakan, the mighty wind, passed over the universe, still wrapped in gloom. He cried out "Earth" and the solid land appeared. Then the chief gods took counsel and decided to make the mother and father gods. Later animals were created; then it was decreed that man should be formed. The gods made a number of mannikins carved out of wood. But these afterward be came irreverent and angered the gods, who resolved to bring about their downfall. First a mighty flood came upon the earth, then thick resinous rain. Their eyes were destroyed, and all their body was ground to powder. Everything both great and small abused the mannikins. The household utensils and domestic animals jeered at them. The dogs and hens bit them. The millstones in revenge said, "You tormented us, making us screech, screech by day and night, now we will grind you." The cups and platters said, "Pain and misery you gave us, smoking our tops and sides, burning and hurting us, now we will bind you."

The poor mannikins ran hither and thither in their despair. They mounted upon the roofs of the houses, but the houses crumbled beneath their feet; they tried to climb to the tops of the trees, but the trees hurled them down; they were even repulsed by the caves, which closed before them. Thus were they all destroyed, the only vestiges of them that remain are certain of their offspring, the little monkeys, which dwell in the woods.

VUKUB-CAKIX, THE GREAT MACAW

ERE the earth was quite recovered from the wrathful flood which had descended upon it there lived a being orgulous and full of pride, called Vukub-Cakix (Seven-times-the-colour-of-fire—the Kiche name for the great macaw bird). His teeth were of emerald, and other parts of him shone with the brilliance of gold and silver. He boasted dreadfully, and his conduct so irritated the other gods that they resolved upon his destruction. His two sons, Zipacna and Cabrakan (Cockspur or Earth-heaper, and Earthquake), were earthquake-gods. These also were prideful and arrogant, and to cause their downfall the gods dispatched the heavenly twins Hun-Apu and Xbalanque to earth, with instructions to chastise the trio.

Vukub-Cakix prided himself upon his possession of the wonderful nanze-tree, the tapal, bearing a fruit round, yellow, and aromatic, upon which he break fasted every morning. One morning he mounted to its summit, whence he could best espy the choicest fruits, when he was surprised and infuriated to observe that two strangers had arrived there before him, and had almost denuded the tree of its produce. On seeing Vukub, Hun-Apu raised a blow-pipe to his mouth and blew a dart at the giant. It struck him on the mouth, and he fell from the top of the tree to the ground. Hun-Apu leapt down upon Vukub and grappled with him, but the giant in terrible anger seized the god by the arm and wrenched it from the body. He then returned to his house, where he was met by his wife, Chimalmat, who inquired for what reason he roared with pain. In reply he pointed to his mouth, and so full of anger was he against Hun-Apu that he took the arm he had wrenched from him and hung it over a blazing fire. He then threw himself down to bemoan his injuries, consoling himself, however, with the idea that he had avenged himself upon the disturbers of his peace.

Whilst Vukub-Cakix moaned and howled with the dreadful pain which he felt in his jaw and teeth (for the dart which had pierced him was probably poisoned) the arm of Hun-Apu hung over the fire, and was turned round and round and basted by Vukub's spouse, Chimalmat. The sun-god rained bitter imprecations upon the interlopers who had penetrated to his paradise and had caused him such woe, and he gave vent to dire threats of what would happen if he succeeded in getting them into his power.

But Hun-Apu and Xbalanque were not minded that Vukub-Cakix should escape so easily, and the recovery of Hun-Apu's arm must be made at all hazards. So they went to consult two great and wise magicians, Xpiyacoc and Xmucane, who advised them to proceed with them in disguise to the dwelling of Vukub, if they wished to recover the lost arm. The old magicians resolved to disguise themselves as doctors, and dressed Hun-Apu and Xbalanque in other garments to represent their sons.

Shortly they arrived at the mansion of Vukub, and while still some way off they could hear his groans and cries. Presenting themselves at the door, they accosted him. They told him that they had heard some one crying out in pain, and that as famous doctors they considered it their duty to ask who was suffering.

Vukub appeared quite satisfied, but closely questioned the old wizards concerning the two young men who accompanied them.

"They are our sons," they replied.

"Good," said Vukub. "Do you think you will be able to cure me?"

"We have no doubt whatever upon that head," answered Xpiyacoc. "You have sustained very bad injuries to your mouth and eyes."

"The demons who shot me with an arrow from their blow-pipe are the cause of my sufferings," said Vukub. "If you are able to cure me shall reward you richly."

"Your Highness has many bad teeth, which must be removed," said the wily old magician. "Also the balls of your eyes appear to me to be diseased." Vukub appeared highly alarmed, but the magicians speedily reassured him.

"It is necessary," said Xpiyacoc, "that we remove your teeth, but we will take care to replace them with grains of maize, which you will find much more agreeable in every way."

The unsuspicious giant agreed to the operation, and very quickly Xpiyacoc, with the help of Xmucane, removed his teeth of emerald, and replaced them by grains of white maize. A change quickly came over the Titan. His brilliancy speedily vanished, and when they removed the balls of his eyes he sank into insensibility and died.

All this time the wife of Vukub was turning Hun-Apu's arm over the fire, but Hun-Apu snatched the limb from above the brazier, and with the help of the magicians replaced it upon his shoulder. The discomfiture of Vukub was then complete. The party left his dwelling feeling that their mission had been accomplished.

THE EARTH GIANTS

BUT in reality it was only partially accomplished, because Vukub's two sons, Zipacna and Cabrakan, still remained to be dealt with. Zipacna was daily employed in heaping up mountains, while Cabrakan, his brother, shook them in earthquake. The vengeance of Hun-Apu and Xbalanque [1] was first directed against Zipacna, and they conspired with a band of young men to bring about his death. The young men, four hundred in number, pretended to be engaged in building a house. They cut down a large tree, which they made believe was to be the roof-tree of their dwelling, and waited in a part of the forest through which they knew Zipacna must pass. After a while they could hear the giant crashing through the trees. He came into sight, and when he saw them standing round the giant tree-trunk, which they could not lift, he seemed very much amused.

"What have you there, O little ones?" he said, laughing.

---

[1] Little Tiger.

"Only a tree, your Highness, which we have felled for the roof-tree of a new house we are building."

"Cannot you carry it?" asked the giant disdainfully.

"No, your Highness," they made answer; "it is much too heavy to be lifted even by our united efforts."

With a good-natured laugh the Titan stooped and lifted the great trunk upon his shoulder. Then, bidding them lead the way, he trudged through the forest, evidently not disconcerted in the least by his great burden. Now the young men, incited by Hun-Apu and Xbalanque, had dug a great ditch, which they pretended was to serve for the foundations of their new house. Into this they requested Zipacna to descend, and, scenting no mischief, the giant readily complied. On his reaching the bottom his treacherous acquaintances cast huge trunks of trees upon him, but on hearing them coming down he quickly took refuge in a small side tunnel which the youths had constructed to serve as a cellar beneath their house. Imagining the giant to be killed, they began at once to express their delight by singing and dancing, and to lend colour to his stratagem Zipacna dispatched several friendly ants to the surface with strands of hair, which the young men concluded had been taken from his dead body. Assured by the seeming proof of his death, the youths proceeded to build their house upon the tree-trunks which they imagined covered Zipacna's body, and, producing a quantity of *pulque*,[2] they began to make merry over the end of their enemy. For some hours their new dwelling rang with revelry.

All this time Zipacna, quietly hidden below, was listening to the hubbub and waiting his chance to revenge himself upon those who had entrapped him.

Suddenly arising in his giant might, he cast the house and all its inmates high in the air. The dwelling was utterly demolished, and the band of youths were hurled with such force into the sky that they remained there, and in the stars we call the Pleiades we can still discern them wearily waiting an opportunity to return to earth.

THE UNDOING OF ZIPACNA

BUT Hun-Apu and Xbalanque, grieved that their comrades had so perished, resolved that Zipacna must not be permitted to escape so easily. He, carrying the mountains by night, sought his food by day on the shore of the river, where he wandered catching fish and crabs. The brothers made a large artificial crab, which they placed in a cavern at the bottom of a ravine. They then cunningly undermined a huge mountain, and awaited events.

---

[2] The universal Mexican beverage.

Very soon they saw Zipacna wandering along the side of the river, and asked him where he was going.

"Oh, I am only seeking my daily food," said the giant.

"And what may that consist of?" asked the brothers.

"Only of fish and crabs," replied Zipacna.

"Oh, there is a crab down yonder," said the crafty brothers, pointing to the bottom of the ravine. "We espied it as we came along. Truly, it is a great crab, and will furnish you with a capital breakfast."

"Splendid!" cried Zipacna, with glistening eyes. "I must have it at once," and with one bound he leapt down to where the cunningly contrived crab lay in the cavern.

No sooner had he reached it than Hun-Apu and Xbalanque cast the mountain upon him; but so desperate were his efforts to get free that the brothers feared he might rid himself of the immense weight of earth under which he was buried, and to make sure of his fate they turned him into stone. Thus at the foot of Mount Meahüan, near Vera Paz, perished the proud Mountain-Maker.

THE DISCOMFITURE OF CABRAKAN

NOW only the third of this family of boasters remained, and he was the most proud of any.

"I am the Overturner of Mountains!" said he.

But Hun-Apu and Xbalanque had made up their minds that not one of the race of Vukub should be left alive. At the moment when they were plotting the overthrow of Cabrakan he was occupied in moving mountains. He seized the mountains by their bases and, exerting his mighty strength, cast them into the air; and of the smaller mountains he took no account at all. While he was so employed he met the brothers, who greeted him cordially.

"Good day, Cabrakan," said they. "What may you be doing?"

"Bah! nothing at all," replied the giant. "Cannot you see that I am throwing the mountains about, which is my usual occupation? And who may you be that ask such stupid questions? What are your names?"

"We have no names," replied they. "We are only hunters, and here we have our blow-pipes, with which we shoot the birds that live in these mountains. So you see that we do not require names, as we meet no one."

Cabrakan looked at the brothers disdainfully, and was about to depart when they said to him: "Stay; we should like to behold these mountain-throwing feats of yours."

This aroused the pride of Cabrakan.

"Well, since you wish it," said he, "I will show you how I can move a really great mountain. Now, choose the one you would like to see me destroy, and before you are aware of it I shall have reduced it to dust."

Hun-Apu looked around him, and espying a great peak pointed toward it. "Do you think you could overthrow that mountain?" he asked.

"Without the least difficulty," replied Cabrakan, with a great laugh. "Let us go toward it."

"But first you must eat," said Hun-Apu. "You have had no food since morning, and so great a feat can hardly be accomplished fasting."

The giant smacked his lips. "You are right," he said, with a hungry look. Cabrakan was one of those people who are always hungry. "But what have you to give me?"

"We have nothing with us," said Hun-Apu.

"Umph!" growled Cabrakan, "you are a pretty fellow. You ask me what I will have to eat, and then tell me you have nothing," and in his anger he seized one of the smaller mountains and threw it into the sea, so that the waves splashed up to the sky.

"Come," said Hun-Apu, "don't get angry. We have our blow-pipes with us, and will shoot a bird for your dinner."

On hearing this Cabrakan grew somewhat quieter. "Why did you not say so at first?" he growled. "But be quick, because I am hungry."

Just at that moment a large bird passed overhead, and Hun-Apu and Xbalanque raised their blow-pipes to their mouths. The darts sped swiftly upward, and both of them struck the bird, which came tumbling down through the air, falling at the feet of Cabrakan.

"Wonderful, wonderful!" cried the giant. "You are clever fellows indeed," and, seizing the dead bird, he was going to eat it raw when Hun-Apu stopped him.

"Wait a moment," said he. "It will be much nicer when cooked," and, rubbing two sticks together, he ordered Xbalanque togather some dry wood, so that a fire was soon blazing.

The bird was then suspended over the fire, and in a short time a savoury odour mounted to the nostrils of the giant, who stood watching the cooking with hungry eyes and watering lips. Before placing the bird over the fire to cook, however, Hun-Apu had smeared its feathers with a thick coating of mud.[1] But Hun-Apu had done this with a purpose. The mud that he spread on the feathers was that of a poisoned earth, called *tizate,* the elements of which sank deeply into the flesh of the bird. When the savoury mess was cooked, he handed it to Cabrakan, who speedily devoured it.

---

[1] The Indians in some parts of Central America still do this, so that when the mud dries with the heat of the fire the feathers will come off with it, leaving the flesh of the bird quite ready to eat.

THE DISCOMFITURE OF CABRAKAN

"Now," said Hun-Apu, "let us go toward that great mountain and see if you can lift it as you boast."

But already Cabrakan began to feel strange pangs.

"What is this?" said he, passing his hand across his brow. "I do not seem to see the mountain you mean."

"Nonsense," said Hun-Apu. "Yonder it is, see, to the east there."

"My eyes seem dim this morning," replied the giant.

"No, it is not that," said Hun-Apu. "You have boasted that you could lift this mountain, and now you are afraid to try."

"I tell you," said Cabrakan, "that I have difficulty in seeing. Will you lead me to the mountain?"

"Certainly," said Hun-Apu, giving him his hand, and with several strides they were at the foot of the eminence.

"Now," said Hun-Apu, "see what you can do, boaster."

Cabrakan gazed stupidly at the great mass in front of him. His knees shook together so that the sound was like the beating of a war drum, and the sweat poured from his forehead and ran in a little stream down the side of the mountain.

"Come," cried Hun-Apu derisively, "are you going to lift the mountain or not?"

"He cannot," sneered Xbalanque. "I knew he could not."

Cabrakan shook himself into a final effort to regain his senses, but all to no purpose. The poison rushed through his blood, and with a groan he fell dead before the brothers.

Thus perished the last of the earth-giants of Guatemala, whom Hun-Apu and Xbalanque had been sent to destroy.

V. THE PUEBLO INDIANS

THE Tay Tay was the aged story-teller of the Pueblo Indians of the Rio Grande Valley of New Mexico. They derive their name from the communal houses in which they used to live at the time of the first Spanish exploration. *Pueblo* is the Spanish word for 'people.' The Indians lived in houses two or three stories high, all joined so as to form one or two large, irregular, flat-topped buildings, with an open courtyard somewhere inside.

The people are superstitious and fatalistic. They deify and worship the forces of nature, believing in the immortality of animal as well as human hearts, except when the hearts are burned.

The wording of the songs introduced is generally meaningless. The physical life, especially of animals, seems to be a kind of masquerade to be put on and off at will. As in other stories one meets old friends and types, but the humour and guile banish any idea of monotony.

THE PINE GUM BABY

A LONG time ago a beautiful river, that ran through the Indian village of Taos, went dry; for no rain had fallen for months and months and months. There was no water anywhere to drink, except in one little spring; and that little spring belonged to a coyote.

One morning a rabbit passed by the coyote's spring.

"Good morning, Rabbit-man," said the coyote, "how are you getting along this dry weather? You must get very thirsty."

"Oh, no," replied the rabbit, "I get along fine. I have plenty of water, for I drink the dew from the cabbage leaves."

"But suppose the drought takes all the dew from the cabbage leaves, then what will you do?"

"I will find water somewhere else," replied the rabbit; and he hopped away.

Still there was no rain and everything was as dry as could be, except the coyote's spring. The rabbit grew very thirsty; so four days later when the coyote was away from home, the rabbit went to the coyote's spring and drank and drank the water. Later in the day the coyote met him: "Good day, Rabbit-man, how are you enjoying the dew from the cabbage leaves these days? Are you finding very much?" And the coyote threw back his head and laughed.

"Oh, I am finding enough!" and again the rabbit hopped away.

The next day the rabbit waited until the coyote went out to hunt for his dinner, then he went to the spring and drank and drank.

When the coyote came back home, he went to his spring for a There was very little water left in it. "Who has been taking my water?"[1] he growled. And then he saw rabbit tracks around the spring.

"So Rabbit-man has been stealing my water! That is why he is getting along so well this dry weather. I shall have to put an end to him."

So the coyote went out and found a piece of wood and cut out of it a baby animal. Then he got gum from the piñon trees and smeared it all over the baby. He put the gum baby beside the spring and hid himself in the bushes.

Very soon the rabbit came along for a drink at the coyote's spring. When he saw the gum baby, he bowed and said, "Hello, what are you doing here?" But the gum baby just sat still and said nothing. This made Mr. Rabbit angry.

"I say 'hello,' and if you don't speak to me politely I'll push you into the spring."

The gum baby did not say anything. Mr. Rabbit grew so angry that he grabbed the gum baby and pushed him into the water.

But the gum on the baby made the rabbit stick hard and fast to him; and when

---

[1] Note the value of water—it was considered a crime to steal water.

he fell into the spring, Mr. Rabbit fell in, too, and got a good ducking that he did not soon forget.

THE COYOTE AND THE FOX

O-WAY-WAY-HAM-BY-JOH, which means long time ago, a fox felt very hungry, so he went down into prairie-dog town and caught a fine fat prairie dog. Then he built a fire of dry rabbit brush. When the brush had all burned up and left a pile of coals, Mr. Fox took his prairie dog and covered him all up with the hot ashes. That was the way he always roasted meat for his dinner. It required some time for the prairie dog to roast, so Mr. Fox lay down and went to sleep.

Very soon Mr. Coyote came along. *Sniff! sniff!* he could smell meat roasting and it smelt very delicious. He saw Mr. Fox fast asleep; so he slipped quietly over to the pile of ashes, stuck his paw in and pulled out the prairie dog. He ran behind a bush and ate all of the meat off, but he left the bones. Then he took a bone and greased the fox's mouth all around with a greasy end of it. After that he put the bones back under the hot ashes and ran away.

When Mr. Fox awoke, he could smell prairie-dog grease. He licked his tongue out and tasted grease all around his mouth. "Surely I have not eaten the prairie dog while I was asleep. No, I feel too hungry; but where did this grease come from on my mouth, if I did not eat him?" Mr. Fox was very much puzzled. He went over to the ashes and caught hold of a prairie-dog foot and pulled. Out came a long leg bone without any meat on it. "This is funny," thought he.

Just then he spied some tracks in the sand. "Oho!" said he. "Now I understand it all. Coyote-man has played a trick on me and eaten my prairie dog. I'll catch him and kill him for this."

So Mr. Fox trotted off, following the coyote tracks. He found the coyote by a high cliff. Mr. Coyote saw Mr. Fox coming and he knew he was angry. He did not have time to run away, so he just leaned against the cliff and called, "Oh, Fox-man, come here quick and help me! Look up there, this cliff is falling! It will kill us both!" Mr. Fox looked up. The clouds were passing over the cliff and made the cliff look as if it were really falling. Mr. Fox jumped quickly over by Mr. Coyote and leaned against the cliff just as hard as he could to hold it up. As soon as Mr. Fox leaned on the cliff, Mr. Coyote jumped away. He made a big jump, just as if the cliff might really fall on him.

"Hold the cliff up, Fox-man, while I go to get a stick to prop it with."

Then Mr. Coyote ran away and left Mr. Fox leaning hard against the cliff.

Mr. Fox stayed there all day waiting for Mr. Coyote to come with the stick. Late that evening he looked up and there were no clouds passing, so he could see that the cliff was not falling. He knew that the coyote had played another trick on him, and he was angrier than ever.

Again he followed the coyote tracks and found the coyote down by the river.

When Mr. Coyote saw Mr. Fox coming, he called: "Oh, Fox-man, come quick and see what I have for you. I found a cheese and I saved half of it for you; but it has fallen into the river. Look!"

And Mr. Fox looked down into the water. There was the reflection of the half-moon in the water. It looked just like the half of a round cheese and Mr. Fox's mouth began to water for a taste of it. He was very hungry.

"I wonder how I can get that cheese!" he said. "I'll tell you how. Let me tie the end of this rope"—for Mr. Coyote had a rope all ready—"around your tail and tie the other end to this big stone. Then you can jump into the river and get the cheese. When you have got hold of it, call me, and I will pull you out."

Mr. Fox thought that was a good scheme, so he let Mr. Coyote tie the rope around his tail and around the stone. Then Mr. Fox jumped into the river with a big splash.

As soon as he did, Mr. Coyote threw the stone in after him, and if the rope had not slipped off of Mr. Fox's tail when it got wet, that would have been the end of poor old Mr. Fox.

THE COYOTE AND THE TURTLE

EARLY one morning, once upon a time, when the ground was cool and damp, a turtle crawled up out of his home in the river. He crawled along, hunting things to eat. He found so many good things that he crawled farther and farther away from the river. He forgot all about old Father Sun, who would come peeping up over the hills after a while. If he had been a wise little turtle, he would not have wandered so far from home. River turtles have to keep themselves damp. If they become too dry they cannot walk, and if the sun shines too hot upon them, they die.

Now while this little turtle was trudging slowly along, the sun came up and shone right down upon him. He turned around and started back to the river; but turtles travel so slowly and the sun was so hot, that he could only get half way there. When he saw what trouble he was in, he climbed into a shady hole in a big rock and began to cry.

He cried so hard and so loud that a coyote, who was passing near by heard him. The coyote's ears were not very keen so he thought it was somebody singing.

"I must find out who that is singing," said Mr. Coyote, "and get him to teach me that song."

So Mr. Coyote peeped round the rock and found the turtle with big tears in his eyes.

"Good day," said Mr. Coyote, "that was a nice song you were singing. Won't you teach it to me ?"

"I was not singing," replied the turtle.

"I know you were, for I heard you and I want to learn your song. If you do not teach it to me I will swallow you whole!"

"That cannot do me any harm," said the turtle, "for I have a hard shell that will hurt your throat."

"Well, if you do not sing for me I'll throw you in the hot sun!"

"That cannot harm me either," said the turtle, "for I can crawl under my shell."

"Well, then," said Mr. Coyote, "I will throw you into the river if you do not sing."

"Oh, please, Coyote-man, do not throw me into the river. I might drown if you do. Please do not throw me in!"

"Yes, I will!" and Mr. Coyote took up the turtle in his mouth and threw him into the river.

The little turtle swam out under the water where the coyote could not reach him. Then he stuck his head up out of the water:

"Thank you very much, Coyote-man, for throwing me into the river. This is my home. I had no way to get here. Thank you for helping me."

And old Mr. Coyote trotted away very angry.

THE FOX AND THE TURKEY

O-WAY-WAY-HAM-BY-JOH, long time ago, a fox went out to hunt. He had such a good place to hunt in, for just north of his den was a stretch of woods, where wild turkeys and many kinds of animals lived. He and Mrs. Fox had been living on cow sinews for many days, so he was hungry for something different to eat.

He hunted for a long time until he grew tired. When suddenly he found—what do you suppose?—a big fat turkey. He was just ready to stick his sharp teeth into the turkey to drag him to his den, when the turkey said: "Wait, Fox-man, are you ill, you look so pale? You look as if you will faint. Don't you want to take a nap? You lie down and go to sleep and I'll go down to your house and tell Mrs. Fox to cook me for your dinner. Poor fellow, you look so weary!" This made Mr. Fox really feel ill.

"That will be kind of you, Turkey-man."

So the turkey started off toward the fox's den and the fox watched him until he reached the door, then he lay down under a tree and went to sleep.

When the turkey reached the door of the fox's den, he knocked loudly. "Who's there?" asked Mrs. Fox.

"Just a friend with a message for you."

"Won't you come in?"

"No, thank you, I am in a hurry. Mr. Fox asked me to come by to tell you that he will be back soon. He is very hungry and wants you to cook him a mess of cow sinews for his dinner."

And then the turkey ran away.

Mrs. Fox got busy and cooked some cow sinews.

Very soon Mr. Fox came home smacking his lips. He was so pleased to think what a delicious turkey dinner he was going to have.

Mrs. Fox brought the dinner and set it on the table before Mr. Fox. He bit off a big piece and began to chew.

"This is the toughest turkey I have ever tasted," said he. "It tastes more like cow sinews than turkey to me. What is the matter with it?"

"Turkey!" exclaimed Mrs. Fox. "Why, I have no turkey! These are cow sinews. Someone knocked at the door this morning. He told me you were hungry and wanted me to cook cow sinews for your dinner right away."

"Oh," groaned Mr. Fox, "that must have been the turkey!"

VI. SOUTH CAROLINA

THE quaint humour of these tales reminds one of the Uncle Remus stories, and the fact that they are written in negro language gives them an added charm. Familiar types are met with but the local setting makes them delightfully fresh and entertaining.

BER RABBIT AND BER WOLF

ONCE upon a time Ber Rabbit and Ber Wolf made a plan together, and promised not to break it.. "Let us go out into the woods and catch any cow that we can catch, and milk it, and set the milk!" And after the milk has been set and turn to hard milk or clabber, then they would churn it together. They had wanted a kagful of butter to put up. So after they had churned the milk and the butter came they put the butter up into the kag and buried it into a woods. And both of them promised faithfully not to walk the road that led by the side which the butter was buried. Ber Rabbit is a very schemy man. He told that he would not go that road, don't care what happen, through the woods.

So one day Brother Wolf was standing in his door, looking out, studying what he was going to find to eat that day, when to his eyes he saw Ber Rabbit just a-coming down the road in full speed.

"Heh, there, Ber Rabbit!" said Ber Wolf, "where are you going in that road ?"

"O Ber Wolf!" said Ber Rabbit, "my sister had a pretty girl-child, the finest child you have ever seen."

"What is the child's name?" said Ber

"Her name is Just-Begin. You must excuse me for coming this side, but my sister said that I must be sure and come."

And he went into the wood and scrape off the top of the earth off the kag, and started into the butter. He took a good deal of it, to last a week or two. And he did this over and over again until Ber Wolf said, "Well, Ber Rabbit, let us go see how the butter is getting on!"

Ber Wolf's wife told him, "See here! that brother of yours who is Ber Rabbit is just eating all of that butter, because his sister she cannot have children so fast."

And so Ber Wolf and Ber Rabbit went to the woods and started to dig. They dug and dug until they came to the kag. And when they sounded the kag, it sounds as if it is empty. Ber Wolf did not say any thing, but took the top off.

And while he was taking it off, Ber Rabbit got a pain in his stomach and beg for excuse to go. And Ber Wolf said, "No, not now." And he said, "I must go. Do let me go!" So he went; and while he was away, Ber Wolf open the kag, and the kag was empty. And Ber Wolf tried to catch him; but all Ber Rabbit said was, "Your sister is a fool! Your mother and father are fools, your whole family are fools, and you are the biggest fool! Ha, ha!"

FATAL IMITATION

ONCE there was Ber Rabbit an' the rooyster. Every night when Ber Rabbit goin' home from work, he would see how de rooyster had only one leg an' no head at all. An' in de mornin' he would have his head an' two legs. So Ber Rabbit asked Ber Rooyster why he cut his head an' leg off at night, an' put it back in the mornin'. So Ber Rooyster tol' Ber Rabbit he rested dat way. So he wen' home an' tol' his wife to cut off three of his leg an' his head, so that he can rest. So, when Ber Rabbit wife cut Bet Rabbit head off, Ber Rabbit began to *jump*. So Ber Rooyster hold up his leg an' took his head from under his wing, an' clap his wings, an' said, "I have my head! I have my head!"

TELL TALE GREASE

D E rabbit eat up a jar of butter f'om de turtle. An' when eat up dis jar of butter f'om Brother Turtle, Brother Turtle had invited all his frien's aroun' to have a butter dinner. He invited de fox to keep peace. He invited de rabbit to dance. An' during de same time he invited Brother Squirrel to call de figgers fo' Brother rabbit to do de dancin'. An' Brother Turtle say, "while we was gettin' our party together, you know, Brother Fox, you got to keep peace yere."

"Ah know dat, Brother Turtle."

"An' keep your eyes on Brother Rabbit, 'cause I know him."

Buddy Rabbit, he had been dere de day befo' den, an' eat up de butter. An' now he went back on de day of de dance to dance. An' so when B'oder Rabbit got dere, dey hadn' looked in de jar fo' de butter, 'cause dey had it in de spring, where 'twould keep cool. An' Buddy Rabbit said, "Man, Brother Turtle, why donsh yer start dis dance, 'cause Ah'm sure goin' ter eat dat butter to-day.

An' so Buddy Rabbit he danced aroun' an' made like he was so hongry, 'til he didn' know what to do. An' he had eat dat butter de day befo'.

Now, when Brother Turtle got to go down to de spring, Brother Rabbit said, "You better hab me go wid yer, Brother Turtle, 'cause I can smell better dan you. If any dawgs been roun' dere, I can smell dem, 'cause you goin' to let Brother Squirrel pervide somet'in to eat."

"No, I ain't, Brother Rabbit, Ah'm goin' diwide dis myself."

"What dat you got, Brother Turtle, outside de butter?"

"I ain't got nothin'." He siad, "If you ain't got nothin', don'give me much butter. I don't like butter much."

Den, when he said dat, B'oder Turtle say, "Well, ef you don' like it, I will give you some for you wife an' chillun."

Brother Turtle went on down to de spring. He see de rabbit tracks. He looked in de jar, an' didn' fin' no butter. He paid good 'tension to de rabbit-tracks, an' he come on back with de jar. Brother Rabbit met him at de do'.

"Law'! Law'! Dat's goin' to be greasy to-day all right fo' dis ol' big jar o' butter."

So Brother Turtle ssaid, "People, Ah'm sorry 'cause Ah'm about to cry. I believe Brother Rabbit eat my butter."

"How come you believe dat?"

"'Cause I see de rabbit-track down to de spring."

"I declare I didn' eat dat butter. If you think I eat dat butter, I blow my breath in your face three times; an' ef I eat dat butter, you can smell it."

Buddy Rabbit blow in his face three times, an' he didn' smell it. So said, "Well, le's go down to de spring an' fit dis trap an' see if dis is Brother Rabbit track." So dey said to de fox, "Brother Fox, you hol' Brother Rabbit 'til us come back. B'oder

Fox grab B'oder Rabbit, an he hol' 'em. B'oder Rabbit beg to get loose. "O Brother Fox! if you tu'n me loose, Ah will tell you wha' green patch." He could get all de turnip-greens he want. He said, "No, Ah'm goin' to hol' yer."

"Ah don' care if you did, Ah didn't eat de butter." So he held him until dey all come back. An' Brother Rabbit say he didn' eat de butter. So dat was his cousin's track, 'cause his cousin was tellin' about some butter las' night. Says, "It wasn' on me. If you all t'ink 'twas me, you can do anything with me you want. You see one rabbit's tracks, an' you think it's me. 'Cause a whole lot o' rabbits in dis worl'. 'Cause my cousin was here from Brother Dove's plantation."

"I kyan' help it, Brother Rabbit, I know it was you."

"Wait, don' kill me yet, don' kill me!"

B'oder Fox said, "Ah'm de peace-man. Brother Rabbit say he didn' eat it."

B'oder Squirrel say, "Don' pay 'tention to Brother Fox, 'cause he goes with Brother Rabbit daughter." B'oder Rabbit said, "Ah don' kyare what you do Wid me ef you prove it, Brother Turtle." Brother Terrapin [1] he said, "Well, le's make up a big ol' fire, an' all us lie down by dat fire an' go to sleep. De one who de grease run out de mout', dat's who eat de butter."

Dey made up a great big fire, an' B'oder Turtle he give all um piece o' boa'd to lie on. Whosever boa'd was greasy, dat's de one eat de butter. Ev'ybody went to sleep. An' de turtle firs' one woke up. An' Brother Rabbit was de nex' one. Brother Turtle woke Brother Rabbit up by cryin'. Brother Rabbit he jumped up an' holiered. Said, "Brother Turtle done slip de greasy boa'd under me." An' dey grab Brother Rabbit, an' dey said, "Ah knowed you eat dat butter." Said, "No, Ah didn', 'cause my boa'd was a straight boa'd, an' Bro' Turtle slip his boa'd under me." An' said, "No, you eat de butter. We go bu'n you up." An' B'oder Rabbit say, "I'd rather fo' you to bu'n me up dan fo' you to do anything else, dan t'row me in dat big ol' thick briar-thicket ower dere. Dem briars would stick me an' get me all sore, an' I lay sick a long time an' suffer befo' I die. An' ef you t'row me in de fire, all dis butter I eat will melt an' drown dat fire out." An' B'oder Turtle say, "T'row him in de briar-patch, Brother Fox."

Brother Rabbit says, "P'ease don', Brother Fox. T'row me in de fire, so I can drown it out!"

So dey got mad at um, an' take him an' t'row him in de briar-patch. Brother Rabbit says, "Shoo!" after he hit de briar-patch. "Dis where I was bred an' born. Ah eat de butter, an' you t'rowed me home."

---

[1] *I.e.*, Turtle.

ARABIA

THE ARABIAN NIGHTS' ENTERTAINMENTS

THE *Arabian Nights' Entertainments* is the best known and most remarkable product of Arabian literature. Part of it can be traced from the Sanskrit through the Persian, but much of both the form and matter appears to be Arabian. Among the Arabs the tales are elegant, pointed with a moral, and adorned with episodes and diversions.

The occasion of the telling is as follows: A certain king, believing that no woman was virtuous, used to marry a new bride every day and put her to death the next morning. One wife was Shahrazad who had understanding and discretion. As they sat together she began a tale, and late at night she broke it off at a particularly interesting point so that the king next morning spared her life, and at night begged her to continue her tale. This she did for a thousand nights. At length the king honoured her and gave her his lasting love.

SHAHRIAR AND SHAHRAZAD

THERE was in ancient times a King of the countries of India and China, possessing numerous troops, and guards, and servants; and he had two sons, who were both brave horsemen; but especially the elder, who inherited the kingdom of his father, and governed his subjects with such justice that the inhabitants of his country and whole empire loved him. He was called King Shahriar; his younger brother was named Shah Zeman, and was King of Samarkand. They ruled for the space of twenty years with the utmost enjoyment and happiness.

At the end of this time, the elder King felt a strong desire to see his brother, and ordered his Vizier to repair to him, and bring him.

Orders were given to prepare handsome presents, such as horses adorned with gold and costly jewels, and slaves, and beautiful maidens, and expensive stuffs. He then wrote a letter to his brother, expressing his great desire to see him; and having sealed it, he gave it to the Vizier, together with the presents above mentioned, and bade him strain his nerves and tuck up his skirts, and hasten on his journey. The Vizier answered without delay, "I hear and obey," and forthwith prepared for the journey.

He proceeded night and day; and each of the kings under the authority of King Shahriar by whose residence he passed came forth to meet him, with costly presents, and gifts of gold and silver, and entertained him three days; after which, on the fourth day, he accompanied him one day's journey, and took leave of him. Thus he continued on his way until he drew near to the city of Samarkand, when he sent forward a messenger to inform King Shah-Zeman of his approach. Then the King ordered the chief officers of his court, and the great men of his kingdom, to go forth a day's journey to meet him; and they did so; and when they met him they welcomed him and walked by his stirrups until they returned to the city. The Vizier then presented himself before the King Shah-Zeman, greeted him with a prayer for the divine assistance in his favour, kissed the ground before him, and informed him of his brother's desire to see him; after which he handed to him the letter. The King took it, read it, and addressed the Vizier thus, "I will not go until I have entertained thee three days." Accordingly, he lodged him in a palace befitting his rank, accommodated his troops in tents, and appointed them all things that they needed; so they remained three days. On the fourth day the King equipped himself for the journey, made ready his baggage, and collected costly presents for his brother.

He then sent forth his tents and camels and mules and servants and guards, appointed his Vizier to be governor of the country during his absence, and set out towards his brother's dominions.

Shahriar, rejoicing at the tidings of his approach, went forth to meet him, saluted him, and welcomed him with the utmost delight. He then ordered that the city should be decorated on the occasion, and sat down to entertain his brother with cheerful conversation.

But the mind of King Shah-Zeman was troubled because his wife no longer had love in her heart toward him and King Shahriar suffered also because his wife was unfaithful to him, and he said, "Arise, and let us travel whither we please, and see if a like evil hath befallen any other person."

So they went out from a private door of the palace, and journeyed continually, days and nights, until they arrived at a tree in the midst of a meadow, by a spring of water, on the shore of the sea. They drank of this spring, and sat down to rest; and when the day had a little advanced, the sea became troubled before them, and there arose from it a black pillar, ascending toward the sky, and approaching the meadow. Struck with fear at the sight, they climbed up into the tree, which was lofty; and thence they gazed to see what this might be; and behold, it was a Genie of gigantic stature, broad-fronted and bulky, bearing on his head a chest. He landed, and came to the tree into which the two Kings had climbed, and, having seated himself beneath it, opened the chest and took out of it another box which he also opened; and there came forth from it a young woman, fair and beautiful, like the shining sun. When the Genie cast his eyes upon her he said, "O lady of noble race, whom I carried off on thy wedding-night, I have a desire to sleep a little"; and he placed his head upon her knee, and slept. The damsel then raised her head toward the tree, and saw there the two Kings; upon which she removed the head of the Genie from her knee, and, having placed it on the ground, stood under the tree, and made signs to the two Kings, as though she would say, Come down and fear not this Afrite; if ye do not come, I will rouse him, and he shall put you to a cruel death. So, being afraid, they came down to her; and, after they had remained with her a while, she took from her pocket a purse, and drew out from this a string, upon which were ninety-eight seal-rings. "The owners of these rings," said she, "have all spoken with me, unknown to this foolish Afrite, and have given me their rings—therefore give me your two rings, ye brothers!"

So they gave her their two rings from their fingers. Then said she to them, "This evil Afrite carried me off on my wedding-night, and put me in the box, and placed the box in the chest, and affixed to the chest seven locks, and deposited me, thus imprisoned, in the bottom of the roaring sea, beneath the dashing waves; not knowing that, while he sleeps one day, I shall slay him, for scarce any man can resist woman's treachery."

When the two Kings heard these words from her lips, they were struck with the utmost astonishment, and said, one to the other, "If this Afrite cannot withstand her power, what will happen to us if we keep not safe from women?" Immediately they departed and returned to the 'city.

As soon as they had entered the palace Shahriar caused his wife to be beheaded, and thenceforth he made it his custom to wed a new wife every day and have her beheaded the morning after the wedding feast. Thus he continued to do for three years; and the people raised an outcry against him, and fled with their daughters. Such was the case when the King ordered the Vizier to bring him a bride according to custom. The Vizier went forth and searched and found none; and he went back to his house enraged and vexed, fearing what the King might do unto him. Now the Vizier had two daughters; the elder of whom was named Shahrazad; and the younger, Dunyazad. Shahrazad had collected together many books concerning the histories of ancient kings and the works of poets. When she saw that her father was sorrowful she said, "Why do I see thee thus changed, and oppressed with care?" Then the Vizier related to her all that had happened to him; upon which she said, "O my father, give me in marriage to this King; either I shall die, and be a ransom for one of the daughters of my race or I shall live and be the cause of their deliverance from him." "1 conjure thee," exclaimed he, "that thou expose not thy self to such peril." But she said, "It must be so," and at length he arrayed her and went to King Shahriar. Now she had given directions to her young sister, saying, "When I have gone to the King, I will send to request thee to come; and when thou comest to me, and seest a convenient time, do thou say to me, 'O my sister, relate to me some strange story to beguile our waking hour,' and I will relate to thee a story that shall, if it be the will of God, be the means of deliverance from death."

Her father, the Vizier, took her to the King, who, when he saw him, was rejoiced, and said, "Hast thou brought me what I desired?" He answered, "Yes." When the King therefore introduced himself to her, she wept; and he said to her, "What aileth thee?" She answered, "O King, I have a young sister, and I wish to take leave of her."

So the King sent to her; and she came to her sister, and embraced her, and sat near her. After she had waited for a proper opportunity, she said, "O my sister, relate to us a story to beguile the waking hour of our night." "Most willingly," answered Shahrazad, "if this virtuous King permit me." The King, hearing these words and being restless, was pleased with the idea of listening to the story; and thus, on the first night of the thousand and one, Shahrazad commenced her stories.

THE STORY OF THE FISHERMAN
AND THE GENIE

THERE was a certain fisherman who had a wife and three children; and though he was poor, it was his custom to cast his net every day no more than four times. One day he went forth at the hour of noon to the shore of the sea, and put down his basket, and cast his net, and waited until it was motionless in the water, when he drew together its strings and found it to be heavy: he pulled, but could not draw it up; so he took the end of the cord, and knocked a stake into the shore, and tied the cord to it. He then stripped himself, and dived round the net, and continued to pull until he drew it out: whereupon he rejoiced, and put on his clothes; but when he came to examine the net, he found in it the carcass of an ass. At the sight of this he exclaimed, "This is a strange piece of fortune!"

He then disencumbered his net of the dead ass, and wrung it out; after which he spread it and descended into the sea, and cast it again, and waited till it had sunk and was still, when he pulled it and found it more heavy and more difficult to raise than on the former occasion. He therefore concluded that it was full of fish; so he tied it and stripped and plunged and dived, and pulled until he raised it, and drew it upon the shore; when he found in it only a large jar, full of sand and mud; on seeing which he was troubled and said hasty words. He threw aside the jar and wrung out and cleansed his net; and, begging the forgiveness of God for his impatience, returned to the sea the third time, and threw the net and waited till it had sunk and was motionless; he then drew it out and found in it a quantity of broken jars and pots.

Upon this he raised his head toward heaven and said, "O God, Thou knowest that I cast not my net more than four times; and I have now cast it three times!" Then exclaiming, "in the name of God!" he cast the net again into the sea, and waited till it was still; when he attempted to draw it up, but could not, for it clung to the bottom. So he stripped himself again and dived round the net, and pulled it until he raised it upon the shore; when he opened it and found in it a bottle of brass filled with something, and having its mouth closed with a stopper of lead, bearing the impression of the seal of our lord Solomon. At the sight of this, the fisherman was rejoiced, and said, "This I will sell in the copper-market; for it is worth ten pieces of gold." He then shook it, and found it to be heavy, and said, "I must open it, and see what is in it, and store it in my bag; and then I will sell the bottle in the copper-market." So he took out a knife, and picked at the lead until he extracted it from the bottle. He then laid the bottle on the ground, and shook it, that its contents might pour out; but there came forth from it nothing but smoke, which ascended toward the sky, and spread over the face of the earth; at which he wondered excessively. And after a little while, the smoke collected together, and was condensed, and then became agitated, and became an Afrite, whose head was in the clouds, while his feet rested upon the ground; his head was like a dome; his hands were like winnowing forks; and his legs, like masts; his mouth resembled a cavern; his teeth were like stones; his nostrils, like trumpets; and his eyes, like lamps; and he had dishevelled and dust-coloured hair.

When the fisherman beheld this Afrite, the muscles of his sides quivered, his teeth were locked together, his spittle dried up, and he saw not his way. The Afrite, as soon as he perceived him, exclaimed, "There is no deity but God. Solomon is the Prophet of God. Receive news, O fisherman!" "Of what?" said the fisherman, "dost thou give me news?" He answered, "Of thou being instantly put to a most cruel death." The fisherman exclaimed, "And wherefore wouldst thou kill me? and what requires thy killing me, when I have liberated thee from the bottle, and rescued thee from the bottom of the sea, and brought thee up upon the dry land?" The Afrite answered, "Choose what kind of death thou wilt die, and in what manner thou shalt be killed." "What is my offence," said the fisherman, "that this should be my reward from thee?" The Afrite replied, "Hear my story, O fisherman." "Tell it then," said the fisherman, "and be short in thy words; for my soul hath sunk down to my feet." "Know then," said he, "that I am one of the heretical Genii: I rebelled against Solomon, the son of David, and he sent to me his Vizier, Asaf, who came upon me forcibly, and took me to him in bonds, and placed me before him; and when Solomon saw me, he offered up a prayer for protection against me, and exhorted me to embrace the faith and to submit to his authority; but I refused; upon which he called for this bottle, and confined me in it, and closed it upon me with the leaden stopper, which he stamped with the Most Great Name; he then gave orders to the Genie, who carried me away, and threw me into the midst of the sea. There I remained a hundred years; and I said in my heart, `Whosoever shall liberate me, I will enrich him for ever' :—but the hundred years passed over me, and no one liberated me. I entered upon another hundred years; and I said, `Whosoever shall liberate me, I will open to him the treasures of the earth.'—But no one did so. Four hundred years more passed over me, and I said, `Whosoever shall liberate me, I will perform for him three wishes'—but still no one liberated me. I then fell into a violent rage, and said within myself, 'Whosoever shall liberate me now, I will kill him; and only suffer him to choose in what manner he will die.' And lo, now thou hast liberated me, and I have given thee thy choice of the manner in which thou wilt die."

When the fisherman had heard the story of the Afrite he exclaimed, "O Allah! that I should not have liberated thee but in such a time as this," and to the Afrite he said, "Pardon me, and kill me not, by way of gratitude." Then to himself he said, "This is a Genie, and I am a man; and God hath given me sound reason; therefore I will now plot his destruction with my art and reason." So he said to the Afrite, "By the Most Great Name engraved upon the seal of Solomon, I will ask thee one question; and wilt thou answer it to me truly?" On hearing the mention of the Most Great Name, the Afrite trembled and replied, "Yes; ask and be brief." The fisherman then said, "How wast thou in the bottle? It will not contain thy hand or thy foot; how then can it contain thy whole body.?" "Dost thou not believe that I was in it?" said the Afrite. The fisherman answered, "I will never believe thee until I see thee in it." Upon this, the Afrite shook, and became converted again into smoke, which rose to the sky and then became condensed, and entered the bottle by little and little, until it was all enclosed; when the fisherman hastily snatched the sealed leaden stopper, and, having replaced it in the mouth of the bottle, called out to the Afrite and said, "Choose in what manner of death thou shalt die. I will assuredly throw thee here into the sea, and build me a house on this spot; and whosoever shall come here, I will prevent his fishing in this place, and will say to him, 'Here is an Afrite who, to any person that liberates him, will propose various kinds of death, and then give him his choice of one of them.'" On hearing these words of the fisherman, the Afrite endeavoured to escape, but could not. The fisherman then took the bottle to the brink of the sea. The Aftire exclaimed, "Nay! Nay!" To which the fisherman replied, "Yea, without fail! Yea, without fail! I will throw thee into the sea; and if thou hast been there a thousand and eight hundred years, I will make thee to remain there until the hour of judgment!" "Open to me," said the Aftire, "that I may confer benefits upon thee" The fisherman replied, "Thou liest, thou accursed! I and thou art like the Vizier of the Greek King and the sage Douban." "What," said the Afrite, "was the case of the Vizier of the Greek King and the sage Douban, and what is their story?" The fisherman answered as follows:

THE STORY OF THE GRECIAN KING
AND THE SAGE DOUBAN

KNOW, O Afrite, that there was, in former times, a monarch who was King of the Grecians, possessing great treasures and numerous forces and valiant troops of every description; but he was afflicted with leprosy, which the physicians and sages had failed to remove; neither their potions, nor powders, nor ointments were of any benefit to him; and none of the physicians was able to cure him. At length there arrived at the city of this king a great sage, stricken in years, who was called the sage Douban. He was acquainted with ancient books and with medicine and astrology and was learned in the wisdom of the philosophers.

After this sage had arrived in this city, and remained in it a few days, he heard of the case of the King, and of the leprosy which afflicted him, and that the physicians had failed to cure him. In consequence of this information he passed the next night in deep study; and when the morning came, he attired himself in the richest of his apparel, and presented himself before the King. Having kissed the ground before him, he informed him who he was, and said, "O King, I have heard of the disease which hath attacked thee, and that none can remove it. I will cure thee without giving thee to drink any potion, or anointing thee with ointment." When the King heard these words, he wondered, and said to him, "How wilt thou do this? If thou cure me, I will enrich thee and thy children's children, and I will heap favours upon thee, and whatever thou shalt desire shall be thine, and thou shalt be my companion and my friend."

He then bestowed upon him a robe of honour, and other presents, and said to him, "Wilt thou cure me of this disease without potion or ointment?" He answered, "Yes; I will cure thee." And the King was extremely astonished, and said, "O Sage, at what time, and on what day, shall that which thou hast proposed to me be done? Hasten it, O my son." He answered, "I hear and obey."

He then went out from the presence of the King, and hired a house, in which he placed his books, and medicines, and drugs. Having done this, he selected certain of his medicines and drugs, and made a golf-stick, with a hollow handle, into which he placed them; after which he made a ball for it, skilfully fashioned.

On the following day, he went again to the King, and kissed the ground before him, and directed him to repair to the horse-course, and to play with the ball and golf-stick. The King, attended by his Emirs and Chamberlains, and Viziers, went thither, and, as soon as he arrived there, the sage Douban handed to him the golf-stick, saying, "Take this golf-stick, and grasp it thus, and ride along the horse-course, and strike the ball with it with all thy force, until the palm of thy hand and thy whole body become moist with perspiration, when the medicine will penetrate into thy hand, and pervade thy whole body. Then return to thy palace and wash thyself, and sleep, and thou shalt find thyself cured; and peace be on thee."

So the King took the golf-stick from the sage, and grasped it in his hand, and mounted his horse, and the ball was thrown before him, and he urged his horse after it until he overtook it, when he struck it with all his force; and when he had continued this as long as was necessary, he bathed and slept, and not a vestige of the leprosy remained. Upon this he rejoiced exceedingly and was full of happiness. On the following morning he entered the council-chamber, and sat upon his throne; and the Chamberlains and great officers of his court came before him. The sage Douban also presented himself; and when the King saw him, he rose to him in haste, and seated him by his side. Food was then spread before them, and the sage ate with the King, and remained as his guest all the day; and when the night approached, the King gave him two thousand pieces of gold, besides dresses of honour and other presents and mounted him on his own horse, and so the sage returned to his house.

Again, the next morning, the King went as usual to his council-chamber. Now there was, among his Viziers, one of ill-aspect, and of evil star; sordid, avaricious, and of an envious and malicious disposition.

When he saw that the King had made the sage Douban his friend, and bestowed upon him these favours he envied him and meditated evil against him. So he approached the King, and kissed the ground before him, and said, "O King, whose goodness extendeth to all men, permit me to give thee important advice. I have seen the King in a way that is not right, since he hath bestowed favours upon his enemy, and upon him who desireth the downfall of his dominions; he hath treated him with kindness, and honoured him with highest honours; and I fear, for the King, the consequence of this conduct." At this the King was troubled, and his countenance changed, and he said, "Who is he whom thou regardest as mine enemy, and to whom I shew kindness?" He replied, "O King, if thou hast been asleep, awake! It is the sage Douban." The King said, "He is my dearest friend, for he cured me of my disease, which the physicians were unable to remove, and there is not now to be found one like to him in the whole world, from west to east. If I gave him a share of my kingdom it were but a small thing to do unto him."

"Nay, O King," said the Vizier, "if thou trust in this sage, he will plot thy destruction. Dost thou not see that he hath cured thee of thy disease by a thing that thou heldest in thy hand and may even plot to kill thee by a thing that thou shalt hold in the same manner?" Then answered the King, "Thou hast spoken truth, the case is as thou hast said, it is probable that this sage came as a spy to accomplish my death, and now, O Vizier, what shall be done respecting him?" The Vizier answered, "Send to him immediately, and desire him to come hither; and when he is come, strike off his head; betray him, before he betray thee."

Immediately, therefore, the King sent for the sage, who came, full of joy, not knowing what was to befall him.

Then said the King, "Knowest thou wherefore I have summoned thee?" The sage answered, "None knoweth what is secret but God, whose name be exalted!" Then said the King, "I have summoned thee that I may take away thy life, for it hath been told to me that thou art a spy, and hast come hither to kill me; but I will prevent thee by killing thee first."

"O King," said the sage, "is this my reward from thee? Dost thou return evil for good?" But the King answered, "Thou must be slain without delay." The executioner then advanced, and bandaged his eyes, and, having drawn his sword, said, "Give permission." Upon this the sage wept and said, "Spare me and so may God spare thee, and destroy me not, lest God destroy thee. Wouldst thou return me the recompense of the crocodile?"

"What," said the King, "is the story of the crocodile?" The sage answered, "I cannot relate it while in this condition." Then one of the officers of the King arose, and said, "O King, give up to me the blood of this sage, for we have not seen him commit any offence against thee; nor have we seen him do aught but cure thee of thy disease, which wearied the other physicians and sages." But the King answered, "I must kill him, and then shall I feel myself safe."

The sage seeing there was no way of escape said, "O King, grant me some respite, that I may return to my house, and bid my family farewell and dispose of my books; among my books is one of especial value, which I offer as a present to thee, that thou mayest treasure it in thy library. It contains things not to be told. When thou hast cut off my head, if thou open this book, and count three leaves, and then read three lines on the page to the left, the head will speak to thee, and answer whatever thou shalt ask." At this the King was exceedingly astonished, and shook with delight. He sent the sage in the custody of guards; and the sage descended to his house, and settled all his affairs on that day; and on the following day he went up to the court; and the Emirs, and Viziers, and Chamberlains and all the great officers of the state, went thither also; and the court resembled a flower-garden. And when the sage had entered, he presented himself before the King, bearing an old book, and a small pot containing a powder; and he sat down, and said, "Bring me a tray." So they brought him one; and he poured out the powder into it, and spread it. He then said, "O King, take this book, and do nothing with it till thou hast cut off my head; when thou hast done so, place it upon this tray, and order some one to press it down upon the powder; then open the book."

As soon as the sage had said this, the King gave orders to strike off his head, and it was done. The King then opened the book, and found that its leaves were stuck together; so he put his finger to his mouth, and moistened it, and opened the first leaf, and the second, and the third; but the leaves were not opened without difficulty. He opened six leaves, and looked at them; but found upon them no writing. So he said, "O sage, there is nothing written in it." The head of the sage answered, "Turn over more leaves." The King did so, and in a little while, the poison penetrated into his system; for the book was poisoned, and the King fell back, and cried out, "The poison hath penetrated into me." Upon this, the head of the sage replied:

"They made use of their power, and used it tyrannically; and soon it became as though it never had existed. This is the reward of your conduct, and fortune is blameless."

And when the head of the sage Douban had uttered these words, the King immediately fell down dead.

MORE ABOUT THE FISHERMAN AND THE GENIE

"NOW, O Afrite," continued the fisherman, "know that if the King of the Grecians had spared the sage Douban, God had spared him; but he refused, and desired his destruction; therefore God destroyed him; and thou, O Afrite, if thou hadst spared me, God had spared thee, and I had spared thee; but thou desiredst my death; therefore will I put thee to death imprisoned in this bottle, and will throw thee here into the sea." The Afrite, upon this, cried out, and said, "I conjure thee by Allah, O fisherman, that thou do it not; spare me in generosity and be not angry with me for what I did; and l vow that I will never do thee harm, but, on the contrary, will do thee a service that shall enrich thee for ever."

Upon this, the fisherman accepted his word and when he had bound him by oaths and vows, and made him swear by the Most Great Name of God, he opened to him; and the smoke ascended until it had all come forth, and then collected together, and became, as before, an Afrite of hideous form. The Afrite then kicked the bottle into the sea. When the fisher man saw him do this, he made sure of destruction, and said, "This is no sign of good," but afterward he took courage.

The Afrite laughed, and, walking on before him, said, "O fisherman, follow me." The fisherman did so, not believing in his escape, until they had quitted the neighbourhood of the city, and ascended a mountain, and descended into a wide desert tract in the midst of which was a lake of water. Here the Afrite stopped, and ordered the fisherman to cast his net and take some fish; and the fisherman, looking into the lake, saw in it fish of different colours, white and red and blue and yellow; at which he was astonished; and he cast his net, and drew it in, and found in it four fish, each fish of a different colour from the others, at the sight of which he rejoiced. The Afrite then said to him, "Take them to the Sultan, and present them to him, and he will give thee what will enrich thee; and for the sake of God accept my excuse, for, at present, I know no other way of rewaruing thee, having been in the sea a thousand and eight hundred years, and not seen the surface of the earth until now; but take not fish from the lake more than once each day; and now I commend thee to the care of God." Having thus said, he struck the earth with his feet, and it clove asunder, and swallowed him.

The fisherman then went back to the city, wondering at all that had befallen him with the Afrite, and carried the fish to his house; and he took an earthen bowl, and, having filled it with water, put the fish into it; and they struggled in the water.

When he had done this, he placed the bowl upon his head, and repaired to the King's palace, as the Afrite had commanded him, and, going up unto the King, presented to him the fish; and the King was excessively astonished at them, for he had never seen any like them in the course of his life; and he said, "Give these fish to the slave cook-maid and bid her fry them, and give to the fisherman four hundred pieces of gold." So the Vizier gave them to him, and he took them in his lap, and returned to his home and his wife, joyful and happy, and bought what was needful for his family.

Such were the events that befell the fisherman; now we must relate what happened to the maid. She took the fish, and cleaned them, and arranged them in the frying-pan, and left them until one side was cooked, when she turned them upon the other side; and lo, the wall of the kitchen clove asunder, and there came forth from it a damsel of tall stature, smooth-cheeked, of perfect form, beautiful in countenance, wearing a head-dress interwoven with blue silk; with rings in her ears, and bracelets on her wrists, and rings set with precious jewels on her fingers; and in her hand was a rod of Indian cane.

She dipped the end of the rod in the frying-pan, and said, "O fish, are ye remaining faithful to your covenant?" At the sight of this, the cook-maid fainted. The damsel then repeated the same words a second and a third time; after which the fish raised their heads from the frying-pan, and answered, "Yes, yes." They then repeated the following verse:

> "If thou return, we return.
> If thou come, we come.
> If thou forsake, we verily do the same."

Upon this the damsel overturned the frying-pan, and departed by the way she had entered, and the wall of the kitchen closed up again. The cook-maid then arose, and beheld the four fish burnt like charcoal. As she sat reproaching herself, she beheld the Vizier standing at her head; and he said to her, "Bring the fish to the Sultan": and she wept, and told him what had happened.

The Vizier was astonished at her words, and exclaimed, "This is indeed a wonderful event." He sent for the fisherman, and when he was brought, he said to him, "O fisherman, thou must bring to us four fish like those which thou broughtest, before." The fisherman accordingly went forth to the lake, and threw his net, and when he had drawn it in he found in it four fish as before; and he took them to the Vizier, who went with them to the maid, and said to her, "Rise, and fry them in my presence." The maid, therefore, prepared the fish, and put them in the frying-pan, and they had remained but a little while, when the wall clove asunder, and the damsel appeared, clad as before, and holding the rod; and she dipped the end of the rod in the frying-pan, and said, "O fish, O fish, are ye remaining faithful to your covenant?" Upon which they raised their heads, and answered as before; and the damsel overturned the frying-pan with the rod, and returned by the way she had entered, and the wall closed up again.

The Vizier then said, "This must be told to the King"; so he went to him, and informed him of what had happened. The King said, "I must see with mine own eyes." He sent, therefore, to the fisherman, and commanded him to bring four fish like the former; granting him a delay of three days. The fisherman repaired to the lake, and brought the fish thence to the King, who ordered again that four hundred pieces of gold should be given to him. Then, turning to the Vizier, the King said, "Cook the fish thyself here before me." The Vizier answered, "I hear and obey."

He brought the frying-pan, and, after he had cleaned the fish, threw them into it; and as soon as he had turned them, the wall clove asunder, and there came forth from it a negro, in size like a bull, or like one of the tribe of 'Ad,[1] having in his hand a branch of a green tree; and he said with a clear but terrifying voice, "O fish, O fish, are ye remaining faithful to your covenant?" Upon which they raised their heads, and answered as before, "Yes, yes:

> "If thou return, we return.
> If thou come, we come.
> If thou forsake, we verily do the same."

The black then approached the frying-pan, and overturned it with the branch, and the fish became charcoal, and he went away as he had come. When he had thus disappeared from before their eyes, the King said, "There must be some strange story connected with these fish." He then ordered the fisherman to come before him and said to him, "Whence came these fish?" The fisherman answered, "From a lake between four mountains behind this mountain which is without thy city." The King said to him, "How many days' journey distant?" He answered, "O our lord the Sultan! a journey of half-an-hour." And the Sultan was astonished, and set out at once with his own troops and the fisherman. They ascended the

---

[1] The smallest of the ancient Arab tribe of 'Ad is said to have been sixty cubits high

mountain, and descended into a wide desert tract which they had never before seen in their whole lives. And between four mountains was a lake in which were fish of four colours, red and white, yellow and blue. The King paused in astonishment, and said to the troops, "Hath any one of you before seen this lake in this place?" They all answered, "No." Then said the King, "I will not enter my city, nor will I sit upon my throne, until I know the true history of this lake, and of its fish."

So the King gave the Vizier charge of the troops and having disguised himself, set out secretly by night. He journeyed until the morning and continued thus for the space of two days, when there appeared before him, in the distance, something black, at the sight of which he rejoiced, and said, "Perhaps I shall find there some person who will inform me of the history of the lake and its fish." When he approached this black object, he found it to be a palace built of black stones, and overlaid with iron; and one of the leaves of its door was open, and the other shut. The King was glad, and knocked gently, but heard no answer; he knocked a second and a third time, but again heard no answer; then he knocked a fourth time with violence; but no one answered. Then he took courage, and entered from the door into the passage and cried out, but heard no answer. In the courtyard was a fountain, with four lions of red gold, which poured forth the water from their mouths, like pearls and jewels: around this were birds; and over the top of the palace was a net, which prevented their flying out. But there was no one to tell him concerning the lake and the fish.

He then sat down between the doors, reflecting upon these things; and as he sat, he heard the sound of lamentation and sorrow coming from the direction of a curtain hung before the door of a chamber; he raised it and beheld behind it a young man sitting on a couch. He was a handsome youth, clad with a vest of silk embroidered with gold. The King was rejoiced and saluted him, and the young man replied, "O my master, excuse my not rising!" "O youth!" said the King, "tell me the meaning of the lake and its fish, and of this palace, and the reason of thy being alone in it, and of thy grief!" When the young man heard these words, tears trickled down his cheeks, and he wept bitterly, and stretched forth his hand, and lifted up the skirts of his clothing; and lo, half of him, from his waist to the soles of his feet, was stone. He then said, "Know, O King, that the story of the fish is extraordinary!" and he related it to the King.

AUSTRALIA

THE natives of Australia may be considered as a race without a history. They are older perhaps than the inhabitants of Egypt, yet they offer little evidence of development. They have been wanderers and their life has been a continual search for food and water. So much is clearly shown by their stories. They have been neither herdsmen nor tillers of the soil, and they have been subject to no higher authority than that of custom. There are no traces of pottery, pictures, palaces, or cities. The stories they tell by the camp-fire or under the gum-tree's shade are pictures of savage life. There are no distinctions of wealth or rank, hence there are no tales like "Cinderella" or "Puss in Boots." They do not possess the humour of the "Uncle Remus" type—they are more leisurely, less dramatic, and somewhat burdened with repetitions. Yet there is in them a naturalness and charm that makes their realism romantic. It is interesting, by the way, to compare the story in which a lasting supply of clear and refreshing water is given to Australia through the sacrifices of the chief's wife with that of the gift of maize to the Indian tribes by means of the sacrifices of an Indian brave.

HOW THE SELFISH GOANNAS LOST THEIR WIVES

LONG, long ago a great drought visited the country. There was no rain, and all the dams and rock holes became dry. The porcupine and the emu tribes did not know what to do, because among their members there were many aged and infirm. Some were sick, and a great many had little children; so that they were in great difficulties. They were not able to move down on the river Murray, where they would have been well and comfortable.

The drought did not affect the goanna tribe, as they had a secret reservoir with a supply of water that would last them for very many years. The cries of the little children, and the distress of the aged and sick, touched the hearts of the wives of the goannas, and they would secretly go among the other tribes and do all they could to supply their wants and relieve their sufferings. One day they asked their husbands to tell them where the great rock hole reservoir was, as they were anxious to supply water to the aged and the sick and the children of the porcupine and emu families. But the selfish goannas refused, and, what was worse, they said to their wives, "Since you are taking such an interest in the needs of others, we will give you only just sufficient water to slake your own thirst."

The wives found that it was useless to plead with their obstinate husbands; but they were determined that, although they had given way to many objections before, and had willingly suffered the indignity of refusals, they would not let this insult pass. So they began to search for the reservoir. They would take up their yam-sticks that their husbands should believe that they were going to dig yams and roots of plants and shrubs. But they would track the footprints of their husbands, which led them to the mountain. At the foot of the mountain they would lose all trace of the footprints, so they would return to the valley and gather a few yams and herbs, and then go to their homes. They would cook the yams in the hot ashes, and then sit down with their husbands and families to eat.

Sometimes a goanna would ask his wife where she had been for such an unusually long time. He would say, "I notice a speck of dirt that comes from the mountain. Have you been there?" The wife would reply, "What do you think, you silly? Do you imagine that we go searching for yams on the mountain-top? We find and dig yams in the low, flat country, not on rocky mountains. Now why do you ask such questions?" The goanna, without another word, would lie down upon his opossum skin.

In the morning, just as the sun rose over the eastern range of mountains, the men of the goanna tribe were out looking for food, and their wives were up too. They had met to discuss what to do in order to discover the secret of the reservoir. One, more thoughtful than the others, said, "It would be a wise plan to go up the mountain and make a *mia-mia* (native hut) and camp there and make observations. Now who amongst us has courage? Let us sit a while and think who will go."

So they sat in silence for a few moments, and then one rose. All eyes became fixed on her. She was the wife of the chief. She said, "Sisters, I take the responsibility. I offer to go. I consider it is my duty as wife of a chief. Who will come and help me with my camp necessaries?"

Two young wives stood up, and said, "We will go with you"

So they made haste and rolled up the belongings of the chief's wife, and the three women hurried away to the mountain before the chief and the other goannas returned from their hunting. Half-way up the side of the mountain there was a spot which gave a good view of the surrounding valley, and especially of the goanna camping-ground. After making the *mia-mia* the two young women returned home, leaving the chief's wife on the mountain. In the evening the young chief summoned the goannas to his *mia-mia* and asked them whether anyone had seen his wife, or had any knowledge regarding her disappearance. All expressed great sorrow, and said they had no knowledge of the matter, nor could they suggest any reason why she should leave the camp. They told their chief that they would do all in their power to assist him to recover his wife, if she had been taken a captive to some other home.

Then the chief summoned the teal teal,[1] the wives of the goannas. They were closely questioned by the chief and the elders, but they remained standing with their heads bowed, and would not make any reply. The questioners tried by threats to make them speak, but they shook their heads and remained silent. The chief of the goannas then ordered that the wives should return to their *mia-mia*. When the teal teal were safely home the chief said to the men, "I have a suspicion that the emus have come to our home while we were out hunting, and have taken my wife, and have given her to the young chief of the tribe. So to-morrow, before the sun rises beyond the mountain-peak, every one that is able to fight will take with him three *kaikes*,[2] four *waddies*,[3] four *panketyes*,[4] and a *nulla-nulla*,[5] and we will march into their land and seek my wife. Then, if she be not there, we will return and march into the land of the porcupines. So to-night let every one go to his *mia-mia* and wait for the cry, 'Rise at once !'"

So every goanna man went straight home to bed and slept soundly. They rose early, and marched into the country of the emu. As soon as the goannas had left home the teal teal rose and met to consider what they should do. One thought it would be well if the two young women who had accompanied the chief's wife hurried away and told her that her absence had caused a stir. So while the chief with his army was marching into the land of the emus, thinking that it was they who had captured his wife and made her the wife of the young emu chief, the young teal teal girls were running to the mountain to tell the chief's wife what was taking place. She sat quietly and listened to what they had to tell, and then in reply she said, "Now is our deliverance. We have been given in marriage to these beings who are not of our race and kind. I have made a discovery. At the dawn of day I was fast asleep, and a Tuckonie [6] came into the *mia-mia* and sat beside the fire warming himself. Suddenly I awoke and saw him comfortably seated there. I became so alarmed that I shrieked with fear; and he turned his eyes upon me and said, 'Do not be afraid. I am your friend, and the friend of all that are in trouble or distress. I and my companion saw you and the two others come up from the plain, and some of my brothers have visited your camping-ground and know all about you. You are in search of a water-hole, and you have been guided by the mind of my tribe to this spot. You have been sleeping. If you will follow me when I come again I will show you the opening on the top of this mountain.'"

When the Tuckonie returned the wife of the chief of the goannas rose and followed him up the mountain. When they arrived at the top he bade her sit down

---

[1] A small kind of duck.   [2] Reed spears.   [3] Weapons for hunting kangaroos.

[4] Boomerangs.   [5] Battle clubs.

[6] These are little men who live in thickly timbered country. The aboriginals believe that these queer little people visited the camping-grounds and became acquainted with all the ways of the people.

and rest. The little spirit man went away a few paces and gave a call somewhat like the *coo-ee*[7] and like a flash out of space there came many little men. Their bodies were striped with red ochre and white pipeclay. They had white cockatoo feathers decorating their heads and tied round their wrists like bracelets. In their hands they held their spears, about two feet long. Each one wore a belt of opossum-skin round his waist, and in this belt there were placed three tiny boomerangs and *waddies*. They circled round their leader, eager to receive his instructions. After a little talk they made way for him, and he came out from their midst and walked toward the wife of the goanna and stood beside her. They followed him, and he addressed his bodyguard thus, "Hear, O my brothers; we have been appointed by the unseen beings that are about—the Spirit of Good, the Spirit of Water, the Spirit of Food, the Spirit of Pleasure, the Spirit of Lightning and Thunder and Wind and Rainstorm, and lastly the Spirit of Sunshine. The goannas have withheld from the tribes that inhabit this country the long-needed water that is locked up in this mountain, they have used this gift for their own selfish ends, and have refused to share it with the aged and the infirm, and the children of other tribes. And, what is more, they have refused to supply the necessities of their own wives. Give this woman the help she requires in order to let loose the water that is contained in the mountain."

The little spirit man turned to the wife of the chief and took her a few paces farther on to a basin-like hole in the rock. He asked her to look into it. She looked and saw sparkling water, clear as crystal. "Drink," he said, and she drank until she was satisfied. "Now," he said, "you must descend, and when you reach the foot of the mountain you will meet two young women. You must ask them to hurry back to their camp and instruct the others that they must all stand on the northern side of the valley toward the porcupine boundary and await your coming."

So she went and did as she had been told. The two young women also hurried back to the camp to deliver their message, and the other teal teal, as they were asked, stood waiting on the northern side of the valley. Meantime the chief's wife stood at the base of the mountain, waiting for further instructions. Presently the Tuckonie stood beside her, and said, "O woman, these good and great spirits have given you the privilege of letting loose the waters that are anxious to be freed from the bonds that have held them prisoner these many, many years. You shall be a blessing to all the animal, bird, reptile, and insect tribes. You must keep this great event in remembrance. Tell your children of the privilege that the Spirit of Water conferred on you. Take this." He handed her a grass-tree stick, and said, "At a given signal thrust it into the mountain-side, and the water shall be let loose."

Again the Tuckonie disappeared. The chief's wife stood there alone, thinking

[7] An Australian bush-cry.

over this strange happening. She pinched her arm and struck her leg to see whether she was asleep. She felt the pinch and the blow. "I am very much awake," she said. "What a wonderful experience!" Then a voice said, "Thrust the stick into the mountain." She placed the point of the stick against the mountain-side, and pushed hard. It gradually went in farther and farther, until it had gone its whole length. Then the voice of the Tuckonie said, "Now flee for your life to where your sisters are." She sped down the valley as fast as her feet could carry her. When she had gone half the distance a loud noise, as of a mighty wind, broke the still air. It was the sound of the water leaping forth out of its prison, and thundering down the valley with the speed of a mighty wind. The chief's wife arrived among her teal teal sisters, and breathlessly told them that the water from the mountain would be flowing down the valley. While she was speaking they saw dust rising from the hill-side, and the water tearing its way through the valley, and huge trees being uprooted and carried along. They looked with amazement as the water rushed past them on its way to join the Murray river. When it reached the Murray it settled down to be a flowing river. The teal teal came to its bank, and sat in the shade of the trees, watching their children sporting and splashing in the water.

Next day the goannas returned, and were making their way to the camp when they beheld with wonder that a river separated them from their wives and children. They were greatly annoyed. The chief called to the women across the river and asked where this flowing stream of water came from. He was answered by the familiar voice of his wife, "From the rock hole that you and the goannas have kept secret from us and the other tribes, and used for your own selfish purposes. But I, O chief, your wife, discovered your secret, and let loose the water, this great gift and blessing that belongs to all beings. So we, who were your wives, have decided that we shall no longer belong to you. Henceforth our home will be in the trees. And we do not wish to be, and we will not be, your wives."

So this separation came about through the selfishness of the goannas, and since that time the teal teal have refused to become the wives of the goannas. To keep in memory that long, long ago event of the release of the water they make their homes in the limbs or branches of the gumtrees, and they make their nests of mud or clay shaped like the mountain that contained the water. And in these small mountain-shaped homes they lay their eggs, and when these are hatched and the little birds come to see the light and the home, the mother in bird-language tells them of the long, long ago when she was in distress, seeking water to quench her thirst, and how a little man helped her in her search and showed her where it was to be found, and promised that their tribe should throughout their generations have a home as a memorial, and rear their children in it. As for the goannas, because of their rough natures and their stealing from others who endure the difficulties, hardships, and dangers of hunting, they are doomed not only to carry upon their bodies the marks received as a punishment for their misdeeds, but to endure a much more grievous punishment for their selfishness to all around them, and more especially to their wives, the teal teal, in that they have lost that great pride of their heart, the wonderful rock hole which contained a lasting supply of clear and refreshing water. And beyond this their strictly guarded prize has become a great barrier separating them from their wives and children for ever. And in sorrow they have wandered to all parts of Australia, and in certain seasons of the year they dig a hole in the ground and bury themselves in it, and weep during the dark, cold wintry nights, until they fall into a deep sleep, which lasts until spring calls them forth to take up their burden of life once more. And, in revenge for the loss of their wives, they rob the nests of the teal teal of their eggs, thinking that by devouring the eggs they may put an end to the existence of their former wives.

DINEWAN THE EMU, AND WAHN THE CROWS

DINEWAN and his two wives, the Wahn, were camping out. Seeing some clouds gathering, they made a bark humpy. It came on to rain, and they all took shelter under it. Dinewan, when his wives were not looking, gave a kick against a piece of bark at one side of the humpy, knocked it down, then told his wives to go and pick it up again. While they were outside putting it up, he gave a kick, and knocked down a piece on the other side; so no sooner were they in again than out they had to go. This he did time after time, until at last they suspected him, and decided that one of them would watch. The one who was watching saw Dinewan laugh to himself and go and knock down the bark they had just put up, chuckling at the thought of his wives having to go out in the wet and cold, to put it up, while he had his supper dry and comfortably inside. The one who saw him told the other, and they decided to teach him a lesson. So in they came, each with a piece of bark filled with hot coals. They went straight up to Dinewan, who was lying down, laughing. "Now," they said, "you shall feel as hot as we did cold." And they threw the coals over him. Dinewan jumped up, crying aloud with the pain, for he was badly burnt. He rolled himself over, and ran into the rain; and his wives stayed inside, and laughed aloud at him.

GOOLAHWILLEEL, THE TOPKNOT PIGEONS

YOUNG Goolahwilleel used to go out hunting every day. His mother and sisters always expected that he would bring home kangaroo and emu for them. But each day he came home without any meat at all. They asked him what he did in the bush, as he evidently did not hunt. He said that he did hunt.

"Then why," said they, "do you bring us nothing home ?"

"I cannot catch and kill what I follow," he said.

"You hear me cry out when I find kangaroo or emu; is it not so ?"

"Yes; each day we hear you call when you find something, and each day we get ready the fire, expecting you to bring home the spoils of the chase, but you bring nothing."

"To-morrow," he said, "you shall not be disappointed. I will bring you a kangaroo."

Every day, instead of hunting, Goolahwilleel had been gathering wattle-gum, and with this he had been modelling a kangaroo—a perfect model of one, tail, ears, and all complete. So the next day he came towards the camp carrying this kangaroo made of gum. Seeing him coming, and also seeing that he was carrying the promised kangaroo, his mother and sisters said: "Ah, Goolahwilleel spoke truly. He has kept his word, and now brings us a kangaroo. Pile up the fire. To-night we shall eat meat."

About a hundred yards away from the camp Goolahwilleel put down his model, and came on without it. His mother called out: "Where is the kangaroo you brought home?"

"Oh, over there." And he pointed toward where he had left it.

The sisters ran to get it, but came back, saying: "Where is it? We cannot see it."

"Over there," he said, pointing again.

"But there is only a great figure of gum there."

"Well, did I say it was anything else? Did I not say it was gum?"

"No, you did not. You said it was a kangaroo."

"And so it is a kangaroo. A beautiful kangaroo that I made all by myself." And he smiled quite proudly to think what a fine kangaroo he had made.

But his mother and sisters did not smile. They seized him, and gave him a good beating for deceiving them. They told him he should never go out alone again, for he only played instead of hunting, though he knew they starved for meat. They would always in the future go with him.

And so forever the Goolahwilleels went in flocks, nevermore singly, in search of food.

THE FIRE-MAKERS

IN the days when Bootoolgah, the crane, married Goonur, the kangaroo rat, there was no fire in their country. They had had to eat their food raw or just dry it in the sun. One day when Bootoolgah was rubbing two pieces of wood together, he saw a faint spark sent forth and then a slight smoke. "Look," he said to Goonur, "see what comes when I rub these two pieces of wood together— smoke! Would it not be good if we could make fire for ourselves with which to cook our food, so as not to have to wait for the sun to dry it ?"

Goonur looked, and, seeing the smoke, she said: "Great indeed would be the day when we could make fire. Split your stick, Bootoolgah, and place in the opening bark and dried grass that even one spark may kindle a light."

And hearing wisdom in her words, even as she said Bootoolgah did. And lo! after much rubbing, from the opening came a small flame. For as Goonur had said it would, the spark lit the grass, the bark smouldered and smoked, and so Bootoolgah the crane, and Goonur the kangaroo rat, discovered the art of fire-making.

"This we will keep secret," they said, "from all the tribes. When we make a fire to cook our fish we will go into a Bingahwingul scrub. There will we make a fire and cook our food in secret. We will hide our fire-sticks in the open-mouthed seeds of the Bingahwinguls; one fire-stick we will always carry hidden in our comebee."[1]

Bootoolgah and Goonur cooked the next fish they caught, and found it very good. When they went back to the camp they took some of their cooked fish with them. The blacks noticed it looked quite different from the usual sun-dried fish, so they asked, "What did you to that fish?,"

"Let it lie in the sun," said they.

"Not so," said the other.

But that the fish was sun-dried Bootoolgah and Goonur persisted. Day by day passed, and after catching their fish, these two always disappeared, returning with their food looking quite different from that of the others. At last, being unable to extract any information from them, it was determined by the tribe to watch them. Boolooral, the night owl, and Quarrian, the parrot, were appointed to follow the two when they disappeared, to watch where they went, and find out what they did. Accordingly after the next fish were caught, when Bootoolgah and Goonur gathered up their share and started for the bush, Boolooral and Quarrian followed on their tracks. They saw them disappear into a Bingahwingul scrub, where they lost sight of them. Seeing a high tree on the edge of the scrub, they climbed up it, and from there they saw all that was to be seen. They saw Bootoolgah and Goonur

---

[1] A bag made of kangaroo skin.

throw down their load of fish, open their comebee and take from it a stick, which stick, when they had blown upon it, they laid in the midst of a heap of leaves and twigs, and at once from this heap they saw a flame leap, which flame the fire-makers fed with bigger sticks. Then, as the flame died down, they saw the two place their fish in the ashes that remained from the burnt sticks. Then back to the camp of their tribes went Boolooral and Quarrian, back with the news of their discovery. Great was the talk amongst the blacks, and many the queries as to how to get possession of the comebee with the fire stick in it, when next Bootoolgah and Goonur came into the camp. It was at length decided to hold a corrobboree,[2] and it was to be one on a scale not often seen, probably never before by the young of the tribes. The greybeards proposed to so astonish Bootoolgah and Goonur as to make them forget to guard their precious comebee. As soon as they were intent on the corrobboree and off guard, someone was to seize the comebee, steal the fire-stick, and start fires for the good of all. Most of them had tasted the cooked fish brought into camp by the fire-makers and, having found it good, hungered for it. Beeargah, the hawk, was told to feign sickness, to tie up his head, and to lie down near wherever the two sat to watch the corrobboree. Lying near them he was to watch them all the time, and when they were laughing and unthinking of anything but the spectacle before them, he was to steal the comebee. Having arranged their plan of action, they all prepared for a big corrobboree. They sent word to all the surrounding tribes, asking them to attend, especially they begged the Bralgahs to come, as they were celebrated for their wonderful dancing, which was so wonderful as to be most likely to absorb the attention of the fire-makers.

All the tribes agreed to come, and soon all were engaged in great preparations. Each determined to outdo the other in the quaintness and brightness of their painting for the corrobboree. Each tribe as they arrived gained great applause; never before had the young people seen so much diversity in colouring and design. Beeleer, the black cockatoo tribe, came with bright splashes of orange-red on their black skins. The Pelicans came as a contrast, almost pure white, only a touch here and there of their black skin showing where the white paint had rubbed off. The Black Divers came in their black skins, but these polished to look like satin. Then came the Millears, the beauties of the Kangaroo Rat family, who had their home on the Morillas. After them came the Buckandeer or Native Cat tribe, painted in dull colours, but in all sorts of patterns. Mairas or Paddymelons came too in haste to take part in the great corrobboree. After them, walking slowly, came the Bralgahs, looking tall and dignified as they held up their red heads, painted so in contrast to their French-grey bodies, which they deemed too dull a colour, unbrightened, for such a gay occasion. Amongst the many tribes there, too

---

[2] A dance.

numerous to mention, were the rose and grey painted Galahs,[3] the green and crimson painted Billai: [4] most brilliant were they with their bodies grass green, and their sides bright crimson, so afterward gaining them the name of crimson wings. The bright little Gidgereegahs [5] came too.

Great was the gathering that Bootoolgah, the crane, and Goonur, the kangaroo rat, found assembled as they hurried on to the scene. Bootoolgah had warned Goonur that they must only be spectators, and take no active part in the corrobboree, as they had to guard their comebee. Obedient to his advice, Goonur seated herself beside him and slung the comebee over her arm. Bootoolgah warned her to be careful and not forget she had it. But as the corrobboree went on, so absorbed did she become that she forgot the comebee, which slipped from her arm. Happily, Bootoolgah saw it do so, replaced it, and bade her take heed, so baulking Beeargah, who had been about to seize it, for his vigilance was unceasing, and, deeming him sick almost unto death, the two whom he was watching took no heed of him. Back he crouched, moaning as he turned, but keeping ever an eye on Goonur. And soon was he rewarded. Now came the turn of the Bralgahs to dance, and every eye but that of the watchful one was fixed on them as slowly they came into the ring. First they advanced, bowed and retired, then they repeated what they had done before, and again, each time getting faster and faster in their movements, changing their bows into pirouettes, craning their long necks and making such antics as they went through the figures of their dance, and replacing their dignity with such grotesqueness, as to make their large audience shake with laughter, they themselves keeping throughout all their grotesque measures a solemn air, which only seemed to heighten the effect of their antics.

And now came the chance of Beeargah the hawk. In the excitement of the moment Goonur forgot the comebee as did Bootoolgah. They joined in the mirthful applause of the crowd, and Goonur threw herself back helpless with laughter. As she did so the comebee slipped from her arm. Then up jumped the sick man from behind her, seized the comebee with his combo, cut it open, snatched forth the fire-stick, set fire to the heap of grass ready near where he had lain, and all before the two realized their loss. When they discovered the precious comebee was gone, up jumped Bootoolgah and Goonur. After Beeargah ran Bootoolgah, but Beeargah had a start and was fleeter of foot, so distanced his pursuer quickly. As he ran he fired the grass with the stick he still held. Bootoolgah, finding he could not catch Beeargah, and seeing fires everywhere, retired from the pursuit, feeling it was useless now to try to guard their secret, for it had become the common property of all the tribes there assembled.

---

[3] Cockatoos.   [4] Parrots.   [5] Small parrots.

WAYAMBEH THE TURTLE

OOLAH, the lizard, was out getting yams on a Mirrieh flat. She had three of her children with her. Suddenly she thought she heard some one moving behind the big Mirrieh bushes. She listened. All of a sudden out jumped Wayambeh from behind a bush and seized Oolah, telling her not to make a noise and he would not hurt her, but that he meant to take her off to his camp to be his wife. He would take her three children too and look after them. Resistance was useless, for Oolah had only her yam-stick, while Wayambeh had his spears and boondees. Wayambeh took the woman and her children to his camp. His tribe when they saw him bring home a woman of the Oolah tribe, asked him if her tribe had given her to him. He said, "No, I have stolen her."

"Well," they said, "her tribe will soon be after her; you must protect yourself; we shall not fight for you. You had no right to steal her without telling us. We had a young woman of our own tribe for you, yet you go and steal an Oolah and bring her to the camp of the Wayambeh. On your head be the consequences."

In a short time the Oolahs were seen coming across the plain which faced the camp of the Wayambeh. And they came not in friendship or to parley, for no women were with them, and they carried no boughs of peace in their hands, but were painted as for war, and were armed with fighting weapons.

When the Wayambeh saw the approach of the Oolah, their chief said: "Now, Wayambeh, you had better go out on to the plain and do your own fighting; we shall not help you."

Wayambeh chose the two biggest boreens that he had; one he slung on him, covering the front of his body, and one on the back; then, seizing his weapons, he strode out to meet his enemies.

When he was well out on to the plain, though still some distance from the Oolah, he called out, "Come on." The answer was a shower of spears and boomerangs. As they came whizzing through the air Wayambeh drew his arms inside the boreens, and ducking his head down between them, so escaped.

As the weapons fell harmless to the ground, glancing off his boreen, out again he stretched his arms and held up again his head, shouting, "Come on, try again, I'm ready.".

The answer was another shower of weapons, which he met in the same way. At last the Oolahs closed in round him, forcing him to retreat toward the creek.

Shower after shower of weapons they slung at him, and were getting at such close quarters that his only chance was to dive into the creek. He turned toward the creek, tore the front boreen off him, flung down his weapons and plunged in.

The Oolah waited, spears poised in hand, ready to aim directly his head appeared above water, but they waited in vain. Wayambeh, the black fellow, they never saw again, but in the water-hole wherein he had dived they saw a strange creature, which bore on its back a fixed structure like a boreen, and which, when they went to try and catch it, drew in its head and limbs, so they said, "It is Wayambeh." And this was the beginning of Wayambeh, or turtle, in the creeks.

GOOLOO THE MAGPIE AND THE WAHROOGAH

GOOLOO was a very old woman, and a very wicked old woman too, as this story will tell. During all the past season, when the grass was thick with seed, she had gathered much doonburr,[1] which she crushed into meal as she wanted it for food. She used to crush it on a big flat stone with a small flat stone— the big stone was called a dayoorl. Gooloo ground a great deal of the doonburr seed to put away for immediate use, the rest she kept whole, to be ground as required.

Soon after she had finished her first grinding, a neighbouring tribe came along and camped near where she was. One day the men all went out hunting, leaving the women and children in the camp. After the men had been gone a little while, Gooloo the magpie came to their camp to talk to the women. She said, "Why do you not go hunting too? Many are the nests of the wurranunnahs[2] round here, and thick is the honey in them. Many and ripe are the bumbles hanging now on the bumble trees; red is the fruit of the grooees,[3] and opening with ripeness the fruit of the guiebets.[4] Yet you sit in the camp and hunger, until your husbands return with the dinewan and bowrah[5] they have gone forth to slay. Go, women, and gather of the plenty that surrounds you. I will take care of your children, the little Wahroogahs."

"Your words are wise," the women said. "It is foolish to sit here and hunger, when near at hand yams are thick in the ground, and many fruits wait but the plucking. We will go and fill quickly our comebees and goolays, but our children we will take with us."

"Not so," said Gooloo, "foolish indeed were you to do that. You would tire the little feet of those that run, and tire yourselves with the burden of those that have to be carried. No, take forth your comebees and goolays empty, that ye may bring back the more. Many are the spoils that wait only the hand of the gatherer. Look ye, I have a durrie[6] made of fresh doonburr seed, cooking just now on that bark between two fires; that shall your children eat, and swiftly shall I make them another. They shall eat and be full ere their mothers are out of sight. See, they come to me now, they hunger for durrie, and well will I feed them. Haste ye then, that

---

[1] Grass seed.	[2] Bees.	[3] Trees with fruit like a plum.
[4] A thorny creeper.	[5] Kangaroo.	[6] Bread.

ye may return in time to make ready the fires for cooking the meat your husbands will bring. Glad will your husbands be when they see that ye have filled your goolays and comebees with fruits, and your wirrees with honey. Haste ye, I say, and do well."

Having listened to the words of Gooloo, the women decided to do as she said, and, leaving their children with her, they started forth with empty comebees, and armed with combos, with which to chop out the bees' nests and opossums, and with yam-sticks to dig up yams.

When the women had gone, Gooloo gathered the children round her and fed them with durrie, hot from the coals. Honey too, she gave them, and bumbles [7] which she had buried to ripen. When they had eaten, she hurried them off to her real home, built in a hollow tree, a little distance away from where she had been cooking her durrie. Into her house she hurriedly thrust them, followed quickly herself, and made all secure. Here she fed them again, but the children had already satisfied their hunger, and now they missed their mothers and began to cry. Their crying reached the ears of the women as they were returning to their camp. Quickly they came at the sound which is not good in a mother's ears. As they quickened their steps they thought how soon the spoils that lay heavy in their comebees would comfort their children. And happy they, the mothers, would feel when they fed the Wahroogahs with the dainties they had gathered for them. Soon they reached the camp, but, alas! where were their children? And where was Gooloo the magpie ?

"They are playing wahgoo," [8] they said, "and have hidden themselves."

The mothers hunted all round for them, and called aloud the names of their children and Gooloo. But no answer could they hear and no trace could they find. And yet every now and then they heard the sound of children wailing. But seek as they would they found them not. Then loudly wailed the mothers themselves for their lost Wahroogahs, and, wailing, returned to the camp to wait the coming of the black fellows. Heavy were their hearts, and sad were their faces when their husbands returned. They hastened to tell the black fellows when they came, how Gooloo had persuaded them to go hunting, promising if they did so that she would feed the hungry Wahroogahs, and care for them while they were away, but—and here they wailed again for their poor Wahroogahs. They told how they had listened to her words and gone; truth had she told of the plenty round, their comebees and goolays were full of fruits and spoils they had gathered, but, alas, they came home with them laden only to find their children gone and Gooloo gone too. And no trace could they find of either, though at times they heard a sound as of children wailing.

---

[7] A fruit like a wild orange.   [8] Hiding.

Then wroth were the men, saying: "What mothers are ye to leave your young to a stranger, and that stranger a Gooloo, ever a treacherous race? Did we not go forth to gain food for you and our children? Saw ye ever your husbands return from the chase empty handed? Then why, when ye knew we were gone hunting, must ye too go forth and leave our helpless ones to a stranger? Oh, evil, evil indeed is the time that has come when a mother forgets her child. Stay ye in the camp while we go forth to hunt for our lost Wahroogahs. Heavy will be our hands on the women if we return without them."

The men hunted the bush round for miles, but found no trace of the lost Wahroogahs, though they too heard at times a noise as of children's voices wailing.

But beyond the wailing which echoed in the mothers' ears forever, no trace was found of the children. For many days the women sat in the camp mourning for their lost Wahroogahs, and beating their heads because they had listened to the voice of Gooloo.

BASQUE TALES

THE Basques represent a very old stratum of European ethnology. Their language, as regards the mass of the people, is largely unwritten, and legends appear in a purer and older form than among many other European peoples. The preservation of primitive ideas has been fostered by the isolation of the people. One feels they really believed in a time when all animals could speak. It is strange, however, to note that the old and the new often go hand in hand, e.g., there is a mention of cannon and bullets in the Tartaro's story. The Tartaro is really the Basque Cyclops—he was a monster with cannibal habits, but was almost always beaten in his contests with men, because of his intellectual inferiority.

ACHERIA THE FOX

ONE day a fox was hungry. He did not know what to think. He saw a shepherd pass every day with his flock, and he said to himself that he ought to steal his milk and his cheese, and to have a good feast; but he needed some one to help him in order to effect anything. So he goes off to find a wolf, and he says to him: "Wolf, wolf! we ought to have a feast with such a shepherd's milk and cheese. You, you shall go to where the flocks are feeding, and from a distance you must howl, 'Uhur, uhur uhur.' The man, after having milked his sheep, drives them into the field, with his dog, very early in the morning, and he stops at home to do his work, and then he makes his cheese; and, when you have begun to howl, 'Uhur, uhur,' and the dog to bark, the shepherd will leave everything else, and will go off full speed. During this time I will steal the milk, and we will share it when you come to me."

The wolf agreed to have a feast, and set out. He did just what the fox had told him. The dog began to bark when the wolf approached. And when the man heard that, he went off, leaving everything, and our fox goes and steals the vessel in which the curdled milk was. What does he do then, before the arrival of the wolf? He gently, gently takes off the cream, thinly, thinly, and he eats all the contents of the jug. After he has eaten all, he fills it up with dirt, and puts back the cream on the top, and he awaits the wolf at the place where he had told him. The fox says to him, since it is he who is to make the division, that as the top is much better than the underneath part, the one who should choose that should have *only* that, and the other all the rest. "Choose now which you would like."

The wolf says to him:
"I will not have the top; I prefer what is at the bottom."

111

The fox then takes the top, and gives the poor wolf the vessel full of dirt. When he saw that, the wolf got angry; but the fox said to him, "It is not my fault. Apparently the shepherd makes it like that."

And the fox goes off well filled.

Another day he was again very hungry, and did not know what to contrive. Every day he saw a boy pass by on the road with his father's dinner. He says to the blackbird:

"Blackbird, you don't know what we ought to do? We ought to have a good dinner. A boy will pass by here directly. You will go in front of him, and when the boy goes to catch you, you will go on a little farther, limping, and when you shall have done that a little while the boy will get impatient, and he will put down his basket in order to catch you quicker. I will take the basket, and will go to such a spot, and we will share it, and will make a good dinner."

The blackbird says to him, "Yes."

When the boy passes, the blackbird goes in front of the boy, limping, limping. When the boy stoops (to catch him), the blackbird escapes a little further on. At last the boy, getting impatient, puts his basket on the ground, in order to go quicker after the blackbird. The fox, who kept watching to get hold of the basket, goes off with it, not to the place agreed upon, but to his hole, and there he stuffs himself, eating the blackbird's share as well as his own.

Then he says to himself:

"I shall do no good stopping here. The wolf is my enemy, and the blackbird too. Something will happen to me if I stay here. I must go off to the other side of the water."

He goes and stands at the water's edge. A boatman happened to pass, and he said to him:

"Ho! man, ho! Will you, then, cross me over this water? I will tell you three truths."

The man said to him, "Yes."

The fox jumps into the boat, and he begins to say:

"People say that maize bread is as good as wheaten bread. That is a falsehood. Wheaten bread is better. That is one truth."

When he was in the middle of the river, he said:

"People say, too, 'What a fine night; it is just as clear as the day!' That's a lie. The day is always clearer. That is the second truth."

And he told him the third as they were getting near the bank.

"Oh! man, man, you have a bad pair of trousers on, and they will get much worse, if you do not pass over people who pay you more than I."

"That's very true," said the man; and the fox leapt ashore.

(Then I was by the side of the river, and I learnt these three truths, and I have never forgotten them since.)

ERRUA THE MADMAN

L IKE many others in the world, there was a man and a woman who had a son. He was very wicked, and did nothing but mischief. His parents decided that they must send him away, and the lad was quite willing to set off.

He set out then, and goes far, far, far away. He comes to a city, and asks if they want a servant. They wanted one in a certain house. He goes there. They settle their terms at so much a month, and that the one who is not satisfied should strip the skin off the other's back.

The master sends his servant to the forest to get the most crooked pieces of wood that he can find. Near the forest there was a vineyard. What does the servant do but cut it all up, and carries it to the house. The master asks him where the wood is. He shows him the vine wood cut up. The master said nothing to him, but he was not pleased.

Next day the master says to him, "Take the cows to such a field, and don't break any hole in the fence."

What does the lad do? He cuts all the cows into little pieces, and throws them bit by bit into the field. The master was still more angry; but he could not say anything, for fear of having his skin stripped off. So what does he do? He buys a herd of pigs, and sends his servant to the mountain with the herd.

The master knew quite well that there was a Tartaro in this mountain, but he sends him there all the same.

Our madman goes walking on, on, on. He arrives at a little hut. The Tartaro's house was quite close to his. The pigs of the Tartaro and those of the madman used to go out together. The Tartaro said one day to him:

"Will you make a wager as to who will throw a stone farthest?"

He accepted the wager. That evening our madman was very sad. While he was at his prayers, an old woman appeared to him, and asks him: "What is the matter with you? Why are you so sad?"

He tells her the wager that he has made with the Tartaro. The old woman says to him: "If it is only that, it is nothing."

And so she gives him a bird and says to him: "Instead of a stone, throw this bird."

The madman was very glad at this. The next day he does as the old woman told him. The Tartaro's stone went enormously far, but at last it fell; but the madman's bird never came down at all.

The Tartaro was astonished that he had lost his wager, and they make another—which of the two should throw a bar of iron the farthest. The madman accepted again. He was in his little house sadly in prayer. The old woman appears again. She asks him:

"What's the matter with you?"

"I have made a wager again, which of the two will throw the bar of iron the farthest, and I am very sorry."

"If it is only that, it is nothing. When you take hold of the bar of iron, say, 'Rise up, bar of iron, here and Salamanca.'"

Next day the Tartaro takes his terrible bar of iron, and throws it fearfully far. The young man could hardly lift up one end, and he says: "Rise up, bar of iron, here and Salamanca."

When the Tartaro heard that he cried out: "I give up my wager—you have won," and he takes the bar of iron away from him. "My father and my mother live at Salamanca; don't throw, I beg of you. I implore you—you will crush them."

Our madman goes away very happy.

The Tartaro says to him again:

"I will pull up the biggest oak in the forest, and you pull up another."

He says, "Yes." And the later it grew in the day, the sadder he became. He was at his prayers. The old woman comes to him again, and says to him:

"What's the matter with you ?"

He tells her the wager he has made with the Tartaro, and how he will pull up an oak. The old woman gives him three balls of thread, and tells him to begin and tie them to all the oaks in the forest.

Next day the Tartaro pulls up his oak, an enormously, enormously big one; and the madman begins to tie, and to tie, and to tie.

The Tartaro asks him:

"What are you doing that for!"

"You pulled up one, but I all these."

The Tartaro replies:

"No! No! No! What shall I do to fatten my pigs with, without acorns? You have won; you have won the wager."

Our madman goes off then with his hogs. He goes walking on, on, on, with all his pigs. He comes to a town where it was just market day, and sells them all except two, keeping, however, all the tails, which he put in his pockets.

He went on to his master's. Near the house there was a marsh quite full of mud. He puts his live pigs into it and all the tails too. He enters the house, and says to the master that he is there with his pigs. The master is astounded to see him.

He asks him, "Where are the pigs, then?"

He says to him, "They have gone into the mud they were so tired."

Both go out, and begin to get the real pig out, and between the two they pull it out very well. They try to do the same thing with the others; but they kept pulling out nothing but tails.

The madman says, "You see how fat they are; that is why the tails come out alone."

He sends the servant to fetch the spade and the hoe. Instead of bringing them he begins to beat the mistress, *whack! whack!* and he cries to the master, "One or both ?"

The master says to him, "Both, both."

And then he beats the servant maid almost to pieces. He goes then to the master, taking with him the spade and the hoe, and he sets to beating him with the spade and the hoe, until he can no longer defend himself, and then he thrashes the skin off his back, and takes his pig and goes off home to his father and mother.

BOHEMIA

THE stories that follow were translated from the language of the Slavonic inhabitants of Bohemia. In them are introduced superhuman dwellers in the wood. As in Russian tales there are two waters, one of death and one of life. The "dead water" heals the wounds of a corpse and the dead body must then be brought to life by the "living water."

THE THREE GOLDEN HAIRS OF GRANDFATHER ALLKNOW

THERE was once upon a time a king who delighted in hunting wild animals in forests. One day he chased a stag to a great distance and lost his way. He was all alone; night came on, and the king was only too glad to find a cottage in a clearing. A charcoal-burner lived there. The king asked him whether he would guide him out of the forest to the road, promising to pay him well for it. "I would gladly go with you," said the charcoal-burner, "but, you see, my wife is ill; I cannot go away. And whither would you go at this time of night? Lie down on some hay on the garret floor, and to-morrow morning I will be your guide."

Soon afterward a baby boy was born to the charcoal-burner. The king was lying on the floor and couldn't sleep. At midnight he observed a kind of light in the keeping-room below. He peeped through a chink in the boarding and saw the charcoal-burner asleep, his wife lying in a dead faint, and three old hags, all in white, standing by the baby, each with a lighted taper in her hand. The first said: "My gift to this boy is, that he shall come into great dangers." The second said: "My gift to him is, that he shall escape from them all and live long." And the third said: "And I give him to wife the baby daughter who has this day been born to that king who is lying upstairs on the hay." Thereupon the hags put out their tapers, and all was still again. They were the Fates.

The king felt as if a sword had been thrust into his breast. He didn't sleep till morning, thinking over what to do, and how to do it, to prevent that coming to pass which he had heard. When day dawned the child began to cry. The charcoal-burner got up and saw that his wife had gone to sleep for ever. "Oh, my poor little orphan," whimpered he; "what shall I do with you now?" "Give me the baby," said the king; "I'll take care that it shall be well with it, and will give you so much money that you needn't burn charcoal as long as you live." 'The charcoal-burner was delighted at this, and the king promised to send for the baby. When he arrived at his palace they told him, with great joy, that a beautiful baby daughter had been

116

born to him on such and such a night. It was the very night on which he saw the three Fates. The king frowned, called one of his servants, and told him: "Go to such a place in the forest; a charcoal-burner lives there in a cottage. Give him this money, and he will give you a little child. Take the child and drown it on your way back. If you don't drown it, you shall drink water yourself." The servant went, took the baby and put it into a basket, and when he came to a narrow foot-bridge, under which flowed a deep and broad river, he threw the basket and all into the water. "Good night, uninvited son-in law!" said the king, when the servant told him what he had done.

The king thought that the baby was drowned, but it wasn't. It floated in the water in the basket as if it had been its cradle, and slept as if the river were singing to it, till it floated down to a fisherman's cottage. The fisher man was sitting by the bank mending his net. He saw something floating down the river, jumped into his boat, and went to catch it, and out of the water he drew the baby in the basket. He carried it to his wife, and said: "You've always wanted a little son, and here you have one. The water has brought him to us." The fisherman's wife was delighted, and brought up the child as her own. They named him "Floatling," because he had floated to them on the water.

The river flowed on and years passed on, and from a boy he became a handsome youth, the like of whom was not to be found far and wide. One day in the summer it came to pass that the king rode that way all alone. It was hot, and he was thirsty, and beckoned to the fisherman to give him a little fresh water. When Floatling brought it to him, the king looked at him with astonishment. "You've a fine lad, fisherman!" said he; "is he your son ?"

"He is and he isn't," replied the fisherman; "just twenty years ago he floated, as a little baby, down the river in a basket, and we brought him up." A mist came before the king's eyes; he became as pale as a whitewashed wall, perceiving that it was the child he had ordered to be drowned. But he soon recollected himself, sprang from his horse, and said: "I want a messenger to my palace, and have nobody with me. Can this youth go thither for me?" "Your majesty has but to command and the lad will go," said the fisherman. The king sat down and wrote a letter to his queen: "Cause this young man whom I send you to be run through with a sword at once; he is a dangerous enemy of mine. Let it be done before I return. Such is my will." He then folded the letter, fastened and sealed it with his signet.

Floatling started at once with the letter. He had to go through a great forest, but missed the road and lost his way. He went from thicket to thicket till it began to grow dark. Then he met an old hag, who said to him: "Whither are you going, Floatling?" "I am going with a letter to the king's palace, and have lost my way. Can't you tell me, mother, how to get into the right road ?" "Anyhow, you won't get there to-day," said the hag; "it's dark. Stay the night with me. You won't be with a stranger. I am your godmother." The young man allowed himself to be persuaded, and they hadn't gone many paces when they saw before them a pretty little house, just as if it had grown all at once out of the ground. In the night, when the lad was asleep, the hag took the letter out of his pocket and put another in its place, in which it was written thus: "Cause this young man whom I send you to be married to our daughter at once; he is my destined son-in-law. Let it be done before I return. Such is my will."

When the queen read the letter, she immediately ordered arrangements to be made for the wedding, and neither she nor the young princess could gaze enough at the bridegroom, so delighted were they with him; and Floatling was similarly delighted with his royal bride. Some days after, the king came home, and when he found what had happened, he was violently enraged at his queen for what she had done. "Anyhow, you ordered me yourself to have him married to our daughter before you returned," answered the queen, and gave him the letter. The king took the letter and looked it through—writing, seal, paper, everything was his own. He had his son-in-law called, and questioned him about what had happened on his way to the palace.

Floatling related how he had started and had lost his way in the forest, and stayed the night with his old godmother. "What did she look like?" "So and so." The king perceived from his statement that it was the same person that had, twenty years before, assigned his daughter to the charcoal burner's son. He thought and thought, and then he said: "What's done can't be altered; still, you can't be my son-in-law for nothing. If you want to have my daughter, you must bring me for a dowry three golden hairs of Grandfather Allknow." He thought to himself that he should thus be quit of his distasteful son-in-law.

Floatling took leave of his bride and went—which way, and whither? I don't know; but, as a Fate was his godmother, it was easy for him to find the right road. He went far and wide, over hills and dales, over fords and rivers, till he came to a black sea. There he saw a boat, and in it a ferryman. "God bless you, old ferryman!" "God grant it, young pilgrim! Whither are you travelling?" "To Grandfather Allknow, for three golden hairs." "Ho, ho! I have long been waiting for such a messenger. For twenty years I've been ferrying here, and nobody's come to set me free. If you promise me to ask Grandfather Allknow when the end of my work will be, I will ferry you over." Floatling promised, and the ferryman ferried him across.

After this he came to a great city, but it was decayed and sad. In front of the city he met an old man, who had a staff in his hand, and could scarcely crawl. "God bless you, aged grandfather!" "God grant it, handsome youth! Whither are you going?" "To Grandfather Allknow, for three golden hairs." "Ah! ah! we've long been waiting for some such messenger; I must at once conduct you to our lord the king." When they got there the king said: "I hear that you are going on an errand to Grandfather Allknow. We had an apple-tree here that bore youth-producing apples. If anybody ate one, though he were on the brink of the grave, he got young again, and became like a young man. But for the last twenty years our apple-tree has produced no fruit. If you promise me to ask Grandfather Allknow whether there is any help for us, I will requite you royally." Floatling promised, and the king dismissed him graciously. After that he came again to another great city, which was half ruined. Not far from the city a son was burying his deceased father, and tears, like peas, were rolling down his cheek. "God bless you, mournful grave digger!" said Floatling. "God grant it, good pilgrim! Whither are you going?" "I am going to Grandfather Allknow, for three golden hairs." "To Grandfather Allknow? It's a pity you didn't come sooner! But our king has long been waiting for some such messenger; I must conduct you to him." When they got there, the king said: "I hear that you are going on an errand to Grandfather Allknow. We had a well here, out of which sprang living water; if anybody drank it, even were he at the point of death, he would get well at once; nay, were he already a corpse, if this water were sprinkled upon him, he would immediately rise up and walk. But for the last twenty years the water has ceased to flow. If you promise me to ask Grandfather Allknow whether there is any help for us, I will give you a royal reward." Floatling promised, and the king dismissed him graciously.

After this he went far and wide through a black forest, and in the midst of that forest espied a large green meadow, full of beautiful flowers, and in it a golden palace. This was Grandfather Allknow's palace; it glittered as if on fire. Floatling went into the palace, but found nobody there but an old hag sitting and spinning in a corner. "Welcome, Floatling!" said she; "I am delighted to see you again." It was his godmother, at whose house he had spent the night when he was carrying the letter. "What has brought you here?" "The king would not allow me to be his son-in-law for nothing, so he sent me for three golden hairs of Grandfather Allknow." The hag smiled, and said: "Grandfather Allknow is my son, the bright Sun; in the morning he is a little lad, at noon a grown man, and in the evening an old grandfather. I will provide you with the three golden hairs from his golden head, that I too mayn't be your godmother for nothing. But, my boy! you can't remain as you are. My son is certainly a good soul, but when he comes home hungry in the evening, it might easily happen that he might roast and eat you for his supper. Yonder is an empty tub; I will cover you over with it." Floatling begged her also to question Grandfather Allknow about the three things concerning which he had promised on the road to bring answers. "I will," said the hag, "and do you give heed to what he says."

All at once a wind arose outside and in flew the Sun, an old grandfather with a golden head, by the west window, into the room. "A smell, a smell of human flesh!" says he; "have you anybody here, Mother?" "Star of the day! whom could I have here without your seeing him? But so it is; you're all day long flying over God's world, and your nose is filled with the scent of human flesh; so it's no wonder that you still smell it when you come home in the evening." The old man said nothing in reply, and sat down to his supper. After supper he laid his golden head on the hag's lap and began to slumber. As soon as she saw that he was sound asleep, she pulled out a golden hair and threw it on the ground. It rang like a harp-string. "What do you want, Mother?" said the old man. "Nothing, Sonny, nothing! I was asleep, and had a marvellous dream." "What did you dream about?" "I dreamt about a city, where they had a spring of living water; when anybody was ill and drank of it, he got well again; and if he died and was sprinkled with this water, he came to life again. But for the last twenty years the water has ceased to flow; is there any help that it may flow again?" "Quite easy; there's a toad sitting on the spring in the well that won't let the water flow. Let them kill the toad and clean out the well; the water will flow as before." When the old man fell asleep again, the hag pulled out a second golden hair and threw it on the ground. "What ails you again, Mother?" "Nothing, Sonny, nothing; I was asleep, and again had a marvellous dream. I dreamt of a city where they had an apple-tree which bore youth restoring apples; when anybody grew old and ate one he became young again. But for the last twenty years the apple-tree has borne no fruit; is there any help?" "Quite easy; under the tree there lies a snake that exhausts its powers; let them kill the snake and transplant the apple-tree; it will bear fruit as before." The old man then fell asleep again, and the hag pulled out a third golden hair. "Why won't you let me sleep, Mother?" said the old man crossly, and wanted to get up. "Lie still, Sonny, lie still! Don't be angry. I didn't want to wake you. But a heavy sleep fell upon me, and I had another marvellous dream. I dreamt of a ferryman on a black sea; for twenty years he has been ferrying across it, and no one has come to set him free. When will his work have an end?" "He's the son of a stupid mother. Let him give the oar into another person's hand and jump ashore himself; the other will be ferryman in his stead. But let me be quiet now; I must get up early to-morrow and go to dry the tears which the king's daughter sheds every night for her husband, the charcoal-burner's son, whom the king has sent for three golden hairs of mine."

In the morning a wind again arose outside, and on the lap of its old mother awoke, instead of the old man, a beautiful golden-haired child, the divine Sun, who bade farewell to his mother and flew out by the east window. The hag turned up the tub and said to Floatling: "There are the three golden hairs for you, and you also know what Grandfather Allknow has answered to those three things. Go; and good-bye! You will see me no more; there is no need of it." Floatling thanked the hag gratefully, and departed. When he came to the first city, the king asked him what news he brought him. "Good news," said Floatling. "Have the well cleaned out, and kill the toad which sits on the spring, and the water will flow again as aforetime." The king had this done without delay, and when he saw the water bubbling up with a full stream, he presented Floatling with twelve horses white as swans, and on them as much gold and silver as they could carry.

When he came to the second city the king asked him again what news he brought. "Good news!" said Floatling. "Have the apple-tree dug up; you will find a snake under the roots; kill it; then plant the apple-tree again, and it will bear fruit as aforetime." The king had this done at once, and during the night the apple-tree was clothed with bloom, just as if it had been bestrewn with roses. The king was delighted, and presented Floatling with twelve horses as black as ravens, and on them as much riches as they would carry.

Floatling travelled on, and when he came to the black sea, the ferryman asked him whether he had learnt when he would be liberated. "I have," said Floatling. "But ferry me over first, and then I will tell you." The ferryman objected, but when he saw that there was nothing else to be done, he ferried him over with his four-and-twenty horses. "Before you ferry anybody over again," said Floatling, "put the oar into his hand and jump ashore, and he will be ferryman in your stead."

The king didn't believe his eyes when Floatling brought him the three golden hairs of Grandfather Allknow; and his daughter wept, not from sorrow, but from joy at his return. "But where did you get these beautiful horses and this great wealth?" asked the king. "I earned it," said Floatling, and related how he had helped one king again to the youth-restoring apples, which made young people out of old ones; and another to the living water, which makes sick people well and dead people living. "Youth-restoring apples! living water!" repeated the king quietly to himself. "If I ate one I should become young again; and if I died I should be restored to life by that water?" Without delay he started on the road for the youth-restoring apples and the living water—and hasn't returned yet.

Thus the charcoal-burner's son became the king's son-in-law, as the Fate decreed; and as for the king, maybe he is still ferrying across the black sea.[1]

---

[1] This story is a variant of Grimm's "Giant with the Three Golden Hairs." But, whereas in Grimm there is nothing to indicate who the giant is, or whether he has three golden hairs and three only, in the Bohemian tale it is plain that "Grandfather Allknow" is the Sun, and that the three golden hairs are three sunbeams.

THE JEZINKAS

THERE was a poor orphan lad who had neither father nor mother, and was compelled to go out to service to get his living. He travelled a long way without being able to obtain an engagement, till one day he came to a hovel all by itself under a wood. On the threshold sat an old man, who had dark caverns in his head instead of eyes. The goats were bleating in the stall, and the old man said: "I wish I could take you, poor goats, to pasture, but I can't, I am blind; and I have nobody to send with you." "Daddy, send me," answered the lad; "I will pasture your goats, and also be glad to wait upon you." "Who are you? and what is your name?" The lad told him all, and that they called him Johnny. "Well, Johnny, I will take you; but drive out the goats for me to pasture first of all. But don't lead them to yon hill in the forest; the Jezinkas will come to you, will put you to sleep, and will then tear out your eyes, as they have mine." "Never fear, Daddy," answered Johnny; "the Jezinkas won't tear out *my* eyes." He then let the goats out of the stall, and drove them to pasture. The first and second day he pastured them under the forest, but the third day he said to himself: "Why should I be afraid of the Jezinkas? I'll drive them where there is better pasture." He then broke off three green shoots of bramble, put them into his hat, and drove the goats straight on to the hill in the forest. There the goats wandered about for pasture, and Johnny sat down on a stone in the cool. He had not sat long, when all of a sudden, how it came about he knew not, a beautiful damsel stood before him, all dressed in white, with her hair— raven-black—prettily dressed and flowing down her back, and eyes like sloes. "God bless you, young goatherd!" said she. "See what apples grow in our garden! Here's one for you; I'll give it you, that you may know how good they are." She offered him a beautiful rosy apple. But Johnny knew that if he took the apple and ate it he would fall asleep, and she would afterward tear out his eyes, so he said: "I am much obliged to you, beautiful damsel! My master has an apple-tree in his garden, on which still handsomer apples grow; I have eaten my fill of them." "Well, if you'd rather not, I won't compel you," said the damsel, and went away.

After a while came another, still prettier, damsel, with a beautiful red rose in her hand, and said:"God bless you, young goatherd! See what a beautiful rose I've just plucked off: the hedge. It smells so nice; smell it yourself." "I am much obliged to you, beautiful damsel. My master has still handsomer roses in his garden; I have smelt my fill of them." "Well, then, if you won't, let it alone!" and the damsel, quite enraged, turned round, and retired. After a while, a third damsel, the youngest and prettiest of them all, came up. "God bless you, young goatherd!" "Thank you, beautiful damsel!" "Indeed, you're a fine lad," said the damsel, "but you'd be still handsomer if you had your hair nicely combed and dressed. Come, I'll comb it for you."

Johnny said nothing, but when the damsel came up to him to comb his hair, he took his hat from his head, drew out a bramble-shoot, and *pop!* struck her on both hands. The damsel screamed, "Help, help!" and began to weep, but was unable to move from the place. Johnny cared naught for her weeping, and bound her hands together with the bramble. Then up ran the other two damsels, and, seeing their sister a captive, began to beg Johnny to unbind her and let her go. "Unbind her yourselves," said Johnny. "Alas! we can't, we have tender hands, we should prick ourselves." But when they saw that the lad would not do as they wished, they went to their sister and wanted to unfasten the bramble.

Thereupon Johnny leapt up, and *pop!pop!* struck them too with a spray, and then bound both their hands together. "See, I've got you, you wicked Jezinkas! Why did you tear out my master's eyes!" After this, he went home to his master, and said, "Come, Daddy, I've found somebody who will give you your eyes again." When they came to the hill, he said to the first Jezinka, "Now tell me where the old man's eyes are. If you don't tell me, I shall throw you at once into the water." The Jezinka made excuse that she didn't know, and Johnny was going to throw her into the river, which flowed hard by under the hill. "Don't, Johnny, don't!" entreated the Jezinka, "and I'll give you the old man's eyes." She conducted him into a cavern, where was a great heap of eyes, large and small, black, red, blue, and green, and took two out of the heap. But when Johnny placed them in the old man's sockets, the poor man began to cry: "Alas, alas! these are not my eyes. I see nothing but owls." Johnny became exasperated, seized the Jezinka, and threw her into the water. He then said to the second: "Tell me, you, where the old man's eyes are." She, too, began to make excuses that she didn't know; but when the lad threatened to throw her, too, into the water, she led him again to the cavern, and took out two other eyes. But the old man cried again: "Alas! these are not my eyes. I see nothing but wolves." The same was done to the second Jezinka as to the first; the water closed over her. "Tell me, you, where the old man's eyes are," said Johnny to the third and youngest Jezinka. She, too, led him to the heap in the cavern, and took out two eyes for him. But when they were inserted, the old man cried out again that they were not his eyes. "I see nothing but pike." Johnny saw that she, too, was cheating him, and was going to drown her as well; but the Jezinka besought him with tears: "Don't, Johnny, don't! I will give you the old man's proper eyes." She took them from under the whole heap. And when Johnny inserted them into the old man's sockets, he cried out joyfully: "These, these are my eyes! Praise be to God! Now I see well again!" Afterward Johnny and the old man lived together happily; Johnny pastured the goats, and the old man made cheeses at home, and they ate them together; but the Jezinka never showed herself again on that hill.

BRITTANY

THE Breton mind is of a grim and somewhat morbid mould. In their folk-lore can be traced ideas of sun-worship, and of the cult of the ancestor. The light, diminutive sprite or fairy of the English tales is not found in Breton stories, where the fairies live a life not far removed, in many ways, from that of mortals.

The Margot-la-Fée is the land-fairy, who dwells in a cavern by the seashore, and is friendly to human beings. The Mary Morgans are sea-fairies and are enemies of mortals, perhaps because the sea indicates something sinister to the Bretons. These Morgans are seldom found in the open sea, the coast-shallows are their home, and here they lure old and young to their doom. Special features of Breton life are the "Pardons"—days of solemn celebration. They are the relics of the ancient "Feasts of the Dead" of Druidism. The Pardons include a long service in or around the chapel of the local saint, a grand procession, vespers, then games, dancing, and the lighting of bonfires. Crowds of beggars are seen at these times in the town and by the roadside, and the visitor who spurns them should remember the Breton tradition that beggars are considered in a special sense the children of God, gifted with powers denied to the wise and prudent. For this reason they should receive kindly consideration from the passers-by. "The Beggar's Curse" is specially interesting from this point of view.

ST. YVES THE TRUTH-GIVER

FOREMOST among the native saints is St. Yves, who combines the *rôles* of patron saint of the poor and patron saint of lawyers; for during his lifetime he followed the law, and it is said that after his death this profession closed to him the Gates of Paradise until God Himself intervened on his behalf.

It is as patron saint of the poor that St. Yves the Truth-giver is widely honoured. His house was regularly patronized by every sort of vagabond and outcast, some of whom accepted his hospitality until their death; for never would St. Yves consent to their being turned out, where they might fall prey to the cruelty of the rich who lived, at that time, in the parish of St. Michel.

But only after St. Yves's death did he feel it necessary to deal drastically with the parish. Every year the poor folk from the surrounding country flocked to his Pardon; and many had perforce to pass along the roads of the rich men. These rich men grew at last weary of the ragged procession, and issued a joint proclamation declaring the roads through the parish of St. Michel to be toll roads and the price of passage to be one gold piece.

So the poor had to trudge round many weary miles, while the servants of the rich men laughed at them. But one day, these servants, whom we may imagine on the watch for casual amusement, caught a poor pilgrim within the forbidden area.

"A gold piece," demanded the servants.

The poor pilgrim laughed bitterly.

"Do you expect gold pieces from blind beggars such as I?" he asked them; for he was indeed blind and unable to see the proclamation giving notice of the toll.

"Come before our masters," cried the servants, and laying hold of him, they dragged him before the rich men.

The rich men were delighted at the opportunity of making an example; for the poor had hitherto humbly accepted the situation and avoided the toll roads.

"Hang him from the church steeple," commanded the rich men.

"Mercy," implored the blind beggar. But they laughed at him and went to see the sport, joking as they followed the whining prisoner to his scaffold.

With a long pull and a strong pull the blind beggar was hoisted up . . . .

A great black cloud descended upon the parish of St. Michel. Earthquakes, rain, hail, wind, thunder, lightning, smoke, flame, made the place a horror. Fiery serpents darted forth their heads from the clouds, and great monsters appeared from the earth. And when at last the cloud lifted, what had been the richest parish in Tréguier was but a blackened desert, a parched wilderness. Only the steeple of the church remained. The rich men, their families, and their servants were never seen again.

As for the blind beggar, he found himself walking safe and sound toward his destination—the Pardon of St. Yves.

THE MIRACULOUS FISH

ST. CORENTIN lived in a simple hermit's cell upon the spot where now stands the city of Quimper; beside his forest hut a pool was scooped out of the rock and filled with clear spring water. A fish lived in this pool, and every day the fish used to gaze with reverence at Corentin at his devotions. But one day, after a fast of more than usual severity, the saint, in a moment of temptation, seized the fish, ate it, and threw the bones back into the pool. To his surprise, the bones took on flesh once more; and so Corentin was able every day to enjoy the fish and, throwing back the bones in the pool, watch another one appear for his consumption upon the morrow.

Now it chanced that King Gralon (most revered of all the Breton kings) passed with his train of attendants the cell of Corentin.

"Good hermit," cried the King, "we are hungry. Can you feed us all, to the number of fifty?"

Corentin laughed.

"Sire," answered he, "cease the jest, I pray you. Here, in this pool, I have one small fish which succours my own daily needs. Beyond that I have nothing."

And he told the King the story of the miraculous fish.

Now Gralon, at that time, still worshipped the gods of his fathers; but he was impressed by the narrative of the holy man.

"Let us test this God of yours," he commanded; and, calling round him his attendants, he bade them prepare the fish for dinner.

Amid much mirth they did so; but mirth died upon their lips when it was found that for every mouthful of the fish eaten another took its place, and that there was ample for the King and for all his fifty followers. Marvelling much, Gralon bade Corentin tell him more of the God that could bring to pass such wonders; and so great was the power of Corentin's preaching that, as the sun sank through the forest trees, King Gralon was baptized at the fountain.

"Corentin," he declared, as he kissed the hermit, "here shall be my capital. And here, before my very eyes, is my bishop."

Thus it came to pass that upon the site of the hermit's cell rose the city and the cathedral of Quimper, over which the kindly Saint still holds his protecting hand.

THE BEGGAR'S CURSE

THERE was once a peasant of the Forêt du Laz, near Châteauneuf- du-Faou, who visited, as he was bound to do, the Pardon of Rumengol, near Quimerch. He was not noted for the evenness of his temper, this peasant; and as he drew near the scene of the Pardon he became increasingly irritated by the beggars who lined the roadside.

"Payez le droit des pauvres," they cried.

One he met who came near to nauseating him. Sores, boils and ulcers did the beggar exhibit to awaken his charity; and very repulsive was the reek of the beggar's unwashed body as it followed him along the dusty highway. "Payez le droit des pauvres," whined the beggar. At last the quick-tempered peasant, raising his stick, struck the beggar heavily, rolling him in the ditch.

"May you wander to Rumengol for seven years," yelled the beggar in fury. "And on your return to your fireside may fresh trouble await you."

The Pardon over, the peasant set out on his tramp home. But imagine his surprise when, on turning a sharp bend in the road, he found himself entering Rumengol once more. With an expression of disgust at his carelessness in taking the wrong path, he retraced his steps; yet after scarcely half a league found himself again on the outskirts of the village.

He slept that night under a hedge, determining to pursue his homeward journey next day. But every path he took led him back to Rumengol. Terrified, dejected, exhausted, he continued mechanically to walk, week in, week out, month in, month out. His wooden *sabots* wore thin, the substance of them peeling from his feet like paper; he walked barefoot; the skin reddened, blistered. And still, in agony, he walked. His clothes, in sun and rain, hung upon his figure like sacks; they too fell gradually to pieces until only his shirt was left. And still, in heat and cold, in sunshine and in storm, he walked. Food became scarce; he grew first hungry, then famished, then ravenous; became lean and haggard and wild-eyed, a creature despairing of very existence. And still, in starvation, he walked. For seven long years he fled from Rumengol only to find himself, a dozen times a day, on the point of re-entering it.

At the end of his strength, he sank one night into a ditch to sleep: with the morning came a thought which was like sweet cider to the drought of his mind.

"To-day I am going home."

Infused by a new spirit he rose, and after washing his face in a brook set about his journey. Scarecrow though he was, he sang blithely; but his voice failed him and his lips became parched with joy as he at length beheld once more the little cottage in the Forêt du Laz he had left seven years previously. A group of people clustered round its door; and from within came a tiny wailing voice as of a new-born child.

"Away with you, tatterdemalion," exclaimed one of the watchers at the door.

"What then goes forward inside?" asked the peasant, amazed at this unexpected reception.

"Mind your own business," retorted the watcher.

"For pity's sake, tell me," persisted the distraught peasant.

"Since you seem so anxious then, know that the good-wife has just given birth to a child—a bonny boy."

"But her husband?" cried the peasant in an agony of soul.

"Is at her bedside," answered the watcher.

The peasant could contain himself no longer. "Fools," he cried, "I am her husband. Let me go to her."

And he made for the door.

"Fool yourself," retorted the watcher, restraining him. "Her first husband has been dead these seven years, killed by a wolf as he returned from the Pardon of Rumengol. He who is with her now is her second."

In vain did the peasant tell them his pitiable story. They laughed at him. Finally they drove him from the door.

"Is there any man more miserable than I?" wailed the peasant. With a great sorrow upon him, he walked blindly into the forest; and was never seen nor heard of again. Beware, therefore, how you spurn God's children of the poor.

MONA AND THE MORGAN

IT used to be told in the Ile d'Ouessand off the western coast of Finestère, that as she gathered shells one day from the seashore, a girl named Mona was seized by the King of the Morgans and carried away to his palace beneath the waves. Here the King's son fell in love with her; but the King forbade him to marry anyone who was not a Morgan, chose for him a suitable bride, and even went with the couple to the church. Mona, meanwhile, was left in the palace to prepare the wedding-feast, under penalty of death should it be late; but she was given nothing but empty pots.

Now the King's son cunningly pretended on his way to church to have forgotten the ring; he hurried back to Mona whom he found weeping. "Dry your eyes, dear Mona," said he when she had told him of her plight; and uttering magic words he filled the pots with good things. The feast was on the table to the second—and a sumptuous feast it was.

The King, of course, was angry that Mona should have found means of frustrating his wishes; and at night, when the bridal pair retired to their chamber, he ordered Mona to hold a lighted candle in the room, with the threat that when the candle burned out the girl's head should be cut off.

Presently the King's son, who had heard the threat, called from his bed: "Is the candle yet burning low?"

And Mona, choking back her fears, replied: "Not yet."

Several times did he ask the same question; and at length Mona answered: "Yes, it is very low."

Then the King's son awakened his bride and said: "Do you hold the candle for a short time, for the girl who has held it is perished with cold."

He hurried his bride out of bed and compelled her to hold the candle while Mona hid in a corner of the room; and suddenly the candle went out.

The King's son rushed to the chamber where his father slept, crying that the candle was out and that she who held it must die.

Whereupon the King, seizing his sword, made his way to the bridal chamber and without waiting to see on whom it fell brought it down with all his force upon the head of the bride. Then he went back to bed and slept peacefully.

In the morning the King's son went to his father. "Father," said he, "I come to ask your permission to get married."

The King stared at him incredulously. "But were you not married yesterday?"

"True, but my bride is dead."

"Unhappy man! What caused you to kill her?"

"It was not I who killed her. It was you."

"I!"

"Yes"—and the King's son recounted how it had come about.

"And if you do not believe me," he added, "go for yourself and see her corpse. It is where you left it."

Then the King understood that his son really loved Mona; and gave his consent to their marriage.

The young husband was full of consideration for his new wife. He gave her succulent fish to eat—for you must not forget that this happened at the bottom of the sea—loaded her with pearl necklaces and coral ornaments and decorated her palace with the rarest sea-flowers known to him. But in spite of these attentions, Mona grew weary of her life and longed to return to her parents on earth; and at last the Morgan promised to allow her to visit her home on the condition that she should return to him before sunset and that she should permit no one to touch her hand. Her parents and brothers and sisters—who, of course, had long since given her up for dead—were overcome with joy at seeing her; and she in her turn did not require great inducement to stay with them overnight, although she would permit no one to touch her hand. One night she stayed, and two and three; she resumed the interrupted thread of her earthly life and forgot all about her Morgan husband. Then came young men to ask her in marriage; and although she refused them she did not rebuke them—for she had forgotten even that she was already a wife.

But gradually she became aware outside her window at night of a plaintive crying and moaning. More and more distinct did it become, more and more distressed and distressing; and as she lay awake one night, uneasy at she knew not what, she heard the moaning and the crying resolve itself into words.

"Oh, I have waited so long, my darling, and still you come not.... Mona, Mona, I am lonely...."

Then, with a great leap of the heart, she remembered and desired her Morgan husband beneath the sea. She leapt out of the window of the cottage and threw herself into his arms. Together they sank below the waves; and nobody on this earth ever saw Mona afterward.

LOÏK GUERN

SORCERERS are frequently met with in Brittany. Some live in castles, others in forests, some scour the night sea in shadowy boats—others again become armies of washerwomen, who spend hours of darkness in working harm to anyone who loiters near streams or washing places.

One of the most widely known is Comorre; he is said to have had his heart in an egg, in a pigeon—in a hare—in a wolf—in his brother, who dwelt a thousand leagues away. Comorre was a kind of "bluebeard" and one of his castles is the Château de Carnoët. A short distance below it, is the Ferry of Carnoët, where the sorcerer Milliguet used to take the form of a ferryman and lure souls to their destruction. Pardon time he was specially busy.

●   ●   ●   ●   ●   ●   ●

One evening Loïk Guern and his sweetheart Marahit came to the ferry to be taken across; and, since he enjoyed tobacco almost as greatly as he enjoyed his sweetheart's society, Loïk stepped into a little cottage by the riverside to light his pipe. Milliguet saw his opportunity.

"If you wish to cross, jump in quickly, my pretty lass," he muttered to Marahit.

Thinking that Loïk was but a few steps behind, Marahit did so; but before she could remonstrate, the boat had been pushed from the bank and was flying downstream, the ferryman sitting idly in the stern.

"Stop, stop," cried Marahit, "we must wait for Loïk."

But the ferryman kept silently to his place; and the boat, caught in the currents, swirled rapidly into the dark forest. As she gazed wildly about her, Marahit could see upon the banks ghostly forms that wandered sadly to and fro and stretched their pale arms invitingly or threateningly toward the boat. They were the murdered wives of Comorre beckoning from the Shore of the Dead.

"Loïk, Loïk," cried terror-stricken Marahit; and fell lifeless in the bottom of the boat.

Loïk, when he came from the cottage and found his beloved gone—when, moreover, he learned her fate—was broken-hearted. Day after day he sat by the side of the ferry imploring passers-by to tell him how he might reach her.

One day, an old beggar-woman hobbled down to the river's edge.

"Would you in truth go to her?" she asked. "For it is a perilous journey."

"Old mother, I would give my life to save hers," replied the distracted man.

"Then listen, my son. You must take a branch of holly from the fairies' village and dip it in the holy-water stoup of your church. At dusk, go with it to the ferry. When the boat sets off with the ferryman at the helm, look neither to right nor to left nor behind you, but tell your beads, Loïk, tell your beads, and make the sign of the Cross reverently. When you come to the thirty-third bead, rise boldly in the boat, and showing your holly branch to the ferryman, command him to take you living to the Shore of the Dead. If you perform these things faithfully—and on these conditions only—will your Marahit be restored to you."

And the beggar-woman vanished.

Full of hope, Loïk managed to procure a holly branch from the fairies' village and dipped it in the holy-water stoup of his church. At dusk he went down to the ferry.

But when the boat got under way, poor Loïk was so overcome at the thought of finding his lost sweetheart that he forgot to tell his beads; and they slipped from his trembling hands into the water.

Immediately cries resounded along the banks, and the wives of Comorre beckoned or threatened him from the dark shades of the trees.

Then he remembered the holly branch; and drawing it forth he held it before the impassive face of the ferryman; but again agitation overcame him and he forgot the injunctions of the beggar-woman.

"Take me to the Shore of the Dead," he cried. "Take me to Marahit."

He had omitted the word "living."

The ferryman gave no sign and the boat sped on; whereat an uncontrollable rage seized the young man and with his full strength he struck Milliguet across the face with the holly branch.

With a terrible cry, the sorcerer-ferryman slipped from his seat and plunged into the water, leaving the boat unguided in its mad course. On it sped faster and faster, whirled hither and thither by currents and eddies, tossed by the waves which rebounded from half-hidden rocks. Loïk screamed in his terror. Darker and darker it grew as the boat penetrated deeper into the forest. Loïk tried to throw himself overboard, but some hidden power held him back. At last, with appalling suddenness, the boat struck against a rock in mid-stream, shuddered, and foundered.

And the murdered wives of Comorre held out their arms and wailed in the darkness as another soul seemed on the verge of joining their company.

But for many years afterward, the Pardons of the neighbourhood were attended by an idiot man carrying a holly branch, dishevelled and pale and dressed in tatters, who cried piteously, "Take me to the Shore of the Dead. Give me back my Marahit."

THE STONES OF PLOUVINEC

IN the little village of Plouvinec there once lived a poor stone-cutter named Bernet.

Bernet was an honest and industrious young man, and yet he never seemed to succeed in the world. Work as he might, he was always poor. This was a great grief to him, for he was in love with the beautiful Madeleine Pornec, and she was the daughter of the richest man in Plouvinec.

Madeleine had many suitors, but she cared for none of them except Bernet. She would gladly have married him in spite of his poverty, but her father was covetous as well as rich. He had no wish for a poor son in-law, and Madeleine was so beautiful he expected her to marry some rich merchant, or a well-to-do farmer at least. But if Madeleine could not have Bernet for a husband, she was determined that she would have no one.

There came a winter when Bernet found himself poorer than he had ever been before. Scarcely anyone seemed to have any need for a stonecutter, and even for such work as he did get he was poorly paid. He learned to know what it meant to go without a meal and to be cold as well as hungry.

As Christmas drew near, the landlord of the inn at Plouvinec decided to give a feast for all the good folk of the village, and Bernet was invited along with all the rest.

He was glad enough to go to the feast, for he knew that Madeleine was to be there, and even if he did not have a chance to talk to her, he could at least look at her, and that would be better than nothing.

The feast was a fine one. There was plenty to eat and drink, and all was of the best, and the more the guests feasted, the merrier they grew. If Bernet and Madeleine ate little and spoke less, no one noticed it. People were too busy filling their own stomachs and laughing at the jokes that were cracked. The fun was at its height when the door was pushed open, and a ragged, ill-looking beggar slipped into the room.

At the sight of him the laughter and merriment died away. This beggar was well known to all the people of the village, though none knew whence he came nor where he went when he was away on his wanderings. He was sly and crafty, and he was feared as well as disliked, for it was said that he had the evil eye. Whether he had or not, it was well known that no one had ever offended him without having some misfortune happen soon after.

"I heard there was a great feast here to-night," said the beggar in a humble voice, "and that all the village had been bidden to it. Perhaps, when all have eaten, there may be some scraps that I might pick up."

"Scraps there are in plenty," answered the landlord, "but it is not scraps that I am offering to anyone to-night. Draw up a chair to the table, and eat and drink what you will. There is more than enough for all." But the landlord looked none too well pleased as he spoke. It was a piece of ill-luck to have the beggar come to his house this night of all nights, to spoil the pleasure of the guests.

The beggar drew up to the table as the landlord bade him, but the fun and merriment were ended. Presently the guests began to leave the table, and after thanking their host, they went away to their own homes.

When the beggar had eaten and drunk to his heart's content, he pushed back his chair from the table.

"I have eaten well," said he to the landlord. "Is there not now some corner where I can spend the night?"

"There is the stable," answered the landlord grudgingly. "Every room in th house is full, but if you choose to sleep there among the clean hay, I am not the one to say you nay."

Well, the beggar was well content with that. He went out to the stable, and there he snuggled down among the soft hay, and soon he was fast asleep. He had slept for some hours, and it was midnight, when he suddenly awoke with a startled feeling that he was not alone in the stable. In the darkness two strange voices were talking together.

"Well, brother, how goes it since last Christmas?" asked one voice.

"Poorly, brother, but poorly," answered the other. "Methinks the work has been heavier these last twelve months than ever before."

The beggar, listening as he lay in the hay, wondered who could be talking there at this hour of the night. Then he discovered that the voices came from the stalls near by; the ox and the donkey were talking together.

The beggar was so surprised that he almost exclaimed aloud, but he restrained himself. He remembered a story he had often heard, but had never before believed, that on every Christmas night it is given to the dumb beasts in the stalls to talk in human tones for a short time. It was said that those who had been lucky enough to hear them at such times had sometimes learned strange secrets from their talk. Now the beggar lay listening with all his ears, and scarcely daring to breathe lest he should disturb them.

"It has been a hard year for me too," said the ox, answering what the donkey had just said. "I would our master had some of the treasure that lies hidden under the stones of Plouvinec. Then he could buy more oxen and more donkeys, and the work would be easier for us."

"The treasure! What treasure is that?" asked the donkey.

The ox seemed very much surprised. "Have you never heard? I thought every one knew of the hidden treasure under the stones."

"Tell me about it," said the donkey, "for I dearly love a tale."

The ox was not loath to do this. At once it began:

"You know the barren heath just outside of Plouvinec, and the great stones that lie there, each so large that it would take more than a team of oxen to drag it from its place?"

Yes, the donkey knew that heath, and the stones too. He had often passed by them on his journeys to the neighbouring town.

"It is said that under those stones lies hidden an enormous treasure of gold," said the ox. "That is the story; it is well known. But none has seen that treasure; jealously the stones guard it. Once in every hundred years, however, the stones go down to the river to drink. They are only away for a few minutes; then they come rolling back in mad haste to cover their gold again. But if anyone could be there on the heath for those few minutes, it is a wonderful sight that he would see while the stones are away. It is now a hundred years, all but a week, since the stones went down to drink."

"Then a week from to-night the treasure will be uncovered again?" asked the donkey.

"Yes, exactly a week from now, at midnight."

"Ah, if only our master knew this," and the donkey sighed heavily. "If only we could tell him! Then he might go to the heath and not only see the treasure, but gather a sack full of it for himself."

"Yes, but even if he did, he would never return with it alive. As I told you, the stones are very jealous of their treasure, and are away for only a few minutes. By the time he had gathered up the gold and was ready to escape, the stones would return and would crush him to powder."

The beggar, who had become very much excited at the story, felt a cold shiver creep over him at these words.

"No one could ever bring away any of it then?" asked the donkey.

"I did not say that. The stones are enchanted. If anyone could find a five-leaved clover, and carry it with him to the heath, the stones could not harm him, for the five-leaved clover is a magic plant that has power over all enchanted things, and those stones are enchanted."

"Then all he would need would be to have a five-leaved clover."

"If he carried that with him, the stones could not harm him. He might escape safely with the treasure, but it would do him little good. With the first rays of the sun the treasure would crumble away unless the life of a human being had been sacrificed to the stones there on the heath before sunrise."

"And who would sacrifice a human life for a treasure!" cried the donkey. "Not our master, I am sure."

The ox made no answer, and now the donkey too was silent. The hour had passed in which they could speak in human voices. For another year they would again be only dumb brutes.

As for the beggar, he lay among the hay, shaking all over with excitement. Visions of untold wealth shone before his eyes. The treasure of Plouvinec! Why, if he could only get it, he would be the richest man in the village. In the village? No, in the country—in the whole world! Only to see it and handle it for a few hours would be something. But before even that were possible and safe it would be necessary to find a five-leaved clover.

With the earliest peep of dawn the beggar rolled from the hay, and, wrapping his rags about him, stole out of the stable and away into the country. There he began looking about for bunches of clover. These were not hard to find; they were everywhere, though the most of them were withered now. He found and examined clump after clump. Here and there he found a stem that bore four leaves, but none had five. Night came on, and the darkness made him give up the search; but the next day he began anew. Again he was unsuccessful. So day after day passed by, and still he had not found the thing he sought so eagerly.

The beggar was in a fever of rage and disappointment. Six days slipped by. By the time the seventh dawned he was so discouraged that he hunted for only a few hours. Then, though it was still daylight, he determined to give up the search. With drooping head he turned back toward the village. As he was passing a heap of rocks he noticed a clump of clover growing in a crevice. Idly, and with no hope of success, he stooped and began to examine it leaf by leaf.

Suddenly he gave a cry of joy. His legs trembled under him so that he was obliged to sink to his knees. The last stem of all bore five leaves. He had found his five-leaved clover!

With the magic plant safely hidden away in his bosom the beggar hurried back toward the village. He would rest in the inn until night. Then he would go to the heath, and if the story the ox had told were true, he would see a sight such as no one living had ever seen before.

His way led him past the heath. Dusk was falling as he approached it. Suddenly the beggar paused and listened. From among the stones sounded a strange tap-tapping. Cautiously he drew nearer, peering about among the stones. Then he saw what seemed to him a curious sight for such a place and such a time. Before the largest stone of all stood Bernet, busily at work with hammer and chisel. He was cutting a cross upon the face of the rock.

The beggar drew near to him so quietly that Bernet did not notice him. He started as a voice suddenly spoke close to his ear.

"That is a strange thing for you to be doing," said the beggar. "Why should you waste your time in cutting a cross in such a lonely place as this?"

"The sign of the cross never comes amiss, wherever it may be," answered Bernet. "And as for wasting my time, no one seems to have any use for it at present. It is better for me to spend it in this way than to idle it away over nothing."

Suddenly a strange idea flashed into the beggar's mind—a thought so strange and terrible that it made him turn pale. He drew nearer to the stone-cutter and laid his hand upon his arm.

"Listen, Bernet," said he; "you are a clever workman and an honest one as well, and yet all your work scarcely brings you in enough to live on. Suppose I were to tell you that in one night you might become rich-richer than the richest man in the village—so that there would be no desire that you could not satisfy; what would you think of that?"

"I would think nothing of it, for I would know it was not true," answered Bernet carelessly.

"But it *is* true; it is *true,* I tell you," cried the beggar. "Listen, and I will tell you."

He drew still nearer to Bernet, so that his mouth almost touched the stone-cutter's ear, and in a whisper he repeated to him the story he had heard the ox telling the donkey—the story of the treasure that was buried under the stones of Plouvinec. But it was only a part of the story that he told after all, for he did not tell Bernet that anyone who was rash enough to seek the treasure would be crushed by the stones unless he carried a five-leaved clover; nor did he tell him that if the treasure were carried away from the heath it would turn to ashes unless a human life had been sacrificed to the stones. As Bernet listened to the story he became very grave. His eyes shone through the fading light as he stared at the beggar's face.

"Why do you tell me this?" he asked. "And why are you willing to share the treasure that might be all your own? If you make me rich, what do you expect me to do for you in return?"

"Do you not see?" answered the beggar. "You are much stronger than I. I, as you know, am a weak man and slow of movement. While the stones are away we two together could gather more than twice as much as I could gather myself. In return for telling you this secret, all I ask is that if we go there and gather all we can, and bring it away with us, you will make an even division with me—that you will give me half of all we get."

"That seems only just," said Bernet slowly. "It would be strange if this story of the hidden treasure proved to be true. At any rate, I will come with you to the heath to-night. We will bring with us some large bags, and if we manage to secure even a small part of the gold you talk of I shall never cease to be grateful to you."

The beggar could not answer. His teeth were chattering, half with fear and half with excitement. The honest stone-cutter little guessed that the beggar was planning to sacrifice him to the stones in order that he himself might become a rich man.

It was well on toward midnight when Bernet and the beggar returned to the heath with the bags. The moon shone clear and bright, and by its light they could see the stones towering up above them, solid and motionless. It seemed impossible to believe that they had ever stirred from their places, or ever would again. In the moonlight Bernet could clearly see the cross that he had carved upon the largest stone.

He and the beggar lay hidden behind a clump of bushes. All was still except for the faint sound of the river some short distance away. Suddenly a breath seemed to pass over the heath. Far off, in the village of Plouvinec, sounded the first stroke of twelve.

At that stroke the two men saw a strange and wonderful thing happen. The motionless stones rocked and stirred in their places. With a rending sound they tore themselves from the places where they had stood for so long. Then down the slope toward the river they rolled, bounding faster and faster, while there on the heath an immense treasure glittered in the moonlight.

"Quick! quick!" cried the beggar in a shrill voice. "They will return! We have not a moment to waste."

Greedily he threw himself upon the treasure. Gathering it up by handfuls he thrust it hurriedly into a sack. Bernet was not slow to follow his example. They worked with such frenzy that soon the two largest sacks were almost full. In their haste everything but the gold was forgotten.

Some sound, a rumbling and crashing, made Bernet look up. At once he sprang to his feet with a cry of fear.

"Look! look!" he cried. "The stones are returning. They are almost on us. We shall be crushed."

"You, perhaps; but not I," answered the beggar. "You should have provided yourself with a five-leaved clover. It is a magic herb, and the stones have no power to touch him who holds it."

Even as the beggar spoke the stones were almost upon them. Trembling, but secure, he held up the five-leaved clover before them. As he did so the ranks of stones divided, passing around him a rank on either side; then, closing together, they rolled on toward Bernet.

The poor stone-cutter felt that he was lost. He tried to murmur a prayer, but his tongue clove to the roof of his mouth with fear.

Suddenly the largest stone of all, the one upon which he had cut the cross, separated itself from the others. Rolling in front of them, it placed itself before him as a shield. Grey and immovable it towered above him. A moment the others paused as if irresolute, while Bernet cowered close against the protecting stone. Then they rolled by without touching him and settled sullenly into their places.

The beggar was already gathering up the sacks. He believed himself safe, but he wished to leave the heath as quickly as possible. He glanced fearfully over his shoulder. Then he gave a shriek, and, turning, he held up the five-leaved clover. The largest stone was rolling toward him. It was almost upon him.

But the magic herb had no power over a stone marked with a cross. On it rolled, over the miserable man, and into the place where it must rest again for still another hundred years.

It was morning, and the sun was high in the heavens when Bernet staggered into the inn at Plouvinec. A heavy, bulging sack was thrown over one shoulder; a second sack he dragged behind him. They were full of gold—the treasure from under the stones of Plouvinec.

From that time Bernet was the richest man in Plouvinec. Madeleine's father was glad enough to call him son-in-law and to welcome him into his family. He and Madeleine were married, and lived in the greatest comfort and happiness all their days. But for as long as he lived Bernet could never be induced to go near the heath nor to look upon the stones that had so nearly caused his death.

COSSACK TALES

THE language of the Cossacks or Ruthenians is intermediate between that of the Russians and Poles. Their land lies between the Carpathians and the Dnieper and the Sea of Azov.

The people cling to traditional usages and customs and have a leaning to fatalism and melancholy. In physique and religion the Cossacks have been mainly Russian. Yet they have lived in a comparative isolation which has favoured the preservation of their folk-tales. Hence these have retained far more of fresh spontaneity and naive simplicity than the Russian *Skazki*. The magic cattle-teeming eggs and the magic handkerchief are elements peculiar and original in this folk-lore.

THE STRAW OX

THERE was once upon a time an old man and an old woman. The old man worked in the fields as a pitch-burner, while the old woman sat at home and spun flax. They were so poor that they could save nothing at all; all their earnings went in bare food, and when that was gone there was nothing left. At last the old woman had a good idea. "Look now, husband," cried she, "make me a straw ox, and smear it all over with tar."

"Why, you foolish woman!" said he, "what's the good of an ox of that sort?"

"Never mind," said she, "you just make it. I know what I am about." What was the poor man to do? He set to work and made the ox of straw, and smeared it all over with tar.

The night passed away, and at early dawn the old woman took her distaff, and drove the straw ox out into the steppe to graze, and she herself sat down behind a hillock, and began spinning her flax, and cried,

"Graze away, little ox, while I spin my flax!
Graze away, little ox, while I spin my flax!"

And while she spun, her head drooped down, and she began to doze, and while she was dozing, from behind the dark wood and from the back of the huge pines a bear came rushing out upon the ox and said, "Who are you? Speak and tell me!"

And the ox said, "A three-year-old heifer am I, made of straw and smeared with tar."

"Oh!" said the bear, "stuffed with straw and smeared with tar, are you? Then give me of your straw and tar, that I may patch up my ragged fur again!"

"Take some," said the ox, and the bear fell upon him and began to tear away at the tar. He tore and tore, and buried his teeth in it till he found he couldn't let go again. He tugged and he tugged, but it was no good, and the ox dragged him gradually off goodness knows where. Then the old woman awoke and there was no ox to be seen. "Alas! old fool that I am!" cried she, "perchance it has gone home." Then she quickly caught up her distaff and spinning board, threw them over her shoulders, and hastened off home, and she saw that the ox had dragged the bear up to the fence, and in she went to the old man. "Dad, dad!" she cried, "look, look! the ox has brought us a bear. Come out and kill it!" Then the old man jumped up, tore off the bear, tied him up, and threw him in the cellar.

Next morning, between dark and dawn, the old woman took her distaff and drove the ox into the steppe to graze. She herself sat down by a mound, began spinning, and said,

"Graze away, little ox, while I spin my flax!
Graze away, little ox, while I spin my flax!"

And while she spun, her head drooped down and she dozed. And, lo! from behind the dark wood, from the back of the huge pines, a grey wolf came rushing out upon the ox and said, "Who are you? Come, tell me!"

"I am a three-year-old heifer, stuffed with straw and trimmed with tar," said the ox.

"Oh! trimmed with tar, are you? Then give me of your tar to tar my sides, that the dogs and the sons of dogs tear me not!"

"Take some," said the ox. And with that the wolf fell upon him and tried to tear the tar off. He tugged and tugged, and tore with his teeth, but could get none off. Then he tried to let go, and couldn't; tug and worry as he might, it was no good. When the old woman woke, there was no heifer in sight. "Maybe my heifer has gone home!" she cried; "I'll go home and see." When she got there she was astonished, for by the palings stood the ox with the wolf still tugging at it. She ran and told her old man, and her old man came and threw the wolf into the cellar also.

On the third day the old woman again drove her ox into the pastures to graze, and sat down by a mound and dozed off. Then a fox came running up. "Who are you?" it asked the ox.

"I'm a three-year-old heifer, stuffed with straw and daubed with tar."

"Then give me some of your tar to smear my sides with, when those dogs and sons of dogs tear my hide!"

"Take some," said the ox. Then the fox fastened her teeth in him and couldn't draw them out again. The old woman told her old man, and he took and cast the fox into the cellar in the same way. And after that they caught Pussy Swift-foot [1] likewise.

---

[1] The hare.

So when he had got them all safely, the old man sat down on a bench before the cellar and began sharpening a knife. And the bear said to him:

"Tell me, daddy, what are you sharpening your knife for?"

"To flay your skin off, that I may make a leather jacket for myself and a pelisse for my old wife."

"Oh! don't flay me, daddy dear! Rather let me go, and I'll bring you a lot of honey."

"Very well, see you do it," and he unbound and let the bear go. Then he sat down on the bench and again began sharpening his knife. And the wolf asked him, "Daddy, what are you sharpening your knife for?"

"To flay off your skin, that I may make me a warm cap against the winter."

"Oh! don't flay me, daddy dear, and I'll bring you a whole herd of little sheep."

"Well, see that you do it," and he let the wolf go. Then he sat down and began sharpening his knife again. The fox put out her little snout and asked him, "Be so kind, dear daddy, and tell me why you are sharpening your knife!"

"Little foxes," said the old man, "have nice skins that do capitally for collars and trimmings, and I want to skin you!"

"Oh! don't take my skin away, daddy dear, and I will bring you hens and geese."

"Very well, see that you do it!" and he let the fox go. The hare now alone remained, and the old man began sharpening his knife on the hare's account. "Why do you do that?" asked puss, and he replied:

"Little hares have nice little soft warm skins, which will make me gloves and mittens against the winter!"

"Oh, daddy dear! don't flay me, and I'll bring you kale and good cauliflower, if only you let me go!" Then he let the hare go also.

Then they went to bed, but very early in the morning, when it was neither dusk nor dawn, there was a noise in the doorway like "Durrrrr!"

"Daddy," cried the old woman, "there's some one scratching at the door, go and see who it is!" The old man went out, and there was the bear carrying a whole hive full of honey. The old man took the honey from the bear, but no sooner did he lie down than again there was another "Durrrrr!" at the door. The old man looked out and saw the wolf driving a whole flock of sheep into the yard. Close on his heels came the fox, driving before her geese and hens and all manner of fowls; and last of all came the hare, bringing cabbage and kale and all manner of good food. And the old man was glad, and the old woman was glad. And the old man sold the sheep and oxen and got so rich that he needed nothing more. As for the straw-stuffed ox, it stood in the sun till it fell to pieces.

THE FOX AND THE CAT

IN a certain forest there once lived a fox, and near to' the fox lived a man who had a cat that had been a good mouser in its youth, but was now old and half blind. The man didn't want puss any longer, but not liking to kill it, took it out into the forest and lost it there. Then the fox came up and said, "Why, Mr. Shaggy Matthew! How d'ye do! What brings you here?"

"Alas!" said Pussy, "my master loved me as long as I could bite, but now that I can bite no longer and have left off catching mice—and I used to catch them finely once—he doesn't like to kill me, but he has left me in the wood where I must perish miserably."

"No, dear Pussy!" said the fox; "you leave it to me, and I'll help you to get your daily bread."

"You are very good, dear little sister foxy!" said the cat, and the fox built him a little shed with a garden round it to walk about in.

Now one day the hare came to steal the man's cabbage. "Kreem kreem-kreem!" he squeaked. But the cat popped his head out of the window, and when he saw the hare, he put up his back and stuck up his tail and said, "Ft-t-t-t—Frrrrrrr!" The hare was frightened and ran away and told the bear, the wolf, and the wild boar all about it. "Never mind," said the bear, "I tell you what, we'll all four give a banquet, and invite the fox and the cat, and do for the pair of them. Now, look here! I'll steal the man's mead; and you, Mr. Wolf, steal his fat-pot; and you, Mr. Wildboar, root up his fruit-trees; and you, Mr. Bunny, go and invite the fox and the cat to dinner."

So they made everything ready as the bear had said, and the hare ran off to invite the guests. He came beneath the window and said, "We invite your little ladyship Foxy-Woxy, together with Mr. Shaggy Matthew, to dinner"—and back he ran again—

"But you should have told them to bring their spoons with them," said the bear.

"Oh, what a head I've got! If I didn't quite forget!" cried the hare, and back he went again, ran beneath the window and cried, "Mind you bring your spoons!"

"Very well," said the fox.

So the cat and the fox went to the banquet, and when the cat saw the bacon, he put up his back and stuck out his tail, and cried, "Mee-oo, Mee-oo!" with all his might. But they thought he said, "Malo, malo!" [1]

"What!" said the bear, who was hiding behind the beeches with the other beasts, "here have we four been getting together all we could, and this pig-faced cat calls it too little! What a monstrous cat he must be to have such an appetite!"

---

1 "What a little! "What a little!

So they were all four very frightened, and the bear ran up a tree, and the others hid where they could.

But when the cat saw the boar's bristles sticking out from behind the bushes, he thought it was a mouse, and put up his back again and cried, "Ft! ft! ft! Frrrrrrr!"

Then they were more frightened than ever. And the boar went into a bush still farther off, and the wolf went behind an oak, and the bear climbed up into a bigger one, and the hare ran right away. But the cat remained in the midst of all the good things and ate away at the bacon, and the little fox gobbled up the honey, and they ate and ate till they couldn't eat any more, and then they both went home licking their paws.

OH, THE TSAR OF THE FOREST

T HE olden times were not like the time we live in. In the olden times all manner of Evil Powers walked abroad. The world itself was not then as it is now: now there are no such Evil Powers among us. I'll tell you a *kazka* [1] of Oh, the Tsar of the Forest, that you may know what manner of being he was.

Once upon a time, long, long ago, beyond the times that we can call to mind, ere yet our great-grandfathers or their grandfathers had been born into the world, there lived a poor man and his wife, and they had one only son, who was not as an only son ought to be to his old father and mother. So idle and lazy was that only son that Heaven help him! He would do nothing, he would not even fetch water from the well, but lay on the stove all day long and rolled among the warm cinders. If they gave him anything to eat, he ate it; and if they didn't give him anything to eat, he did without. His father and mother fretted sorely because of him, and said, "What are we to do with thee, O son? for thou art good for nothing. Other people's children are a stay and a support to their parents, but thou art but a fool and dost consume our bread naught."

But it was of no use at all. He would do nothing but sit on the stove and play with the cinders. So his father and mother grieved over him for many a long day, and at last his mother said to his father, "What is to be done with our son? Thou dost see that he has grown up and yet is of no use to us, and he is so foolish that we can do nothing with him. Look now, if we can send him away, let us send him away; if we can hire him out, let us hire him out; perchance other folk may be able to do more with him than we can." So his father and mother laid their heads together, and sent him to a tailor's to learn tailoring. There he remained three days, but then he ran away home, climbed up on the stove, and again began playing with

---

[1] A folk-tale.

the cinders. His father then gave him a sound drubbing and sent him to a cobbler's to learn cobbling, but again he ran away home. His father gave him another drubbing and sent him to a blacksmith's to learn smith's work. But there too he did not remain long, but ran away home again, so what was that poor father to do? "I'll tell thee what I'll do with thee, thou son of a dog!" said he. "I'll take thee, thou lazy lout, into another kingdom. There, perchance, they will be able to teach thee better than they can here, and it will be too far for thee to run home." So he took him and set out on his journey.

They went on and on, they went a short way and they went a long way, and at last they came to a forest so dark that they could see neither earth nor sky. They went through this forest, but in a short time they grew very tired, and when they came to a path leading to a clearing full of large tree-stumps, the father said, "I am so tired out that I will rest here a little," and with that he sat down on a tree-stump and cried, "Oh, how tired I am!" He had no sooner said these words than out of the tree-stump, nobody could say how, sprang such a little, little old man, all so wrinkled and puckered, and his beard was quite green and reached right down to his knee.

"What dost thou want of me, O man?" he asked.

The man was amazed at the strangeness of his coming to light, and said to him, "I did not call thee; begone!"

"How canst thou say that when thou didst call me?" asked the little old man.

"Who art thou, then?" asked the father.

"I am Oh, the Tsar of the Woods," replied the old man; "why didst thou call me, I say?"

"Away with thee, I did not call thee," said the man.

"What! thou didst not call me when thou saidst 'Oh'?"

"I was tired, and therefore I said 'Oh'!" replied the man.

"Whither art thou going?" asked Oh.

"The wide world lies before me," sighed the man. "I am taking this sorry blockhead of mine to hire him out to somebody or other. Perchance other people may be able to knock more sense into him than we can at home; but send him whither we will, he always comes running home again!"

"Hire him out to me. I'll warrant I'll teach him," said Oh. "Yet I'll only take him on one condition. Thou shalt come back for him when a year has run, and if thou dost know him again, thou mayst take him; but if thou dost not know him again, he shall serve another year with me."

"Good!" cried the man. So they shook hands upon it, had a good drink to clinch the bargain, and the man went back to his own home, while Oh took the son away.

Oh took the son away with him, and they passed into the other world, the world beneath the earth, and came to a green hut woven out of rushes, and in this hut everything was green; the walls were green and the benches were green, and Oh's wife was green and his children were green—in fact, everything there was green. And Oh had water-nixies for serving-maids, and they were all as green as rue.

"Sit down now!" said Oh to his new labourer, "and have a bit of something to eat." The nixies then brought him some food, and that also was green, and he ate of it.

"And now," said Oh, "take my labourer into the courtyard that he may chop wood and draw water." So they took him into the courtyard, but instead of chopping any wood he lay down and went to sleep.

Oh came out to see how he was getting on, and there he lay a-snoring. Then Oh seized him, and bade them bring wood and tie his labourer fast to the wood, and set the wood on fire till the labourer was burnt to ashes.

Then Oh took the ashes and scattered them to the four winds, but a single piece of burnt coal fell from out of the ashes, and this coal he sprinkled with living water, whereupon the labourer immediately stood there alive again and somewhat handsomer and stronger than before. Oh again bade him chop wood, but again he went to sleep. Then Oh again tied him to the wood, and burnt him, and scattered his ashes to the four winds and sprinkled the remnant of the coal with living water, and instead of the loutish clown there stood there such a handsome and stalwart Cossack [2] that the like of him can neither be imagined nor described but only told in tales. There, then, the lad remained for a year, and at the end of the year the father came for his son. He came to the self-same charred stumps in the self-same forest, sat him down, and said, "Oh!"

Oh immediately came out of the charred stump and said, "Hail! O man!"

"Hail to thee, Oh!"

"And what dost thou want, O man?" asked Oh.

"I have come," said he, "for my son."

"Well, come then! If thou dost know him again, thou shalt take him away; but if thou dost not know him, he shall serve with me yet another year."

So the man went with Oh. They came to his hut, and Oh took whole handfuls of millet and scattered it about, and myriads of cocks came running up and pecked it. "Well, dost thou know thy son again?" said Oh.

The man stared and stared. There was nothing but cocks, and one cock was just like another. He could not pick out his son. "Well," said Oh, "as thou dost not know him, go home again; this year thy son must remain in my service." So the man went home again.

The second year passed away, and the man again went to Oh. He came to the charred stumps and said, "Oh!" and Oh popped out of the tree stump again.

---

[2] Ideal human hero.

"Come!" said he, "and see if thou canst recognize him now." Then he took him to a sheep pen, and there were rows and rows of rams, and one ram was just like another. The man stared and stared, but he could not pick out his son. "Thou mayst as well go home then," said Oh, "but thy son shall live with me yet another year." So the man went away, sad at heart.

The third year also passed away, and the man came again to find Oh. He went on and on till there met him an old man all as white as milk, and the raiment of this man was glistening white. "Hail to thee, O man!" he.

"Hail to thee also, my father!"

"Whither doth God lead thee?"

"I am going to free my son from Oh."

"How so?"

Then the man told the old white father how he had hired out his son to Oh and under what conditions.

"Aye, aye!" said the old white father, "'tis a vile pagan thou hast to deal with; he will lead thee about by the nose for a long time."

"Yes," said the man, "I perceive that he is a vile pagan; but I know not what in the world to do with him. Canst thou not tell me then, dear father, how I may recover my son?"

"Yes, I can," said the old man.

"Then prythee tell me, darling father, and I will pray for thee to God all my life, for though he has not been much of a son to me, he is still my own flesh and blood."

"Hearken, then!" said the old man; "when thou dost go to Oh, he will let loose a multitude of doves before thee, but choose not one of these doves. The dove thou shalt choose must be the one that comes not out, but remains sitting beneath the pear-tree pruning its feathers; that will be thy son." Then the man thanked the old white father and went on.

He came to the charred stumps. "Oh!" cried he, and out came Oh and led him to his sylvan realm. There Oh scattered about handfuls of wheat and called his doves, and there flew down such a multitude of them that there was no counting them, and one dove was just like another.

"Dost thou recognize thy son?" asked Oh. "An thou knowest him again, he is thine; an thou knowest him not, he is mine." Now all the doves there were pecking at the wheat, all but one that sat alone beneath the pear-tree, sticking out its breast, and pruning its feathers.

"That is my son," said the man.

"Since thou hast guessed him, take him," replied Oh. Then the father took the dove, and immediately it changed into a handsome young man, and a handsomer was not to be found in the wide world. The father rejoiced greatly and embraced and kissed him. "Let us go home, my son!" said he. So they went.

As they went along the road together they fell a-talking, and his father asked him how he had fared at Oh's. The son told him. Then the father told the son what he had suffered, and it was the son's turn to listen. Furthermore the father said, "What shall we do now, my son? I am poor and thou art poor: hast thou served these three years and earned nothing?"

"Grieve not, dear dad, all will come right in the end. Look! there are some young nobles hunting after a fox. I will turn myself into a grey hound and catch the fox, then the young noblemen will want to buy me of thee, and thou must sell me to them for three hundred roubles—only, mind thou sell me without a chain; then we shall have lots of money at home, and will live happily together!"

They went on and on, and there, on the borders of a forest, some hounds were chasing a fox. They chased it and chased it, but the fox kept on escaping, and the hounds could not run it down. Then the son changed himself into a greyhound, and ran down the fox and killed it. The noblemen thereupon came galloping out of the forest.

"Is that thy greyhound?"

"It is."

"'Tis a good dog; wilt sell it to us?"

"Bid for it!"

"What dost thou require?"

"Three hundred roubles without a chain."

"What do we want with *thy* chain, we would give him a chain of gold. Say a hundred roubles!"

"Nay!"

"Then take thy money and give us the dog."

They counted down the money and took the dog and set off hunting. They sent the dog after another fox. Away he went after it and chased it right into the forest, but then he turned into a youth again and rejoined his father.

They went on and on, and his father said to him, "What use is this money to us after all? It is barely enough to begin housekeeping with and repair our hut."

"Grieve not, dear dad, we shall get more still. Over yonder are some young noblemen hunting quails with falcons. I will change myself into a falcon, and thou must sell me to them; only sell me for three hundred roubles, and without a hood."

They went into the plain, and there were some young noblemen casting their falcon at a quail. The falcon pursued but always fell short of the quail, and the quail always eluded the falcon. The son then changed himself into a falcon, and immediately struck down its prey. The young noblemen saw it and were astonished. "Is that thy falcon?"

"'Tis mine."

"Sell it to us, then!"

"Bid for it!"

"What dost thou want for it?"

"If ye give three hundred roubles, ye may take it, but it must be without the hood."

"As if we want *thy* hood! We'll make for it a hood worthy of a Tsar."

So they higgled and haggled, but at last they gave him the three hundred roubles. Then the young nobles sent the falcon after another quail, and it flew and flew till it beat down its prey; but then he became a youth again, and went on with his father.

"How shall we manage to live with so little?" said the father.

"Wait a while dad, and we shall have still more," said the son. "When we pass through the fair, I'll change myself into a horse, and then thou must sell me. They will give thee a thousand roubles for me, only sell me without a halter." So when they got to the next little town, where they were holding a fair, the son changed himself into a horse, a horse as supple as a serpent, and so fiery that it was dangerous to approach him. The father led the horse along by the halter; it pranced about and struck sparks from the ground with its hoofs. Then the horse-dealers came together and began to bargain for it. "A thousand roubles down," said he, "and you may have it, but without the halter."

"What do we want with *thy* halter? We will make for it a silver-gilt halter. Come, we'll give thee five hundred!"

"No!" said he.

Then up there came a gipsy, blind of one eye.

"O man! What dost thou want for that horse?" said he.

"A thousand roubles without the halter."

"Nay! but that is dear, little father! Wilt thou not take five hundred with the halter?"

"No, not a bit of it!"

"Take six hundred, then!"

Then the gipsy began higgling and haggling, but the man would not give way.

"Come, sell it," said he, "with the halter."

"No, thou gipsy, I have a liking for that halter."

"But, my good man, when didst thou ever see them sell a horse without a halter? How then can one lead him off?"

"Nevertheless, the halter must remain mine."

"Look now, my father, I'll give thee five roubles extra, only I must have the halter."

The old man fell a-thinking.

"A halter of this kind is worth but three *grivni* [3] and the gipsy offers me five roubles for it; let him have it."

So they clinched the bargain with a good drink, and the old man went home with the money, and the gipsy walked off with the horse. But it was not really a gipsy, but Oh, who had taken the shape of a gipsy. Then Oh rode off on the horse, and the horse carried him higher than the trees of the forest, but lower than the clouds of the sky. At last they sank down among the woods, and came to Oh's hut, and Oh went into his hut and left his horse outside on the steppe.

"This son of a dog shall not escape from my hands so quickly a second time," said he to his wife. At dawn Oh took the horse by the bridle and led it away to the river to water it. But no sooner did the horse get to the river and bend down its head to drink than it turned into a perch and began swimming away. Oh, without more ado, turned himself into a pike and pursued the perch. But just as the pike was almost up with it, the perch gave a sudden twist and stuck out its spiky fins and turned its tail toward the pike, so that the pike could not lay hold of it. So when the pike came up to it, it said, "Perch! perch! turn thy head toward me, I want to have a chat with thee!"

"I can hear thee very well as I am, dear cousin, if thou art inclined to chat," said the perch. So off they set again, and again the pike overtook the perch.

"Perch! perch! turn thy head round toward me, I want to have a chat with thee!"

Then the perch stuck out its bristly fins again and said, "If thou dost wish to have a chat, dear cousin, I can hear thee just as well as I am." So the pike kept on pursuing the perch, but it was of no use. At last the perch swam ashore, and there was a Tsarivna whittling an ash twig. The perch changed itself into a gold ring set with garnets, and the Tsarivna saw it and fished up the ring out of the water. Full of joy she took it home, and said to her father, "Look, dear papa! what a nice ring I have found!" The Tsar kissed her, but the Tsarivna did not know which finger it would suit best, it was so lovely.

About the same time they told the Tsar that a certain merchant had come to the palace. It was Oh, who had changed himself into a merchant. The Tsar went out to him and said, "What dost thou want, old man?"

"I was sailing on the sea in my ship," said Oh, "and carrying to the Tsar of my own land a precious garnet ring, and this ring I dropped into the water. Has any of thy servants perchance found this precious ring?"

"No, but my daughter has," said the Tsar.

So they called the damsel, and Oh began to beg her to give it back to him, "For

---

[3] The tenth part of a rouble about 2½d., or 5 cents.

I may not live in this world if I bring not the ring," said he. But it was of no avail, she would not give it up.

Then the Tsar himself spoke to her. "Nay, but, darling daughter, give it up, I say!" Then Oh begged and prayed her yet more, and said, "Take what thou wilt of me, only give me back the ring."

"Nay, then," said the Tsarivna, "it shall be neither mine nor thine," and with that she tossed the ring upon the ground, and it turned into a heap of millet-seed and scattered all about the floor. Then Oh, without more ado, changed into a cock, and began pecking up all the seed. He pecked and pecked till he had pecked it all up. Yet there was one single little grain of millet which rolled right beneath the feet of the Tsarivna, and that he did not see. When he had done pecking he got upon the window-sill, opened his wings, and flew right away.

But the one remaining grain of millet-seed turned into a most beauteous youth, a youth so beauteous that when the Tsarivna beheld him she fell in love with him on the spot, and begged the Tsar and Tsaritsa right piteously to let her have him as her husband.

"With no other shall I ever be happy," said she; "my happiness is in him alone!" For a long time the Tsar wrinkled his brows at the thought of giving his daughter to a simple youth; but at last he gave them his blessing, and they crowned them with bridal wreaths, and all the world was bidden to the wedding-feast. And I too was there, and drank beer and mead, and what my mouth could not hold ran down over my beard, and my heart rejoiced within me.

CELTIC TALES

THE folk-lore of the Celts has kindled the imagination of many poets. It abounds in superstition and all types of fairy-lore. The lively elves, the dainty Queen Mab and her courtiers, the mischievous brownie, the domestic banshee, the magical dwarf, the fantastic little leprechaun, the wilful Puck, the little hill-people, and the good little people all play important parts in the stories as well as the grotesque and terrible ogre, the giant, and the dragon.

The English tales, naturally, are more akin to the Norse than those of the true Celtic type. They are quaint, pleasing, and full of wonder and magic. There is many a touch of humour in them, but they are characterized mainly by a delightful charm both of incident and setting.

A more serious and romantic note is emphasized in the Scottish tales, as shown by such stories as "The Seal Maiden," and "The Tale of the Hoodie." They are, however, usually lacking in humour.

The popular tales of Ireland possess a special interest. As the country has not been repeatedly overrun by alien tribes the old forms of expression have been retained more firmly than in England. The stories have more of the primitive elements. They point to the East for origin, and, as compared with the English fairy-tales, have a weird, old-world touch. The Irish peasant is a mystic and is sensitive and impressionable. His nature cherishes the supernatural and rejoices in the presence of spirits—the "good people"—whose rights he never fails to respect. He loves all that has in it the breath of vitality—youth, beauty, the feast, and the dance—yet his strong yearnings for the mystical and unknown show that he believes the true fruit of life to be a spiritual reality. We see this in such a story as "Etain." There is an abundance of humour in the Irish tales, while many are pervaded by an almost enchanting pathos.

I. ENGLISH AND WELSH

CAP O' RUSHES

WELL, there was once a very rich gentleman, and he'd three daughters, and he thought he'd see how fond they were of him. So he says to the first, "How much do you love me, my dear?"

"Why," says she, "as I love my life."

"That's good," says he.

So he says to the second, "How much do *you* love me, my dear?"

'Why," says she, "better nor all the world."

"That's good," says he.

So he says to the third, "How much do *you* love me, my dear?"

"Why, I love you as fresh meat loves salt," says she.

Well, but he *was* angry. "You don't love me at all," says he, "and in my house you stay no more." So he drove her out there and then, and shut the door in her face.

Well, she went away on and on till she came to a fen, and there she gathered a lot of rushes and made them into a kind of a sort of a cloak with a hood, to cover her from head to foot, and to hide her fine clothes. And then she went on and on till she came to a great house.

"Do you want a maid?" says she.

"No, we don't," said they.

"I haven't nowhere to go," says she, "and I ask no wages, and do any sort of work," says she.

"Well," said they, "if you like to wash the pots and scrape the saucepans you may stay," said they.

So she stayed there and washed the pots and scraped the saucepans and did all the dirty work. And because she gave no name they called her "Cap o' Rushes."

Well, one day there was to be a great dance a little way off, and the servants were allowed to go and look on at the grand people. Cap o' Rushes said she was too tired to go, so she stayed at home. But when they were gone she offed with her cap o' rushes, and cleaned herself, and went to the dance. And no one there was so finely dressed as she.

Well, who should be there but her master's son, and what should he do but fall in love with her the minute he set eyes on her. He wouldn't dance with anyone else.

But before the dance was done Cap o' Rushes slips off, and away she went home. And when the other maids came back she was pretending to be asleep with her cap o' rushes on.

Next morning, they said to her, "You did miss a sight, Cap o' Rushes!"

"What was that?" says she.

"Why, the beautifullest lady you ever see, dressed right gay and ga'. The young master, he never took his eyes off her."

"Well, I should have liked to have seen her," says Cap o' Rushes.

"Well, there's to be another dance this evening, and perhaps she'll be there."

But, come the evening, Cap o' Rushes said she was too tired to go with them. Howsoever, when they were gone she offed with her cap o' rushes and cleaned herself, and away she went to the dance. The master's son had been reckoning on seeing her, and he danced with no one else, and never took his eyes off her. But, before the dance was over, she slipt off, and home she went, and when the maids came back she pretended to be asleep with her cap o' rushes on.

Next day they said to her again, "Well, Cap o' Rushes, you should ha' been there to see the lady. There she was again, gay and ga', and the young master he never took his eyes off her."

"Well, there," says she, "I should ha' liked to ha' seen her."

"Well," says they, "there's a dance again this evening, and you must go with us, for she's sure to be there." Well, come this evening, Cap o' Rushes said she was too tired to go, and do what they would she stayed at home. But when they were gone she offed with her cap o' rushes and cleaned herself, and away she went to the dance.

The master's son was rarely glad when he saw her. He danced with none but her, and never took his eyes off her. When she wouldn't tell him her name, nor where she came from, he gave her a ring and told her if he didn't see her again he should die. Well, before the dance was over, off she slipped, and home she went, and when the maids came home she was pretending to be asleep with her cap o' rushes on.

Well, next day they says to her, "There, Cap o' Rushes, you didn't come last night, and now you won't see the lady, for there's no more dances."

"Well, I should have rarely liked to have seen her," says she.

The master's son he tried every way to find out where the lady was gone, but go where he might, and ask whom he might, he never heard anything about her. And he grew worse and worse for the love of her till he had to keep his bed.

"Make some gruel for the young master," they said to the cook. "He's dying for the love of the lady." The cook she set about making it when Cap o' Rushes came in.

"What are you doing?" says she.

"I'm going to make some gruel for the young master," says the cook, "for he's dying for love of the lady."

"Let me make it," says Cap o' Rushes.

The cook wouldn't at first, but at last she said yes, and Cap o' Rushes made the gruel. And when she had made it she slipped the ring into it on the sly before the cook took it upstairs.

The young man drank it and then he saw the ring at the bottom.

"Send for the cook," says he.

So up she comes.

"Who made this gruel?" says he.

"I did," says the cook, for she was frightened.

And he looked at her.

"No, you didn't," says he. "Say who did it, and you won't be harmed."

"Well, then, 'twas Cap o' Rushes," says she.

"Send Cap o' Rushes here," says he.

So Cap o' Rushes came.

"Did you make my gruel ?" says he.

"Yes, I did," says she.

"Where did you get this ring?" says he.

"From him that gave it me," says she.

"Who are you, then?" says the young man.

"I'll show you," says she. And she offed with her cap o' rushes, and there she was in her beautiful clothes.

The master's son was well very soon, and they were to be married in a little time. It was to be a very grand wedding, and every one was asked far and near. And Cap o' Rushes' father was asked. But she never told anybody who she was.

Before the wedding, however, she went to the cook and says she:

"I want you to dress every dish without a grain o' salt."

"That'll be rare nasty," says the cook.

"That doesn't matter," says she.

"Very well," says the cook.

Well, the wedding-day came, and they were married. And afterward all the company sat down to the dinner. When they began to eat the meat, it was so tasteless that they couldn't touch it. Cap o' Rushes' father tried first one dish and then another and then began to weep.

"What is the matter?" said the master's son to him.

"Oh!" says he, "I had a daughter. And I asked her how much she loved me. And she said, 'As much as fresh meat loves salt.' And I turned her from my door, for I thought she didn't love me. And now I see she loved me best of all. And she may be dead for aught I know."

"No, father, here she is!" says Cap o' Rushes. And she goes up to him and puts her arms round him.

And so they were all happy ever after.

LAZY JACK

ONCE upon a time there was a boy whose name was Jack, and he lived with his mother on a dreary common. They were very poor, and the old woman got her living by spinning, but Jack was so lazy that he would do nothing but bask in the sun in the hot weather, and sit by the corner of the hearth in the winter-time. So they called him lazy Jack. His mother could not get him to do any work for her, and was obliged at last to tell him that if he did not begin to work for his porridge, she would turn him out to get his living as best he could.

Roused by this, Jack went out and hired himself for the day to a neighbouring farmer for a penny; but as he was coming home, never having had any money of his own before, he lost it in passing over a brook.

"You stupid boy," said his mother, "you should have put it in your pocket."
"I'll do so another time," replied Jack.

The next day Jack went out again and hired himself to a cowkeeper, who gave him a jar of milk for his day's work. Jack took the jar and put it into the large pocket of his jacket, spilling it all long before he got home.

"Dear me!" said the old woman; "you should have carried it. on your head."
"I'll do so another time," replied Jack.

The following day Jack hired himself again to a farmer, who agreed to give him a cream cheese for his services. In the evening Jack took the cheese, and went home with it on his head. By the time he reached home the cheese was completely spoilt, part of it being lost, and part matted with his hair.

"You stupid lout," said his mother, "you should have carried it very carefully in your hands."
"I'll do so another time," replied Jack.

The day after this Jack again went out, and hired himself to a baker, who would give him nothing for his work but a large tom-cat. Jack took the cat, and began carrying it very carefully in his hands, but in a short time pussy scratched him so much that he was compelled to let it go.

When he got home, his mother said to him: "You silly fellow, you should have tied it with a string, and dragged it along after you."
"I'll do so another time," said Jack.

The next day Jack hired himself to a butcher, who rewarded him by the handsome present of a shoulder of mutton. Jack took the mutton, tied it to a string, and trailed it along after him in the dirt, so that by the time he reached home, the meat was completely spoilt. His mother was this time quite out of patience with him, for the next day was Sunday, and she was obliged to content herself with cabbage for her dinner.

"You ninney-hammer, said she to her son, "you should have carried it on your shoulder."
"I'll do so another time," replied Jack.

On the next Monday, Lazy Jack went once more and hired himself to a cattle-keeper, who gave him a donkey for his trouble. Although Jack was very strong, he found it very difficult to hoist the donkey on to his shoulders, but at length he managed it, and began walking slowly home with his prize.

Now, it happened that in the course of his journey there lived a rich man with his only daughter, a beautiful girl, but deaf and dumb. She had never laughed in her life, and the doctors said she would never speak till somebody made her laugh. This young lady happened to be looking out of the window when Jack was passing with the donkey on his shoulders, with the legs sticking up in the air, and the sight was so comical that she burst out into a great fit of laughter, and at once recovered her speech and hearing. Her father was overjoyed, and fulfilled his promise by marrying her to Jack, who was thus made a fine gentleman. They lived in a large house, and Jack's mother lived with them in great happiness until she died.

MR. VINEGAR

MR. and Mrs. Vinegar lived in a vinegar bottle. Now, one day, when Mr. Vinegar was from home, Mrs. Vinegar, who was a very good housewife, was busily sweeping her house, when an unlucky thump of the broom brought the whole house *clitter-clatter, clitter-clatter,* about her ears. In an agony of grief she rushed forth to meet her husband. On seeing him she exclaimed, "O Mr. Vinegar, Mr. Vinegar, we are ruined, we are ruined: I have knocked the house down, and it is all to pieces!"

Mr. Vinegar then said:" My dear, let us see what can be done. Here is the door; I will take it on my back, and we will go forth to seek our fortune."

They walked all that day, and at nightfall entered a thick forest. They were both very, very tired, and Mr. Vinegar said: "My love, I will climb up into a tree, drag up the door, and you shall follow." He accordingly did so, and they both stretched their weary limbs on the door, and fell fast asleep. In the middle of the night Mr. Vinegar was disturbed by the sound of voices underneath, and to his horror and dismay found that it was a band of thieves met to divide their booty. "Here, Jack" said one, "here's five pounds for you; here, Bill, here's ten pounds for you; here, Bob, here's three pounds for you." Mr. Vinegar could listen no longer; his terror was so great that he trembled and trembled, and shook down the door on their heads. Away scampered the thieves, but Mr. Vinegar dared not quit his retreat till broad daylight. He then scrambled out of the tree, and went to lift up the door. What did he see but a number of golden guineas. "Come down, Mrs. Vinegar," he cried; "come down, I say; our fortune's made, our fortune's made! Come down, I say." Mrs. Vinegar got down as fast as she could, and when she saw the money she jumped for joy. "Now, my dear," said she, "I'll tell you what you shall do. There is a fair at the neighbouring town; you shall take these forty guineas and buy a cow. I can make butter and cheese, which you shall sell at market, and we shall then be able to live very comfortably." Mr. Vinegar joyfully agrees, takes the money, and off he goes to the fair. When he arrived, he walked up and down, and at length saw a beautiful red cow. It was an excellent milker, and perfect in every way. "Oh," thought Mr. Vinegar, "if I had but that cow, I should be the happiest man alive." So he offers the forty guineas for the cow, and the owner said that, as he was a friend, he'd oblige him. So the bargain was made, and he proudly drove the cow backward and forward to show it. By-and-by he saw a man playing the bagpipes—Tweedle-dum, tweedle-dee. The children followed him, and he appeared to be pocketing money on all sides.

"Well," thought Mr. Vinegar, if I had but that beautiful instrument I should be the happiest man alive—my fortune would be made." So he went up to the man. "Friend," says he, "what a beautiful instrument that is, and what a deal of money you must make." " Why, yes," said the man, "I make a great deal of money, to be sure, and it is a wonderful instrument." "Oh!" cried Mr. Vinegar, "how I should like to possess it!" "Well," said the man, "as you are a friend, I don't much mind parting with it; you shall have it for that red cow." "Done!" said the delighted Mr. Vinegar. So the beautiful red cow was given for the bagpipes. He walked up and down with his purchase; but it was in vain he tried to play a tune, and instead of pocketing pence, the boys followed him, hooting, laughing and pelting.

Poor Mr. Vinegar, his fingers grew very cold, and, just as he was leaving the town, he met a man with a fine thick pair of gloves. "Oh, my fingers are so very cold," said Mr. Vinegar to himself. "Now if I had but those beautiful gloves I should be the happiest man alive." He went up to the man, and said to him: "Friend, you seem to have a capital pair of gloves there." "Yes, truly," cried the man; "and my hands are as warm as possible this cold November day." "Well," said Mr. Vinegar, "I should like to have them." "What will you give?" said the man; "as you are a friend, I don't mind letting you have them for those bagpipes." "Done!" cried Mr. Vinegar. He put on the gloves, and felt perfectly happy as he trudged homeward.

At last he grew very tired, when he saw a man coming toward him with a good stout stick in his hand.

"Oh," said Mr. Vinegar, "that I had but that stick! I should then be the happiest man alive." He said to the man: "Friend! what a rare good stick you have there." "Yes," said the man; "I have used it for many a long mile, and a good friend it has been; but if you have a fancy for it, as you are a friend, I don't mind giving it to you for that pair of gloves." Mr. Vinegar's hands were so warm, and his legs so tired, that he gladly made the exchange. As he drew near to the wood where he had left his wife, he heard a parrot on a tree calling out his name. "Mr. Vinegar, you foolish man, you blockhead, you simpleton; you went to the fair, and laid out all your money in buying a cow. Not content with that, you changed it for bagpipes, on which you could not play, and which were not worth *one-tenth* of the money. You fool, you—you had no sooner got the bagpipes than you changed them for the gloves, which were not worth *one quarter* of the money; and when you had got the gloves, you changed them for a miserable stick; and now for your forty guineas, cow, bagpipes, and gloves, you have nothing to show but that poor miserable stick, which you might have cut in any hedge." On this the bird laughed and laughed, and Mr. Vinegar, falling into a violent rage, threw the stick at its head.

The stick lodged in the tree, and he returned to his wife without money, cow, bagpipes, gloves, or stick, and she instantly gave him such a sound cudgelling that she almost broke every bone in his skin.

THE CAT AND THE MOUSE

The cat and the mouse
Play'd in the malt-house:

THE cat bit the mouse's tail off. "Pray, puss, give me my tail." "No," says the cat, "I'll not give you your tail, till you go to the cow, and fetch me some milk."

First she leapt, and then she ran,
Till she came to the cow, and thus began:

"Pray, Cow, give me milk, that I may give cat milk, that cat may give me my own tail again." "No," said the cow, "I will give you no milk, till you go to the farmer and get me some hay."

First she leapt, and then she ran,
Till she came to the farmer, and thus began:

"Pray, Farmer, give me hay, that I may give cow hay, that cow may give me milk, that I may give cat milk, that cat may give me my own tail again." "No," says the farmer, "I'll give you no hay, till you go to the butcher and fetch me some meat."

First she leapt, and then she ran,
Till she came to the butcher, and thus began:

"Pray, Butcher, give me meat, that I may give farmer meat, that farmer may give me hay, that I may give cow hay, that cow may give me milk, that I may give cat milk, that cat may give me my own tail again." "No," says the butcher, "I'll give you no meat, till you go to the baker and fetch me some bread."

First she leapt, and then she ran,
Till she came to the baker, and thus began:

"Pray, Baker, give me bread, that I may give butcher bread, that butcher may give me meat, that I may give farmer meat, that farmer may give me hay, that I may give cow hay, that cow may give me milk, that I may give cat milk, that cat may give me my own tail again."

"Yes," says the baker, "I'll give you some bread,
But if you eat my meal, I'll cut off your head."

Then the baker gave mouse bread, and mouse gave butcher bread, and butcher gave mouse meat, and mouse gave farmer meat, and farmer gave mouse hay, and mouse gave cow hay, and cow gave mouse milk, and mouse gave cat milk, and cat gave mouse her own tail again!

MOLLY WHUPPIE

ONCE upon a time there was a man and a wife who had too many children, and they could not get meat for them, so they took the three youngest and left them in a wood. They travelled and travelled and could see never a house. It began to be dark, and they were hungry. At last they saw a light and made for it; it turned out to be a house. They knocked at the door, and a woman came to it, who said: "What do you want?" They said: "Please let us in and give us something to eat." The woman said: "I can't do that, as my man is a giant, and he would kill you if he comes home." They begged hard. "Let us stop for a little while," said they, "and we will go away before he comes." So she took them in, and set them down before the fire, and gave them milk and bread; but just they had begun to eat a great knock came to the door, and a dreadful voice said:

> "Fee, fie, fo, fum,
> I smell the blood of some earthly one.

Who have you there?" "Eh," said the wife, "it's three poor lassies cold and hungry, and they will go away. Ye won't touch 'em, man." He said nothing, but ate up a big supper and ordered them to stay all night. Now he had three lassies of his own, and they were to sleep in the same bed with the three strangers. The youngest of the three strange lassies was called Molly Whuppie, and she was very clever. She noticed that before they went to bed the giant put straw ropes round her neck and her sisters', and round his own lassies' necks he put gold chains. So Molly took care and did not fall asleep, but waited till she was sure every one was sleeping sound. Then she slipped out of the bed, and took the straw ropes off her own and her sisters' necks, and took the gold chains off the giant's lassies. She then put the straw ropes on the giant's lassies and the gold on herself and her sisters, and lay down. And in the middle of the night up rose the giant, armed with a great club, and felt for the necks with the straw. It was dark. He took his own lassies out of bed on to the floor, and battered them until they were dead, and then lay down again, thinking he had managed finely. Molly thought it time she and her sisters were off and away, so she wakened them and told them to be quiet, and they slipped out of the house. They all got out safe, and they ran and ran, and never stopped till morning, when they saw a grand house before them. It turned out to be a king's house; so Molly went in, and told her story to the king. He said: "Well, Molly, you are a clever girl, and you have managed well; but if you would manage better, go back, and steal the giant's sword that hangs on the back of his bed, I would give your eldest sister my eldest son to marry." Molly said she would try. So she went back, and managed to slip into the giant's house, and crept in below the bed. The giant came home, and ate up a great supper, and went to bed. Molly waited until he was snoring, and she crept out, reached over the giant, and got down the sword; but just as she got it over the bed it gave a rattle, and up jumped the giant, and Molly ran out at the door and the sword with her; and she ran, and he ran, till they came to the "Bridge of one hair"; she got over, but he couldn't, and he said, "Woe worth ye, Molly Whuppie! never ye come again." And she said: "Twice yet, carle, I'll come to Spain." So Molly took the sword to the king, and her sister was married to his son.

Well, the king he said: "Ye've managed well, Molly; but if ye would manage better, and steal the purse that lies below the giant's pillow, I would marry your second sister to my second son." And Molly said she would try. So she set out for the giant's house, and slipped in, and hid again below the bed, waited till the giant had eaten his supper, and was snoring, sound asleep. She crept out and slipped her hand below the pillow, and got out the purse; but just as she was going out the giant wakened, and ran after her; and she ran, and he ran, till they came to the "Bridge of one hair"; she got over, but he couldn't, and he said, "Woe worth ye, Molly Whuppie! never you come again." "Once yet, carle," quoth she, "I'll come to Spain." so Molly took the purse to the king, and her second sister was married to the king's second son.

After that the king said to Molly: "Molly, you are a clever girl, but if you would do better yet, and steal the giant's ring that he wears on his finger, I will give you my youngest son for yourself." Molly said she would try.

So back she goes to the giant's house, and hides herself below the bed. The giant wasn't long ere he came home, and, after he had eaten a great big supper, he went to his bed, and shortly was snoring loud. Molly crept out and reached over the bed, got hold of the giant's hand, and she pulled and she pulled until she got off the ring; but just as she got it off the giant got up, and gripped her by the hand, and he says: "Now I have caught you, Molly Whuppie, and, if I had done as much ill to you as ye have done to me, what would ye do to me?"

Molly says: "I would put you into a sack, and I'd put the cat inside wi' you, and the dog aside you, and a needle and thread and a shears, and I'd hang you up upon the wall, and I'd go to the wood, and choose the thickest stick I could get, and I would come home, and take you down, and bang you till you were dead."

"Well, Molly," says the giant, "I'll just do that to you."

So he gets a sack, and puts Molly into it, and the cat and the dog beside her, and a needle and thread and shears, and hangs her up upon the wall, and goes to the wood to choose a stick.

Molly she sings out: "Oh, if ye saw what I see."

"Oh," says the giant's wife, "what do ye see, Molly?"

But Molly never said a word but, "Oh, if ye saw what I see!"

The giant's wife begged that Molly would take her up into the sack till she could see what Molly saw. So Molly took the shears and cut a hole in the sack, and took out the needle and thread with her, and jumped down and helped the giant's wife up into the sack, and sewed up the hole. The giant's wife saw nothing, and began to ask to get down again; but Molly never minded, and hid herself at the back of the door. Home came the giant, and a great big tree in his hand, and he took down the sack, and began to batter it. His wife cried, "It's me, man"; but the dog barked and the cat mewed, and he did not know his wife's voice. But Molly came out from the back of the door, and the giant saw her, and he after her; and he ran and she ran, till they came to the "Bridge of one hair," and she got over but he couldn't; and he said, "Woe worth you, Molly Whuppie! never you come again." "Never more, carle," quoth she, "will I come again to Spain."

So Molly took the ring to the king, and she was married to his youngest son, and she never saw the giant again.

JOHNNY-CAKE

ONCE upon a time there was an old man, and an old woman, and a little boy. One morning the old woman made a Johnny-cake, and put it in the oven to bake. "You watch the Johnny-cake while your father and I go out to work in the garden." So the old man and the old woman went out and began to hoe potatoes, and left the little boy to tend the oven. But he didn't watch it all the time, and all of a sudden he heard a noise, and he looked up and the oven door popped open, and out of the oven jumped Johnny-cake, and went rolling along end over end, toward the open door of the house. The little boy ran to shut the door, but Johnny-cake was too quick for him and rolled through the door, down the steps, and out into the road long before the little boy could catch him. The little boy ran after him as fast as he could clip it, crying out to his father and mother, who heard the uproar, and threw down their hoes and gave chase too. But Johnny-cake outran all three a long way, and was soon out of sight, while they had to sit down, all out of breath, on a bank to rest. On went Johnny-cake, and by-and-by he came to two well diggers who looked up from their work and called out: "Where ye going, Johnny-cake ?"

He said: "I've outrun an old man, and an old woman, and a little boy, and I can outrun you too-o-o!"

"Ye can, can ye? We'll see about that!" said they; and they threw down their picks and ran after him, but couldn't catch up with him, and soon they had to sit down by the roadside to rest.

On ran Johnny-cake, and by-and-by he came to two ditch-diggers who were digging a ditch. "Where ye going, Johnny-cake?" said they. He said, "I've outrun an old man, and an old woman, and a little boy, and two well-diggers, and I can outrun you too-o-o!"

"Ye can, can ye? We'll see about that!" said they; and they threw down their spades, and ran after him too. But Johnny-cake soon outstripped them also, and seeing they could never catch him, they gave up the chase and sat down to rest.

On went Johnny-cake, and by-and-by he came to a bear. The bear said: "Where are ye going, Johnny-cake?"

He said: "I've outrun an old man, and an old woman, and a little boy, and two well-diggers, and two ditch-diggers, and I can outrun you too-o-o!"

"Ye can, can ye?" growled the bear. "We'll see about that!" and trotted as fast as his legs could carry him after Johnny-cake, who never stopped to look behind him. Before long the bear was left so far behind that he saw he might as well give up the hunt first as last, so he stretched himself out by the roadside to rest.

On went Johnny-cake, and by-and-by he came to a wolf. The wolf said: "Where ye going, Johnny-cake?" He said: "I've outrun an old man, and an old woman, and a little boy, and two well-diggers, and two ditch-diggers, and a bear, and I can outrun you too-o-o!"

"Ye can, can ye?" snarled the wolf. "We'll see about that!" And he set into a gallop after Johnny-cake, who went on and on so fast that the wolf too saw there was no hope of overtaking him, and he too lay down to rest.

On went Johnny-cake, and by-and-by he came to a fox that lay quietly in a corner of the fence. The fox called out in a sharp voice, but without getting up: "Where ye going, Johnny-cake?" He said: "I've outrun an old man, and an old woman, and a little boy, and two well-diggers, and two ditch-diggers, and a bear, and a wolf, and I can outrun you too-o-o!"

The fox said: "I can't quite hear you, Johnny-cake; won't you come a little closer?" turning his head a little to one side.

Johnny-cake stopped his race for the first time, and went a little closer, and called out in a very loud voice: *"I've outrun an old man, and an old woman, and a little boy, and two well-diggers, and two ditch-diggers, and a bear, and a wolf, and I can outrun you too-o-o!"*

"Can't quite hear you; won't you come a *little* closer?" said the fox in a feeble voice, as he stretched out his neck toward Johnny-cake, and put one paw behind his ear.

Johnny-cake came up close, and leaning toward the fox screamed out: "I'VE OUTRUN AN OLD MAN, AND AN OLD WOMAN, AND A LITTLE BOY, AND TWO WELL-DIGGERS, AND TWO DITCH-DIGGERS, AND A BEAR, AND A WOLF, AND I CAN OUTRUN YOU TOO-O-O!"

"You can, can you?" yelped the fox, and he snapped up the Johnny-cake in his sharp teeth in the twinkling of an eye.

TITTY MOUSE AND TATTY MOUSE

TITTY MOUSE and Tatty Mouse both lived in a house,
      Titty Mouse went a leasing and Tatty Mouse went a leasing,
            So they both went a leasing.
Titty Mouse leased an ear of corn, and Tatty Mouse leased an ear of corn,
            So they both leased an ear of corn.
Titty Mouse made a pudding, and Tatty Mouse made a pudding,
            So they both made a pudding.
And Tatty Mouse put her pudding into the pot to boil,
But when Titty went to put hers in, the pot tumbled over, and scalded her to
            death.

Then Tatty sat down and wept; then a three-legged stool said: "Tatty, why do you weep?" "Titty's dead," said Tatty, "and so I weep." "Then," said the stool, "I'll hop," so the stool hopped.

Then a broom in the corner of the room said, "Stool, why do you hop?" "Oh!" said the stool, "Titty's dead, and Tatty weeps, and so I hop." "Then," said the broom, "I'll sweep," so the broom began to sweep.

"Then," said the door, "Broom, why do you sweep?" "Oh!" said the broom, "Titty's dead, and Tatty weeps, and the stool hops, and so I sweep." "Then," said the door, "I'll jar," so the door jarred. "Then," said the window, "Door, why do you jar?" "Oh!" said the door, "Titty's dead, and Tatty weeps, and the stool hops, and the broom sweeps, and so I jar."

"Then," said the window, "I'll creak," so the window creaked. Now there was an old form outside the house, and when the window creaked, the form said: "Window, why do you creak?" "Oh!" said the window, "Titty's dead, and Tatty weeps, and the stool hops, and the broom sweeps, the door jars, and so I creak?'

"Then," said the old form, "I'll run round the house." Then the old form ran round the house. Now there was a fine large walnut-tree growing by the cottage, and the tree said to the form: "Form, why do you run round the house.?" "Oh!" said the form, "Titty's dead, and Tatty weeps, and the stool hops, and the broom sweeps, the door jars, and the window creaks, and so I run round the house."

"Then," said the walnut-tree, "I'll shed my leaves," so the walnut-tree shed all its beautiful green leaves. Now there was a little bird perched on one of the boughs of the tree, and when all the leaves fell, it said: "Walnut-tree, why do you shed your leaves?" "Oh!" said the tree, "Titty's dead, and Tatty weeps, the stool hops, and the broom sweeps, the door jars, and the window creaks, the old form runs round the house, and so shed my leaves."

"Then," said the little bird, "I'll moult all my feathers," so he moulted all his pretty feathers. Now there was a little girl walking below, carrying a jug of milk for her brothers' and sisters' supper, and when she saw the poor little bird moult all its feathers, she said: "Little bird, why do you moult all your feathers?" "Oh!" said the little bird, "Titty's dead, and Tatty weeps, the stool hops, and the broom sweeps, the door jars, and the window creaks, the old form runs round the house, the walnut-tree sheds its leaves, and so I moult all my feathers."

"Then," said the little girl, "I'll spill the milk," so she dropt the pitcher and spilt the milk. Now there was an old man just by on the top of a ladder thatching a rick, and when he saw the little girl spill the milk, he said: "Little girl, what do you mean by spilling the milk? Your little brothers and sisters must go without their supper." Then said the little girl: "Titty's dead, and Tatty weeps, the stool hops, and the broom sweeps, the door jars, and the window creaks, the old form runs round the house, the walnut-tree sheds all its leaves, the little bird moults all its feathers, and so I spill the milk."

"Oh!" said the old man, "then I'll tumble off the ladder and break my neck," so he tumbled off the ladder and broke his neck; and when the old man broke his neck, the great walnut-tree fell down with a crash, and upset the old form and house, and the house falling knocked the window out, and the window knocked the door down, and the door upset the broom, and the broom upset the stool, and poor little Tatty Mouse was buried beneath the ruins.

ROBIN GOODFELLOW

ONCE upon a time, a great while ago, when men did eat and drink less, and were more honest, and knew no knavery, there was wont to walk many harmless spirits called fairies, dancing in brave order in fairy rings on green hills with sweet music. Sometimes they were invisible, and sometimes took divers shapes. Many mad pranks would they play, as pinching of untidy damsels black and blue, and misplacing things in ill-ordered houses; but lovingly would they use good girls, giving them silver and other pretty toys, which they would leave for them, sometimes in their shoes, other times in their pockets, sometimes in bright basins and other clean vessels. Now it chanced that in those happy days, a babe was born in a house to which the fairies did like well to repair. This babe was a boy, and the fairies, to show their pleasure, brought many pretty things thither, coverlets and delicate linen for his cradle; and capons, woodcock and quail for the christening, at which there was so much good cheer that the clerk had almost forgot to say the babe's name—Robin Goodfellow. So much for the birth and christening of little Robin.

When Robin was grown to six years of age, he was so knavish that all the neighbours did complain of him; for no sooner was his mother's back turned, but he was in one knavish action or other, so that his mother was constrained (to avoid the complaints) to take him with her to market, or wheresoever she went or rode. But this helped little or nothing, for if he rode before her, then would he make mouths and ill-favoured faces at those he met: if he rode behind her, then would he clap his hand on the tail; so that his mother was weary of the many complaints that came against him. Yet knew she not how to beat him justly for it, because she never saw him do that which was worthy blows. The complaints were daily so renewed that his mother promised him a whipping. Robin did not like that cheer, and therefore, to avoid it, he ran away, and left his mother a-sorrowing for him.

After Robin had travelled a good day's journey from his mother's house he sat down, and being weary he fell asleep. No sooner had slumber closed his eyelids, but he thought he saw many goodly proper little personages in antic measures tripping about him, and withal he heard such music, as he thought that Orpheus, that famous Greek fiddler (had he been alive), compared to one of these, had been but a poor musician.

As delights commonly last not long, so did those end sooner than Robin would willingly they should have done; and for very grief he awaked, and found by him lying a scroll wherein was written these lines following in golden letters:

Robin, my only son and heir,
How to live take thou no care:
By nature thou hast cunning shifts,
Which I'll increase with other gifts.
Wish what thou wilt, thou shall it have;
And for to fetch both fool and knave,
Thou hast the power to change thy shape,
To horse, to hog, to dog, to ape.
Transformed thus, by any means
See none thou harm'st but knaves and queanes:
But love thou those that honest be,
And help them in necessity.
Do thus and all the world shall know
The pranks of Robin Goodfellow,
For by that name thou called shalt be
To age's last posterity;
And if thou keep my just command,
One day thou shalt see Fairy Land!

Robin, having read this, was very joyful, yet longed he to know whether he had the power or not, and to try it he wished for some meat; presently a fine dish of roast veal was before him. Then wished he for plum-pudding; he straightway had it. This liked him well, and because he was weary, he wished himself a horse; no sooner was his wish ended, but he was changed into as fine a nag as you need see, and leaped and curveted as nimbly as if he had been in stable at rack and manger a full month. Then he wished himself a black dog, and he was so; then a green tree and he was so. So from one thing to another, till he was quite sure that he could change himself to anything whatsoever he liked.

Thereupon, full of delight at his new powers, Robin Goodfellow set out, eager to put them to the test. As he was crossing a field, he met with a red-faced carter's clown, and called to him to stop.

"Friend," quoth he, "what is a clock?"

"A thing," answered the clown, "that shows the time of the day."

"Why then," said Robin Goodfellow, "be thou a clock and tell me what time of the day it is."

"I owe thee not so much service," answered the clown again, "but because thou shalt think thyself beholden to me, know that it is the same time of the day as it was yesterday at this time!"

These shrewd answers vexed Robin Goodfellow, so that in himself he vowed to be revenged of the clown, which he did in this manner.

Robin Goodfellow turned himself into a bird, and followed this fellow who was going into a field a little from that place to catch a horse that was at grass. The horse being wild ran over dyke and hedge, and the fellow after, but to little purpose, for the horse was too swift for him. Robin was glad of this occasion, for now or never was the time to have his revenge.

Presently Robin shaped himself exactly like the horse that the clown followed, and so stood right before him. Then the clown took hold of the horse's mane and got on his back, but he had not ridden far when, with a stumble, Robin hurled his rider over his head, so that he almost broke his neck. But then again he stood still, and let the clown mount him once more.

By the way which the clown now would ride was a great pond of water of a good depth, which covered the road. No sooner did he ride into the very middle of the pond, than Robin Goodfellow turned himself into a fish, and so left him with nothing but the packsaddle on which he was riding betwixt his legs. Meanwhile the fish swiftly swam to the bank. And then Robin, changed to a naughty boy again, ran away laughing *"Ho, ho, hoh,"* leaving the poor clown half drowned and covered with mud. As Robin took his way then along a green hedgeside he fell to singing:

> "And can the doctor make sick men well?
> And can the gipsy a fortune tell
> Without lily, germander, and cockle-shell?
>   With sweet-brier,
>   And bon-fire,
>   And straw-berry wine,
>   And columbine."

> "When Saturn did live, the sun did shine,
> The king and the beggar on roots did dine,
> With lily, germander, and sops in wine.
>   With sweet-brier,
>   And bon-fire,
>   And straw-berry wine,
>   And columbine."

And when he had sung this over, he fell to wondering what he should next turn himself into. Then as he saw the smoke rise from the chimneys of the next town, he thought to himself, it would be to him great sport to walk the streets with a broom on his shoulder, and cry "Chimney-sweep." But when presently Robin did this, and one did call him, then did Robin ran away, laughing, *"Ho, ho, hoh!"*

Next he set about to counterfeit a lame beggar—begging very pitifully, but when a stout chandler came out of his shop to give Robin an alms, again he skipped off nimbly, laughing, as his naughty manner was.

That same night, he did knock at many men's doors, and when the servants came out, he blew out their candle and straightway vanished in the dark street, with his *"Ho, ho, hoh!"*

All these mirthful tricks did Robin play, that day and night, and in these humours of his he had many pretty songs, one of which I will sing as perfect as I can. He sang it in his chimney-sweeper's humour:

> "Black I am from head to foot,
> And all doth come by chimney soot.
> Then, maidens, come and cherish him
> That makes your chimneys neat and trim."

But it befell that, on the very next night to his playing the chimney-sweep, Robin had a summons from the land where there are no chimneys. For King Oberon, seeing Robin Goodfellow do so many merry tricks, called him out of his bed with these words, saying:

> "Robin, my son, come quickly rise:
> First stretch, then yawn, and rub your eyes;
> For thou must go with me to-night,
> And taste of Fairy Land's delight."

Robin, hearing this, rose and went to him. There did King Oberon show Robin Goodfellow many secrets, which he never did open to the world. And there, in Fairy Land, doth Robin Goodfellow abide now this many a long year.

THE WISE MEN OF GOTHAM

OF SENDING RENT

O NCE on a time the men of Gotham had forgotten to pay their landlord. One said to the other, "To-morrow is our pay-day, and what shall we find to send our money to our landlord?"

The one said, "This day I have caught a hare, and he shall carry it, for he is light of foot."

"Be it so," said all; "he shall have a letter and a purse to put our money in, and we shall direct him the right way." So when the letters were written and the money put in a purse, they tied it round the hare's neck, saying, "First you go to Lancaster, then thou must go to Loug borough, and Newarke is out landlord, and commend us to him, and there is his dues."

The hare, as soon as he was out of their hands, ran on along the contrary way. Some cried, "Thou must go to Lancaster first."

"Let the hare alone," said another; "he can tell a nearer way than the best of us all. Let him go."

Another said, "It is a subtle hare, let her alone; she will not keep the highway for fear of dogs."

OF DROWNING EELS

When Good Friday came, the men of Gotham cast their heads together what to do with their white herrings, their red herrings, their sprats, and other salt fish. One consulted with the other, and agreed that such fish should be cast into their pond (which was in the middle of the town), that they might breed against the next year, and every man that had salt fish left cast them into the pool.

"I have many white herrings," said one.

"I have many sprats," said another.

"I have many red herrings," said the other.

"I have much salt fish. Let all go into the pond or pool, and we shall fare like lords next year."

At the beginning of next year following, the men drew the pond to have their fish, and there was nothing but a great eel. "Ah," said they all, "a mischief on this eel, for he has eaten up all our fish."

"What shall we do to him?" said one to the other.

"Kill him," said one.

"Chop him into pieces," said another. "Not so," said another; "let us drown him."

"Be it so," said all. And they went to-another pond, and cast the eel into the pond. "Lie there and shift for yourself, for no help thou shalt have from us"; and they left the eel to drown.

OF SENDING CHEESE

There was a man of Gotham who went to the market at Nottingham to sell cheese, and as he was going down the hill to Nottingham bridge, one of his cheeses fell out of his wallet and rolled down the hill. "Ah, gaffer," said the fellow, "can you run to market alone? I will send one after another after you."

Then he laid down his wallet and took out the cheeses, and rolled them down the hill. Some went into one bush, and some went into another.

"I charge you all to meet me near the market place"; and when the fellow came to the market to meet his cheeses, he stayed there till the market was nearly done. Then he went about to inquire of his friends and neighbours, and other men, if they did see his cheeses come to the market.

"Who should bring them?" said one of the market men.

"Marry, themselves," said the fellow; "they know the way well enough."

He said, "A vengeance on them all. I did fear, to see them run so fast, that they would run beyond the market. I am now fully persuaded that they must be now almost at York." Whereupon he forthwith hired a horse to ride to York, to seek his cheeses where they were not, but to this day no one can tell him of his cheeses.

OF BUYING OF SHEEP

There were two men of Gotham, and one of them was going to market to Nottingham to buy sheep, and the other came from the market, and they both met together upon Nottingham bridge.

"Where are you going?" said the one who came from Nottingham.

"Marry," said he that was going to Nottingham, "I am going to buy sheep."

"Buy sheep?" said the other, "and which way will you bring them home ?"

"Marry," said the other, "I will bring them over this bridge."

"By Robin Hood," said he that came from Nottingham, "but thou shalt not."

"By Maid Marion," said he that was going thither, "but I will."

"You will not," said the one.

"I will," said the other.

Then they beat their staves against the ground one against the other, as if there had been a hundred sheep between them.

"Hold in," said one; "beware lest my sheep leap over the bridge."

"I care not," said the other; "they shall not come this way."

"But they shall," said the other.

Then the other said: "If that thou make much to-do, I will put my fingers in thy mouth."

"Will you?" said the other.

Now, as they were at their contention, another man of Gotham came from the market with a sack of meal upon a horse, and seeing and hearing his neighbours at strife about sheep, though there were none between them, said:

"Ah, fools! will you ever learn wisdom? Help me, and lay my sack upon my shoulders."

They did so, and he went to the side of the bridge, unloosened the mouth of the sack, and shook all his meal out into the river.

"Now, neighbours," he said, "how much meal is there in my sack?"

"Marry," said they, "there is none at all."

"Now, by my faith," said he, "even as much wit as is in your two heads to stir up strife about a thing you have not."

Which was the wisest of these three persons, judge yourself.

THE LOST FISHER

ON a certain time there were twelve men of Gotham who went a-fishing, and some waded in the water, and some stayed on dry land. When they went homeward one said to the others: "We have ventured much in wading, I pray that none of us be drowned." "Marry," said the other, "let us then count ourselves." And they counted, but each forgot himself, and so could count only eleven. "Alas," they said, "one of us *must* be drowned." They went back to the brook, and sought up and down with much weeping. Soon a courtier came riding by and asked why they were troubled. To him they told their sad story. "Well," said the Courtier, "what will you give me if I find you the twelfth man?" "Sir," said they, "all the money we have." "In truth," replied he, giving one of them a sound blow on the shoulder, "here is the first."

In like manner he served each one, and at the last cried: "And here is the twelfth man!" "God's blessing on your heart," said all the company, "that you have found our neighbour."

THE GOLDEN BALL

THERE were two lasses, daughters of one mother, and as they came home from t' fair, they saw a right bonny young man stand it house-door before them. They niver seed such a bonny man afore. He had gold on t' cap, gold on t' finger, gold on t' neck, a red gold watch chain—Eh! but he had brass. He had a golden ball in each hand. He gave a ball to each lass, and she was to keep it, and if she lost it, she was to be hanged. One o' the lasses, 't was t' youngest, lost her ball. (I'll tell thee how. She was by a park-paling, and she was tossing her ball, and it went up, and up, and up, till it went fair over t' paling; and when she climbed up to look, t' ball ran along green grass, and it went raite forward to t' door of t' house, and t' ball went in, and she saw 't no more.)

So she was taken away to be hanged by t' neck till she were dead, a cause she'd lost her ball. But she had a sweetheart, and he said he would get ball. So he went to t' park-gate, but 't was shut; so he climbed hedge, and when he got tut top of hedge, an old woman rose up out of t' dyke afore him, and said, if he would get ball, he must sleep three nights in t' house. He said he would.

Then he went into t' house, and looked for ball, but could na find it. Night came on and he heard spirits move it courtyard; so he looked o' t' window, and t' yard was full of them, like maggots in rotten meat.

Presently he heard steps coming upstairs. He hid behind door, and was as still as a mouse. Then in came a big giant five times as tall as he were, and giant looked round but did not see t' lad, so he went tut window and bowed to look out; and as he bowed on his elbows to see spirits it yard, t' lad stepped behind him, and wi' one blow of his sword he cut him in twain, so that the top part of him fell in the yard, and t' bottom part stood looking out of t' window.

There was a great cry from t' spirits when they saw half the giant come tumbling down to them, and they called out, "There come half our master, give us t' other half." So the lad said, "It's no use of thee, thou pair of legs, standing aloan at window, as thou hast no een to see with, so go join thy brother"; and he cast the bottom part of t' giant after top part. Now when the spirits had gotten all t' giant they were quiet.

Next night t' lad was at the house again, and now a second giant came in at door, and as he came in t' lad cut him in twain, but the legs walked on tut chimney and went up them. "Go, get thee after thy legs," said t' lad tut head, and he cast t' head up chimney too.

The third night t' lad got into bed, and he heard spirits striving under the bed, and they had t' ball there, and they were casting it to and fro.

Now one of them has his leg thrussen out from under bed, so t' lad brings his sword down and cuts it off. Then another thrusts his arm out at other side of the bed, and t' lad cuts that off. So at last he had maimed them all, and they all went crying and wailing off, and forgot t' ball, but he took it from under t' bed, and went to seek his truelove.

Now t' lass was taken to York to be hanged; she was brought out on t' scaffold, and t' hangman said, "Now, lass, tha' must hang by t' neck till tha' be'st dead." But she cried out:

> "Stop, stop, I think I see my mother coming!
> O mother, hast brought my golden ball
> And come to set me free?"

> "I've neither brought thy golden ball
> Nor come to set thee free,
> But I have come to see thee hung
> Upon this gallows-tree."

Then the hangman said, "Now, lass, say thy prayers, for tha' must dee." But she said:

> "Stop, stop, I think I see my father coming!
> O father, hast brought my golden ball
> And come to set me free?"

> "I've neither brought thy golden ball
> Nor come to set thee free,
> But I have come to see thee hung
> Upon this gallows-tree."

Then the hangman said, "Hast thee done thy prayers? Now, lass, put thy head intut noo-is." But she answered, "Stop, stop, I think I see my brother coming!", etc. After which, she excused herself because she thought she saw her sister coming, then her uncle, then her aunt, then her cousin, each of which was related in full; after which the hangman said, I wee-nt stop no longer, tha's making gam of me. Tha' must be hung at once."

But now she saw her sweetheart coming through the crowd, and he had over head i' t' air her own golden ball; so she said:

> "Stop, stop, I see my sweetheart coming!
> Sweetheart, hast brought my golden ball
> And come to set me free?"

> "Aye, I have brought thy golden ball
> And come to set thee free;
> I have not come to see thee hung
> Upon this gallows-tree."

THE HISTORY OF TOM THUMB

IN the days of King Arthur, Merlin, the famous enchanter, was once upon a long journey; when, feeling very weary, he stopped at the cottage of an honest ploughman to ask for some food. The ploughman's wife immediately brought him some milk and some brown bread, setting it before him with great civility.

Merlin could not help seeing that, although everything was very neat and clean, and the ploughman and his wife did not seem to be in want, yet they looked very sad; so he asked them to let him know the cause of their grief, and found that they were unhappy because they had no children.

"Ah me!" said the forlorn woman, "if I had but a son, although he were no longer than my husband's thumb, I should be the happiest woman in the world!"

Now Merlin was much amused at the thought of a boy no bigger than a man's thumb, and, as soon as he got home, he sent for the queen of the fairies, who was a great friend of his, and told her of the night he spent at the ploughman's hut, and of the strange wish of the poor woman, and he asked her to grant her the tiny child she so earnestly wished. The thought amused the queen, and she promised that his wish should be granted.

And so it turned out that the ploughman's wife had a son, who, to the wonder of all the country people, was just the size of his father's thumb.

One day, while the happy mother was sitting up in bed, smiling on its pretty face, and feeding it out of the cup of an acorn, the queen came in at the window, and kissing the child, gave it the name of Tom Thumb. She then told the other fairies to dress her favourite.

> An oak-leaf he had for his crown,
> His shirt, it was by spiders spun;
> With doublet wove of thistle-down,
> His trousers up with points were done;
> His stockings of apple-rind, they tie
> With eyelash plucked from his mother's eye;
> His shoes were made of a mouse's skin,
> Nicely tanned, with the hair within.

Tom never grew bigger than his father's thumb; but, as he grew older, he became very cunning and full of mischievous tricks. Thus, when he was old enough to play cherry-stones with other boys, and had lost his own, he used to creep into other boys' bags, fill his pockets, and come out again to play. But one day as he was getting out of a bag, the owner chanced to see him.

"Ah ha! my little Tom Thumb," said the boy, "so I have caught you at your tricks at last; now I will pay you off for your thieving."

Then drawing the string around his neck, he shook the bag so heartily that the cherry-stones bruised Tom's limbs and body sadly, which made him beg to be let out, and promised never to be guilty of such doings any more. He was soon let off, but this cured him of pilfering.

One day Tom's mother was beating up a batter pudding, and she placed him in an egg-shell to be out of harm's way. Tom crept out, however, and climbed to the edge of the bowl, when his foot slipped, and he fell over head and ears into the batter. His mother, not seeing him, stirred him into the pudding, which she next put into the pot to boil. Tom soon felt the scalding water, which made him kick and struggle.

His mother, seeing the pudding turn round and round in the pot in such a furious manner, thought it was bewitched; and as a tinker came by just at the time, she quickly gave him the pudding, which he put into his budget, and went away.

As soon as Tom could get the batter out of his mouth, he began to cry aloud. This so frightened the poor tinker that he flung the pudding over the hedge, and ran away as fast as he could. The pudding being broken by the fall, Tom was set free, so he walked home to his mother, who kissed him and put him to bed.

Another time, Tom Thumb's mother took him with her when she went to milk the cow, and as it was a very windy day, she tied him with a needleful of thread to a thistle, that he might not be blown away.

The cow, liking his oak-leaf hat, picked him and the thistle up at one mouthful. When the cow began to chew the thistle, Tom was dreadfully frightened at her great teeth, and cried out, "Mother! mother!"

"Where are you, Tommy, my dear Tommy?" cried the mother, in great alarm.

"Here, mother, here, in the red cow's mouth!"

The mother began to cry and wring her hands; but the cow, surprised at such odd noises in her throat, opened her mouth and let him drop out. His mother caught him in her apron, and ran home with him.

One day, as Tom Thumb's father was in the fields with him, Tom begged to be allowed to take home the horse and cart. The father laughed at the thought of little Tom driving a horse, and asked him how he would hold the reins.

"Oh," said Tom, "I will sit in the horse's ear, and call out which way he is to go."

The father consented, and off Tom set, seated in the ear of the horse. "Yeo hup! yeo hup!" cried Tom, as he passed some country people, who, not seeing Tom, and thinking the horse was bewitched, ran off very fast.

Tom's mother was greatly surprised when she saw the horse arrive at the cottage door, with no one to guide it, and she ran out to look after it; but Tom called out, "Mother, mother, take me down, I am in the horse's ear!"

Tom's mother was very glad that her little son could be so useful, and she lifted him gently down, and gave him half a blackberry for his dinner.

After this, Tom's father made him a whip of barley-straw, that he might sometimes drive the cattle; and as he was driving them home one day, he fell into a deep furrow. A raven picked up the straw, with Tom too, and carried him to the top of a giant's castle, by the sea-side, and there left him.

Soon afterward old Grumbo, the giant, came out to walk on the terrace. Grumbo took the child up between his finger and thumb, and, opening his great mouth, he tried to swallow Tom like a pill. But Tom so danced in the red throat of the giant, that he soon cast him into the sea, where a large fish swallowed him in an instant.

This fish was soon after caught, and sent as a present to King Arthur. When it was cut open, everybody was delighted with the sight of Tom Thumb, who was found inside. The king made him his dwarf, and he was soon a very great favourite; for his tricks and gambols, and lively words amused the queen and the Knights of the Round Table.

When the king rode out, he frequently took Tom in his hand, and if rain fell, he used to creep into the king's pocket, and sleep till the rain was over.

One day, the king asked Tom concerning his parents, and finding they were very poor, the king led Tom into his treasury, and told him he might pay them a visit, and take with him as much money as he could carry.

Tom bought a small purse, and putting a three-penny piece into it, with much difficulty got it upon his back, and after travelling two days and two nights, reached his father's cottage.

His mother met him at the door, almost tired to death, having travelled forty-eight hours without resting, with a huge silver three-penny piece upon his back.

His parents were glad to see him, especially when he was the bearer of so large a sum of money. They placed him in a walnut shell by the fireside, and feasted him on a hazel-nut for three days.

When Tom recovered his strength, his duty told him it was time to return to court; but there had been such a heavy fall of rain that he could not travel; so his mother opened the window, when the wind was blowing in the proper direction, and gave him a puff, which soon carried him to the king's palace. There Tom exerted himself so much at tilts and tournaments, for the diversion of the king, queen, and nobility, that he brought on a fit of sickness, and his life was despaired of.

The queen of the fairies having heard of this, came in a chariot, drawn by flying mice, and placing Tom by her side, she drove back through the air, without stopping, to her own home.

The child soon recovered health and strength in fairy-land, and much enjoyed the diversions which were prepared for his amusement in that happy country.

After a while the queen sent him back to the king, floating upon a current of air, which she caused to be ready for the journey. Just as Tom was flying over the palace yard, the cook passed along with a great bowl of the king's favourite dish, furmenty, and poor Tom fell plumb into the middle of it, and splashed the hot furmenty into the cook's eyes, making him let fall the bowl.

"Oh, dear! oh, dear!" cried Tom.

"Murder! murder!" cried the cook, as the king's dainty furmenty ran into the dog's kennel.

The cook was a red-faced, cross fellow, and swore to the king that Tom had done it out of some evil design; so he was taken up, tried for high treason, and sentenced to be beheaded.

Just as this dreadful sentence was given, it happened that a miller was standing by, with his mouth wide open; so Tom took a good spring and jumped down his throat, unseen by anyone, even by the miller himself.

The culprit being now lost, the court broke up and the miller went back to his home. But Tom did not leave him long at rest; he began to roll and tumble about, so that the miller thought himself bewitched and sent for a doctor.

When the doctor came, Tom began to dance and sing. The doctor was more frightened than the miller, and he sent in a hurry for ten other doctors and twenty wise men, who began to discuss the matter at great length, each insisting that his own explanation was the true one.

The miller could not refrain from a hearty yawn, upon which Tom seized the lucky chance, and, with another bold jump, he alighted safely upon his feet on the middle of the table. The miller, in a fury, seized Tom, and threw him out of the window into the mill-stream, where he was once more swallowed up by a fish.

As happened before, the fish was caught and sold in the market to the steward of a great lord. The nobleman, seeing such a fine fish, sent it as a present to the king, who ordered it to be cooked for dinner.

When the fish was opened, Tom found himself once more in the hands of the cook, who immediately ran with him to the king; but the king being busy with state affairs, ordered him to be brought another day. The cook, to be sure of the prisoner, put him into a mouse-trap, where he remained seven days.

After that, the king sent for him, forgave him for throwing down the furmenty, ordered him a new suit of clothes, gave him a spirited hunter, and knighted him.

> His shirt was made of butterflies' wings;
> His boots were made of chickens' skins;
> His coat and breeches were made with pride;
> A tailor's needle hung by his side;
> A mouse for a horse he used to ride.

Thus dressed and mounted, he rode a-hunting with the king and nobility, who all laughed heartily at Tom and his fine prancing steed.

One fine day, as they passed an old farmhouse, a large black cat jumped out and seized both Tom and his steed, and began to devour the poor mouse. Tom drew his sword, and boldly attacked the cat.

The king and his nobles seeing Tom in danger, went to his assistance, and one of the lords bravely saved him just in time; but poor Tom was sadly scratched, and his clothes were torn by the claws of the cat.

In this condition he was carried in the palace and laid on a bed of down in a beautiful ivory cabinet. The queen of the fairies then came and took him to fairy-land again, where she kept him for some years; after which, dressing him in bright green, she sent him once more flying through the air to the earth.

People flocked far and near to look at Tom Thumb, and he was carried before King Thunstone, who had succeeded to the throne, King Arthur being dead .

The king asked him who he was, whence he came, and where he lived. Tom answered:

> "My name is Tom Thumb,
> From the fairies I've come.
> When King Arthur shone,
> This court was my home;
> In me he delighted,
> By him I was knighted;
> Did you never once hear of Sir Thomas Thumb?"

The king was charmed with this speech. He caused a little chair to be made, in order that Tom might sit on his table; and also a palace of gold a span high, with a door an inch wide, for little Tom to live in. He also gave him a coach, drawn by six small mice. This made the queen angry, because she had not got a coach also. She made up her mind to ruin Tom, and told the king that he had been very insolent to her; when the king sent for Tom in a great rage. To escape his fury, Tom hid himself in an empty snail-shell, where he lay till he was nearly starved.

At last, peeping out, he saw a fine butterfly settle on the ground. He now ventured forth, and got astride the butterfly, which took wing and mounted into the air with little Tom on his back.

Away they went from field to field, and from flower to flower, till the butterfly, attracted by the light streaming from the king's dining-room, flew in at the open window. The king, queen, and nobles all strove to catch the butterfly, but could not.

At length poor Tom, having neither saddle nor bridle, slipped from his seat into a sweet dish called whitepot, and was nearly drowned. The queen was bent on having him punished, and he was once more put in a mouse-trap. Here the cat, seeing something stir, and thinking a mouse was there, so rolled about the trap with her claws, that she broke it, and the prisoner escaped.

Soon afterward a large spider, taking poor Tom for a big fly, made a spring at him. Tom drew his sword, and fought with courage, but the poisonous breath of the spider overcame him.

> He fell dead on the ground where late he had stood,
> And the spider sucked up the last drop of his blood.

King Thunstone and all his court wept for the loss of the little favourite. They wore mourning for him for three years. He was buried under a rosebush, and a marble head-stone was raised over his grave, bearing these words:

> Here lies Tom Thumb, King Arthur's knight,
>   Who died by spider's cruel bite;
> He was well known in Arthur's court,
>   Where he afforded gallant sport.
>
> He rode a tilt and tournament,
>   And on a mouse a-hunting went;
> Alive, he filled the court with mirth,
>   His death to sorrow soon gave birth;
> Wipe, wipe your eyes, and shake your head,
>   And cry, "Alas! Tom Thumb is dead!"

HENNY-PENNY

ONE fine summer morning a hen was picking peas in a farm-yard under a pea-stack, when a pea fell on her head with such a thump that she thought the sky was falling. And she thought she would go to the court and tell the king that the sky was falling: so she gaed, and she gaed, and she gaed, and she met a Cock. And the Cock said:

"Where are you going to-day, Henny-penny?"

And she said:

"Oh, Cocky-locky, the sky is falling, and I am going to tell the king."

And Cocky-locky said:

"I will go with you, Henny-penny."

So Cocky-locky and Henny-penny they gaed, and they gaed, and they gaed till they met a Duck. So the Duck said:

"Where are you going to-day, Cocky-locky and Henny-penny?"

And they said:

"Oh, Ducky-daddles, the sky is falling, and we are going to tell the king."

"I will go with you, Cocky-locky and Henny-penny."

So Ducky-daddles, and Cocky-locky, and Henny-penny they gaed, and they gaed, and they gaed till they met a Goose. So the Goose said:

"Where are you going to-day, Ducky-daddles, Cocky-locky, and Henny-penny?"

And they said:

"Oh, Goosie-poosie, the sky is falling, and we are going to tell the king."

And Goosie-poosie said:

"I will go with you, Ducky-daddles, Cocky-locky, and Henny-penny."

So Goosie-poosie, and Ducky-daddles, and Cocky-locky, and Henny-penny they gaed, and they gaed, and they gaed till they met a Turkey. So the Turkey said:

"Where are you going to-day, Goosie-poosie, Ducky-daddles, Cocky-locky, and Henny-penny ?"

And they said:

"Oh, Turkey-lurky, the sky is falling, and we are going to tell the king."

And Turkey-lurky said:

"I will go with you, Goosie-poosie, Ducky-daddles, Cocky-locky, and Henny-penny."

So Turkey-lurky, and Goosie-poosie, and Ducky-daddles, and Cocky-locky, and Henny-penny they gaed, and they gaed, and they gaed till they met a Fox. So the Fox said:

"Where are you going to-day, Turkey-lurky, Goosie-poosie, Ducky-daddles, Cocky-locky, and Henny-penny?"

And they said:

"Oh, Mr. Fox, the sky is falling, and we are going to tell the king."

And the Fox said:

"Come with me, Turkey-lurky, Goosie-poosie, Ducky-daddles, Cocky locky, and Henny-penny, and I will show you the road to the king's house."

So they all gaed, and they gaed, and they gaed till they came to the Fox's hole, and the Fox took them all into his hole, and his young cubs eat up first poor Henny-penny, then poor Cocky-locky, then poor Ducky-daddles, then poor Goosie-poosie, and then poor Turkey-lurky; and so they never got to the king to tell him that the sky had fallen on the head of poor Henny-penny.

RED JACKET; OR THE NOSE TREE

THERE were once three poor soldiers, who on being disbanded after the war journeyed home together, begging their bread as they went along. It was hard to be thus turned adrift without any provision for their old age, and our wanderers were dejected enough at the weary prospect that lay before them; but as there was no help for it, they struggled on as best they might, and trusted to Providence for their daily support. One evening they reached a thick, gloomy wood, and night having presently surprised them, they had no other alternative than to lie down and go to sleep, without having tasted a morsel of anything like supper. For fear of being torn to pieces by wild beasts, they agreed that one should keep sentry in true military style, while the other two slept; and as soon as the one that watched grew tired, he was to wake another, who would relieve guard.

Two of the soldiers were presently fast asleep, while the other kindled a fire beneath the trees, and sat down to warm himself. He had not been there long before a diminutive being in a red jacket suddenly appeared before him, saying: "Who is there?" "A poor soldier, who will not harm you," replied our friend; "so you had better come and sit down and warm yourself." "And how fares it with you, my brave fellow?" said the little being. "But poorly," replied the soldier, "for my comrades and I possess nothing in the world beyond the clothes we stand in." "Well, then, my good fellow," said little Red Jacket, "take this cloak, and whenever you put it on and wish for anything it shall be granted directly."

So saying, he disappeared as he had come.

When it became the second soldier's turn to keep watch, little Red Jacket appeared again, and handed him a purse, which he told him should be always full of gold, let him draw upon it as often as he pleased.

It was now the third soldier's turn to keep sentry; and little Red Jacket did not forget him, but presented him with a magic horn, that possessed the property of summoning crowds at a blast, and of making people forget their cares and dance to its sound.

When morning dawned, the three friends had each a wonderful tale to tell, and they presently agreed that, as they had shared each other's adversity, so would they now enjoy together the prosperity that had so unexpectedly befallen them, and resolved to travel for their amusement, and make use of the inexhaustible purse. They now spent their time very pleasantly, till at last they grew tired of roaming about, when two of the comrades requested their companion to wish for a beautiful castle to serve as their home. This was accordingly set before them, with as little fuss as a waiter brings a glass of beer. The castle was, moreover, surrounded by delightful gardens and luxuriant pastures, where countless flocks were seen grazing; and the gates flew open to give passage to a stately carriage drawn by three dapple-grey horses, that soon fetched them home.

After enjoying a very quiet life for a time, they began to be as much cloyed by continued rest as they had been heretofore by their journeyings to and fro; so they thought they would make a change, and accordingly they ordered the carriage, and, taking with them a quantity of fine clothes and costly jewels, they proceeded on a visit to a neighbouring monarch. The king, who had an only daughter, seeing such magnificent strangers, concluded they must be princes in disguise, and welcomed them accordingly. It happened one day that the second soldier was walking with the princess, when she remarked the purse in his hand, and asked what it was. The soldier was weak enough to tell her, which, to be sure, though very foolish in him, did not make much difference, as she was a fairy, and already knew what wonderful gifts the three comrades held in their keeping. So she set to work to make a purse exactly similar to the stranger's, and when it was completed she took an opportunity of offering him some wine that she had drugged for the purpose, which made him fall into a dead sleep, when she gently drew his purse from his pocket, and placed her own in its stead.

On the following day, the soldiers returned homeward; and not long after they reached their stately castle they happened to want some money, and applied to the purse, whose contents, indeed, they emptied; but oh, disaster of disasters! no fresh gold came to fill it! The owner of the purse then speedily perceived that the princess had played him false, and began to lament over his lost riches. "Nay," said the first soldier, "be not downcast: I shall soon be able to get your purse back again." So he put on his cloak, and wished he were in the princess's room.

No sooner was he transported thither, than he found her busy drawing gold from the purse, till it lay in heaps about her. Instead of at once securing the prize, the soldier was imprudent enough to stand watching her, till she happened to turn round, and on seeing him, began to call out: "A thief! a thief!" as loud as she could, till all the courtiers and household rushed in to help her. The soldier was so taken aback that, in his alarm and confusion, he never thought of wishing himself a hundred miles off, but ran to the window and jumped out in such haste that he left his cloak dangling to the balcony, much to the delight of the cunning princess, who thus secured another gift.

The poor soldier returned home on foot in the most sad mood possible, and informed his comrades what a heavy misfortune had befallen him. "Never mind," said the third soldier, "keep up your spirits, for we have still a remedy left." And, taking up his horn, he blew a loud blast, which brought countless troops of soldiers, infantry and cavalry, with whom they set forth to besiege the king's palace. Before they drew their swords, however, they informed the king that if he gave up the purse and the cloak they would withdraw thir army; but, if he persisted in keeping them, they would destroy the palace to its foundations. The king therefore went and tried to persuade his daughter to avert such a misfortune; but, as she was very unwilling to part with their treasures, she replied, "Cunning may overcome force"; and bade her father wait for the result of a scheme she had laid, which should drive away the whole army like chaff before the wind. Accordingly, she dressed herself up as a fruit-girl, and, taking a basket on her arm, went out, accompanied by her maid, at nightfall, and took a roundabout way to reach the enemy's camp. When morning came, she rambled about amongst the tents, offering her wares for sale, and singing with so wonderful a voice that the soldiers crowded round her, to listen to her songs. Presently she saw the owner of the magic horn amongst the throng, and made a sign to her maid, who stole away to his tent, and while he was engrossed with listening to the music, she took possession of the precious horn. No sooner was this accomplished than the princess returned to the palace; and sure enough, the army vanished, as she had told her father it would, while she kept all the fairy gifts; and the three luckless soldiers found themselves once more as desolate and as poor as when little Red Jacket had been the maker of their fortunes.

They now held a council as to what they should do next, when the second soldier, who had once owned the purse, proposed they should each seek their bread separately. He then turned to the right, while the other two, who wished to keep together, turned to the left. The second soldier wandered on till he came to the self-same wood where they had met with such unexpected luck; and when night came he felt so tired that he fell asleep beneath a tree. On awaking next morning, he was delighted to see that the tree was laden with beautiful apples; having gathered some, he began eating first one, then another, and then a third. He now began to feel a queer sensation in his nose, and, on attempting to put another apple in his mouth, there seemed to be something in the way; to his horror he found that his nose had grown to such an enormous length that it reached to his waist. "Where will this end?" cried he in alarm. And well he might say so, for the thought was no sooner uttered than his nose had grown down to the ground, and kept stretching onward like a stream, till it meandered through the wood, and on over hill and dale beyond. Meanwhile, his comrades, who had journeyed onward since the morning, now stumbled over something which they at first mistook for a kind of bridge; then they thought it looked more like a nose, especially as it felt like flesh; and at last they determined to follow it up, to find who could be the owner of this strange nose. They were much shocked on reaching the tree to find that it belonged to their unhappy comrade, who was lying quite exhausted on the ground. The two soldiers tried to raise him, but found it quite impossible; and they were all three giving way to despair, when, to their great relief, their little friend Red Jacket once more popped in upon them. "You are in a sad plight indeed, my good friend," cried he, laughing; "but luckily there is a cure near at hand." He then told the two others to gather a pear from a neighbouring tree; and no sooner had their comrade eaten of it, than his nose was at once restored to its proper size.

"Now," said little Red Jacket, "I'll give you a piece of advice. Gather some of these pears and apples, go to the princess and offer her some of the latter, when her nose will grow twenty times longer than yours did; then make the best bargain you can for your gifts to be returned before you let her have the cure."

The three friends thanked Red Jacket with heartfelt gratitude and left the wood. They then agreed that Nosey, as his comrades now nicknamed him, should disguise himself as a gardener, and go to the king's palace, and offer the apples for sale. Accordingly, Nosey made his way thither, and he had no sooner displayed his tempting wares than everyone wished to buy some of his fruit. But he declared that these apples were so rare as to be fit only for the princess; the moment she heard this she sent to purchase his whole stock. They tasted so well that the princess ate a whole dozen, when suddenly she had the same alarming feelings as the soldier had had. Her nose soon reached the window, and from thence the garden, and then began to wander into the wide world.

The king, greatly terrified, offered a large reward to whoever should cure her of this strange illness. The soldier then dressed himself as a physician, and offered his help. At first he began by giving her a dose containing more apple chopped up very small, which of course made matters worse. After leaving her thus for a whole day he gave her a little of the pear, which made her nose grow shorter. As, however, he wanted to frighten her well, before curing her, he caused the nose to grow smaller and larger by turns. At last he said, "Princess, my knowledge tells me that there is some evil at work to spoil the effect of my medicines, and I am sure that you have about you stolen goods; until these are returned, I cannot cure you." The princess at first denied any such thing, but when the king heard what the physician had said, he went to his daughter and entreated her to restore the cloak, the purse, and the horn to their right owners.

So, as there was no help for it, she returned them all to the physician, to give to the soldiers. In exchange he gave her a whole pear, which brought back her nose to its pretty little shape again. Then the soldier wished himself back with his comrades; and from that time all three lived happily together.

II. SCOTTISH

AINSEL

MISTRESS ARMSTRONG, a canny widow, and her son Parcie [Percy], who was a little boy then, lived together in a cottage near Rothley. One winter's night, Parcie refused to go to bed with his mother, as he wished to sit up for a while longer, "For," says he, "I am not a bit sleepy."

His mother told him that if he sat up by himself the old fairy-wife would most certainly come and take him away. But the boy laughed at this, and his mother went to bed, leaving him sitting by the fire.

He had not been there long, watching the fire and enjoying its ruddy blaze, when a bonny little figure, about the size of a bairn's doll, hopped down the chimney and alighted on the hearth. Parcie, poor little fellow, was like to be startled at first, but the Brownie's smile as it hopped to and fro before him soon overcame his fears. At last he inquired:

"What do they ca' thou?"

"Ainsel," answered the little thing, tossing its wee head.

After a bit it turned to Parcie with just the same question: "And what do they call thou?"

"*My* ainsel," answers Parcie.

So they began playing together like any two wee bairns. Their gambols went on till the fire began to grow dim; when Parcie took up the poker to stir it, and a hot cinder accidentally fell upon the foot of his playmate. Her mouse voice was instantly raised to a most terrific yell, and Parcie had scarce time to crouch into the box-bed behind his mother before the voice of the old fairy-wife was heard shouting:

"Who's done it? Who's done it?"

"Hoots! it was 'my ainsel'!" said the boggart bairn.

"Why, then," said the mother, as she kicked her up the chimney, "what's all this noise for; there's nyon [*i.e.,* no one] to blame but thine ainsel!"

THE TALE OF THE HOODIE

THERE was ere now a farmer, and he had three daughters. They were waulking[1] clothes at a river. A hoodie[2] came round and he said to the eldest one, "M-POS-U-MI, wilt thou wed me, farmer's daughter?" "I won't wed thee, thou ugly brute. An ugly brute is the hoodie," said she. He came to the second one on the morrow, and he said to her, "M-POS-U-MI, wilt thou wed me?" "Not I, indeed," said she; "an ugly brute is the hoodie." The third day he said to the youngest, "M-POS-U-MI, wilt thou wed me, farmer's daughter?" "I will wed thee," said she; "a pretty creature is the hoodie," and on the morrow they married. The hoodie said to her, "Whether wouldst thou rather that I should be a hoodie by day, and a man at night; or be a hoodie at night, and a man by day?" "I would rather that thou wert a man by day, and a hoodie at night," says she. After this he was a splendid fellow by day, and a hoodie at night. A few days after they married he took her with him to his own house.

At the end of three quarters they had a son. In the night there came the very finest music that ever was heard about the house. Every man slept, and the child was taken away. Her father came to the door in the morning, and he asked how

---

[1] A method of washing clothes practised in the Highlands—viz., by dancing on them barefoot in a tub of water.

[2] Hoodie—the Royston crow—a sly, familiar, knowing bird common in the Highlands.

were all there. He was very sorrowful that the child should be taken away, for fear that he should be blamed for it himself.

At the end of three quarters again they had another son. A watch was set on the house. The finest of music came, as it came before, about the house; every man slept, and the child was taken away. Her father came to the door in the morning. He asked if everything was safe; but the child was taken away, and he did not know what to do for sorrow.

Again, at the end of three quarters, they had another son. A watch was set on the house as usual. Music came about the house as it came before; every one slept, and the child was taken away. When they rose on the morrow they went to another place of rest that they had, himself and his wife, and his sister-in-law. He said to them by the way, "See that you have not forgotten anything." The wife said, "I FORGOT MY COARSE COMB." The coach in which they were fell a withered faggot, and he went away as a hoodie. Her two sisters returned home, and she followed after him. When he would be on a hill top, she would follow to try and catch him; and when she would reach the top of a hill, he would be in the hollow on the other side. When night came, and she was tired, she had no place of rest or dwelling; she saw a little house of light far from her, and though far from her she was not long in reaching it.

When she reached the house she stood deserted at the door. She saw a little laddie about the house, and she yearned to him exceedingly. The housewife told her to come up, that she knew her cheer and travel. She laid down, and no sooner did the day come than she rose. She went out, and when she was out, she was going from hill to hill to try if she could see a hoodie. She saw a hoodie on a hill, and when she would get on the hill, the hoodie would be in the hollow, when she would go to the hollow, the hoodie would be on another hill. When the night came she had no place of rest or dwelling. She saw a little house of light far from her, and if far from her she was not long in reaching it. She went to the door. She saw a laddie on the floor to whom she yearned right much. The housewife laid her to rest. No earlier came the day than she took out as she used. She passed this day as the other days. When the night came she reached a house. The housewife told her to come up, that she knew her cheer and travel, that her man had but left the house a little while, that she should be clever, that this was the last night she would see him, and not to sleep, but to strive to seize him. She slept, he came where she was, and he let fall a ring on her right hand. Now when she awoke she tried to catch hold of him, and she caught a feather of his wing. He left the feather with her, and he went away. When she rose in the morning she did not know what she should do. The housewife said that he had gone over a hill of poison over which she could not go without horseshoes on her hands and feet. She gave her man's clothes, and she told her to go to learn smithying till she should be able to make horseshoes for herself.

She learned smithying so well that she made horseshoes for her hands and feet. She went over the hill of poison. That same day after she had gone over the hill of poison, her man was to be married to the daughter of a great gentleman that was in the town.

There was a race in the town that day, and every one was to be at the race but the stranger that had come over the poison hill. The cook came to her, and he said to her, would she go in his place to make the wedding meal, and that he might get to the race.

She said she would go. She was always watching where the bridegroom would be sitting.

She let fall the ring and the feather in the broth that was before him. With the first spoon he took up the ring, with the next he took up the feather. When the minister came to the fore to make the marriage, he would not marry till he should find out who had made ready the meal. They brought up the cook of the gentleman, and he said that *this* was not the cook who made ready the meal.

They brought up now the one who had made ready the meal. He said, "That now was his married wife." The spells went off him. They turned back over the hill of poison, she throwing the horseshoes behind her to him, as she went a little bit forward, and he following her. When they came back over the hill, they went to the three houses in which she had been. These were the houses of his sisters, and they took with them the three sons, and they came home to their own house, and they were happy.

THE SEAL MAIDEN

A Tale of the Hebrides

THE King of the Sea had a beautiful Queen, and they loved each other dearly. They had delight in many children, who were all straight-limbed, brown-eyed, eager-hearted, and their happiness was greater than any tongue can tell.

Suddenly dark sorrow fell upon this King. His wife tarried too long on the level white sands; a great storm arose before she could reach safety in the pearl palaces of the sea, and she was trampled to death by the wild sea-horses as they rushed and bounded over the grey granite ledges of the isles.

Lonely in his soul and grieving for his children, the King sought the cave of the sea-witch. Thinking she would care for his children, he married her, but when she saw their surpassing loveliness green envy and black hatred surged within her. One night when the moon was hidden behind dark massy clouds, and the sea moaned with its swelling pain, she distilled a magic from the yellow berries of deadly sea-grape that grew on its pale green sickly stem around the entrance of the cave.

This magic enchanted the children of the sea, so that they became seals. But each year for one day and one night, from sun-down to sun-down, they could take and enjoy their own shapes again.

So it chanced that a young fisher-lad toiling in the early dawn saw a sweet maid playing in the white foam, and loved her. All that day long they roamed together among the moon-flowers, hearing the music of the murmuring tide. When evening came they watched the rising moon cast its silver pathway over the lulling sea. Then a little sobbing wind began to creep over the surface of the deep. The maiden grew strange and shy, and presently she slipped away among the black shadows of the great grey rocks on the shimmering sands. Puzzled and angry, the fisher sought for her, but found only at last a lonely seal, whose eyes were brown and kind and loving. They say that madness came upon him. Madly he sailed away in the teeth of a lowering storm. His frail boat was dashed to pieces on the cruel rocks over the cave of the sea-witch, where grow the deadly yellow berries of the sea-grape on its pale sickly stem.

THE RED BULL OF NORROWAY

ONCE upon a time there lived a king who had three daughters—the two eldest were proud and ugly, but the youngest was the gentlest and most beautiful ever seen, and the pride not only of her father and mother, but of all in the land. As it fell out, the three princesses were talking one night of whom they would marry. "I will have no one lower than a king," said the eldest princess; the second would take a prince, or a great duke even. "Pho, pho," said the youngest, laughing, "you are both so proud; now, I would be content with 'The Red Bull o' Norroway.'"

Well, they thought no more of the matter till the next morning, when, as they sat at breakfast, they heard the most dreadful bellowing at the door, and what should it be but the Red Bull come for his bride. You may be sure they were all terribly frightened at this, for the Red Bull was one of the most horrible creatures ever seen in the world. And the king and queen did not know how to save their daughter. At last they determined to send him off with the old hen-wife. So they put her on his back, and away he went with her till he came to a great black forest, when, throwing her down, he returned roaring louder and more frightfully than ever; they then sent, one by one, all the servants, then the two eldest princesses, but not one of them met with any better treatment than the old hen-wife, and at last they were forced to send their youngest and favourite child.

On travelled the lady and the bull through many dreadful forests and lonely wastes, till they came at last to a noble castle, where a large company was assembled. The lord of the castle pressed them to stay, though much he wondered at the lovely princess and her strange companion. When they went in among the company, the princess espied a pin sticking in the bull's hide, which she pulled out, and to the surprise of all, there appeared, not a frightful wild beast, but one of the most beautiful princes ever beheld. You may believe how delighted the princess was to see him fall at her feet, and thank her for breaking his cruel enchantment. There was great rejoicing in the castle at this; but, alas! at that moment he suddenly disappeared, and though every place was sought he was nowhere to be found. The princess, however, determined to seek through all the world for him, and many weary ways she went, but nothing could she hear of her lover. Travelling once through a dark wood, she lost her way, and as night was coming on, she thought she must now certainly die of cold and hunger; but seeing a light through the trees, she went on till she came to a little hut where an old woman lived, who took her in, and gave her both food and shelter. In the morning, the old wife gave her three nuts, that she was not to break till her heart was like to break, "and ower again like to break"; so, showing her the way, she bade God speed her, and the princess once more set out on her wearisome journey.

She had not gone far till a company of lords and ladies rode past her, all talking merrily of the fine doings they expected at the Duke o' Norroway's wedding. Then she came up to a number of people carrying all sorts of fine things, and they, too, were going to the duke's wedding. At last she came to a castle, where nothing was to be seen but cooks and bakers, some running one way and some another, and all so busy, they did not know what to do first. Whilst she was looking at all this to-do, she heard a noise of hunters behind her, and some one cried out, "Make way for the Duke o' Norroway," and who should ride past but the prince and a beautiful lady. You may be sure her heart was now like to break, "and ower again like to break" at this sad sight, so she broke one of the nuts, and out came a *wee wifie carding*. The princess then went into the castle and asked to see the lady; who no sooner saw the wee wifie so hard at work, than she offered the princess anything in her castle for it. "I will give it to you," said she, "only on condition that you put off for one day your marriage with the Duke o' Norroway, and that I may go into his room alone to-night." So anxious was the lady for the nut, that she consented. And when dark night was come, and the duke fast asleep, the princess was put alone into his chamber. Sitting down by his bedside, she began singing—

"Far hae I sought ye, near am I brought to ye,
   Dear Duke o' Norroway, will ye no turn and speak to me?"

Though she sung this over and over again, the duke never wakened, and in the morning the princess had to leave him without his knowing she had ever been there. She then broke the second nut, and out came a *wee wifie spinning*, which so delighted the lady, that she readily agreed to put off her marriage another day for it; but the princess came no better speed the second night than the first; and almost in despair she broke the last nut, which contained a *wee wifie reeling*, and on the same condition as before the lady got possession of it. When the duke was dressing in the morning, his man asked him what the strange singing and moaning that had been heard in his room for two nights meant. "I heard nothing," said the duke; "it could only have been your fancy." "Take no sleeping draught to-night, and be sure to lay aside your pillow of heaviness," said the man, "and you also will hear what for two nights has kept me awake." The duke did so, and the princess coming in, sat down sighing at his bedside, thinking this the last time she might ever see him. The duke started up when he heard the voice of his dearly loved princess; and with many endearing expressions of surprise and joy, explained to her that he had long been in the power of an enchantress, whose spells over him were now happily ended by their once again meeting. The princess, happy to be the instrument of his second deliverance, consented to marry him; and the enchantress, who fled that country, afraid of the duke's anger, has never since been heard of. All was again hurry and preparation in the castle; and the marriage which now took place, at once ended the adventures of the Red Bull o' Norroway and the wanderings of the king's daughter.

WHIPPETY STOURIE

THERE was once a gentleman that lived in a very grand house, and he married a young lady that had been delicately brought up. In her husband's house she found everything that was fine—fine tables and chairs, fine looking-glasses, and fine curtains; but then her husband expected her to be able to spin twelve hanks o' thread every day, besides attending to her house; and, to tell the even-down truth, the lady could not spin a bit. This made her husband glunchy with her, and, before a month had passed, she found hersel very unhappy.

One day the husband gaed away upon a journey, after telling her that he expected her, before his return, to have not only learned to spin, but to have spun a hundred hanks o' thread. Quite downcast, she took a walk along the hill side, till she cam to a big flat stane, and there she sat down and grat. By and by, she heard a strain o' fine sma' music, coming as it were frae aneath the stane, and, on turning it up, she saw a cave below, where there were sitting six wee ladies in green gowns, ilk ane o' them spinning on a little wheel, and singing,

> "Little kens my dame at hame,
> That Whippety Stourie is my name."

The lady walked into the cave and was kindly asked by the wee bodies to take a chair and sit down, while they still continued their spinning.

She observed that ilk ane's mouth was thrawn away to ae side, but she dinna venture to speer the reason. They asked her why she looked so unhappy, and she telt them that it was because she was expected by her husband to be a good spinner, when the plain truth was that she could not spin at all, and found herself quite unable for it, having been so delicately brought up; neither was there any need for it, as her husband was a rich man. "Oh, is that a'?" said the little wifies, speaking out at their cheeks like [imitate a person with a wry mouth].

"Yes, and is it not a very good a' too?" said the lady, her heart like to burst wi' distress.

"We could easily quit ye o' that trouble," said the wee women. "Just ask us a' to dinner for the day when your husband is to come back. We'll then let you see how we'll manage him." So the lady asked them all to dine with herself and her husband, on the day when he was to come back.

When the gudeman cam hame, he found the house so occupied with preparations for dinner, that he had nae time to ask his wife about her thread; and, before ever he had ance spoken to her on the subject, the company was announced at the hall door. The six wee ladies all came in a coach and six, and were as fine as princesses, but still wore their gowns of green. The gentleman was very polite, and showed them up the stair with a pair of wax candles in his hand. And so they all sat down to dinner, and conversation went on very pleasantly, till at length the husband, becoming familiar with them, said, "Ladies, if it be not an uncivil question, I should like to know how it happens that all your mouths are turned away to one side?"

"Oh," said ilk ane at ance, "it's with our constant *spin-spin-spinning?* [Here speak with the mouth turned to one side!.]

"Is that the case?" cried the gentleman; "then, John, Tam, and Dick,. fye, go haste and burn every rock, and reel, and spinning-wheel, in the house, for I'll not have my wife to spoil her bonnie face with *spin-spin spinning.* "

And so the lady lived happily with her gudeman all the rest of her days.

JOCK AND HIS MOTHER

YE see, there was a wife had a son, and they ca'd him Jock; and she said to him, "You are a lazy fallow; ye maun gang awa' and do something for to help me." "Weel," says Jock, "I'll do that." So awa' he gangs, and fa's in wi' a packman. Says the packman, "If you carry my pack a' day, I'll gie you a needle at night." So he carried the pack, and got the needle; and as he was gaun awa' hame to his mither, he cuts a burden o' brakens, and put the needle into the heart o' them. Awa' he gaes hame. Says his mither, "What hae ye made o' yoursel the day?" Says Jock, "I fell in wi' a packman, and carried his pack a' day, and he gae me a needle for 't; and ye may look for it amang the brakens."

"Hout," quo' she, "ye daft gowk, you should hae stuck it into your bonnet, man." "I'll mind that again," quo' Jock.

Next day, he fell in wi' a man carrying plough socks. "If ye help me to carry my socks a' day, I'll gie ye ane to yersel at night." "I'll do that," quo' Jock. Jock carries them a' day, and gets a sock, which he sticks in his bonnet. On the way home Jock was dry, and gaed away to tak a drink out o' the burn; and wi' the weight o' the sock, it fell into the river, and gaed out o' sight. He gaed hame, and his mither says, "Weel, Jock, what hae you been doing a' day?" And then he tells her. "Hout," quo' she, "ye should hae tied a string to it, and trailed it behind you." "Weel," quo' Jock, "I'll mind that again."

Awa' he sets, and he fa's in wi' a flesher. "Well," says the flesher, "if ye'll be my servant a' day, I'll gie yea leg o' mutton at night." "I'll be that," quo' Jock. He gets a leg o' mutton at night; he ties a string to it, and trails it behind him the hale road hame. "What hae ye been doing?" said his mither. He tells her. "Hout, you fool, ye should hae carried it on your shouther." "I'll mind that again," quo' Jock.

Awa' he goes next day, and meets a horse-dealer. He says, "If you will help me wi' my horses a' day, I'll gie you ane to yersel at night." "I'll do that," quo' Jock. So he served him, and got his horse, and he ties its feet; but as he was not able to carry it on his back, he left it lying on the roadside. Hame he comes, and tells his mither. "Hout, ye daft gowk, ye'll never turn wise! Could ye no hae loupen on it, and ridden it?" "I'll mind that again," quo' Jock.

Aweel, there was a grand gentleman, wha had a daughter wha was very subject to melancholy; and her father gae out that whaever should mak her laugh would get her in marriage. So it happened that she was sitting at the window ae day, musing in her melancholy state, when Jock, according to the advice o' his mither, cam flying up on the cow's .back, wi' the tail ower his shouther. And she burst out into a fit o' laughter. When they made inquiry wha made her laugh, it was found to be Jock riding on the cow. Accordingly Jock is sent for to get his bride. Weel, Jock is married to her, and there was a great supper prepared. Amongst the rest o' the things, there was some honey, which Jock was very fond o'. After supper, they were bedded, and the auld priest that married them sat up a' night by the fireside. So Jock waukens in the night-time, and says, "Oh, wad ye gie me some o' yon nice sweet honey that we got to our supper last night?" "Oh, ay," says his wife, "rise and gang into the press, and ye'll get a pig fou o't." Jock rises and thrusts his hand into the honey pig for a nievefu' o't; and he could not get it out. So he cam awa' wi' the pig on his hand, like a mason's mell, and says, "Oh, I canna get my hand out." "Hout," quo' she, "gang awa' and break it on the cheek-stane." By this time, the fire was dark, and the auld priest was lying snoring wi' his head against the chimney-piece, wi' a huge white wig on. Jock gaes awa', and gae him a whack wi' the honey pig on the head, thinking it was the cheek-stane, and knocks it a' in bits. The auld priest roars out, "Murder!" Jock taks down the stair, as hard as he can bicker, and hides himsel amang the bees' skeps.

That night, as luck wad have it, some thieves cam to steal the bees' skeps, and in the hurry o' tumbling them into a large grey plaid, they tumbled Jock in alang wi' them. So aff they set, wi' Jock and the skeps on their backs. On the way, they had to cross the burn where Jock lost his bannet. One o' the thieves cries, "Oh, I hae fand a bannet!" and Jock, on hearing that, cries out, "Oh, that's mine!" They thocht they had got the deil on their backs. So they let a' fa' in the burn; and Jock, being tied in the plaid, couldna get out; so he and the bees were a' drowned thegither.

If a' tales be true, that's nae lee.

III. IRISH

JACK THE CUNNING THIEF

THERE was a poor farmer who had three sons, and on the same day the three boys went to seek their fortune. The eldest two were sensible, industrious young men; the youngest never did much at home that was any use. He loved to be setting snares for rabbits, and tracing hares in the snow, and inventing all sorts of funny tricks to annoy people at first and then set them laughing.

The three parted at cross-roads, and Jack took the lonesomest. The day turned out rainy, and he was wet and weary, you may depend, at nightfall, when he came to a lonesome house a little off the road.

"What do you want?" said a blear-eyed old woman, that was sitting at the fire.

"My supper and a bed, to be sure," said he.

"You can't get it," said she.

"What's to hinder me?" said he.

"The owners of the house is," said she, "six honest men that does be out mostly till three or four o'clock in the morning and if they find you here they'll skin you alive at the very least."

"Well, I think," said Jack, "that their very most couldn't be much worse. Come, give me something out of the cupboard, for here I'll stay. Skinning is not much worse than catching your death of cold in a ditch or under a tree such a night as this."

Begonius she got afraid, and gave him a good supper; and when he was going to bed he said if she let any of the six honest men disturb him when they came home she'd sup sorrow for it. When he awoke in the morning, there were six ugly-looking spalpeens standing round his bed. He leaned on his elbow, and looked at them with great contempt.

"Who are you" said the chief "and what's your business?" .

"My name" says he, "is Master Thief, and my business just now is to find apprentices and workmen. If I find you any good, maybe I'll give you a few lessons."

Bedah they were a little cowed, and says the head man, "Well, get up, and after breakfast, we'll see who is to be the master, and who the journeyman."

They were just done breakfast, when what should they see but a farmer driving a fine large goat to market.

"Will any of you," says Jack, "undertake to steal that goat from the owner before he gets out of the wood, and that without the smallest violence?"

"I couldn't do it," says one; and "I couldn't do it," says another.

"I'm your master," says Jack, "and I'll do it."

He slipped out, went through the trees to where there was a bend in the road, and laid down his right brogue in the very middle of it. Then he ran on to another bend, and laid down his left brogue and went and hid himself.

When the farmer sees the first brogue, he says to himself, "That would be worth something if it had the fellow, but it is worth nothing by itself."

He goes on till he comes to the second brogue.

"What a fool I was," says he, "not to pick up the other! I'll go back for it."

So he tied the goat to a sapling in the hedge and returned for the brogue. But Jack, who was behind a tree had it already on his foot, and when the man was beyond the bend he picked up the other and loosened the goat, and led him off through the wood.

Ochone! the poor man couldn't find the first brogue, and when he came back he couldn't find the second, nor neither his goat.

"Mile mollacht!" says he, "what will I do after promising Johanna to buy her a shawl? I must only go and drive another beast to the market unknownst. I'd never hear the last of it if Joan found out what a fool I made of myself."

The thieves were in great admiration at Jack, and wanted him to tell them how he had done the farmer, but he wouldn't tell them.

By-and-by, they see the poor man driving a fine fat wether the same way.

"Who'll steal that wether," says Jack, "before it's out of the wood, and no roughness used?"

"I couldn't," says one; and "I couldn't," says another.

"I'll try," says Jack. "Give me a good rope."

The poor farmer was jogging along and thinking of his misfortune, when he sees a man hanging from the bough of a tree.

"Lord save us!" says he, "the corpse wasn't there an hour ago." He went on about half a quarter of a mile, and there was another corpse again hanging over the road.

"God between us and harm," said he, "am I in my right senses?"

There was another turn about the same distance, and just beyond it the third corpse was hanging.

"Oh, murdher!" said he; "I'm beside myself. What would bring three hung men so near one another? I must be mad. I'll go back and see if the others are there still."

He tied the wether to a sapling, and back he went.

But when he was round the bend, down came the corpse, and loosened the wether, and drove it home through the wood to the robber's house.

You all may think how the poor farmer felt when he could find no one dead or alive going or coming, nor his wether, nor the rope that fastened him.

"Oh, misfortunate day!" cried he, "what'll Joan say to me now? My morning gone, and the goat and wether lost! I must sell something to make the price of the shawl. Well, the fat bullock is in the nearest field. She won't see me taking it."

Well, if the robbers were not surprised when Jack came into the bawn with the wether!

"If you do another trick like this," said the captain, "I'll resign the command to you."

They soon saw the farmer going by again, driving a fat bullock this time.

"Who'll bring that fat bullock here," says Jack, "and use no violence?"

"I couldn't," says one; and "I couldn't," says another.

"I'll try," says Jack, and away he went into the wood.

The farmer was about the spot where he saw the first brogue, when he heard the bleating of a goat off at his right in the wood.

He cocked his ears, and the next thing he heard was the maaing of a sheep.

"Blood alive!" says he, "maybe these are my own that I lost." There was more bleating and more maaing.

"There they are as sure as a gun," says he, and he tied his bullock to a sapling that grew in the hedge, and away he went into the wood. When he got near the place where the cries came from, he heard them a little before him, and on he followed them. At last, when he was about half a mile from the spot where he tied the beast, the cries stopped altogether. After searching and searching till he was tired, he returned for his bullock; but there wasn't the ghost of a bullock there, nor anywhere else that he searched.

This time, when the thieves saw Jack and his prize coming into the bawn, they couldn't help shouting out, "Jack must be our chief." So there was nothing but feasting and drinking hand to fist the rest of the day. Before they went to bed, they showed Jack the cave where their money was hid, and all their disguises in another cave, and swore obedience to him.

One morning, when they were at breakfast, about a week after, said they to Jack, "Will you mind the house for us to-day while we are at the fair of Mochurry? We hadn't a spree for ever so long: you must get your turn whenever you like."

"Never say't twice," says Jack, and off they went.

After they were gone says Jack to the wicked housekeeper, "Do these fellows ever make you a present?"

"Ah, catch them at it! indeed, and, they don't, purshuin to 'em."

"Well, come along with me, and I'll make you a rich woman."

He took her to the treasure cave; and while she was in raptures, gazing at the heaps of gold and silver, Jack filled his pockets as full as they could hold, put more into a little bag, and walked out, locking the door on the old hag, and leaving the key in the lock. He then put on a rich suit of clothes, took the goat, and the wether, and the bullock, and drove them before him to the farmer's house. Joan and her husband were at the door; and when they saw the animals, they clapped their hands and laughed for joy.

"Do you know who owns them bastes, neighbours?"

"Maybe we don't! sure they're ours."

"I found them straying in the wood. Is that bag with ten guineas in it that's hung round the she goat's neck yours?"

"Faith, it isn't."

"Well, you may as well keep it for a Godsend, I don't want it."

"Heaven be in your road, good gentleman!"

Jack travelled on till he came to his father's house in the dusk of the evening. He went in. "God save all here!"

"God save you kindly, sir!"

"Could I have a night's lodging here?"

"Oh, sir, our place isn't fit for the likes of a gentleman such as you."

"Oh, musha, don't you know your own son?"

Well, they opened their eyes, and it was only a strife to see who'd have him in their arms first.

"But, Jack asthore, where did you get the fine clothes?"

"Oh, you may as well ask me where I got all that money," said he, emptying his pockets on the table.

Well, they got in a great fright, but when he told them his adventures, they were easier in mind, and all went to bed in great content.

"Father," says Jack, next morning, "go over to the landlord, and tell him I wish to be married to his daughter."

"Faith, I'm afraid he'd only set the dogs at me. If he asks me how you made your money, what'll I say?"

"Tell him I am a master thief, and that there is no one equal to me in the three kingdoms; that I am worth a thousand pounds, and all taken from the biggest rogues unhanged. Speak to him when the young lady is by."

"It's a droll message you're sending me en: I'm afraid it won't end well."

The old man came back in two hours.

"Well, what news?"

"Droll news, enough. The lady didn't seem a bit unwilling: I suppose it's not the first time you spoke to her; and the squire laughed, and said you would have to steal the goose off o' the spit in his kitchen next Sunday, and he'd see about it."

"Oh! that won't be hard anyway."

Next Sunday, after the people came from early Mass, the Squire and all his people were in the kitchen, and the goose turning before the fire.. The kitchen door opened, and a miserable old beggar man with a big wallet on his back put in his head.

"Would the mistress have anything for me when dinner is over, your honour?"

"To be sure. We have no room here for you just now; sit in the porch for a while."

"God bless your honour's family, and yourself!"

Soon some one that was sitting near the window cried out, "Oh, sir, there's a big hare scampering like the divil round the bawn. Will we run out and pin him?"

"Pin a hare indeed! Much chance you'd have; sit where you are."

That hare made his escape into the garden, but Jack that was in the beggar's clothes soon let another out of the bag.

"Oh, master, there he is still pegging round. He can't make his escape; let us have a chase. The hall door is locked on the inside, and Mr. Jack can't get in."

"Stay quiet, I tell you."

In a few minutes he shouted out again that the hare was there still, but it was the third that Jack was just after giving its liberty. Well, by the laws, they couldn't be kept in any longer. Out pegged every mother's son of them, and the squire after them.

"Will I turn the spit, your honour, while they're catching the *hareyeen*?" says the beggar.

"Do, and don't let anyone in for your life."

"Faith, an' I won't, you may depend on it."

The third hare got away after the others, and when they all came back from the hunt, there was neither beggar nor goose in the kitchen.

"Purshuin' to you, Jack," says the landlord, "you've come over me this time."

Well, while they were thinking of making out another dinner, a messenger came from Jack's father to beg that the squire, and the mistress, and the young lady would step across the fields, and take share of what God sent. There was no dirty mean pride about the family, and they walked over, and got a dinner with roast turkey, and roast beef, and their own roast goose; and the squire had like to burst his waistcoat with laughing at the trick, and Jack's good clothes and good manners did not take away any liking the young lady had for him already. While they were taking their punch at the old oak table in the nice clean little parlour with the sanded floor, says the squire, "You can't be sure of my daughter, Jack, unless you steal away my six horses from under the six men that will be watching them to-morrow night in the stable."

"I'll do more than that," says Jack, "for a pleasant look from the young lady"; and the young lady's cheeks turned as red as fire.

Monday night the six horses were in their stalls, and a man on every horse, and a good glass of whisky under each man's waistcoat, and the door was left wide open for Jack. They were merry enough for a long time, and joked and sung, and were pitying the poor fellow. But the small hours crept on, and the whisky lost its power, and they began to shiver and wish it was morning. A miserable old colliach, with half a dozen bags round her, and a beard half an inch long on her chin came to the door.

"Ah, then, tendher-hearted Christians," says she, "would you let me in, and allow me a wisp of straw in the corner; the life will be froze out of me, if you don't give me shelter."

Well, they didn't see any harm in that, and she made herself as snug as she could, and they soon saw her pull out a big black bottle, and take a sup. She coughed and smacked her lips, and seemed a little more comfortable, and the men couldn't take their eyes off her.

"Gorsoon," says she, "I'd offer you a drop of this, only you might think it too free making."

"Oh, hang all impedent pride," says one, "we'll take it, and thankee."

So she gave them the bottle, and they passed it round, and the last man had the manners to leave half a glass in the bottom for the old woman. They all thanked her, and said it was the best drop ever passed their tongue.

"In throch, agras," said she, "it's myself that's glad to show how I value your kindness in giving me shelter; I'm not without another *buideal,* and you may pass it round while myself finishes what the dasent man left me."

Well, what they drank out of the other bottle only gave them a relish for more, and by the time the last man got to the bottom, the first man was dead asleep in the saddle, for the second bottle had a sleepy posset mixed with the whisky. The beggar woman lifted each man down, and laid him in the manger, or under the manger, snug and sausty, drew a stocking over every horse's hoof, and led them away without any noise to one of Jack's father's outhouses. The first thing the squire saw next morning was Jack riding up the avenue, and five horses stepping after the one he rode.

"Confound you, Jack!" says he, "and confound the numskulls that let you outwit them!"

He went out to the stable, and didn't the poor fellows look very lewd o' themselves, when they could be woke up in earnest!

"After all," says the squire, when they were sitting at breakfast, "it was no great thing to outwit such ninny-hammers. I'll be riding out on the common from one to three to-day, and if you can outwit me of the beast I'll be riding, I'll say you deserve to be my son-in-law?'

"I'd do more than that," says Jack, "for the honour, if there was no love at all in the matter," and the young lady held up her saucer before her face.

Well, the squire kept riding about and riding about till he was tired, and no sign of Jack. He was thinking of going home at last, when what should he see but one of his servants running from the house as if he was mad.

"Oh, masther, masther," says he, as far as he could be heard, "fly home, if you wish to see the poor mistress alive! I'm running for the surgeon. She fell down two flights of stairs, and her neck, or her hips, or both her arms are broke, and she's speechless, and it's a mercy if you find the breath in her. Fly as fast as the baste will carry you."

"But hadn't you better take the horse? It's a mile and a half to the surgeon's."

"'Oh, anything you like, master. Oh, *Vuya, Vuya!* misthress *alanna,* I should ever see the day! and your purty body disfigured as it is!" "Here, stop your noise, and be off like wildfire! Oh, my darling, my darling, isn't this a trial?" He tore home like a fury, and wondered to see no stir outside, and when he flew into the hall, and from that to the parlour, his wife and daughter that were sewing at the table screeched out at the rush he made, and the wild look that was on his face.

"Oh, my darling," said he, when he could speak, "how's this? Are you hurt? Didn't you fail down the stairs? What happened at all? Tell me!"

"Why, nothing at all happened, thank God, since you rode out; where did you leave the horse?"

Well, no one could describe the state he was in for about a quarter of an hour, between joy for his wife, and anger with Jack, and *sharoose* for being tricked. He saw the beast coming up the avenue, and a little gorsoon in the saddle with his feet in the stirrup leathers. The servant didn't make his appearance for a week; but what did he care with Jack's ten golden guineas in his pocket.

Jack didn't show his nose until next morning, and it was a queer reception he met.

"That was all foul play you gave," says the squire. "I'll never forgive you for the shock you gave me. But then I am so happy ever since, that I think I'll give you only one trial more. If you will take away the sheet from under my wife and myself to-night, the marriage may take place to-morrow."

"We'll try," says Jack, "but if you keep my bride from me any longer, I'll steal her away if she was minded by fiery dragons."

When the squire and his wife were in bed, and the moon shining in through the window, he saw a head rising over the sill to have a peep, and then bobbing down again.

"That's Jack," says the squire; "I'll astonish him a bit," says the squire, pointing a gun at the lower pane.

"Oh, Lord, my dear!" says the wife, "sure you wouldn't shoot the brave fellow?"

"Indeed, an' I wouldn't for a kingdom; there's nothing but powder in it."

Up went the head, bang went the gun, down dropped the body, and a great souse was heard on the gravel walk.

"Oh, Lord," says the lady, "poor Jack is killed or disabled for life." "I hope not," says the squire, and down the stairs he ran. He never minded to shut the door, but opened the gate and ran into the garden. His wife heard his voice at the room door, before he could be under the window and back, as she thought.

"Wife, wife," says he from the door, "the sheet, the sheet! He is not killed, I hope, but he is bleeding like a pig. I must wipe it away as well as I can, and get some one to carry him in with me." She pulled it off the bed, and threw it to him. Down he ran like lightning, and he had hardly time to be in the garden, when he was back, and this time he came back in his shirt as he went out.

"High hanging to you, Jack," says he, "for an arrant rogue!"

"Arrant rogue?" says she. "Isn't the poor fellow all cut and bruised?"

"I didn't much care if he was. What do you think was bobbing up and down at the window, and tossed down so heavy on the walk? A man's clothes stuffed with straw, and a couple of stones."

"And what did you want with the sheet just now, to wipe his blood if he were only a man of straw?"

"Sheet, woman! I wanted no sheet."

"Well, whether you wanted it or not, I threw it to you, and you standing outside o' the door."

"Oh, Jack, Jack, you terrible tinker!" says the squire, "there's no use in striving with you. We must do without the sheet for one night. We'll have the marriage to-morrow to get ourselves out of trouble."

So married they were, and Jack turned out a real good husband. And the squire and his lady were never tired of praising their son-in-law, "Jack the Cunning Thief."

THE FARMER OF LIDDESDALE

THERE was in Liddesdale (in Morven) a Farmer who suffered great loss within the space of one year. In the first place, his wife and children died, and shortly after their death the Ploughman left him. The hiring-markets were then over, and there was no way of getting another ploughman in place of the one that left. When spring came his neighbours began ploughing; but he had not a man to hold the plough, and he knew not what he should do.

The time was passing, and he was therefore losing patience. At last he said to himself in a fit of passion, that he would engage the first man that came his way, whoever he should be. Shortly after that a man came to the house. The Farmer met him at the door, and asked him whither was he going, or what was he seeking. He answered that he was a ploughman, and that he wanted an engagement. "I want a ploughman, and if we agree about the wages, I will engage thee. What dost thou ask from this day to the day when the crop will be gathered in?"

"Only as much of the corn when it shall be dry as I can carry with me in one burden-withe."

"Thou shalt get that," said the Farmer, and they agreed.

Next morning the Farmer went out with the Ploughman, and showed him the fields which he had to plough. Before they returned, the Ploughman went to the wood, and having cut three stakes, came back with them, and placed one of them at the head of each one of the fields. After he had done that he said to the Farmer, "I will do the work now alone, and the ploughing need no longer give thee anxiety."

Having said this, he went home and remained idle all that day. The next day came, but he remained idle as on the day before. After he had spent a good while in that manner, the Farmer said to him that it was time for him to begin work now, because the spring was passing away, and the. neighbours had half their work finished. He replied, "Oh, our land is not ready yet."

"How dost thou think that?"

"Oh, I know it by the stakes."

If the delay of the Ploughman made the Farmer wonder, this answer made him wonder more. He resolved that he would keep his eye on him, and see what he was doing.

The Farmer rose early next morning, and saw the Ploughman going to the first field. When he reached the field, he pulled the stake at its end out of the ground, and put it to his nose. He shook his head and put the stake back in the ground. He then left the first field and went to the rest. He tried the stakes, shook his head, and returned home. In the dusk he went out the second time to the fields, tried the stakes, shook his head, and after putting them again in the ground, went home.

Next morning he went out to the fields the third time. When he reached the first stake he pulled it out of the ground and put it to his nose as he did on the foregoing days. But no sooner had he done that than he threw the stake from him, and stretched away for the horses with all his might.

He got the horses, the withes, and the plough, and when he reached the end of the first field with them, he thrust the plough into the ground, and cried:

> "My horses and my leather-traces, and mettlesome lads,
> The earth is coming up!"

He then began ploughing, kept at it all day at a terrible rate, and before the sun went down that night there was not a palm-breadth of the three fields which he had not ploughed, sowed, and harrowed. When the farmer saw this he was exceedingly well pleased, for he had his work finished as soon as his neighbours.

The Ploughman was quick and ready to do everything that he was told, and so he and the Farmer agreed well until the harvest came. But on a certain day when the reaping was over, the Farmer said to him that he thought the corn was dry enough for putting in. The Ploughman tried a sheaf or two, and answered that it was not dry yet. But shortly after that day he said that it was now ready.

"If it is," said the Farmer, "we better begin putting it in."

"We will not until I get my share out of it first," said the Ploughman. He then went off to the wood, and in a short time returned, having in his hand a withe scraped and twisted. He stretched the withe on the field, and began to put the corn in it. He continued putting sheaf after sheaf in the withe until he had taken almost all the sheaves that were in the field. The Farmer asked of him what he meant. "Thou didst promise me as wages as much corn as I could carry with me in one burden-withe, and here I have it now," said the Ploughman, as he was shutting the withe.

The Farmer saw that he would be ruined by the Ploughman, and therefore said:

> "'Twas in the Màrt I sowed,
> 'Twas in the Màrt I baked,
> 'Twas in the Màrt I harrowed.
> Thou Who hast ordained the three Màrts,
> Let not my share go in one burden-withe."

Instantly the withe broke, and it made a loud report, which echo answered from every rock far and near. Then the corn spread over the field, and the Ploughman went away in a white mist in the skies, and was seen no more.

DREAM OF OWEN O'MULREADY

HERE was a man long ago living near Ballaghadereen named Owen
O'Mulready, who was a workman for the gentleman of the place, and was
a prosperous, quiet, contented man. There was no one but himself and his wife
Margaret, and they had a nice little house and enough potatoes in the year, in
addition to their share of wages, from their master. There wasn't a want or anxiety
on Owen, except one desire, and that was to have a dream—for he had never had
one.

One day when he was digging potatoes, his master—James Taafe—came out
to his ridge, and they began talking, as was the custom with them. The talk fell on
dreams, and said Owen that he would like better than anything if he could only
have one.

"You'll have one to-night," says his master, "if you do as I tell you."

"Musha, I'll do it, and welcome," says Owen.

"Now," says his master, "when you go home to-night, draw the fire from the
hearth, put it out, make your bed in its place and sleep there to-night, and you'll
get your enough of dreaming before the morning."

Owen promised to do this. When, however, he began to draw the fire out,
Margaret thought that he had lost his senses, so he explained everything James
Taafe had said to him, had his own way, and they went to lie down together on
the hearth. Not long was Owen asleep when there came a knock at the door.

"Get up, Owen O'Mulready, and go with a letter from the master to America."

Owen got up, and put his feet into his boots, saying to himself, "It's late you
come, messenger."

He took the letter, and he went forward and never tarried till he came to the foot
of Sliabh Charn, where he met a cow-boy, and he herding cows.

"The blessing of God be with you, Owen O'Mulready," says the boy.

"The blessing of God and Mary be with you, my boy," says Owen. "Every one
knows me, and I don't know any one at all."

"Where are you going this time of night?" says the boy.

"I'm going to America, with a letter from the master; is this the right road?"
says Owen.

"It is; keep straight to the west; but how are you going to get over the water?"
says the boy.

"Time enough to think of that when I get to it," replied Owen.

He went on the road again, till he came to the brink of the sea; there he saw a
crane standing on one foot on the shore.

"The blessing of God be with you, Owen 'O'Mulready," says the crane.

"The blessing of God and Mary be with you, Mrs. Crane," says Owen.
"Everybody knows me, and I don't know any one."

"What are you doing here?"

Owen told her his business, and that he didn't know how he'd get over the water.

"Leave your two feet on my two wings, and sit on my back, and I'll take you to the other side," says the crane.

"What would I do if tiredness should come on you before we got over?" says Owen.

"Don't be afraid, I won't be tired or wearied till I fly over."

Then Owen went on the back of the crane, and she arose over the sea and went forward, but she hadn't flown more than half-way, when she cried out:

"Owen O'Mulready, get off me; I'm tired."

"That you may be seven times worse this day twelve-months, you rogue of a crane," says Owen; "I can't get off you now, so don't ask me."

"I don't care," replied the crane, "if you'll rise off me a while till I'll take a rest!"

With that they saw threshers over their heads, and Owen shouted:

"Och! thresher, thresher, leave down your flail at me, that I may give the crane a rest!"

The thresher left down the flail, but when Owen took a hold with his two hands, the crane went from him, laughing and mocking.

"My share of misfortune go with you!" said Owen. "It's you've left me in a fix hanging between the heavens and the water in the middle of the great sea."

It wasn't long till the thresher shouted to him to leave go the flail.

"I won't let it go," said Owen; "shan't I be drowned?"

"If you don't let it go, I'll cut the whang."

"I don't care," says Owen; "I have the flail"; and with that he looked away from him, and what should he see but a boat a long way off.

"O sailor dear, sailor, come, come; perhaps you'll take my lot of bones," said Owen.

"Are we under you now?" says the sailor.

"Not yet, not yet," says Owen.

"Fling down one of your shoes, till we see the way it falls," says the captain.

Owen shook one foot, and down fell the shoe.

"Uill, uill, puil, uil, liu—who is killing me?" came a scream from Margaret in the bed. "Where are you, Owen?"

"I didn't know whether 'twas you were in it, Margaret."

"Indeed, then it is," says she. "Who else would it be?"

She got up and lit the candle. She found Owen half-way up the chimney, climbing by the hands on the crook, and he black with soot! He had one shoe on, but the point of the other struck Margaret, and 'twas that which awoke her. Owen came down off the crook and washed himself, and from that out there was no envy on him ever to have a dream again.

THE PIPER AND THE PÚCA

IN the old times, there was a half fool living in Dunmore, in the county Galway, and although he was excessively fond of music, he was unable to learn more than one tune, and that was the "Black Rogue." He used to get a good deal of money from the gentlemen, for they used to get sport out of him. One night the piper was coming home from a house where there had been a dance, and he half drunk. When he came to a little bridge that was up by his mother's house, he squeezed the pipes on, and began playing the "Black Rogue." The Púca came behind him, and flung him up on his own back. There were long horns on the Púca, and the piper got a good grip of them, and then he said—

"Destruction on you, you nasty beast, let me home. I have a ten-penny piece in my pocket for my mother, and she wants snuff."

"Never mind your mother," said the Púca, "but keep your hold. If you fall, you will break your neck and your pipes." Then the Púca said to him, "Play up for me the 'Shan Van Vocht.'"

"I don't know it," said the piper.

"Never mind whether you do or you don't," said the Púca. "Play up, and I'll make you know."

The piper put wind in his bag, and he played such music as made himself wonder.

"Upon my word, you're a fine music-master," says the piper then; "but tell me where you're for bringing me."

"There's a great feast in the house of the Banshee, on the top of Croagh Patric to-night," says the Púca, "and I'm for bringing you there to play music, and, take my word, you'll get the price of your trouble."

"By my word, you'll save me a journey, then," says the piper, "for Father William put a journey to Croagh Patric on me, because I stole the white gander from him last Martinmas."

The Púca rushed him across hills and bogs and rough places, till he brought him to the top of Croagh Patric. Then the Púca struck three blows with his foot, and a great door opened, and they passed in together, into a fine room.

The piper saw a golden table in the middle of the room, and hundreds of old women sitting round about it. The women rose up, and said, "A hundred thousand welcomes to you, you Púca of November. Who is this you have with you?"

"The best piper in Ireland," says the Púca.

One of the old women struck a blow on the wall, and what should the piper see coming out but the white gander which he had stolen from Father William.

"By my conscience, then," says the piper, "myself and my mother ate every taste of that gander, only one wing, and I gave that to Red Mary, and it's she told the priest I stole his gander."

The gander cleaned the table, and carried it away, and the Púca said, "Play up music for these ladies."

The piper played up, and the old women began dancing, and they were dancing till they were tired. Then the Púca said to pay the piper, and every old woman drew out a gold piece, and gave it to him.

"By the tooth of Patric," said he, "I'm as rich as the son of a lord."

"Come with me," says the Púca, "and I'll bring you home."

They went out then, and just as he was going to ride on the Púca, the gander came up to him, and gave him a new set of pipes. The Púca was not long until he brought him to Dunmore, and he threw the piper off at the little bridge, and then he told him to go home, and says to him, "You have two things now that you never had before—you have sense and music."

The piper went home, and he knocked at his mother's door, saying, "Let me in, I'm as rich as a lord, and I'm the best piper in Ireland."

"You're drunk," said the mother.

"No, indeed," says the piper, "I haven't drunk a drop."

The mother let him in, and he gave her the gold pieces, and "Wait now," says he, "till you hear the music I'll play."

He buckled on the pipes, but instead of music, there came a sound as if all the geese and ganders in Ireland were screeching together. He wakened the neighbours, and they were all mocking him, until he put on the old pipes, and then he played melodious music for them; and after that he told them all he had gone through that night.

The next morning, when his mother went to look at the gold pieces, there was nothing there but the leaves of a plant.

The piper went to the priest, and told him his story, but the priest would not believe a word from him, until he put the pipes on him, and then the screeching of the ganders and geese began.

"Leave my sight, you thief," says the priest.

But nothing would do the piper, till he would put the old pipes on him to show the priest that his story was true.

He buckled on the old pipes, and he played melodious music, and from that day till the day of his death, there was never a piper in the county Galway was as good as he was.

MUNACHAR AND MANACHAR

THERE once lived a Munachar and a Manachar, a long time ago, and it is a long time since it was, and if they were alive then they would not be alive now. They went out together to pick raspberries, and as many as Munachar used to pick Manachar used to eat. Munachar said he must look for a rod to make a gad (a withy band) to hang Manachar, who ate his raspberries every one; and he came to the rod. "God save you," said the rod. "God and Mary save you." "How far are you going?" "Going looking for a rod, a rod to make a gad, a gad to hang Manachar, who ate my raspberries every one."

"You will not get me," said the rod, "until you get an axe to cut me."

He came to the axe. "God save you," said the axe. "God and Mary save you." "How far are you going?" "Going looking for an axe, an axe to cut a rod, a rod to make a gad, a gad to hang Manachar, who ate my raspberries every one." "You will not get me," said the axe, "until you get a flag to edge me."

He came to the flag.

"God save you," said the flag. "God and Mary save you." "How far are you going?" "Going looking for a flag, a flag to edge axe, an axe to cut a rod, a rod to make a gad, a gad to hang Manachar, who ate my raspberries every one." "You will not get me," says the flag, "till you get water to wet me."

He came to the water.

"God save you," says the water. "God and Mary save you." "How far are you going?" "Going looking for water, water to wet flag, flag to edge axe, axe to cut a rod, a rod to make a gad, a gad to hang Manachar, who ate my raspberries every one." "You will not get me," the water, "until you get a deer who will swim me."

He came to the deer.

"God save you," says the deer. "God and Mary save you." "How far are you going?" "Going looking for a deer, deer to swim water, water to wet flag, flag to edge axe, axe to cut a rod, a rod to make a gad, a gad to hang Manachar, who ate my raspberries every one." "You will not get me," said the deer, "until you get a hound who will hunt me."

He came to the hound.

"God save you," says the hound. "God and Mary save you." "How far are you going?" "Going looking for a hound, hound to hunt deer, deer to swim water, water to wet flag, flag to edge axe, axe to cut a rod, a rod to make a gad, a gad to hang Manachar, who ate my raspberries every one." "You will not get me," said the hound, "until you get a bit of butter to put in my claw."

He came to the butter.

"God save you," says the butter. "God and Mary save you." "How far are you going?" "Going looking for butter, butter to go in claw of hound, hound to hunt deer, deer to swim water, water to wet flag, flag to edge axe, axe to cut a rod, a rod to make a gad, a gad to hang Manachar, who ate my raspberries every one." "You will not get me," said the butter, "until you get a cat who shall scrape me."

He came to the cat.

"God save you," said the cat. "God and Mary save you." "How are you going?" "Going looking for a cat, cat to scrape butter, butter to go in claw of hound, hound to hunt deer, deer to swim water, water to wet flag, flag to edge axe, axe to cut a rod, a rod to make a gad, a gad to hang Manachar, who ate my raspberries every one." "You will not get me," said the cat, "until you will get milk, which you will give me."

He came to the cow.

"God save you," said the cow. "God and Mary save you." "How far are you going?" "Going looking for a cow, cow to give me milk, milk I will give to the cat, cat to scrape butter, butter to go in claw of hound, hound to hunt deer, deer to swim water, water to wet flag, flag to edge axe, axe to cut a rod, a rod to make a gad, a gad to hang Manachar, who ate my raspberries every one."

"You will not get any milk from me," said the cow, "until you bring me a whisp of straw from those threshers yonder."

He came to the threshers.

"God save you," said the threshers. "God and Mary save ye." "How far are you going?" "Going looking for a whisp of straw from ye to give to the cow, the cow to give me milk, milk I will give to the cat, cat to scrape butter, butter to go in claw of hound, hound to hunt deer, deer to swim water, water to wet flag, flag to edge axe, axe to cut a rod, a rod to make a gad, a gad to hang Manachar, who ate my raspberries every one." "You will not get any whisp of straw from us," said the threshers, "until you bring us the makings of a cake from the miller over yonder."

He came to the miller.

"God save you," said the miller. "God and Mary save you." "How far are you going?" "Going looking for the makings of a cake, which I will give to the threshers, the threshers to give me a whisp of straw, the whisp of straw I will give to the cow, the cow to give me milk, milk I will give to the cat, cat to scrape butter, butter to go in claw of hound, hound to hunt deer, deer to swim water, water to wet flag, flag to edge axe, axe to cut a rod, a rod to make a gad, a gad to hang Manachar, who ate my raspberries every one."

"You will not get any makings of a cake from me," said the miller, "till you bring me the full of that sieve of water from the river over there."

He took the sieve in his hand, and went over to the river, but as often as ever he would stoop and fill it with water, the moment he raised it the water would run out of it again, and sure, if he had been there from that day till this, he never could have filled it. A crow went flying by him over his head. "Daub! daub!" said the crow. "My soul to God, then," said Munachar, "but it's the good advice you have," and he took the red clay and the daub that was by the brink, and he rubbed it to the bottom of the sieve, until all the holes were filled, and then the sieve held the water, and he brought the water to the miller, and the miller gave him the makings of a cake, and he gave the makings of a cake to the threshers, and the threshers gave him a whisp of straw, and he gave the whisp of straw to the cow, and the cow gave him milk, the milk he gave to the cat, the cat scraped the butter, the butter went into the claw of the hound, the hound hunted the deer, the deer swam the water, the water wet the flag, the flag sharpened the axe, the axe cut the rod, and the rod made a gad, and when he had it ready—I'll go bail that Manachar was far enough away from him.

THE HORNED WOMEN

A RICH woman sat up late one night carding and preparing wool, while all the family and servants were asleep. Suddenly a knock was given at the door, and a voice called—"Open! open!"

"Who is there?" said the woman of the house.

"I am the Witch of the one Horn," was answered.

The mistress, supposing that one of her neighbours had called and required assistance, opened the door, and a woman entered, having in her hand a pair of wool carders, and bearing a horn on her forehead, as if growing there. She sat down by the fire in silence, and began to card the wool with violent haste. Suddenly she paused, and said aloud: "Where are the women? They delay too long."

Then a second knock came to the door, and a voice called as before, "Open! open!"

The mistress felt herself constrained to rise and open to the call, and immediately a second witch entered, having two horns on her forehead, and in her hand a wheel for spinning wool.

"Give me place," she said, "I am the Witch of the two Horns," and she began to spin as quick as lightning.

And so the knocks went on, and the call was heard, and the witches entered, until at last twelve women sat round the fire—the first with one horn, the last with twelve horns.

And they carded the thread, and turned their spinning wheels, and wound and wove.

All singing together an ancient rhyme, but no word did they speak to the mistress of the house. Strange to hear, and frightful to look upon, were these twelve women with their horns and their wheels; and the mistress felt near to death, and she tried to rise that she might call for help, but she could not move, nor could she utter a word or a cry, for the spell of the witches was upon her.

Then one of them called to her in Irish, and said—"Rise, woman, and make us a cake." Then the mistress searched for a vessel to bring water from the well that she might mix the meal and make the cake, but she could find none.

And they said to her, "Take a sieve and bring water in it."

And she took the sieve and went to the well; but the water poured from it, and she could fetch none for the cake, and she sat down by the well and wept. Then a voice came by her and said, "Take yellow clay and moss, and bind them together, and plaster the sieve so that it will hold."

This she did, and the sieve held the water for the cake; and the voice said again—

"Return, and when thou comest to the north angle of the house, cry aloud three times and say, 'The mountain of the Fenian women and the sky over it is all on fire.'" And she did so.

When the witches inside heard the call, a great and terrible cry broke from their lips, and they rushed forth with wild lamentations and shrieks, and fled away to Slievenamon (mountains of the women) where was their chief abode. But the Spirit of the Well bade the mistress of the house to enter and prepare her home against the enchantments of the witches if they returned again.

And first, to break their spells, she sprinkled the water in which she had washed her child's feet (the feet-water) outside the door on the threshold; secondly, she took the cake which the witches had made in her absence, of meal mixed with the blood drawn from the sleeping family, and she broke the cake in bits, and placed a bit in the mouth of each sleeper, and they were restored; and she took the cloth they had woven and placed it half in and half out of the chest with the padlock; and lastly, she secured the door with a great crossbeam fastened in the jambs, so that they could not enter, and having done these things she waited.

Not long were the witches in coming back, and they raged and called for vengeance.

"Open! open!" they screamed, "open, feet-water!"

"I cannot," said the feet-water, "I am scattered on the ground, and my path is down to the Lough."

"Open, open, wood and trees and beam!" they cried to the door.

"I cannot," said the door, "for the beam is fixed in the jambs and I have no power to move."

"Open, open, cake that we have made and mingled with blood!" they cried again.

"I cannot," said the cake, "for I am broken and bruised, and my blood is on the lips of the sleeping children."

Then the witches rushed through the air with great cries, and fled back to Slievenamon, uttering strange curses on the Spirit of the Well, who had wished their ruin; but the woman and the house were left in peace, and a mantle dropped by one of the witches in her flight was kept hung up by the mistress as a sign of the night's awful contest; and this mantle was in possession of the same family from generation to generation for five hundred years after.

THE KING'S DAUGHTER OF FRANCE

THERE was once an old man of Ireland who was terrible poor, and he lived by his lone in a small wee house by the roadside. At the morning of the day he would go for to gather sticks in a wood was convenient to that place, the way he'd have a clear fire to be sitting at of an evening.

It fell out one time, of a cold night, that Paddy heard a knock at the door. He went over, and when he opened it he seen a little boy in a red cap standing without.

"Let you come in and take an air to the fire," says he, for he always had a good reception for every person.

The boy with the red cap walked in, and he stopped for a good while conversing. He was the best of company, and the old man didn't find the time passing until he rose for to go. "Let you come in and rest yourself here any evening you are out in these parts," says he.

The very next night the little fellow was in it again, and the night after that, warming himself at the clear fire and talking away.

"Paddy," says he, the evening he was in for the third time, "Paddy, I do be thinking it is bitter poor you are!"

"I am, surely," says the old man.

"Well, let you pay attention to me, it is the truth I'm speaking, you'll have more gold than ever you'll contrive for to spend."

"I could go through a fair share of gold," says Paddy.

"I am determined for to make a rich man of you," the little boy goes on. "There is a lady at the point of death, and she is the King's daughter of France. I have a bottle here in my pocket, and that is the cure for the disease is on her. I'll be giving it to you, and let you set out for France at the morning of the day. When you come to the King's palace the servants will bid you be gone for an ignorant beggar, but let you not be heeding them at all. Don't quit asking to see the King, and in the latter end they'll give in to you. It is with himself the most difficulty will be, for that man will think it hard to believe the likes of a poor old Irishman could have a better cure nor all the doctors in the world. A power of them [1] allowed they'd have her right

---
[1] A large number of them.

well in no time, and it is worse they left her. The King is after giving out that the
next person coming with a false cure be to lose their life. Let you not be scared
at that decree, for you are the man shall succeed. You may promise to have the
lady fit to ride out hunting in nine days. Three drops from the bottle is all you have
to give her, and that for three mornings after other."

Paddy paid great heed to all the boy in the red cap was telling him. He took the
wee bottle that was to make him a rich man, and he made ready for to set out at
the morning of the day. He was a long time travelling the world before he came
to the palace where the King's daughter of France was lying at the point of death.
The servants made a great mock of the poor old Irishman, but he paid no attention
to their words at all. In the latter end he got seeing the King, and that gentleman
allowed [2] the likes of Paddy could never succeed when the doctors of the world
were after failing.

"I'd only be having the head cut off you, my poor old man!" says he.

"I'm not the least bit in dread, your honour," says Paddy. "The lady is bound
to be ready to ride out hunting in nine days, if she uses my medicine."

His perseverance and courage won over the King of France, and permission
was given for a trial of the cure.

The first morning, after taking the three drops from the bottle, the lady turned
in her bed. The second morning, after the treatment, she sat up and ate her food.

The third morning, when she had taken the three drops, the King's daughter of
France rose from her bed. And in nine days she was ready to ride out hunting.

They could not do enough for Paddy, there was great gratitude in them. Well,
the reward he accepted was a big sack of gold, and that was the load he brought
home to his cabin in Ireland.

The first evening he was sitting by his clear fire, the little boy came in at the
door.

"Didn't I do well for you, Paddy?" says he.

"You did surely. I have more gold in that sack than ever I'll contrive for to
spend."

"Ah, not at all! It is twice as much I'll be getting for you."

"Is it another King's daughter has need of a cure?" asks Paddy.

"No, but a different business entirely. There is a great bully to be fought in the
City of Dublin, and yourself is the man shall win it."

"Do you tell me so!" says Paddy.

"In troth I do. The man you have to fight is a big, fierce fellow no one can get
the better of. He has the youth of the world battered to pieces, the way no person
comes forward against him any more. There is a fine purse of money put up for
to entice a champion to face him; and there will be great laughter when yourself

---

[2] Declared.

puts in an appearance. They will ask if you are wishful to fight with gloves on your hands, but it is your bare fists are the best. Let you say you'll toss for which it is to be, but toss with the half-crown I give you, and you are certain to win. Myself is coming to that place for to second you, and it's bound to be the grandest bully was seen in the City of Dublin."

With that the little fellow went away out of the house. And at the morning of the day my brave old Paddy started for Dublin. He wasn't too long on the road, for he got a lift from a man was driving there to see the bully. Well, there was odious laughter and cheering when the crowd saw the champion was come to accept the challenge. The big man was after battering the youth of the world, allowed he had no notion of striving against the likes of Paddy. But when no person else came forward they were bound for to accept him, and they asked would he wear gloves on his fists.

"We'll be tossing for that," says he, bringing out the half-crown he had from the little boy in the red cap.

He won the toss, sure enough, and he allowed it was bare-handed he'd strive. All the time he was looking round, anxious like, but he could see no sign of the one that was to second him. He went into the ring in odious dread; but then the little fellow came and stood beside him. My brave Paddy let out and he struck the champion one blow, and didn't he lay him dead at his feet.

It was then there was roaring and cheering for the old man. And in all the confusion the little lad got away; Paddy never seen where he went. The whole crowd took up a terrible great collection of money for the champion was after destroying the man with a single blow. That lot of gold, along with the purse was promised for the fight, filled a sack as full as it could hold. So Paddy went home well rewarded, and not a bit the worse of his jaunt to the City of Dublin.

The first evening he was sitting by his own fireside, the little boy in the red cap came in at the door.

"Didn't I do well for you, Paddy?" says he.

"You did, surely. It is rich for life I am, owing to your contrivances."

"Then will you be doing me a service in return for all?" asks the little fellow.

"Indeed then, I will," says Paddy.

"We have all arranged for to cross over to France this night. We intend for to bring away the lady you cured, the King's daughter of that country," says the boy. "But we cannot contrive for to accomplish the like unless we have flesh and blood along with us. Will you come?"

"Aye, surely!" says Paddy.

With that the two went out at the door and across the road into a field. It was thronged with regiments of the Good People, past belief or counting. They were running every way through the field, calling out:

"Get me a horse, get me a horse!"

And what were they doing only cutting down the bohlans [3] and riding away on them.

"Get me a horse, get me a horse!" says old Paddy, calling out along with them. But the fellow in the red cap came over to him looking terrible vexed.

"Don't let another word out of you," says he, "except one of ourselves speaks first. Mind what I'm telling you or it will be a cause of misfortune."

"I'll say no more except in answer to a question," says Paddy.

With that they brought him a white yearling calf, and put him up for to ride upon it. He thought it was a queer sort of a horse, but he passed no remarks. And away they rode at a great pace, the Good People on the bohlans and Paddy on the yearling calf.

They made grand going, and it wasn't long before they came to a big lake had an island in the middle of it. With one spring the whole party landed on the island and with another they were safe on the far shore.

"Dam, but that was a great lep for a yearling calf," says Paddy.

With that one of the Good People struck him a blow on the head, the way the sense was knocked out of him and he fell on the field. At daylight the old man came to himself, and he lying on the field by the big lake. He was a long journey from home, and he was weary travelling round the water and over the hills to his own place. But the worst of all was the sacks of gold: didn't every bit of the fortune melt away and leave him poor, the way he was before he came in with the Good People.

FAIRY GOLD

IT happened one time that a poor man dreamt three nights after other of a sack of fairy gold was buried in under the roots of a lone bush [1] and it growing in a field convenient to his house.

"It may be there is nothing in it," says he to himself. "But I will be digging in that place and if I find a treasure it will be a big reward for the labour."

He never let on a word of his intentions to any person, nor did he evenly pass any remark on the strange dreams were after coming to him. At the fall of the day he took a loy [2] in his hand and set out for the lone bush. He was not a great while at work before the steel blade struck against a substance that had no feel of clay, and the man was full sure it was not a stone he was after striking against. He

---

[3] Ragweed.

[1] A hawthorn growing at a distance from all other trees. The lone bushes are dedicated to the fairies and must not be cut down.

[2] A sort of spade peculiar to the west and north-west of Ireland.

wrought hard to bring whatever was in it to light—and what had he only a powerful fine sack of pure gold and splendid jewels. He raised it up on his shoulders and set out for home, staggering under the load. It was maybe a hundred-weight of treasure he had with him, and he went along planning out the uses of that wealth. Sure the burden was a rejoicement to him and no hardship at all evenly if it had him bent double like an aged and crippled man.

When he came to his own place he went to the byre, and it was there he put down the sack in front of three cows were standing in the bails. For he was not wishful to be making a display of that splendour before the neighbours all, and it was likely he would find some person within making their cailee.[3]

Sure enough when he went in on the door of the house he seen two men sitting by the fire and they in no haste to depart. Now the strangers had the English only, and the people of the house spoke Irish with one another.

Says himself, using the Gaelic, "I have a beautiful treasure without—bars of fine gold are in it, and jewels would be the delight of a queen of the world."

"Oh, bring it into the house," says she. "Sure it will rise my heart to be looking on the like; the hunger of it is put on my eyes by your words speaking."

"I have better wit than to make display of my fortune to every person is living in the land," says he. "Let you content yourself until the two men have departed, and then we'll fetch the sack in from the byre where I left it in front of the cows."

When the man and woman of the house were shut of the company they went out to the yard, and they fair wild with delight. Himself told the story of the three dreams and the finding of the gold in under the roots of the lone bush.

"Did you spit on it?" she inquires.

"I did not," says he.

With that she allowed he was after making a big mistake.

"How could that be?" he asks.

"My father had great knowledge of the like," says herself. "I often heard him tell of how those treasures do be enchanted, and power is on them for to melt away. But if a man was to spit on fairy gold he'd get keeping it surely."

"Amn't I after bringing it this far," says he, "and the weight of it destroying my shoulders with bruises and pains. Not the least sign of melting was on yon article and it a warrant to bring down the scales at a hundred and more."

With that they went into the byre, and they seen the three cows were striving to break out of the bails.

"They are in dread of what's lying there in front," says herself. "The cattle of the world have good wisdom surely, and they do the looking on more nor the eye of man gets leave to behold."

---

[3] A visit.

"Quit raving about the cows," says he. "Look at my lovely sack and it bulging full."

When the two went up to the head of the bails the woman let a great cry out of her. "What are you after bringing to this place from among the roots of the lone bush? It has the movement of life in it—and how could the like be treasure at all!"

"Hold your whisht, woman," says her husband, and he middling vexed at her words.

"Will you look at the bag is turning over on the ground?" says she. He seen there was truth in her words, but all the while he would not give in to be scared.

"It is likely a rat is after creeping in," he allows, "and he is having his own times striving to win out."

"Let you open the sack, and I will be praying aloud for protection on us—for it is no right thing is in it at all," says herself. With that he went over and he turned the hundredweight of treasure until he had it propped up against the bails. When he began for to open the bag the cows went fair wild, striving and roaring and stamping to get away from the place entirely.

The head of a great eel looked out from under the man's hand where he was groping for the treasure. The eyes of it were the colour of flame and as blinding to the sight as the naked sun at noon of a summer's day. The man gave one lep that carried him to the door and there the paralysis of dread held him down. Herself let a scream could be heard in the next townland, but she never asked to stir from where she was standing. The appearance of the eel twisted itself out of the sack and travelled along the ground, putting the six feet of its length into the awfullest loops and knots were ever seen. Then it reared up its head and neck to stand swaying for a while, a full half of it in the air. The man and woman were convenient to the door but the both were too scared to go out on it; they watched the eel and they seen it twist up round a bail until the head of it was touching the roof. Didn't it break away out through the thatch, and whether it melted off the face of the earth or travelled to other parts was never heard tell. But the likeness of that beast was the whole and only treasure came out of the sack the poor man dug from under the roots of the lone bush where the fairy gold was hid.

THE ENCHANTED HARE

THERE was a strong farmer one time and he had nine beautiful cows grazing on the best of land. Surely that was a great prosperity, and you'd be thinking him the richest man in all the country-side. But it was little milk he was getting from his nine lovely cows, and no butter from the milk. They'd be churning in that house for three hours or maybe for five hours of a morning, and at the end of all a few wee grains of butter would be floating on the top of the milk. Evenly that much did not remain to it, for when herself ran the strainer in under them they melted from the churn. There were great confabulations held about the loss of the yield, but the strength of the spoken word was powerless to restore what was gone. Herself allowed that her man be to have the evil eye, and it was overlooking his own cattle he was by walking through them and he fasting at the dawn of day.

The notion didn't please him too well, indeed he was horrid vexed at her for saying the like, but he went no more among the cows until after his breakfast time. Sure that done no good at all—it was less and less milk came in each day. And butter going a lovely price in the market, to leave it a worse annoyance to have none for to sell.

The man of the house kept a tongue hound that was odious wise. The two walked the cattle together, and it happened one day that they came on a hare was running with the nine cows through the field. The hound gave tongue and away with him after the hare, she making a great offer to escape.

"Maybe there is something in it," says the man to himself. "I have heard my old grandfather tell that hares be's enchanted people; let it be true or no, I doubt they're not right things in any case."

With that he set out for to follow his tongue hound, and the hunt went over the ditches and through the quick hedges and down by the lake.

"Begob it's odious weighty I am to be diverting myself like a little gosoon," says the man. And indeed he was a big, hearty farmer was leaving powerful gaps behind him where he burst through the hedges.

There was a small, wee house up an old laneway, and that was where the hunt headed for. The hare came in on the street not a yard in front of the tongue hound, and she made a lep for to get into the cabin by a hole on the wall convenient to the door. The hound got a grip of her and she rising from the ground. But the farmer was coming up close behind them and didn't he let a great crow out of him.

"Hold your hold, my bully boy! Hold your hold!" The tongue hound turned at the voice of the master calling, and the hare contrived for to slip from between his teeth. One spring brought her in on the hole in the wall, but she splashed it with blood as she passed, and there was blood on the mouth of the hound.

The man came up, cursing himself for spoiling the diversion, but he was well determined to follow on. He took the coat off his back and he stuffed it into the opening the way the hare had no chance to get out where she was after entering, then he walked round the house for to see was there any means of escape for what was within. There wasn't evenly a space where a fly might contrive to slip through, and himself was satisfied the hunt was shaping well.

He went to the door, and it was there the tongue hound went wild to be making an entry, but a lock and a chain were upon it. The farmer took up a stone and he broke all before him to get in after the hare they followed so far.

"The old house is empty this long time," says he, "and evenly if I be to repair the destruction I make—sure what is the price of a chain and a lock to a fine, warm man like myself!" With that he pushed into the kitchen, and there was neither sight nor sign of a hare to be found, but an old woman lay in a corner and she bleeding.

The tongue hound gave the mournfullest whine and he juked [1] to his master's feet, it was easy knowing the beast was in odious dread. The farmer gave a sort of a groan and he turned for to go away home.

"It's a queer old diversion I'm after enjoying," says he. "Surely there's not a many in the world do be hunting hares through the fields and catching old women are bleeding to death."

When he came to his own place the wife ran out of the house.

"Will you look at the gallons of beautiful milk the cows are after giving this day," says she, pulling him in on the door.

Sure enough from that out there was a great plenty of milk and a right yield of butter on the churn.

THE BRIDGE OF THE KIST

THERE was once a man the name of Michael Hugh, and he was tormented with dreams of a kist was buried in under a bridge in England. For a while he took no heed to the visions were with him in the stillness of the night, but at long last the notion grew in his mind that he be to visit that place and find out was there anything in it.

"I could make right use of a treasure," thinks he to himself.. "For 'tis heart scalded I am with dwelling in poverty, and a great weariness is on me from toiling for a miserable wage." Then he bethought of the foolishness of making the journey if all turned out a deceit.

"Sure I'll be rid of belief in the dreams are driving me daft with their grandeur and perseverance," says he. "Evenly failure will bring a sort of satisfaction for I'll get fooling whatever spirit does be bringing the vision upon me."

So my brave Michael Hugh took an ash plant in his hand, and away with him oversea to England to discover the bridge of the kist. He was a twelvemonth travelling and rambling with no success to rise his heart, and he began for to consider he had better return to his own place. But just as he was making ready to turn didn't he chance on a strong flowing river, and the sight near left his eyes when he found it was spanned by the bridge he was after dreaming of.

Well, Michael Hugh went over and he looked down on the black depth of water was flowing in under the arch.

---

[1] Darted.

"It'll be a hard thing surely to be digging for a kist in that place" says he. "I'm thinking a man would find a sore death and no treasure at all if he lepped into the flood. But maybe it's laid out for me to gather my fortune here, and some person may come for to give me instruction."

With that he walked up and down over the bridge, hoping for further advice since he could not contrive a wisdom for his use. There was a house convenient to the river, and after a while a man came from it.

"Are you waiting on any person in this place?" says he to Michael Hugh. "It's bitter weather to be abroad and you have to be as hardy as a wild duck to endure the cold blast on the bridge."

"I'm hardy surely," Michael Hugh makes his answer. "But 'tis no easy matter to tell if I'm waiting on any person."

"You're funning me," says the Englishman. "How would you be abroad without reason, and you having a beautiful wise countenance on you?" With that Michael Hugh told him the story of the dreams that brought him from Ireland, and how he was expectant of a sign to instruct him to come at the kist. The Englishman let a great laugh.

"You're a simple fellow," says he. "Let you give up heeding the like of visions and ghosts, for there is madness in the same and no pure reason at all. There's few has more nor better knowledge than myself of how they be striving to entice us from our work, but I'm a reasonable man and I never gave in to them yet."

"Might I make so free as to ask," says Michael Hugh, "what sort of a vision are you after resisting?"

"I'll tell you and welcome," says the Englishman. "There isn't a night of my life but I hear a voice calling: 'Away with you to Ireland, and seek out a man the name of Michael Hugh. There is treasure buried in under a lone bush in his garden, and that is in Breffny of Connacht."[1]

The poor Irishman was near demented with joy at the words, for he understood he was brought all that journey to learn of gold was a stone's throw from his own little cabin door.

But he was a conny sort of a person, and he never let on to the other that Michael Hugh was the name of him, nor that he came from Breffny of Connacht.

The Englishman invited him into his house for to rest there that night, and he didn't spare his advice that dreams were a folly and sin.

"You have me convinced of the meaning of my visions," says Michael Hugh. "And what's more I'll go home as you bid me."

Next morning he started out, and he made great haste with the desire was on him to get digging the gold.

When he came to his own place in Connacht he made straight for a loy and then

---

[1] The counties of Cavan and Leitrim, originally part of Connaught, though Cavan is now in Ulster.

for the lone bush. Not a long was he digging before he hoked out a precious crock full of treasure, and he carried it into the house. There was a piece of a flag stone lying on top of the gold, and there was a writing cut into it. What might be the meaning of that Michael Hugh had no notion, for the words were not Gaelic nor English at all.

It happened one evening that a poor scholar came in for to make his cailee.

"Can you read me that inscription, mister?" asks Michael Hugh, bringing out the flag.

"Aye, surely," says the poor scholar. "That is a Latin writing, and I am well learned in the same."

"What meaning is in it?" asks the other.

"'The same at the far side,'" says the scholar. "And that is a droll saying surely when it gives no information beyond."

"Maybe it will serve my turn, mister!" says Michael Hugh, in the best of humour.

After the scholar was gone on his way, didn't himself take the loy and out to the garden. He began for to dig at the far side of the lone bush, and sure enough he found a second beautiful kist the dead spit of the first.

It was great prosperity he enjoyed from that out. And he bought the grandest of raiment, the way the neighbours began for to call him Michael Hughie the Cock.

THE CHILD AND THE FIDDLE

THERE was a woman one time, and she had the fretfullest child in all Ireland. He lay in the cradle and lamented from morning to night and from dark to the dawn of day. There was no prosperity nor comfort in that house from he came to it. All things went astray within in the kitchen and without upon the farm: the cattle fell sick, the potatoes took a blight, there was not a taste of butter on the churn, and evenly the cat began for to dwine and dwine away. But of all the misfortunes that come the woefullest was the continual strife between the man and woman of the house, and they a couple that were horrid fond aforetime.

It happened when the child was about eighteen months of age that a strange man was hired to work on the farm. Surely he'd never have ventured into the place if he had heard tell of the ill luck was in it, but he was from distant parts and didn't know a heth.

One day he chanced to be in from the work a while before the master of the house, and herself was gone to the spring for water. The hired man sat down by the kitchen fire, taking no heed of the child was watching him from the cradle. The little fellow quit his lamenting; he sat up straight, with a countenance on him like a wise old man.

"I will be playing you a tune on the fiddle, for I'm thinking 'tis fond of the music you are," says he. The man near fell into the fire with wonderment to hear the old-fashioned talk. He didn't say one word in answer, but he waited to see what would be coming next.

The small weak infant pulled a fiddle out from under the pillow of the cradle, and he began for to play the loveliest music was ever heard in this world. He had reels and jigs, songs and sets; merry tunes would rise the heart of man and mournful tunes would fill the mind with grief.

The man sat listening, and he was all put through other, thinking the child was no right thing.

After a time the little lad quit playing, he put back the fiddle where he took it from and began at his old whimpering again. Herself came in at the door with a bucket of water in her hand. Well the man walked out and he called her after him.

"That is a strange child you have, mistress," says he.

"A strange child, surely, and a sorrowful," she makes answer.

"It is tormented with his roaring you are, no person could be enduring it continually."

"Did ever he play on the fiddle in your hearing?" asks the man. "Is it raving you are?" says she.

"I am not, mistress," he answers. "He is after giving me the best of entertainment with reels and marches and jigs."

"Let you quit funning me!" says she, getting vexed.

"I see you are doubting my words," he replies. "Do you stand here without where he'll not be looking on you at all. I'll go into the kitchen, and maybe he'll bring out the fiddle again." With that he went in, leaving herself posted convenient to the window.

Says he to the child, "I'm thinking there's not above a score of fiddlers in all Ireland having better knowledge of music nor yourself. Sure that is a great wonder and you but an innocent little thing."

"Maybe it's not that innocent I am," says the child. "And let me tell you there isn't one fiddler itself to be my equal in the land."

"You're boasting, you bold wee coley," says the man.

The child sat up in a great rage, pulled the fiddle from under the pillow and began for to play a tune was grander nor the lot he gave first.

The man went out to herself.

"Are you satisfied now?" he asks.

"My heart beats time to his reels," says she. "Run down to the field and send the master to this place that he may hear him too."

The man of the house came up in a terrible temper.

"If it's lies you are telling me, I'll brain the pair of you with the loy," says he, when he heard the news of the fiddle.

"Put your ear to the window, it's soft he is playing now," says his wife.

But the words weren't out of her mouth before a blast of loud music was heard. Himself ran in on the door, and he seen the gosoon sitting up playing tunes.

"Let you be off out of this," says he, "or I'll throw you at the back of the fire, for you are no right thing at all."

With that the little fellow made a powerful great lep out of the cradle, across the floor and away with him out over the fields. But he left his fiddle behind, and the master of the house threw it down on the burning turf. And that was no true fiddle at all, only a piece of an old bog stick was rotten with age.

"GOOD NIGHT, MY BRAVE MICHAEL"

THERE was a big gathering of neighbours sitting round a fire, telling stories of an evening, and some person says:

"There's the strongest bolt and lock in all Ireland on the door there beyond, and it couldn't be broken at all."

With that the Good People were listening outside began for to laugh. Didn't they whip the lock off the door and sway with them through the fields?

Says the man of the house: "I'm thinking there's danger abroad; let the lot of you stop here till dawn."

But there was a big, venturesome man in it and he allowed he'd go home no spite of the fairies.

He started off by his lone, and he had a wet sort of field to pass through with a great shaking scraw [1] to one side. It was an awful and dangerous place to any person not used to the like, but he knew his way by the pass.

He was travelling at a good speed when all on a sudden he heard the tramping of a score of horses behind him. Then they came up round himself, but he seen no person at all nor a sign of a horse, or an ass.

"The fairies are in it," says he.

With that one of them took a hold of him by the collar and turned him round on the path.

"Good night, my brave Michael," says the horsemen.

Then another of them took him by the shoulder and faced him away round again.

"Good night, my brave Michael," says he. Well the whole score of fairies kept turning him round until he seen the stars dropping down from the sky and his ears were deafened with a sound like the sea. And every one that took him by the shoulder would say: "Good night, my brave Michael, good night!"

---

[1] Bog.

The poor fellow didn't know what in under the shining Heaven was he to do. He seen they were setting him astray, but he couldn't continue for to keep on the path, and he was in odious dread they'd furl him into the shaking scraw where he'd sink from the sight of man.

A sudden thought struck his mind of a saying he heard from his ma. He whipped the coat off his back and he put it on with the wrong side turned out. And then he found he was standing alone in the field, on the edge of the scraw, and no person near him at all. So he went away home without any mishap, but indeed he was trembling with dread.

THE LAD AND THE OLD LASSIE'S SONG

THERE was a young lad living in these parts, not long since at all, and his name was Francis John.

It chanced of a May morning that water was scarce for the tea, the way his mother put a bucket in his hand and hunted him off to the spring.

Now an old lassie lived by her lone in a little wee house was built right close to the path. The door stood open that morning, and my brave Francis John looked in when he went on his way to the well. He seen the old girl sitting on a small creepy stool by the fire, with a row of clay images baking in front of the turf. Wasn't she singing a song—and a queer cracked voice was her own—every word of it came good and plain to the ears of the lad.

> Ye that I bake before the fire,
> Bring me the milk from my neighbour's byre;
> Gather the butter from off the churn
> And set it forenenst me before you burn.

Francis John didn't ask to disturb her diversions at all, so he went on his way and filled up his can at the spring. But all the road home the old lassie's song tormented his mind, and as he came in at the door he began for to sing:

> Ye that she bakes before the fire,
> Bring me the milk from the neighbour's byre;
> Gather the butter from off the churn
> And set it forenenst me before you burn.

With the power of the words coming from him didn't the boots on his feet fill up with sweet milk, and it running out on the lace holes.

"Man, but that's an enchanted song," says he. And what did he do only step into four pounds of butter that fell on the threshold before him, for he never remarked it at all!

THE BASKET OF EGGS

THERE was a woman one time, and she on her way to the market, counting the price of her basket of eggs.

"If eggs are up," says she, "I'll be gaining a handful of silver, and evenly if prices be down I'll not do too badly at all for I have a weighty supply."

With that she remarked a little wee boy sitting down by the hedge, he stitching away at a brogue.

"If I had a hold of yon lad," says she, "I'd make him discover a treasure—for the like of him knows where gold does be hid."

She juked up behind him, like a cat would be after a bird, and she caught a strong grip of his neck.

Well, he let an odious screech out of him, for he was horrid surprised.

"I have you, my gosoon," says she.

"Oh surely you have, mam," he answers. "The strength of your thumb is destroying my thrapple this day."

"Will you show me a treasure?" says she.

"I'd have you to know," he replies, "that the pot of gold I could convey you in sight of is guarded by the appearance of a very strange frog."

"What do I care for the creeping beasts of the world?" says she. "Worse nor a frog wouldn't scare me at all."

"You're a terrible fine woman, mistress dear," says the leprachaun. "I've travelled a power of the earth and I never came in with your equal."

"Go on with your old-fashioned chat," she replies, but she was middling well pleased all the same.

"I'm a small little fellow," says he, "and I couldn't keep up with yourself! But it's light in the body I am, the way I'd be never a burden at all and I sitting up on the handle of the basket."

"Up with you," she answers, "for I'll soon put you down to walk by my side if you are not speaking the truth."

But she didn't find the least burden more on the basket when himself was on the handle.

He was a great warrant to flatter, and he had her in humour that day all the while he was watching out for a chance to escape, but she kept a hold of his ear.

What did he do only put his two wee hands down into the basket and he began for to bail out the eggs. She fetched him a terrible clout, but the harder she beat him the faster he threw out the eggs.

"Oh mam! oh mam!" says he, "what for are you skelping my head?"

"To make you quit breaking my eggs, you unmannerly coley," says she.

"Sure it's doing you favour I am," he replies. "I'd have you to know when I spill an egg on the ground a well-grown spring chicken leps out."

"Quit raving," says she.

"If you doubt my word," he makes answer, "let you turn and look back at the chickens are flocking along."

With that she turned her head, and the leprachaun slipped from her grasp. He made one spring from the basket into the hedge, and he vanished away from the place.

"The wee lad has fooled me entirely," says she, "and my beautiful eggs are destroyed—but I am the finest woman he's seen, and that is a good thing to know!"

THE MONSTER OF BAYLOCK

IT is well known that the destiny and fate of the people of Ireland has at all times been different from the destiny and fate of all other peoples and nations in the world. For this reason not even the wisest of men could ever foretell what would happen in Ireland. Many a time they set themselves to reason out, and explain, the things that would come to pass. Yet for all their wisdom, and all their thought, it was always a different thing that happened from the thing they foretold. When they prophesied war there was peace, and when they prophesied peace, there was war. It was only the seers who have vision and foresight and knowledge that come, not through the seven senses, but by looking into empty space, who ever knew the things that must be, and it was few they found to believe their words. As it has been in the past so it must be to the end of time. It is known to them that have the understanding, that Ireland will never wait for fire and brimstone on the Last Day, but will be devoured, on the day before all other nations are delivered over to the everlasting flame, by a giant born of her own people.

The giant that is to devour Ireland has been born, and is in hiding, waiting and longing for the day before the final perdition, when he can gulp and swallow the whole country that is hiding him, alive, since ancient times.

The people in times past lived like they do now for the most part in the valleys and plains. On the sides of the mountains and in the hills it was only a few people there were, fighting for their living against the wild beasts and against the ferns and bushes that were at all times destroying their fields. It happened that there lived a man and his wife in a little rough cabin of a place, high up on the side of the Knockmealdowns. For many years they had no child and worked by themselves for their living in a place where the nearest neighhour was a mile away and where few had occasion to go unless hunting or getting fuel for their fires.

At last the woman had a son and the two of them had great rejoicings the day he was born. It happened a few days after that the woman of the house had left the baby snug in a box, that served for a cradle, and had gone out to milk the cow, before the man of the house came home from the woods. When she came back into the house she thought to herself that the baby looked queer. She went over to the box and, sure enough, you could see him growing. Before long he was too big to stay in the box and got out on the floor. He took a cake that was lying on the hearth and swallowed it, hot as it was, in one gulp. Not a word he said, but looked round the place for more to eat. The woman of the house had never heard of the queer fellow that was to devour Ireland on the day before the Last Day, but she knew by the way the lad was carrying on that he was not right. With the fright that seized her, the woman of the house let a shriek from the door. At most times there would have been no one to hear, but this day it happened that there was an old man passing, who used to wander by himself in the mountains, talking to himself and looking into the future, the way he would know the things that would happen to Ireland. When he heard the yell he came to the door and asked the woman was there anything astray. "Anything astray," says she. "Will you look at that lad that is after growing out of the cradle and eating the loaf?"

Hardly were the words out of her mouth before the child ran out of the house and killed and swallowed two whole bullocks before their eyes. "That must be the giant," said the old man, "who will gulp and swallow the whole of Ireland on the day before the final perdition. "If he can eat two bullocks at five days old, to swallow the country should be no trouble when he is grown to be a man." "Unless the right spell is put on that fella," said the old man, "he will have damage done before the day is out."

The old man began to say spells and incantations and to make charms and symbols of bits of straw he pulled from the roof. He fastened up charms in the house which had the power, as the queer lad soon found, to turn him from the door. When he tried to get into the house, the power of the charms and spells turned him back three times from the open door as if it was shut, and he began to take the steep path up the mountainside. The old man followed after him. All the time the lad was growing and by this time he had become a terrible monster. He was walking with heavy steps because of the spells that were upon him, but his mind was raging to devour the world. The great fury that was in him made his appearance terrible to see. The clap of his heart against his ribs could be heard like the yelp of a dog. There was a rain cloud of poison over his head. His hair bristled like a thorn bush in the gap of a hedge. If a bag of apples were shaken on his crown very few of them would have reached the ground for one would have stuck on every hair, so great was the anger that raised it on his head.

So it was he went up the path before the old man and the woman of the house, until he reached the mountain lake of Baylock. As they had been going up the path the wind was rising and black clouds had been gathering on the hills. When the monstrous giant reached the shore of the lake, a wild blast of wind shrieked through the hills. A wild, furious, dark, frightful, voracious, merciless vulture arose from the rocks, and fluttered screaming over the water. There arose also the idiots and maniacs of the valleys and the witches and the goblins and the ancient birds and the destroying demons of the air, and the feeble phantom host, and they screamed together with the great whirlwind that blew from the mountains. The old man and the woman hid themselves in the rocks, but the whirlwind caught the giant and carried him out into the middle of the lake. As he sunk, the wind fell, the water became calm and the silence of death hung over Baylock. Those who had no understanding, when they heard the story, believed that the monster was drowned and lost, never to return, but the like of him is never drowned. With the spells that are on him, and the nature of his fate, he must await his time in the bottom of Baylock.

Once in every year, as the shepherds in the mountains well know, the same wind blows through the Knockmealdowns and the demon hosts break loose and screech over the lake. When the monster hears that noise he puts up his head and says in a voice that shakes the rocks, "Is it the day before the Last Day yet?"

Sometime back they thought to bring water from the Baylock into the town of Cloheen. The pipes were brought and the men, with their picks and shovels, went up to start work on the shore of the lake. When the first man dug his pick in the ground, the ganger that was with them, shouted, "Look at Cloheen!" They all turned in time to see the town bursting into flames. They dropped their tools and ran down to put out the fire, but when they got back to the town, not a house had been alight. They knew by that, that the fairies had made the appearance of fire on the town, so that they should not draw off the waters of the lake that are covering the monster, who will devour the land, and let him loose on the country before the day before the destruction of the world.

ETAIN

YOCHAY was the High King of Ireland in the days long, long ago. He pleased his people in all things save one—he did not take a wife. This was not because he did not desire a queen, but because he longed for a maid more beautiful than any in the world. Soon he grew lonely and restless. No longer did he take delight in council, Court, or chase. Nothing now would please him but he must go in quest of a queen—a maid more beautiful than any in the world. The Spirit of Dreams warned Yochay that a mortal must pay a great, great price if he gained his heart's desire. But Yochay would not turn back. One night, therefore, in a peasant's lonely hut on the shores of the great grey sea Yochay took shelter from the storm, and there he saw Etain.

Her eyes were deep as a forest pool in moonlight, and wistful, because she did not understand how came she here on earth at all. Her lips were red as the sunset's heart; and in her dark braided hair, blue-glossy as a raven's wing, were entwined the pale berries of the mystic mistletoe. This should have warned Yochay, for no one save the high gods might wear the sacred berry, but he saw only the fear in her eyes and the love on her lips. Here was his queen—for Etain was more beautiful than any other in the world.

So they lived for the space of time that mortals call a year. Then appeared a stranger, asking if he might sing a little song to Yochay's fair queen.

She laid aside her courtly robes of gold, and in her little sea-green dress, with the mystic mistletoe twined in her long dark hair, she came to hear the stranger's song. Yochay sat amazed. He could not move or speak as he watched the glad light wake in Etain's face. She moved with outstretched hands toward the kingly singer; as he sang the stranger drew backward out of the great hall toward the setting sun, Etain following with parted lips and glad eyes. For this was Midir, King of the Land of Youth, the Land of Heart's Desire, come to claim his queen Etain. He had missed her but an hour.

Yochay sat on his lonely throne as the song died away. To him it sounded as cruel, mocking laughter, for he had lost his heart's desire. No, not quite lost, for there was left his little daughter. Her name too was Etain. Her eyes were deep as a forest pool. Her lips were red as the sunset's heart. Her long dark hair was blue-glossy as a raven's wing. But never did she braid in it the pale berries of the mystic mistletoe.

CHINA

THE Chinese tales are somewhat lacking in the sparkle and vivacity which gives such charm to the folk-stories of other races. They are often fantastic and deal largely in magic. Yet there is much in them that is monotonous and mediocre. In Chinese literature there is no counterpart of the sagas and eddas of the North, and there is nothing of the grand manner about the telling of the Chinese stories. The benefits which the Chinese have derived from their ancient culture seem, to a large extent, to have been neutralized by the fact that for so many centuries they lived in isolation. The result is seen in a certain restriction of the imaginative powers and a lack of constructive ability.

THE TALKING BIRD

THERE was a man who had a pet bird, very like a starling, which he taught to talk; and the bird was in the habit of travelling about with him all over the country as his companion. This went on for some years, until once he found himself far away from home with all his money spent and without means of getting home. He was in a great state of perplexity, when suddenly the bird said to him, "Why not sell me? Try to get me into the prince's palace; I ought to fetch a good sum, and then you will have enough to get home with." To this the man said, "My dear bird, I couldn't do it; I couldn't bear to part with you." "Never mind that," said the bird. "Wait for me under the big tree a little way out of the city." So he took the bird along, chattering together as they went, until he was seen by a servant of the palace, who promptly reported to the prince. The prince at once sent for the man and offered to buy the bird; but the man said that he and the bird were leading their lives together and could not possibly be parted. Then the prince turned to the bird and said, "Would you like to live here?" "Very much indeed," replied the bird; "give my master ten ounces of silver for me, not more."

The prince was delighted with the bird, and immediately gave orders for the ten ounces to be weighed out and given to the man, who went away grumbling at his bad luck. The prince had a long conversation with the bird, and by and by sent for some meat for it to eat. After this, the bird said, "Please, your Highness, may I have a bath?" At this the prince told his servants to bring water in a golden bowl, and he opened the cage door for the bird to come out. The bird splashed about in the bath; and when it had finished, flew up and perched on the eaves of the palace, where it shook itself and smoothed its feathers, talking all the time to the prince. When it was quite dry it suddenly said, "Good-bye, your Highness; I'm off!" And in half a moment the bird was out of sight. The prince was very angry, and

227

immediately sent out to call the man back; but he had disappeared. Later on some people saw the man and the bird back again in their own old house.

THE WONDERFUL PEAR-TREE

ONCE upon a time a countryman came into the town on market-day, and brought a load of very special pears with him to sell. He set up his barrow in a good corner, and soon had a great crowd round him; for every one knew he always sold extra fine pears, though he did also ask an extra high price. Now, while he was crying up his fruit, a poor, old, ragged, hungry-looking priest stopped just in front of the barrow, and very humbly begged him to give him one of the pears. But the countryman, who was very mean and very nasty-tempered, wouldn't hear of giving him any, and as the priest didn't seem inclined to move on, he began calling him all the bad names he could think of. "Good sir," said the priest, "you have got hundreds of pears on your barrow. I only ask you for one. You would never even know you had lost one. Really, you needn't get angry."

"Give him a pear that is going bad; that will make him happy," said one of the crowd. "The old man is quite right; you'd never miss it."

"I've said I won't, and I won't!" cried the countryman; and all the people close by began shouting, first one thing, and then another, until the constable of the market, hearing the hubbub, hurried up; and when he had made out what was the matter, pulled some *cash* out of his purse, bought a pear, and gave it to the priest. For he was afraid that the noise would come to the ears of the mandarin who was just being carried down the street.

The old priest took the pear with a low bow, and held it up in front of the crowd, saying, "You all know that I have no home, no parents, no children, no clothes of my own, no food, because I gave up everything when I became a priest. So it puzzles me how any one can be so selfish and so stingy as to refuse to give me one single pear. Now I am quite a different sort of man from this countryman. I have got here some perfectly exquisite pears, and I shall feel most deeply honoured if you will accept them from me."

"Why on earth didn't you eat them yourself, instead of begging for one?" asked a man in the crowd.

"Ah," answered the priest, "I must grow them first"

So he ate up the pear, only leaving a single pip. Then he took a pick which was fastened across his back, dug a deep hole in the ground at his feet, and planted the pip, which he covered all over with earth. "Will some one fetch me some hot water to water this?" he asked. The people, who were crowding round, thought he was only joking, but one of them ran and fetched a kettle of boiling water and gave it to the priest, who very carefully poured it over the place where he had sowed the pip. Then, almost while he was pouring, they saw, first a tiny green sprout, and then another, come pushing their heads above the ground; then one leaf uncurled, and then another, while the shoots kept growing taller and taller; then there stood before them a young tree with a few branches with a few leaves; then more leaves; then flowers; and last of all clusters of huge, ripe, sweet-smelling pears weighing the branches down to the ground! Now the priest's face shone with pleasure, and the crowd roared with delight when he picked the pears one by one until they were all gone, handing them round with a bow to each man present. Then the old man took the pick again, hacked at the tree until it fell with a crash, when he shouldered it, leaves and all, and with a final bow, walked away.

All the time this had been going on, the countryman, quite forgetting his barrow and pears, had been in the midst of the crowd, standing on the tips of his toes, and straining his eyes to try to make out what was happening. But when the old priest had gone, and the crowd was getting thin, he turned round to his barrow, and saw with horror that it was quite empty. Every single pear had gone! In a moment he understood what had happened. The pears the old priest had been so generous in giving away were not his own; they were the countryman's! What was more, one of the handles of his barrow was missing, and there was no doubt that he had started from home with two! He was in a towering rage, and rushed as hard as he could after the priest; but just as he turned the corner he saw, lying close to the wall, the barrow-handle itself, which without any doubt was the very pear-tree which the priest had cut down. All the people in the market were simply splitting their sides with laughter; but as for the priest, no one saw him any more.

THE COUNTRY OF GENTLEMEN

MORE than a thousand years ago there lived an Empress of China, who was a very bold and obstinate woman. She thought she was powerful enough to do anything. One day, she even gave orders that every kind of flower throughout the country was to be out in full bloom on a certain day. Being a woman herself, she thought that women would govern the empire much better than men; so she actually had examinations for women and gave them all the important posts. This made a great many men extremely angry; especially a young man named Tang, who was very clever and had taken many prizes. He said he couldn't live in such a country any more; and sailed away with an uncle of his and another friend, on a long voyage to distant parts of the world. They visited many extraordinary nations, in one of which the people all had heads of dogs; in another, they flew about like birds; in another, they had enormously long arms with which they reached down into the water to catch fish. Then there was the country of tall men, where everybody was about twenty feet in height; the country of dwarfs, where the people were only one foot in height, and their funny little children were not more than four inches. In another place, the people all had large holes in the middle of their bodies; and rich persons were carried about by servants who pushed long sticks through the holes. After a time, they came to a land which they were told was the Country of Gentlemen. They went ashore, and walked up to the capital. There they found the people buying and selling, and strange to say they were all talking the Chinese language. They also noticed that everybody was very polite, and the foot-passengers in the streets were very careful to step aside and make room for one another. In the market-place they saw a man who was buying things at a shop. Holding the things in his hand, the man was saying to the shopkeeper, "My dear sir, I really cannot take these excellent goods at the absurdly low price you are asking. If you will oblige me by doubling the amount, I shall do myself the honour of buying them; otherwise I shall know for certain that you do not wish to do business with me to-day." The shopkeeper replied, "Excuse me, sir, I am already very much ashamed at having asked you so much for these goods; they really are not worth more than half. If you insist upon paying such a high price, I must really beg you, with all possible respect, to go and buy in some other shop." At this, the man who wanted to buy got rather angry, and said that trade could not be carried on at all if all the profit was on one side and all the loss on the other, adding that the shopkeeper was not going to catch him in a trap like that. After a lot more talk, he put down the full price on the counter, but only took half the things. Of course the shopkeeper would not agree to this, and they would have gone on arguing forever had not two old gentlemen who happened to be passing stepped aside and arranged the matter for them by deciding that the purchaser was to pay the full price but only to receive three-quarters of the goods. Tang heard this sort of thing going on at every shop he passed. It was always the buyer who wanted to give as much as possible, and the seller to take as little.

In one case a shopkeeper called after a customer who was hurrying away with the goods he had bought and said, "Sir, sir, you have paid me too much, you have paid me too much." "Pray don't mention it," replied the customer, "but oblige me by keeping the money for another day when I come again to buy some of your excellent goods." "No, no," answered the shopkeeper; "you don't catch old birds with chaff; that trick was played on me last year by a gentleman who left some money with me, and to this day I have never set eyes on him again, though I have tried all I can to find out where he lives."

But soon they had to say good-bye to this wonderful country and started once more upon their voyage. They next came to a very strange land where the people did not walk, but moved about upon small clouds of different colours, about half a foot from the ground. Meeting with an old priest, who seemed rather a queer man, Tang asked him to be kind enough to explain the meaning of the little clouds upon which the people rode. "Ah, sir," said the priest, "these clouds show what sort of a heart is inside the persons who are riding on them. People can't choose their own colours; clouds striped like a rainbow are the best; yellow are the second best, and black are the worst of all."

Thanking the old man, they passed on and among those who were riding on clouds of green, red, blue and other colours, they saw a dirty beggar riding on a striped cloud. They were much astonished at this because the old priest had told them that the striped cloud was the best. "I see why that was," said Tang, "the old rascal had a striped cloud himself." Just then the people in the street began to fall back, leaving a passage in the middle; and by and by they saw a very grand officer pass along in great state with a long procession of servants carrying red umbrellas, gongs, and other things. They tried to see what colour his cloud was, but to their disappointment it was covered up with a curtain of red silk.

"Oho!" said Tang, "this gentleman has evidently got such a bad colour for his cloud that he is ashamed to let it be seen. I wish we had clouds like these in our country so that we could tell good people from bad by just looking at them. I don't think there would be so many wicked people about then."

Soon after this, news reached them that the Empress who had been so troublesome in their own country had been obliged to give up the throne. So they went no further on their travels but turned their ship round toward home, where their families were very glad to see them again.

THE MAGIC PILLOW

ONE day, an old priest stopped at a wayside inn to rest, spread out his mat, and sat down with his bag. Soon afterward, a young fellow of the neighbourhood also arrived at the inn; he was a farm-labourer and wore short clothes, not a long robe like the priest and men who read books. He took a seat near to the priest and the two were soon laughing and talking together. By and by, the young man cast a glance at his own rough dress and said with a sigh, "See, what a miserable wretch I am." "You seem to me well fed and healthy enough," replied the priest; "why in the middle of our pleasant chat do you suddenly complain of being a miserable wretch?" "What pleasure can I find," retorted the young man, "in this life of mine, working every day as I do from early morn to late at night? I should like to be a great general and win battles, or to be a rich man and have fine food and wine, and listen to good music, or to be a great man at court and help our Emperor and bring prosperity to my family;—that is what I call pleasure. I want to rise in the world, but here I am a poor farm-labourer; if you don't call that miserable wretchedness, what is it?" He then began to get sleepy, and while the landlord was cooking a dish of millet-porridge, the priest took a pillow out of his bag and said to the young man, "Lay your head on this and all your wishes will be granted."

The pillow was made of porcelain; it was round like a tube, and open at each end. When the young man put his head down toward the pillow, one of the openings seemed so large and bright inside that he got in, and soon found himself at his own home.

Shortly afterward he married a beautiful girl, and began to make money. He now wore fine clothes and spent his time in study. In the following year he passed his examination and was made a magistrate; and in two or three years he had risen to be Prime Minister. For a long time the Emperor trusted him in everything, but the day came when he got into trouble; he was accused of treason and sentenced to death. He was taken with several other criminals to the place of execution; he was made to kneel on both knees, and the executioner approached with his sword. Too terrified to feel the blow, he opened his eyes, to find himself in the inn. There was the priest with his head on his bag; and there was the landlord still stirring the porridge, which was not quite ready. After eating his meal in silence, he got up and bowing to the priest, said, "I thank you, sir, for the lesson you have taught me; I know now what it means to be a great man!" With that, he took his leave and went back to his work.

THE STONE MONKEY

LONG, long ago, on the top of a mountain called the Flower-and-Fruit Mountain, there lay all by itself a queer-shaped stone egg. No one knew what bird had laid it, or how it had got there; no one ever saw it, for there was nobody there to see. The egg lay all by itself on some green grass, until one day it split with a crack, and out came a stone monkey, a monkey whose body was of shining polished stone. Before long, this wonderful stone monkey was surrounded by a crowd of other monkeys, chattering to one another as hard as they could. By and by they seemed to have settled something in their minds, and one of them came forward and asked the stone monkey to be their king. This post he accepted at once, having indeed already thrown out hints that he thought himself quite fit to rule over them.

Soon after this, he determined to travel in search of wisdom, and to see the world. He went down the mountain, until he came to the sea-shore, where he made himself a raft, and sailed away.

Reaching the other side of the great ocean, he found his way to the abode of a famous magician, and persuaded the magician to teach him all kinds of magical tricks. He learned to make himself invisible, to fly up into the sky, and to jump many miles at a single jump. At last he began to think himself better and stronger than anybody else, and determined to make himself Lord of the Sky.

.   .   .   .   .   .

"Have you heard of the new king of the monkeys?" said the Dragon prince to the Lord Buddha one day, as they were sitting together in the palace of the sky. "No," answered the Lord Buddha. "What is there to hear about him?" "He has been doing a lot of mischief," replied the Dragon prince. "He has learnt all kinds of magical tricks, and knows more than anybody else in the whole world. He now means to turn the Lord of the Sky out of his place, and be Lord of the Sky himself. I promised I would ask you to help us against this impudent stone monkey. If you will be good enough to do so, I feel sure we should conquer him."

The Lord Buddha promised to do his best, and the two went together to the cloud palace of the Lord of the Sky, where they found the stone monkey misbehaving himself, and insulting everybody who dared to interfere with him. The Lord Buddha stepped forward, and in a quiet voice said to him, "What do you want?" "I want," answered the stone monkey, "to be Lord of the Sky. I could manage things much better than they are managed now. See how I can jump!" Then the stone monkey jumped a big jump. In a moment he was out of sight, and in another moment he was back again.

"Can you do that?" he asked the Lord Buddha; at which the Lord Buddha only smiled and said, "I will make a bargain with you. You shall come outside the palace with me and stand upon my hand. Then, if you can jump out of my hand, you shall be Lord of the Sky, as you wish to be; but if you cannot jump out of my hand, you shall be sent down to earth, and never be allowed to come up to the sky any more." The stone monkey laughed loudly when he heard this, and said, "Jump out of your hand, Lord Buddha! Why, of course I can easily do that."

So they went outside the palace, and the Lord Buddha put down his hand, and the stone monkey stepped on to it. He then gave one great jump, and again he was away far out of sight. On and on he went in his jump, until he came to the end of the earth. There he stopped; and while he was chuckling to himself that he would soon be Lord of the Sky, he caught sight of five great red pillars standing on the very edge with nothing but empty space beyond; and now he thought he would leave a mark to show how far he had really jumped. So he scratched a mark on one of the pillars, meaning to bring the Lord Buddha there to see it for himself. When he had done this, he took another big jump, and in the twinkling of an eye he was back again in the Lord Buddha's hand. "When are you going to begin to jump?" the Lord Buddha asked, as the monkey stepped down on to the ground.

"When!" cried the monkey sarcastically. "Why, I have jumped—jumped to the very end of the earth. If you want to know how far I have been, you have only to get on my back, and I'll take you there to see. There are five red pillars there, and I've left a mark on one of them." "Look here, monkey," the Lord Buddha said, holding out his hand; "look at this." The stone monkey looked. On one of the fingers of the Lord Buddha's hand there was the very mark which he himself had made on the red pillar. "You see," said the Lord Buddha; "the whole world lies in my hand. You could never have jumped out of it. When you jumped and thought you were out of sight, my hand was under you all the time. No one, not even a stone monkey, can ever get beyond my reach. Now go down to earth, and learn to keep in your proper place."

THE BOY WHO BECAME EMPEROR

FAR away in the hill country of China once lived a boy named Yu Shin, with his father, mother, and younger brother. Yu Shin was a good boy, but for some strange reason his parents mistreated him sadly. It was to the younger child, a spoiled and sickly lad, that they gave all their favours, while poor Yu Shin was lucky if he got through a single day without a beating.

The boy would have run away from such a cruel home, but for the advice of his teacher, a wise old man who taught the precepts of Confucius which command all Chinese boys and girls, no matter what happens, to love and obey their parents. So Yu Shin came to believe that all parents were harsh to their older children, and that a big boy like himself must learn to take all these beatings without a murmur. Whenever he saw a boy whose father treated him kindly, he thought the man peculiar, and his eyes would follow him with wonder and doubt.

One day, it is true, in early childhood, after an unusually hard beating given for no offence whatever, except that he was present when his father was angry, Yu Shin ran to the white-haired master whom he considered his best friend and, pouring the story into his ears, asked him why men treated their sons in such a cruel fashion.

"My dear boy," exclaimed the elder sadly, stroking the child with his wrinkled hand, "the question you ask is as old as this old world itself. Ever since man was first created there has been evil in his heart. Not all men are like your father, but, alas! too many lay the hand of hate upon the innocent and weak. My son, resolve to live in such a manner that, some day, if your father is still living, he will be ashamed to think of how he acted. Resolve to rise to such a level that you will be far above all the petty trials you are now enduring."

"But my younger brother," urged Yu Shin, "why should they treat him differently from me? He disobeys them every day, runs away from home, refuses to work when they set him a task, and you know well his record here at school; yet they favour him as if he were a god and I a beggar."

"Alas! my boy, too true. It is well known that while merit is frequently a slow horse, in the end it always wins the race. At first the wicked may be as fleet as the wind, but they are sure to stumble, they are sure to fall. Cheer up, do not let your heart be envious of your brother. Mark my words, he will die unknown, while you—there is no telling what you may accomplish, no limit to the station to which you may sometime rise."

Yu Shin left his master much comforted. He resolved, no matter what befell, to bear it like a man.

Strange to say, on the very night after he had made this resolution he overheard his father and mother plotting some evil against him.

"The boy is a curse to my sight," complained the mother. "I can endure him no longer."

"Nor I," answered his father roughly; "he's not for such a family as ours. To-morrow let us make away with him."

"Why not sell him to the travelling players?" suggested the mother. "Might as well get a little money while we are about the business."

"That would be all right, if we were sure he would not escape and turn up when we least expect it. No, we'd better make sure of it."

After that, try as he would, Yu Shin could make out nothing of their plans. Trembling with fear, he lay on his hard bed thinking over the dreadful words that had been spoken. He tried to think of some plan for escaping on the morrow. Was there not some power which would protect him? There in his bed he breathed forth his petitions to the gods for help. Then he fell into a sweet slumber, and in his sleep he had a dream in which a fairy floated above his couch, touching him lightly upon the brow and saying, "Yu Shin, Yu Shin, be not afraid; your heart is good, and you need never fear."

In the morning the boy awoke and went about his duties, calm and unafraid. Presently his father ordered him to go after a tool which had fallen into an abandoned well, long since gone dry.

Although fearful that this command had some connection with the plot against him, without a moment's hesitation Yu Shin slid down a rope, after fastening it securely about the trunk of a tree. No sooner had he arrived at the bottom of the well than he heard a taunting voice above, and, looking up, saw that his brother was pulling up the rope. A moment later the lad in the pit was horrified to see a millstone tumbling down upon him. He had no time to think of escape, even had this been possible. Closing his eyes, he awaited the blow which he knew would crush him to the earth.

Just then he heard a voice speaking, "Yu Shin, have no fear. Gaze upward and behold."

He looked, and was astonished to find that the round white stone had been changed suddenly into a fairy, who floated over him with outstretched arms, saying, "Put your hands in mine, and all is well."

Yu Shin did not wait to be told twice. No sooner had he touched the fairy's hands than he was whisked to the mouth of the well, in time to see his brother, who had been too much frightened to linger, dashing into the cottage. Full of gratitude toward his deliverer, he turned to thank him, but saw instead the stone lying where it formerly had, by the mouth of the well; but on the top of it was a beautiful white flower. Picking this up, he found these words written upon the petals:

HAVE COURAGE

The rope was lying in a heap upon the ground where his brother had left it. Gathering this up, Yu Shin started for the house. As he entered, he heard his father laughing at the younger son for being so frightened, while the mother was dishing out millet into bowls for their dinner.

"The pick was not in the well, father," said Yu Shin, calmly, laying the rope in one corner of the room as if nothing unusual had happened, and taking his place at the table.

"And did you see nothing there?" asked his brother, trembling and gazing blankly at him.

"Nothing but the worn-out millstone we used to sit on," he replied. "I thought you might want it, so I left it lying by the well."

Now, although Yu Shin did not tell his father that he had lifted the great stone from the bottom of the pit, the latter believed this to be true, and thought his son must have been aided by some demon. More than ever was he determined to kill him. He could not afford to have a son who was stronger than he; there was no telling when the boy would rebel against him. But he said nothing to Yu Shin of his evil thoughts. On the contrary, he spoke more civilly than was his wont, thinking in this manner to deceive the boy.

For some days Yu Shin was allowed to go about his daily tasks. He felt sure that he had nothing further to fear from his younger brother, as the latter, being a coward, henceforth would be afraid to injure him. He knew, however, that his parents were still plotting against him, for although they now spoke smoothly enough, they scarcely gave him time to rest, day or night. One day he had toiled hard since early morning in an outhouse cutting straw. It was extremely hot, and he was compelled to rest now and then from his labour. During one of these moments, he sank down upon the straw, and went sound asleep.

Awaking with a start, he found the whole interior of the building one mass of flames. The passage to the only door was entirely blocked by fire, and as there was no other outlet he came near giving up all as lost. His father and his brother, he well knew, would make no effort to rescue him. In fact he felt sure that they had started the fire. But one thought came to comfort him, the fairy's words, "Have courage." At the very instant when the flames seemed ready to seize him, a voice spoke to him, saying, "Lie down, Yu Shin, the fire shall harm you not." Sinking to the ground, he found with amazement that, although the air a few feet from him was scorching, the space wherein he lay was cool as if a March breeze were fanning him. Again the voice addressed him:"Sleep on, Yu Shin, and fear not."

Calmly he closed his eyes, and in the midst of that fiery furnace fell asleep.

On awaking, he beheld his father and his brother standing over him, awestruck when they saw that he was still alive.

"Why, what's happened, father?" he said coolly. "Has there been a fire? I dreamed I was lying on the seashore fanned by the waves of the ocean."

Father and brother looked at him in amazement. Clearly this boy was of a different clay from that of which they were constructed; clearly the gods held him as in the hollow of their hands. So they gave over their plots to kill him.

On the morrow the father called his son before him, and said: "This place is much too small for us all to live upon comfortably. You are now old enough to take a wife and have a home of your own. Now, I want you to go over and take charge of some property I own on the edge of the mountain. Cultivate it and get all you can out of it. I'll give you a deed to the place, and what you make is yours. It will be much better for you than to remain at home."

Although Yu Shin knew that this farm was the stoniest, most worthless piece of ground in all the Middle Kingdom, he agreed to go at once. He knew that his father, in sending him there, believed it impossible for him to make a living, and thought that he would thus get rid of him easily; while the younger brother would receive the main property worth a hundred times more.

The next day, after bidding his parents and brother farewell, and without one word of complaint at this unjust treatment, Yu Shin set out for his new home. Arriving there, he found the place even worse than he had imagined. Twenty men working night and day could not clear the ground of its stones, roots and stumps to make it yield a crop large enough for one man's support. Yu Shin saw this plainly, but went resolutely to work, while he sent a silent prayer to his good fairy to aid him. All at once he saw a cloud of dust in the distance and a black shadow forming overhead. Nearer and nearer came the dust-cloud; closer and closer hovered the shadow, until at last he saw to his amazement a herd of elephants approaching, and above, a flock of magpies. Then he heard a voice speaking in his ear, "Behold, the beasts of the field and the birds of the air are at your beck and call. Command, and they will serve you; lead, and they will follow."

Yu Shin thanked the fairy and went into the fields attended by his host of helpers. Under his direction the elephants tore up huge rocks from their lodgment and piled them along the boundary lines to form a wall. Patiently they rooted up the stumps, clearing the field completely. In the meantime the busy magpies, not to be outdone, tore from the soil every vestige of small root and weed and ended by breaking up the clods with their beaks. So unceasing was their activity that within the short space of an hour the entire farm, which before would not have produced food enough to support one able-bodied man, had been converted into an immense ploughed field of excellent quality, with sufficient cleared land to make its owner prosperous.

When the elephants and the magpies had completed their labour, the big beasts marched slowly by Yu Shin in single file, with heads lowered in reply to his hearty thanks, till they had passed out of sight; while the birds, after circling thrice about his head, disappeared as quickly as they had come.

Offering up a prayer of thanksgiving, Yu Shin turned to enter his humble cottage, when lo and behold, he saw that it too had been transformed, and was now a handsome dwelling! Just as he was passing through the door, he looked toward the front of the field and was surprised to see nine sturdy youths walking up the pathway, followed by a beautiful maiden riding. When these newcomers had reached the entrance, they knelt before Yu Shin, touching their foreheads to the ground.

"Arise," said the young man, filled with wonder; "I am no man of rank that you should treat me thus."

"Oh, mighty one," said the oldest of the men, advancing, "we pray you to accept our services. Your fields need cultivating and your walls must be repaired. Command us, and we shall do your bidding."

Too much surprised even to question them, Yu Shin bade his guests enter the new dwelling, and there he feasted them right nobly with what he found spread out in readiness upon the tables.

On the following day he took the maiden to be his wife, while to each of the nine assistants he assigned his place and station; and for many moons thereafter this happy household lived together in harmony and concord, ruled by the wisdom and kindness of Yu Shin. The fame of his wonderful farm and great crops soon, spread abroad, and everybody was rejoiced at his prosperity, except his parents and brother. You could hardly imagine their amazement and chagrin, but they dared not lift another finger against him. One day a retinue of soldiers approached the dwelling and asked for the master of the estate. Yu Shin made himself known, and the leader of the company presented him a summons from the august Emperor of China to appear at once before the Dragon Throne.

Knowing nothing of what was about to happen, and yet without a tremor in his heart, Yu Shin obeyed the command. Accompanied by his wife and nine servants, he followed the soldiers, who gave him much honour, treating him at all times as though he were a king instead of a simple farmer.

Eleven days and nights they travelled, and on the twelfth day his faithful followers pointed out to him in the distance the walls of the Imperial City. Now, for the first time, Yu Shin began to tremble, in spite of the knowledge that he was innocent of evil.

Then within him once more spoke the fairy, "Let your heart be at peace, Yu Shin. All is well."

With a firm step he approached the palace, entered its sacred courts, and at last arrived in the presence of the Emperor himself. Then he pressed his head to the ground before the throne, while the nine retainers, also on their knees, ranged themselves behind him in a semicircle.

"Yu Shin," said the monarch, addressing him by name, "here into the imperial presence we have summoned you that we may confer the highest honour in our keeping. Throughout the trials of your childhood our royal eyes have been upon you. Your wise old teacher was one of my ministers, sent out to find a son who could be wise, obedient, and industrious. Just as the fairies sent the beasts of the fields and the birds of the air to aid you, we, as a test, bestowed our nine sons and daughter to your keeping. You have ruled your household with a hand so skilful, with a mind so full of wisdom, with a heart so swayed by love, that one and all have sung your praises and concurred with us in our august decision.

"Know that we the ruler of the Ancient Kingdom have grown so old in years that cares of state rest heavily upon us. Therefore rise up, Yu Shin, to the Dragon Throne, for upon your head we choose to place the crown of this imperial domain. May you, who have ruled your past life so nobly, rule this country no less wisely and well."

And thus did Yu Shin, the farmer's son, win the fame his teacher promised, and thus did his name become "worthy of being handed down through myriads of ages," among the greatest rulers of China.

DENMARK

D ANISH tales are bold and outspoken. The humour is of the broad and spontaneous kind—very different from the more insidious wit which is the product of a cultured mind. The people, as revealed in these stories, are hearty, simple souls, headstrong and uncouth at times, but always intensely human. The general view of human nature which they take is good and kindly. In the midst of difficulty and danger there is always the idea of making the best of everything. We see a great homeliness and a love of domesticity existing side by side with the ravages of dragons, imps, and Old Eric. In plot many of these tales have counterparts in the folk-lore of other European nations, and the frequent transformation of men into beasts is a striking feature.

VIRTUE ITS OWN REWARD

T HERE was once a man who went to the forest for firewood. He walked about a long time and looked at one tree after the other, but they were all too good for his purpose; they would make fine timber if they were allowed to grow. At last he found a tree which was more suitable, as it was crooked and withered, and he began to cut it down.

Then he heard some one saying to him: "Help me, good friend, and set me free!" He looked to find out who it might be, and he saw a large viper tightly wedged in a crevice of the tree and unable to free itself. "No, I will not help you," said the man; "you would be sure to sting me." The viper replied that it would not hurt him, if he would only set it free, so the man slipped his axe very carefully into the crevice below the viper, so that it could get out. But no sooner was it at liberty than it curled itself up, showed its poisoned fangs, and threatened to sting him.

"Did I not tell you," said the man, "that you were an evil creature, and would repay good, with evil !" "Oh," answered the viper, "it is all very well for you to talk, but is it not the way of the world, that good deeds are ill requited?" "I don't believe that," said the man; "good deeds reap their own reward." "You are wrong there," said the viper; "I know better what happens in the world." "Let us ask somebody else," suggested the man. "Oh, very well!" replied the viper, and, as it would not leave him, the man had to go through the forest with it, until they met a worn-out old horse grazing in a meadow. It was quite lame and its back was sore from the hard saddle; in one eye it was blind, and there were hardly any teeth left in its mouth.

To this animal they put the question, whether good deeds were well rewarded in this world or not. "They are indeed very badly rewarded," said the horse. "I have served my master faithfully for twenty years, carried him on my back and drawn his carriage, have carefully watched every step so that I might not stumble and cause him injury. So long as was I young and strong I had a good time, was well fed and watered and groomed, had a comfortable stable, and always clean straw; but now that I have grown old and weak, I work in the treadmill, and am left out here day and night in all sorts of weather and get no food but what I can find for myself. No, no, good deeds are very ill requited." "Did I not tell you so?" said the viper, "and now I will sting you." "Oh! no," said the man, "do wait another moment; here comes old Reynard the fox; let us ask his opinion." Reynard came trotting along, stopped and looked at them; he could see quite well that the man was in a bad fix. Then the viper asked him whether it was a fact that good deeds were badly rewarded, or whether he thought that they were sometimes well rewarded. "Say well!" whispered the man, "and I will give you two fat geese." The viper did not hear what the man had said, but the fox did, and he replied: "Good deeds are well rewarded," and at the same moment he leaped at the viper and bit it in the neck so that it fell to the ground. But before dying it had time to say: "No; good deeds are ill requited. I have just had proof of that, for I have spared the man's life and lost my own."

Now the viper was dead and the man was free. He said to the fox: "Come home with me and get your geese." "No, thank you," said Reynard, "I am not going to the village, because you would set your dogs at me." "Very well, then, wait here until I bring them to you!" said the man, and he ran home to his wife and said to her hastily: "Be quick, wife, and put two fat geese into a sack; I have promised them to Reynard for his breakfast." The wife did take a sack and put something into it. It was not geese, however, but two fierce little terriers. Then the man ran with the sack to the fox and said: "Here is the reward that I promised you." "Thanks," said the fox, "I did speak the truth, after all, when I said that good deeds are well rewarded." Saying this, he took the sack on his back and ran off to his lair. "These geese are really heavy," said the fox, as he sat down and bit through the string of the sack with his sharp teeth, and prepared to enjoy his meal. At that moment the two dogs darted out of the sack and leaped at his throat, and as he could not shake them off they worried him to death. Before he died he had just time to say: "It was a lie, after all, for good deeds are indeed ill requited."

OLAF THE MERMAID'S SON

IN Furreby, on the Skager Rack, there lived once upon a time a blacksmith, called Rasmus Natzen. He was a young man, and a handsome strong fellow into the bargain, but he had married quite early and had a number of young children, and as there was not much trade in the place, he made but a scant living.

He was industrious and hardworking and when there was nothing to do in the smithy he would go out fishing or would pick up wreckage on the seashore.

Now it once happened that he had set out all by himself, in his little boat, to fish for cod. He did not return that night or the next day, and everybody thought that he had perished at sea. But on the third day Rasmus landed again with his boat full of fish, larger and finer than had ever been seen before, and he himself was quite well, complaining neither of hunger nor of thirst. He explained that he had suddenly found himself in a thick mist and had lost his bearings, but he did not say where he had been during his absence; that only came to light six years afterward. Then it was discovered that when he was far out at sea he had been caught by a mermaid and had been her guest for some days. After that he never went fishing again, nor did he need to do so, for the sea offered him rich booty in the shape of all kinds of wreckage. Many valuable things came to his hand, and as in those days everybody was allowed to keep what he found, the blacksmith soon became a well-to-do man.

When seven years had gone by since his last voyage, there came one morning to Rasmus, when he was in his smithy repairing a plough, a handsome young lad who said, "Good morning, Father! My mother the Mermaid sends greetings to you. She said, as she had kept me for six years, you could now look after me in your turn for the next six." This stranger was a queer lad, more like a boy of eighteen than of six, and he was much bigger and stronger even than ordinary boys of that age. "Are you hungry?" asked the smith, and when Olaf, for that was the boy's name, said "Yes," the smith asked his wife to cut a slice of bread for the lad. She did so, and the boy put it into his mouth all at once and went back to his father, who asked him whether he had been given enough to eat. "No," said Olaf, "I had only a bite." So his father went indoors, took a whole loaf of bread, cut it through lengthways, put butter and cheese on each half and handed it to the boy. Olaf came back to the smithy in a short time, and his father asked him whether he had eaten enough now. "No," said the boy, "I am not half satisfied yet; I think I had better look out for another place where they will feed me more generously, for I can see I shall never get my hunger satisfied here."

He meant to start at once, as soon as his father had made him a good stick of iron to lean upon; it would have to be strong, to last him for some time. The smith handed him a rod of iron as thick as an ordinary walking-stick, but Olaf twisted it round his finger; it was no good. Then the smith dragged along another rod, as thick as the pole of a farm waggon, but when Olaf bent it across his knee, it broke like a reed, and so the smith had to take all the iron he had in his smithy and weld it together into a huge bar. Olaf held it while his father forged out of it a cudgel that was heavier than the anvil. Then Olaf lifted the cudgel and thanked his father for his trouble. "Now, I will start, father! I have got my inheritance from you";

and saying this he stepped out into the country. The smith was heartily glad to be rid of this boy who would have eaten him out of house and home.

Olaf found his way to a large farm, and it so happened that the farmer himself was standing outside. "Where are you going?" he asked Olaf. "I am looking for a place where they need strong men and give them plenty to eat," replied Olaf. "Well," said the farmer, "I usually employ twenty-four men at this season of the year, but I have only twelve, so that I can give you work." "You may risk that," replied Olaf, "for I can easily do the work of twelve men, if you will give me as much food as they would eat." The farmer agreed to that and took Olaf into the kitchen, where he told the servants that the new farm hand was to have as much to eat as the other twelve men together.

It was toward evening when Olaf arrived at the farm, so he had no work to do that day, and when he had finished his supper, which consisted of a huge pot of porridge, he felt fairly satisfied and went to bed. He slept well and long, and when the other labourers were already at their work Olaf was still sleeping like a sack of flour. The farmer was also about and he was anxious to learn how the new servant was getting on. As he could not see him anywhere he went into the men's sleeping-room and called out: "Get up, Olaf! You have overslept yourself." Olaf woke up and rubbed his eyes, saying: "Why, so I have! I must get up and eat my breakfast." Then he dressed and went into the kitchen, where he ate a huge cauldron of soup, and then inquired about his work.

It happened to be threshing day, and the other twelve men were already hard at work. There were twelve threshing-floors and six of them were occupied, two men to each floor. Olaf was told to thresh what the other six floors could hold, so he went in, took a flail and watched how the others used theirs, but when he tried to imitate them he smashed the flail into little bits with the very first stroke. There were several flails hanging on the wall, and Olaf tried one after the other, but it was of no use; at the first stroke they all went to pieces. He looked about for something stouter with which to thresh and found a large wooden beam. To this he nailed a horse's hide that happened to be hanging at the barn door to dry, and by means of another beam he managed to construct a flail, and finally set to work. Things seemed all right now, but unfortunately there was not room enough to wield the flail, for he hit the walls of the barn with each stroke. However, he knew how to get over that difficulty; he simply lifted the roof from the barn and put it out in the field, then he carried all the sheaves into the middle of the floor and started threshing. Whenever he had finished a bundle he threw it outside and took the next that came handy, and so it happened that he threshed all the farmer's grain, rye and wheat, buckwheat and oats pell-mell, and threw it all into one tremendous heap. Then he picked up the roof, put it back in its place, and went indoors to tell the farmer that he had finished his task.

The farmer refused to believe that the work could have been done in such a short time, and went out to see for himself, but he was terribly angry when he found all his good grain mixed up in this ruinous fashion. When, however, he saw the flail that Olaf had used, and learned how he had made room for himself to work in comfort, he was so frightened at the strength of his new servant that he dared not find fault with him. He merely told Olaf that he was glad he had finished his threshing, and that he would now have to winnow what he had threshed. Olaf asked what this meant, and was told that the corn must now be separated from the chaff, as they were now mixed up from floor to ceiling.

Olaf tried in several ways to accomplish this, but did not succeed at all, so at last he opened the doors on either side of the barn, then lay down at one end of the building and blew as hard as he could. In a moment all the chaff lay outside, like a huge sand-bank, while the grain was quite clean; then he went and informed his master that he had finished his task. The farmer said that he was satisfied and that he had no other work for him that day, so Olaf went into the kitchen where he was given as big a meal as he could eat. Then he slept soundly till supper-time.

But the farmer was sorely troubled, and asked his wife to suggest a plan by which they could get rid of that terrible fellow, for he did not dare to dismiss him. They sent for the steward, and among them they planned that next day, when all the men went into the forest to cut down trees, it should be given out that he who came home last with his load would be hanged, and surely it could easily be arranged that Olaf should be the victim. It was only necessary that they should start early in the morning and let Olaf sleep as long as he usually did. Accordingly, in the evening, when all the servants were sitting together in the kitchen, they began talking about their next day's work, and how hard it would be. One of them suggested that they should start very early in the morning, and, as an encouragement to get the work done as quickly as possible, they agreed that the one who came home last should lose his life on the gallows. Olaf laughed quietly, but had no objection to this plan.

Next morning the twelve men were up and stirring long before sunrise. They took all the best horses and carts, and started for the forest. But Olaf was still sleeping soundly, and his master rubbed his hands in glee, thinking to himself: "Let him sleep as long as he likes." However, at last Olaf awoke and thought it was time to get up, so he dressed himself and partook of his breakfast in his usual leisurely fashion. Then he went to the stables to get his cart ready, but as the others had taken all the good vehicles, Olaf was compelled to hunt about until he found four old cart-wheels, which he fixed to an ancient cart-frame. He then yoked two sorry old nags to his wretched vehicle and started. When he came to the gate at the entrance to the forest he happened to break it, so he picked up a large stone, seven yards long and seven yards broad, and put it into the opening instead of a gate. When he joined the others they laughed and jeered at him, for they had been hard at work since sunrise, and had helped each other to cut down the heavy trees and to load them on their carts, which were all fully laden, with the exception of one. Now Olaf set to work: he seized an axe and tried to fell a tree, but that was no good, the blade bent and the handle broke in two. He then threw aside the axe, put his arms around one of the largest trees, and pulled it out, root and all; he next threw this tree on his cart, and then a second and a third and so on, until his cart was full. The other servants had forgotten all about their work. They stood and gaped in wonderment at this new method of tree-cutting, but suddenly they pulled themselves together, filled their last cart, whipped up their horses and drove home as fast as they could. When they had gone, Olaf yoked his horses to his cart and started to follow, but the cart was far too heavily laden, and the horses could not drag it from the spot. Olaf then unyoked them again, tied a rope round the cart and the tree-trunks, and put the whole load on his back, but the horses he led behind by the bridle. When he came to the end of the wood, he found the other twelve men with their carts waiting there. They had not been able to get through owing to the heavy stone that Olaf had put into the opening. "What," he said, "are twelve men not able to lift that stone ?" and he picked it up and flung it aside. He then walked on with his load on his back and his horses behind him, and arrived home long before the others. There stood the farmer peering down the road, for he was anxious to know how it would all end, and who would come home first. All at once he caught sight of Olaf with his load on his back, and his horses walking behind, and he was so frightened that he quickly shut the big gate and shot home the bolts. Olaf laid down his load and knocked, but nobody came to open, and so he took the tree-trunks one after the other, and flung them over the wall into the courtyard; then he threw the cart after them, so that the four wheels rolled away in different directions. When the farmer saw this, he thought: "Well, if I do not open the gate, he will throw over the horses in the same way"; and so he unfastened the gate. "Good day, master," said Olaf; and then, after leading the horses into the stable, he went into the kitchen to have a meal. After a while the others came home too with their loads, and Olaf said to them: "Do you remember what we arranged last night? Which of you is to be hanged?" But they said that had only been a joke and did not mean anything. "Ah well, I don't mind," said Olaf; and that was the end of that day's work.

But the farmer and his wife and the bailiff sat up talking that night about their terrible servant and how they might get rid of him. The bailiff suggested that on the next day, when they were to clean out the deep draw-well, they might manage it; they would try to get Olaf down first and then roll a huge mill-stone on the top of him; that was sure to make an end of him. Then they could simply fill up the well, which would save funeral expenses. The farmer and his wife thought that this was an excellent plan, and they rejoiced in the anticipation of thus getting rid of Olaf once and for all in an easy way.

Olaf, however, had a tougher life than his master thought, and slept very soundly till late into the next day, so that they had to waken him. As usual he rubbed his eyes quite unconcernedly and said: "Oh, yes, it's time to get up and breakfast." He got up, dressed himself and ate a hearty meal, and then asked what he was expected to do that day. When he was told that he would have to clean the well, along with the other men, he went out, and found the others already waiting for him. Olaf told them to choose what they preferred to do: either they might go down into the well and fill the buckets and he would draw them up, or if they liked, he would go down and fill the buckets and they could draw them up. They answered that they preferred to stay above as there was not enough room for them all at the bottom of the well. Accordingly Olaf went down and began to clean out the well, but the men did as they had arranged beforehand; each of them brought a stone as large as he could carry, and threw it down on top of Olaf, thinking that that would surely kill him. Olaf, however, did not mind this a bit, but merely cried up to them to drive away the fowls that were scraping sand on his head. Then the other servants saw that these little stones were of no use, and so they armed themselves with poles, ropes, and levers and rolled the big millstone to the edge of the well. It took all their strength to throw the huge stone down. Now, they thought, Olaf is surely settled for ever. But the stone fell in such a lucky way that Olaf got his head right through the hole in the middle and it fitted round his neck like a collar. However, Olaf was angry now and would not stay in the well any longer; he went straight to the farmer and complained that the other men had been trying to make a fool of him; then, lowering his head, he shook off the mill stone so that it fell on the farmer's toes and crushed them flat.

The poor man limped indoors to his wife and then, sending for the bailiff, told him that he must suggest some way to get rid of that terrible fellow who was playing ducks and drakes with everything; what they had tried so far had been of no use and they must discover some more successful method. After a while the bailiff said: "I know one more plan that might help us. We will send him out this evening to the devil's pool to fish, and from there he will never come back alive, for old Eric allows no one to approach him at night-time." The farmer and his wife thought that was really good advice, and then the farmer limped back to Olaf and told him he would punish the men for having played him that mean trick. Meanwhile, however, he would be obliged, if Olaf would do a little job for him where he would be sure that those spiteful fellows could not disturb him. He might row out in the evening to the devil's pool and fish, and in return for that he would have no work to do next day. "Very well," said Olaf, "I am quite agreeable to that, but I must have a good meal to take with me: an ovenful of bread, a quarter of a hundred-weight of butter, a cask of beer and a gallon of brandy; it must not be any less." His master told him that he would give him that with pleasure, and Olaf had the whole lot packed up, hung it on the end of his stick, slung it over his shoulder and set out to the devil's pool. When he got there he entered the boat, rowed out on the lake, and prepared to fish. When he was right out on the water he thought it would be better to have a meal first, before starting work. He had just begun, when old Eric rose out of the water, seized him by the neck and pulled him to the bottom of the pool. Luckily, Olaf had taken his stick with him, and just before he felt old Eric's claws at his neck, he seized the stick and took it down with him. When they reached the bottom, Olaf said: "Stop a little, we are on solid ground now"; and he seized old Eric by the neck with one hand, while with the other he pummelled him with his iron stick so hard on the back that his back soon was as flat as a pancake. Then old Eric began to moan and lament, and begged Olaf to let him go, promising that he would never come near the pool again. "No, my dear friend," said Olaf, "you won't get off, unless you promise to bring all the fish that are in this pool to my master's farm to-morrow morning." Old Eric promised gladly to do this if Olaf would only let him free. Olaf then rowed ashore, ate the rest of his supper, and went home to bed.

Next morning, when the farmer opened the front door, fish began to tumble in until the yard was full of them, and the heap was sky-high. Then he ran in to his wife again and said: "Whatever are we going to do with the fellow? Old Eric has not done him any harm; I am sure there are no fish left in the lake, for the courtyard is covered with them." "That is terrible," she said. "You must persuade him to travel to the infernal regions to collect the interest that is due to us." The farmer now wished to go across to Olaf's bedroom to have a talk with him, but he was obliged to keep close to the wall, because he could hardly get past all the fish that Olaf had procured. Then he told Olaf that he was much obliged to him for his grand catch, and that he now had a task for him, with which he could entrust only a reliable servant. He wished him to go underground to old Eric's regions and collect the interest that was due to him for three years. "I will do that with pleasure," said Olaf; "but what is the way to the place ?"

Then the farmer was at his wits' end, and did not know what to say, so he ran indoors again to ask his wife's advice. "Fool that you are," she said; "tell him to go straight in front of him to the south, through the large forest! Whether he gets there or not does not matter, if only we get rid of him." The farmer went back to Olaf and told him that the way led straight on to the south through the woods. Olaf again demanded enough food to last him for the journey: two ovensful of bread, two quarters of a hundredweight of butter, two barrels of beer and two gallons of brandy. They gave him all that with pleasure; he packed it again in a bundle, flung it on the end of his stick over his shoulder, and then walked away toward the south.

When he came through the wood, he found that there were several roads and he was in doubt which to take, so he sat down and undid his bundle. But, unluckily, he had left his knife at home, and so he picked up a ploughshare that he found in a field and began to cut his bread with it. While he was sitting there a man came riding past. Olaf stopped eating and asked him: "Where are you going?" "To call on old Eric," answered the man. "Then just wait a minute, I have business there too." But the man was in a hurry and would not wait, so Olaf went after him and seized the horse by the tail, so that it stood on its hind legs, and the man flew right into a ditch. "Just wait a minute, I am going the same way," said Olaf. Then he tied up his bundle again and put it on the horse's back, took the horse by the bridle, and said to the man: "Now, we can both walk." On the way Olaf told the man his business, and also the fun he had had with old Eric; the other man did not say much but he evidently knew the road well, for it was not long before they came to the gate of old Eric's domain. But just as they got there both man and horse vanished and Olaf stood at the gate by himself. "They'll soon come and open it," he thought; but no one came. Then he knocked at the gate, but still no one came, so that he grew tired of waiting and began hammering at the gate with his iron stick, until he had smashed the gate to pieces, and entered. Then a swarm of little imps came rushing at him, and asked him what he wanted. He told them that he was there to present his master's compliments, and to demand the interest due for the last three years. Then they roared at him and began to seize him and drag him to the ground, but when he had given them a few blows with his cudgel, they let him go and roared even louder than before, calling at the same time to old Eric, who, however, was still lying on his bed after the terrible treatment he had received from Olaf at the bottom of the pool. They said there was a farmer's messenger who had come to collect three years' interest, and that he had broken the gate with his cudgel and had broken their arms and legs as well.

"Give him the interest for ten years, for all I care," said old Eric, "only do not let him come near me!" Then all the little imps came with so much gold and silver that it was almost terrible to behold. Olaf filled his big bag with it, slung it over his shoulder, and then walked back to the farm. There they were all exceedingly frightened at the sight of him, but Olaf was tired of his greedy master and would work no longer for him. Therefore he gave him half of the money he had brought with him, and took the other half to his father the blacksmith at Furreby. Then he bade him farewell, also, telling him that he was tired of living on shore and serving human folk; and that he would much rather go back to his mother the Mermaid. And no one ever saw Olaf, the Mermaid's son, again.

THE LITTLE PONY

THERE was, once upon a time, a King who had an only son. He was the handsomest young man anyone could see. He also had a good heart, and a good intellect. But he was conceited about his position, his intellect, and his good looks. As he was handsome, he loved everything handsome, anything ugly was more than he could stand; he said it made him very ill to see any one who was deformed.

It so happened one day when he was out hunting with his courtiers, they threw themselves down close to a farm road to have their breakfast, and an old man came riding along on a very sorry horse; he was wrinkled, one-eyed and crooked-necked as well as poor and very ill-clad; and his horse was not much better; it was a little long-haired farm pony, which had gone lame on one of its fore-feet.

"Oh lor," said the Prince, "turn that ugly old fellow and his ugly pony off the road for me, I can't bear to see anything so hideous." The courtiers sent for the shabby rider without delay and made him get off the road so that he was out of sight.

But the old man was not what he appeared to be: he was a great and mighty Troll, who did not always appear in such a mean form. One day, the Prince went quite alone out into the wood, when the old one-eyed man stood before him, touched him with his stick and said: "Now you will see what it is like to be a pony like mine. And so you will remain until a guileless King's daughter shall call you her 'Ever dearest Friend.' The moment he said that the handsome Prince immediately became an ugly little pony like the one he could not bear to look at.

In the Prince's home there was great trouble. The King's son had disappeared and no one knew what had become of him.

And so he went into the wood as a little mean-looking farm pony, very ill satisfied with himself. It was no use for him to go home to his father's castle, for he knew that no one would know him. Well, when he had been in the wood a couple of days, it so happened that there came along a little farmer's boy, who was out gathering firewood. He saw the little pony grazing there; he went up to him and patted him and took a fancy to him, and the pony followed him where he went, and so came home with him to his father, who had a little homestead outside the wood. "See, father," said he, "here you have a new pony instead of the old one, which died yesterday"

"It is only a very sorry beast," said the father, "hardly worth his feed, but we will try him."

So the pony was put into the stable. On the next day the farmer harnessed him to his little plough, and he drew it fairly well. "The pony is not so bad as he appeared to be," said the farmer to Hans—so the boy was called—"You may feed him well, and so we will at any rate get some good out of him." Hans became very fond of his little pony, as he called it; he currycombed him and was right good to him. He also got much benefit from the good fodder which the farmer had ordered he should have. One day the farmer said to Hans: "You can ride the pony into the market town in the morning, and have two shoes, and no more, put on him, as now I will sell him."

Hans did not like this, as he would not see his little pony again.

When he came to the town he had the pony shod with two shoes, and there came a one-eyed man and had a chat with him as to whether he would sell the horse. "It would cost 200 Daler," said Hans in jest. "That is too much for him," said the man, "but never mind, you shall have it." "No," said Hans, "I cannot sell him, as he does not belong to me but to my father." "Then you can go home and ask him whether you may," said the man. But Hans would not. He mounted his little pony and rode home, but said nothing to his father about his having been able to get 200 Daler for him.

A short time after this the horse fair at the market town came round, and so the farmer said to Hans: "You must groom the pony, he shall go to market to-day." Hans became very sad and begged that he might go to the fair with the little pony, but his father chose to go himself. "You should ask 300 Daler for him, father," said Hans. "You are mad, boy," said the father, "I know well enough what the pony is worth; he is not worth 100 Daler." Then Hans told him he had been offered 200 Daler for the pony. "Then you are a great booby," said the father, and he gave Hans a box on the ear. So he mounted and rode to market with the animal. He thought, however, about what Hans had said to him, and when any one asked him what he wanted for the horse, he said at once, "300 Daler." The buyers laughed at him and said, "That is a fine price for a brute that is not worth 100 Daler; but the farmer would knock nothing off the price, and, at last, there came an old one-eyed man, who did not bargain about the price, but gave the 300 Daler, and so got the pony. The farmer went home and was not a little pleased with the good bargain, but Hans wept and was very sad. His father looked for him next morning, but could not find him. "He has surely run after the pony," said the mother, and with that they were satisfied.

Hans had really and truly run after his dear pony. He found out by inquiring in the market town that the man who had bought the horse had travelled to a town which lay 100 miles away.[1] He was a rich man, they said, and a man of rank, and was employed about the King's castle. Hans started on the road at once, and thus he at last covered all the hundred miles, and then he went straight to the King's castle, and asked them to give him work as a stable boy, but he did not find the pony in the King's stables; but one day Hans saw a little sledge in the castle square,

---

[1] About 450 English miles

and the sledge horse was none other than his own dear little pony. Hans was indeed glad, and he went over and patted him. At the same time it happened that the King's youngest daughter, who was still a child, came running past, and when she saw Hans standing with the little pony, she said, "Such a little horse would I gladly have, then could I both drive and ride. Don't you think so, Hans?"

Hans said he knew the horse and it was the smartest and likeliest little animal there was.

She ran up to her father, the King, and asked him to buy the little horse for her. "It is an ugly little beast," said the King. "You may take which horse you will in my stable, there are good horses enough." But she had taken such a fancy to the little horse, and kept on asking till the King said "Yes," and bought it for her. "Now, Hans, take right good care of him," said the little Princess, and he willingly promised to do so, and kept his promise, so that the little pony became smarter every day, and the little Princess both drove with it, and rode it, and became very fond of it.

When some time had passed by, it so happened that the King's eldest daughter—for the King had two daughters and no sons—had been out fishing, and had lost a finger ring which had been left her by her mother. It was of great value and also was a lucky ring. Both she and her father, the King, thought it very unlucky to have lost the ring, and the King did everything he could to search for it, but could not find it. At last the King issued a proclamation that whoever should bring back the Princess's ring should have her in marriage, and half the kingdom with her. There were many dukes, earls and noblemen from the country and foreign lands, who came to look for the ring; many gave up their whole lives to it, but none could find it.

The youngest Princess in the meantime made her little horse dearer every day that went by. She put four beautiful gold shoes under him, and kissed and patted him.

One day, Hans the stable boy went with the little horse to water, when the pony kicked a beautiful goldfish out of the water. Hans sprang after it, but could not catch it. But it happened that a couple of days after that he again watered the pony, who again kicked the same goldfish out of the water.

Hans took the fish up to the King's kitchen and every one came down to see it; when it was cut up there was the Princess's ring inside it. So the King said to his eldest daughter: "Of course you must now take Hans the stable boy in marriage, he has brought back your ring." The Princess also was willing to do so. Hans said, "Yes," or rather he didn't say, "No"; but he added that it was not properly to him that the honour should come for having found the ring, but to the little Princess's horse, who had scratched it to land with his golden shoe.

When the little Princess heard that, she ran down at once to the stable to her little horse, and took him by the neck, and kissed him and said: "No, you shall not have my sister; she can have Hans the stable boy, for you will I keep always, for you are my ever dearest friend," and in the same moment she said that, there was no longer a horse there, but a beautiful young Prince stood before her. He thanked her and told her everything; how he had been both punished and rewarded, and then they went to the King; they had their wedding on the same day that Hans the stable boy married the eldest Princess. The handsome Prince travelled home with his Princess to his father's kingdom, where there was joy without measure at seeing him again. He has now quite given up his pride and lives in happiness and splendour with his ever dearest friend; and Hans the stable boy has also a good time with the eldest Princess. He now has the whole of her father's kingdom since the old King is dead.

EGYPT

THERE is a grave and learned air about the Egyptian stories and a gloomy mysticism pervades many of them. It is singular that with the exception of the Osirian saga, Egyptian mythology can hardly be said to exist. There are few or no legends about the gods. Their characters are differentiated but their exploits remain unsung. There are no records which tell of the origin of this great nation, of its childhood, or of its development, hence it is impossible to say whether they ever possessed "folk-tales" in the generally accepted meaning of the term.

THE STORY OF THE TWO BROTHERS

ANAPOU and Bitou were two brothers who lived in Egypt a long time ago. To Anapou, as the elder, belonged house, cattle, and fields; and Bitou, the younger, worked for him. Bitou was marvellously clever in his management of the cattle and in all things relating to agriculture—he could even tell what the cattle said to him and to each other. One day, as the brothers were working in the fields, Anapou sent Bitou home for a large quantity of seed, as he saw the time had come for sowing. Bitou went and got the seed, and after their day's work the two returned, to find Anapou's wife lying moaning, and saying she had been thrashed by Bitou until she was sore because she would not yield him something he had asked of her when he came for the seed. Then Anapou sought to kill Bitou by stealth, but Bitou, warned by the cattle, fled. His brother overtook him, but the god Phra-Harmakhis caused a wide stream full of crocodiles to arise between them, and Bitou asked his brother to wait till break of day, when he would explain all that had happened. When day broke Bitou told Anapou the truth, refusing at the same time ever to return to the house where Anapou's wife was. "I shall go," he said, "to the Vale of the Acacia. Now listen to what will happen. I shall tear out my heart by magic so as to place it on the topmost bough of the acacia, and when the acacia is cut down, and my heart will fall to the ground, you will come to look for it. After you have looked for seven years, do not be discouraged, but put it in a vessel of cold water; that will bring me to life again. I shall certainly live again and be revenged on my enemies. You will know that something of moment is about to happen to me when a jug of beer is given you and the froth shall run over. They will then give you a jug of wine of which the sediment will rise to the top. Rest no more when these things come about."

He went to the valley and his brother returned home, killed his wife, and mourned for Bitou.

Bitou, in the valley, spent his days in hunting, and at night slept under the acacia, on top of which his heart was placed. One day he met the nine gods, who gave him the daughter of the gods for his wife; but the Seven Hathors swore she should die by the sword. He told her about his heart, and that whoever should find the acacia would have to fight with him.

Pharaoh, hearing of this beautiful woman, desired to take possession of her, and sent armed men into the valley, all of whom Bitou killed. Pharaoh at last enticed her away and made her his chief favourite. She told him her husband's secret and bade him cut down the acacia-tree, which was accordingly done, and Bitou fell down dead at the same moment.

Then what Bitou had foretold happened to his brother. Beer that foamed was brought to him, and then wine which became muddy while he held the cup. By these signs he knew that the time had come to act, and taking his clothes and sandals and weapons, he set off for the valley. When he got there he found his brother lying dead on his bed. He went to the acacia to look for the heart, but could find only a berry, which, however, was the heart. He placed it in cold water, and Bitou was restored to life. They embraced each other, and Bitou said to his brother, "1 shall now become a sacred bull [Apis]. Lead me, then, to Pharaoh, who will reward you with gold and silver for having brought me. I shall then find means to punish my wife for having betrayed me." Anapou did as Bitou directed, and when the sun rose again next day, Bitou having then assumed the form of a bull, he led him to court. There were great rejoicings over the miraculous bull, and Pharaoh rewarded Anapou richly and preferred him before any other man.

Some days after, the bull entered the harem and addressed his former wife. "You see, I am still alive, after all," he said. "Who are you?" she replied. He said, "I am Bitou. You knew well what you were doing when you got Pharaoh to have the acacia cut down."

Then she was very much afraid, and begged Pharaoh to grant her any request she would make.

Pharaoh, who loved her so much that he could refuse her nothing, consented. "Then!" she said, "give me the liver of the sacred bull to eat, for nothing else will satisfy me."

Pharaoh was very much grieved at this, but he had sworn, and one day when the people were offering up sacrifices to the bull he sent his butchers to kill it.

When the bull was being killed two big drops of blood fell from his neck, and flowing till they were opposite Pharaoh's doorway, they sprang up in the form of two great trees, one at either side of the portal.

At this second miracle all the people rejoiced again and offered sacrifices to the two trees.

A long time after, Pharaoh, in his crown of lapis-lazuli, with a garland of flowers round his neck, got into his electrum chair and was carried out to look at the two trees. His chief favourite—Bitou's wife—was brought after him and they were set down, one under each tree.

Then Bitou, the tree under which his wife was seated, whispered to her, "Faithless woman! I am Bitou, and I am still alive in spite of you. You made Pharaoh cut down the acacia, and killed me. Then I became a bull and you had me slain.

Afterward, when she was seated again with Pharaoh at table, she made him swear another oath to do whatever she asked him, and Pharaoh swore again. Then she said, "Cut me down these two trees and make them into two good beams."

What she demanded was done, but as the trees were being cut down a chip flew into her mouth.

In time she had a little son who was none other than Bitou restored to life—though she did not know it. Pharaoh loved the child and made him Prince of the Upper Nile, and when Pharaoh died, Bitou succeeded him. Then he summoned all the great officials of the court, had his wife brought before him, and told them all that had happened. So she was put to death. Bitou lived and reigned for twenty years, and then his brother, Anapou, whom he had made his successor, reigned in his stead.

THE DOOMED PRINCE

THERE was once a king who was sore in heart because no son had been born to him. He prayed the gods to grant his desire, and they decreed that as he had prayed, so it should be. And his wife had a son. When the Hathors came to decide his destiny they said, "His death shall be by the crocodile, or by the serpent, or by the dog." And those who stood round, upon hearing this, hurried to tell the king, who was much grieved thereat and feared greatly.

And because of what he had heard he caused a house to be built in the mountains and furnished richly and with all that could be desired, so that the child should not go abroad. When the boy was grown he went one day upon the roof, and from there he saw dog following a man upon the road. Then he turned to his attendant and said, "What is that which follows the man coming along the road?" And he was told that it was a dog.

And the child at once wished to possess a dog, and when the king was told of his desire he might not deny him, lest his heart should be sad.

As time went on and the child became a man he grew restive, and, being told of the decree of the Hathors, at once sent a message to his father, saying, "Come, why and wherefore am I kept a prisoner? Though I am fated to three evil fates, let me follow my desires. Let God fulfil His will."

And after this he was free and did as other men. He was given weapons and his dog was allowed to follow him, and they took him to the east country and said to him, "Behold, thou art free to go wheresoever thou wilt."

He set his face to the north, his dog following, and his whim dictated his path. Then he lived on all the choicest of the game of the desert. And then he came to the chief of Nahairana. And this chief had but one child, a daughter. For her had been built a house with seventy windows seventy cubits from the ground. And here the chief had commanded all the sons of the chiefs of the country of Khalu to be brought, and he said to them, "He who climbs and reaches my daughter's windows shall win her for wife."

And some time after this the prince arrived, and the people of the chief of Nahairana took the youth to the house and treated him with the greatest honour and kindness. And as he partook of their food they asked him whence he had come. He answered them, saying, "I come from Egypt; I am the son of an officer of that land. My mother died and my father has taken another wife, who, when she bore my father other children, grew to hate me. Therefore have I fled as a fugitive from her presence." And they were sorry for him and embraced him.

Then one day he asked the climbing youths what it was they did there. And when they told him that they climbed the height that they might win the chief's daughter for wife, he decided to make the attempt with them, for afar off he beheld the face of the chief's daughter looking forth from her window and turned toward them.

And he climbed the dizzy height and reached her window. So glad was she that she kissed and embraced him.

And thinking to make glad the heart of her father, a messenger went to him, saying, "One of the youths hath reached thy daughter's window." The chief inquired which of the chief's sons had accomplished this, and he was told that it was the fugitive from Egypt.

At this the chief of Nahairana was wroth and vowed that his daughter was not for an Egyptian fugitive. "Let him go back whence he came!" he cried.

An attendant hurried to warn the youth, but the maiden held him fast and would not let him go. She swore by the gods, saying, "By the being of Ra Harakhti, if he is taken from me, I will neither eat nor drink and in that hour I shall die !"

And her father was told of her vow, and hearing it he sent some to slay the youth while he should be in his house. But the daughter of the chief divined this and said again, "By the great god Ra, if he be slain, then I shall die ere the set of sun. If I am parted from him then I live no longer!"

Again her words were carried to the chief. He caused his daughter and the youth to be brought before him, and at first the young man was afraid, but the chief of Nahairana embraced him affectionately, saying, "Tell me who thou art, for now thou art as a son to me." He answered him, "I come from Egypt; I am the son of an officer of that land. My mother died and my father has taken another wife, who, when she bore my father children, grew to hate me. Therefore have I fled as a fugitive from her presence!"

Then the chief gave him his daughter to wife; he gave him a house and slaves, he gave him lands and cattle and all manner of good gifts.

The time passed. One day the youth told his wife of his fate, saying to her, "I am doomed to three evil fates—to die by a crocodile, a serpent, or a dog."

And her heart was filled with a great dread. She said to him, "Then let one kill the dog which follows thee." But he told her that could not be, for he had brought it up from the time it was small.

At last the youth desired to travel to the land of Egypt, and his wife, fearing for him, would not let him go alone, so one went with him. They came to a town, and the crocodile of the river was there. Now in that town was a great and mighty man, and he bound the crocodile and would not suffer it to escape. When it was bound the mighty man was at peace and walked abroad. When the sun rose the man went back to his house, and this he did every day for two months. After this as the days passed the youth sat at ease in his house. When the night came he lay on his couch and sleep fell upon him. Then his wife filled a bowl of milk and placed it by his side. Out from a hole came a serpent, and it tried to bite the sleeping man, but his wife sat beside him watching and unsleeping. And the servants, beholding the serpent, gave it milk so that it drank and was drunk and lay helpless on its back. Seeing this, with her dagger the wife dispatched it. Upon this her husband woke and, understanding all, was astonished. "See," she said to him, "thy god hath given one of thy dooms into thy hand. Surely he shall also give thee the others!"

And then the youth made sacrifices to his god and praised him always.

One day after this the youth walked abroad in his fields, his dog following him. And his dog chased after the wild game, and he followed after the dog, who plunged into the river. He also went into the river, and then out came the crocodile, who took him to the place where the mighty man lived. And as he carried him the crocodile said to the youth, "Behold, I am thy doom, following after thee . . . .

[At this point the papyrus is so extensively mutilated that in all probability we shall never know what happened to the prince. Was he at last devoured by the crocodile? or perchance did his faithful dog lead him into still graver danger? Let every one concoct his own ending to the tale!]

THE STORY OF RA AND ISIS

IN those far distant days before history begins, it is said that there lived in Egypt a woman of great knowledge called Isis. She was well skilled in all arts and magic, and her wisdom and learning were equal to those of the gods. This superiority over her fellow-creatures made her desirous of yet more power and honour. "Why should I not," she said to herself, "make myself mistress of all the earth, and become like unto a goddess in heaven? Did I know the secret name of Ra, verily I could accomplish this."

Now when Ra, the greatest of the gods, was created, his father had given him a secret name, so awful that no man dared to seek for it, and so pregnant with power that all the other gods desired to know and possess it too. That they might not find it out by spells and enchantments it was hidden within the body of the Sun-god himself. But what man dared not, and the gods had failed to do, Isis resolved to achieve.

Every morning Ra came forth from the land of darkness and travelled across the sky in his Boat of Millions of Years. Now Isis had noticed that water fell from his mouth; so she took some of this and the earth on which it had fallen and fashioned them in the form of a sacred serpent, which, by reason of its being made from the spittle of a god, came to life when she uttered over it one of her magic spells. The serpent she then laid carefully in the path of Ra, in such wise that he should not see it and yet he must pass over it. Thus, indeed, it fell out. On his next journey as he passed by the place where the serpent lay hid, the reptile bit him. The pain was intense, and Ra began to cry aloud. "What is it?" asked the gods who attended on him. "Wherefore criest thou thus as if in pain?" But Ra found no words wherewith to answer them. His limbs shook, his teeth chattered, his face became pale, and his whole body was rapidly being suffused with the poison.

At length the Sun-god called his companions to him. "Come hither, ye gods," he cried, "and hear what hath befallen me. I have been bitten by something deadly. My eyes have not seen it, nor did I make it; it is not one of my creatures. But never have I felt pain so mortal. I am God, the son of God, and I was travelling through my lands to see them and my people, when the creature arose in my path and wrought me this ill. Go quickly, therefore, to the other gods, and bring those who are skilled in spells and enchantments that they may take away this pain."

Soon the company of the gods, especially those versed in the use of magical words, were assembled about the boat of Ra; and with them came the woman Isis. In vain did Ra's companions use their talismans and utter their spells; the poison continued to burn within him. Then Isis approached, and said, "What is this, O Ra? Surely some serpent hath bitten thee; some one of thy creatures hath dared to raise its head against the hand that made it. Tell me thy name, I pray thee, thy secret name, that by its power I may cast out the poison and thou shalt be whole."

"I am the maker of heaven and earth," answered Ra, "and without me was nothing made that is made. When I open my eye, behold, it is light; and when I close it again, then darkness reigns. My word brings the flood into the Nile to water the land of Egypt. I make the hours, the days, and the yearly festivals. I am he who was, and is, and ever shall be."

"Verily thou hast told me who thou art," said Isis, "but not yet hast thou spoken thy secret name. Wouldst thou be healed, thou must divulge it to me, that by its power and my lore I may overcome the evil wrought unto thee."

Meanwhile the poison was coursing through the body of Ra, and making him very ill indeed; for you must remember that the serpent was a magic serpent, and also that it had not been created by Ra himself; for which reasons, though he was the greatest of the gods, he could not destroy the effects of its venom. One moment his body burnt as with fire, and the next it was icy cold, as the fever raged through and through him.

Finally he could no longer stand, and he sank down in the boat.

Then he called Isis to him. "I consent," he said to the company around him. "I consent to be searched out by Isis, and that my name be yielded up unto her." So Ra and Isis went apart, lest the assembled gods should also hear the secret name, and Ra confessed that which the woman so greatly longed to know.

As soon as she had obtained her wish, Isis began to utter her magic spells, and here her ancient wisdom stood her in good stead. Then she cried aloud, "Come out, poison, depart from the body of Ra. Let Ra live! May Ra live! Poison, depart from the body of Ra."

At the words a change came over the mighty god. No longer did he seem about to die. Quickly his strength returned, and ere long he was whole again, ready to continue his journey in the Boat of Millions of Years. And Isis, who by her wit had learnt what neither man nor god ever knew, was granted her desire, and henceforth was known as the mistress of the gods.

What was the secret name, do you ask? Ah! that I cannot tell you. It is what wise men have been seeking for thousands of years. Some few have found it, but the strange thing is that no one can tell it to anyone else. He can help others on the way to discover it for themselves, but that is all; and very often people neglect to hear it when it is whispered to them. They let it pass, borne away on the wings of the wind, and the opportunity comes not again. But to those who do find out the secret name, it is all-sufficient. They need nothing more, for it is the greatest gift that heaven or earth can bestow.

FINLAND

THE following delightful stories are dramatic, picturesque, and full of local colour. Mr. Parker Fillmore has rendered the somewhat stiff, bald, and monotonous wording of these Finnish tales in captivating language. The themes may be traced in the folk-lore of other countries, yet the stories possess an individuality which is distinctive.

The humour of the little cycle of animal stories is very pleasing; the tales are full of the liveliest traits of nature and may be considered in the light of Fables. The animals represent plain, downright Finnish peasants, sometimes stupid, often dull, frequently amusing and always very human.

In "Olli" one meets the troll, so evident in Norse mythology. These trolls were supernatural dwellers of the woods and hills; to them belongs the untold wealth of the mineral world. In caves and clefts of the mountainside they guard heaps of gold and silver and precious things. They stride off into the dark forests by day, returning home at nightfall to feast and sleep. The sight of the sun is fatal to them. Should any gaze full in its face, they would be overcome by its glory and burst.

THE TERRIBLE OLLI

THERE was once a wicked rich old Troll who lived on a mountain that sloped down to a bay. A decent Finn, a farmer, lived on the opposite side of the bay. The farmer had three sons. When the boys had reached manhood he said to them one day:

"I should think it would shame you three strong youths that that wicked old Troll over there should live on year after year and no one trouble him. We work hard like honest Finns and are as poor at the end of the year as at the beginning. That old Troll with all his wickedness grows richer and richer. I tell you, if you boys had any real spirit you'd take his riches from him and drive him away !"

His youngest son, whose name was Olli, at once cried out:

"Very well, father, I will!"

But the two older sons, offended at Olli's promptness, declared:

"You'll do no such thing! Don't forget your place in the family! You're the youngest and we're not going to let you push us aside. Now, father, we two will go across the bay and rout out that old Troll. Olli may come with us if he likes and watch us while we do it."

Olli laughed and said: "All right!" for he was used to his brothers treating him like a baby.

So in a few days the three brothers walked around the bay and up the mountain

260

and presented themselves at the Troll's house. The Troll and his old wife were both at home. They received the brothers with great civility.

"You're the sons of the Finn who lives across the bay, aren't you?" the Troll said. "I've watched you boys grow up. I am certainly glad to see you for I have three daughters who need husbands. Marry my daughters and you'll inherit my riches."

The old Troll made this offer in order to get the young men into his power.

"Be careful!" Olli whispered.

But the brothers were too delighted at the prospect of inheriting the Troll's riches so easily to pay any heed to Olli's warning. Instead they accepted the Troll's offer at once.

Well, the old Troll's wife made them a fine supper and after supper the Troll sent to bed with his three daughters. But first he put red caps on the three youths and white caps on the three Troll girls. He made a joke about the caps. "A red cap and a white cap in each bed!" he said.

The older brothers suspected nothing and soon fell asleep. Olli, too, pretended to fall asleep, and when he was sure that none of the Troll girls were still awake he got up and quietly changed the caps. He put the white caps on himself and his brothers and the red caps on the Troll girls. Then he crept back to bed and waited.

Presently the old Troll came over to the beds with a long knife in his hand. There was so little light in the room that he couldn't see the faces of the sleepers, but it was easy enough to distinguish the white caps from the red caps. With three swift blows he cut off the heads under the red caps, thinking of course they were the heads of the three Finnish youths. Then he went back to bed with the old Troll wife and Olli could hear them both chuckling and laughing. After a time they went soundly to sleep as Olli could tell from their deep regular breathing and their loud snores.

Olli now roused his brothers and told them what had happened, and the three of them slipped quietly out of the Troll house and hurried home to their father on the other side of the bay.

After that the older brothers no longer talked of despoiling the Troll. They didn't care to try another encounter with him.

"He might have cut our heads off!" they said, shuddering to think of the awful risk they had run.

Olli laughed at them.

"Come on!" he kept saying to them day after day. "Let's go across the bay to the Troll's!"

"We'll do no such thing!" they told him. "And you wouldn't suggest it either if you weren't so young and foolish!"

"Well," Olli announced at last, "if you won't come with me I'm going alone.

I've heard that the Troll has a horse with hairs of gold and silver. I've decided I want that horse."

"Olli," his father said, "I don't believe you ought to go. You know what your brothers say. That old Troll is an awfully sly one!"

But Olli only laughed.

"Good-bye!" he called back as he waved his hand. "When you see me again I'll be riding the Troll's horse!"

The Troll wasn't at home but the old Troll wife was there. When she saw Olli she thought to herself: "Mercy me, here's that Finnish boy again, the one that changed the caps! What shall I do? I must keep him here on some pretext or other until the Troll comes home!"

So she pretended to be very glad to see him. "Why, Olli," she said, "is that you? Come right in!"

She talked to him as long as she could and when she could think of nothing more to say she asked him would he take the horse and water it at the lake.

"That will keep him busy," she thought to herself, "and long before he gets back from the lake the Troll will be here."

But Olli, instead of leading the horse down to the lake, jumped on its back and galloped away. By the time the Troll reached home, he was safely on the other side of the bay.

When the Troll heard from the old Troll wife what had happened, he went down to the shore and hallooed across the bay:

"Olli! Oh, Olli, are you there?

Olli made a trumpet of his hands and called back: "Yes, I'm here! What do you want?"

"Olli, have you got my horse?"

"Yes, I've got your horse, but it's my horse now!"

"Olli! Olli!" his father cried. "You mustn't talk that way to the Troll! You'll make him angry!" And his brothers looking with envy at the horse with gold and silver hairs warned him sourly: "You better be careful, young man, or the Troll will get you yet!"

A few days later Olli announced:

"I think I'll go over and get the Troll's money-bag."

His father tried to dissuade him.

"Don't be foolhardy, Olli! Your brothers say you had better not go to the Troll's house again."

But Olli only laughed and started gaily off as though he hadn't a fear in the world.

Again he found the old Troll wife alone.

"Mercy me!" she thought to herself as she saw him coming, "here is that terrible Olli again! Whatever shall I do? I mustn't let him off this time before the Troll gets back! I must keep him right here with me in the house."

So when he came in she pretended that she was tired and that her back ached and she asked him would he watch the bread in the oven while she rested a few minutes on the bed.

"Certainly I will," Olli said.

So the old Troll wife lay down on the bed and Olli sat quietly in front of the oven. The Troll wife really was tired and before she knew it she fell asleep.

"Ha!" thought Olli, "here's my chance!"

Without disturbing the Troll wife he reached under the bed, pulled out the big money-bag, full of silver pieces, threw it over his shoulder, and hurried home.

He was measuring the money when he heard the Troll hallooing across to him:

"Olli! Oh, Olli, are you there ?"

"Yes," Olli shouted back; "I'm here! What do you want?"

"Olli, have you got my money-bag ?"

"Yes, I've got your money-bag, but it's my money-bag now!"

A few days later Olli said:

"Do you know, the Troll has a beautiful coverlet woven of silk and gold. I think I'll go over and get it."

His father as usual protested but Olli laughed at him merrily and went. He took with him an auger and a can of water. He hid until it was dark, then climbed the roof of the Troll's house and bored a hole right over the bed. When the Troll and his wife went to sleep he sprinkled some water on the coverlet and on their faces. The Troll woke with a start.

"I'm wet!" he said, "and the bed's wet, too!"

The old Troll wife got up to change the covers.

"The roof must be leaking," she said. "It never leaked before. I suppose it was that last wind."

She threw the wet coverlet up over the rafters to dry and put other covers on the bed.

When she and the Troll were again asleep, Olli made the hole a little bigger, reached in his hand, and got the coverlet from the rafters.

The next morning the Troll hallooed across the bay:

"Olli! Oh, Olli, are you there ?"

"Yes," Olli shouted back, "I'm here! What do you want?"

"Have you got my coverlet woven of silk and gold?"

"Yes," Olli told him, "I've got your coverlet but it's my coverlet now!"

A few days later Olli said:

"There's still one thing in the Troll's house that I think I ought to get. It's a golden bell. If I get that golden bell then there will be nothing left that had better belong to an honest Finn."

So he went again to the Troll's house, taking with him a saw and an auger. He hid until night and, when the Troll and his wife were asleep, he cut a hole through the side of the house through which he reached in his hand to get the bell. At the touch of his hand the bell tinkled and woke the Troll. The Troll jumped out of bed and grabbed Olli's hand.

"Ha! Ha!" he cried. "I've got you now and this time you won't get away!"

Olli didn't try to get away! He made no resistance while the Troll dragged him into the house.

"We'll eat him—that's what we'll do!" the Troll said to his wife. "Heat the oven at once and we'll roast him!"

So the Troll wife built a roaring fire in the oven.

"He'll make a fine roast!" the Troll said, pinching Olli's arms and legs. "I think we ought to invite the other Troll folk to come and help us eat him up. Suppose I just go over the mountain and gather them in. You can manage here without me. As soon as the oven is well heated just take Olli and slip him in and close the door and by the time we come he'll be done."

"Very well," the Troll wife said, "but don't be too long! He's young and tender and will roast quickly!"

So the Troll went out to invite to the feast the Troll folk who lived on the other side of the mountain and Olli was left alone with the Troll wife.

When the oven was well heated she raked out the coals and said to Olli:

"Now then, my boy, sit down in front of the oven with your back to the opening and I'll push you in nicely."

Olli pretended he didn't quite understand. He sat down first one way and then another, spreading himself out so large that he was too big for the oven door.

"Not that way!" the Troll wife kept saying. "Hunch up little, straight in front of the door!"

"You show me how," Olli begged.

So the old Troll wife sat down before the oven directly in front of the opening, and she hunched herself up very compactly with her chin on her knees and her arms around her legs.

"Oh, that way!" Olli said, "so that you can just take hold of me and push me in and shut the door!"

And as he spoke he took hold of her and pushed her in and slammed the door! And that was the end of the old Troll wife!

Olli let her roast in the oven till she was done to a turn. Then he took her out and put her on the table all ready for the feast. Then he filled a sack with straw and dressed the sack up in some of the old Troll wife's clothes. He threw the dressed-up sack on the bed and, just to glance at it, you'd suppose it was the Troll wife asleep. Then Olli took the golden bell and went home.

Well, presently the Troll and all the Troll folk from over the mountain came trooping in.

"Yum! Yum! It certainly smells good!" they said as they got their first whiff from the big roast on the table.

"See !" the Troll said, pointing to the bed. "The old woman's asleep! Well, let her sleep! She's tired! We'll just sit down without her!"

So they set to and feasted and feasted.

"Ha! Ha!" said the Troll. "This is the way to serve a troublesome young Finn!" Just then his knife struck something hard and he looked down to see what it was.

"Mercy me!" he cried, "if here isn't one of the old woman's beads! What can that mean? You don't suppose the roast is not Olli after all but the old woman! No! No! It can't be!" He got up and went over to the bed. Then he came back shaking his head sadly.

"My friends," he said, "we've been eating the old woman! However, we've eaten so much of her that I suppose we might as well finish her!"

So the Troll folk sat all night feasting and drinking.

At dawn the Troll went down to the water and hallooed across:

"Olli! Oh, Olli, are you there?"

Olli, who was safely home, shouted back:

"Yes, I'm here! What do you want?"

"Have you got my golden hell?"

"Yes, I've got your golden bell, but it's my golden bell now!"

"One thing more, Olli: did you roast my old woman?"

"Your old woman?" Olli echoed. "Look! Is that she?"

Olli pointed at the rising sun which was coming up behind the Troll.

The Troll turned and looked. He looked straight at the sun and then, of course, he burst!

So that was the end of him!

Well, after that no other Troll ever dared settle on that side of the mountain. They were all too afraid of the Terrible Olli!

THE ANIMALS TAKE A BITE

A FARMER once dug a pit to trap the Animals that had been stealing his grain. By a strange chance he fell into his own pit and was killed.

The Ermine found him there.

"H'm," thought the Ermine, "that's the Farmer himself, isn't it? I better take him before any one else gets him."

So the Ermine dragged the Farmer's body out of the pit, put it on a sledge, and then, after taking a bite, began hauling it away.

Presently he met the Squirrel, who clapped his hands in surprise.

"God bless you, brother!" the Squirrel exclaimed, "what's that you're hauling behind you?"

"It's the Farmer himself," the Ermine explained. "He fell into the pit that he had digged for us poor forest folk and serve him right, too! Take a bite of him and then come along and help me pull."

"Very well," the Squirrel said.

He took a bite of the Farmer and then marched along beside the Ermine, helping him to pull the sledge.

Presently they met Jussi, the Hare. Jussi looked at them in amazement, his eyes popping out of his head.

"Mercy me!" he cried, "what's that you two are hauling?"

"It's the Farmer," the Ermine explained. "He fell into the pit that he digged for us poor forest folk and serve him right, too! Take a bite of him, Jussi, and then come along and help us pull."

So Jussi, the Hare, took a bite of the Farmer and then marched along beside the Ermine and the Squirrel, helping them to pull the sledge.

Next they met Mikko, the Fox.

"Goodness me!" Mikko said, "what's that you three are hauling ?"

The Ermine again explained:

"It's the Farmer. He fell into the pit that he had digged for us poor forest folk and serve him right, too! Take a bite of him, Mikko, and then come along and help us pull."

So Mikko, the Fox, took a bite and then marched along beside the Ermine and the Squirrel and the Hare, helping them to pull the sledge.

Next they met Pekka, the Wolf.

"Good gracious!" Pekka cried, "what's that you four are hauling?"

The Ermine explained:

"It's the Farmer. He fell into the pit that he had digged for us poor forest folk and serve him right, too! Take a bite of him, Pekka, and then help us pull."

So Pekka, the Wolf, took a bite and then marched along beside the Ermine, the Squirrel, the Hare, and the Fox, helping them to pull the sledge.

Next they met Osmo, the Bear.

"Good heavens!" Osmo rumbled, "what's that you five are hauling?"

"It's the Farmer," the Ermine explained. "He fell into the pit that he had digged for us poor forest folk and serve him right, too! Take a bite of him, Osmo, and then help us pull."

So Osmo, the Bear, took a bite and then marched along beside the Ermine, the Squirrel, the Hare, the Fox, and the Wolf, helping them to pull the sledge.

Well, they pulled and they pulled and whenever they felt tired or hungry they stopped and took a bite until the Farmer was about finished.

Then Pekka, the Wolf, said:

"See here, brothers, we've eaten up every bit of the Farmer except his beard. What are we going to eat now ?"

Osmo, the Bear, grunted out:

"Huh! That's easy! We'll eat the smallest of us next!"

He had no sooner spoken than the Squirrel ran up a tree and the Ermine slipped under a stone.

Pekka, the Wolf, said:

"But the smallest have escaped!" Osmo, the Bear, grunted again:

"Huh! The smallest now is that pop-eyed Jussi! Let's—"

At mention of his name the Hare went loping across the field and was soon at a safe distance.

Osmo, the Bear, put his heavy paw on the Fox's shoulder.

"Mikko," he said, "it's your turn now for you're the smallest of the three."

Mikko, the Fox, pretended not to be at all afraid.

"That's true," he said, "I'm the smallest. All right, brothers, I'm ready. But before you eat me I wish you'd take me to the top of the hill. Down here in the valley it's so gloomy."

"Very well," the others agreed, "we'll go where you say. It is more cheerful there."

As they climbed the hill the Fox whispered to the Wolf:

"Sst! Pekka! When you eat me, whose turn will it be then? Who will be the smallest then?"

"Mercy me!" the Wolf cried, "it will be my turn then, won't it?"

The terror of the thought quite took his appetite away.

"See here, Osmo," he said to the Bear, "I don't think it would be right for us to eat Mikko. You and I and Mikko ought to be friends and live together in peace. Now let's take a vote on the matter and we'll do whatever the majority says. I vote that we three be friends. What do you say, Mikko?"

The Fox said that he agreed with the Wolf. It would be much better all around if they three were friends.

"Well," grunted Osmo, the Bear, "it's no use my voting, for you two make a majority. But I must say I'm sorry to have you vote this way, for I'm hungry."

So the three animals, the Bear, the Wolf, and the Fox, agreed hence forward to be friends and planned to live near each other in the woods behind the Farm.

THE PARTNERS

THE Bear and the Wolf and the Fox made houses quite close together, and the Wolf and the Fox decided to go into partnership.

"The first thing we ought to do," said Pekka, the Wolf, "is make a clearing in the forest and plant some crops."

The Fox agreed and the very next day they started out to work. Each had a crock with three pats of butter for his dinner. They left their crocks in the cool water of a little spring in the forest not far from the place where they had decided to make a clearing.

It was hard work felling trees and the Fox, soon tiring of it, made some sort of excuse to run off. When he came back he said to the Wolf: "Pekka, the folks at the Farm are having a christening and have sent me an invitation to attend."

"It's too bad we're so busy to-day," the Wolf said. "Another day you might have gone."

"But I must go," the Fox insisted. "They've been good neighbours to us and they'd be insulted if I refused."

"Very well," the Wolf said, "if you feel that way about it you better go. But hurry back for we have a lot to do."

So the Fox trotted off but he got no farther than the spring where the butter crocks were cooling. He took the Wolf's crock and licked off the top layer of butter. Then after a while he went back to the clearing.

"Well, Mikko," the Wolf said, "is the christening over?"

"Yes, it's over."

"What did they name the child?"

"They named it Top."

"Top? That's a strange name!"

In a few moments the Fox again ran off and returned with the announcement that there was to be another christening at the Farm and again they wanted him to attend.

"Another christening!" the Wolf exclaimed. "How can that be?"

"This time the daughter has a baby."

"You're not going, are you, Mikko! You can't always be going to christenings."

"That's true, Pekka, that's true," said the Fox, "but I think I must go this time."

The Wolf sighed.

"You will hurry back, won't you? This work is too much for me alone."

"Yes, Pekka dear," the Fox promised, "I'll hurry back as quickly as I can."

So he trotted off again to the spring and the Wolf's butter crock. This time he ate the middle pat of the Wolf's butter, then slowly sauntered back to the clearing.

"Well," said the Wolf, pausing a moment in his work, "what did they name the baby this time?"

"This one they named Middle."

"Middle? That's a strange name to give a baby!"

For a few moments the Fox pretended to work hard. Then he ran off again. When he came back, he said:

"Pekka, do you know they're having another christening at the Farm and they say that I just must come!"

"Another christening! Now, Mikko, that's too much! How can they be having another christening?"

"Well, this time it's the daughter-in-law that has a baby."

"I don't care who it is," the Wolf said, "you just can't go. You've got some work to do, you have!"

The Fox agreed:

"You're right, Pekka, you're right! I'm entirely too busy to be running off all the time to christenings! I'd say, 'No!' in a minute if it wasn't that we are new settlers and they are our nearest neighbours. As it is I'm afraid they'd think it wasn't neighbourly if I didn't come. But I'll hurry back, I promise you!"

So for the third time the Fox trotted off to the little spring and this time he licked the Wolf's butter crock clean to the bottom. Then he went slowly back to the clearing and told the Wolf about the christening and the baby.

"They've named this one Bottom," he said.

"Bottom!" the Wolf echoed. "What funny names they give children nowadays!"

The Fox pretended to work hard for a few minutes, then threw himself down exhausted.

"Heigh ho!" he said, with a yawn, "I'm so tired and hungry it must be dinner time!"

The Wolf looked at the sun and said:

"Yes, I think we had better rest now and eat."

So they went to the spring and got their butter crocks.

The Wolf found that his had already been licked clean.

"Mikko!" he cried, "have you been at my butter?"

"Me?" the Fox said in a tone of great innocence. "How could I have been at your butter when you know perfectly well that I've been working right beside you all morning except when I was away at the christenings? You must have eaten up your butter yourself!"

"Of course I haven't eaten it up myself!" the Wolf declared. "I just bet anything you took it!"

The Fox pretended to be much aggrieved.

"Pekka, I won't have you saying such a thing! We must get at the bottom of this! I tell you what we'll do: we'll both lie down in the sun and the heat of the sun will melt the butter and make it run. Now then, if butter runs out of my nose then I'm the one that has eaten your butter; if it runs out of your nose, then you've eaten it yourself. Do you agree to this test?"

The Wolf said, yes, he agreed, and at once lay down in the sun. He had been working so hard that he was very tired and in a few moments he was sound asleep. Thereupon the Fox slipped over and daubed a little lump of butter on the end of his nose. The sun melted the butter and then, of course, it looked as if it were running out of the Wolf's nose.

"Wake up, Pekka! Wake up!" the Fox cried. "There's butter running out of your nose!"

The Wolf awoke and felt his nose with his tongue.

"Why, Mikko," he said in surprise, "so there is! Well, I suppose I must have eaten that butter myself but I give you my word for it I don't remember doing it!"

"Well," said the Fox, pretending still to feel hurt, "you shouldn't always suspect me."

When they went back to the clearing, the Wolf began pulling the brush together to burn it up and the Fox slipped away and lay down behind some brushes.

"Mikko! Mikko!" the Wolf called. "Aren't you going to help me burn the brush?"

"You set it afire," the Fox called back, "and I'll stay here to guard against any flying sparks. We don't want to burn down the whole forest !"

So the Wolf burned up all the brush while the Fox took a pleasant nap.

Then when he was ready to plant the seed in the rich wood ashes, the Wolf again called out to the Fox to come and help him.

"You do the planting, Pekka," the Fox called back, "and I'll stay here and frighten off the birds. If I don't they'll come and pick up every seed you plant."

So Mikko, the rascal, took another nap while the poor Wolf planted the field he had already cleared and burned.

THE HARVEST

WELL, the time came when the field of barley which the Fox and the Wolf had planted together was ready to harvest. So the two friends cut the grain and carried the sheaves to the threshing barn where they spread them out to dry.

When it was time to thresh the grain, they asked Osmo, the Bear, to come and help them.

"Certainly," Osmo said.

At the time agreed the three animals met at the threshing barn.

"Now the first thing to decide," Pekka said, "is how to divide the work."

The Fox climbed nimbly up to rafters.

"I'll stay up here," he called down, "and support the beams and the rafters. In that way there won't be any danger of their falling and injuring either of you. You two work down there without any concern. Trust me! I'll take care of you!"

So Osmo, the Bear, used the flail, and Pekka, the Wolf, winnowed the chaff from the grain. Mikko, the rascal, occasionally dropped down upon them a hunk of wood.

"Take care!" they'd call out. "Do you want to kill us?"

"Indeed, brothers, you have no idea how hard it is for me to hold up all these rafters!" Mikko would say. "You're very lucky it's only a little piece that drops on you now and then! If it weren't for me, you'd certainly be killed, both of you!"

Well, the Bear and the Wolf worked steadily. When they were finished Mikko, the rascal, leaped down from the rafters and stretched himself as though he had been working the hardest of them all.

"I'm glad that job of mine is finished!" he said. "I couldn't have held things up much longer!"

"Well, now," Pekka asked, "how shall we divide this our harvest?" "I'll tell you how," Mikko said. "Here are three of us and, see, here on the floor is our harvest already divided into three heaps. The biggest heap will naturally go to the biggest of us. That's Osmo, the Bear. The middle-sized heap will go to you, Pekka. I'm the smallest, so the smallest heap comes to me."

The Bear and the Wolf, stupid old things, agreed to this. So Osmo took the great heap of straw, Pekka the pile of chaff, and Mikko, the rascal, got for his share the little mound of clean grain. Together they all went to the mill to grind their meal.

As the millstone turned on Mikko's grain, it made a rough rasping sound.

"Strange," Osmo said to Pekka, "Mikko's grain sounds different from ours."

"Mix some sand with yours," Mikko said, "then yours will make the same sound."

So the Bear and the Wolf poured some sand in their straw and their chaff, and sure enough, when they turned their millstones again, they, too, got a rough rasping sound. This satisfied them and they went home feeling they hid just as good a winter's supply of food as Mikko.

THE PORRIDGE

WELL, it was only natural that they should all want to see at once what kind of porridge their meal would make.

Osmo's came out black and disgusting. Greatly disturbed, he ambled over to Mikko's house for advice. The Fox was stirring his own porridge which was white and smooth.

"What's the matter with my porridge?" the Bear asked. "Yours is white and smooth but mine is black and horrid."

"Did you wash your meal before you put it into the pot?" the Fox asked.

"Wash it? No! How do you wash meal?"

"You take it to the river and drop it in the water. Then when it's clean you take it out."

The Bear at once went home and got his ground-up straw and took it to the river. He dropped it in the water and of course it spread out far and wide and the current carried it off. So that was the end of Osmo's share of the harvest.

Pekka, the Wolf, had as little luck with his porridge. Soon he, too, came to Mikko for advice. "I don't know what's the matter with me," he said. "I don't seem to be able to make good porridge. Look at yours all white and smooth! I must watch you how you make it. Won't you let me hang my pot on your crane? Then I'll do just as you do."

"Certainly," the Fox said. "Hang your pot on this chain and the two pots can then cook side by side."

"Yours is so white to begin with," Pekka said, "and mine looks no better than dirt."

"Before you came I climbed up the chain and hung over the pot," the Fox said. "The heat of the fire melted the fat in my tail and it dripped down into the pot. It's that fat that makes my porridge look so white."

Poor gullible Pekka immediately suspended himself on the chain above his porridge. But he didn't stay there long. The flames scorched him and he fell down, hurting his side. If you notice, to this day any Wolf that you meet has stiff sides that make it hard for him to turn and twist, and to this day all Wolves smell of burnt hair.

Well, Pekka, after he had got his breath, tasted his porridge again to see if it was any better. But it wasn't. It was as bad as ever.

"I don't see any difference in it," he said. "Let me taste yours, Mikko."

The Fox artfully scooped up a spoonful of the Wolf's porridge and dropped it into his own pot.

"Help yourself," he said. "Take some out of that spot there. That's good."

The place he pointed to was, of course, the place where he had dropped some of the Wolf's own porridge.

So poor old stupid Pekka only sampled his own porridge again when he thought he was tasting Mikko's.

"Strange," he said, "your porridge doesn't taste good to me either. I don't believe anything tastes good to me to-day. The truth is I don't believe I like porridge."

He went home sad and discouraged, while Mikko, the rascal, chuckled to himself and said:

"I wonder why Pekka doesn't like porridge. It tastes awful good to me!"

THE BEAR SAYS "NORTH"

ONE day while Osmo, the Bear, was prowling about the woods he caught a Grouse.

"Pretty good!" he thought to himself. "Wouldn't the other animals be surprised if they knew old Osmo had caught a Grouse!"

He was so proud of his feat that he wanted all the world to know of it. So, holding the Grouse carefully in his teeth without injuring it, he began parading up and down the forest ways.

"They'll all certainly envy me this nice plump Grouse," he thought. "And they won't be so ready to call me awkward and lumbering after this, either!"

Presently Mikko, the Fox, sauntered by. He saw at once that Osmo was showing off and he determined that the Bear would not get the satisfaction of any admiration from him. So he pretended not to see the Grouse at all. Instead he pointed his nose upward and sniffed.

"Um! Um!" grunted Osmo, trying to attract attention to himself.

"Ah," Mikko remarked, casually, "is that you, Osmo? Which way is the wind blowing to-day? Can you tell me?"

Osmo, of course, could not answer without opening his mouth, so he grunted again, hoping that Mikko would have to notice why he couldn't answer. But the Fox didn't glance at him at all. With his nose still pointing upward he kept sniffing the air.

"It seems to me it's from the South," he said. "Isn't it from the South, Osmo?

"Um! Um! Um!" the Bear grunted.

"You say it is from the South, Osmo? Are you sure?"

"Um! Um!" Osmo repeated, growing every moment more impatient.

"Oh, not from the South, you say. Then from what direction is it blowing?"

By this time the Bear was so exasperated by Mikko's interest in the wind when he should have been admiring the Grouse that he forgot himself, opened his mouth, and roared out:

"North!"

Of course the instant he opened his mouth, the Grouse flew away.

"Now see what you've done!" he stormed angrily. "You've made me lose my fine plump Grouse!"

"I?" Mikko asked. "What had I to do with it?"

"You kept asking me about the wind until I opened my mouth—that's what you did."

The Fox shrugged his shoulders.

"Why did you open your mouth?"

"Well, you can't say 'North!' without opening your mouth, can you?" the Bear demanded.

The Fox laughed heartily.

"See here, Osmo, don't blame me. Blame yourself. If I had had that Grouse in my mouth and you had asked me about the wind, I should never have said 'North!'"

"What would you have said?" the Bear asked.

Mikko, the rascal, laughed harder than ever. Then he clenched his teeth and said:

"East!"

FIJI ISLANDS

THE dwellers in these islands are in race akin to the Papuans, but there is an admixture from Tonga and elsewhere. Before the introduction of Christianity, the Fijians were ferocious cannibals, but religious after their kind, and possessing a strong belief in a future life. The people unite the character of childhood with the passions and strength of men. Beneath a simple and childlike exterior there have often been terrible cruelty and revolting ideas. Even before the white man's arrival, the Fijians were advancing toward civilization. Weapons were carved, pottery made, houses built, and canoes fashioned to hold a hundred warriors, the only tools being a stone hatchet, a pointed shell, and a firestick.

The stories given below were not originally written for publication. The chief informant was Taliai-tupou, the King of Lakemba—a talkative old gentleman with a lively imagination. Of him it was said, "A thing is always bigger when it comes out of his mouth than it was when it went in at his ears." There is a simplicity and dignity about the language which is captivating, and the reader will do well to seek to visualize the picturesque setting of these delightful stories.

HOW THE TONGANS CAME TO FIJI

Told by Taliai-tupou, Lord of Naiau

THIS is the account of how the Tonga men came to Fiji. In the old days a Samoan went out in his canoe to fish; and, while he was fishing, a great storm, which drove him far out to sea, came near to swamping his canoe in the waves.

Then, when the sun went down, and the land was dark, he said, "Why do I kill myself with baling? It is useless. Let me now sink down in the waters and die." So he left off baling, and the canoe filled with water; but, just as it was ready to sink, a great wave lifted it and threw it against a rock, to which the man clung, while his canoe floated away till it was dashed to pieces.

Then this Samoan, whose name was Lekambai, climbed and climbed up this rock; but still he could find no dwelling place, nor food, nor drink, excepting he found, here and there, a little water in the hollows of the rock; so, after climbing many days, he was weak and ready to die.

Now was the earth hidden from his sight because of the great height to which he had climbed; and he could see nothing but the sun by day, and the moon and the stars by night, while the clouds lay far beneath his feet; and still, as bending his head backward he looked up, he could see no end to the great black rock. Yet, however, he went climbing on, higher and ever higher, till in the middle of the night his strength failed him; and, fainting, he fell to the ground.

275

When his spirit came back to him again he looked up, and saw that he was in a pleasant land, full of trees and sweet-smelling flowers, whereon the sun was shining brightly; but there were no coconut trees, nor could he see any man. Then he began to weep bitterly, as he thought of his home and his friends, and how that he would see them no more.

Now this land to which he had climbed was the Sky; and the Sky-king heard his weeping, and said, "You wretched man there! Why are you weeping !"

"I am weeping, sir," answered he, "because I am a stranger in a strange land. My country is Samoa, and I know that I shall see it no more forever."

Then did the Sky-king pity him, and said, "Weep not, for you shall see your land again, and your wife, and your children, and your friends. See this turtle. Get on its back, and it will carry you safe to Samoa. Only mind this, when it begins to move, do you hide your face in your hands, and look not up again till the turtle crawls ashore. Know now that, if you do not follow my words, a great and terrible evil will befall you. And when you reach your land remember to give the turtle a coconut and a coconut-leaf mat, of the kind called 'tambakau,' that we may plant the nut, and learn how to make mats out of its leaves; for we have none in this our country. Go now, the turtle is ready."

So Lekambai thanked the Sky-king and promised faithfully to remember all his words; then, hiding his face in his hands, he mounted upon the turtle's back, whereupon it leapt at once with him down into the sea, into which they fell with a great splash, sinking down deep into the midst of the waters, till Lekambai was nearly choked for want of breath; but still he remembered the words of the Sky-king, and kept his hands tight over his eyes.

Then the turtle rose again to the surface, and went swimming swiftly over the waves with Lekambai on its back, covering his eyes with his hands, lest he should look up and die. Many voices sounded in his ears persuading him to uncover his eyes; but he would not. The sharks called after him, and said, "We are coming! We, the sharks, are coming to eat you!" but still he covered his eyes. The wind howled past him, screaming into his ears, "I am strong! I will blow you off into the sea." The waves roared, as he went sailing over them, "Yet will we swallow you up," and the dolphin, more cunning than any other fish, leaped high out of the water close to him, and said, "See! Here comes sailing a canoe from your own land, from Samoa. It is your friends looking for you"; but still Lekambai covered his eyes tightly with his hands, for he feared the words of Sky-king.

All night they went on swiftly over the waters; and when morning dawned a great bird flew past, crying aloud, "Lekambai! Lekambai! Look up, for Samoa is in sight." But he would not; and presently his feet struck against the ground, and the turtle crawled up on the beach. Then he looked up and found that he had landed close to his own town; so he leaped to the ground and ran in amongst his friends, who welcomed him back as one from the dead, weeping over him for joy that he had returned once more—he whom they had mourned as lost for so long a time.

So it fell out that he forgot the turtle, thinking of nothing but his wife and his children and his friends who were thronging around, kissing him and weeping over him and asking many questions, so that it was long before he thought again of the turtle; and then he remembered the mat and the coconut which he had promised to the Sky-king: whereupon he ran down again to the beach and found that the turtle was gone, for it had grown tired of waiting, and hungry, and had therefore swum off a little way along the reef (as far, perhaps, as from here to Nuku-nuku) to look for some seaweed to eat; and there some of the townsfolk saw it, and speared it, and killed it.

Now Lekambai, when he could not find the turtle, ran along the beach in great fear, looking for it; and when he came to the place where the fishing canoes were at anchor, he found it lying dead upon the beach, while his townsmen were heating an oven wherein to cook it.

Then was he very sorry; great was his grief; and he said, "What is this you have done, my friends? An evil thing, a wretched thing! You have killed my friend—he who brought me hither over the sea. What shall I do? How can I now send my gifts to the Sky-king? Iau-e, Iau-e! A miserable man am I!" And they wept together.

Then said Lekambai, "Useless now is our weeping. Put out the fire in the oven, and let us dig it deeper down to form a grave, and therein let us bury the turtle that you have killed. Oh, evil day!"

So they dug the grave, digging it deep—very deep, such as had never been dug before; for they were five days digging it, and they had to put down the stem of a tall coconut palm as a ladder whereon they might climb up with the earth from the grave; and at the bottom, on the sixth day, they laid the turtle, burying also therewith a mat and a coconut, which were the gifts asked for by the Sky-king.

Now all this time the Sky-king was wondering that the turtle did not come back again, after carrying Lekambai to Samoa; therefore he sent a sandpiper to see what was the matter; and the sandpiper came by just as they were covering in the grave. So he swept down amongst the crowd, brushing with his wings the head of a lad called Lavai-pani, and then returned to make his report to the Sky-king.

Now from that time Lavai-pani remained a child. That generation passed away, and the next, and a third, and still he was the same as on the day when the turtle was buried in the deep grave, and when the sandpiper brushed his head with its wings. Little children grew old and grey-headed, and died; their children also, and their grandchildren passed away, but Lavai-pani was still but a boy, and so, when many years were gone by, the Samoans forgot where the turtle was buried; for he only among them all knew the place of its grave, and he was silent.

Then, in the after days, this tale came to the ears of the King of Tonga; and he said to his people, "Sail now away to Samoa, and bring me the shell of that turtle, that I may make therewith fish hooks, such as our grandfathers formerly employed. Good enough for *you* are the shells of turtles which we find in our land; but for *me,* the great King, let there be hooks made from the shell of the turtle which came down from heaven."

So a big canoe sailed, full of men, and the messenger reported the words of the King to the people of Samoa, but they laughed and said, "It is an idle tale. Your sailing is in vain. There is not one among us who knows the place where the turtle is buried; and how, then, can we find its shell?"

Therefore, the Tongas went back again to their land and reported this to their King. But when he heard their report his rage was great; and he said, "You, O disobedient ones! Loose not your sail from the mast to bring it ashore; but hoist it again at once and bring me the shell of that turtle. Why should you wish to die?" So they sailed away in sorrow and great fear.

When they came again to Samoa, all the people gathered together and inquired of the old men as to where the grave of the turtle which had come down from heaven, but none of them knew. This only they knew—that their fathers had told them how it had brought Lekambai over the waters to their land, but as to its burial-place, not one of them could tell where it was. Then Lavai-pani, the silent one, stood up and said, "Let not your souls be small, ye chiefs from Tonga. I can show you the grave of the turtle, for I was there when it was buried."

But they were angry and cried out, "What words are these? Have you brought this lad hither to mock us? Here are men whose heads are grey, they can remember nothing about the turtle; and this impudent one—a boy, a child—tells us that he saw it buried. What words perchance are these?"

Then said the Samoans, "We know not whether he be child or not. He is not one of this generation. When our old men were boys, he was a boy among them; and their fathers said he was the same in their time also. Let us listen to his words, for never before have we heard him speak."

When the Tongans heard this, they wondered and were silent; but the boy said, "Come, let us go to the grave of the turtle." And he took them to the place, saying, "Here was the turtle buried. Dig here, and you will find its shell."

So they dug till the sun went down, but found nothing; and cried out in anger, "This is a deceiver. He is mocking us. Where, then, is the turtle-shell, that we may take it to our King and live?"

But Lavai-pani laughed and turned to his people, saying, "See, now, the foolishness of these Tongans! Twice have they sailed hither across the waters from their land to get this shell, and now they have not patience to dig for it. Five days were our fathers in digging this grave, and do you expect to find the shell to-day? Dig four days more, and you will find it."

So they continued digging, and on the evening of the fifth day they found the shell and the bones of the turtle; and great then was their joy, for they said, "Now we live!"

Then they went sailing back to Tonga, carrying with them the shell. Twelve pieces thereof they gave to the King, but the thirteenth they kept for themselves, hiding it. So the King was angry and said, "Here are only twelve pieces. Where, then, is the thirteenth? See, here is one piece missing, for the shell is not whole." And they said, "It is true, sir, that there were thirteen pieces, but the men of Samoa said to us, 'Take you these twelve to the great chief, your King, and let the thirteenth stay with us?' But we answered, 'Not so; we will have all the shell.' Then were they angry and said to us, 'Take your twelve pieces and go. Why should we kill you?' So we feared, for they were many; and the thirteenth piece is still with them."

But the King glowed with anger, and cried aloud, "Go back this very day and bring me the piece you have left behind."

So they sailed again in great fear, and when they were outside the reef they said, "What shall we do? We cannot go back to Samoa, and if we return to our own land the King will kill us; let us, therefore, follow the wind and perhaps it will take us to some land where we may live. Oh, evil day! Why did we hide the thirteenth piece and not give it up to our lord the King?"

So they kept away before the wind which was then blowing, and when it shifted, they did not sheet home their sail, but steered always before the wind and so it fell out that, after many days, they came to Kandavu near Fiji.

Now, Kandavu was then subject to Rewa, and the King of Rewa took them away, giving them land near his town, where their children dwell at this day. A turtle shell also was the god they worshipped till the "lotu"[1] of the white men spread over all these lands.

And this is how the men of Tonga came down to Fiji.

HOW THE MOSQUITOES CAME TO ONEATA

Told by the Lord of Oneata

IN the old days there were no mosquitoes in Oneata. Happy times were those; for then we were not tormented by their bitings, and our women also were blest, in that they were not weary with beating out tree-bark for cloths to make curtains withal, as in this our day. Moreover, we had then the Kekeo, that excellent shellfish, in such numbers that the beach was covered with them. Our fathers ate them every day, and were full; but now, you might search the whole island over and not one would you find.

---

[1] The name given to Christianity.

A foolish god was the root of this evil; even Wākuli-kuli, who was the god of Oneata in the olden time, and who dwelt here, as a chief, ruling his people.

A great stay-at-home was he; and indeed there was no sailing about in those days, for there were no canoes. But when the great Serpent-god brought the great flood upon the tribe of the Mataisau (or "Boat-builders") because they killed Turu-kawa, his dove, then certain of them drifted to Kambara. Twelve of them were they who drifted thither; and they had tied themselves to a big tree, which floated with them over the waters. Ten were living and two were dead, having been killed by the sharks as they drifted over the sea. So these ten landed at Kambara, and begged their lives of the chiefs, who spared them, making them their carpenters; and this was the beginning of our having canoes up here to Windward.

Now the men of Kambara, in those days, were eaten up by mosquitoes. No rest had they, day or night, because of them; and the noise of the beating was heard continually in every house, as the women beat the bark into cloth to make mosquito-curtains, till their arms ached and were sore weary. Neither had they the Kekeo, that excellent shellfish; though in those days it was found all along the beach and the inland lake at Vuang-gāva (near Kambara) is full of it, while never a mosquito is there to wake them out of their sleep. And that which brought about this blessed change was the wisdom of their god Tuwara, who dwelt with them in the olden time, ruling them as chief; even as the god of our fathers ruled here at Oneata.

Happy is the country where the gods are wise; but woe to the land whose god is a fool! A wise one and cunning was Tuwara; therefore he rejoiced greatly when the Boat-builders drifted to his land and told him of the wonderful vessels which they could build; wherein men could sail across the seas, even in stormy weather, and live. Glad of heart was he, because he saw what good things might come out of his sailing; he saw, moreover, that his land was full of splendid timber; and he set the ten carpenters to work at once, giving them food and houses and wives that they might forget their weeping for those who were lost; for their beautiful town which was swallowed up by the waves; and for the great and mighty kingdom, now gone from them forever. So they settled down at Kambara, with their wives, and (in due time) with their little ones, working hard every day at the double canoe that they were building for the god.

Two years and more were they in building it; for in those days there were no knives, nor hatchets, nor gouges, nor saws, nor gimlets in Fiji. Weary then was the work of canoe-building; for sharp stones were our only hatchets; and we used to burn the logs with fire, on the side which we wanted to cut, chopping off the charcoal with our stone axes, and then burning again; so that many were the burnings, and many the choppings before so much as one plank was finished; while, for boring holes, we had nothing but a pointed shell and a small firebrand.

Nevertheless the canoe was finished at last and dragged down to the sea. Great then were the rejoicings in Kambara, and rich the feast that was made for the Boat-builders: but Tuwara could not rest till he had sailed away beyond the reef out into the open sea. So he hurried on the work; and, when all was ready—mast, sail, ropes, sculls, steering-oars, poles; even all the fittings—then went he on board, with the ten carpenters as his crew, and a great crowd of his people besides; and sailed away before a pleasant breeze; all the Kambarans, who were on board, singing a merry song, while their friends, who stayed behind, ran along the beach, shouting after them.

But when the canoe began to pitch and roll among the waves outside it was not long before the merry chant was changed into a chorus of groans; and all the singers lay sprawling along the deck, not a man of them being able so much as to lift his head; for they were all very sick.

"Here, now, is a terrible thing!" moaned Tuwara. "What is this, ye carpenters? What is this fearful sickness? Oh, my soul is gone. Villains that you are, to bring me into this evil case!"

But the Boat-builders only laughed. "Let not your soul be small, my lord," said they. "Wait a little while and your trouble will be over. It is always thus when we first put to sea." Wherewith Tuwara comforted himself as best he might, and the canoe went swiftly onward before the pleasant breeze till Oneata rose out of the waters in their course.

Then said Malani, the greybeard, eldest of the Boat-builders, "There is land, sir, ahead. Shall we steer for it; or whither do you wish to go.?"

"Steer for it, by all means," groaned Tuwara. "Let me but get to land once more!"

So they went to Oneata and, when our fathers saw them coming, they were sore afraid and hid themselves in the forest; for they took the canoe for some great living sea-monster coming to devour them. Wherefore the town was empty when the strangers landed, and Tuwara threw himself down on the mats in the king's house, saying, "Now I live!" But when, peeping out from their hiding-places, they saw that the Kambarans were men, even as themselves, and that they went about peaceably doing no harm, their souls came back to them again and, when they had heard the strangers' report, they took courage and went down to the beach to see the canoe, whereat they wondered greatly.

Many days did Tuwara stay at Oneata, living in great peace and friendship with the god of that island, for the Kambarans were loth to depart from so good a land as ours, where no mosquitoes drank their blood by night and where they ate the shellfish every day to the filling of their stomachs. And, when they went away, they took the god of Oneata with them, that he might see their land, and that they might return to him and to his men the kindness wherewith they had been treated at Oneata. So these two gods sailed and were seasick together, though the wind was light—so light that the sun was near going down into the waters when they reached Kambara. Then they landed and went up to the great house, where a rich feast was all made ready and waiting for them, the people having seen them coming afar off.

After they had eaten their fill and when the *kava* bowl was empty, the god of Oneata began to yawn; for he was tired and sleepy.

"Come with me, friend," said Tuwara. And he took him within the great mosquito-curtain.

"What is this?" asked the Oneata god, in great surprise at the bigness thereof, and the beauty of the painting. "A wonderful piece of cloth is this! We have none such in my land. But why do you keep it thus hung up, Tuwara? What, then, is its use?"

"Its use," answered the other—"its use, do you ask? It is a useful thing. It is useful as a—yes, as a screen to hide me when I wish to sleep. Therefore do I keep it thus hung up in the midst of the house. And, moreover, it is very useful when the wind blows strong and cold. But let us sleep now, and in the morning I will show you the town."

Thus spake Tuwara, because he was ashamed of the mosquitoes; for he knew that there were none at Oneata, and he wanted to hide from his companion the thing which was the plague of his land. Wherefore he lied to him about the curtain.

Not long was it after darkness had closed in before the house was full of mosquitoes, and the god of Oneata heard them buzzing in thousands outside the curtain, just as he was dozing off to sleep.

"What is that?" cried he. "What sweet sound is that?"

"What can I say to him now?" thought Tuwara in great perplexity; and not being able to think of anything, he pretended to be asleep and answered only with a snore.

"Hi! Tuwara!" shouted the Oneata god, punching him into wakefulness. "Wake up, Tuwara, and tell me what sweet sounds are these?"

"Eh? What? What's the matter?" said Tuwara with a yawn.

"What are those pleasant sounds? Truly a sweet and soothing note is that which I now hear."

"Pleasant sounds? Ah, yes—the buzzing. Oh, that's only the mosquitoes."

"And what are mosquitoes?" asked his companion.

"They are little insects that fly in the air by night and buzz. I keep them to sing me to sleep," said the artful Tuwara.

"A treasure indeed!" cried the other god. "Woe is me that there are none at Oneata. Give them to me, Tuwara."

"Give you my mosquitoes! I dare not, indeed. My people would never forgive me. They would hate me and rebel. Wretched indeed should we be if there were no mosquitoes in Kambara."

"Well, then, give me some of them," pleaded his companion. "Give me some, and keep some yourself, that we may both have them."

"It is impossible," replied the cunning one. "They are a loving tribe. If I send even a few of them away, all the rest will leave me. Truly my soul is sore in that I must refuse you, Wākuli-kuli; but refuse you I must. And now let us sleep, for my word is spoken."

"No, no!" whined the foolish god, in a voice that was neighbour to crying, "refuse me not, I beseech you. Give me the mosquitoes, that I may take them to our land; and, when we hear their song in the night, we shall think of you, and say to our children, 'Great is the love of Tuwara.'"

"That, indeed, is a tempting thought," said the Kambara god. "Glad should I be for you to hold us in loving remembrance. But what am I to say to my people? How can I appease their anger when they rage against me, saying, 'Our god has given away *for nothing* our dear mosquitoes'?" And his voice fell heavy on the words "for nothing."

"For nothing!" cried the other. "No, truly! All that I have is yours. Name anything that you saw in my land, and you shall have it; only let the insects be mine that sing this pleasant song."

"Well, then—I do not ask for myself. Gladly would I give you freely anything that is mine; but my people, friend, my people! You know these children of men, and their ways, how covetous they are. And what *is* there in your land that would satisfy them? Of a truth I cannot think of anything at all. Ah, yes! There is the shellfish! That will do. That is the very thing for these people. Fill but their stomachs, and you can do anything with them. Give me the shellfish, friend, and my mosquitoes are yours."

"Willingly, willingly!" cried the other in an eager voice. "It's a bargain, Tuwara. And now let us lift up the curtain and let some of them in, that I may see them."

"Forbear!" cried Tuwara, starting up in a great fright, lest the mosquitoes should get at his companion and bite him, and he thereby repent of his bargain. "Forbear! Lift not the curtain, friend, lift it not! A modest tribe and a bashful are they; nor can they bear to be looked upon; therefore do they hide themselves by day, and it is in the darkness only that they sing their pleasant song."

"*Wou! Wou!*" exclaimed the silly one. "Wonderful things do I hear! The curtain shall remain unlifted."

"And now, do let us sleep," said Tuwara; "for it is far into the night, and we will sail together in the morning, taking with us the mosquitoes."

So they ceased talking, but neither of them slept; for he of Oneata was listening all night to the song of the biters; and Tuwara was chuckling to himself over the good bargain he had made; being, moreover, fearful that the foolish god would find him out before he could get the shellfish. "I must not let him rise too early," thought he, "lest there should perhaps be still some of them flying about the house."

But his companion was stirring with the first streak of dawn. "Wake, Tuwara, wake!" cried he. "Give me the mosquitoes, and let us go."

"*Isa, isa!*" said the other, with a great yawn. "What a restless one you are! Here you have kept me awake all night with your talking; and now you want me to rise before it is day! Lie still, Wākuli-kuli; lie still yet for a little while. This is just about the time when the mosquitoes are gathering together to fly away to the cave, where they sleep till night comes again over the land; and, if we go among them now, we shall disturb them, causing them to flee hither and thither, so that we shall not be able to catch them for you to-day."

"That would indeed be an unlucky chance," said he from Oneata. "Let us by all means lie still, and wait till they be fairly asleep."

But so great was his eagerness that he could not rest. Sorely did he plague Tuwara; starting up every little while, and crying out, "Do you think they are asleep yet, Tuwara?" or "Surely by this time they are all in the cave"; and with many suchlike foolish words did he vex the soul of the Kambara god, till he waxed very wroth and would have smitten him with his club but for his hope of the shellfish. Therefore he kept his temper, putting the silly one off from time to time with soothing words till it was broad day; and then he said, "Now will they be all asleep. Come, friend, rise and let us sail."

How he got the mosquitoes together we do not know, but our fathers said he shut them all up in a big basket, which was lined inside, and covered with fine mats, through the plait whereof not even a little one could crawl. And when this basket was carried on board the canoe they hoisted the sail, and went out, through the passage, into the open sea, steering for Oneata. Terribly seasick were they both, but neither of them cared so much for it this time, he of Oneata being cheered by the thought of his sweet singers and Tuwara because he was now well rid of them, and moreover because of the shellfish; wherefore were they both content to suffer.

The sun was still high in the heavens when they furled their sail at Oneata, and the Oneata god leaped on shore, crying aloud, "Come hither, my people. Come hither, all of you, and see the good things I have brought. Hand down the basket, Tuwara, that the hearts of my people may be glad."

"Not so!" answered the cunning Tuwara. "The mosquitoes are a loving folk, as I told you before, and if we were to let them go while I am in sight they will not leave the canoe; for they love me, friend, they love me. Give me therefore the shellfish, and I will depart, leaving the great basket with you. And if you are wise you will not open it till I am beyond the reef, lest the mosquitoes should fly after me and leave you."

"True!" quoth the foolish god. "True are your words, Tuwara. A wise god are you, for you think of everything. Come from the beach, from the sea, from the rocks, ye shellfish! Come! for your lord is calling!"

Then from the rocks, from the sea, from the beach, came the shellfish, crawling over the sand, a great multitude. And the Boat-builders threw them into the canoe, our fathers also helping, till it was full and heaped high above the deck, and there was not one shellfish left on land.

"Go now, Tuwara," cried his companion, "give me the basket and go, for the shellfish are all on board."

So Tuwara handed down the basket, while the Boat-builders hoisted the great sail and soon the canoe was gliding swiftly away toward the passage; while the Oneata men crowded round the basket, asking their god all manner of eager questions as to its contents. "It must be something wonderful," said they, "or our lord would never have parted with the shellfish."

"Wait and see," quoth the god, with a self-satisfied smile.

As soon as the canoe had cleared the reef, he untied the fastenings of the basket and lifted the mat wherewith it was covered.

"Here is our treasure," cried the foolish god. Then up rose the mosquitoes in a cloud, fierce and angry; and Tuwara could hear the screams and yells of our fathers, as they smarted under the sharp bites of the savage insects.

"The god of Oneata's sweet singers have begun their song," said he, as soon as he could speak for laughing. "Many fools have I met with among the children of men, but never such a fool as the god of Oneata."

Many were the schemes which the miserable god tried to rid himself of the plague he had bought so dearly; but they were all in vain, for the mosquitoes increased in numbers day by day; and their night-song, that sounded so sweetly in his ears when he first heard it at Kambara, became more fearful to him than the war-cry of an enemy.

Many plots also did he lay to get back the shellfish; but what chance had such an one as he in plotting against Tuwara! Once, indeed, after some years, when he had a canoe of his own, he went over to Kambara in the night, making sure of getting them. And standing on the beach he cried aloud: "Come from the shore, from the sea, from the rocks, ye shellfish! Come, for your lord is calling!" but not one of them came—it was as if they heard him not. There was one, however, who heard him—even Tuwara, who had seen him coming, and lain in wait for him. Creeping therefore softly up behind him, he smote him full on the head with his club, crying aloud: "O villainous god! Would you steal my shellfish?" and drove him howling down to his canoe.

Thus the Kekeo, that excellent shellfish, was lost to us; and thus it was that "The Mosquitoes came to Oneata."

FRANCE

MUCH of the folk-lore of France is so familiar that many of the stories are regarded by English readers as their own. The French tales combine vivacity and a certain artistic feeling with a measure of laboriousness. One misses the pleasant spontaneity of the Norse legends, the poetry of the Celtic stories, and the intensity of the Scottish ballads. One feels that the simple freshness of the peasant's life among woods and fields and hills has given place to the complicated and somewhat unreal life of the court and ballroom. A kind of refined mockery overshadows the outlook on life.

CINDERELLA, OR THE LITTLE GLASS SLIPPER

ONCE there was a gentleman who married, for his second wife, the proudest and most haughty woman that was ever seen. She had by a former husband, two daughters of her own humour, who were, indeed, exactly like her in all things.

He had, likewise, by another wife, a young daughter, but of unparalleled goodness and sweetness of temper, which she took from her mother, who was the best creature in the world.

No sooner were the ceremonies of the wedding over but the stepmother began to show herself in her colours. She could not bear the good qualities of this pretty girl; and the less, because they made her own daughters appear the more odious.

She employed her in the meanest work of the house; she scoured the dishes, tables, and cleaned madam's room and the rooms of the misses, her daughters; she lay up in a sorry garret, upon a wretched straw bed, while her sisters lay in fine rooms, with floors all inlaid, upon beds of the very newest fashion, and where they had looking-glasses so large, that they might see themselves at their full length, from head to foot.

The poor girl bore all patiently, and dared not tell her father, who would have rattled her off, for his wife governed him entirely. When she had done her work, she used to go into the chimney-corner, and sit down among cinders and ashes, which made her commonly called Cinder-wench; but the youngest, who was not so rude and uncivil as the eldest, called her Cinderella.

However, Cinderella, notwithstanding her mean apparel, was a hundred times handsomer than her sisters, though they were always dressed very richly.

It happened that the king's son gave a ball, and invited all persons of fashion to it. Our young misses were also invited, for they cut a very grand figure among the quality. They were mightily delighted at this invitation, and wonderfully busy in choosing out such gowns, petticoats, and head-clothes as might best become them. This was a new trouble to Cinderella; for it was she who ironed her sisters' linen, and plaited their ruffles; they talked all day long of nothing but how they should be dressed.

"For my part," said the eldest, "I will wear my red velvet suit with French trimmings."

"And I," said the youngest, "shall only have my usual petticoat; but then, to make amends for that, I will put on my gold-flowered manteau, and my diamond stomacher, which is far from being the most ordinary one in the world."

They sent for the best tire-woman they could get, to make up their head-dresses, and they had their patches from the very best maker.

Cinderella was likewise called up to them to be consulted in all these matters, for she had excellent notions, and advised them always for the best; nay, and offered her service to dress their heads, which they were very willing she should do. As she was doing this they said to her:

"Cinderella, would you not be glad to go to the ball?"

"Ah!" said she, "you only jeer at me; it is not for such as I am to go thither."

"Thou art in the right of it," replied they; "it would make the people laugh to see a cinder-wench at a ball?"

Any one but Cinderella would have dressed their heads awry, but she was very good, and dressed them perfectly well. They were almost two days without eating, so much they were transported with joy. They broke above a dozen of laces in trying to be laced up close, that they might have a fine slender shape, and they were continually at their looking-glass.

At last the happy day came; they went to court, and Cinderella followed them with her eyes as long as she could, and when she had lost sight of them, she fell a-crying.

Her godmother, who saw her all in tears, asked her what was the matter.

"I wish I could—l wish I could—" She was not able to speak the rest, being interrupted by her tears and sobbing.

This godmother of hers, who was a fairy, said to her:

"Thou wishest thou couldest go to the ball, is it not so?"

"Y-es," cried Cinderella with a great sigh.

"Well," said her godmother, "be but a good girl, and I will contrive that thou shalt go."

Then she took her into her chamber and said to her, "Run into the garden, and bring me a pumpkin."

Cinderella went immediately to gather the finest she could get, and brought it to her godmother, not being able to imagine how this pumpkin could make her go to the ball.

Her godmother scooped out all the inside of it, having left nothing but the rind;

which done, she struck it with her wand, and the pumpkin was instantly turned into a fine coach, gilded all over with gold.

She then went to look into her mouse-trap, where she found six mice, all alive, and ordered Cinderella to lift up a little the trap-door, when giving each mouse, as it went out, a little tap with her wand, the mouse was that moment turned into a fair horse, which all together made a very fine set of six horses of a beautiful mouse-coloured dapple-grey.

Being at a loss for a coachman, "I will go and see," says Cinderella, "if there be never a rat in the rat-trap, that we may make a coachman of him."

"Thou art in the right," replied her godmother, "go and look."

Cinderella brought the trap to her, and in it there were three huge rats. The fairy made choice of one of the three, which had the largest beard, and, having touched him with her wand, he was turned into a fat, jolly coachman, who had the smartest whiskers eyes ever beheld.

After that, she said to her, "Go again into the garden, and you will find six lizards behind the watering pot; bring them to me."

She had no sooner done so, than her godmother turned them into six footmen, who skipped up immediately behind the coach, with their liveries all bedecked with gold and silver, and clung as close behind each other, as if they had done nothing else their whole lives. The fairy then said to Cinderella:

"Well, you see here an equipage fit to go to the ball with; are you not pleased with it?"

"Oh, yes," cried she, "but must I go thither as I am, in these filthy rags ? "

Her godmother only just touched her with her wand, and, at the same instant, her clothes were turned into cloth of gold and silver, all beset with jewels. This done, she gave her a pair of glass slippers, the prettiest in the whole world.

Being thus decked out, she got up into her coach; but her godmother, above all things, commanded her not to stay till after midnight, telling her, at the same time, that if she stayed at the ball one moment longer, her coach would be a pumpkin again, her horses mice, her coachman a rat, her footmen lizards, and her clothes become just as they were before.

She promised her godmother she would not fail of leaving the ball before midnight; and then away she drives, scarce able to contain herself for joy.

The king's son, who was told that a great princess, whom nobody knew, was come, ran out to receive her; he gave her his hand as she alighted from the coach, and led her into the hall among all the company. There was immediately a profound silence, they left off dancing, and the violins ceased to play, so attentive was every one to contemplate the singular beauties of this unknown new-comer. Nothing was then heard but a confused noise of, "Ha! how handsome she is! Ha! how handsome she is!"

The king himself, old as he was, could not help ogling her and telling the queen softly that it was a long time since he had seen so beautiful and lovely a creature.

All the ladies were busied in considering her clothes and head-dress, that they might have some made next day after the same pattern, provided they could meet with such fine materials and as able hands to make them.

The king's son conducted her to the most honourable seat, and afterward took her out to dance with him. She danced so very gracefully that they all more and more admired her.

A fine collation was served up, whereof the young prince ate not a morsel, so intently was he busied in gazing on her. She went and sat down by her sisters, showing them a thousand civilities, giving them part of the oranges and citrons which the prince had presented her with; which very much surprised them, for they did not know her.

While Cinderella was thus amusing her sisters, she heard the clock strike eleven and three quarters, whereupon she immediately made a courtesy to the company, and hasted away as fast as she could.

Being got home, she ran to seek out her godmother; and after having thanked her, she said she could not but heartily wish she might go next day to the ball, because the king's son had desired her. As she was eagerly telling her godmother whatever had passed at the ball, her two sisters knocked at the door, which Cinderella ran and opened.

"How long you have stayed!" cried she, gaping, rubbing her eyes, and stretching herself as if she had been just awaked out of her sleep; she had not, however, any manner of inclination to sleep since they went from home.

"If thou hadst been at the ball," says one of her sisters, "thou wouldest not have been tired with it. There came thither the finest princess, the most beautiful ever seen with mortal eyes; she showed us a thousand civilities, and gave us oranges and citrons." Cinderella seemed very indifferent in the matter; indeed, she asked them the name of the princess, but they told her they did not know it, and that the king's son was very uneasy on her account, and would give all the world to know who she was.

At this Cinderella, smiling, replied, "She must then be very beautiful indeed! How happy have you been! Could not I see her? Ah! dear Miss Charlotte, do lend me your yellow suit of clothes, which you wear every day."

"Ay, to be sure," cried Miss Charlotte, "lend my clothes to such a dirty cinder-wench as thou art! Who's the fool then?"

Cinderella, indeed, expected some such answer, and was very glad of the refusal; for she would have been sadly put to it, if her sister had lent her what she asked for jestingly.

The next day the two sisters were at the ball, and so was Cinderella, but dressed more magnificently than before.

The king's son was always by her side, and never ceased his compliments and amorous speeches to her; to whom all this was so far from being tiresome that she quite forgot what her godmother had recommended to her, so that she at last counted the clock striking twelve when she took it to be no more than eleven; she then rose up, and fled as nimble as a deer.

The prince followed, but could not overtake her. She left behind one of her glass slippers, which the prince took up most carefully. She got home, but quite out of breath, without coach or footmen, and in her old cinder clothes, having nothing left of all her finery but one of the little slippers, fellow to that she dropped.

The guards at the palace gate were asked if they had not seen a princess go out. They said they had seen nobody go out but a young girl, very meanly dressed, and who had more the air of a poor country wench than a gentlewoman.

When the two sisters returned from the ball, Cinderella asked them if they had been well diverted, and if the fine lady had been there.

They told her yes, but that she hurried away immediately when it struck twelve, and with so much haste that she dropped one of her little glass slippers, the prettiest in the world, which the king's son had taken up; that he had done nothing but look at her all the time of the ball, and that most certainly he was very much in love with the beautiful person who owned the little slipper.

What they said was very true; for a few days after, the king's son caused to be proclaimed by sound of trumpets that he would marry her whose foot this slipper would just fit.

They whom he employed began to try it on upon the princesses, then the duchesses, and all the court, but in vain; it was brought to the two sisters, who did all they possibly could to thrust their foot into the slipper, but they could not effect it.

Cinderella, who saw all this, and knew her slipper, said to them, laughing, "Let me see if it will not fit me!"

Her sisters burst out laughing, and began to banter her.

The gentleman who was sent to try the slipper looked earnestly at Cinderella, and finding her very handsome, said it was but just that she should try, and that he had orders to let every one make trial. He obliged Cinderella to sit down, and putting the slipper to her foot, he found it went in very easily, and fitted her as if it had been made of wax.

The astonishment her two sisters were in was excessively great, but still abundantly greater, when Cinderella pulled out of her pocket the other slipper and put it on her foot.

Thereupon, in came her godmother, who having touched, with her wand, Cinderella's clothes, made them richer and more magnificent than any of those she had before.

And now her two sisters found her to be that fine beautiful lady whom they had seen at the ball. They threw themselves at her feet, to beg pardon for all the ill treatment they had made her undergo. Cinderella took them up, and as she embraced them, cried that she forgave them with all her heart, and desired them always to love her. She was conducted to the young prince, dressed as she was. He thought her more charming than ever, and a few days after, married her.

PUSS IN BOOTS

THERE was once a miller who left no more estate to the three sons he had than his mill, his ass, and his cat. The division was soon made. Neither the clerk nor the lawyer was sent for. They would soon have eaten up all the poor patrimony. The eldest had the mill, the second the ass, and the youngest nothing but the cat.

The poor young fellow was quite comfortless at having so poor a lot. "My brothers," said he, "may get their living handsomely enough by joining their stocks together; but for my part, when I have eaten up my cat, and made me a muff of his skin, I must die with hunger."

The cat, who heard all this, but made as if he had not, said to him with a grave and serious air: "Do not thus afflict yourself, my good master; you have nothing else to do but to give me a bag and get a pair of boots made for me, that I may scamper through the dirt and the brambles, and you shall see that you have not so bad a portion of me as you imagine."

Though the cat's master did not build very much upon what he said, he had, however, often seen him play a great many cunning tricks to catch rats and mice; as when he used to hang by the heels, or hide himself in the meal and make as if he was dead; so that he did not altogether despair of his affording him some help in his miserable condition.

When the cat had what he asked for, he booted himself very gallantly; and putting his bag about his neck, he held the strings of it in his two fore paws, and went into a warren where was great abundance of rabbits.

He put bran and sow-thistle into his bag, and stretching himself out at length, as if he had been dead, he waited for some young rabbits, not yet acquainted with the deceits of the world, to come and rummage his bag for what he had just put into it.

Scarce was he lain down but he had what he wanted; a rash and foolish young rabbit jumped into his bag, and master Puss, immediately drawing close the strings, took and killed him without pity. Proud of his prey, he went with it to the palace, and asked to speak with his majesty. He was shown upstairs into the king's apartment, and, making a low reverence, said to him:

"I have brought you, sir, a rabbit of the warren which my noble lord, the marquis of Carabas" (for that was the title which Puss was pleased to give his master) "has commanded me to present to your majesty from him."

"Tell thy master," said the king, "that I thank him, and that he gives me a great deal of pleasure."

Another time he went and hid himself among some standing corn, holding still his bag open; and when a brace of partridges ran into it, he drew the strings, and so caught them both.

He went and made a present of these to the king, as he had done before of the rabbit which he took in the warren. The king, in like manner, received the partridges with great pleasure, and made him a gift of money.

The cat continued for two or three months thus to carry his majesty, from time to time, game of his master's taking.

One day in particular, when he knew for certain that he was to take the air, along the riverside, with his daughter, the most beautiful princess in the world, he said to his master: "If you will follow my advice, your fortune is made; you have nothing else to do but go and wash yourself in the river, in that part I shall show you, and leave the rest to me."

The marquis of Carabas did what the cat advised him to, without knowing why or wherefore.

While he was washing, the king passed by, and the cat began to cry out as loud as he could, "Help, help! my lord marquis of Carabas is going to be drowned."

At this noise the king put his head out of his coach-window, and finding it was the cat who had so often brought him such good game, he commanded his guards to run immediately to the assistance of his lordship, the marquis of Carabas.

While they were drawing the poor marquis out of the river, the cat came up to the coach, and told the king that while his master was washing there came by some rogues, who went off with his clothes, though he had cried out, "Thieves, thieves," as loud as he could.

This cunning cat had hidden them under a great stone. The king immediately commanded the officers of his wardrobe to run and fetch one of his best suits for the lord marquis of Carabas.

The king caressed him after a very extraordinary manner; and as the fine clothes he had given him extremely set off his good mien (for he was well made, and very handsome in his person), the king's daughter took a secret inclination to him, and the marquis of Carabas had no sooner cast two or three respectful and somewhat tender glances, but she fell in love with him to distraction. The king would needs have him come into his coach, and take part of the airing.

The cat, quite overjoyed to see his project begin to succeed, marched on before, and meeting with some countrymen who were mowing a meadow, he said to them, "Good people, you who are mowing, if you do not tell the king, who will soon pass this way, that the meadow you mow belongs to my lord marquis of Carabas, you shall be chopped as small as herbs for the pot."

The king did not fail asking of the mowers to whom the meadow they were mowing belonged: "To my lord marquis of Carabas," answered they, all together, for the cat's threats had made them terribly afraid.

"You see, sir," said the marquis, "this is a meadow which never fails to yield a plentiful harvest every year."

The master-cat, who went still on before, met with some reapers, and said to them, "Good people, you who are reaping, if you do not tell the king, who will presently go by, that all this corn belongs to the marquis of Carabas, you shall be chopped as small as herbs for the pot."

The king, who passed by a moment after, would needs know to whom all that corn, which he then saw, did belong: "To my lord marquis of Carabas," replied the reapers; and the king was very well pleased with it, as well as the marquis, whom he congratulated thereupon.

The master-cat, who went always before, said the same words to all he met; and the king was astonished at the vast estates of my lord marquis of Carabas.

Master Puss came at last to a stately castle, the owner of which was an ogre, the richest had ever been known; for all the lands which the king had then gone over belonged to this castle.

The cat, who had taken care to inform himself who the ogre was, and what he could do, asked to speak with him, saying he could not pass so near his castle without having the honour of paying his respects to him.

The ogre received him as civilly as an ogre could do, and made him sit down. "I have been assured," said the cat, "that you have the gift of being able to change yourself into all sorts of creatures you have a mind to; you can, for example, transform yourself into a lion, or elephant, and the like."

"This is true," answered the ogre, very briskly, "and to convince you, you shall see me now become a lion."

Puss was so sadly terrified at the sight of a lion so near him, that he immediately got into the gutter, not without abundance of trouble and danger, because of his boots, which were of no use at all to him in walking upon the tiles. A little while after, when Puss saw that the ogre had resumed his natural form, he came down and owned he had been very much frightened.

"I have been, moreover, informed," said the cat, "but I know not how to believe it, that you have also the power to take on you the shape of the smallest animals; for example, to change yourself into a rat or a mouse; but I must own to you, I take this to be impossible."

"Impossible!" cried the ogre, "you shall see that presently," and at the same time changed himself into a mouse, and began to run about the floor.

Puss no sooner perceived this but he fell upon him, and ate him up.

Meanwhile the king, who saw, as he passed, this fine castle of the ogre's, had a mind to go into it. Puss, who heard the noise of his majesty's coach running over the drawbridge, ran out and said to the king, "Your majesty is welcome to this castle of my lord marquis of Carabas."

"What! my lord marquis!" cried the king, "and does this castle also belong to you? There can be nothing finer than this court, and all the stately buildings which surround it; let us go into it, if you please."

They passed into a spacious hall, where they found a magnificent collation which the ogre had prepared for his friends, who were that very day to visit him, but dared not to enter, knowing the king was there.

His majesty was perfectly charmed with the good qualities of my lord marquis of Carabas, as was his daughter, who had fallen in love with him; and seeing the vast estate he possessed, said to him, while they sat at the feast, "It will be owing to yourself only, my lord marquis, if you are not my son-in-law."

The marquis, making several low bows, accepted the honour which his majesty conferred upon him, and forthwith, that very same day, married the princess.

Puss became a great lord, and never ran after mice any more but for his diversion.

LITTLE RED RIDING HOOD

IN a very pretty village, far away, there once lived a nice little girl. She was one of the sweetest children ever seen.

Her mother loved her very much, and her grandmother said that she was the light of her eyes and the joy of her heart.

To show her love for the child, this good old dame had made her a little red hood, and after a time the little girl was known as Little Red Riding Hood.

One day her mother baked some cakes and made some fresh butter. "Go," she said to Little Red Riding Hood, "and take this cake and a pot of butter to your grandmother; for she is ill in bed."

Little Red Riding Hood was a willing child, and liked to be useful; and, besides, she loved her grandmother dearly.

So she put the things in a basket, and at once set out for the village, on the other side of the wood, where her grandmother lived.

Just as she came to the edge of the wood, Little Red Riding Hood met a wolf, who said to her, "Good morning, Little Red Riding Hood."

He would have liked to eat her on the spot; but some woodmen were at work near by, and he feared they might kill him.

"Good morning, Master Wolf," said the little girl, who had no thought of fear.

"And where are you going?" said the wolf.

"I am going to my grandmother's," said Little Red Riding Hood, "to take her a cake and a pot of butter; for she is ill,"

"And where does poor grandmother live?" asked the wolf.

"Down past the mill, on the other side of the wood," said the child.

"Well, I think that I will go and see her too," said the wolf. "So I will take this road, and do you take that, and we shall see which of us will be there first."

The wolf knew that his way was the nearer, for he could dash through the trees, and swim a pond, and so by a very short cut get to the old dame's door.

The wolf ran on as fast as he could, and was very soon at the cottage. He knocked at the door with his paw, "Thump! thump!"

"Who is there?" cried grandmother.

"It is Little Red Riding Hood. I have come to see how you are, and to bring you a cake and a pot of butter," said the wolf, as well as he could.

He made his voice sound like that of the little girl.

"Pull the bobbin, and the latch will fly up," called the grandmother from her bed.

The wolf pulled the bobbin, and in he went. Without a word he sprang upon the old woman and ate her up, for he had not tasted food for three days.

Then he shut the door, and got into the grandmother's bed. But first he put on her cap and night-gown.

He laughed to think of the trick he was to play upon Little Red Riding Hood, who must soon be there.

All this time Little Red Riding Hood was on her way through the wood.

She stopped to listen to the birds that sang in the trees; and she picked the sweet flowers that her grandmother liked, and made a pretty nosegay of them.

A wasp buzzed about her head, and lighted on her flowers. "Eat as much as you like," she said; "only do not sting me." He buzzed louder, but soon flew away.

And a little bird came and pecked at the cake in her basket. "Take all you want, pretty bird," said Little Red Riding Hood. "There will still be plenty left for grandmother and me." "Tweet, tweet," sang the bird, and was soon out of sight.

And now she came upon an old dame who was looking for cresses. "Let me fill your basket," she said, and she gave her the bread she had brought to eat by the way.

The dame rose, and patting the little maid on the head, said, "Thank you, Little Red Riding Hood. If you should meet the green huntsman as you go, pray tell him from me that there is game in the wind."

Little Red Riding Hood looked all about for the green huntsman. She had never seen or heard of such a person before.

At last she passed by a pool of water, so green that you would have taken it for grass. There she saw a huntsman, clad all in green. He stood looking at some birds that flew above his head.

"Good morning, Mr. Huntsman," said Little Red Riding Hood; "the water-cress woman says there is game in the wind."

The huntsman nodded. He bent his ear to the ground to listen. Then he took an arrow and put it in his bow. "What can it mean?" thought the little girl.

Little Red Riding Hood at last came to her grandmother's cottage, and gave a little tap at the door.

"Who is there?" cried the wolf.

The hoarse voice made Little Red Riding Hood say to herself, "Poor grand-mother is very ill, she must have a bad cold."

"It is I, your Little Red Riding Hood," she said. "I have come to see how you are, and to bring you a pot of butter and a cake from mother."

"Pull the bobbin, and the latch will fly up," called the wolf. Little Red Riding Hood did so, the door flew open, and she went at once into the cottage.

"Put the cake and butter on the table," said the wolf. "Then come and help me to rise." He had hid his head under the bed-clothes.

She took off her things, and went to the bed to do as she had been told.

"Why, grandmother," she said, "what long arms you have!"

"The better to hug you, my dear," said the wolf.

"And, grandmother, what long ears you have!"

"The better to hear you, my dear."

"But, grandmother, what great eyes you have!"

"The better to see you, my dear."

"But, grandmother, what big teeth you have!"

"The better to eat you with, my dear," said the wolf.

He was just going to spring upon poor Little Red Riding Hood, when a wasp flew into the room and stung him upon the nose.

The wolf gave a cry, and a little bird outside sang, "Tweet! tweet!" This told the green huntsman it was time to let fly his arrow, and the wolf was killed on the spot.

BEAUTY AND THE BEAST

A VERY wealthy merchant was left, at his wife's death, with a family of three sons and three daughters.

As he was a highly intelligent man, he determined to give his children the best education that money could procure for them, and he spared no expense to engage the very best masters to teach them.

The three daughters were exceedingly handsome both in face and person, but the youngest was especially admired for the sweetness of her countenance. When she was only a very little girl everyone called her the beauty of the family, and as she grew up the name was still used, and all friends addressed her as "My Beauty," to the disgust of her elder sisters, who were jealous of her.

Beauty was not only prettier than her sisters but she had a very much finer character, being good-tempered, gentle-mannered, obliging, and considerate.

The sisters, on the contrary, were haughty and purse-proud. They liked to imagine themselves great ladies, and they despised the daughters of the other merchants, refusing to visit them or to receive their visits. They spent all their time driving in the park or going to balls and theatres, and they amused themselves by making game of their younger sister because she spent her leisure painting, studying her music, or reading the works of the best authors.

As every one knew of their great wealth, these young ladies had many suitors from among the families of the other rich merchants, but when these gentlemen asked them in marriage, the two sisters replied contemptuously that no one less than a duke, or at the very least an earl, need take the trouble to propose to them. When any gentleman proposed marriage to Beauty, she thanked him politely for the honour he did her, but told him she was too young to marry, and wished to stay at home to cheer her father for some years yet.

Quite suddenly the merchant lost the whole of his great fortune, and all he had left was a few acres of land with a small cottage on it, quite far away in the country.

Almost broken-hearted, he called his children together and told them of the calamity, and that they must prepare to leave town and accompany him to the cottage, where, by industry and hard work, they would be able to live plainly, like the peasants, and pay their way honestly.

The two elder daughters laughed scornfully at the idea of living in such a place, and replied that they had lovers enough desirous of marrying them for their beauty, even if they had not a penny. They were woefully disappointed, however, for these very lovers refused to look at them now that they were poor. As they had always been so disdainful in their treatment of their neighbours, no one was sorry for them.

"They do not deserve to be pitied. It is a good thing to know their pride is humbled," was all one heard, but with regard to the youngest sister it was quite different, and on all sides one heard:

"Oh! how sorry we are for poor Beauty—she was always so gentle and kind, and she was so polite when she spoke to us!"

There were even several gentlemen who came, now when she had not a farthing, to ask if she would marry them; but while she thanked them from her heart, she told them that she could not leave her father in his misfortune, but would go with him to the country, where she would grudge no trouble to try to make him comfortable, and to help him all she could in his work.

Poor Beauty had certainly been grieved by the loss of their wealth—it could not have been otherwise; but when she felt inclined to cry over it, she said to herself:

"Why should I cry? An ocean of tears would not mend matters. I must try and be happy without riches, like the people I see round about me."

When they were settled in their country cottage, the merchant and his three sons set to work to dig and cultivate their land. Beauty rose at four o'clock every morning and busied herself cleaning the house and preparing and cooking food for the family.

At first she found it all very difficult, but it gradually became easier, and at the end of a few months she did not think it a trouble at all. Also, she was very much stronger—air and exercise had given her perfect health, so that she became more beautiful than ever. When she had finished her household tasks she read, played on the harpsichord, or sang to herself while spinning.

Her two sisters, on the contrary, were bored to death with their surroundings. They did not get out of bed till ten o'clock, and spent their time wandering aimlessly about, talking to each other about their former grandeur, and regretting their fine clothes and gay companions. They twitted their sister with being mean and poor-spirited because she was contented in her poverty. Their father did not think as they did. He knew that Beauty was better fitted than they were to shine in a high position. He greatly admired the character of his youngest daughter, and especially her gentle patience with her sisters, who not only left all the housework for her to do, but constantly insulted her while she was doing it.

When the family had lived about a year at the cottage, the merchant got a letter informing him that a ship in which he had valuable cargo had just arrived safely in port. The two elder girls nearly lost their heads with joy at the news, thinking that now they would be able to leave the cottage where time had hung so heavy on their hands, and when their father was ready to start upon the journey which he must make to town, they gave him a list of the dresses, mantles, and hats that he was to bring them. Beauty asked for nothing, thinking to herself that the price of the cargo would hardly pay for all the things her sisters had asked.

"Do you not want me to bring you anything?" said her father.

"Oh! thank you!" said Beauty. "I should be so glad to have a rose, if you can get one, for there are none in our little garden."

It was not really that Beauty wanted a rose so much, but she did not want to look superior to her sisters for fear of hurting their feelings, and she knew a rose would not cost much.

The good father set off with hope in his heart, but when he arrived in town some one brought a lawsuit against him, and though he won his case, it took all the money he had received to pay the lawyers, so that after all his trouble he had to return home as poor as when he went away, and very much sadder. But he comforted himself with the thought that he would soon be among his own family again, and urged his horse on as quickly as it could go.

When he was only thirty miles from home it began to snow heavily, so that he could only see a few yards before him. The road lay through a large forest, with many paths branching in different directions. He took a wrong turning and soon found himself completely lost. The wind had risen to a furious gale, and he was twice blown off his horse. Then darkness came down, and the thought of spending the night in the forest, with the wolves already howling in the distance, filled him with dismay. Also he was stiff with cold and very hungry. Leading his tired horse he almost groped his way, but he felt safer on foot, as the swaying branches were too high to hurt him. All of a sudden he saw a distant light and going in its direction soon found himself in a long avenue, at the end of which were many lights. Thanking God for such a deliverance, he mounted his horse. The intelligent animal also saw the lights and needed no urging to gallop toward them. They came from the windows of a great castle, but though it was illuminated as if for a feast, there was no sign or sound of life anywhere around it.

From the court they could see the open door of a great stable, toward which the horse turned of its own accord, and, finding both corn and hay there, the tired, hungry animal attacked them without hesitation and made a good meal.

The merchant tied him up for the night and turned toward the house, but no one was to be seen. He entered the open door and found himself in a great dining-hall, with a good fire blazing on the hearth, and a fine dinner already on the table, but with only one cover laid. As he was wet to the skin, he stood up before the fire, saying to himself:

"Both master and servants will pardon me, under the circumstances, and no doubt they will soon be here."

He waited long, but no one came, and when the clock struck eleven o'clock he could resist no longer, for he was faint with hunger, so he took some chicken from a dish and ate it greedily, but trembling with fear of the consequences. As no one came, he filled a glass of wine for himself and drank it off, then another, and another. His courage returned, he went from the dining-hall, through one splendid apartment after another, all magnificently furnished, and soon found himself in a beautiful bedroom, evidently prepared for a guest, and as it was past midnight, and he was greatly fatigued, he made up his mind to lock the door of the room and go to bed.

He did not wake till ten o'clock next morning, and the first thing his eye fell on was a fine new suit of clothes laid where his wet, muddy garments had been the night before.

"Surely," said he to himself, "this palace must belong to some good fairy, who has taken pity on me in my misery."

He rose and looked out of the window. The snow was all gone, and under a bright sun lawns of velvety grass, avenues of shady trees, and arbours of roses, with fountains and flowers, enchanted the eye.

He dressed and went down to the great hall where he had supped the previous night, and there, on a small table, was a cup of delicious cbocolate and some crisp toast.

"Thank you, my lady fairy," said he, "for having had the goodness to think of my breakfast."

When he had taken his chocolate, the good man went out to the stable for his horse, and, as he passed under a bower of roses, Beauty's request came to his mind, so he broke off a branch which had several roses on it. As he did so, a sudden fearful sound arose, and, looking round, he saw coming toward him a beast so horrible in appearance that he almost fainted.

"Monster of ingratitude!" said the Beast in a terrible voice. "I saved your life by receiving you into my castle, and, for my thanks, you rob me of my roses, which I love above all else in the world! Your life is the price you must pay for such a deed. I give you one quarter of an hour to prepare for your death!"

The merchant, clasping his bands, threw himself on his knees before the monster and cried:

"Pardon me, my lord, I did not dream of offending you. I was only gathering a rose for one of my daughters who had asked me to take her one."

"I am not called 'my lord,' but 'the Beast,'" replied the odious creature. "I hate compliments, and only wish people to say what they really think, so you need not try to make me change my mind by your flatteries.

"You say, however, that you have daughters, so if one of them will come, of her own free will, to die in your stead, I am willing to pardon you—no arguing!— I have told you my will—off with you! And if none of your daughters will die for you, give me your oath that you will return yourself three months from this day."

The good man had no intention of letting any one of his daughters sacrifice herself for him, but he saw the opportunity of seeing his family once more, and of bidding them farewell, so he promised, and the Beast told him he was free to go at any hour that suited him, adding:

"I do not wish you, however, to leave my house empty-handed. Go back to the room you slept in. There you will see a large empty chest. You may fill it with whatever you see around you, and I shall see that it is taken to your cottage." Then the Beast disappeared.

The merchant consoled himself a little by thinking that, if he had to die, he would now be able to provide his children with something to help them to live, so he returned to the bedroom. Looking around him, he discovered quite a heap of gold coins lying on the floor. With these he quickly filled the chest and locked it; then, taking his horse from the stable, he remounted, and left the palace with a very heavy heart.

The horse, of its own accord, took the shortest way to the cottage, where they arrived in a few hours.

On his arrival the family crowded round him, kissing him and welcoming him home, but instead of returning their caresses he burst into tears.

He held the rose branch in his hand, and when he could speak he turned to his daughter, and gave it to her saying:

"My Beauty, take the roses—they are going to cost your unfortunate father very dear"

Then he told his family the dire strait in which he found himself.

On hearing his story, the two elder daughters uttered piercing shrieks, and heaped insults and bad names on poor Beauty, who did not shed a tear.

"Only think what the pride of that small creature has brought about!" said they. "Why could she not ask for useful garments, like us? But no! the young lady wished to distinguish herself. Look, she does not even cry for causing the death of her father!"

"That would be a very useless thing to do," said Beauty. "Why should I weep for my father's death? He shall not die! Since the monster is willing to accept one of his daughters in his place, I shall give myself up to it, and shall be proud if by the sacrifice of my life I can save that of my dear father."

"No! my dear sister," cried the three brothers, with one voice. "We shall go and find this monster, and we shall1 kill him or perish ourselves."

"Do not indulge in such hopes," said the merchant. "The power of this Beast is so great that I have no hope of anyone being able to kill him. I am charmed with the kind heart of my Beauty, but I cannot let her risk her life. I am old, and, at best, could only live a few years longer. I have nothing to regret but leaving you alone, my dear children."

"I assure you, dearest Father," said Beauty, "that you shall not go to the Beast's palace without me. You could not possibly hinder me from following you. Although I am young, life has no great attractions for me, and I prefer being devoured by the monster to dying of grief for the loss of my father."

It was useless to try to dissuade her. Beauty was quite determined to go with her father when the time should come for him to return to the palace, and the jealous sisters could hardly hide their pleasure at her decision.

The merchant was so grieved at the thought of perhaps losing his favourite daughter that he quite forgot to speak of the chest of gold coins which the Beast had promised to send, but on going to bed he found it there at his bedside.

He made up his mind not to tell his two eider daughters about it, as he felt sure they would want to go back to their extravagant life in town, and he had determined to spend what of his life might still be before him in the country. He, however, confided the secret to Beauty, who at once remembered to tell him that during his absence two gentlemen who had made their acquaintance had fallen in love with her sisters, and, in the goodness of her heart, she advised her father to use a great part of the money in getting them married and comfortably provided for. The sweet-tempered girl cherished no resentment against them for their daily unkindness to her. She wanted to see them happy.

When the sisters saw Beauty ready to start with her father, at the date fixed, they rubbed their eyelids with an onion to make them look as if they were weeping; but the brothers, as well as their father, wept in earnest, not knowing what might happen. Beauty alone did not cry, for she did not wish to add to their grief.

They set off on horseback, Beauty riding on a pillion behind her father. The horse took the road to the palace without being guided, and they arrived in the evening, finding the whole place brilliantly lighted as before. They alighted at the entrance. The horse went to the stable, while the father and daughter entered the dining-hall, where they found a magnificently spread table, with covers for two. The merchant was too sad to care to eat, but Beauty made a great effort not to seem afraid, and sitting down, began to help him to the different dishes which he preferred. While they were eating, Beauty remarked to herself:

"The Beast must wish to fatten me before eating me, as he has provided such a feast."

Just when they had finished their supper they heard a strange noise, and the merchant, feeling sure it was the Beast, bade his daughter adieu, weeping bitterly.

Beauty could not help shuddering when she saw the horrible face of the frightful creature, but she made a brave effort to overcome her fear, and when the monster asked her if it was really of her own free will that she had come, although she was trembling from head to foot she answered, "Yes."

"You are a good girl, and I am much obliged to you," said the Beast; then he turned to the father and said:

"Good man, leave this palace to-morrow morning, and do not take it into your head to return.

"Good night, my Beauty."

"Good night, Beast," the maiden replied, and the Beast withdrew.

"Oh, my child," said the merchant, embracing his daughter, "I am half dead already with horror. Hear me! Let me stay."

"No, dear Father," said she firmly; "you will go home to-morrow, and you will leave me to the care of kind Providence, who will perhaps take pity on me."

They parted to go to their bedrooms; neither of them expected to sleep that night, but their heads were no sooner on their pillows than they fell into a deep slumber.

During her sleep, Beauty dreamt she saw a lady, who said to her:

"Beauty, I am charmed with your tenderness of heart. Your kind action in giving your life to save your father's will not go unrewarded."

In the morning Beauty told the dream to her father, and it comforted him a little, but it did not keep him from crying aloud in his distress when the moment came for parting with his beloved daughter.

When he was out of sight, Beauty could not help throwing herself on a couch and sobbing as if her heart would break. This relieved her feelings, and, being of a brave nature, she sat up, commended herself to the care of God, and though she quite expected to be eaten by the Beast that evening, she resolved not to waste the few last hours of her life by meeting her trouble halfway.

She therefore took a walk through the lovely grounds, and then began to explore the interior of the castle. She could not help admiring the magnificent decorations and priceless tapestries, as well as the costly furniture.

She came to a door on which was written:

BEAUTY'S BOUDOIR

Extremely surprised, she quickly opened the door, and was dazzled by the brilliance of her surroundings—every comfort and luxury she could desire was there.

One of the first things that caught her eye was an exquisite bookcase, filled with handsome editions of her favourite books, and near it was a harpsichord with an abundance of music.

"The Beast does not want me to weary," said she in a low voice; then she thought to herself, "If I had only one day to live, he would surely not have provided so much for my entertainment." This thought gave her courage. She opened the bookcase, and took out a volume with a very long title in gold letters; it was this:

Desire Command.
You are Lady and Mistress Here.

"Alas!" thought she, with a sigh, "I desire nothing but to see my poor father, and to know what he is doing just now."

She laid down the book without speaking a word. Judge then of her surprise, when, in a great mirror on the opposite wall, she saw the cottage where her father was just arriving, broken down with grief. Her sisters came out to meet him, pretending to be sorry, but, in spite of their false grimaces, joy was visible in their eyes to see him returning without her. Then it all disappeared, and, standing there, she could not help thinking how considerate and kind the Beast seemed to have been in trying to make her happy, and in her heart she felt she need not be so much afraid of him.

At noon an excellent dinner was on the table, and while she was eating she listened to a fine band playing lovely music, but no one was visible.

In the evening, as she sat down to supper, she heard the peculiar noise made by the Beast, and she could not help trembling violently when he appeared.

"Beauty," said the monster, "are you willing to let me look at you while you sup?"

"You are master here," said Beauty, in a tremulous voice.

"No!" replied the Beast, "you alone are mistress here. You have only to bid me go away if my presence annoys you and I shall go at once. Tell me frankly—do you not think me extremely ugly?"

"I do indeed," said Beauty, "for I cannot tell an untruth, but I think you are very kind."

"You are right," said the monster, "but besides being ugly, I am very stupid. I know quite well that I am only a fool."

"No one is really stupid who thinks he is not clever. No fool ever considers himself one."

"Enjoy your supper, then, Beauty," said the monster, "and try not to feel weary in your own house, for all you see is yours, and it would grieve me much to see you unhappy."

"You are very kind," said Beauty, "and your goodness of heart gives me great pleasure. Indeed, when I think how good you are, I do not seem to see you so ugly."

"Oh! for that part," said the Beast, "my heart is tender enough, but it does not hinder me from being a monster."

"There are many men far worse monsters than you are," said Beauty, "and I prefer you with the face you have to many men I have met, who, behind a handsome face, hide a false, bad heart."

"If I had wit enough I should pay you a great compliment to thank you for the pleasure your words give me," said the Beast, "but, being so stupid, all I can say is that I am greatly obliged to you."

Beauty took a hearty supper, and quite forgot her fear of the Beast, but she was again in an agony of terror when he suddenly said to her: "Beauty, will you be my wife?"

It was some time before she could find words to reply, but at last she answered simply:

"No, Beast."

At this the poor monster heaved a dreadful sigh, which seemed more like a shriek, and the whole palace shook with the sound. Beauty thought her last hour had come. The Beast, however, only said gently: "Good night, then, Beauty," and went slowly to the door, turning his head time to time to look wistfully at her as he went.

Left alone, Beauty felt a great wave of pity rising within her.

"What a pity it is that he is so ugly!" said she. "He is so very good and kind !"

Three months passed thus in the palace, without any special event. Every evening Beauty received a visit from the Beast, who did his best to entertain her during supper with his simple talk, which never lacked good sense, but which was far from being what is called, in society, brilliant conversation. Every day Beauty noticed some new token of the goodness which lay below the repulsive outward appearance of the monster. She was becoming accustomed to his ugliness, and instead of dreading his visits she often found herself looking at her watch as nine o'clock drew near, for that was the hour when he made his appearance. There was only one thing which really distressed her. It was that the monster, before leaving her, never failed to ask her if she would become his wife, and never seemed less pained at her refusal.

One evening, Beauty said to him:

"Beast, you grieve me greatly. I only wish I could bring myself to marry you, but I am too sincere to pretend to you that I can ever do so. I shall always be your friend—will you not try to be contented with that ?"

"I suppose I must," said the Beast. "I can judge justly, and I know how horribly ugly I am, only I love you greatly. I ought to be very thankful that you are willing to remain here to keep me company. Promise me, I entreat you, that you will never leave me."

Beauty blushed deeply at these words. That afternoon she had seen in her mirror that her father was very ill from his grief at losing her, and she wished greatly to visit him, and reassure him.

"I could readily promise," said she, "never to leave you altogether, but I wish so much to see my father again that I shall die of grief if I may not do so."

"I would rather die myself than grieve you," said the monster. "I shall send you home to your father, you will stay there, and your poor Beast will die of grief."

"Oh, no!" said Beauty, weeping. "I love you too much to wish to cause your death. I promise you to return in eight days. You have enabled me to see that my sisters are both married, and that my brothers have joined the army. My father is quite alone. Let me stay with him for a week, I beg of you."

"You shall be there to-morrow morning," said the Beast, "but do remember your promise. When you are ready to return, you have only to lay your ring on the table when you go to bed. Good-bye, Beauty."

The Beast sighed, in his usual fearful way, when he said these words, and Beauty went to bed, much grieved at having hurt him. She awoke next morning in her father's house. She rang a bell which was on the table by the side of her bed, and it was answered by the servant-maid, who gave a great cry of astonishment when she saw her. The father went quickly upstairs to know what had happened, and was beside himself with joy when he saw his dear daughter. He clasped her in his arms and they embraced each other long and tenderly.

When she got up to dress, Beauty remembered that she had no clothes to put on, but the maid told her that she had just found a chest in the next room, and on opening it she saw it was filled with magnificent robes of costly materials, trimmed with gold lace and embroidered with jewels, and Beauty felt most grateful to the kind Beast for his attentions. She chose the plainest of these beautiful dresses; then she asked the maid to lock the chest, as she wished to give the others to her sisters, but she had hardly said the words when the chest disappeared. Her father said it looked as if the Beast only intended the dresses for herself, and at these words the chest was again in its place.

While Beauty was dressing, word of her arrival was sent to her sisters, who appeared soon after with their husbands. Both of them were miserably unhappy. One had married a man who was exceedingly handsome, but who was so vain that he thought of nothing but his own good looks, and took no notice whatever of his wife. The other had married a man who was extraordinarily clever, but the only use he made of his brains was to utter sarcastic remarks to every one, and particularly to his wife.

These sisters were very envious when they saw Beauty looking prettier than ever and dressed like a princess. In vain she kissed and fondled them; they could not hide their jealousy, which increased as they saw how happy she was. They both went into the garden to vent their spite, and to complain to each other.

"Why," said they, "is that creature so much happier than we? Are we not as deserving of happiness as she is?"

"Sister," said the eldest, "I have an idea; let us persuade her to overstay her time. Her stupid Beast will be enraged with her for not keeping her word, and probably he will devour her."

"What a clever plan!" said the other. "We must pretend to be very fond of her and make a great fuss about her."

With this wicked thought in their minds they went back into the cottage, and were so very loving in their speech and manner that poor Beauty almost wept for joy. At the end of the eight days, they made such a show of grief, tearing their hair and wringing their hands, that Beauty consented to stay another week, not without being very sorry for the disappointment she was causing her poor Beast, whom she had grown so fond of, and whom she was longing to see again. On the tenth night of her visit, she dreamt she was in the palace garden, where she saw the Beast lying prone upon the grass, dying, and reproaching her for her ingratitude. She awoke with a start; then she began to weep.

"How wicked I am!" she said to herself. "How could I grieve the poor Beast who has been so good to me? Is it his fault that he is ugly and not clever? He is good, and that is worth more than cleverness or good looks. Why could I not marry him? I should have been much happier with him than my sisters are with their husbands. It is neither the good looks nor the cleverness of her husband that can make a woman happy; it is kindness of heart, uprightness, and readiness to oblige, and my poor Beast has all these good qualities. I may not be in love with him, but my heart is full of respect, friendship, and gratitude whenever I think of him. Come! I must not make him unhappy. I should reproach myself all my life if I did."

Beauty got up, put her ring on the table, and went back to bed. She quickly fell asleep, and when she awoke next morning she was pleased to find herself back in the palace of the Beast. She dressed herself magnificently to give him pleasure, and found the day pass all too slowly, waiting for nine o'clock. At last the hour struck, but the Beast did not make his appearance.

Beauty was greatly alarmed, fearing lest she had caused his death. She ran from room to room, calling him loudly, but she got no answer. She was almost in despair when she suddenly remembered her dream. Quick as thought, she turned and ran toward the garden. There, on the very spot she had seen in her sleep, lay her poor Beast, prone on the grass near the brook, quite unconscious and apparently dead. In an agony of grief she threw herself down over his body, without any sense of horror; then, finding that his heart was still beating, she brought water from the stream and bathed his temples. This revived him a little, and at length he opened his eyes.

After a little, the Beast found strength to speak.

"You forgot your promise," said he, gazing at Beauty. "My grief at losing you was so great that I determined to starve myself to death, but I shall die happy now that I have had the great pleasure of seeing you again."

"No, my dear Beast, you shall not die," cried Beauty. "You must live to become my husband. From this moment I am yours. I imagined I had no stronger feeling for you than friendship, but now I know that I cannot live without you."

Just as Beauty finished this speech, the whole palace was brilliantly illuminated, while fireworks and music showed that some great event was being celebrated. Beauty looked up for a moment, but immediately turned again toward her dear Beast, for whose life she trembled. But where was he ? What did it all mean ? At her feet knelt a young Prince, handsome as Adonis, who was gratefully thanking her for having broken the spell of his enchantment. Although this Prince well deserved her attention, she quickly asked him:

"Where is my Beast?"

"You see him at your feet," was the reply. "A wicked fairy had condemned me to remain in that dreadful form till a beautiful young lady should, of her own free will, consent to marry me, and I was strictly forbidden to show my intelligence. You alone of all those I have met were touched by my kindness of disposition in spite of my forbidding appearance, and in offering you my crown and my heart I do not pretend to be able to repay all I owe to you."

Beauty held out her hand to the Prince, in a dream of delighted surprise. He rose and clasped her hand in his, and they walked together to the palace. On entering the great hall, Beauty was overjoyed to see her dear father and all the family there. The beautiful lady whom she had seen in her dream had transported them there from the cottage.

This lady, who was a great fairy, now came forward.

"Beauty," said she, "come and receive the reward of your wise choice. You preferred high character to mere beauty, or even cleverness; you deserve to find all these united in one person. You are going to be a great queen. I hope that the throne will not alter your character."

"As for you, ladies," said the fairy to the sisters, "I know the malice which fills your hearts. You shall become statues, but you shall retain your reason inside the stone which imprisons you. You shall be placed one on each side of the door of your sister's palace, where your only punishment will be seeing your sister's happiness. When you recognize your faults and repent of them, you will be restored to your human forms, but I fear you are likely to remain statues. One may correct oneself of pride, bad temper, greed, or sloth, but to change an evil, envious heart is little short of a miracle."

Then, with one touch of her wand, she transported the whole company to the kingdom of the Prince, whose subjects received him with joy. Beauty and he were married with great pomp, the festivities lasting many days. The union was a very happy one, and at the end of a long life their love for each was still undiminished.

GEORGIA

THE early history of the Georgians is wrapped in fable. Georgia is bounded by the Caucasian Mountains on the north and by the Armenian Mountains on the south. The people have gained much from the Byzantine Empire on the one side and from Persia and Turkey on the other. Thus they owe something both to Christendom and to Islam. Their literature is by no means negligible. There are Georgian manuscripts now in existence which date from about the year 946. The Georgians first appear in history in the time of Alexander the Great, reaching their zenith in the twelfth century. After this they were long subjected to oppression and this has had an effect upon their character.

The elemental ideas of the stories are like those of other folk-tales, but their development is different. "The Serpent and the Peasant" is a beautiful parable which deserves a high place in folk-lore.

THE PRINCE WHO BEFRIENDED THE BEASTS

THERE was a king, and he had three sons. Once he fell ill, and became blind in both eyes. He sent his sons for a surgeon. All the surgeons agreed that there was a fish of a rare kind by the help of which the king might be cured. They made a sketch of the fish, and left it with the sick monarch.

The king commanded his eldest son to go and catch that fish in the sea. A hundred men with their nets were lost in the sea, but nought could they find like the fish they sought. The eldest son came home to his father and said: "I have found nothing." .This displeased the king, but what could he do? Then the second son set out, taking with him a hundred men also, but all his men were lost too, and he brought back nothing.

After this, the youngest brother went. He had recourse to cunning; he took with him a hundred kilas [1] of flour and one man. He came to the sea, and every day he strewed flour in the water, near the shore, until all the flour was used up; the fishes grew fat on the flour, and said: "Let us do a service to this youth since he has enabled us to grow fat"; so, as soon as the youth threw a net into the sea, he at once drew out the rare fish he sought. He wrapped it up in the skirt of his robe, and went his way.

As he rode along, some distance from his companion, he heard a voice that said: "O youth, I am dying!" But on looking round he saw no man, and continued his

---

[1] Kila, a measure of flour = about 36-40 pounds.

309

journey. After a short time, he again heard the same words. He looked round more carefully, but saw nothing. Then he glanced at the skirt of his robe, and saw that the fish had its mouth open, and was dying. The youth said to it: "What dost thou want?" The fish answered: "It will be better for thee if thou wilt let me go, some day I shall be of use to thee." The youth took it and threw it into the water, saying to his comrade:" I hope thou wilt not betray me."

When he reached home, he told his father that he had been unsuccessful. Some time passed. Once the prince quarrelled with his comrade, and the latter ran off and told the king how his son had deceived him. When the king heard this, he ordered his son to be taken away and killed. He was taken out, but when they were about to kill him, the youth entreated them, saying: "What doth it profit you if you slay me? If you let me go, 'twill be a good deed, and I shall flee to foreign lands." The executioners took pity on him, and set him free; he thanked them and departed.

He went, he went, he went, he went farther than anybody ever went—he came to a great forest. As he went through the forest, he saw a deer running, in a great state of alarm. The youth stopped, and fixed his gaze on it; then the deer came up and fell on its face before him. The youth asked: "What ails thee?" "The prince pursues me, and on thee depends my safety." The youth took the deer with him and went on. A huntsman met him, and asked: "Whither art thou leading the deer?" The youth replied: "One king has sent it as a gift to another king, and, lo! I am taking it." The youth thus saved the deer from death, and the deer said: "A time will come when I shall save thy life."

The youth went on his way: he went, he went, he went, so far he went, good sir, that the "three day colt" (of fable) could not go so far. He looked, and, lo! a frightened eagle perched on his shoulder, and said: "Youth, on thee depends my safety!" The youth protected it also from its pursuer. Then the eagle said to him: "Some day I shall do thee a service."

The youth went on: he went through the forest, he went, he went, he went, he went farther than he could, he went a week, two weeks, a year and three months. Then he heard some fearful rumbling, roaring, thunder and lightning—something was coming through the forest, breaking down all the trees. A great jackal appeared, and ran up to the youth, saying: "If thou wilt thou canst protect me; the prince is pursuing me with all his army." The youth saved the jackal, as he had saved the other animals. Then the jackal said: "Some day I shall help thee."

The youth went on his way, and, when he was out of the wood, came to a town. In this town he found a castle of crystal, in the courtyard of which he saw a great number of young men, some dying and some dead. He asked the meaning of this, and was told: "The king of this land has a daughter, a maiden queen; she has made a proclamation that she will wed him that can hide himself from her; but no man can hide himself from her, and all these men has she slain, for he that cannot hide himself from her is cast down from the top of the castle."

When the youth heard this, he at once arose, and went to the maiden. They bowed themselves each to the other. The maiden asked him: "Wherefore art thou come hither?" The youth answered: "I come for that which others have come for." She immediately called her viziers together, and they wrote out the usual contract. The youth went out from the castle, came to the seashore, sat down, and was soon buried in thought. Just then, something made a great splash in the sea, came and swallowed the youth, carried him into the Red Sea, there they were hidden in the depths of the sea, near the shore. The youth remained there all that night.

When the maiden arose next morning she brought her mirror and looked in it, but she found nothing in the sky, she looked on the dry land, and found nothing there, she looked at the sea—and then she saw the youth in the belly of the fish, which was hiding in the deep waters. After a short time, the fish threw up the youth on the place where it had found him. He went merrily to the maiden. She asked: "Well, then, didst thou hide thyself?" "Yes, I hid myself." But the maiden told him where he had been, and how he got there, and added: "This time I forgive thee, for the cleverness thou hast shown."

The youth set out again, and sat down in a field. Then something fell upon him, and took him up into the air, lifted him up into the sky, and covered him with its wing. When the maiden arose next morning, she looked in her mirror, she gazed at the mountain, she gazed at the earth, but she found nothing, she looked at the sky, and there she saw how the eagle was covering the youth. The eagle carried the youth down, and put him on the ground. He was joyful, thinking that the maiden could not have seen him; but when he came to her she told him all.

Then he fell into deep melancholy, but the maiden, being struck with wonder at his cunning in hiding himself, told him that she again forgave him. He went out again, and, as he was walking in the field, the deer came to him and said:" Mount on my back." He mounted, and the deer carried him away, away, away over all the mountains that were there, and put him in a lair. When the maiden rose next morning, she found him, and when he came back to her she said: "Young man, it seems that thou hast many friends, but thou canst not hide thyself from me; yet this day also I forgive thee." The youth went sadly away; he had lost confidence.

When he sat down in the field, an earthquake began, the town shook, lightning flashed, thunder rolled, and when a thunderbolt had fallen, there leapt out from it his friend the gigantic jackal, and said to him:

"Fear not, O youth!"

The jackal had recourse to its wonted cunning; it began to scrape at the earth: it dug, it dug, it dug, and burrowed right up to the place where the maiden dwelt, and then it said to the youth: "Stay thou here, she will look at the sky, the mountain, the sea, and when she cannot find thee she will break her mirror; when thou hearest this, then strike thy head through the ground and come out."

This advice, of course, pleased the youth. When the maiden arose in the morning, she looked at the sea, she found him not, she looked at the mountain, she looked at the sky, and still she could not see him, so she broke the mirror. Then the youth pushed his head through the floor, bowed, and said to the maiden: "Thou art mine and I am thine!" They summoned the viziers, sent the news to the king, and a great feast began.

THE STRONG MAN AND THE DWARF

THERE came from far-off lands a strong man who had nowhere met his match, and challenged anyone in the whole kingdom to wrestle with him.

The king gathered his folk together, but, to his wonder, could not for a long time find anybody ready to face the strong man, till, at last, there stood forth a weak insignificant-looking dwarf, who offered to wrestle with the giant. Haughtily looking down on his adversary, the giant carelessly turned away, thinking that he was befooled. But the dwarf asked that his strength should be put to the proof before the struggle began.

The giant angrily seized a stone, and, clasping it in his fingers, squeezed moisture out of it.

The dwarf cunningly replaced the stone by a sponge of the same appearance, and squeezed still more moisture out of it.

The giant then took another stone, and threw it so violently on the ground that it became dust.

The dwarf took a stone, hid it under the ground, and threw on the ground a handful of flour, to the great astonishment of the giant.

Stretching forth his hand to the dwarf, the giant said: "I never expected to find so much strength in such a small man, I will not wrestle with you; but give me your hand in token of friendship and brotherhood."

After this, the giant asked the dwarf to go home with him. But first he asked the dwarf why he had not pressed his hand in a brotherly manner. The dwarf replied that he was unable to moderate the force of his pressure, and that more than one man had already died from the fearful force of his hand. The new brothers then set out together. On their way to the giant's house, they came to a stream which had to be forded.

The dwarf, fearing to be carried away by the current, told the strong man that he was suffering from belly-ache, and did not therefore wish to go into the cold water, so he asked to be carried over.

In the midst of the stream, the strong man, with the dwarf on his shoulders, suddenly stopped and said: "I have heard that strong people are heavy, but I do not feel you on my shoulders. Tell me how this is, for God's sake."

"Since we have become brothers," replied the dwarf, "I have no right to press with all my weight upon you, and did I not support myself by holding on to the sky with one hand, you could never carry me."

But the strong man, wishing to test his strength, asked the dwarf to drop his hand for a moment, whereupon the dwarf took from his pocket two nails, and stuck the sharp points of them into the shoulders of the strong man. The giant could not endure the pain, and begged the dwarf to lighten his burden at once, *i.e.*, to lay hold of heaven again with one hand.

When they had reached the other side, the two new friends soon came to the strong man's house. The giant, wishing to give a dinner to the dwarf, proposed that they should share the work of getting it ready, that one of them should take the bread out of the oven, while the other went to the cellar for wine.

The dwarf saw in the oven an immense loaf which he could never have lifted, so he chose to go to the cellar for wine. But when he had descended he was unable even to lift the weights on the top of the jars, so, thinking that by this time the giant would have taken the loaf out of the oven, he cried: "Shall I bring up all the jars?"

The giant, alarmed lest the dwarf should spoil his whole year's stock of wine, by digging the jars out of the ground, where they were buried, rushed into the cellar, and the dwarf went upstairs.

But great was the astonishment of the dwarf when he found that the bread was still in the oven, and that he must take it out, willy-nilly. He succeeded with difficulty in dragging a loaf to the edge of the oven, but then he fell with the hot bread on top of him, and, being unable to free himself, was almost smothered.

Just then the giant came in, and asked what had happened. The dwarf replied: "As I told you this morning, I am suffering from a stomach-ache, and, in order to sooth the pain, I applied the hot loaf as a plaster." . . . Then the giant came up, and said: "Poor fellow! How do you feel now, after your plaster?" "Better, thank God," replied the dwarf, "I feel so much better that you can take off the loaf." . . .

The giant lifted the loaf, and the two then sat down to dinner. Suddenly the giant sneezed so hard that the dwarf was blown up to the roof, and seized a beam, so that he should not fall down again. The giant looked up with astonishment, and asked: "What does this mean?" The dwarf angrily replied: "If you do such a vulgar thing again I shall pull this beam out and break it over your stupid head." The giant made humble excuses, and promised that he would never sneeze again during dinner time; he then brought a ladder by which the dwarf came down.

A WITTY ANSWER

A CERTAIN king was angry with one of his lords, and put him in prison; wishing to keep him there, he said he would only set him free if he could bring to the court a horse which was neither grey, nor black, brown nor bay, white nor roan, dun, chestnut, nor piebald—and, in short, the king enumerated every possible colour that a horse could be. The imprisoned lord promised to get such a horse if the king would set him free at once. As soon as he was at liberty, the lord asked the king to send a groom for the horse, but begged that the groom might come neither on Monday nor Tuesday, Wednesday nor Thursday, Friday, Saturday, nor Sunday, but on any other day of the week that suited His Majesty.

THE KING AND THE APPLE

THERE was and there was not at all (of God's best may it be!), there was a king. When the day of his death was drawing nigh, he called his son to him, and said: "In the day when thou goest to hunt in the east, take this coffer, but only open it when thou art in dire distress."

The king died, and was buried in the manner he had wished. The prince fell into a state of grief, and would not go outside the door. At last the ministers of state came to the new king, and proposed to him that he should go out hunting. The king was delighted with the idea, and set out for the chase with his suite.

They went eastward, and killed a great quantity of game. On their way home, the young monarch saw a tower near the road, and wished to know what was in it. He asked one of his viziers to go and try to find out about it. He obeyed, but first said:

"I hope to return in three days, and if I do not I shall be dead."

Three days passed, and the vizier did not return. The king sent a second, a third, a fourth, but not one of them came back. Then he rose and went himself. When he arrived he saw written over the door: "Enter and thou wilt repent; enter not and thou wilt repent."

"I must do one or the other," said the king to himself, "so I shall go in."

He opened the door and went in. Behold! there stood twelve men with drawn swords. They took his hand and led him into twelve rooms. When he was come into the twelfth, he saw a golden couch, on which was stretched a boy of eight or nine years of age. His eyes were closed, and he did not utter a word. The king was told: "Thou mayst ask him three questions, but if he does not understand and answer all of them, thou must lose thy head."

The king became very sad, but at last remembered the coffer his father had given him. "What greater misfortune can I have than to lose my head?" said he to himself. He took out the coffer, and opened it; from it there fell out an apple, which rolled toward the couch. "What help can this be to me?" said the king.

But the apple began to speak, and told the following tale to the boy: "A certain man was travelling with his wife and brother, when night fell, and they had no food. The woman's brother-in-law went into a neighbouring village to buy bread; on the way he met brigands, who robbed him and cut off his head. When his brother did not return, the man went to look for him; he met the same fate. The next day the unhappy woman went to seek them, and there she saw her husband and her brother-in-law lying in one place with their heads cut off. The woman sat down, tore her hair, and began to weep bitterly.

"At that moment there jumped out a little mouse. The woman took a stone, threw it at the mouse, and killed it. Then the mouse's mother came out and said: look at me, I can bring my child back to life, but what canst thou do for thy husband and his brother?' She pulled up an herb, applied it to the little mouse, and it was restored to life. Then they both disappeared in their hole. The woman rejoiced greatly when she saw this; she also plucked of the same herb, put the heads on the bodies, and applied it to them. Her husband and brother-in-law both came back to life, but alas! she had put the wrong heads on the bodies. Now, my sage youth! tell me, which was the woman's husband?" concluded the apple.

He opened his eyes, and said: "Certainly it was he who had the right head."

The king was very glad.

"A joiner, a tailor, and a priest were travelling together at one time," began the apple. "Night came on when they were in a wood; they lighted a huge fire, had their supper, and then said: 'Do not let us be deprived of employment, each of us shall in turn watch, and do something in his trade.'

"The joiner's turn came first. He cut down a tree, and out of it he fashioned a man. Then he lay down, and went to sleep, while the tailor mounted guard. When he saw the wooden man, he took off his clothes and put them on it. Last of all, the priest acted as sentinel. When he saw the man he said: 'I will pray to God that he may give this man a soul.' He prayed, and his wish was granted.

"Now, my boy, canst thou tell me who made the man?"

"He who gave him the soul?"

The king was pleased, and said to himself, "That is two." The apple went on again: "There were a diviner, a physician, and a swift runner. The diviner said: 'There is a certain prince who is ill with such and such a disease.' The physician said:' I know a cure for it.' 'I will run with it,' said the swift runner. The physician prepared the medicine, and the man ran with it. Now tell me who cured the king's son?" said the apple.

"He who made the medicine," replied the boy. When he had given the three answers, the apple rolled back into the casket, and the king put it in his pocket. The boy arose, embraced the king, and kissed him: "Many men have been here, but I have not been able to speak before: now tell me what thou wishest, and I will do it." The king asked that his viziers might be restored to life, and they all went away with rich presents.

TEETH AND NO TEETH

SHAH ALl desired to see the hungriest man in his kingdom, and find out how much of the daintiest food such a man could eat at a meal. So he let it be known that on a certain day he would dine with his courtiers in the open air, in front of the palace. At the appointed hour, tables were laid and dinner was served, in the presence of a vast crowd. After the first course, the shah mounted a daïs, and said: "My loyal subjects! You see what a splendid dinner I have. I should like to share it with those among you who are really hungry, and have not eaten for a long time, so tell me truly which is the hungriest of you all, and bid him come forward."

Two men appeared from the crowd: an old man of fifty and a young man of twenty-seven. The former was grey-haired and feeble, the latter was fresh and of athletic build.

"How is it that you are hungry?" asked the shah of the old man. "I am old, my children are dead, toil has worn me out, and I have eaten nothing for three days." "And you?" said the shah, turning to the young man. "I could not find work, and as I am a hearty young man I am ashamed to beg, so I too have not eaten for three days."

The shah ordered them to be given food, on one plate, and in small portions. The hungry men eagerly ate, watching each other intently.

Suddenly the old man and the young one both stopped and began to weep. "Why do you weep?" asked the shah in astonishment. "I have no teeth," said the old man, "and while I am mumbling my food this young man eats up everything." "And why are you weeping?" "He is telling lies, your Majesty; while I am chewing my meat, the old man gulps down everything whole . . . . "

GERMANY

GERMAN folk-lore is bound up inextricably with the names of the brothers Grimm, who collected so great a number of traditional tales and formed a foundation for the study of comparative folk-lore. The brothers Grimm early found a startling similarity in the substance of stories. Certain plots, incidents, and basic elements appear everywhere, *e.g.*, the youngest son is wiser than the other two, the youngest daughter is generally ill-treated, the false bride is substituted for the true one, a supernatural husband or wife chooses a human wife or husband, inanimate things are transformed and made capable of speech and action. They collected a great number of folk and fairy stories—a work which carried their name all over the civilized world and ensured for them the happiest and most enduring kind of immortality.

HANSEL AND GRETHEL

ONCE upon a time there dwelt near a large wood a poor woodcutter, with his wife and two children by his former marriage, a little boy called Hansel, and a girl named Grethel. He had little enough to break or bite; and once, when there was a great famine in the land, he could not procure even his daily bread; and as he lay thinking in his bed one evening, rolling about for trouble, he sighed, and said to his wife, "What will become of us? How can we feed our children, when we have no more than we can eat ourselves?"

"Know, then, my husband," answered she, "we will lead them away, quite early in the morning, into the thickest part of the wood, and there make them a fire, and give them each a little piece of bread; then we will go to our work, and leave them alone, so they will not find the way home again, and we shall be freed from them."

"No, wife," replied he, "that I can never do. How can you bring your heart to leave my children all alone in the wood? for the wild beasts will soon come and tear them to pieces."

"Oh, you simpleton!" said she, "then we must all four die of hunger; you had better plane the coffins for us." But she left him no peace till he consented, saying, "Ah, but I shall regret the poor children."

The two children, however, had not gone to sleep for very hunger, and so they overheard what the stepmother said to their father. Grethel wept bitterly, and said to Hansel, "What will become of us?" "Be quiet, Grethel," said he; do not cry— I will soon help you." And as soon as their parents had fallen asleep, he got up, put on his coat, and, unbarring the back door, slipped out. The moon shone brilliantly, and the white pebbles which lay before the door seemed like silver pieces, they glittered so brightly. Hansel stooped down, and put as many into his pocket as it would hold; and then going back, he said to Grethel, "Be comforted, dear sister, and sleep in peace; God will not forsake us." And so saying, he went to bed again.

The next morning, before the sun arose, the wife went and awoke the two children. "Get up, you lazy things; we are going into the forest to chop wood." Then she gave them each a piece of bread, saying, "There is something for your dinner; do not eat it before the time, for you will get nothing else." Grethel took the bread in her apron, for Hansel's pocket was full of pebbles; and so they all set out upon their way. When they had gone a little distance, Hansel stood still, and peeped back at the house; and this he repeated several times, till his father said, "Hansel, what are you peeping at, and why do you lag behind? Take care, and remember your legs."

"Ah, father," said Hansel, "I am looking at my white cat sitting upon the roof of the house, and trying to say good-bye." "You simpleton!" said the wife, "that is not a cat; it is only the sun shining on the white chimney." But in reality Hansel was not looking at a cat; but every time he stopped, he dropped a pebble out of his pocket upon the path.

When they came to the middle of the forest, the father told the children to collect wood, and he would make them a fire, so that they should not be cold. So Hansel and Grethel gathered together quite a little mountain of twigs. Then they set fire to them; and as the flame burnt up high, the wife said, "Now, you children, lie down near the fire, and rest yourselves, while we go into the forest and chop wood; when we are ready, I will come and call you."

Hansel and Grethel sat down by the fire, and when it was noon, each ate the piece of bread; and because they could hear the blows of an axe, they thought their father was near; but it was not an axe, but a branch which he had bound to a withered tree, so as to be blown to and fro by the wind. They waited so long, that at last their eyes closed from weariness, and they fell fast asleep. When they awoke, it was quite dark, and Grethel began to cry, "How shall we get out of the wood?" But Hansel tried to comfort her by saying, "Wait a little while till the moon rises, and then we will quickly find the way." The moon soon shone forth, and Hansel, taking his sister's hand, followed the pebbles, which glittered like new-coined silver pieces, and showed them the path. All night long they walked on, and as day broke they came to their father's house. They knocked at the door, and when the wife opened it, and saw Hansel and Grethel, she exclaimed, "You wicked children! why did you sleep so long in the wood? We thought you were never coming home again." But their father was very glad, for it had grieved his heart to leave them all alone.

Not long afterward there was again great scarcity in every corner of the land;

and one night the children overheard their stepmother saying to their father, "Everything is again consumed; we have only half a loaf left, and then the song is ended: the children must be sent away. We will take them deeper into the wood, so that they may not find the way out again; it is the only means of escape for us."

But her husband felt heavy at heart, and thought, "It were better to share the last crust with the children." His wife, however, would listen to nothing that he said, and scolded and reproached him without end.

He who says A must say B too; and he who consents the first time must also the second.

The children, however, had heard the conversation as they lay awake, and as soon as the old people went to sleep Hansel got up, intending to pick up some pebbles as before; but the wife had locked the door, so that he could not get out. Nevertheless he comforted Grethel, saying, "Do not cry; sleep in quiet; the good God will not forsake us."

Early in the morning the stepmother came and pulled them out of bed, and gave them each a slice of bread, which was still smaller than the former piece. On the way, Hansel broke his in his pocket, and, stooping every now and then, dropped a crumb upon the path. "Hansel, why do you stop and look about?" said the father; "keep in the path." "I am looking at my little dove," answered Hansel, "nodding a good-bye to me." "Simpleton!" said the wife, "that is no dove, but only the sun shining on the chimney." But Hansel still kept dropping crumbs as he went along.

The mother led the children deep into the wood, where they had never been before, and there making an immense fire, she said to them, "Sit down here and rest, and when you feel tired you can sleep for a little while. We are going into the forest to hew wood, and in the evening, when we are ready, we will come and fetch you."

When noon came Grethel shared her bread with Hansel, who had strewn his on the path. Then they went to sleep; but the evening arrived and no one came to visit the poor children, and in the dark night they awoke, and Hansel comforted his sister by saying, "Only wait, Grethel, till the moon comes out, then we shall see the crumbs of bread which I have dropped, and they will show us the way home." The moon shone and they got up, but they could not see any crumbs, for the thousands of birds which had been flying about in the woods and fields had picked them all up. Hansel kept saying to Grethel, "We will soon find the way"; but they did not, and they walked the whole night long and the next day, but still they did not come out of the wood; and they got so hungry, for they had nothing to eat but the berries which they found upon the bushes.

Soon they got so tired that they could not drag themselves along, so they lay down under a tree and went to sleep.

It was now the third morning since they had left their father's house, and they still walked on; but they only got deeper and deeper into the wood, and Hansel saw that if help did not come very soon they would die of hunger. At about noonday they saw a beautiful snow-white bird sitting upon a bough, which sang so sweetly that they stood still and listened to it. It soon left off, and spreading its wings flew off; and they followed it until it arrived at a cottage, upon the roof of which it perched; and when they went close up to it they saw that the cottage was made of bread and cakes, and the window-panes were of clear sugar.

"We will go in there," said Hansel, "and have a glorious feast. I will eat a piece of the roof, and you can eat the window. Will they not be sweet?" So Hansel reached up and broke a piece off the roof, in order to see how it tasted, while Grethel stepped up to the window and began to bite it. Then a sweet voice called out in the room, "Tip-tap, tip-tap, who raps at my door?" and the children answered, "The wind, the wind, the child of heaven"; and they went on eating without interruption. Hansel thought the roof tasted very nice, and so he tore off a great piece; while Grethel broke a large round pane out of the window, and sat down quite contentedly. Just then the door opened, and a very old woman, walking upon crutches, came out. Hansel and Grethel were so frightened that they let fall what they had in their hands; but the old woman, nodding her head, said, "Ah, you dear children, what has brought you here? Come in and stop with me, and no harm shall befall you"; and so saying she took them both by the hand, and led them into her cottage. A good meal of milk and pancakes, with sugar, apples, and nuts, was spread on the table, and in the back room were two nice little beds, covered with white, where Hansel and Grethel laid themselves down, and thought themselves in heaven. The old woman behaved very kindly to them, but in reality she was a wicked witch who waylaid children, and built the bread-house in order to entice them in, but as soon as they were in her power she killed them, cooked and ate them, and made a great festival of the day. Witches have red eyes, and cannot see very far; but they have a fine sense of smelling, like wild beasts, so that they know when children approach them. When Hansel and Grethel came near the witch's house she laughed wickedly, saying, "Here come two who shall not escape me." And early in the morning, before they awoke, she went up to them, and saw how lovingly they lay sleeping, with their chubby red cheeks, and she mumbled to herself, "That will be a good bite." Then she took up Hansel with her rough hands, and shut him up in a little cage with a lattice-door; and although he screamed loudly it was of no use. Grethel came next, and, shaking her till she awoke, the witch said, "Get up, you lazy thing, and fetch some water to cook something good for your brother, who must remain in that stall and get fat; when he is fat enough I shall eat him." Grethel began to cry, but it was all useless, for the old witch made her do as she wished. So a nice meal was cooked for Hansel, but Grethel got nothing but a crab's claw.

Every morning the old witch came to the cage and said, "Hansel, stretch out your finger that I may feel whether you are getting fat." But Hansel used to stretch out a bone, and the old woman, having very bad sight, thought it was his finger, and wondered very much that he did not get fatter. When four weeks had passed, and Hansel still kept quite lean, she lost all her patience, and would not wait any longer. "Grethel," she called out in a passion, "get some water quickly; be Hansel fat or lean, this morning I will kill and cook him." Oh, how the poor little sister grieved, as she was forced to fetch the water, and fast the tears ran down her cheeks! "Dear good God, help us now!" she exclaimed. "Had we only been eaten by the wild beasts in the wood, then we should have died together." But the old witch called out, "Leave off that noise; it will not help you a bit."

So early in the morning Grethel was forced to go out and fill the kettle, and make a fire. "First, we will bake, however," said the old woman; "I have already heated the oven and kneaded the dough"; and so saying, she pushed poor Grethel up to the oven, out of which the flames were burning fiercely. "Creep in," said the witch, "and see if it is hot enough, and then we will put in the bread; but she intended when Grethel got in to shut up the oven and let her bake, so that she might eat her as well as Hansel. Grethel perceived what her thoughts were, and said, "I do not know how to do it; how shall I get in?" "You stupid goose," said she, "the opening is big enough. See, I could even get in myself!" and she got up, and put her head into the oven. Then Grethel gave her a push, so that she fell right in, and then shutting the iron door she bolted it. Oh! how horribly she howled; but Grethel ran away, and left the ungodly witch to burn to ashes.

Now she ran to Hansel, and, opening his door, called out, "Hansel, we are saved; the old witch is dead!" So he sprang out, like a bird out of his cage when the door is opened; and they were so glad that they fell upon each other's neck, and kissed each other over and over again. And now, as there was nothing to fear, they went into the witch's house, where in every corner were caskets full of pearls and precious stones. "These are better than pebbles," said Hansel, putting as many into his pocket as it would hold; while Grethel thought, "I will take some home too," and filled her apron full. "We must be off now," said HanseL, "and get out of this enchanted forest." But when they had walked for two hours they came to a large piece of water. "We cannot get over," said Hansel; "I can see no bridge at all." "And there is no boat either," said Grethel; "but there swims a white duck, I will ask her to help us over." And she sang:

> "Little Duck, good little Duck,
>   Grethel and Hansel, here we stand;
> There is neither stile nor bridge,
>   Take us on your back to land."

So the duck came to them, and Hansel sat himself on, and bade his sister sit behind him. "No," answered Grethel, "that will be too much for the duck; she shall take us over one at a time." This the good little bird did, and when both were happily arrived on the other side, and had gone a little way, they came to a well-known wood, which they knew the better every step they went, and at last they perceived their father's house. Then they began to run, and, bursting into the house, they fell into their father's arms. He had not had one happy hour since he had left the children in the forest; and his wife was dead. Grethel shook her apron, and the pearls and precious stones rolled out upon the floor, and Hansel threw down one handful after the other out of his pocket. Then all their sorrows were ended, and they lived together in great happiness.

My tale is done. There runs a mouse; whoever catches her may make a great, great cap out of her fur.

HANS IN LUCK

HANS had served his master seven years, and at the end of that time he said to him, "Master, since my time is up, I should like to go home to my mother; so give me my wages, if you please."

His master replied, "You have served me truly and honestly, Hans, and such as your service was, such shall be your reward," and with these words he gave him a lump of gold as big as his head. Hans thereupon took his handkerchief out of his pocket, and wrapping the gold up in it, threw it over his shoulder and set out on the road toward his native village. As he went along, carefully setting one foot to the ground before the other, a horseman came in sight, trotting gaily and briskly along upon a capital animal. "Ah," said Hans aloud, "what a fine thing that riding is! one is seated, as it were, upon a stool, kicks against no stones, spares one's shoes, and gets along without any trouble!"

The Rider, overhearing Hans making these reflections, stopped and said, "Why, then, do you travel on foot, my fine fellow?"

"Because I am forced," replied Hans, "for I have got a bit of a lump to carry home; it certainly is gold, but then I can't carry my head straight, and it hurts my shoulder."

"If you like we will exchange," said the Rider; "I will give you my horse, and you can give me your lump of gold."

"With all my heart," cried Hans; "but I tell you fairly you undertake a very heavy burden."

The man dismounted, took the gold, and helped Hans on to the horse, and, giving him the reins into his hands, said, "Now, when you want to go faster, you must chuckle with your tongue and cry, 'Gee up! gee up!'"

Hans was delighted indeed when he found himself on the top of a horse, and riding along so freely and gaily. After a while he thought he should like to go rather quicker, and so he cried, "Gee up! gee up!" as the man had told him. The horse soon set off at a hard trot, and before Hans knew what he was about he was thrown head over heels into a ditch which divided the fields from the road. The horse, having accomplished this feat, would have bolted off it he had not been stopped by a Peasant who was coming that way, driving a cow before him. Hans soon picked himself up on his legs, but he was terribly put out, and said to the country man, "That is bad sport, that riding, especially when one mounts such a beast as that, which stumbles and throws one off so as nearly to break one's neck: I will never ride on that animal again. Commend me to your cow: one may walk behind her without any discomfort, and besides one has, every day for certain, milk, butter, and cheese. Ah! what would I not give for such a cow!"

"Well," said the Peasant, "such an advantage you may soon enjoy; I will exchange my cow for your horse."

To this Hans consented with a thousand thanks, and the Peasant, swinging himself upon the horse, rode off in a hurry.

Hans now drove his cow off steadily before him, thinking of his lucky bargain in this wise:" I have a bit of bread, and I can, as often as I please, eat with it butter and cheese; and when I am thirsty I can milk my cow and have a draught; and what more can I desire?"

As soon, then, as he came to an inn he halted, and ate with great satisfaction all the bread he had brought with him for his noonday and evening meals, and washed it down with a glass of beer, to buy which he spent his two last farthings. This over, he drove his cow farther, but still in the direction of his mother's village. The heat meantime became more and more oppressive as noonday approached, and just then Hans came to a common which was an hour's journey across. Here he got into such a state of heat that his tongue clave to the roof of his mouth, and he thought to himself, "This won't do; I will just milk my cow, and refresh myself." Hans, therefore, tied her to a stump of a tree, and, having no pail, placed his leathern cap below, and set to work, but not a drop of milk could he squeeze out. He had placed himself, too, very awkwardly, and at last the impatient cow gave him such a kick on the head that he tumbled over on the ground, and for a long time he knew not where he was. Fortunately, not many hours after, a Butcher passed by, trundling a young pig along upon a wheelbarrow. "What trick is this!" exclaimed he, helping up poor Hans; and Hans told him all that had passed. The Butcher then handed him his flask, and said, "There, take a drink; it will revive you. Your cow might well give no milk: she is an old beast, and worth nothing at the best but for the plough or the butcher!"

"Eh! eh!" said Hans, pulling his hair over his eyes, "who would have thought it? It is all very well when one can kill a beast like that at home, and make a profit of the flesh; but for my part I have no relish for cow's flesh; it is too tough for me! Ah! a young pig like yours is the thing that tastes something like, let alone the sausages!"

"Well now, for love of you," said the Butcher, "I will make an exchange, and let you have my pig for your cow."

"Heaven reward you for your kindness!" cried Hans; and, giving up the cow, he untied the pig from the barrow, and took into his hand the string with which it was tied.

Hans walked on again, considering how everything had happened just as he wished, and how all his vexations had turned out for the best after all! Presently a Boy overtook him, carrying a fine white goose under his arm, and after they had said "Good day" to each other, Hans began to talk about his luck, and what profitable exchanges he had made. The Boy on his part told him that he was carrying the goose to a christening feast. "Just lift it," said he to Hans, holding it up by its wings, "just feel how heavy it is; why, it has been fattened up for the last eight weeks, and whoever bites it when it is cooked will have to wipe the grease from each side of his mouth!"

"Yes," said Hans, weighing it with one hand, "it is weighty, but my pig is no trifle either."

While he was speaking the Boy kept looking about on all sides, and shaking his head suspiciously, and at length he broke out, "I am afraid it is not all right about your pig. In the village through which I have just come one has been stolen out of the sty of the mayor himself; and I am afraid, very much afraid, you have it now in your hand! They have sent out several people, and it would be a very bad job for you if they found you with the pig; the best thing you can do is to hide it in some dark corner!"

Honest Hans was thunderstruck, and exclaimed, "Ah, Heaven help me in this fresh trouble! You know the neighbourhood better than I; do you take my pig and let me have your goose," said he to the Boy.

I shall have to hazard something at that game," replied the Boy, "but still I do not wish to be the cause of your meeting with misfortune"; and, so saying, he took the rope into his own hand, and drove the pig off quickly by a side path, while Hans, lightened of his cares, walked on homeward with the goose under his arm. "If I judge rightly," thought he to himself, "I have gained even by this exchange: first there is the good roast; then the quantity of fat which will drip out will make goose broth for a quarter of a year; and then there are the fine white feathers, which, once I have put them into my pillow, I warrant will make me sleep without rocking. What pleasure my mother will have!"

As he came to the last village on his road there stood a Knife-grinder, with his barrow by the hedge, whirling his wheel round, and singing:

> "Scissors and razors and suchlike I grind,
>   And gaily my rags are flying behind"

Hans stopped and looked at him, and at last he said, "You appear to have a good business, if I may judge by your merry song?"

"Yes," answered the Grinder, "this business has a golden bottom! A true knife-grinder is a man who, as often as he puts his hand into his pocket, .feels money in it! But what a fine goose you have got; where did you buy it?"

I did not buy it at all," said Hans, "but took it in exchange for my pig." "And the pig?" "I exchanged for my cow." "And the cow?" "I exchanged a horse for her." "And the horse?" "For him I gave a lump of gold as big as my head." "And the gold?" "That was my wages for a seven years' servitude." "And I see you have known how to benefit yourself each time," said the Grinder; "but could you now manage that you heard the money rattling in your pocket as you walked, your fortune would be made." "Well! how shall I manage that?" asked Hans.

"You must become a grinder like me; to this trade nothing peculiar belongs but a grindstone, the other necessaries find themselves. Here is one which is a little worn, certainly, and so I will not ask anything more for it than your goose; are you agreeable?"

"How can you ask me?" said Hans; "why, I shall be the luckiest man in the world; having money as often as I dip my hand into my pocket, what have I to care about any longer?"

So saying, he handed over the goose, and received the grindstone in exchange.

"Now," said the Grinder, picking up an ordinary big flint stone which lay near, "now, there you have a capital stone, upon which only beat them long enough and you may straighten all your old nails! Take it, and use it carefully!"

Hans took the stone and walked on with a satisfied heart, his eyes glistening with joy. "I must have been born," said he, "to a heap of luck; everything happens just as I wish, as if I were a Sunday-child."

Soon, however, having been on his legs since daybreak, he began to feel very tired, and was plagued too with hunger, since he had eaten all his provision at once in his joy about the cow bargain. At last he felt quite unable to go farther, and was forced, too, to halt every minute, for the stones encumbered him very much. Just then the thought overcame him, what a good thing it were if he had no need to carry them any longer, and at the same moment he came up to a stream. Here he resolved to rest and refresh himself with a drink, and so that the stones might not hurt him in kneeling, he laid them carefully down by his side on the bank. This done, he stooped down to scoop up some water in his hand, and then it happened that he pushed one stone a little too far, so that both presently went plump into the water. Hans, as soon as he saw them sinking to the bottom, jumped up for joy, and then kneeled down and returned thanks, with tears in his eyes, that so mercifully, and without any act on his part, and in so nice a way, he had been delivered from the heavy stones, which alone hindered him from getting on.

"So lucky as I am," exclaimed. Hans, "is no other man under the sun!" Then with a light heart, and free from every burden, he leaped gaily along till he reached his mother's house.

BEARSKIN

THERE was once upon a time a young fellow who enlisted for a soldier; and became so brave and courageous that he was always in the front ranks when it rained blue beans.[1] As long as the war lasted all went well, but when peace was concluded he received his discharge, and the captain told him he might go where he liked. His parents meanwhile had died, and as he had no longer any home to go to he paid a visit to his brothers, and asked them to give him shelter until war broke out again. His brothers, however, were hard-hearted, and said, "What could we do with you? We could make nothing of you; see to what you have brought yourself"; and so turned a deaf ear. The poor Soldier had nothing but his musket left; so he mounted this on his shoulder and set out on tramp. By and by he came to a great heath with nothing on it but a circle of trees, under which he sat down, sorrowfully considering his fate. "I have no money," thought he; "I have learnt nothing but soldiering, and now, since peace is concluded, there is no need of me. I see well enough I shall have to starve." All at once he heard a rustling, and as he looked round he perceived a stranger standing before him, dressed in a grey coat, who looked very stately, but had an ugly cloven foot. "I know quite well what you need," said this being; "gold and other possessions you shall have, as much as you can spend; but first I must know whether you are a coward or not, that I may not spend my money foolishly."

"A soldier and a coward!" replied the other, "that cannot be; you may put me to any proof."

"Well, then," replied the stranger, "look behind you."

The Soldier turned and saw a huge bear, which eyed him very ferociously. "Oho!" cried he, "I will tickle your nose for you, that you shall no longer be able

[1] Small shot.

to grumble"; and, raising his musket, he shot the bear in the forehead, so that he tumbled in a heap upon the ground, and did not stir afterward. Thereupon the stranger said, "I see quite well that you are not wanting in courage; but there is yet one condition which you must fulfil." "If it does not interfere with my future happiness," said the Soldier, who had remarked who it was that addressed him; "if it does not interfere with that, I shall not hesitate."

"That you must see about yourself!" said the stranger. "For the next seven years you must not wash yourself, nor comb your hair or beard, neither must you cut your nails nor say one paternoster. Then I will give you this coat and mantle, which you must wear during these seven years; and if you die within that time you are mine, but if you live you are rich, and free all your life long."

The Soldier reflected for a while on his great necessities, and, remembering how often he had braved death, he at length consented, and ventured to accept the offer. Thereupon the Evil One pulled off the grey coat, handed it to the Soldier, and said, "If you at any time search in the pockets of your coat when you have it on, you will always find your hand full of money." Then also he pulled off the skin of the bear, and said, "That shall be your cloak and your bed; you must sleep on it, and not dare to lie in any other bed, and on this account you shall be called 'Bearskin.'" Immediately the Evil One disappeared.

The Soldier now put on the coat, and dipped his hands into the pockets, to assure himself of the reality of the transaction. Then he hung the bear skin around himself, and went about the world chuckling at his good luck, and buying whatever suited his fancy which money could purchase. For the first year his appearance was not very remarkable, but in the second he began to look quite a monster. His hair covered almost all his face, his beard appeared like a piece of dirty cloth, his nails were claws, and his countenance was so covered with dirt that one might have grown cresses upon it if one had sown seed! Whoever looked at him ran away; but because he gave the poor in every place gold coin they prayed that he might not die during the seven years; and because he paid liberally every-where, he found a night's lodging without difficulty. In the fourth year he came to an inn where the landlord would not take him in, and refused even to give him a place in his stables, lest the horses should be frightened and become restive. However, when Bearskin put his hand into his pocket and drew it out full of gold ducats the landlord yielded the point, and gave him a place in the outbuildings, but not till he had promised that he would not show himself, for fear the inn should gain a bad name.

While Bearskin sat by himself in the evening, wishing from his heart that the seven years were over, he heard in the corner a loud groan. Now the old Soldier had a compassionate heart, so he opened the door and saw an old man weeping violently and wringing his hands. Bearskin stepped nearer, but the old man jumped up and tried to escape; but when he recognized a human voice he let

himself be persuaded, and by kind words and soothings on the part of the old
Soldier he at length disclosed the cause of his distress. His property had dwindled
away by degrees, and he and his daughters would have to starve, for he was so poor
that he had not the money to pay the host, and would therefore be put into prison.

"If you have no care except that," replied Bearskin, I have money enough"; and
causing the landlord to be called, he paid him, and put a purse full of gold besides
into the pocket of the old man. The latter, when he saw himself released from his
troubles, knew not how to be sufficiently grateful, and said to the Soldier, "Come
with me; my daughters are all wonders of beauty, so choose one of them for a wife.
When they hear what you have done for me they will not refuse you. You appear
certainly an uncommon man, but they will soon put you to rights."

This speech pleased Bearskin, and he went with the old man. As soon as the
eldest daughter saw him, she was so terrified at his countenance that she shrieked
and ran away. The second one stopped and looked at him from head to foot; but
at last she said, "How can I take a husband who has not a bit of a human
countenance? The grizzly bear would have pleased me better who came to see us
once, and gave himself out as a man, for he wore a hussar's hat, and had white
gloves on besides."

But the youngest daughter said, "Dear father, this must be a good man who has
assisted you out of your troubles; if you have promised him a bride for the service
your word must be kept."

It was a pity the man's face was covered with dirt and hair, else one would have
seen how glad at heart these words made him. Bearskin took a ring off his finger,
broke it in two, and, giving the youngest daughter one half, he kept the other for
himself. On her half he wrote his name, and on his own he wrote hers, and begged
her to preserve it carefully. Thereupon he took leave, saying, "For three years
longer I must wander about; if I come back again, then we will celebrate our
wedding; but if I do not, you are free, for I shall be dead. But pray to God that he
will preserve my life."

When he was gone the poor bride clothed herself in black, and whenever she
thought of her bridegroom burst into tears. From her sisters she received nothing
but scorn and mocking. "Pay great attention when he shakes your hand," said the
eldest, "and you will see his beautiful claws!" "Take care!" said the second, "bears
are fond of sweets, and if you please him he will eat you up, perhaps!" "You must
mind and do his will," continued the eldest, "or he will begin growling!" And the
second daughter said further, "But the wedding will certainly be merry, for bears
dance well!" The bride kept silence, and would not be drawn from her purpose
by all these taunts; and meanwhile Bearskin wandered about in the world, doing
good where he could, and giving liberally to the poor, for which they prayed
heartily for him. At length the last day of the seven years approached, and Bearskin
went and sat down again on the heath beneath the circle of trees. In a very short

time the wind whistled, and the Evil One presently stood before him and looked at him with a vexed face. He threw the Soldier his old coat and demanded his grey one back. "We have not got so far as that yet," replied Bearskin; "you must clean me first." Then the Evil One had, whether he liked it or no, to fetch water, wash the old Soldier, comb his hair out, and cut his nails. This done, he appeared again like a brave warrior, and indeed was much handsomer than before.

As soon as the Evil One had disappeared, Bearskin became quite lighthearted; and going into the nearest town he bought a fine velvet coat, and hired a carriage drawn by four white horses, in which he was driven to the house of his bride. Nobody knew him; the father took him for some celebrated general, and led him into the room where his daughters were. He was compelled to sit down between the two eldest, and they offered him wine, and heaped his plate with the choicest morsels; for they thought they had never seen anyone so handsome before. But the bride sat opposite to him dressed in black, neither opening her eyes nor speaking a word. At length the Soldier asked the father if he would give him one of his daughters to wife, and immediately the two elder sisters arose, and ran to their chambers to dress themselves out in their most becoming clothes, for each thought she should be chosen. Meanwhile the stranger, as soon as he found himself alone with his bride, pulled out the half of the ring and threw it into a cup of wine, which he handed across the table. She took it, and as soon as she had drunk it and seen the half ring lying at the bottom her heart beat rapidly, and she produced the other half, which she wore round her neck on a riband. She held them together, and they joined each other exactly, and the stranger said, "I am your bride groom, whom you first saw as Bearskin; but through God's mercy I have regained my human form, and am myself once more." With these words he embraced her and kissed her; and at the same time the two eldest sisters entered in full costume. As soon as they saw that the very handsome man had fallen to the share of their youngest sister, and heard that he was the same as "Bearskin," they ran out of the house full of rage and jealousy.

THE POOR MILLER'S BOY AND THE CAT

ONCE upon a time there lived in a mill an old Miller who had neither wife nor children, but three apprentices instead; and after they had been with him several years, he said to them one day, "I am old, and shall retire from business soon; do you all go out, and whichever of you brings me home the best horse to him will I give the mill, and, moreover, he shall attend me in my last illness."

The third of the apprentices was a small lad despised by his brothers, and so much so that they did not intend that he should ever have the mill, even after them. But all three went out together, and as soon as they got away from the village the two eldest brothers said to the stupid Hans, "You may as well remain here; in all your lifetime you will never find a horse." Nevertheless Hans went with them, and when night came on they arrived at a hollow where they lay down to sleep. The two clever brothers waited till Hans was fast asleep, and then they got up and walked off, leaving Hans snoring. Now they thought they had done a very clever thing, but we shall see how they fared. By and by the sun arose and awoke Hans, who, when he found himself lying in a deep hollow, peeped all around him, and exclaimed, "Oh Heavens! where have I got to?" He soon got up and scrambled out of the hollow into the forest, thinking to himself, "Here am I all alone, what shall I do to get a horse?" While he ruminated, a little tortoise-shell Cat came up, and asked in a most friendly manner, "Where are you going, Hans?" "Ah! can you help me?" said Hans. "Yes, I know very well what you wish," replied the Cat; "you want a fine horse, come with me, and for seven years be my faithful servant, and then I will give you a handsomer steed than you ever saw."

"Well," thought Hans to himself, "this is a wonderful Cat! But still I may as well see if this will be true."

So the Cat took him into her enchanted castle, where there were many other cats who waited upon her, jumping quickly up and down the steps, and bustling about in first-rate style. In the evening when they sat down to table three cats had to play music; one played the violoncello, a second the violin, and a third blew a trumpet so loudly that its cheeks seemed as if they would burst. When they had finished dinner the table was drawn away, and the Cat said, "Now, Hans, come and dance with me." "No, no," replied he, "I cannot dance with a Cat! I never learned how!"

"Then take him to bed." cried the Cat to her attendants; and they lighted him at once to his sleeping apartment, where one drew off his shoes, another his stockings, while a third blew out the light. The following morning the servant-cats made their appearance again, and helped him out of bed: one drew on his stockings, another buckled on his garters, a third fetched his shoes, a fourth washed his face, and a fifth wiped it with its tail. "That was done well and gently," said Hans to the last. But all day long Hans had to cut wood for the Cat, and for that purpose he received an axe of silver and wedges and saws of the same metal, while the mallet was made of copper.

Here Hans remained making himself useful. Every day he had good eating and drinking, but he saw nobody except the tortoise-shell Cat and her attendants. One day the Cat said to him, "Go and mow my meadow and dry the grass well," and she gave him a scythe made of silver and a whetstone of gold, which she bade him bring back safely. Hans went off and did what he was told; and, when it was finished, he took home the scythe, whetstone, and hay, and asked the Cat if she would not give him a reward? "No," said the Cat, "you must first do several things for me. Here are beams of silver, binding clamps, joists, and all that is necessary, all of silver, and of these you must first build me a small house." Hans built it, and when it was done he reminded the Cat he had still no horse, although his seven years had passed like half the time. The Cat asked him whether he wished to see her horses. "Yes," said Hans. So they went out of the house, and as they opened the door there stood twelve horses, very proud creatures, pawing the ground impatiently. Hans was glad enough to see them, but as soon as he looked at them for a minute the Cat gave him his dinner, and said, "Go home; I shall not give you your horse now, but in three days I will come to you and bring it with me." So Hans walked off, and the cats showed him the way to the mill; but as they had not furnished him with new clothes he was forced to go in his old ragged ones, which he had taken with him, and which during the seven years had become much too short for him. When he arrived at home he found his two other brothers had preceded him, and each had bought a horse; but the one was blind and the other lame. "Where is your horse, Hans?" inquired they. "It will follow me in three days," he replied. At this they laughed, and cried, "Yes, Hans, and when it does come it will be something wonderful, no doubt." Hans then went into the parlour, but the old Miller said he should not sit at table because he was so ragged and dirty; they would be ashamed of him if any one came in. So they gave him something to eat out of doors, and when bed time came the two brothers refused Hans a share of the bed, and he was obliged to creep into the goose-house and stretch himself upon some hard straw. The next morning was the third day mentioned by the Cat, and as soon as Hans was up there came a carriage drawn by six horses, which shone from their sleek condition, and a servant besides, who led a seventh horse, which was for the poor Miller's boy. Out of the carriage stepped a beautiful Princess, who went into the mill, and she was the tortoise-shell Cat whom poor Hans had served for seven years. She asked the Miller where the mill-boy, her little slave, was, and he answered, "We could not take him into the mill, he was so ragged and dirty; he lies now in the goose-house." The Princess bade him fetch Hans, but before he could come the poor fellow had to draw together his smock-frock in order to cover himself. Then the servant drew forth some elegant clothes, and, after washing, Hans put them on, so that no king could have looked more handsome. Thereupon the Princess desired to see the horses which the other apprentices had brought home, and one was blind and the other lame. When she had seen them she ordered her servant to bring the horse he had in his keeping, and as soon as the Miller saw it he declared that such an animal had never before been in his farmyard. "It belongs to the youngest apprentice," said the Princess. "And the mill too," rejoined the Miller; but the Princess said he might keep that and the horse as well for himself. With these words she placed her faithful Hans in the carriage with her and drove away. They went first to the little house which Hans had built with the silver tools and which had become a noble castle wherein everything was of gold and silver. There the Princess married him, and he was so very rich that he had enough for all his life.

GIPSY TALES

GIPSIES are spread widely over the world, and many folk-tales have been transmitted by them. The general theory is that they quitted India at an unknown but very early date, probably taking with them some scores of Indian folk-tales, as they certainly took many Indian words. By way of Persia and Armenia they arrived in the Greek-speaking Balkan Peninsula, and tarried there for three centuries, probably disseminating their Indian folk-tales and themselves absorbing others of Greek origin. Since 1417 they have spread to Siberia, Norway, Scotland, Wales, Spain, Brazil, and elsewhere, giving out and gathering up folk-stories.

One of their finest tales is "The Red King and the Witch." It compares with the story of Rip Van Winkle, of Tara Urashima, and others, but it is nobler. "The Seer" reminds one of the Aladdin type.

In these folk-tales there is a frequent change from the past tense to the present, and from the present to past. Another distinctive feature is the form of question and answer introduced into the narrative. There is also a "crisp," almost disjointed, effect produced by the omission of some words, or connecting phrases, and by the use of short sentences.

THE SEER

THEY say there was an emperor, and he had three sons. And he gave a ball; all Bukowina came to it. And a mist descended, and there came a dragon, and caught up the empress, and carried her into the forests to a mountain, and set her down on the earth. There in the earth was a palace. Now after the ball the men departed home.

And the youngest son was a seer; and his elder brothers said he was mad. Said the youngest, "Let us go after our mother, and seek for her in Bukowina."

The three set out, and they came to a place where three roads met. And the youngest said, "Brothers, which road will you go?"

And the eldest said, "I will keep straight on." And the middle one went to the right, and the youngest to the left. The eldest one went into the towns, and the middle one into the villages, and the youngest into the forests. They had gone a bit when the youngest turned back and cried, "Come here. How are we to know who has found our mother? Let us buy three trumpets, and whoever finds her must straightway blow a blast, and we shall hear him, and return home."

The youngest went into the forests. And he was hungry, and he found an apple-tree with apples, and he ate an apple, and two horns grew. And he said, "What God

332

has given me I will bear." And he went onward, and crossed a stream, and the flesh fell away from him. And he kept saying, "What God has given me I will bear. Thanks be to God." And he went further, and found another apple-tree. And he said, "I will eat one more apple, even though two more horns should grow." When he ate it the horns dropped off. And he went further, and again found a stream. And he said, "God, the flesh has fallen from me, now will my bones waste away; but even though they do, yet will I go." And he crossed the stream; his flesh grew fairer than ever. And he went up into a mountain. There was a rock of stone in a spot bare of trees. And he reached out his hand, and moved it aside, and saw a hole in the earth. He put the rock back in its place, and went back, and began to wind his horn.

His brothers heard him and came.

"Have you found my mother?"

"I have; come with me."

And they went to the mountain to the rock of stone.

"Remove this rock from its place."

"But we cannot."

"Come, I will remove it."

He put his little finger on it, and moved it aside. "Hah!" said he, "here is our mother. Who will let himself down?"

And they said, "Not I."

The youngest said, "Come with me into the forest, and we will strip off bark and make a rope."

They did so, and they made a basket.

"I will lower myself down, and when I jerk the rope haul me up."

So he let himself down, and came to house No. 1. There he found an emperor's daughter, whom the dragon had brought and kept prisoner.

And she said, "Why are you here? The dragon will kill you when he comes." And he asked her, "Didn't the dragon bring an old lady here?"

And she said, "I know not, but go to No. 2; there is my middle sister."

He went to her; she too said, "Why are you here? The dragon will kill you when he comes."

And he asked, "Didn't he bring an old lady?"

And she said, "I know not, but go to No. 3; there is my youngest sister."

She said, "Why are you here? The dragon will kill you when he comes."

And he asked, "Didn't he bring an old lady here?"

And she said, "He did, to No. 4."

He went to his mother, and she said, "Why are you here ? The dragon will kill you when he comes."

And he said, "Fear not, come with me. And he led her, and put her in the basket, and said to her, "Tell my brothers they've got to pull up three maidens." He jerked the rope, and they hauled their mother up.

He put the eldest girl in the basket, and they hauled her up; then the middle one jerked the rope, and they hauled her up. And while they are hauling, he made the youngest swear that she will not marry "till I come." She swore that she will not marry till he comes; he put her also in the basket, jerked the rope and they hauled her up.

And he found a stone, and put it in the basket, and jerked the rope. "If they haul up the stone, they will also haul up me." And they hauled it half-way up, and the rope broke, and they left him to perish, for they thought he was in the basket. And he began to weep. And he went into the palace where the dragon dwelt, and pulled out a box, and found a rusty ring. And he is cleaning it; out of it came a lord, and said, "What do you want, master?"

"Carry me out into the world."

And he took him up on his shoulders, and carried him out. And he took two pails of water. When he washed himself with one his face was changed; and when with the other it became as it was before. And he brought him to a tailor in his father's city.

And he washed himself with the water, and his face was changed. And he went to that tailor; and that tailor was in his father's employment. And he hired himself as a prentice to the tailor for a twelvemonth, just to watch the baby in another room. The tailor had twelve prentices. And the tailor did not recognize him, nor did his brothers.

The eldest brother proposed to the youngest sister, whom the seer had saved from the dragon. And she said, "No, I have sworn not to marry until my own one comes." The middle son also proposed. She said, "I will not, until my own one comes."

So the eldest son married the eldest girl; the middle son married the middle girl; and they called the tailor to make them wedding garments, and gave him cloth.

And the emperor's son said, "Give it me to make."

"No, I won't, you wouldn't fit him properly."

"Give it me. I'll pay the damage if I don't sew it right."

The tailor gave it him, and he rubbed the ring. Out came a little lord, and said, "What do you want, master?"

"Take this cloth, and go to my eldest brother and take his measure, so that it mayn't be too wide, or too narrow, but just an exact fit. And sew it so that the thread mayn't show."

And he sewed it so that one couldn't tell where the seam came. And in the morning he brought them to the tailor.

"Carry them to them."

And when they saw them, they asked the tailor, "Who made these clothes? For you never made so well before."

"I've a new prentice made them."

"Since the youngest would not have us, we'll give her to him, that he may work for us."

They went and got married. After the wedding they called the prentice, called too the maiden, and bade her go to him.

She said, "I will not," for she did not know him.

The emperor's eldest son caught hold of her to thrash her. She said, "Go to him I will not."

"You've got to."

"Though you cut my throat, I won't."

Said the youngest son, "I'll tell you what, Prince, let me go with her into a side-room and talk with her."

He took her aside, and washed himself with the other water, and his face became as it was.

She knew him.

"Come, now I'll have you."

He washed himself again with the first water, and his face was changed once more, and he went back to the emperor.

And he asked her, "Will you have him ?"

"I will."

"The wedding is to be in twelve days."

And they called the old tailor, and commanded him, "In twelve days' time be ready for the wedding." And they departed home.

Six days are gone, and he takes no manner of trouble, but goes meanly as ever. Now ten are gone, and only two remain. The tailor called the bridegroom. "And what shall we do, for there's nothing ready for the wedding?"

"Ah! don't fret, and fear not! God will provide."

Now but one day remained; and he, the bridegroom, went forth, and rubbed the ring. And out came a little lord and asked him, "What do you want, master?"

"In a day's time make me a three-story palace, and let it turn with the sun on a screw, and let the roof be of glass, and let there be water and fish there, the fish swimming and sporting in the roof, so that the lords may look at the roof, and marvel what magnificence is this. And let there be victuals and golden dishes and silver spoons, and one cup being drained and one cup filled."

That day it was ready.

"And let me have a carriage and six horses, and a hundred soldiers for outriders, and two hundred on either side."

On the morrow he started for the wedding, he from one place, and she from another; and they went to the church and were married, and came home. His brothers came and his father, and a heap of lords. And they did drink and eat, and all kept looking at the roof.

When they had eaten and drunk, he asked the lords, "What they would do to him who seeks to slay his brother?"

His brothers heard. "Such a one merits death."

Then he washed himself with the other water, and his face became as it was. Thus his brothers knew him. And he said, "Good day to you, brothers. You fancied I had perished. You have pronounced your own doom. Come out with me, and toss your swords up in the air. If you acted fairly by me, it will fall before you, but if unfairly it will fall on your head."

The three of them tossed up their swords, and that of the youngest fell before him, but theirs both fell òn their head, and they died.

THE RED KING AND THE WITCH

IT was the Red King, and he bought ten ducats' worth of victuals. He cooked them, and he put them in a press. And he locked the press, and from night to night posted people to guard the victuals.

In the morning, when he looked, he found the platters bare; he did not find anything in them. Then the king said, "I will give the half of my kingdom to whoever shall be found to guard the press, that the victuals may not go amissing from it."

The king had three sons. Then the eldest thought within himself, "God! What, give half the kingdom to a stranger! It were better for me to watch. Be it unto me according to God's will."

He went to his father. "Father, all hail. What, give the kingdom to a stranger! It were better for me to watch."

And his father said to him, "As God will, only don't be frightened by what you may see."

Then he said, "Be it unto me according to God's will."

And he went and lay down in the palace. And he put his head on the pillow, and remained with his head on the pillow till toward dawn. And a warm sleepy breeze came and lulled him to slumber. And his little sister arose. And she turned a somersault, and her nails became like an axe and her teeth like a shovel. And she opened the cupboard and ate up everything. Then she became a child again and returned to her place in the cradle. The lad arose and told his father that he had seen nothing. His father looked in the press, found the platters bare—no victuals, no anything. His father said, "It would take a better man than you, and even he might do nothing."

His middle son also said, "Father, all hail. I am going to watch to-night."

"Go, dear, only play the man."

"Be it unto me according to God's will."

And he went into the palace and put his head on a pillow. And at ten o'clock came a warm breeze and sleep seized him. Up rose his sister and unwound herself from her swaddling-bands and turned a somersault, and her teeth became like a shovel and her nails like an axe. And she went to the press and opened it, and ate off the platters what she found. She ate it all, and turned a somersault again and went back to her place in the cradle. Day broke and the lad arose, and his father asked him and said, "It would take a better man than you, and even he might do nought for me if he were as poor a creature as you."

The youngest son arose. "Father, all hail. Give me also leave to watch the cupboard by night."

"Go, dear, only don't be frightened with what you see."

"Be it unto me according to God's will," said the lad.

And he went and took four needles and lay down with his head on the pillow; and he stuck the four needles in four places. When sleep seized him he knocked his head against a needle, so he stayed awake until ten o'clock. And his sister arose from her cradle, and he saw, and she turned a somersault, and he was watching her. And her teeth became like a shovel and her nails like an axe. And she went to the press and ate up everything. She left the platters hare. And she turned a somersault, and became tiny again as she was; went to her cradle. The lad, when he saw that, trembled with fear; it seemed to him ten years till daybreak. And he arose and went to his father. "Father, all hail."

Then his father asked him, "Didst see anything, Peterkin?"

"What did I see? What did I not see? Give me money and a horse, a horse fit to carry the money, for I am away to marry me."

His father gave him a couple of sacks of ducats, and he put them on his horse. The lad went and made a hole on the border of the city. He made a chest of stone, and put all the money there and buried it. He placed a stone cross above and departed. And he journeyed eight years and came to the queen of all the birds that fly. And the queen of the birds asked him, "Whither away, Peterkin ?"

"Thither, where there is neither death nor old age, to marry me."

The queen said to him, "Here is neither death nor old age."

Then Peterkin said to her, "How comes it that here is neither death nor old age."

Then she said to him, "When I whittle away the wood of all this forest, then death will come and take me and old age."

Then Peterkin said, "One day and one morning death will come and old age, and take me."

And he departed further, and journeyed on eight years, and arrived at a palace of copper. And a maiden came forth from that palace and took him and kissed him. She said, "I have waited long for thee."

She took the horse and put him in the stable, and the lad spent the night there. He arose in the morning and placed his saddle on the horse.

Then the maiden began to weep, and asked him, "Whither away, Peterkin ?"

"Thither, where there is neither death nor old age."

Then the maiden said to him, "Here is neither death nor old age."

Then he asked her, "How comes it that here is neither death nor old age?"

"Why, when these mountains arc levelled, and these forests, then death will come."

"This is no place for me," said the lad to her. And he departed further.

Then what said his horse to him? "Master, whip me four times, and twice yourself, for you are come to the Plain of Regret. And Regret will seize you and cast you down, horse and all. So spur your horse, escape, and tarry not."

He came to a hut. In that hut he beholds a lad, as it were ten years old, who asked him, "What seekest thou, Peterkin, here?"

"I seek the place where there is neither death nor old age."

The lad said, "Here is neither death nor old age. I am the Wind."

Then Peterkin said, "Never, never will I go from here." And he dwelt there a hundred years and grew no older.

There the lad dwelt, and he went out to hunt in the Mountains of Gold and Silver, and he could scarce carry home the game.

Then what said the Wind to him? "Peterkin, go unto all the Mountains of Gold and unto the Mountains of Silver; but go not to the Mountain of Regret or to the Valley of Grief."

He heeded not, but went to the Mountain of Regret and the Valley of Grief. And Grief cast him down, he wept till his eyes were full.

And he went to the Wind. "I am going home to my father. I will not stay longer."

"Go not, for your father is dead, and brothers you have no more left at home. A million years have come and gone since then. The spot is not known where your father's palace stood. They have planted melons on it; it is but an hour since I passed that way."

But the lad departed thence, and arrived at the maiden's whose was the palace of copper. Only one stick remained, and she cut it and grew old. As he knocked at the door, the stick fell and she died. He buried her, and departed thence. And he came to the queen of the birds in the great forest. Only one branch remained, and that was all but through. When she saw him she said, "Peterkin, thou art quite young."

Then he said to her, "Dost thou remember telling me to tarry here?"

As she pressed and broke through the branch, she, too, fell and died.

He came where his father's palace stood and looked about him. There was no palace, no anything. And he fell to marvelling: "God, Thou art mighty!" He only recognized his father's well, and went to it. His sister, the witch, when she saw him, said to him, "I have waited long for you, dog." She rushed at him to devour him, but he made the sign of the cross and she perished.

And he departed thence, and came on an old man with his beard down to his belt. "Father, where is the palace of the Red King? I am his son."

"What is this," said the old man, "thou tellest me, that thou art his son? My father's father has told me of the Red King. His very city is no more. Dost thou not see it is vanished? And dost thou tell me that thou art the Red King's son?"

"It is not twenty years, old man, since I departed from my father, and dost thou tell me that thou knowest not my father?" (It was a million years since he had left his home.)

"Follow me if thou dost not believe me."

And he went to the cross of stone; only a palm's breadth was out of the ground. And it took him two days to get at the chest of money. When he had lifted the chest out and opened it, Death sat in one corner groaning, and Old Age groaning in another corner.

Then what said Old Age? "Lay hold of him, Death."

"Lay hold of him yourself."

Old Age laid hold of him in front, and Death laid hold of him behind.

The old man took and buried him decently, and planted the cross near him. And the old man took the money and also the horse.

GREECE

IT is interesting to compare the old Greek tales with those of more recent times. To the old Greeks each god was beautiful. Earth, air, sea sky, storm, forest, and flowers were manifestations of an all-pervading spiritual power. Freedom, art, and joy were elements of the Greek religion, and these were reflected in their stories. There is throughout a radiance of beauty.

The Greeks modified the primitive sun-worship of the Aryan tribes and began to think of such things as sun and wind as real persons. From this developed the belief in many gods and goddesses. Everything was alive. Even the quiet places of the earth were the abode of nymphs, fauns, and satyrs. The heroes, too, they regarded as supreme because they were endowed with supernatural powers.

The modern Greek folk-lore is more human and less classical. It deals not with gods but with dragons, beasts, magic, and craft. It is a strange admixture of East and West, reminding one at times of the *Arabian Nights' Entertainments* and at others of the old Norse tales.

I. ANCIENT GREECE

CERES AND PROSERPINE

IN the island of Sicily, high up among the mountains, there was once a beautiful valley, called the valley of Enna. It was seldom that a human being, even a shepherd, climbed so high; but the goats, being able to climb by the steepest and most slippery paths, over the roughest rocks, knew well what soft, sweet grass grew there. Sheep, too, and sometimes wild swine, found their way to this spot.

Not another mountain valley anywhere was quite like this one. It was never visited by any of the winds except Zephyrus, who was always mild and gentle. The grass was always green and the flowers were always in bloom. There were shady groves on every side, and numberless fountains of sparkling water. It would have been hard to find a pleasanter spot.

This valley of Enna was the home of Ceres, the Earth-mother, one of the wisest of the goddesses. In fact, the valley owed its beauty to the presence of Ceres, and the wonderful vegetation which covered the whole island of Sicily was due to her influence; for she was the goddess of all that grows out of the earth, and knew the secret of the springing wheat and the ripening fruits. She watched over the flowers, the lambs in the fields, and the young children. The springs of water, too, which came from hidden places of the earth, were hers.

One day Proserpine, the little daughter of Ceres, was playing in the meadows of Enna. Her hair was as yellow as gold, and her cheeks had the delicate pink of an apple blossom. She seemed like a flower among the other flowers of the valley.

She, and the daughters of the valley-nymphs, who were children of about her own age, had taken off their sandals and were running about on the soft grass in their bare feet. They were as light-hearted as the little lambs and kids.

Soon they began to gather the flowers that grew so thick on every side—violets, hyacinths, lilies, and big purple irises. They filled their baskets, and then their dresses, and twisted long sprays of wild roses around their shoulders.

Suddenly, Proserpine saw a flower which made her forget everything else. This flower seemed to be a strange, new kind of narcissus. It was of gigantic size, and its one flower-stalk held at least a hundred blossoms. Its fragrance was so powerful that it filled the entire island, and might be noticed even out at sea.

Proserpine called to her playmates to come and see this wonderful flower, and then she noticed, for the first time, that she was alone; for she had wandered from one flower to another till she had left the other children far behind. Running quickly forward to pick this strange blossom, she saw that its stalk was spotted like a snake, and feared that it might be poisonous. Still it was far too beautiful a flower to be left by itself in the meadow, and she therefore tried to pluck it. When she found that she could not break the stalk, she made a great effort to pull the whole plant up by the roots.

All at once, the black soil around the plant loosened, and Proserpine heard a rumbling underneath the ground. Then the earth suddenly opened, a great black cavern appeared, and out from its depths sprang four magnificent black horses, drawing a golden chariot. In the chariot sat a king with a crown on his head, but under the crown was the gloomiest face ever seen.

When this strange king saw Proserpine standing there by the flower, too frightened to run away, he checked his horses for an instant and, bending forward, snatched the poor child from the ground and placed her on the seat by his side. Then he whipped up his horses and drove away at a furious rate.

Proserpine, still holding fast to her flowers, screamed for her mother.

Helios, the sun-god, saw how the gloomy-faced king had stolen Proserpine away, and Hecate, who sat near by in her cave, heard the scream and the sound of wheels. No one else had any suspicion of what had happened.

Ceres was far away across the sea in another country, overlooking the gathering in of the harvests. She heard Proserpine's scream, and like a sea-bird when it hears the distressed cry of its young, came rushing home across the water.

She filled the valley with the sound of her calling, but no one answered to the name of Proserpine. The strange flower had disappeared. A few roses lay scattered on the grass, and near them were a child's footprints. Ceres felt sure that these were the traces of Proserpine's little bare feet, but she could not follow them far, because a herd of swine had wandered that way and left a confusion of hoofprints behind them.

Ceres could learn nothing about her daughter from the nymphs. She sent out her own messenger, the big white crane that brings the rain; but although he could fly very swiftly and very far on his strong wings, he brought back no news of Proserpine.

When it grew dark, the goddess lighted two torches at the flaming summit of Mount Ætna, and continued her search. She wandered up and down for nine days and nine nights. On the tenth night, when it was nearly morning, she met Hecate, who was carrying a light in her hand, as if she, too, were looking for something. Hecate told Ceres how she had heard Proserpine scream, and had heard the sound of wheels, but had seen nothing. Then she went with the goddess to ask Helios, the sun-god, whether he had not seen what happened that day, for the sun-god travels around the whole world, and must see everything.

Ceres found Helios sitting in his chariot, ready to drive his horses across the sky. He held the fiery creatures in for a moment, while he told Ceres that Pluto, the king of the underworld, had stolen her daughter and had carried her away to live with him in his dark palace.

When Ceres heard this, she knew that Proserpine was lost to her, and she kept away from the other gods and hid herself in the dark places of the earth. She liked to keep away from the earth's people as well as from the gods, for wherever she went she was sure to see some happy mother with her children around her, and the sight made her feel very lonely. She sometimes envied the poorest peasants, or even the little birdmothers in the trees.

One day she sat down by the side of the road, near a well, in the shade of an olive tree. While she was sitting there, the four daughters of Celeus, carrying golden pitchers on their shoulders, came down from their father's palace to draw water. Seeing a sad old woman sitting by the well, they spoke to her in a kindly way. Not wishing them to know that she was a goddess, Ceres told the four young princesses that she had been carried away from her home by pirates, and had escaped from being sold for a slave by running away the instant that the pirates' ship reached the shore.

"I am old, and a stranger to every one here," she said, "but I am not too old to work for my bread. I could keep house, or take care of a young child."

Hearing this, the four sisters ran eagerly back to the palace, and asked permission to bring the strange woman home with them. Their mother told them that they might engage her as nurse for their little brother, Demophoon.

Therefore Ceres became an inmate of the house of Celeus, and the little Demophoon flourished wonderfully under her care.

Ceres soon learned to love the human baby who was her charge, and she wished to make him immortal. She knew only one way of doing this, and that was to bathe him with ambrosia, and then, one night after another, place him in the fire, until his mortal parts should be burned away. Every night she did this, without saying a word to any one. Under this treatment Demophoon was growing wonderfully god-like; but one night, his mother being awake very late, and hearing some one moving about, drew the curtains aside a very little, and peeped out. There, before the fireplace, where a great fire was burning, stood the strange nurse, with Demophoon in her arms. The mother watched in silence until she saw Ceres place the child in the fire, then she gave a shriek of alarm.

The shriek broke the spell. Ceres took Demophoon from the fire and laid him on the floor. Then she told the trembling mother that she had meant to make her child immortal, but that now this could not be. He would have to grow old and die like other mortals. Then, throwing off her blue hood, she suddenly lost her aged appearance, and all at once looked very grand and beautiful. Her hair, which fell down over her shoulders, was yellow, like the ripe grain in the fields. Demophoon's mother knew by these signs that her child's nurse must be the great Ceres, but she saw her no more, for the goddess went out into the dark night.

After this Ceres continued her lonely wandering, not caring where she went. One day, as she stooped to drink from a spring, Abas, a freckled boy who stood near, mocked her because she looked sad and old. Suddenly he saw Ceres stand up very straight, with a look that frightened him. Then he felt himself growing smaller and smaller, until he shrunk into a little speckled water-newt, when he made haste to hide himself away under a stone.

Unlike Abas, most of the people whom Ceres met with felt sorry her. One day, while she was sitting on a stone by the side of a mountain road in Greece, feeling very sorrowful, she heard a childish voice say, "Mother, are you not afraid to stay all alone here on the mountain?"

Ceres looked up, pleased to hear the word "mother"; and saw a little peasant girl, standing near two goats that she had driven down from the mountain-pastures.

"No, my child," said she, "I am not afraid."

Just then, out from among the trees came the little girl's father, carrying a bundle of firewood on his shoulder. He invited Ceres to come to his cottage for the night. Ceres at first refused, but finally accepted the invitation.

"You are happier than I," said Ceres, as the three walked toward the cottage. "You have your little daughter with you, but I have lost mine."

"Alas! I have sorrow enough," said the peasant. "I fear that my only son, little Triptolemus, lies dying at home."

"Let us hope that he may yet be cured," said Ceres, and stooping, she gathered a handful of poppies. Soon they came into the little cottage, where they found the mother beside herself with grief for her boy.

Ceres bent over the child and kissed him softly on both cheeks. As she did so, the poppies in her hands brushed lightly against his face. Then his groans ceased, and the child fell into a quiet sleep. In the morning Triptolemus woke strong and well; and when Ceres called her winged dragons and drove away through the clouds, she left a happy and grateful family behind her.

THE RETURN OF PROSERPINE

ALL this time, while Ceres had been mourning for her lost Proserpine, she had neglected to look after the little seeds that lay in the brown earth. The consequence was that these little seeds could not sprout and grow; therefore there was no grain to be ground into flour for bread. Not only the seeds but all growing things missed the care of Mother Ceres. The grass turned brown and withered away, the trees in the olive orchards dropped their leaves, and the little birds all flew away to a distant country. Even the sheep that fed among the water-springs in the valley of Enna grew so thin that it was pitiful to see them.

Jupiter saw that without Ceres, the Great Mother, there could be no life on the earth. In time, all men and animals would die for lack of food. He therefore told Iris to set up her rainbow-bridge in the sky, and to go quickly down to the dark cave where Ceres mourned for Proserpine, that she might persuade the goddess to forget her sorrow, and go back to the fields, where she was so much needed.

Iris found Ceres sitting in a corner of her cave, among the shadows, wrapped in dark blue draperies that made her almost invisible. The coming of Iris lighted up every part of the cave and set beautiful colours dancing everywhere, but it did not make Ceres smile.

After this, Jupiter sent the gods, one after another, down to the cave; but none of them could comfort the Earth-mother. She still mourned.

Then Jupiter sent Mercury down into Pluto's kingdom, to see whether he could not persuade that grim king to let Proserpine return to her mother.

When Mercury told his errand to King Pluto, Proserpine jumped up from her throne, all eagerness to see her mother again, and Pluto, seeing how glad she was, could not withhold his consent. So he ordered the black horses and the golden chariot to be brought out to take her back; but before she sprang to the chariot's seat, he craftily asked her if she would not eat one of the pomegranates that grew in his garden.

Proserpine tasted the fruit, taking just four seeds. Then the black horses swiftly carried Mercury and herself into the upper world, and straight to the cave' where Ceres sat.

What a change! How quickly Ceres ran out of the cave when she heard her daughter's voice! No more mourning in shadowy places for her, now! Proserpine told her mother everything—how she had found the wonderful narcissus, how the earth had opened, allowing King Pluto's horses to spring out, and how the dark king had snatched her and carried her away.

"But, my dear child," Ceres anxiously inquired, "have you eaten anything since you have been in the underworld?"

Proserpine confessed that she had eaten the four pomegranate seeds. At that, Ceres beat her breast in despair, and then once more appealed to Jupiter. He said that Proserpine should spend eight months of every year with her mother, but would have to pass the other four—one for each pomegranate seed—in the underworld with Pluto.

So Ceres went back to her beautiful valley of Enna, and to her work in the fields. The little brown seeds that had lain asleep so long sprouted up and grew; the fountains sent up their waters; the brown grass on the hills became green; the olive trees and the grape-vines put out new leaves; the lambs and the kids throve, and skipped about more gayly than ever; and all the hosts of little birds came back with the crane of Ceres to lead them.

During the eight months that Proserpine was with her, Ceres went about again among her peasants, standing near the men while they were threshing the grain, helping women to bake their bread, and having a care over everything that went on. She did not forget the peasant family of Greece, in whose cottage she had been invited to pass the night, and where she had cured little Triptolemus. She visited this family again and taught the young Triptolemus how to plough, to sow, and to reap, like the peasants of her own Sicily. The time came when Proserpine was obliged to go back to King Pluto. Then Ceres went and sat among the shadows in the cave, as she had done before.

All nature slept for a while; but the peasants had no fear now, for they knew that Proserpine would surely come back, and that the great Earth-mother would then care for her children again.

PSYCHE

A CERTAIN king had three daughters who were known far and wide for their beauty. The most beautiful of all was the youngest, Psyche. When this youngest princess went into the temples, many people mistook her for Venus herself, and offered her the garlands which they had brought for the goddess of love and beauty.

The real Venus, much vexed by this, determined to be revenged on poor Psyche, who was in no way to blame. One day she told Eros, the god of love, to wound Psyche with one of his golden-pointed arrows, and make her fall in love with some wretched beggar, the most degraded that could be found.

Eros took his arrows and went down to the earth to do his mother's bidding. As soon as he saw Psyche, he was so startled by her wonderful beauty that he wounded himself with his own arrow; consequently, instead of making Psyche fall in love with some ragged beggar, he himself fell in love with Psyche.

Long before this the two elder of the three beautiful sisters had been married to king's sons, as befitted the rank of princesses; but in spite of her superior beauty, no lovers came to sue for the hand of the youngest sister. The king, suspecting that this might be caused by the wrath of Venus, inquired of the oracle what he should do. The answer that he received allowed him no longer to doubt the anger of the gods. These were the words of the prophetess:

> Dress thy daughter like a bride,
> Lead her up the mountain-side,
> There an unknown wingèd foe,
> Feared by all who dwell below,
> And even by the gods above,
> Will claim her, as a hawk the dove.

The king was overcome with grief, but did not dare to disobey. Therefore one night Psyche's maids of honour dressed her in wedding garments, and a long procession of her father's people escorted her to an exposed rock at the top of a high mountain, where they sadly extinguished their torches, and left her alone in the darkness.

After the last sound of human footsteps has died away, Psyche sat weeping and trembling, fearing every moment that she might hear the rushing wings of some dragon, and feel his claws and teeth. Instead, she felt the cool breath and the downy wings of Zephyrus, the west wind, who lifted her gently from the rock, then puffed out his cheeks, and blew her down into a beautiful green valley, where he laid her softly on a bank of violets.

This moonlit valley was so sweet and peaceful that Psyche forgot her fears and fell asleep. When she woke in the morning, she saw a beautiful grove of tall trees, and in the grove a most wonderful palace, with a fountain in front of it. The great arches of the roof were supported by golden columns, and the walls were covered with silver carving, while the floor was a mosaic of precious stones of all colours.

Psyche timidly entered the doors, and wandered through the great rooms, each of which seemed more splendid than the last. She could see no one, but once or twice thought she heard low voices, as if the fairies were talking together. It might have been voices, or it might have been the trickling of water in the fountain.

Presently, she opened the door of a room, where a table was laid ready for a feast. Evidently only one guest was expected, for there was but one chair and one cover. Psyche, half afraid, seated herself in the chair, and the fairies of the palace, or the nymphs, or whatever beings the voices belonged to, came and waited on her, but not one of them could be seen. She enjoyed a most appetizing repast. After the last dish had been whisked away by invisible hands, she heard music—a chorus of singing voices, and then a single voice, accompanied by a lyre, which seemed to play of itself.

As the light faded away, and night came, Psyche began to tremble, for she feared that the owner of the palace might prove to be the winged monster of the oracle, and that he would come to claim her. There were no locks nor bolts, and the doors and windows stood wide open, as if no thief, nor evil creature of any kind, had ever lived.

When it had grown perfectly dark, so dark that she could not see her own hand, Psyche heard the sound of wings, and then footsteps coming down the great hall. The footsteps came lightly and quickly to the low seat where she was sitting, and then a voice which was sweet and musical said to her: "Beautiful Psyche, this palace and all it holds is yours, if you will consent to live here and be my wife. The voices you have heard are the voices of your hand-maidens, who will obey any commands that you give them. Every night I will spend here with you; but before day comes, I must fly away. Do not ask to see my face, nor to know who I am. Only trust me; I ask nothing more."

This speech took away Psyche's fear of being immediately eaten, at any rate; but still she could not be quite sure that this voice was not the voice of the monster.

Her mysterious lover came to talk to her every night, as he had said he would do. Sometimes she looked forward to his coming with pleasure; at other times the sound of his wings filled her with terror.

One day, while she was gathering roses within sight of the rock from which Zephyrus had blown her into the valley, she saw her two sisters on this rock, weeping, beating their breasts, and crying out as if mourning for the dead. Hearing her own name, she knew that her sisters must be mourning for her, supposing that she had been devoured on this rock. These sisters of Psyche had not always been kind to her; but she now believed that they had really loved her after all.

That night, when her lover came in the dark, Psyche asked him if she might not see her sisters, and let them know that she was alive and happy. She received an unwilling consent.

The next day the sisters came again to the high rock, and Zephyrus blew them down into the valley, just as he had blown Psyche down. They were very much surprised to see the good fortune that had befallen their little sister, but instead of rejoicing at it, as they should have done, they were envious of her. They asked her a great many questions, and were particularly curious about the owner of the palace. Psyche told them that he was away hunting on the mountains. Then Zephyrus, thinking that they were getting too inquisitive, whisked them away to the rock, and that was the end of their visit.

After a time Psyche grew tired of being so much alone, and wished to see her sisters again. Her lover gave his consent a second time, but warned her not to answer or even to listen to any questions about himself, and told her, above all, that if she ever tried to see him face to face, he should be forced to fly away and leave her, and that the palace also would vanish.

The next day Zephyrus brought the sisters into the valley as before. These envious women had brooded over their sister's superior fortune till their minds were full of wicked thoughts, and between them they made a plan by which they meant to destroy Psyche's happiness. They told her that the owner of the palace was, without doubt, a most horrible winged serpent, the nameless monster of the oracle, and that the people who lived the mountain had seen him coming down into that valley, every day toward dusk. "Although he seems so kind," said they, "he is only waiting his time to devour you. He knows that you would be terrified by his ugly scales, and this is the reason he never allows you to see him. But listen to the advice of your sisters, who are older and wiser than you. Take this knife, and while your pretended friend is asleep, light a lamp and look at him. If our words prove to be true, strike off his head, and save yourself from an awful death."

With these words her sisters left Psyche the knife and hurried away. When they had gone, poor Psyche could not rid her mind of the fears their words had raised. Her faith was gone. If all were right, why was her lover so anxious to be hidden in the darkness? Why did he fear her sisters' visits? Why did he have wings? Worst of all, she remembered, with a shudder that she had once or twice heard a sound like the gliding of a serpent over the marble floors.

Soon it grew dark, and she heard her lover coming. That night she would not talk to him, therefore he went into a chamber where there was a couch, lay down and fell asleep.

Then Psyche, trembling with fear, lighted her lamp, took the knife, and stole to the couch where he lay. The light of the lamp fell full on his face, and Psyche saw no scaly serpent, but Eros, or Love himself, the most beautiful of the gods. Golden curls fell back from his wonderful face; his snow-white wings were folded in sleep, while the down on them—as delicate as that on the wings of a butterfly—stirred faintly, set in motion by his quiet breathing. At his feet lay his bow and arrows.

Psyche dropped her knife, in horror at the deed it might have done. Then taking up an arrow curiously, she pricked her finger on its golden point. Holding her lamp high above her head, she turned to look at Eros again, and now for the first time in love with Love, gazed at him in an ecstasy of happiness; but her hand trembled, and a drop of hot oil fell on the shoulder of the god. He opened his eyes, looked at her reproachfully, and then flew away without a word. The beautiful palace vanished, and Psyche found herself alone.

Then Psyche began a long search for her lost Eros. She met Pan, Ceres, and Juno, one after another, but none of them could help her. At last she went to Venus herself, thinking that the mother of Love would be kind to her for Love's sake.

Eros, at this time, lay in the palace of Venus, suffering from the wound caused by the burning oil. Venus knew all that had happened, for a gull had flown to her and told her. She was very angry, and as a punishment imposed certain almost impossible tasks upon Psyche.

First, the goddess pointed to a great heap of seeds, the food of the doves that drew her chariot, and of the little sparrows that accompanied her on her journeys. It was composed of wheat, barley, millet, and other kinds of seed, all mixed carelessly together. "Take these," said Venus, "and separate them grain by grain; place each kind by itself, and finish the task before nightfall."

Poor Psyche had no courage to begin the task, but sat with drooping head and folded hands. Then a little ant ran out from under a stone, and called the whole army of the ant people, who came for Love's sake, and quickly separated the seeds, laying each kind by itself.

When Venus came at the close of the day, and saw that Psyche's task was finished, she was very much surprised, and throwing the poor girl a piece of coarse bread, remarked that a harder task would be set for her in the morning. Accordingly, when morning came, Venus took Psyche to the bank of a broad river, and pointing to a grove on the opposite shore, where a flock of sheep with golden wool were feeding, said, "Bring me some of that wool."

Psyche would have plunged immediately into the river, if some reeds on the bank had not whispered to her: "Do not go near those sheep now. They are fierce creatures when the sun is high. Wait till the song of the river has lulled them to sleep; then go and pick all the wool you like from the bushes, where the sheep have left it clinging." So Psyche waited till the sun was low, then crossed the river and came back with her arms full of golden wool.

Venus, seeing Psyche return in safety, was angrier than ever. "You never did this by yourself," said she. "Now we will see whether you are wise and prudent enough to become the bride of Eros. Take this crystal vase, and fill it with water from the Fountain of Forgetfulness."

This fountain was at the very top of a high mountain. The icy water gushed forth from a smooth rock, far higher than anyone could climb, and as it rushed down its narrow channel it shouted, "Fly from me! Beware! Thou wilt perish!" On either side of the black stream was a cave, and in each cave lived a fierce dragon. When Psyche came to the place and saw all this, she was so horrified that she could not move or speak. Nevertheless, she accomplished this task also; for Jupiter's eagle, to whom Love had been kind, took the crystal vase and filled it for her at the fountain.

Psyche ran back to Venus with the water, hoping to please her this time. But Venus was still angry. "You are a witch," said she, "or you could not do these things. However, here is one task more. Take this box, carry it down into the under-world, and ask Proserpine if you may not bring back to me some of her beauty."

When Psyche heard this, she felt sure that Venus meant to destroy her, and thinking that it was of no use to struggle longer against the persecutions of the goddess, she climbed up the stairway of a lofty tower, intending to throw herself down from the top. But the stones of the tower cried out to her: "Listen, Psyche! From yonder dark chasm, choked with thorns, a path leads down to the under-world. Take a piece of barley-bread in each hand, and two pieces of money in your mouth, then follow this rough path. When you come to the river of the dead, Charon will ferry you over for one of your pieces of money. When you reach the gate of Pluto's palace, where Cerberus keeps watch, give that fierce dog one of the pieces of bread, and he will let you pass. You can then enter the palace where Proserpine is queen. She will give you a portion of her beauty, shutting it into the box, and you can return by the same way, giving the remaining piece of bread to Cerberus, and the remaining piece of money to Charon. One thing more. I charge you, do not, by any means, look into the box."

Psyche was thankful indeed for this advice, and followed it in every particular but one. When she was returning, she forgot the warning about not looking into the box. Since Love had flown away from her, her suffering had been so great that her beauty was nearly gone. Therefore, thinking that it might not be wrong to take a very little of Proserpine's beauty for herself, she raised the lid of the box. Whiff! A strange invisible something rushed from it and overcame her. She fell into a deep sleep, and might never have waked again if Love, cured of his wounds, had not passed by and seen her. The god shook her till she was awake again, then sent her back to his mother with the box, while he flew straight to Mount Olympus, and laid the case before Jupiter.

The king of the gods, after hearing the story, said that Psyche should be made immortal, and should become the bride of Eros.

Mercury was immediately sent to bring Psyche up to Mount Olympus, while the gods all gathered to a great feast. Jupiter himself handed to this mortal maid the cup of sacred nectar, of which whoever drinks will live forever. Psyche drank from the golden cup, and straightway two beautiful butterfly-like wings sprang from her shoulders, and she became like the gods in all things.

After this, she was wedded to Eros, who never flew away from her again. Apollo sang, and Venus, her anger forgotten, danced at the wedding.

II.MODERN GREECE

THE CRAZY PRIESTESS WITH HER CRAZY DAUGHTERS

ONCE upon a time there was a priest who had a wife and three daughters. But I must tell you that all four of them were an even match for each other in point of folly. One day, the eldest daughter, the pride of the family, went outside the town, as soon as church was over, to take a walk. She espies a steep cliff, and at once goes forward and sits on the edge of the cliff, and begins to weep and wail.

"Alas, to think that I shall marry, and have a little child, and he shall come and look over here, and fall over the edge, and get killed. Alas, my darling, my darling!"

The others were waiting for her, and said, "Why, what can have become of our sister?"

The second one goes to fetch her, and sees her sitting on a rock, and lamenting.

"My dear," she says, "what's the matter with you that you weep ?"

"Alas!" replies the other, "don't you see this steep cliff? where—when I am married, and get a little nephew for you, he'll come and tumble down, and be killed?"

Then the other sits down and cries. Lastly, they send the youngest of all. She, too, does the same; so, to avoid repetition, we will add, the mother also comes and bewails the sad fate of her grandson.

The worthy priest runs to look for them, and finds the good women weeping and wailing. When he asks them what's the matter that they are crying in this fashion, they reply that the eldest daughter is going to marry and have a little baby, and it will tumble down that steep cliff!

He replies, "Bless me! bad luck take you all! how long am I to put up with your folly? You never will learn sense! Heaven is my witness that I will get away from here, and leave you to your fate, or you will be the death of me.".

So he packs up and departs, saying to them, "If fortune is kind to you, you most unhappy women, and I chance to find any who are worse fools than you, it may be I shall see you again; otherwise your eyes will lose their lustre, ere ever you look on me again."

Then the priest journeys on and on, until he comes to another village, and in a certain house he hears lamentations, and peeps in to see what is going on; and beholds a woman who had a child in a cradle, and over it against a wall there was a hatchet hanging, and she did nothing but cry. "Alack! my baby, my baby, killed by a hatchet!"

"Good woman," says the priest, addressing her, "what are you weeping about?"

"Why, don't you see, your reverence, that that hatchet will fall and kill my child? And you ask me why I am weeping?"

"Ah, then I'm not the only one!" said the priest to himself; and added aloud, "What will you give me to save it from so sad a fate?"

"Whatever you please, your reverence; my very life, if it was mine to give !"

Thereupon, he moves the cradle to another part of the room. "There, good woman," he says, "now don't cry any more."

Then the good priest receives a handsome fee, and travels further, and soon he comes to a place where he sees a crowd gathered. There were shouts and lamentations. So the priest went to see what was up. And what should he behold but a tall man who was to be married, and the door of the house was rather low, and he would not stoop to enter. But they were considering what they should do, whether they should cut off his feet or his head. For these seemed the only alternatives. At this sight the priest shook his sides with laughter, and then addressed them thus:

"Fellow Christians, what ails you that you weep?"

Then they explain to him the state of the case.

"Oh," says he, "I'll get him in for you. What will you give me?"

"Take whatever you will. Only do us that favour."

Then the priest takes hold of his head. "Stoop a bit, my son," he says, "a little more, a little more," he repeated, until he got him in. Then said he, "There! now lift up your head again, and as often as you go in and out, you must do the same; do you see ?"

Then he takes and marries him into the bargain, after which he takes leave of the company, and goes further. Some way on he sees an old woman who had a sow, which she was washing and decking with diamonds and spangles to go to the wedding; for this, she said, was her daughter.

At length she espies the priest. "Oh, my son," she cries, "pray take my girl to the wedding, for you see I am old and can't go; I'll pay you for the trouble of walking so far."

"Willingly, mother, I shall regard it as a favour to myself," he replied; and here again he had an eye to the main chance. So the good priest takes the sow and drives it on before him. But when he had gone a little way, the old woman seemed uneasy, for she called after the priest:

"Oh, my son, turn round and let me look at you, that I may know you again."

Whereupon the good priest, without more ado, presented his back to her.

"Oh, thank you, thank you!" she cried. "What a handsome round face, and what expressive features! Yes, now I shall know you again. Only please bring me a cake from the feast!"

When the priest had turned the corner, he stripped the sow and took all the gold and silver ornaments, and thus laden with treasures he returned to his wife.

"Welcome home, father," they cried. "Where have you been wandering all this long time? Why, we were almost in despair."

"I thought," said he, "there were none like you in the world; but, as I see, there are others who outstrip you. Henceforth I shall put up with you for better, for worse."

And with the profits he brought home he got his daughters dowered and married, and lived happily with his wife ever after, although she did play a mad freak or two from time to time. And may we be happier still.

THE LION, THE TIGER, AND THE EAGLE

THERE was once a King who had three daughters and three sons. The time came for their father to die, and he said to his sons, "My sons, I am now dying; but do you think to get your sisters married, and afterwards to marry yourselves. As for you," he said to the youngest, "I have a fairy for you shut up in the crystal chamber, and when your sisters are married, see that you get married too."

After giving them further counsel, he died. A few days later the Queen died also, and the children were left orphans. A short time passed and there came a lion, and knocked at the door. "Who is there?" cried the King's children.

"I am the lion," said he, "come to take your eldest sister to wife."

"How far off is your dwelling?" said they.

"For such as me, five days' journey, and for such as you, five years'," said he.

"Five years!" they cried. "We will not let our sister go. If she should ever fall ill, how could we get to see her?"

But the youngest brother took her by the hand and led her to the lion. "Go where your fortune takes you," said he.

So when they had made love to one another, the lion took her and fled. The next day the tiger came and knocked at the door. They asked what he wanted. And he answered, "I want your second sister to wife."

"How far is it to your dwelling?" said they.

"For such as me, ten days, and for such as you, ten years," was the answer.

"Ten years!" said they. "We won't let our sister go." But their' youngest brother again took his sister and gave her to the tiger, as he had done before with the lion.

The next day the eagle came and knocked at the door, and they asked him who was there, and he said, "I am the eagle, and have come to take your youngest sister to wife."

Him too they asked if his dwelling was far. And he answered, "For such as me, fifteen days, and for such as you, fifteen years."

"We won't let our sister go," said they. "One sister we have let go five years' journey away, the other, ten years', and shall we let this one go fifteen ?"

Once more the youngest brother took her too by the hand, and gave her to the eagle.

When the maidens were married, the young men got married too; first the eldest, then the middle one, and lastly the youngest opened the chamber to take thence the fairy. But the fairy at once escaped, and said to him, "If you want to get me, you must make an iron staff and iron shoes, and come

"To the Illinees, the Billinees, the Alamalacusians,[1]
Unto the marble mountains, and unto the crystal meadows."

So he made the iron staff and the iron shoes and went to find her. And when he had gone five years' journey, he came to his sister's house, and sat outside on the stone seat to rest. Then the servant came out to fill her pail with water, and he asked her for a drink from the pail. At first she would not give him one, but after he had entreated her, she did so. And while he drank the water, he dropped his ring into it. The maid brought the water to her mistress. The mistress perceived by the ring that her brother was outside.

"Whom have you given water to?" she asked her maid.

"I have not given to anyone," said the maid.

"Don't be afraid," said her mistress, "tell me who the man was?"

"He is a traveller, he was sitting on the stone seat outside," said the maid, "and he besought me, and I gave him some."

"Go and bid him come in," said she.

And when he was come in, they embraced one another, and his sister asked him: "How did you come hither?"

_____
[1] These names are mere gibberish.

Then he told her all that had befallen him. As they were talking they heard the lion coming. "Let me hide you," said she to her brother, "lest he eat you." And she gave him a pat and he was turned into a broom, and she put him against the door.

When the lion had come in at the door, he said, "I smell kingly blood!"

"Kingly the ways that you walk!" replied the King's daughter, "hence the smell of kingly blood in your nose!" While they were eating bread, the King's daughter said to the lion, "If my eldest brother were to come, what would you do to him?"

"I would rip him up," said he.

"If the second one were to come?"

"I would make mince-meat of him."

"If the youngest came?"

"I would kiss him on his eyes."

"He has come!" said she.

"And you hide him from me?" said he. Then she took the broom and gave it a pat, and it became her brother.

The lion embraced him, kissed him, and asked him wherefore he was come.

Then he told him all that had befallen him, and asked him if he knew where were the

> "Illinees, the Billinees, the Alamalacusians,
>   The mountains made of marble, and the meadows all of crystal."

"I don't know them myself," said he, "but to-morrow I will summon all the beasts, and perhaps one of them may know."

On the morrow he summoned all the beasts, but none of them knew. So he set off the next day to find the "Illiness, Billinees," and after five years he came to the other sister, and sat again on the stone seat, and the maid-servant came to fetch water, and he begged her to give him a little water from the pail to drink.

And when he had drunk, he dropped his ring into the pail, and when his sister saw the ring, she perceived that it belonged to her brother, and she sent, and they called him in.

And when he was come in they embraced and kissed each other, and his sister asked him, "How did you come?" And when he had told her all that had befallen him, they heard the tiger coming. And she gave him a pat, and turned him into a dust-box, so that the tiger might not eat him. As soon as the tiger came in, "I smell kingly blood!" says he.

"Kingly the ways that you walk," said his wife to him, "hence the smell of king's blood in your nostrils. If my eldest brother were to come, what would you do to him?"

"I would rip him up," said he.

"If the second one came?"

"I would make mince-meat of him," said he.

"And if the youngest came ?"

"I would treat him as a brother."

"He has come," said she, "and I was afraid you would eat him, and so I hid him." Then she gave him another pat, and made him into a man. Thereupon the tiger embraced him, and kissed him, and asked him, "Wherefore are you come?"

He asked him whether he knew of the "Illiness, Billinees."

"I don't know them," said he. "To-morrow, I will summon all the beasts, and some of them may know." So in the morning he summoned them, but none of them knew.

So next day he set off, and came to his third sister, who was five years' journey further still. And again he went and sat on the stone seat by his sister's house; and the maid came to fetch water, and he begged a drink, and threw his ring into the pail. And when the King's daughter saw the ring, she perceived that her brother had come, and sent her maid to bid him come in. And when he was come in, they embraced and kissed each other, and she asked him. "Wherefore are you come?" And he told her what had befallen him. Then came the eagle, and asked why he was come.

And he told him, and asked him if he knew of the "Illinees, Billinees."

"I know them not," said he; "but to-morrow I will gather together all the birds, and perhaps one of them may know."

So on the morrow all the birds were gathered together, and the eagle asked them if they knew anything about the "Illinees, Billinees." "We know them not," said they; "but there is a lame she-hawk absent, and perhaps she may know." Then the lame she-hawk came, and she did know. Then said the eagle to her, "Take this man to the 'Illinees, Billinees.'" "I will," said the lame she-hawk. And when they came to the "Illinees, Billinees," the iron shoes were worn to holes. So he came to the "Illinees, Billinees" and found his bride, who was with the other fairies, and he took her and to his palace married her.

THE SNAKE, THE DOG, AND THE CAT

THERE was a poor woman who had one son, and they had no bread to eat. So the lad took a load of oleander and went and sold it for a couple of coppers. And as he was coming back he found some boys, who were about to kill a snake, and said to them, "There's a copper for you; don't kill it." So he gave them the copper, and the boys did not kill it, and the snake followed him. When he came home he told his mother what he had done.

And his mother scolded him, and said, "I send you to get money that we may have something to eat, and you bring me snakes!"

And he said, "Never mind, mother; even this will be of some use to us."

Again the lad took some oleander and sold it; and as he came back he saw some boys who were going to kill a dog, and said to them, "There's a copper for you, don't kill it." The boys took the copper and let the dog go. Then it, too, followed him.

The lad went to his mother and told her what he had done. And again his mother scolded him as before.

Once more he took some oleander, and sold it, and on his way back he found some boys who were going to kill a cat, and said to them, "Don't kill it, and I will give you a copper." So he gave them the copper, and they let the cat go.

And when he came home again, he told his mother what he had done, and she scolded him and said to him, "I send you to get money that we may eat bread, and you bring dogs, and cats, and snakes."

Then said he to her: "Never mind, mother, even they will be of some use to us."

Afterward the snake said to him, "Bring me to my father and mother, and take neither silver nor gold from them, only ask for the signet-ring which my father wears on his finger, and from it you will reap great advantage."

Then he took the snake to its father, and the snake said to its father, "This lad saved me from death."

And the father of the snake said to him. "What shall I give you for the kindness you have shown to my son?"

Then said the lad to the snake's father, "I want neither silver nor gold, I only want the signet-ring which you wear on your finger."

Then said the snake's father to the lad, "It is a great request you make, and more than I can grant."

Then the snake made as though he would follow the boy home, and said to its father, "Since you will not give the signet-ring to him who saved me from death, I will follow him wherever he goes, for I owe my life to him."

Then the father of the snake gave the ring to the boy, and said to him, "Whenever you want anything, press the seal, and there will come a Negro, whom you may bid do whatever you want, and he will do it."

Then the boy left and came to his house. And his mother said to him, "What shall we eat, my darling?" And he said to her, "Go to the cupboard and you will find bread there."

Then said his mother, "My son, I know there is no bread in that cupboard, and yet you tell me to go and find bread there."

And he said, "Go, as I tell you, and you will find some."

And while she was going to the cupboard he pressed the seal, and the Negro came, and said, "What are your orders, Master?" And the lad said to him, "I wish you to fill the cupboard with bread."

And when his mother came to the cupboard she found it full of bread, and took, and ate.

In this way they fared well with the signet-ring.

Once on a time the lad said to his mother, "Mother, go to the King and tell him to give me his daughter in marriage." His mother answered him, "What a pass have things come to that the King should give his daughter in marriage to the likes of us!" But he said, "Go, I tell you."

So the poor woman set off to see the King.

When she was admitted she said to the King, "My son wishes to marry your daughter." Then said the King to her, "I will give her to him if he is able to build a palace larger than mine."

The old woman arose and went to her son, and told him what the King said. And that same night he pressed the seal, and straightway the Negro appeared, and said to him:

"What are your orders, Master?"

And the other said to him, "That you build a castle larger than that of the King," and forthwith he found himself in a large palace.

Then he sent his mother to the King again, and she said to him, "My son has built the castle which you ordered." Said the King to her, "If he is able to pave the street from his palace to mine with gold, then he shall have my daughter in marriage."

Then the old woman went to her son, and told him all these things, and the lad called the Negro, and told him to pave the road all with gold. In the morning the lad got up and found it covered with gold, as the King had required. Then his mother went again to the King, and said to him: "My son has done all that you required." Then the King told her that the wedding should be made ready. And the old woman ran off, and went and told her son what the King had said to her.

The lad then made ready for the wedding. And the King called his daughter, and told her all that had happened, and that she was to get ready for the marriage.

The daughter was delighted, but begged her father to give her a slave to send whithersoever she would, and her father did as she desired. When the wedding was held the bridegroom took the bride, and they lived happily for a long time. At length the Princess fell in love with the slave, and one night she stole the signet-ring from her husband, and ran away with the slave, and they went to the seaside and built a palace with the seal, and lived together there close to the sea.

When the Princess had gone away with the slave, the cat came and purred and mewed and said to her master, "Master, what's the matter?"

"Matter, indeed! puss, this is what has befallen me: One night, while I was asleep, the slave took my ring, and my wife, and ran away with them."

"Peace, Master," said his cat, "I will go and fetch her. Give me the dog to ride, and let me go and fetch the ring."

Then he gives her the dog, and the cat rides him, and crosses the sea. And as she was going along she found a mouse and said to it, "If you wish me to spare your life, go and stick your tail into the slave's nose while he is asleep."

The mouse did so, and then the slave sneezed, and the ring which he had hidden in his mouth, fell out of it. The cat seized it and bestrode the dog, and while they were swimming in the sea, the dog said to the cat:

"As you hope to live, puss, stop, and let me just have a peep at the signet-ring."

"Why should you want to look at it, Coz?" And as the dog took the seal, he let it drop into the sea, and a fish snapped it up and turned all sorts of fine colours. Then said the cat to the dog, "Alack, what have you done to me? How shall I go to my master without the signet? Come along, let's ride you." And she rode him again till she came where the ships were drawn ashore.

And in the ship beside which they stopped the captain had just caught the very fish. So the cat began to purr and mew again, till the captain said, "What a nice cat we have here. This evening when I go home and cook the fish, I will throw her the entrails to eat." So when he was cleaning the fish and throwing her the entrails, the signet falls out, and the cat seizes it, rides the dog, and brings it to her master. And when her master saw her he said, "Well, puss, have you brought the signet?"

"I have," said she, "only you must kill the dog, because he threw it into the sea, and I have had no end of trouble to find it again," and she told him all she had gone through.

Then he took his gun to kill the dog, but now the cat interfered, and said to him, "Spare him this time, because we have taken our meals together so long."

Then he spared him. After that he took the signet and pressed it, and the Negro comes, and says to him, "What are your orders, Master?"

"That you bring hither the castle that is by the sea," said he.

In a moment the Negro brought it.

The lad went in and killed the slave.

Then he took his wife and they lived happily all their lives.

SIR LAZARUS AND THE DRAGONS

THERE was once a cobbler called Lazarus. One day as he was cobbling, a swarm of flies came about him, and he switched a sole at them, and slew forty flies. Then he went and made a sword, and wrote on it, "With one stroke I have taken forty lives."

And when he had made his sword, he set off for foreign parts. After two days' journey from his home he came to a spring, and lay down to sleep there. There the dragons were dwelling. Then one came to fetch water, and found Lazarus asleep. He also saw what was written on his sword, and went and told the rest. They told him to go and propose to him that they should become comrades.

The dragon went and called him, and said, "If he liked they would become comrades."

Lazarus said he was willing. And they went and lived together.

Then the dragons told him they took it in turn to go for water and also for wood. So the dragons went to fetch wood and water. At length the turn of Lazarus came to fetch water. The dragons had a skin in which they took the water, and it held two hundred gallons. It was all that Lazarus could do to carry the skin empty to the well, and since he could not carry the water, he did not fill the skin, but began digging round the well. The dragons, finding Lazarus was a long time away, were afraid something was wrong, and sent one of their number to go and see what had happened.

The dragon went and said to him, "What are you doing there, Sir Lazarus ?"

Says he, "I can't be at the trouble of coming to fetch water every day, am going to bring the whole well at once, to save time."

"For God's sake, Sir Lazarus, don't do that," says the dragon, "for we shall die of thirst; we will go in your stead, when it is your turn."

Next it came to the turn of Lazarus to fetch wood; and as he could not lift a tree like the dragon's he tied all the trees together with thongs. And when it grew late, the dragons again sent one of their number to see what he was doing. "What are you doing there, Sir Lazarus?" said he

"I am going to bring the whole wood at once, to save trouble," said he.

"Don't do that, Sir Lazarus," says the dragon, "or we shall die of cold; we will go in your stead when it is your turn."

So the dragon took the tree and carried it off.

After some time the dragons thought they would kill him, and they resolved that at nightfall they would all fetch him a stroke with an axe. Lazarus heard what they said and when evening came he put a log in his bed, and covered it with his cloak. At nightfall they all struck the log at once, and hewed it in pieces, and thought they had killed him. When the dragons had gone to sleep, Lazarus took the log and threw it away, and lay down, and as day began to dawn he murmured something, and the dragons asked him, saying, "What is the matter?"

And he told them that some fleas had been biting him. The dragons supposed that he thought the axe-blows were flea-bites, and next day they told him that if he had wife and children, and thought well, they would give him a supply of money, and let him go home. Lazarus said he was willing, and that he would take one of the dragons with him to carry the money to his house.

While they were on the way, he said to the dragon, "Stop! let me go and tie up my children, lest they eat you."

He went and tied up his children with some old ropes, and said to them, "When you see the dragon, mind you call out 'Dragon's flesh!'"

And when the dragon came near, the children called out "Dragon's flesh!" The dragon in a great fright left the money and fled.

While he was on his way he met a fox, who asked why he was in such a fright. And he said to him, "That until he had made good his escape, the children of Sir Lazarus were like to eat him." "Are you afraid of Sir Lazarus' children?" said he. "Why, he had two hens, one of them I ate yesterday, and the other I am going to eat now. And if you don't believe me, come along with me and see; tie yourself to my tail."

So the dragon tied himself to the fox's tail, and went to see.

When they neared the house of Sir Lazarus, Sir Lazarus was on the look-out with his gun, for he was afraid of the dragons.

When he saw the fox coming along with the dragon, he said to it, "I didn't tell you only to bring that dragon, but to bring them all."

When the dragon heard that, he made off; and from the great force with which it dragged the fox, it died.

So when Sir Lazarus had got rid of the dragons, he did up his house handsomely, and lived at ease.

HUNGARY

BEFORE the invasion of the Magyars, or Hungarian horsemen, in the ninth century the northern part of Hungary was inhabited by an older Slavonic race, and it is to them that the first story belongs.

The Magyars, who are said to be descended from the Scythians, were at first extremely warlike and even savage. Their folk-tales show points of strong resemblance to those of other races. In "Prince Csihan," we see the "Puss-in-boots" type, while "Fisher Joe" may be compared to Grimm's "The Gold Children."

THE SPEAKING GRAPES, THE SMILING APPLE, AND THE TINKLING APRICOT

THERE was once, I don't know where, beyond seven times seven countries, a king who had three daughters. One day the king was going to the market, and thus inquired of his daughters: "What shall I bring you from the market, my dear daughters?"

The eldest said, "A golden dress, my dear royal father"; the second said, "A silver dress for me"; the third said, "Speaking grapes, a smiling apple, and a tinkling apricot for me."

"Very well, my daughters," said the king, and went. He bought the dresses for his two elder daughters in the market, as soon as he arrived; but, in spite of all exertions and inquiries, he could not find the speaking grapes, the smiling apple, and tinkling apricot. He was very sad that he could not get what his youngest daughter wished, for she was his favourite; and he went home. It happened, however, that the royal carriage stuck fast on the way home, although his horses were of the best breed, for they were such high steppers that they kicked the stars. So he at once sent for extra horses to drag out the carriage; but all in vain, the horses couldn't move either way. He gave up all hope, at last, of getting out of the position, when a dirty, filthy pig came that way, and grunted, "Grumph! grumph! grumph! King, give me your youngest daughter, and I will help you out of the mud." The king, never thinking what he was promising, and over-anxious to get away, consented, and the pig gave the carriage a push with its nose, so that the carriage and horses at once moved out of the mud. Having arrived at home the king handed the dresses to his two daughters, and was now sadder than ever that he had brought nothing for his favourite daughter; the thought also troubled him that he had promised her to an unclean animal.

After a short time the pig arrived in the courtyard of the palace, dragging a wheelbarrow after it, and grunted, "Grumph! grumph! grumph! King, I've come for your daughter."

The king was terrified, and, in order to save his daughter, he had a peasant girl dressed in rich garments, embroidered with gold, sent her down, and had her seated in the wheelbarrow: the pig again grunted, "Grumph! grumph! grumph! King, this is not your daughter"; and, taking the barrow, it tipped her out. The king, seeing that deceit was of no avail, sent down his daughter, as promised, but dressed in ragged, dirty tatters, thinking that she would not please the pig; but the animal grunted in great joy, seized the girl, placed her in the wheelbarrow. Her father wept that through a careless promise, he had brought his favourite daughter to such a fate.

The pig went on and on with the sobbing girl, till, after a long journey, it stopped before a dirty pig-sty and grunted, "Grumph! grumph! grumph! Girl, get out of the wheelbarrow." The girl did as she was told. "Grumph! grumph! grumph!" grunted the pig again; "go into your new home."

The girl, whose tears, now, were streaming like a brook, obeyed; the pig then offered her some Indian corn that it had in a trough, and also its litter which consisted of some old straw, for a resting-place. The girl had not a wink of sleep for a long time, till at last, quite worn out with mental torture, she fell asleep.

Being completely exhausted with all her trials, she slept so soundly that she did not wake till next day at noon. On awakening, she looked round, and was very much astonished to find herself in a beautiful fairy-like palace, her bed being of white silk with rich purple curtains and golden fringes. At the first sign of her waking, maids appeared all round her, awaiting her orders, and bringing her costly dresses. The girl, quite enchanted with the scene, dressed without a word, and the maids accompanied her to her breakfast in a splendid hall, where a young man received her with great affection. "I am your husband, if you will accept me, and whatever you see here belongs to you," said he; and after breakfast led her into a beautiful garden. The girl did not know *whether it was a dream she saw or reality,* and answered all the questions put to her by the young man with evasive and chaffing replies. At this moment they came to that part of the garden which was laid out as an orchard, and the bunches of grapes began to speak, "Our beautiful queen, pluck some of us." The apples smiled at her continuously, and the apricots tinkled a beautiful silvery tune. "You see, my love," said the handsome youth, "here you have what you wished for—and your father could not obtain. You may know now, that once I was a monarch but I was bewitched into a pig and I had to remain in that state till a girl wished for speaking grapes, a smiling apple, and a tinkling apricot. You are the girl and I have been delivered; and if I please you you can be mine forever." The girl was enchanted with the handsome youth and the royal splendour, and consented. They went with great joy to carry the news to their father, and to tell him of their happiness.

FISHER JOE

THERE was once a poor man, who had nothing in the world but his wife and an unhappy son, Joe. His continual and his only care was how to keep them: so he determined to go fishing, and thus to keep them from day to day upon whatever the Lord brought to his net. Suddenly both the old folks died and left the unhappy son by himself; he went behind the oven and did not come out till both father and mother were buried; he sat three days behind the oven, and then remembered that his father had kept them by fishing; so he got up, took his net, and went fishing below the weir: there he fished till the skin began to peel off the palms of his hands, and never caught so much as one fish. At last he said, "I will cast my net for the last time," and drew to shore a golden fish. While he was going home he thought he would give it to the lord of the manor, so that perhaps he might grant a day's wages for it. When he got home he took down a plate from the rack, took the fish from his bag, and laid it upon the plate; but the fish slipped off the plate and changed into a lovely girl, who said, "I am thine, and you are mine, love." The moment after she asked, "Joe, did your father leave you anything?" "We had something," replied her husband; "but my father was poor and he sold everything; but," continued he, "do you see that high mountain yonder? It is not sold yet, for it is too steep and no one would have it." Then said his wife, "Let's go for a walk and look over the mountain." So they went all over it, length and breadth, from furrow to furrow. When they came to a furrow in the middle his wife said, "Let us sit down on a ridge, my love, and rest a little." They sat down, and Joe laid his head on his wife's lap and fell asleep. She then slipped off her cloak, made it into a pillow, drew herself away, and laid Joe upon the pillow without waking him. She rose, went away, uncoiled a large whip and cracked it. The crack was heard over seven times seven countries. In a moment as many dragons as existed came forth. "What are your Majesty's commands?" said they. "My commands are these," replied she: "You see this place—build a palace here, finer than any that exists in the world; and whatever is needed in it must be there: stables for eight bullocks and the bullocks in them, with two men to tend them; stalls for eight horses and the horses in them, and two grooms to tend them; six stacks in the yard, and twelve threshers in the barn." She was greatly delighted when she saw her order completed, and thanked God that He had given her what He had promised.

"I shall go now," said she, "and wake my husband." When she came to him he was still asleep. "Get up, my love," said she, "look after the threshers, the grooms, the oxen, and see that all do their work; and that all the work be done, and give your orders to the labourers; and now, my love, let us go into the house and see that all is right. You give your orders to the men-servants and I will give mine to the maids. We have now enough to live on"; and Joe thanked God for His blessings.

He then told his wife that he would invite the lord of the manor to dine with him on Whit Sunday.

"Don't leave me," replied his wife; "for if he catch sight of me you will lose me. I will see that the table is laid and all is ready; but a maid shall wait on you. I will retire to an inner room lest he should see me."

Joe ordered the carriage and six, seated himself in it, the coachman sat on the box, and away they went to the lord's house. They arrived at the gate, Joe got out, went through the gate, and saw three stonemasons at work in the yard; he greeted them and they returned his greeting. "Just look," remarked one of them, "what Joe has become and how miserable he used to be!" He entered the castle, and went into the lord's room. "Good day, my lord."

"God bless you, Joe, what news?" "I have come to ask your lordship to dine with me on Whit Sunday, and we shall be very pleased to see you." "I will come, Joe"; they then said good-bye and parted.

After Joe had gone the lord came into the courtyard, and the three masons asked him: "What did Joe want?" "He has invited me to dine with him," was the reply, "and I am going." "Of course; you must go," said one of them, "that you may see what sort of a house he keeps."

The lord set out in his carriage and four, with the coachman in front and arrived at the palace. Joe ran out to meet him, they saluted each other, and entered arm in arm. They dined, and all went well till the lord asked, "Well, Joe, and where is your wife?" "She is busy," said Joe.

"But I should like to see her," explained the baron.

"She is rather shy when in men's society," said Joe.

They enjoyed themselves, lighted their pipes and went for a walk over the palace. Then said the baron to his servant, "Order the carriage at once"; it arrived, and Joe and he said, "Farewell." As the baron went through the gate he looked back and saw Joe's wife standing at one of the windows, and at once fell so deeply in love with her that he became dangerously ill; when he arrived at home the footmen were obliged to carry him from his carriage and lay him in his bed.

At daybreak the three masons arrived and began to work. They waited for their master. As he did not appear, "I will go and see what's the matter with him," said one of them. "for he always came out at 8 A.M." So the mason went in and saluted the baron, but got no reply. "You are ill, my lord," said he. "I am," said the baron, "for Joe has such a pretty wife, and if I can't get her I shall die."

The mason went out and the three consulted together as to what was best to be done. One of them proposed a task for Joe, *i.e.*, that a large stone column which stood before one of the windows should be pulled down, the plot planted with vines, the grapes to ripen overnight, and the next morning a goblet of wine should be made from their juice and be placed on the master's table; if this was not done Joe was to lose his wife. So one of them went in to the baron and told him of their plan, remarking that Joe could not do that, and so he would lose his wife. A groom was sent on horseback for Joe, who came at once, and asked what his lordship desired. The baron then told him the task he had to propose and the penalty. Poor Joe was so downcast that he left without even saying good-bye, threw himself into his carriage, and went home.

"Well, my love," asked his wife, "what does he want?"

"Want," replied her husband, "he ordered me to pull down the stone column in front of this window. Since my father was not a workingman, how could I do any work? Nor is that all. I am to plant the place with vines, the grapes have to ripen, and I am to make a goblet of wine, to be placed on his table at daybreak; and if I fail I am to lose you."

"Your smallest trouble ought to be greater than that," said his wife. "Eat and drink, go to bed and have a good rest, and all will be well."

When night came she went out into the farmyard, uncoiled her whip, gave a crack, which was heard over seven times seven countries, and immediately all the dragons appeared. "What are your Majesty's commands?"

She then told them what her husband required, and in the morning Joe had the goblet of wine, which he took on horseback lest he should be late; he opened the baron's window, and, as nobody was there, he placed the goblet on the table, closed the window, and returned home.

At daybreak the baron turned in his bed. The bright light reflected by the goblet met his eyes, and had such an effect on him that he fell back in his bed, and got worse and worse.

The three masons arrived and wondered why their master did not appear. Said the tallest to the middle one, "I taught him something yesterday; now you must teach him something else."

"Well," said the middle one, "my idea is this, that Joe shall build a silver bridge in front of the gate during the night, plant both ends with all kinds of trees, and that the trees be filled with all kinds of birds singing and twittering in the morning. I'll warrant he won't do that, and so he will lose his wife."

When the baron came out they communicated their plan; he at once sent for Joe and told him what he required. Joe went away without even saying good-bye, he was so sad. When he got home he told his wife what the baron wanted this time.

"Don't trouble yourself, my love," said his wife. "Eat and drink and get a good rest, all shall be well." At night she cracked her whip and ordered the dragons to do all that was required, and so at daybreak all was done. The birds made such a noise that the whole of the village was awakened by them. One nightingale loudly and clearly to the baron sang, "Whatever God has given to some one else that you must not covet; be satisfied with what has been given to you." The baron awoke, and turned over, and, hearing the loud singing of the birds, rose and looked out of the window. The glare of the silver bridge opposite the gate blinded him and he fell back in his bed and grew worse and worse.

When the three masons arrived they could not enter, for the splendour of the silver bridge dazzled them, and they were obliged to enter by an other gate.

As they were working, the shortest said to the middle one, "Go and see why his lordship does not come out; perhaps he is worse." He went in and found the baron worse than ever. Then said the shortest, "I thought of something, my lord, which he will never be able to do, and so you will get his wife."

"What is that, mason?" demanded the baron. "It is this, my lord," said the mason, "that he shall ask God to dinner on Palm Sunday, and that he can't do, and so he will lose his wife."

"If you can get Joe's wife for me you shall have all this property," said the baron. "It's ours, then," said they, "for he can't do that."

Joe was sent for, and came at once to know what was required of him.

"My orders are these," replied the baron, "that you invite God to dinner on Palm Sunday to my house; if you do not your wife is lost." Poor Joe went out without saying good-bye, jumped into his carriage, and returned home dreadfully miserable. When his wife asked him what was the matter he told her of the baron's commands. "Go on," said his wife; "bring me that foal, the yearling, the most wretched one of all, put upon it an old saddle and silver harness on its head, and then get on its back." He did so, said good-bye, and the wretched yearling darted off at once straight to heaven. By the time it had arrived there it had become quite a beautiful horse. When Joe reached the gates of Paradise, he tied his horse to a stake, knocked at the door, which opened and he went in. St. Peter received him, and asked him why he had come. "I've come," said he, "to invite God to dinner at my lord's on Palm Sunday." "Tell him from me," said the Deity, "that I will come, and tell him that he is to sow a plot with barley, and that it will ripen, and that I will eat bread made of it at dinner. That a cow is to be taken to the bull to-day, and that I will eat the flesh of the calf for my dinner."

With this Joe took leave, and the foal flew downward. As they went Joe was like to fall head-foremost off. When he arrived at home the barley was waving in the breeze. "Well, wife," said he, "I will go to the baron's and give him the message." So he went, knocked at the door, and entered the room.

"Don't come a step further," cried the baron. "I don't intend to," said Joe. "I've come to tell you I have executed your commands, and mind you don't blame me for what will happen. The Deity has sent you this message: you are to sow a plot with barley, and of it make bread for His dinner. A cow is to go to the bull, and of the calf's flesh He will eat." The baron became thoughtful. "Don't worry yourself, my lord," said Joe, "you have worried me enough, it is your turn now," and so he said good-bye, and went off home. When he got there the barley-bread was baking and the veal was roasting.

At this moment the Deity and St. Peter arrived and were on their way to the baron's, who the moment he saw them called out to his servant, "Lock the gate, and do not let them in." Then said the Deity, "Let us go back to the poor man's home, and have dinner there." When they reached the foot of the mountain St. Peter was told to look back and say what he saw, and lo! the whole of the baron's property was a sheet of water. "Now," said the Deity to St. Peter, "let us go on, for the mountain is high, and difficult to ascend." When they arrived at Joe's he rushed out with outspread arms, fell to the ground, and kissed the sole of the Deity's foot. He entered and sat down to dinner, so did Joe and his wife and also St. Peter. Then said God to Joe, "Set a table in this world for the poor and miserable, and you shall have one laid for you in the world to come; and now good-bye: you shall live in joy, and in each other's love."

They are living still if they have not died since. May they be your guests to-morrow!

PRINCE CSIHAN [1]

THERE was once—I don't know where, at the other side of seven times seven countries, or even beyond them, on the tumble-down side of a tumble-down stove—a poplar-tree, and this poplar-tree had sixty-five branches, and on every branch sat sixty-five crows; and may those who don't listen to my story have their eyes picked out by those crows!

There was a miller who was so proud that had he stept on an egg he would not have broken it. There was a time when the mill was in full work, but once as he was tired of his mill-work he said, "May God take me out of this mill!" Now, this miller had an auger, a saw, and an adze, and he set off over seven times seven countries, and never found a mill. So his wish was fulfilled. On he went, roaming about, till at last he found on the bank of the Gagy, below Martonos, a tumble-down mill, which was covered with nettles. Here he began to build, and he worked, and by the time the mill was finished all his stockings were worn into holes and his garments all tattered and torn. He then stood expecting people to come and have their flour ground; but no one ever came.

---

[1] Nettles.

One day the twelve huntsmen of the king were chasing a fox; and it came to where the miller was, and said to him:

"Hide me, miller, and you shall be rewarded for your kindness."

"Where shall I hide you?" said the miller, "seeing that I possess nothing but the clothes I stand in?"

"There is an old torn sack lying beside that trough," replied the fox; "throw it over me, and, when the dogs come, drive them away with your broom."

When the huntsmen came they asked the miller if he had seen a fox pass that way.

"How could I have seen it; for, behold, I have nothing but the clothes I stand in ?"

With that the huntsmen left, and in a little while the fox came out, and said, "Miller, I thank you for your kindness; for you have preserved me, and saved my life. I am anxious to do you a good turn if I can. Tell me, do you want to get married?"

"My dear little fox," said the miller, "if I could get a wife, who would come here of her own free will, I don't say that I would not—indeed, there is no other way of my getting one; for I can't go among the spinning-girls in these clothes."

The fox took leave of the miller, and, in less than a quarter of an hour, he returned with a piece of copper in his mouth. "Here you are, miller," said he; "put this away, *you will want* it ere long."

The miller put it away, and the fox departed; but, before long, he came back with a lump of gold in his mouth. "Put this away, also," said he to the miller, "as you will need it before long. And now," said the fox, "Wouldn't you like to get married?" "Well, my dear little fox," said the miller, "I am quite willing to do so at any moment, as that is my special desire." The fox vanished again, but soon returned with a lump of diamond in his mouth. "Well, miller," said the fox, "I will not *ask* you any more to get married; I will get you a wife myself. And now give me that piece of copper I gave you." Then, taking it in his mouth, the fox started off over seven times seven countries, and travelled till he came to King Yellow Hammer's.

"Good day, most gracious King Yellow Hammer," said the fox; "my life and death are in your majesty's hands. I have heard that you have an unmarried daughter. I am a messenger from Prince Csihan, who has sent me to ask for your daughter as his wife."

"I will give her with pleasure, my dear little fox," replied King Yellow Hammer; "I will not refuse her; on the contrary, I give her with great pleasure; but I would do so more willingly if I saw to whom she is to be married—even as it is, I will not refuse her."

The fox accepted the king's proposal, and they fixed a day upon which they should fetch the lady. "Very well," said the fox; and, taking leave of the king, set off with the ring to the miller.

"Now then, miller," said the fox, "you are no longer a miller, but Prince Csihan, and on a certain day and hour you must be ready to start; but, first of all, give me that lump of gold I gave you that I may take it to His Majesty King Yellow Hammer, so that he may not think you are a nobody."

The fox then started off to the king. "Good day, most gracious king, my father. Prince Csihan has sent this lump of gold to my father the king that he may spend it in preparing for the wedding, and that he might change it, as Prince Csihan has no smaller change, his gold all being in lumps like this."

"Well," reasoned King Yellow Hammer, "I am not sending my daughter to a bad sort of place, for although I am a king, I have no such lumps of gold lying about in my palace."

The fox then returned home to Prince Csihan. "Now then, Prince Csihan," said he, "I have arrived safely, you see; prepare yourself to start to-morrow."

Next morning he appeared before Prince Csihan. "Are you ready?" asked he. "Oh! yes, I am ready; I can start at any moment, as I got ready long ago."

With this they started over seven times seven lands. As they passed a hedge the fox said, "Prince Csihan, do you see that splendid castle?" "How could I help seeing it, my dear little fox." "Well," replied the fox, "in that castle dwells your wife."

On they went, when suddenly the fox said, "Take off the clothes you have on, let us put them into this hollow tree, and then burn them, so that we may get rid of them." "You are right, we won't have them, nor any like them."

Then said the fox, "Prince Csihan, go into the river and take a bath." Having done so the prince said, "Now I've done." "All right," said the fox; "go and sit in the forest until I go into the king's presence." The fox set off and arrived at King Yellow Hammer's castle.

"Alas! my gracious king, my life and my death are in thy hands. I started with Prince Csihan with three loaded waggons and a carriage and six horses, and I've just managed to get the prince naked out of the water." The king raised his hands in despair, exclaiming, "Where hast thou left my dear son-in-law, little fox?" "Most gracious king, I left him in such-and-such a place in the forest."

The king at once ordered four horses to be put to a carriage, and then looked up the robes he wore in his younger days and ordered them to be put in the carriage; the coachman and footman to take their places, the fox sitting on the box.

When they arrived at the forest the fox got down, and the footman carrying the clothes upon his arm, took them to Prince Csihan. Then said the fox to the servant, "Don't you dress the prince, he will do it more becomingly himself." He then made

Prince Csihan arise, and said, "Come here, Prince Csihan, don't stare at yourself too much when you get dressed in these clothes, else the king will think you are not used to such robes."

Prince Csihan got dressed, and drove off to the king. When they arrived, King Yellow Hammer took his son-in-law in his arms, and said, "Thanks be to God, my dear future son-in-law, for that he has preserved thee from the great waters; and now let us send for a clergyman and let the marriage take place."

The grand ceremony over, they remained at the court of the king. One day, a month or so after they were married, the princess said to Prince Csihan, "My dear treasure, don't you think it would be as well to go and see your realm?"

Prince Csihan left the room in great sorrow, and went toward the stables in great trouble to get ready for the journey he could no longer postpone. Here he met the fox lolling about. As the prince came his tears rolled down upon the straw. "Hollo! Prince Csihan, what's the matter?" cried the fox. "Quite enough," was the reply; "my dear wife insists upon going to see my home." "All right," said the fox, "prepare yourself, Prince Csihan, and we will go."

The prince went off to his castle and said, "Dear wife, get ready; we will start at once." The king ordered out a carriage and six, and three waggons loaded with treasure and money, so that they might have all they needed. So they started off. Then said the fox, "Now, Prince Csihan, wherever I go you must follow."

So they went over seven times seven countries. As they travelled they met a herd of oxen. "Now, herdsman," said the fox, "if you won't say that this herd belongs to the Vasfogu Bába, but to Prince Csihan, you shall have a handsome present." With this the fox left them, and ran straight to the Vasfogu Bába.

"Good day, my mother," said he. "Welcome, my son," replied she; "it's a good thing for you that you called me your mother, else I would have crushed your bones smaller than poppy-seed." "Alas! my mother," said the fox, "don't let us waste our time talking such nonsense, the French are coming!"

"Oh! my dear son, hide me away somewhere!" cried the old woman. "I know of a bottomless lake," thought the fox; and he took her and left her on the bank, saying, "Now, my dear old mother, wash your face here until I return."

The fox then left the Vasfogu Bába, and went to Prince Csihan, whom he found standing in the same place where he left him. He began to swear and rave at him fearfully. "Why didn't you drive on after me? Come along at once."

They arrived at the Vasfogu's great castle, and took possession of a suite of apartments. Here they found everything the heart could wish for, and at night all went to bed in peace.

Suddenly the fox remembered that the Vasfogu Bába had no proper abode yet, and set off to her. "I hear, my dear son," said she, "that the horses with their bells have arrived; take me away to another place." The fox crept up behind her, gave her a push, and she fell into the bottomless lake, and was drowned, leaving all her vast property to Prince Csihan.

"You were born under a lucky star, my prince," said the fox, when he returned; "for see I have placed you in possession of all this great wealth."

In his joy the prince gave a great feast to celebrate his coming into his property, so that the people from Bánczida to Zsukhajna were feasted royally, but he gave them no drink. "Now," said the fox to himself, "after all this feasting I will sham illness, and see what treatment I shall receive at his hands in return for all my kindness to him." So Mr. Fox became dreadfully ill; he moaned and groaned so fearfully that the neighbours made complaint to the prince. "Seize him," said the prince, "and pitch him out on the dunghill." So the poor fox was thrown out on the dunghill. One day Prince Csihan was passing that way. "You a prince!" muttered the fox; "you are nothing else but a miller; would you like to be a householder such as you were at the nettle-mill?"

The prince was terrified by this speech of the fox, so terrified that he nearly fainted. "Oh! dear little fox, do not do that," cried the prince, "and I promise you on my royal word that I will give you the same food as I have, and that so long as I live you shall be my dearest friend and you shall be honoured as my greatest benefactor."

He then ordered the fox to be taken to the castle, and to sit at the royal table, nor did he ever forget him again.

So they lived happily ever after, and do yet, if they are not dead. May they be your guests to-morrow!

THE WISHES

THERE was once, it doesn't matter where: there was once upon a time, a poor man who had a pretty young wife; they were very fond of each other. The only thing they had to complain of was their poverty, as neither of them owned a farthing; it happened, therefore, sometimes, that they quarrelled a little, and then they always cast it in each other's teeth that they hadn't got anything to bless themselves with. But still they loved each other.

One evening the woman came home much earlier than her husband and went into the kitchen and lighted the fire, although she had nothing to cook. "I think I can cook a little soup, at least, for my husband. It will be ready by the time he comes home." But no sooner had she put the kettle over the fire, and a few logs of wood on the fire in order to make the water boil quicker, than her husband arrived home and took his seat by the side of her on the little bench. They warmed themselves by the fire, as it was late in the autumn and cold. In the neighbouring village they had commenced the vintage on that very day. "Do you know the news, wife?" inquired he. "No, I don't. I've heard nothing; tell me what it is."

"As I was coming from the squire's maize-field, I saw in the dark, in the distance, a black spot on the road. I couldn't make out what it was, so I went nearer, and lo! do you know what it was?—A beautiful little golden carriage, with a pretty little woman inside, and four fine black dogs harnessed to it."

"You're joking," interrupted the wife.

"I'm not, indeed, it's perfectly true. You know how muddy the roads about here are; it happened that the dogs stuck fast with the carriage and they couldn't move from the spot; the little woman didn't care to get out into the mud, as she was afraid of soiling her golden dress. At first, when I found out what it was, I had a good mind to run away, as I took her for an evil spirit, but she called out after me and implored me to help her out of the mud; she promised that no harm should come to me, but on the contrary she would reward me.

"So I thought that it would be a good thing for us if she could help us in our poverty; and with my assistance the dogs dragged her carriage out of the mud. The woman asked me whether I was married. I told her I was. And she asked me if I was rich. I replied, not at all; I didn't think, I said, that there were two people in our village who were poorer than we. 'That can be remedied,' replied she. 'I will fulfil three wishes that your wife may propose.' And she left as suddenly as if dragons had kidnapped her: she was a fairy."

"Well, she made a regular fool of you!"

"That remains to be seen; you must try and wish something, my dear wife." Thereupon the woman without much thought said: "Well, I should like to have some sausage, and we could cook it beautifully on this nice fire." No sooner were the words uttered than a frying-pan came down the chimney, and in it a sausage of such length that it was long enough to fence in the whole garden.

"This is grand!" they both exclaimed together. "But we must be more clever with our next two wishes; how well we shall be off! I will at once buy two heifers and two horses, as well as a sucking pig," said the husband. Whereupon he took his pipe from his hatband, took out his tobacco-pouch, and filled his pipe; then he tried to light it with a hot cinder, but was so awkward about it that he upset the frying-pan with the sausage in it.

"Good heavens! the sausage; what on earth are you doing! I wish that sausage would grow on to your nose," exclaimed the frightened woman, and tried to snatch the same out of the fire, but it was too late, as it was already dangling from her husband's nose down to his toes. "My Lord Creator help me!" shouted the woman. "You see, you fool, what you've done, there! now the second wish is gone," said her husband. "What can we do with this thing?"

"Can't we get it off?" said the woman.

"Take off the devil. Don't you see that it has quite grown to my nose; you can't take it off."

"Then we must cut it off," said she, "as we can do nothing else."

"I shan't permit it: how could I allow my body to be cut about? Not for all the treasures on earth; but do you know what we can do, love? There is yet one wish left; you'd better wish that the sausage go back to the pan, and so all will be right." But the woman replied, "How about the heifers and the horses, and how about the sucking pig; how shall we get those ?"

"Well, I can't walk about with this ornament, and I'm sure you won't kiss me again with this sausage dangling from my nose."

And so they quarrelled for a long time, till at last he succeeded in persuading his wife to wish that the sausage go back to the pan. And thus all three wishes were fulfilled; and yet they were as poor as ever.

They, however, made a hearty meal of the sausage; and as they came to the conclusion that it was in consequence of their quarrelling that they had no heifers, nor horses, nor sucking pig, they agreed to live thenceforth in harmony together; and they quarrelled no more after this. They got on much better in the world, and in time they acquired heifers, horses, and a sucking pig into the bargain; because they were industrious and thrifty.

ICELAND

MR. JÓN ARNASON, who collected most of the legends of Iceland, has been called the "Grimm of Iceland." These simple tales show that the manners, sayings, and customs of these pastoral people, who were ever struggling with nature out of doors and poverty within, are different from those of a more refined and leisured people.

Icelandic mythology abounds with stories of elves and trolls. The sea-roving tendencies of the people and their unceasing battle with nature's forces added freshness, life, and originality to their spirit. They are fanciful and imaginative to a high degree. The desolate beauty of their storm-lashed island seems reflected in these vigorous, freedom-loving people. Their stories bear striking resemblances to many others of Northern Europe.

THE MERMAN

LONG ago a farmer lived at Vogar, who was a mighty fisherman, and, of all the farms round about, not one was so well situated with regard to the fisheries as his.

One day, according to custom, he had gone out fishing, and having cast down his line from the boat, and waited awhile, found it very hard to pull up again, as if there were something very heavy at the end of it. Imagine his astonishment when he found that what he had caught was a great fish, with a man's head and body! When he saw that this creature was alive, he addressed it and said, "Who and whence are you ?"

"A merman from the bottom of the sea," was the reply.

The farmer then asked him what he had been doing when the hook caught his flesh. The other replied, "I was turning the cowl of my mother's chimney-pot, to suit it to the wind. So let me go again, will you?"

"Not for the present," said the fisherman. "You shall serve me awhile first."

So without more words he dragged him into the boat and rowed to shore with him.

When they got to the boat-house, the fisherman's dog came to him and greeted him joyfully, barking and fawning on him, and wagging his tail. But his master's temper being none of the best, he struck the poor animal; whereupon the merman laughed for the first time.

Having fastened the boat, he went toward his house, dragging his prize with him, over the fields, and stumbling over a hillock, which lay in his way, cursed it heartily; whereupon the merman laughed for the second time.

When the fisherman arrived at the farm, his wife came out to receive him, and embraced him affectionately, and he received her salutations with pleasure; whereupon the merman laughed for the third time.

Then said the farmer to the merman, "You have laughed three times, and I am curious to know *why* you have laughed. Tell me, therefore."

"Never will I tell you," replied the merman, "unless you promise to take me to the same place in the sea wherefrom you caught me, and there to let me go free again." So the farmer made him the promise.

"Well," said the merman, "I laughed the first time because you struck your dog, whose joy at meeting you was real and sincere. The second time, because you cursed the mound over which you stumbled, which is full of golden ducats. And the third time, because you received with pleasure your wife's empty and flattering embrace, who is faithless to you and a hypocrite. And now be an honest man and take me out to the sea whence you have brought me."

The farmer replied: "Two things that you have told me I have no means of proving, namely, the faithfulness of my dog and the faithlessness of my wife. But of the third I will try the truth, and if the hillock contain gold, then I will believe the rest."

Accordingly he went to the hillock, and having dug it up, found therein a great treasure of golden ducats, as the merman had told him. After this the farmer took the merman down to the boat, and to that place in the sea whence he had caught him. Before he put him in, the latter said to him:

"Farmer, you have been an honest man, and I will reward you for restoring me to my mother, if only you have skill enough to take possession of property that I shall throw in your way. Be happy and prosper."

Then the farmer put the merman into the sea, and he sank out of sight.

It happened that not long after, seven sea-grey cows were seen on the beach, close to the farmer's land. These cows appeared to be very unruly, and ran away directly the farmer approached them. So he took a stick and ran after them, possessed with the fancy that if he could burst the bladder which he saw on the nose of each of them, they would belong to him. He contrived to hit out the bladder on the nose of one cow, which then became so tame that he could easily catch it, while the others leaped into the sea and disappeared. The farmer was convinced that this was the gift of the merman. And a very useful gift it was, for a better cow was never seen nor milked in all the land, and she was the mother of the race of grey cows so much esteemed now.

And the farmer prospered exceedingly, but never caught any more mermen. As for his wife, nothing further is told about her, so we can repeat nothing.

THE MONEY CHEST

IT happened, once upon a time, that a large party of men were travelling together, and pitched their tent, early one Sunday morning, on the fresh sward of a fair green meadow. The weather was bright and warm, and the men being tired with their night's journey, and having tethered their horses, fell asleep, side by side, all round the inside of the tent. One of them, however, who happened to be lying nearest the door, could not, in spite of his fatigue, succeed in getting to sleep, so lay idly watching the other sleepers. As he looked round he discovered a small cloud of pale-blue vapour moving over the head of the man who was sleeping in the innermost part of the tent. Astonished at this he sat up, and at the same moment the cloud flitted out of the tent. Being curious to know what it could be and what would become of it, he jumped up softly, and, without awaking the others, stole out into the sunshine. On looking round he saw the vapour floating slowly over the meadow, so set himself to follow it. After a while it stopped over where lay the blanched skull of a horse upon the grass, in and about which hummed and buzzed a cloud of noisy blue flies. Into this the vapour entered among the flies. After staying awhile, it came out, and took its course over the meadow till it came to a little thread of a rivulet, which hurried through the grass. Here it seemed to be at a loss how to get over the water, and moved restlessly and impatiently up and down the side of it, till the man laid his whip, which he happened to have with him, over it, the handle alone being sufficient to bridge it across. Over this the vapour passed and moved on till it came to a small hillock, into which it disappeared. The man stood by and waited for it to come out again, which it soon did, and returned by the same way as that by which it had come. The man laid his whip as before across the stream and the vapour crossed upon the handle. Then it moved on toward the tent, which it entered, and the man who had followed it saw it hover for a minute over the head of the sleeper, where he had first seen it, and disappear. After this he lay down again, and went to sleep himself.

When the day was far spent and the sun was going down, the men rose, struck the tent, and made preparations for beginning their journey again. While they were packing, and loading the horses, they talked on various things, and, among others, on money.

"Bless me!" said the man who had slept in the innermost part of the tent, "I wish I had what I saw in my dream to-day."

"What was your dream, and what did you see?" asked the man who had followed the vapour.

The other replied, "I dreamt that I walked out from the tent, and across the meadow till I came to a large and beautiful building, into which I went. There I found many people at revel in a vast and noble hall, singing, dancing and making merry. I played some time among them, and when I left them and stepped out from the hall, I saw stretched before me a vast plain of fair green sward. Over this I walked for some time, till I came to an immensely broad and turbulent river, over which I wished to cross, but could find no means of doing so. As I was walking up and down the bank, thinking how I could possibly get over it, I saw a mighty giant greater than any I had ever heard of, come toward me, holding in his hand the trunk of a large tree, which he laid across the river. Thus I was able to get easily to the other side. The river once passed, I walked straight on for a long time till I came to a high mound which lay open. I went into it, thinking to find wonderful treasures, but found only a single chest, which, however, was so full of money that I could neither lift it, nor, though I spent hours over it, count the quarter of its contents. So I gave it up and bent my steps hither again. The giant flung his tree across the river as before, and I came to the tent and went to sleep from sheer weariness."

At hearing this, the other who had followed the vapour was mightily pleased, and, laughing to himself, said, "Come, my good fellow, let us fetch the money. If one could not count it, no doubt two can."

"Fetch the money!" replied the man. "Are you mad? Do you forget that I only *dreamed* about it? Where would you fetch it from?"

But as the other seemed really earnest and determined, he consented to go with him.

So they took the same course as the vapour had taken, and when they came to the skull, "There is your hail of revel," said the man who had followed the mist some hours before.

"And there," he said, when they stepped over the rivulet, "is your broad and turbulent river, and here the trunk the giant threw over it as a bridge." With these words he showed him his whip.

The other was filled with amazement, and when they came to the mound, and having dug a little way into it, really and truly discovered a heavy chest full of golden pieces, his astonishment was not a whit the less. On their way back to the tent with the treasure, his companion told him all about the matter.

Whether they complained of the weight of the money-chest or gave up counting its contents in despair, this story relateth not.

THE SHEPHERD OF SILFRÚNARSTADIR

A MAN named Gudmundur lived once upon a time at a farm called Silfrúnarstadir, in the bay of Skagafjördur. He was rich in flocks, and looked upon by his neighbours as a man of high esteem and respectability. He was married, but had no children.

It happened one Christmas-eve at Silfrúnarstadir, that the herdsman did not return home at night, and, as he was not found at the sheep-pens, the farmer caused a diligent search to be made for him all over the country, but quite in vain.

Next spring Gudmundur hired another shepherd, named Grimur, who was tall and strong, and boasted of being able to resist anybody. But the farmer, in spite of the man's boldness and strength, warned him to be careful how he ran risks, and on Christmas-eve bade him drive the sheep early into the pens, and come home to the farm while it was still daylight. But in the evening Grimur did not come, and though search was made far and near for him, was never found. People made all sorts of guesses about the cause of his disappearance, but the farmer was full of grief, and after this could not get any one to act as shepherd for him.

At this time there lived a very poor widow at Sjavarborg, who had several children, of whom the eldest, aged fourteen years, was named Sigurdur. To this woman the farmer at last applied, and offered her a large sum of money if she would allow her son to act as shepherd for him.

Sigurdur was very anxious that his mother should have all this money, and declared himself most willing to undertake the office; so he went with the farmer, and during the summer was most successful in his new situation, and never lost a sheep.

At the end of a certain time the farmer gave Sigurdur a wether, a ewe, and a lamb as a present, with which the youth was much pleased. Gudmundur became attached to him, and on Christmas-eve begged him to come home from his sheep before sunset.

All day long the boy watched the sheep, and when evening approached, he heard the sound of heavy footsteps on the mountains. Turning round he saw coming toward him a gigantic and terrible troll.

She addressed him, saying, "Good evening, my Sigurdur. I am come to put you into my bag."

Sigurdur answered, "Are you cracked? Do you not see how thin I am? Surely I am not worth your notice. But I have a sheep and a fat lamb here which I will give you for your pot this evening."

So he gave her the sheep and the lamb, which she threw on her shoulder, and carried off up the mountain again. Then Sigurdur went home and right glad was the farmer to see him safe, and asked him whether he had seen anything.

"Nothing whatever, out of the common," replied the boy.

After New Year's Day the farmer visited the flock, and, on looking over them, missed the sheep and lamb which he had given the youth, and asked him what had become of them. The boy answered that a fox had killed the lamb, and that the wether had fallen into a bog; adding, "I fancy I shall not be very lucky with *my* sheep."

When the farmer heard this, the farmer gave him one ewe and two wethers, and asked him to remain another year in his service. Sigurdur consented to do so.

Next Christmas-eve, Gudmundur begged Sigurdur to be cautious, and not run any risks, for he loved him as his own son.

But the boy answered, "You need not fear, there are no risks to run."

When he had got the sheep into the pens about nightfall, the same troll came to him, and said:

"As sure as ever I am a troll, you shall not, this evening, escape being boiled in my pot."

"I am quite at your service," answered Sigurdur, intrepidly; "but you see that I am still very thin; nothing to be compared even to one wether. I will give you, however, for your Christmas dinner, two old and two young sheep. Will you condescend to be satisfied with this offer of mine ?"

"Let me see," said the troll; so the lad showed her the sheep, and she, hooking them together by their horns, threw them on to her shoulder, and ran off with them up the mountain.

Then Sigurdur returned to the farm, and, when questioned, declared, as before, that he had seen nothing whatever unusual upon the mountain. "But," he said, "I have been dreadfully unlucky with *my* sheep, as I said should be."

Next summer the farmer gave him four more wethers. When Chrismas-eve had come again, just as Sigurdur was patting the sheep into their pens, the troll came to him, and threatened to take him away with her. Then he offered her the four wethers, which she took, and hooking them together by their horns, threw them over her shoulder. Not content with this, however, she seized the lad, too, tucked him under her arm, and ran off with her burthen to her cave in the mountains.

Here she flung the sheep down, and Sigurdur after them, and ordered him to kill them and shave their skins. When he had done so, he asked her what task she had now for him to perform.

She said, "Sharpen this axe well, for I intend to cut off your head with it."

When he had sharpened it well, he restored it to the troll, who bade him take off his neckerchief; which he did, without changing a feature of his face.

Then the troll, instead of cutting off his head, flung the axe down on the ground, and said, "Brave lad! I never intended to kill you, and you shall live to a good old age. It was I that caused you to be made herdsman to Gudmundur, for I wished to meet with you. And now I will show you in what way you shall arrive at good fortune. Next spring you must move from Silfrúnarstadir, and go to the house of a silversmith, to learn his trade. When you have learned it thoroughly, you shall take some specimens of silver-work to the farm where the dean's three daughters live; and I can tell you that the youngest of them is the most promising maiden in the whole country. Her elder sisters love dress and ornaments, and will admire what you bring them, but Margaret will not care about such things. When you leave the house, you shall ask her to accompany you as far as the door, and then as far as the end of the grass-field, which she will consent to do. Then you shall give her these three precious things—this handkerchief, this belt, and this ring; and after that she will love you. But when you have seen me in a dream you must come here, and you will find me dead. Bury me, and take for yourself everything of value that you find in my cave."

Then Sigurdur bade her farewell and left her, and returned to the farm, where Gudmundur welcomed him with joy, having grieved at his long absence, and asked him whether he had seen nothing.

"No," replied the boy; and declared that he could answer for the safety of all future herdsmen. But no more questions would he answer, though the family asked him many. The following spring he went to a silversmith's house, and in two years made himself master of the trade. He often visited Gudmundur, his old master, and was always welcome.

Once he went to the trading town of Hofsós, and buying a variety of glittering silver ornaments, took them to Miklïboer, and offered them for sale to the dean's daughters, as the troll had told him. When the elder sisters heard that he had ornaments for sale, they begged him to let them see them first, in order that they might choose the best of them. Accordingly he showed them wares, and they bought many trinkets, but Margaret would not even so much as look at the silver ornaments.

When he took leave, he asked the youngest sister to accompany him as far as the door, and when they got there, to come with him as far as the end of the field. She was much astonished at this request, and asked him what he wanted with her, as she had never seen him before. But Sigurdur entreated her the more the more she held back, and at last she consented to go with him. At the end of the field Sigurdur gave her the belt and handkerchief, and put the ring on to her finger.

This done, Margaret said, "I wish I had never taken these gifts, but I cannot now give them you back."

Sigurdur then took leave and went home. But Margaret, as soon as she had received the presents, fell in love with their giver; and finding after a while that she could not live without him, told her father all about it. Her father bade her desist from such a mad idea, and declared that she should never marry the youth as long as he lived to prevent it. On this Margaret pined away, and became so thin from grief that the father found he would be obliged to consent to her request; and going to the farm at which Sigurdur lived, engaged him as his silversmith.

Not long after, Sigurdur and Margaret were betrothed.

One day the youth dreamed that he saw the old troll, and felt sure from this that she was dead; so he asked the dean to accompany him as far as Silfrúnarstadir, and sleep there one night. When they arrived there, they told Gudmundur that Sigurdur was betrothed to Margaret. When the farmer heard this, he said that it had long been his intention to leave Sigurdur all his property, and offered him the management of the farm the ensuing spring. The youth thanked him heartily, and the dean was glad to see his daughter so soon, and so well, provided for.

Next day Sigurdur asked the farmer and the dean to go with him as far as the middle of the mountain, where they found a cave into which he bade them enter without fear. Inside they saw the troll lying dead on the floor with her face awfully distorted. Then Sigurdur told them all about his interviews with the troll, and asked them to help him to bury her. When they had done so, they returned to the cave and found there as many precious things as ten horses could carry, which Sigurdur took back to the farm.

Not long after, he married the dean's daughter, and prospered to the end of his life, which, as the old troll had prophesied, was a long one.

INDIA

MANY authorities consider that India is the original home of all folk-tales, and that these have been transmitted to other nations through wars, merchants, gipsies, and crusaders, chiefly by way of Byzantium.

As the present anthology shows, however, there are very many identities and similarities that have been discovered among races far removed contact with India, and Andrew Lang urged that the spontaneous generation of like ideas and incidents was not only possible but highly probable.

Whichever theory is accepted, India must be acknowledged as the home of some of the oldest folk-tales of the world. It possesses a fantastic mythology, overlaid by superstition. One misses in it, however, the romantic beauty of such stories as "Psyche" and the delightful fairy element of Celtic literature. There is much subtlety but little boisterous humour; a moral note but not nobility. The Indian mind has been compared to a plant reared in a hot-house—gorgeous in colour, rich in perfume, precocious and abundant in fruit.

I. PANCHATANTRA TALES

THE *Panchatantra* or *The Five Books* is the oldest extant collection of stories in Sanskrit literature. It is believed to have been gathered together about 200 B.C., though the stories themselves are of unknown antiquity. It was composed for the instruction of princes by a Brahman, to whom a king entrusted the education of his three rather indolent sons. The moral tone is clearly manifest. Each of the five books is independent and deals with a definite principle, *e.g.,* the danger of listening to perfidious insinuations concerning one's friends, or the advantages of banding together to help one another.

Though only separate stories have been given in this anthology, the *Panchatantra* tales are inserted in a kind of framing narrative, somewhat in the style of the *Arabian Nights* stories.

THE BRAHMAN, THE THIEF, AND THE GHOST

THERE was once a poor Brahman in a certain place. He lived on presents, and always did without such luxuries as fine clothes, and ointments and perfumes and garlands and gems and betel-gum. His beard and his nails were long, and so was the hair that covered his head and his body. Heat, cold, rain, and the like had dried him up.

Then some one pitied him and gave him two calves. And the Brahman began when they were little and fed them on butter and oil and fodder and other things that he begged. So he made them very plump.

Then a thief saw them and the idea came to him at once: "I will steal these two cows from the Brahman." So he took a rope and set out at night. But on the way he met a fellow with a row of sharp teeth set far apart, with a high-bridged nose and uneven eyes, with limbs covered with knotty muscles, with hollow cheeks, with beard and body as yellow as a fire with much butter in it.

And when the thief saw him, he started with acute fear and said: "Who are you, sir?"

The other said, "I am a ghost named Truthful. It is now your turn to explain yourself."

The thief said: "I am a thief, and my acts are cruel. I am on my way to steal two cows from a poor Brahman."

Then the ghost felt relieved and said, "My dear sir, I take one meal every three days. So I will just eat this Brahman to-day. It is delightful that you and I are on the same errand."

So together they went there and hid, waiting for the proper moment. And when the Brahman went to sleep, the ghost started forward to eat him. But the thief saw him and said: "My dear sir, this is not right. You are not to eat the Brahman until I have stolen his two cows."

The ghost said: "The racket would most likely wake the Brahman. In that case all my trouble would be vain."

"But, on the other hand," said the thief, "if any hindrance arises when you start to eat him, then I cannot steal the two cows either. First I will steal the two cows, then you may eat the Brahman."

So they disputed, each crying, "Me first! Me first!" And when they became heated, the hubbub waked the Brahman. Then the thief said: "Brahman, this is a ghost who wishes to eat you." And the ghost said: "Brahman, this is a thief who wishes to steal your two cows."

When the Brahman heard this, he stood up and took a good look. And by remembering a prayer to his favourite god, he saved his life from the ghost, then lifted a club and saved his two cows from the thief.

HOW SUPERSMART ATE THE ELEPHANT

THERE was once a jackal named Supersmart in a part of a forest. One day he came upon an elephant that had died a natural death in the wood. But he could only stalk about the body; he could not cut through the tough hide.

At this moment a lion, in his wanderings to and fro, came to the spot. And the jackal spying him, obsequiously rubbed his scalp in the dust, clasped his lotus-paws, and said: "My lord and king, I am merely a cudgel-bearer, guarding this elephant in the king's interest. May the king deign to eat it."

Then the lion said: "My good fellow, under no circumstances do I eat what another has killed. I graciously bestow this elephant upon you."

And the jackal joyfully replied: "It is only what our lord and king has taught his subjects to expect."

When the lion was gone, a tiger arrived. And the jackal thought when he saw him: "Well, I sent one rascal packing by doing obeisance. Now, how shall I dispose of this one? To be sure, he is a hero, and therefore can be managed only by intrigue. For there is a saying:

> "Where bribes and flattery would fail,
> Intrigue is certain to avail."

So he took his decision, went to meet the tiger, and slightly stiffening his neck, he said in an agitated tone: "Uncle, how could you venture into the jaws of death? This elephant was killed by a lion, who put me on guard while he went to bathe. And as he went, he gave me my orders. 'If any tiger comes this way,' he said, creep up and tell me. I have to clear this forest of tigers, because once, when I had killed an elephant, a tiger helped himself while my back was turned, and I had the leavings. From that day I have been death on tigers.'"

On hearing this, the tiger was terrified, and said: "My dear nephew, make me a gift of my life. Even if he is slow in returning, don't give him any news of me." With these words he decamped.

When the tiger had gone, a leopard appeared. And the jackal thought when he saw him: "Here comes Spot. He has powerful teeth. So I will use him to cut into this elephant-hide."

With this in mind, he said: "Well, nephew, where have you been this long time? And why do you seem so hungry? You come as my guest, according to the proverb:

> "A guest in need
> Is a guest indeed."

"Now here lies this elephant, killed by a lion who appointed me its guardian. But for all that, you may enjoy a square meal of elephant meat, provided you cut and run before he gets back."

"No, uncle," said the leopard, "if things stand so, this meat is not healthy for me. You know the saying:

> "A man to thrive
> Must keep alive.

"Never eat a thing that doesn't sit well on the stomach. So I will be off." "Don't be timid," said the jackal. "Pluck up courage and eat. I will warn you of his coming while he is yet a long way off." So the leopard did as suggested, and the jackal, as soon as he saw the hide cut through, called out: "Quick, nephew, quick! Here comes the lion." Hearing this, the leopard vanished also.

Now while the jackal was eating meat through the opening cut by the leopard, a second jackal came on the scene in a great rage. And Supersmart, esteeming him an equal whose prowess was a known quantity, recited the stanza:

> "Sway patrons with obeisance;
> In heroes raise a doubt;
> Fling petty bribes to flunkeys;
> With equals, fight it out—"

made a dash at him, tore him with his fangs, made him seek the horizon, and himself comfortably enjoyed elephant-meat for a long time.

HUNDRED-WIT, THOUSAND-WIT, AND SINGLE-WIT

IN a certain pond lived two fishes whose names were Hundred-Wit and Thousand-Wit. And a frog named Single-Wit made friends with them. Thus all three would for some time enjoy at the water's edge the pleasure of conversation spiced with witticisms, then would dive into the water again.

One day at sunset they were engaged in conversation, when fishermen with nets came there, who said to one another on seeing the pond: "Look! This pond appears to contain plenty of fish, and the water seems shallow. We will return at dawn." With this they went home.

The three friends felt this speech to be dreadful as the fall of a thunderbolt, and they took counsel together. The frog spoke first: "Hundred-Wit and Thousand-Wit, my dear friends, what should we do now: flee or stick it out?"

At this Thousand-Wit laughed and said: "My good friend, do not be frightened merely because you have heard these words. An actual invasion is not to be anticipated. Yet should it take place, I will save you and myself by virtue of my wit. For I know plenty of tricks in the water." And Hundred-Wit added: "Yes, Thousand-Wit is quite right. For

> "Where wind is checked, and light of day,
> The wise man's wit soon finds a way.

"One cannot, because he has heard a few mere words, abandon his birthplace, the home of his ancestors. You must not go away. I will save you by virtue of my wit."

"Well," said the frog, "I have only a single wit, and that tells me to flee. My wife and I are going to some other body of water this very night." So spoke the frog, and under cover of night he went to another body of water. At dawn the next day came the fish-catchers, who seemed the servants of Death, and inclosed the pond with nets. And all the fishes, turtles, frogs, crabs, and other water-creatures were caught in the nets and captured. Even Hundred-Wit and Thousand-Wit fell into a net and were killed, though they struggled to save their lives by fancy turns.

On the following day the fishermen gleefully started home. One of them carried Hundred-Wit, who was heavy, on his head. Another carried Thousand-Wit tied to a cord. Then the frog, safe in the throat of a cistern, said to his wife: "Look, darling, look!

> "While Hundred-Wit is on a head,
> While Thousand-Wit hangs limp and dead,
> Your humble Single-Wit, my dear,
> Is padding in the water clear."

THE BRAHMAN'S DREAM

IN a certain town lived a Brahman named Seedy, who got some barley meal by begging, ate a portion, and filled a jar with the remainder. This jar he hung on a peg one night, placed his cot beneath it, and fixing his gaze on the jar, fell into a hypnotic reverie.

"Well, here is a jar full of barley-meal," he thought. "Now, if famine comes, a hundred rupees will come out of it. With that sum I will get two she-goats. Every six months they will bear two more she-goats. After goats, cows. When the cows have calves, I will sell the calves. After cows, buffaloes; after buffaloes, mares. From the mares I shall get plenty of horses. The sale of these will mean plenty of gold. The gold will buy a great house with an inner court. Then some one will come to my house and offer his lovely daughter with a dowry. She will have a son, whom I shall name Moon-Lord. When he is old enough to ride on my knee, I will take a book, sit on the stable roof, and think. Just then Moon-Lord will see me, will jump from his mother's lap in his eagerness to ride on my knee, and will go too near the horses. Then I shall get angry and tell my wife to take the boy. But she will be busy with her chores and will not pay attention to what I say. Then I will get up and kick her."

In his daydream he let fly such a kick that he smashed the jar. And the barley-meal which it contained turned him white all over.

THE UNFORGIVING MONKEY

IN a certain city was a king named Moon, who had a pack of monkeys for his son's amusement. They were kept in prime condition by daily provender and pabulum in great variety.

For the amusement of the same prince there was a herd of rams. One of them had an itching tongue, so he went into the kitchen at all hours of the day and night and swallowed everything in sight. And the cooks would beat him with any stick or any other object within reach.

Now when the chief of the monkeys observed this, he reflected: "Dear me! This quarrel between ram and cooks will mean the destruction of the monkeys. For the ram is a regular guzzler, and when the cooks are infuriated, they hit him with anything handy. Suppose some time they find nothing else and beat him with a firebrand. Then that broad, woolly back will very easily catch fire. And if the ram, while burning, plunges into the stable near by, it will blaze—for it is mostly thatch—and the horses will be scorched. Now the standard work on veterinary science prescribes monkey-fat to relieve burns on horses. This being so, we are threatened with death."

Having reached this conclusion, he assembled the monkeys and said:

> "A quarrel of the ram and cooks
> Has lately come about;
> It threatens every monkey's life.
> Without a shade of doubt.

Therefore let us leave the house and take to the woods before we are all dead."

But the conceited monkeys laughed at his warning and said: "Oho! You are old and your mind is slipping. Your words prove it. We have no intention of foregoing the heavenly dainties which the princes give us with their own hands, in order to eat fruits peppery, puckery, bitter and sour from the trees out there in the forest."

Having listened to this, the monkey chief made a wry face and said: "Come, come! You are fools. You do not consider the outcome of this pleasant life. Just at present it is sweet, at the last it will turn to poison. At any rate I will not behold the death of my household. I am off for that very forest."

With these words, the chief left them all behind, and went to the forest.

One day after he had gone, the ram entered the kitchen. And the cook, finding nothing else, picked up a firebrand, half-consumed and still blazing, and struck him. Whereat, with half his body blazing, he plunged bleating into the stable near by. There he rolled until flames started up on all sides—for the stable was mostly thatch—and of the horses tethered there some died, their eyes popping, while some, half-burned to death and whinnying with pain, snapped their halters, so that nobody knew what to do.

In this state of affairs, the saddened king assembled the veterinary surgeons and said: "Prescribe some method of giving these horses relief from the pain of their burns." And they, recalling the teaching of their science, said: "O King, the blessed master of our craft prescribed for this emergency as follows:

> "Let monkey-fat be freely used;
> Like dark before the dawn,
> The pain that horses feel from burns,
> Will very soon be gone.

"Pray adopt this remedy before they perish miserably."

When the king heard this, he ordered the slaughter of the monkeys. And, not to waste words, every one was killed.

Now the monkey chief did not with his own eyes see this outrage perpetrated on his household. But he heard the story as it passed from one to another, and did not take it tamely.

Now as the elderly monkey wandered about thirsty, he came to a lake made lovely by clusters of lotuses. And as he observed it narrowly, he noticed footprints leading into the lake, but none coming out. Thereupon he reflected, "There must be some vicious beast here in the water. So I will stay at a safe distance and drink through a hollow lotus-stalk."

When he had done so, there issued from the water a man-eating fiend with a pearl necklace adorning his neck, who spoke and said: "Sir, I eat every one who enters the water. So there is none shrewder than you, who drink in this fashion. I have taken a liking to you. Name your heart's desire."

"Sir," said the monkey, "how many can you eat?" And the fiend replied: "I can eat hundreds, thousands, myriads, yes, hundreds of thousands, if they enter the water. Outside, a jackal can overpower me."

"And I," said the monkey, "live in mortal enmity with a king. If you will give me that pearl necklace, I will awaken his greed with a plausible narrative, and will make that king enter the lake along with his retinue." So the fiend handed over the pearl necklace.

Then people saw the monkey roaming over trees and palace-roofs with a pearl necklace embellishing his throat, and they asked him: "Well, chief, where have you spent this long time? Where did you get a pearl necklace like that? Its dazzling beauty dims the very sun."

And the monkey answered: "In a spot in the forest is a shrewdly hidden lake, a creation of the god of wealth. Through his grace, if anyone bathes there at sunrise on Sunday, he comes out with a pearl necklace like this embellishing his throat."

Now the king heard this from somebody, summoned the monkey, and asked: "Is this true, chief?"

"O King," said the monkey, "you have visible proof in the pearl necklace on my throat. If you, too, could find a use for one, send somebody with me, and I will show him."

On hearing this, the king said: "In view of the facts, I will come myself with my retinue, so that we may acquire numbers of pearl necklaces."

"O King," said the monkey, "your idea is delicious."

So the king and his retinue started, greedy for pearl necklaces. And the king in his palanquin clasped the monkey to his bosom, showing him honour as they travelled. For there is wisdom in the saying:

> The educated and the rich,
>   Befooled by greed,
> Plunge into wickedness, then feel
>   The pinch of need.

> The hair grows old with aging years;
>   The teeth grow old, the eyes and ears.
> But while the aging seasons speed,
>   One thing is young forever—greed.

At dawn they reached the lake and the monkey said to the king: "O King, fulfilment comes to those who enter at sunrise. Let all your attendants be told, so that they may dash in with one fell swoop. You, however, must enter with me, for I will pick the place I found before and show you plenty of pearl necklaces." So all the attendants entered and were eaten by the fiend.

Then, as they lingered, the king said to the monkey: "Well, chief, why do my attendants linger?"

And the monkey hurriedly climbed a tree before saying to the king: "You villainous king, your attendants are eaten by a fiend that lives in the water. My enmity with you, arising from the death of my household, has been brought to a happy termination. Now go. I did not make you enter there, because I remembered that you were the king. Thus you plotted the death of my household, and I of yours."

When the king heard this, he hastened home, grief-stricken. And when the king had gone, the fiend, fully satisfied, issued from the water, and gleefully recited a verse:

> "Very good, my monkey-O!
>   You won a friend, and killed a foe,
>   And kept the pearls without a flaw,
>   By sucking water through a straw."

II. THE DECCAN

THESE stories are current in Southern India. They were told by a native *ayah* in 1865-6 to Miss Mary Frere, whose father was Governor of the Bombay Presidency. They formed a great part of the existing beliefs of the lower orders. Notice the humour of "The Valiant Chattee-maker." Hindus do not, as a rule, indulge in humour. The Cobra plays an important part in these popular tales. It rarely goes far from home and is supposed to watch jealously over a hidden treasure. The Rakshas—the most prominent superhuman personage—was a kind of ogre, of giant bulk, with terrible teeth. It feasted on dead bodies yet withal was very simple and stupid, so that a quick-witted mortal could generally gain the victory.

THE VALIANT CHATTEE-MAKER

LONG, long ago, in a violent storm of thunder, lightning, wind, and rain, a Tiger crept for shelter close to the wall of an old woman's hut. This old woman was very poor, and her hut was but a tumble-down place, through the roof of which the rain came *drip, drip, drip,* on more sides than one. This troubled her much, and she went running about from side to side, dragging first one thing and then another out of the way of the leaky places in the roof, and as she did so, she kept saying to herself, "Oh, dear! oh, dear! how tiresome this is! I'm sure the roof will come down! If an elephant, or a lion, or a tiger were to walk in, he wouldn't frighten me half as much as this perpetual dripping."

And then she would begin dragging the bed and all the other things in the room about again, to get them out of the way of the rain. The Tiger, who was crouching down just outside, heard all that she said, and thought to himself, "This old woman says she would not be afraid of an elephant, or a lion, or a tiger, but that this perpetual dripping frightens her more than all. What can this 'perpetual dripping' be? must be something very dreadful." And, hearing her immediately afterward dragging all the things about the room again, he said to himself, "What a terrible noise! Surely that must be the *'perpetual dripping.'*"

At this moment a chattee-maker,[1] who was in search of his donkey which had strayed away, came down the road. The night being very cold, he had, truth to say, taken a little more toddy than was good for him, and seeing, by the light of a flash of lightning, a large animal lying down close to the old woman's hut, mistook it for the donkey he was looking for. So, running up to the Tiger, he seized hold of

---

[1] Potter.

it by one ear, and commenced beating, kicking, and abusing it with all his might and main.

"You wretched creature," he cried, "is this the way you serve me, obliging me to come out and look for you in such pouring rain, and on such a dark night as this? Get up instantly, or I'll break every bone in your body"; and he went on scolding and thumping the Tiger with his utmost power, for he had worked himself up into a terrible rage. The Tiger did not know what to make of it all, but he began to feel quite frightened, and said to himself, "Why, this must be the 'perpetual dripping'; no wonder the old woman said she was more afraid of it than of an elephant, a lion, or a tiger, for it gives most dreadfully hard blows."

The Chattee-maker, having made the Tiger get up, got on his back, and forced him to carry him home, kicking and beating him the whole way (for all this time he fancied he was on his donkey), and then he tied his fore feet and his head firmly together, and fastened him to a post in front of his house, and when he had done this he went to bed.

Next morning, when the Chattee-maker's wife got up and looked out of the window, what did she see but a great big Tiger tied up in front of their house, to the post to which they usually fastened the donkey; she was very much surprised, and running to her husband, awoke him, saying, "Do you know what animal you fetched home last night?"

"Yes, the donkey, to be sure," he answered.

"Come and see," said she, and she showed him the great Tiger tied to the post. The Chattee-maker at this was no less astonished than his wife, and felt himself all over to find out if the Tiger had not wounded him. But no! there he was, safe and sound, and there was the Tiger tied to the post, just as he had fastened it up the night before.

News of the Chattee-maker's exploit soon spread through the village, and all the people came to see him and hear him tell how he had caught the Tiger and tied it to the post; and this they thought so wonderful, that they sent a deputation to the Rajah, with a letter to tell him how a man of their village had, alone and unarmed, caught a great Tiger, and tied it to a post.

When the Rajah read the letter he also was much surprised, and determined to go in person and see this astonishing sight. So he sent for his horses and carriages, his lords and attendants, and they all set off together to look at the Chattee-maker and the Tiger he had caught.

Now the Tiger was a very large one, and had long been the terror of all the country round, which made the whole matter still more extraordinary; and this being represented to the Rajah, he determined to confer every possible honour on the valiant Chattee-maker. So he gave him houses and lands, and as much money as would fill a well, made him lord of his court, and conferred on him the command of ten thousand horse.

It came to pass, shortly after this, that a neighbouring Rajah, who had long had a quarrel with this one, sent to announce his intention of going instantly to war with him; and tidings were at the same time brought that the Rajah who sent the challenge had gathered a great army together on the borders and was prepared at a moment's notice to invade the country.

In this dilemma no one knew what to do. The Rajah sent for all his generals, and inquired which of them would be willing to take command of his forces and oppose the enemy. They all replied that the country was so ill-prepared for the emergency, and the case was apparently so hopeless, that they would rather not take the responsibility of the chief command. The Rajah knew not whom to appoint in their stead. Then some of his people said to him, "You have lately given command of ten thousand horse to the valiant Chattee-maker who caught the Tiger. Why not make him Commander-in-Chief? A man who could catch a Tiger and tie him to a post must surely be more courageous and clever than most."

"Very well," said the Rajah, "I will make him Commander-in-Chief." So he sent for the Chattee-maker and said to him, "In your hands I place all the power of the kingdom; you must put our enemies to flight."

"So be it," answered the Chattee-maker, "but, before I lead the whole army against the enemy, suffer me to go by myself and examine their position; and, if possible, find out their numbers and strength."

The Rajah consented, and the Chattee-maker returned home to his wife, and said, "They have made me Commander-in-Chief, which is a very difficult post for me to fill, because I shall have to ride at the head of all the army, and you know I never was on a horse in my life. But I have succeeded in gaining a little delay, as the Rajah has given me permission to go first alone, and reconnoitre the enemy's camp. Do you, therefore, provide a very quiet pony, for you know I cannot ride, and I will start to-morrow morning."

But before the Chattee-maker had started, the Rajah sent over to him a most magnificent charger, richly caparisoned, which he begged he would ride when going to see the enemy's camp.

The Chattee-maker was frightened almost out of his life, for the charger that the Rajah had sent him was very powerful and spirited, and he felt sure that, even if he ever got on it, he should very soon tumble off; however, he did not dare to refuse it, for fear of offending the Rajah by not accepting his present. So he sent him back a message of dutiful thanks, and said to his wife, "I cannot go on the pony now that the Rajah has sent me this fine horse, but how am I ever to ride it?"

"Oh, don't be frightened," she answered; "you've only got to get upon it, and I will tie you firmly on, so that you cannot tumble off, and if you start at night no one will see that you are tied on."

"Very well," he said.

So that night his wife brought the horse that the Rajah had sent him to the door.

"Indeed," said the Chattee-maker, "I can never get into that saddle, it is so high up."

"You must jump," said his wife.

Then he tried to jump several times, but each time he jumped he tumbled down again.

"I always forget when I am jumping," said he, "which way I ought to turn."

"Your face must be toward the horse's head," she answered.

"To be sure, of course," he cried, and giving one great jump he jumped into the saddle, but with his face toward the horse's tail.

"This won't do at all," said his wife as she helped him down again; "try getting on without jumping."

" I never can remember," he continued, "when I have got my left foot in the stirrup, what to do with my right foot, or where to put it."

"That must go in the other stirrup," she answered; "let me help you."

So, after many trials, in which he tumbled down very often, for the horse was fresh and did not like standing still, the Chattee-maker got into the saddle; and no sooner had he got there than he cried, "O wife, wife! tie me very firmly as quickly as possible, for I know I shall jump down again if I can." Then she fetched some strong rope and tied his feet firmly into the stirrups, and fastened one stirrup to the other, and put another rope round his waist, and another round his neck, and fastened them to the horse's body, and neck, and tail.

When the horse felt all these ropes about him he could not imagine what queer creature had got upon his back, and he began rearing, and kicking, and prancing, and at last set off full gallop, as fast as he could tear, right across country.

"Wife, wife," cried the Chattee-maker, "you forgot to tie my hands."

."Never mind," said she, "hold on by the mane." So he caught hold of the horse's mane as firmly as he could. Then away went horse, away went Chattee-maker, away, away, away, over hedges, over ditches, over rivers, over plains, away, away, like a flash of lightning, now this way, now that, on, on, on, gallop, gallop, gallop, until they came in sight of the enemy's camp.

The Chattee-maker did not like his ride at all, and when he saw where it was leading him he liked it still less, for he thought the enemy would catch him and very likely kill him. So he determined to make one desperate effort to be free, and stretching out his hand as the horse shot past a young banyan-tree, seized hold of it with all his might, hoping the resistance it offered might cause the ropes that tied him to break. But the horse was going at his utmost speed, and the soil in which the banyan-tree grew was loose, so that when the Chattee-maker caught hold of it and gave it such a violent pull, it came up by the roots, and on he rode as fast as before, with the tree in his hand.

All the soldiers in the camp saw him coming, and having heard that an army was to be sent against them, made sure that the Chattee-maker was one of the vanguard. "See," cried they, "here comes a man of gigantic stature on a mighty horse! He rides at full speed across the country, tearing up the very trees in his rage! He is one of the opposing force; the whole army must be close at hand. If they are such as he, we are all dead men." Then, running to their Rajah, some of them cried again, "Here comes the whole force of the enemy" (for the story had by this time become exaggerated); "they are men of gigantic stature mounted on mighty horses; as they come they tear up the very trees in their rage; we can oppose men, but not monsters such as these." These were followed by others, who said, "It is all true," for by this time the Chattee-maker had got pretty near the camp, "they're coming! they're coming! let us fly! let us fly! fly, fly for your lives!"

And the whole panic-stricken multitude fled from the camp (those who had seen no cause for alarm going because the others did, or because they did not care to stay by themselves) after having obliged their Rajah to write a letter to the one whose country he was about to invade, to say that he would not do so, and propose terms of peace, and to sign it, and seal it with his seal. Scarcely had all the people fled from the camp, when the horse on which the Chattee-maker was came galloping into it, and on his back rode the Chattee-maker, almost dead from fatigue, with the banyan-tree in his hand. Just as he reached the camp the ropes by which he was tied broke, and he fell to the ground. The horse stood still, too tired with its long run to go further. On recovering his senses, the Chattee-maker discovered, to his surprise, that the whole camp, full of rich arms, clothes, and trappings, was entirely deserted. In the principal tent, moreover, he found a letter addressed to his Rajah, announcing the retreat of the invading army, and proposing terms of peace.

So he took the letter, and returned home with it as fast as he could, leading his horse all the way, for he was afraid to mount him again.

It did not take him long to reach his house by the direct road, for whilst riding he had gone a more circuitous journey than was necessary, and he got there just at nightfall. His wife ran out to meet him, overjoyed at his speedy return. As soon as he saw her, he said, "Ah, wife, since I saw you last I've been all round the world, and had many wonderful and terrible adventures. But never mind that now, send this letter quickly to the Rajah by a messenger, and also the horse that he sent for me to ride.. He will then see, by the horse looking so tired, what a long ride I've had, and if he is sent on beforehand, I shall not be obliged to ride him up to the palace-door to-morrow morning, as I otherwise should, and that would be very tiresome, for most likely I should tumble off."

So his wife sent the horse and the letter to the Rajah, and a message that her husband would be at the palace early next morning, as it was then late at night. And next day he went down there as he had said he would, and when the people saw him coming, they said, "This man is as modest as he is brave; after having put our enemies to flight, he walks quite simply to the door, instead of riding here in state, as any other man would." (For they did not know that the Chattee-maker walked because he was afraid to ride.)

The Rajah came to the palace-door to meet him, and paid him all possible honour. Terms of peace were agreed upon between the two countries, and the Chattee-maker was rewarded for all he had done by being given twice as much rank and wealth as he had before, and he lived very happily all the rest of his life.

TIT FOR TAT

THERE once lived a Camel and a Jackal who were great friends. One day the Jackal said to the Camel, "I know that there is a fine field of sugar-cane on the other side of the river. If you will take me across I'll show you the place. This plan will suit me as well as you. You will enjoy eating the sugar-cane, and I am sure to find many crabs, bones, and bits of fish by the river-side, on which to make a good dinner."

The Camel consented, and swam across the river, taking the Jackal, who could not swim, on his back. When they reached the other side, the Camel went to eat the sugar-cane, and the Jackal ran up and down the river-bank devouring all the crabs, bits of fish, and bones he could find.

But being so much smaller an animal, he had made an excellent meal before the Camel had eaten more than two or three mouthfuls; and no sooner had he finished his dinner, than he ran round and round the sugarcane field, yelping and howling with all his might.

The villagers heard him; and thought, "There is a Jackal among the sugar-canes; he will be scratching holes in the ground, and spoiling the roots of the plants." And they went down to the place to drive him away. But when they got there, they found to their surprise not only a Jackal, but a Camel who was eating the sugar-canes! This made them very angry, and they caught the poor Camel, and drove him from the field, and beat him till he was nearly dead.

When they had gone, the Jackal said to the Camel, "We had better go home." And the Camel said, "Very well, then, jump upon my back as you did before."

So the Jackal jumped upon the Camel's back, and the Camel began to recross the river. When they had got well into the water, the Camel said, "This is a pretty way in which you have treated me, friend Jackal. No sooner had you finished your own dinner than you must go yelping about the place loud enough to arouse the whole village, and bring all the villagers down to beat me black and blue, and turn me out of the field before I had eaten two mouthfuls! What in the world did you make such a noise for?"

"I don't know," said the Jackal. "It is a custom I have. I always like to sing a little after dinner."

The Camel waded on through the river. The water reached up to his knees—then above them—up, up, up, higher and higher, until he was obliged to swim. Then turning to the Jackal, he said, "I feel very anxious to roll." "Oh, pray don't; why do you wish to do so?" asked the Jackal. "I don't know," answered the Camel; "it is a custom I have. I always like to have a little roll after dinner."

So saying, he rolled over in the water, shaking the Jackal off as he did so. And the jackal was drowned, but the Camel swam safely ashore.

III. THE "TALKING THRUSH" TALES

MANY familiar types may be noted in these stories, but the local setting is unmistakable, and there are many touches of humour. These indigenous beast-stories are little affected by the so-called Aryan influences.

THE VALIANT BLACKBIRD

A BLACKBIRD and his mate lived together on a tree. The Blackbird used to sing very sweetly, and one day the King heard him in passing by, and sent a Fowler to catch him. But the Fowler made a mistake; he did not catch Mr. Blackbird, who sang so sweetly, but Mrs. Blackbird, who could hardly sing at all. However, he did not know the difference, to look at her, nor did the King when he got the bird; but a cage was made for Mrs. Blackbird, and there she was kept imprisoned.

When Mr. Blackbird heard that his dear spouse was stolen, he was very angry indeed. He determined to get her back, by hook or by crook. So he got a long sharp thorn, and tied it at his waist by a thread; and on his head he put the half of a walnut shell for a helmet, and the skin of a dead frog served for body-armour. Then he made a little kettle-drum out of the other half of the walnut shell; and he beat his drum and proclaimed war upon the King.

As he walked along the road, beating his drum, he met a Cat.

"Whither away, Mr. Blackbird?" said the Cat.

"To fight against the King," said Mr. Blackbird.

"All right," said the Cat, "I'll come with you: he drowned my kitten."

"Jump into my ear, then," says Mr. Blackbird. The Cat jumped into the Blackbird's ear, and curled up, and went to sleep: and the Blackbird marched along, beating his drum.

Some way further on he met some Ants.

"Whither away, Mr. Blackbird?" said the Ants.

"To fight against the King," said Mr. Blackbird.

"All right," said the Ants, "we'll come too; he poured hot water down our hole."

"Jump into my ear," said Mr. Blackbird. In they jumped, and away went Blackbird, beating upon his drum.

Next he met a Rope and a Club. They asked him, Whither away? and when they heard that he was going to fight against the King, they jumped into his ear also, and away he went.

Not far from the King's palace, Blackbird had to cross over a River.

"Whither away, friend Blackbird?" asked the River.

Quoth the Blackbird, "To fight against the King."

"Then I'll come with you," said the River.

"Jump into my ear," says the Blackbird.

Blackbird's ears were pretty full by this time, but he found room some where for the River, and away he went.

Blackbird marched along until he came to the palace of the King. He knocked at the door, thump, thump.

"Who's there?" said the Porter.

"General Blackbird, come to make war upon the King, and get back his wife."

The Porter laughed so at the sight of General Blackbird, with his thorn, and his frogskin, and his drum, that he nearly fell off his chair. Then he escorted Blackbird into the King's presence.

"What do you want?" said the King.

"I want my wife," said the Blackbird, beating upon his drum, rub-a dub-dub, rub-a-dub-dub.

"You shan't have her," said the King.

"Then," said the Blackbird, "you must take the consequences." Rub-a dub-dub went the drum.

"Seize this insolent bird," said the King, "and shut him up in the henhouse. I don't think there will be much left of him in the morning."

The servants shut up Blackbird in the henhouse. When all the world was asleep, Blackbird said:

> "Come out, Pussy, from my ear,
>   There are fowls in plenty here;
>   Scratch them, make their feathers fly,
>   Wring their necks until they die."

Out came Pussy-cat in an instant. What a confusion there was in the henhouse. Cluck-cluck-cluck went the hens, flying all over the place; but no use: pussy got them all, and scratched out their feathers, and wrung their necks. Then she went back into Blackbird's ear, and Blackbird went to sleep.

When morning came, the King said to his men, "Go fetch the carcass of that insolent bird, and give the Chickens an extra bushel of corn." But when they entered the henhouse, Blackbird was singing away merrily on the roost, and all the fowls lay round in heaps with their necks wrung.

They told the King, and an angry King was he. "To-night," said he, "you must shut up Blackbird in the stable." So Blackbird was shut up in the stable, among the wild Horses.

At midnight, when all the world was asleep, Blackbird said:

> "Come out, Rope, and come out, Stick,
>   Tie the Horses lest they kick;
>   Beat the Horses on the head,
>   Beat them till they fall down dead."

Out came Club and Rope from Blackbird's ear; the Rope tied the horses, and the Club beat them, till they died. Then the Rope and the Club went back into the Blackbird's ear, and Blackbird went to sleep.

Next morning the King said:

"No doubt my wild Horses have settled the business of that Blackbird once for all. Just go and fetch out his corpse."

The servants went to the wild Horses' stable. There was Blackbird, sitting on the manger, and drumming away on his walnut-shell; and all round lay the dead bodies of the Horses, beaten to death.

If the King was angry before, he was furious now. His horses had cost a great deal of money; and to be tricked by a Blackbird is a poor joke.

"All right," said the King, "I'll make sure work of it to-night. He shall be put with the Elephants."

When night came the Blackbird was shut up in the Elephants' shed. No sooner was all the world quiet, than Blackbird began to sing:

> "Come from out my ear, you Ants,
>   Come and sting the Elephants;
>   Sting their trunk, and sting their head,
>   Sting them till they fall down dead."

Out came a swarm of Ants from the Blackbird's ear. They crawled up inside the Elephants' trunks, they burrowed into the Elephants' brains, and stung them so sharply that the Elephants all went mad, and died.

Next morning, as before, the King sent for the Blackbird's carcass; and, instead of finding his carcass, the servants found the Blackbird rub-a-dub dubbing on his drum, and the dead Elephants piled all round him.

This time the King was fairly desperate. "I can't think how he does it," said he, "but I must find out. Tie him to-night to my bed, and we'll see."

So that night Blackbird was tied to the King's bed. In the middle of the night, the King (who had purposely kept awake) heard him sing:

> "Come out, River, from my ear,
> Flow about the bedroom here;
> Pour yourself upon the bed,
> Drown the King till he is dead."

Out came the River, pour-pour-pouring out of the Blackbird's ear. It flooded the room, it floated the King's bed, the King began to get wet.

"In Heaven's name, General Blackbird," said the King, "take your wife, and begone."

So Blackbird received his wife again, and they lived happily ever after.

THE WISE OLD SHEPHERD

ONCE upon a time, a Snake went out of his hole to take an airing. He crawled about, greatly enjoying the scenery and the fresh whiff of the breeze, until, seeing an open door, he went in. Now this door was the door of the palace of the King, and inside was the King himself, with all his courtiers.

Imagine their horror at seeing a huge Snake crawling in at the door. They all ran away except the King, who felt that his rank forbade him to be a coward, and the King's son. The King called out for somebody to come and kill the Snake; but this horrified them still more, because in that country the people believed it to be wicked to kill any living thing, even snakes, and scorpions, and wasps. So the courtiers did nothing, but the young Prince obeyed his father, and killed the Snake with his stick.

After a while the Snake's wife became anxious, and set out in search of her husband. She too saw the open door of the palace, and in she went. O horror! there on the floor lay the body of her husband, all covered with blood, and quite dead. No one saw the Snake's wife crawl in; she inquired from a white ant what had happened, and when she found that the young Prince had killed her husband, she made a vow, that as he had made her a widow, so she would make his wife a widow.

That night, while all the world was asleep, the Snake crept into the Prince's bedroom, and coiled around his neck. The Prince slept on, and when he awoke in the morning, he was surprised to find his neck encircled with the coils of a Snake. He was afraid to stir, so there he remained, until the Prince's mother became anxious, and went to see what was the matter. When she entered his room, and saw him in this plight, she gave a loud shriek, and ran off to tell the King.

"Call the archers," said the King. The archers came, and the King told them to go into the Prince's room, and shoot the Snake that was coiled about his neck. They were so clever, that they could easily do this without hurting the Prince at all.

In came the archers in a row, fitted the arrows to the bows, the bows were raised and ready to shoot, when, on a sudden, from the Snake there issued a voice, which spoke as follows:

"O archers! wait, and hear me before you shoot. It is not fair to carry out the sentence before you have heard the case. Is not this good law, an eye for an eye, and a tooth for a tooth? Is it not so, O King?"

"Yes," replied the King, "that is our law."

"Then," said the Snake, "I plead the law. Your son has made me a widow, so it is fair and right that I should make his wife a widow."

"That sounds right enough," said the King, "but right and law are not always the same thing. We had better ask somebody who knows."

They asked all the judges, but none of them could tell the law of the matter. They shook their heads, and said they would look up all their law-books, and see whether anything of the sort had ever happened before, and if so, how it had been decided. That is the way judges used to decide cases in that country, though I daresay it sounds to you a very funny way. It looked as if they had not much sense in their own heads, and perhaps that was true. The upshot of all was, that not a judge would give any opinion; so the King sent messengers all over the country-side, to see if they could find somebody somewhere who knew something.

One of these messengers found a party of five Shepherds, who were sitting upon a hill and trying to decide a quarrel of their own. They gave their opinions so freely, and in language so very strong, that the King's messenger said to himself, "Here are the men for us. Here are five men, each with an opinion of his own, and all different." Post haste he scurried back to the King, and told him he had found at last some one ready to judge the knotty point.

So the King and the Queen, and the Prince and the Princess, and all the courtiers, got on horseback, and away they galloped to the hill whereupon the five Shepherds were sitting, and the Snake too went with them, coiled round the neck of the Prince.

When they got to the Shepherd's hill, the Shepherds were dreadfully frightened. At first they thought that the strangers were a gang of robbers; and when they saw that it was the King, their next thought was that one of their misdeeds had been found out, and each of them began thinking what was the last thing he had done, and wondering, was it that? But the King and his court got off their horses, and said good-day in the most civil way. So the Shepherds felt their minds set at ease again. Then the King said:

"Worthy Shepherds, we have a question to put to you, which not all the judges in all the courts of my city have been able to solve. Here is my son, and here, as you see, is a Snake coiled round his neck. Now, the husband of this Snake came creeping into my palace hall, and my son the Prince killed him; so this Snake, who is the wife of the other, says that as my son has made her a widow, so she has a right to widow my son's wife. What do you think about it?"

The first Shepherd said, "I think she is quite right, my lord King. If anyone made my wife a widow, I would pretty soon do the same to him."

This was brave language, and the other Shepherds shook their heads and looked fierce. But the King was puzzled, and could not quite understand it. You see, in the first place, if the man's wife were a widow, the man would be dead; and then it is hard to see how he could do anything. So to make sure, the King asked the second Shepherd whether that was his opinion too.

"Yes," said the second Shepherd; "now the Prince has killed the Snake, the Snake has a right to kill the Prince, if he can."

But that was not of much use either, as the Snake was as dead as a door-nail. So the King passed on to the third.

"I agree with my mates," said the third Shepherd, "because, you see, a Prince is a Prince, but then a Snake is a Snake."

That was quite true, they all admitted; but it did not seem to help the matter much. Then the King asked the fourth Shepherd to say what he thought.

The fourth Shepherd said, "An eye for an eye, and a tooth for a tooth; so I think a widow should be a widow; if so be she don't marry again."

By this time the poor King was so puzzled that he hardly knew whether he stood on his head or his heels. But there was still the fifth Shepherd left, the oldest and wisest of them all; and the fifth Shepherd said:

"O King, I should like to ask two questions."

"Ask twenty, if you like," said the King. He did not promise to answer them, so he could afford to be generous.

"First, I ask the Princess how many sons she has?"

"Four," said the Princess.

"And how many sons has Mistress Snake here?"

"Seven," said the Snake.

"Then," said the old Shepherd, "it will be quite fair for Mistress Snake to kill his Highness the Prince, when her Highness the Princess has had three sons more."

"I never thought of that," said the Snake. "Good-bye, King, and all you good people. Send a message when the Princess has had three more sons, and you may count upon me—I will not fail you." So saying, she uncoiled from the Prince's neck and slid away among the grass.

The King and the Prince and everybody shook hands with the wise old Shepherd, and went home again. And as the Princess never had any more sons at all, she and the Prince lived happily for many years; and if they are not dead they are living still.

HOW THE MOUSE GOT INTO HIS HOLE

A MERCHANT was going along the road one day with a sack of peas on the back of an Ox. The Ox was stung by a Fly, and gave a kick, and down fell the sack. A Mouse was passing by, and the Merchant said, "Mousie, if you will help me up with this sack I will give you a pea." The Mouse helped him up with the sack and got a pea for his trouble. He stole another, and a third he found on the road.

When he got home with his three peas he planted them in front of his hole. As he was planting them he said to them, "If you are not all three sprouting by to-morrow I'll cut you in pieces and give you to the black Ox." The peas were terribly frightened, and the next morning they had already begun to sprout, and each of them had two shoots. Then he said, "If I don't find you in blossom to-morrow I'll cut you in pieces and give you to the black Ox." When he went to look next day they were all in blossom. So he said, "If I don't find ripe peas on you to-morrow I'll cut you in pieces and give you to the black Ox." Next day they had pods full of ripe peas on them.

So every day he used to eat lots of ripe peas, and in this manner he got very fat. One day a pretty young lady Mouse came to see him.

"Good morning, Sleekie," said she; "how are you?"

"Good morning, Squeakie," said he; "I'm quite well, thank you."

"Why, Sleekie," said she, "how fat you are!"

"Am I?" said he. "I suppose that's because I have plenty to eat."

"What do you eat, Sleekie?" asked the pretty young lady Mouse.

"Peas, Squeakie," said the other.

"Where do you get them, Sleekie?"

"They grow all of themselves in my garden, Squeakie."

"Will you give me some, please?" asked the lady Mouse.

"Oh, yes, if you will stay in my garden, you may have as many as you like."

So Squeakie stayed in Sleekie's garden, and they both ate so many peas that they got fatter and fatter every day.

One day Squeakie said to Sleekie, "Let's try which can get into the hole quickest." Squeakie was slim, and she had not been at the peas so long as Sleekie, so she got into the hole easily enough; but Sleekie was so fat that he could not get in at all.

He was very much frightened, and went off in hot haste to the Carpenter, and said to him, "Carpenter, please pare off a little flesh from my ribs, so that I can get into my hole."

"Do you think I have nothing better to do than paring down your ribs ?" said the Carpenter angrily, and went on with his work.

The Mouse went to the King, and said, "O King, I can't get into my hole, and the Carpenter will not pare down my ribs; will you make him do it ?"

"Get out," said the King; "do you think I have nothing better to do than to look after your ribs?"

So the Mouse went to the Queen. Said he, "Queen, I can't get into my hole, and the King won't tell the Carpenter to pare down my ribs. Please divorce him."

"Bother you and your ribs," said the Queen; "I am not going to divorce my husband because you have made yourself fat by eating too much."

The Mouse went to the Snake. "Snake, bite the Queen, and tell her to divorce the King, because he will not tell the Carpenter to pare my ribs down and let me get into my hole."

"Get away," said the Snake; "or I'll swallow you up, ribs and all; the fatter you are, the better I shall be pleased."

He went to the Stick, and said, "Stick, beat the Snake, because she won't bite the Queen, who won't divorce the King and make him tell the Carpenter to pare down my ribs, and let me get into my hole."

"Off with you," said the Stick; "I'm sleepy, because I have just beaten a thief; I can't be worried about your ribs."

He went to the Furnace, and said, "Furnace, burn the Stick, and make it beat the Snake, that she may bite the Queen, and make her divorce the King, who won't tell the Carpenter to pare down my ribs, and let me get into my hole."

"Get along with you," said the Furnace; "I am cooking the King's dinner, and I have no time now to see about your ribs."

He went to the Ocean, and said, "Ocean, put out the Fire, and make it burn the Stick, so that it may beat the Snake, and the Snake may bite the Queen, and she may divorce the King, who won't tell the Carpenter to pare down my ribs, and let me get into my hole."

"Don't bother me," said the Ocean; "it's high tide, and all the fishes are jumping about, and giving me no rest'

He went to the Elephant, and said, "O Elephant, drink up the Ocean, that it may put out the Fire, and the Fire may burn the Stick, and the Stick may beat the Snake, and the Snake may bite the Queen, and the Queen may divorce the King, and make him tell the Carpenter to pare down my ribs, and let me get into my hole."

"Go away, little Mouse," said the Elephant; "I have just drunk up a whole lake, and I really can't drink any more."

He went to the Creeper, and said, "Dear Creeper, do please choke the Elephant, that he may drink up the Ocean, and the Ocean may put out the Fire, and the Fire may burn the Stick, and the Stick may beat the Snake, and the Snake may bite the Queen, and the Queen may divorce the King, and the King may tell the Carpenter to pare down my ribs, and let me get into my hole."

"Not I," says the Creeper; "I am stuck fast here to this tree, and I couldn't get away to please a fat little Mouse."

Then he went to the Scythe, and said, "Scythe, please cut loose the Creeper, that it may choke the Elephant, and the Elephant may drink up the Ocean, and the Ocean may put out the Fire, and the Fire may burn the Stick, and the Stick may beat the Snake, and the Snake may bite the Queen, and the Queen may divorce the King, and the King may tell the Carpenter to pare down my ribs, and let me get into my hole."

"With pleasure," said the Scythe, who is always sharp.

So the Scythe cut the Creeper loose, and the Creeper began to choke the Elephant, and the Elephant ran off and began to drink up the Ocean, and the Ocean began to put out the Fire, and the Fire began to burn the Stick, and the Stick began to beat the Snake, and the Snake began to bite the Queen, and the Queen told the King she was going to divorce him, and the King was frightened, and ordered the Carpenter to pare Sleekie's ribs, and at last Sleekie got into his hole.

IV. BUDDHIST BIRTH-STORIES

PART of the three great divisions of the Buddhist Scriptures consists of Birth stories, or Jataka Tales. The tales are in prose, each expounding a much more ancient poem. They deal with the life of Gotama Buddha during some incarnation in one of his previous existences as a Bodhisatta. The immensely long evolution before he finally became Buddha the Enlightened One is described in detail.

SAKKA'S PRESENTS

ONCE upon a time, when Brahmadatta was reigning in Benares, four brothers, Brahmans, of that kingdom, devoted themselves to an ascetic life; and having built themselves huts at equal distances in the region of the Himalaya mountains, took up their residence there. The eldest of them died, and was reborn as the god Sakka.[1] When he became aware of this, he used to go and render help at intervals every seven or eight days to the others. And one day, having greeted the eldest hermit, and sat down beside him, he asked him: "Reverend Sir, what are you in need of?"

The hermit, who suffered from jaundice, answered: "I want fire!" So he gave him a double-edged hatchet. But the hermit said: "Who is to take this, and bring me firewood?"

Then Sakka spake thus to him: "Whenever, reverend Sir, you want firewood, you should let go the hatchet from your hand and say: 'Please fetch me firewood: make me fire!' And it will do so."

So he gave him the hatchet; and went to the second hermit, and asked: "Reverend Sir, what are you in need of?"

Now the elephants had made a track for themselves close to his hut. And he was annoyed by those elephants, and said: "I am much troubled by elephants; drive them away."

Sakka, handing him a drum, said: "Reverend Sir, if you strike on this side of it, your enemies will take to flight; but if you strike on this side, they will become friendly, and surround you on all sides with an army in fourfold array." [2]

So he gave him the drum; and went to the third hermit, and asked: "Reverend Sir, what are you in need of?"

He was also affected with jaundice, and said, therefore: "I want sour milk."

Sakka gave him a milk-bowl, and said: "If you wish for anything, and turn this bowl over, it will become a great river, and pour out such a torrent, that it will be able to take a kingdom, and give it to you."

And Sakka went away. But thenceforward the hatchet made fire for the eldest hermit; when the second struck one side of his drum, the elephants ran away; and the third enjoyed his curds.

Now at that time a wild boar, straying in a forsaken village, saw a gem of magical power. When he seized this in his mouth, he rose by its magic into the air, and went to an island in the midst of the ocean. And thinking, "Here now I ought to live," he descended, and took up his abode in a convenient spot under an Udumbara-tree. And one day, placing the gem before him, he fell asleep at the foot

---

[1] Not quite the same as Jupiter. Sakka is a very harmless and gentle kind of god, not a jealous god, nor given to spite. Neither is he immortal; he dies from time to time; and, if he has behaved well, is reborn under happy conditions. Meanwhile somebody else, usually one of the sons of men who has deserved it, succeeds, for a hundred thousand years or so, to his name and place and glory. Sakka can call to mind his experiences in his former birth, a gift in which he surpasses most other beings. He was also given to a kind of practical joking, by which he tempted people, and has become a mere beneficent fairy.

[2] That is, infantry, cavalry, chariots of war, and elephants of war. Truly a useful kind of present to give to a pious hermit!

of the tree. Now a certain man of the land of Kāsi had been expelled from home by his parents, who said: "This fellow is of no use to us." So he went to a seaport, and embarked in a ship as a servant to the sailors. And the ship was wrecked; but by the help of a plank he reached that very island. And while he was looking about for fruits, he saw the boar asleep; and going softly up, he took hold of the gem.

Then by its magical power he straightway rose right up into the air! So, taking a seat on the Udumbara-tree, he said to himself: "Methinks this boar must have become a sky-walker through the magic of this gem. That's how he got to be living here! It's plain enough what I ought to do; I'll first of all kill and eat him, and then. I can get away!"

So he broke a twig off the tree, and dropped it on has head. The boar woke up, and not seeing the gem, ran about, trembling, this way and that way. The man seated on the tree laughed. The boar, looking up, saw him, and dashing his head against the tree, died on the spot.

But the man descended, cooked his flesh, ate it, and rose into the air. And as he was passing along the summit of the Himalaya range, he saw a hermitage; and descending at the hut of the eldest hermit, he stayed there two or three days, and waited on the hermit; and thus became aware of the magic power of the hatchet.

"I must get that," thought he. And he showed the hermit the magic power of his gem, and said: "Sir, do you take this, and give me the hatchet." The ascetic, full of longing to be able to fly through the air,[3] did so. But the man, taking the hatchet, went a little way off, and letting it go, said: "O hatchet! cut off that hermit's head, and bring the gem to me!" And it went, and cut off the hermit's head, and brought him the gem.

Then he put the hatchet in a secret place, and went to the second hermit, and stayed there a few days. And having thus become aware of the magic power of the drum, he exchanged the gem for the drum; and cut off *his* head too in the same way as before.

Then he went to the third hermit, and saw the magic power of the milk-bowl; and exchanging the gem for it, caused *his* head to be cut off in the same manner. And taking the gem, and the hatchet, and the drum, and the milk-bowl, he flew away up into the air.

Not far from the city of Benares he stopped and sent by the hand of a man a letter to the king of Benares to this effect: "Either do battle, or give me up your kingdom!"

No sooner had he heard that message than the king sallied forth, saying: "Let us catch the scoundrel!"

---

[3] The power of going through the air is usually considered in Indian legends be the result, and a proof, of great holiness, and long-continued penance. So the hermit thought he would get a fine reputation cheaply.

But the man beat one side of his drum, and a fourfold army stood around him! And directly he saw that the king's army was drawn out in battle array, he poured out his milk-bowl; and a mighty river arose, and the multitude, sinking down in it, were not able to escape! Then letting go the hatchet, he said: "Bring me the king's head!" And the hatchet went, and brought the king's head, and threw it at his feet; and no one had time even to raise a weapon!

Then he entered the city in the midst of his great army, and caused himself to be anointed king, under the name of Dadhivāhana (Bringer of Milk), and governed the kingdom with righteousness.

A LESSON FOR KINGS

[The mixture in this Jataka of earnestness with dry humour is very instructive. The exaggeration in the earlier part of the story; the hint that law depends in reality on false cases; the suggestion that to decide cases justly would by itself put an end not only to "the block in the law courts," but even to all lawsuits; the way in which it is brought about that two mighty kings should meet unattended, in a narrow lane; the cleverness of the first charioteer in getting out of his difficulties; the brand-new method of settling the delicate questions of precedence—a method which, logically carried out, would destroy the necessity of such questions being raised at all;—all this is the amusing side of the Jataka. It throws, and is meant to throw, an air of unreality over the story; and it is none the less humour because it is left to be inferred, because it is only an aroma which might easily escape unnoticed, only the humour of naive absurdity and of clever repartee. But none the less also is the story-teller thoroughly in earnest; he really means that justice is noble, that to conquer evil by good is the right thing, and that goodness is the true measure of greatness. The object is edification also, and not amusement only.]

●   ●   ●   ●   ●   ●   ●

ONCE upon a time, when Brahmadatta was reigning in Benares, the future Buddha returned to life as his son. After his father died he ascended the throne, and ruled the kingdom with righteousness and equity. He gave judgments without partiality, hatred, ignorance, or fear. Since he thus reigned with justice, with justice also his ministers administered the law. Lawsuits being thus decided with justice, there were none who brought false cases. And as these ceased the noise and tumult of litigation ceased in the king's court. Though the judges sat all day in the court, they had to leave without any one coming for justice. It came to this, that the Hall of Justice would have to be closed!

Then the future Buddha thought: "From my reigning with righteousness there are none who come for judgment; the bustle has ceased, and the Hall of Justice will have to be closed. It behoves me, therefore, now to examine into my own faults; and if I find that anything is wrong in me, to put that away, and practise only virtue."

Thenceforth he sought for some one to tell him his faults; but among those around him he found no one who would tell him of any fault, but heard only his own praise.

Then he thought: "It is from fear of me that these men speak only good things, and not evil things," and he sought among those people who lived outside the palace. And finding no fault-finder there, he sought those who lived outside the city, in the suburbs, at the four gates[1] And there, too, finding no one to find fault, and hearing only his own praise, he determined to search the country places.

So he made over the kingdom to his ministers, and mounted his chariot; and taking only his charioteer, left the city in disguise. And searching the country through, up to the very boundary, he found no fault-finder, and heard only of his own virtue; and so he turned back from the outermost boundary, and returned by the high road toward the city.

Now at that time the king of Kosala, Mallika by name, was also ruling his kingdom with righteousness; and when seeking for some fault in himself, he also found no fault-finder in the palace, but only heard of his own virtue! So seeking in country places, he too came to that very spot. And these two came face to face in a low cart-track with precipitous sides, where there was no space for a chariot to get out of the way!

Then the charioteer of Mallika the king said to the charioteer of the king of Benares: "Take thy chariot out of the way!"

But he said: "Take thy chariot out of the way, O charioteer! In this chariot sitteth the lord over the kingdom of Benares, the great king Brahmadatta."

Yet the other replied: "In this chariot, O charioteer, sitteth the lord over the kingdom of Kosala, the great king Mallika. Take thy carriage out of the way, and make room for the chariot of our king!"

Then the charioteer of the king of Benares thought: "They say then that he too is a king! What is now to be done?" After some consideration, he said to himself, "I know a way. I'll find out how old he is, and then I'll let the chariot of the younger be got out of the way, and so make room for the elder."

And when he had arrived at that conclusion, he asked that charioteer what the age of the King of Kosala was. But on inquiry he found that the ages of both were equal. Then he inquired about the extent of his kingdom, and about his army, and

---

[1] N.S.E.W. gates.

his wealth, and his renown, and about the country he lived in, and his caste and tribe and family. And he found that both were lords of a kingdom three hundred leagues in extent; and that in respect of army and wealth and renown, and the countries in which they lived, and their caste and their tribe and their family, they were just on a par!

Then he thought: "I will make way for the most righteous." And he asked: "What kind of righteousness has this king of yours?"

And the other saying: "Such and such is our king's righteousness," and so proclaiming his king's wickedness as goodness, uttered the First Stanza:

> "The strong he overthrows by strength,
> The mild by mildness, Mallika;
> The good by goodness he o'ercomes,
> The wicked by the wicked too.
> Such is the nature of this king!
> Move out of the way, O charioteer!"

But the charioteer of the king of Benares asked him: "Well, have you told all the virtues of your king?"

"Yes," said the other.

"If these are his *virtues,* where are then his faults?" replied he.

The other said: "Well, for the nonce, they shall be faults, if you like! But pray, then, what is the kind of goodness your king has?"

And then the charioteer of the king of Benares called unto him to hearken, and uttered the Second Stanza:

> "Anger he conquers by not-anger,
> By goodness he conquers what is not good;
> The stingy he conquers by giving gifts,
> By truth he meets the speaker of lies;
> Such is the nature of this king!
> Move out of the way, O charioteer!"

And when he had thus spoken, both Mallika the king and his charioteer alighted from their chariot. And they took out the horses, and removed their chariot, and made way for the king of Benares!

But the king of Benares exhorted Mallika the king, saying: "Thus and thus is it right to do." And returning to Benares, he practised charity, and did other good deeds, and so when his life was ended he passed away to heaven.

And Mallika the king took his exhortation to heart; and having in vain searched the country through for a fault-finder, he too returned to his own city, and practised charity and other good deeds; and so at the end of his life he went to heaven.

V. FABLES OF BIDPAI

BIDPAI, or Pilpay, is the reputed author of a number of fables and stories. The original Indian collection is not now in existence, but an Arabic version exists, dating about 750 A.D., and from this, other versions and translations have been made and circulated both in the East and West.

Each chapter forms a story, which is supposed to have been related to a king of India by his philosopher Bidpai, to point some moral. The stories are not so brief as other fables, and they are often somewhat involved.

THE MONKEYS AND THE BEARS

A GREAT number of Monkeys once lived in a country where grew much fruit and life was very happy. It chanced one day that a Bear, travelling there, looked enviously at the Monkeys and said, "Why should I always roam the forests and mountains in search of food, while these creatures live at their ease?" In his anger he rushed among them and killed some; but soon other Monkeys came and by their numbers overcame him, and with great difficulty he escaped. He returned to his friends, roaring and angry. He told them all that had happened, but instead of feeling pity for him, they all laughed at him, saying, "You must indeed be a coward to allow such small creatures to beat you." "Now," said the chief of the Bears, "we must be revenged on the Monkeys." So toward night all the Bears set off over the mountain and surprised the Monkeys who were dreaming happily in the trees. The Bears rushed hither and thither and soon many Monkeys lay dead and the others fled to another region. "Now," said the chief of the Bears, "this land of the Monkeys pleases me well; let us dwell here always." So they feasted to their hearts' content on all the good things they found there.

In the meantime the King of the Monkeys, who had been away hunting several days, discovered what had happened. When he saw his Monkeys wounded and in a strange land, he wept bitter tears and knew not which way to turn. Now among the Monkeys there was one called Maimon, whose learning and cunning made him the King's favourite. Seeing his master sad, he said, "Do not despair, friends, but let each listen to my plan. I am resolved to die, if need be, for you all. My wife and children have been killed by the enemy and life now is bitter to me. So, O King, will you command my ears to be torn from my head, my teeth to be pulled out, and my feet to be cut off. Then take me to a corner of the forest and leave me there alone. You must go two days' journey away and on the third you may return in peace and safety. And may my death bring you blessings."

The King was grieved at Maimon's request, but allowed him to have his way. Accordingly Maimon was left, wounded and alone, in the forest. There he cried loudly for many hours.

On the morrow, the King of the Bears who had been disturbed by Maimon's cries came to see what was wrong.

When he saw the Monkey in such a sad state, his heart was filled with pity, and he asked Maimon who had ill-treated him thus.

Maimon bowed humbly to the King of the Bears and said, "Sir, I am the King of the Monkeys' chief minister. I went some days ago hunting with him, and on our return, we found what harm you had done in our land. I bade him beware of such great foes as the Bears, 'for indeed,' said I, 'they are more powerful than we are.' Then my King became angry with me, and called me a traitor, and commanded me to be thus ill-treated."

When he had said that Maimon wept long and loudly and even so did the Bear himself. At length he asked Maimon where the Monkeys had gone. "Ah," replied Maimon, "they are in a desert called Mardazmay, and are gathering together a huge army, with which to return and attack the Bears."

"Indeed," said the Bear King, inwardly alarmed at this news. "How do you think we shall be able to overcome them?" "Right easily," replied Maimon, "if you are but bold. I would my legs were not broken, then would I destroy many." "Well," said the King, "if you will help us, we will venture forth to their camp. Guide us thither and we will revenge not only ourselves but you." Accordingly Maimon promised and was tied to the head of one of the biggest Bears. Joyous that his trick was succeeding, Maimon guided them into the desert of Mardazmay, where there blew a poisonous wind, and where the heat was so great that no creature could live long in the place. "Hasten," said Maimon, anxious to lead them far into the desert, "for soon we shall be upon the enemy." So he kept them marching till their feet were sore and blistered. The birds even lay dead around them with the heat and everything was barren and deserted with not even one Monkey in sight.

The King of the Bears now turned angrily upon Maimon and said, "Into what ruinous land have you brought us?" Maimon, seeing all were too weak ever to return, said boldly, "Tyrant, your destruction is near, for we are in the desert of death; yonder whirlwind you see approaching is death itself, which will punish you for your cruel ways; none can hope escape."

Even while he was speaking, the whirlwind came and swept them all away.

Two days after this the King of the Monkeys returned to his own land, as Maimon had bidden him, and finding all the enemies gone, reigned happily for many years, ever keeping in remembrance the noble Maimon.

THE FOUR FRIENDS

WHILE the Raven, the Rat, and the Tortoise were talking together they saw a little wild Goat running toward them very swiftly. Judging that some great hunter was pursuing her, they scurried off, each to take care of himself. The Tortoise slipped into the water, the Rat crept into a hole, and the Raven hid in the boughs of a tree near by. Meanwhile the Goat stopped suddenly by the side of the fountain. The Raven, seeing no one around, called to the Tortoise, who peeped up above the water, and seeing the Goat afraid to drink, said, "Drink boldly, the water is clear." When the Goat had done so, the Tortoise continued, "Why ran you so hurriedly and in so great a fright?"

"Indeed," replied the Goat, "with difficulty have I escaped from a Hunter."

"Well," said the Tortoise, "now you are safe, pray stay with us and be of our company." The Raven and the Rat agreed also to befriend her and she gladly promised to remain with them.

All went happily with the four friends for some time, but one day, on meeting at the fountain the Rat, the Tortoise, and the Raven found that the Goat was missing. Sorrowfully they waited and at last decided to seek for her.

The Raven mounted high into the air, and looking round him, discovered the Goat at some distance caught in a Hunter's net.

Hastily he flew down with the sad news to the Rat and the Tortoise.

Together they talked over the matter, wondering how best they could set the Goat free.

At length the Raven said to the Rat, "O excellent friend, you have power to deliver the Goat, but you must act quickly, or the Huntsman will lay hold upon her."

"Indeed, let us lose no time," said the Rat; "carry me thither at once that I may gnaw the net."

The Raven carried the Rat in his bill, and the Rat soon set to work upon the meshes. As he was about to finish the task, the Tortoise arrived. When the Goat saw the Tortoise she lamented thus, "Oh, why have you ventured hither, you are slow of foot and cannot escape the Hunter.

I am now all but free and can run swiftly, the Raven can fly to the trees, the Rat can run into any hole, but for you there is no escape."

At this moment the Hunter appeared; the Goat being loosened ran away; the Raven mounted aloft; the Rat scurried into a hole, but for the Tortoise there was no help.

The Hunter was vexed to find the Goat had escaped, but looking around, spied the Tortoise. "Oh!" cried he, "a good fat Tortoise is better than nothing," whereupon he picked up the Tortoise, put it in his sack and trudged off homeward.

Out came the three friends from their hiding places, and bewailed the loss of their friend. When they had shed many tears, the Raven besought them to find some means of rescuing her. "Ah," said the Rat, "let the Goat run before the Hunter, then he will drop his sack and pursue her."

"Good," replied the Goat, "I will pretend to be lame, and run limping a little distance before him; this will make him follow me; then can the Rat set our friend at liberty."

All agreed to this, and the Goat set off; the Hunter caught sight of her, and thinking her now within his power, lay down the sack and ran after her. Cunningly the Goat led him on, till at last he was tired with his vain chase and returned slowly to the sack. Meantime the Rat had gnawed the string that tied the sack and the Tortoise crawled out and hid near by.

"Well," said the Hunter as he took up the sack, "at any rate I have a good plump Tortoise here." His amazement knew no bounds, however, when he found that the Tortoise too had escaped him. Having been fooled alike by the swift of foot and the slow of foot, he became full of fear, thinking himself in a land of hobgoblins. He ran home with great speed as if pursued by an army of spirits. Then came the four faithful creatures from their hiding places and vowed to be friends till death should separate them.

VI. THE KATHA-SARIT-SAGARA TALES

THE *Katha-sarit-sagara,* or "Ocean of Story," is a gigantic collection of Indian folk-tales. It was composed by one named Somadeva Bhatta about the twelfth century. These stories, which were based on an earlier collection called the *Vrihat Katha* (*i.e.,* "the lengthened story"), were told by Somadeva to amuse his mistress, the Queen of Cashmere. Many are from the *Panchatantra* and the *Fables of Bidpai.*

THE JACKAL AND THE DRUM

LONG ago there lived a jackal in a certain forest district. He was roaming about in search of food, and came upon a plot of ground where a battle had taken place, and hearing from a certain quarter a booming sound, he looked in that direction. There he saw a drum lying on the ground, a thing with which he was not familiar. He thought, "What kind of animal is this, that makes such a sound?" Then he saw that it was motionless, and coming up and looking at it, he came to the conclusion that it was not an animal. And he perceived that the noise was produced by the parchment being struck by the shaft of an arrow, which was moved by the wind. So the jackal laid aside his fear, and he tore open the drum, and went inside, to see if he could get anything to eat in it, but lo ! it was nothing but wood and parchment.

THE MICE THAT ATE AN IRON BALANCE

ONCE on a time there was a merchant's son, who had spent all his father's wealth, and had only an iron balance left to him. Now the balance was made of a thousand *palas* of iron; and depositing it in the care of a certain merchant, he went to another land. And when, on his return, he came to that merchant to demand back his balance, the merchant said to him: "It has been eaten by mice." He repeated: "It is quite true; the iron of which it was composed was particularly sweet, and so the mice ate it." This he said with an outward show of sorrow, laughing in his heart.

Then the merchant's son asked him to give him some food, and he, being in a good temper, consented to give him some. Then the merchant's son went to bathe, taking with him the son of that merchant, who was a mere child, and whom he persuaded to come with him by giving him a dish of *āmalakas*. And after he had bathed, the wise merchant's son deposited that boy in the house of a friend, and returned alone to the house of that merchant. And the merchant said to him: "Where is that son of mine?" He replied: "A kite swooped down from the air and carried him off." The merchant in a rage said: "You have concealed my son." And so he took him into the king's judgment-hall; and there the merchant's son made the same statement. The officers of the court said: "This is impossible; how could a kite carry off a boy?" But the merchant's son answered: "In a country where a large balance of iron was eaten by mice, a kite might carry off an elephant, much more a boy."

When the officers heard this, they asked about it, out of curiosity, made the merchant restore the balance to the owner, and he, for his part, restored the merchant's child.

THE MOUSE THAT WAS TURNED INTO A MAIDEN

FOR once on a time a hermit found a young mouse, which had escaped from the claws of a kite, and pitying it, made it by the might of his asceticism into a young maiden. And he brought her up in his hermitage; and, when he saw that she had grown up, wishing to give her to a powerful husband, he summoned the sun. And he said to the sun: "Marry this maiden, whom I wish to give in marriage to some mighty one." Then the sun answered:" The cloud is more powerful than I; he obscures me in a moment." When the hermit heard that, he dismissed the sun, and summoned the cloud and made the same proposal to him. He replied: "The wind is more powerful than I; he drives me into any quarter of the heaven he pleases." When the hermit got this answer, he summoned the wind, and made the same proposal to him. And the wind replied: "The mountains are stronger than I, for I cannot move them." When the great hermit heard this, he summoned the Himalaya, and made the same proposal to him. That mountain answered him: "The mice are stronger than I, for they dig holes in me."

Having thus got these answers in succession from those wise divinities, the great Rishi summoned a forest mouse, and said to him: "Marry this maiden." Thereupon the mouse said: "Show me how she is to be got into my hole." Then the hermit said: "It is better that she should return to her condition as a mouse." So he made her a mouse again and gave her to that male mouse.

THE FOOLISH TEACHER, THE FOOLISH PUPILS, AND THE CAT

IN Ujjayini there lived in a convent a foolish teacher. And he could not sleep because mice troubled him at night. And wearied with this infliction, he told the whole story to a friend. The friend, who was a Brahman, said to that teacher: "You must set up a cat; it will eat the mice." The teacher said: "What sort of a creature is a cat? Where can one be found? I never came across one." When the teacher said this, the friend replied: "Its eyes are like glass, its colour is brownish grey, it has a hairy skin on its back, and it wanders about in roads. So, my friend, you must quickly discover a cat by these signs and have one brought."

After his friend had said this, he went home. Then that foolish teacher said to his pupils: "You have been present and heard all the distinguishing marks of a cat. So look about for a cat, such as you have heard described, in the roads here."

Accordingly the pupils went and searched hither and thither, but they could not find a cat anywhere. Then at last they saw a Brahman boy coming from the opening of a road, his eyes were like glass, his colour brownish grey, and he wore on his back a hairy antelope-skin. And when they saw him they said: "Here we have got the cat according to the description." So they seized him, and took him to their teacher. Their teacher also observed that he had got the characteristics mentioned by his friend; so he placed him in the convent at night. And the silly boy himself believed that he was a cat, when he heard the description that those fools gave of the animal.

Now it happened that the silly boy was a pupil of that Brahman who out of friendship gave that teacher the description of a cat. And that Brahman came in the morning, and, seeing the boy in the convent, said to those fools: "Who brought this fellow here?" The teacher and his foolish pupils answered: "We brought him here as a cat, according to the description which we heard from you." Then the Brahman laughed, and said: "There is considerable difference between a stupid human being and a cat, which is an animal with four feet and a tail." When the foolish fellows heard this, they let the boy go, and said: "So let us go and search for a cat such as has been now described to us."

And the people laughed at those fools.

VII. INDIAN NIGHTS' ENTERTAINMENTS

AS folk-tales these stories claim the highest possible antiquity. They are essentially tales of the people, stories which form the delight of the village *hujra*, or guest-house, on winter nights.

THE SAGACIOUS LUMBARDAR

A LARGE earthen chatty, or jar, half filled with corn, was once standing in a courtyard of a farmhouse, when a horned sheep coming by thrust his head into it and began to enjoy himself. When he had satisfied his hunger, however, he found himself unable, owing to the size of the neck of the chatty, to draw forth his head again, so that he was thus caught in a trap. The farmer and his servants perceiving this were sadly perplexed. "What's to be done now?" said they. One of them proposed that the lumbardár, or village head-man, whose wisdom was in every one's mouth, should be requested to help them in their difficulty, which was no sooner said than done. The lumbardár was delighted. He at once mounted his camel, and in a few minutes arrived at the spot. But the archway into the yard was low, and he on the top of his camel was high, nor did it occur to him or to anyone else that the camel should be left outside. "I cannot get in there," said he to the farmer; "pray knock the doorway down!" and accordingly the arch was destroyed, and the wise man entered.

Having dismounted and gazed profoundly at the imprisoned ram, he suddenly exclaimed: "This matter is a mere trifle. Fetch me a sword."

So the sword was brought, and taking it in his hand he cut off the animal's head at a single blow. "There," cried he, "is your sheep, and here is your vessel of corn. Take them away."

By this time the whole village had assembled, and every one began to murmur his praises. But a farm-servant, who was reputed cunning, observed: "But the sheep's head is still in the jar. *Now* what are wet o do ?"

"True," answered the lumbardar. "To you this affair seems difficult; but to me the one thing is just as easy as the other."

With this he raised a great stone and smashed the vessel into a thousand pieces, while the people clapped their hands with satisfaction. No one was more astonished than the farmer. It is true his gateway was ruined, his grain spilt, his jar broken, and his stock-ram killed. These things, however, gave him no concern. He had been rescued from a serious difficulty, and so the fame of that lumbardar became the envy of all the surrounding villages.

THE FARMER, HIS WIFE, AND THE OPEN DOOR

ONCE upon a time a poor farmer and his wife, having finished their day's labour and eaten their frugal supper, were sitting by the fire, when a dispute arose between them as to who should shut the door, which had been blown open by a gust of wind.

"Wife, shut the door!" said the man.

"Husband, shut it yourself!" said the woman.

"I will not shut it, and you shall not shut it," said the husband, "but let the one who speaks the first word shut it."

This proposal pleased the wife exceedingly, and so the old couple, well satisfied, retired in silence to bed.

In the middle of the night they heard a noise, and peering out, they perceived that a wild dog had entered the room, and that he was busy devouring their little store of food. Not a word, however, would either of these silly people utter, and the dog, having sniffed at everything, and having eaten as much as he wanted, went out of the house.

The next morning the woman took some grain to the house of a neighhour in order to have it ground into flour.

In her absence the barber entered, and said to the husband: "How is it you are sitting here all alone?"

The farmer answered never a word. The barber then shaved his head, but still he did not speak; then he shaved off half his beard and half his moustache, but even then the man refrained from uttering a syllable. Then the barber covered him all over with a hideous coating of lampblack, but the stolid farmer remained as dumb as a mute. "The man is bewitched!" cried the barber, and he hastily quitted the house.

He had hardly gone when the wife returned from the mill. She, seeing her husband in such a ghastly plight, began to tremble, and exclaimed: "Ah! wretch, what have you been doing?" "You spoke the first word," said the farmer, "so begone, woman, and shut the door."

THE SILLY WEAVER-GIRL

A CERTAIN quarter of a village was inhabited only by weavers. One day a fine young weaver-girl was sweeping out the house, and as she swept she said to herself: "My father and mother, and all my relations belong to this village. It would be a good thing if I married in this village, and settled here too, so that we should always be together. But," continued she, "if I did marry here, and had a son, and if my son were to sicken and die, oh, how my aunts, my sisters, and my friends would come, and how they would all bewail him!" Thinking of this, she laid her broom against the wall, and began to cry. In came her aunts and her friends, and, seeing her in such distress, they all began to cry too. Then came her father, and her uncles and her brothers, and they also began to cry most bitterly; but not one of them had the wit to say, "What is the matter?—for whom is this wailing?" At last, when the noise and the weeping had continued for some time, a neighbour said: "What bad news have you had ? Who is dead here ?"

"I don't know," answered one of the howling uncles. "These women know, ask one of them."

At this point the head-man arrived at the spot, and cried: "Stop, stop this hubbub, good people, and let us find out what is the matter."

Addressing himself to an old woman, he said: "What is all this disturbance in the village for?"

"How can I tell?" answered she. "When I came here, I found this weaver-girl crying about something."

Then the weaver-girl, on being questioned, said: "I was weeping because I could not help thinking how, if I married in this village, and had a son, and if my son were to sicken and die, all my aunts, my sisters, and my friends would come round me, and how we should all bewail him. The thought of this made me cry."

On hearing her answer, the head-man and his followers began to laugh, and the crowd dispersed.

VIII. SANTAL TALES

T HE Santals are an aboriginal tribe of India. They prefer to live on the edges of the great forests and when the ground becomes well cultivated, they seek new districts. In personal appearance they are somewhat like the negroes. They worship the sun as supreme god, while in various ways they seek to counteract the evil powers of other spirits. They have resisted the subtle Hindu influences and have retained their own language, institutions, tribal organization, and religion almost intact.

Most of the folk-tales show the superstitious awe of the people. The first story given here bears a striking resemblance to the better known story of Aladdin.

THE MAGIC LAMP

I N the capital of a certain raja, there lived a poor widow. She had an only son who was of comely form and handsome countenance. One day a merchant from a far country came to her house, and standing in front of the door called out, "*Dada, dada*," (elder brother). The widow replied, "He is no more, he died many years ago." On hearing this the merchant wept bitterly, mourning the loss of his younger brother. He remained some days in his sister-in-law's house, at the end of which he said to her, "This lad and I will go in quest of the golden flowers, prepare food for our journey." Early next morning they set out, taking provisions with them for the way. After they had gone a considerable distance, the boy being fatigued said, "Oh! uncle, I can go no further." The merchant scolded him, and walked along as fast as he could. After some time the boy again said, "I am so tired I can go no further." His uncle turned back and beat him, and he, nerved by fear, walked rapidly along the road. At length they reached a hill, to the summit of which they climbed, and gathered a large pile of firewood. They had no fire with them, but the merchant ordered his nephew to blow with his mouth as if he were kindling the embers of a fire. He blew until he was exhausted, and then said, "What use is there in blowing when there is no fire?" The merchant replied, "Blow, or I shall beat you." He again blew with all his might for a short time, and then stopping, said, "There is no fire, how can it possibly burn?" on which the merchant struck him. The lad then redoubled his efforts, and presently the pile of firewood burst into a blaze. On the firewood being consumed, an iron trap door appeared underneath the ashes, and the merchant ordered his nephew to pull it up. He pulled, but finding himself unable to open it, said, "It will not open." The merchant told him to pull with greater force, and he, being afraid lest he should be again beaten, pulled with all his might, but could not raise it. He again said, "it will not open," whereupon the merchant struck him, and ordered him to try again. Applying himself with all his might, he at length succeeded. On the door being raised, they saw a lamp burning, and beside it an immense quantity of golden flowers.

The merchant then said to the boy, "As you enter do not touch any of the gold flowers, but put out the lamp, and heap on the gold tray as many of the gold flowers as you can, and bring them away with you." He did as he was ordered, and on reaching the door again requested his uncle to relieve him of the gold flowers, but he refused, saying, "Climb up as best you can." The boy replied, "How can I do so, when my hands are full?" The merchant then shut the iron trap door on him, and went away to a distant country.

The boy being imprisoned in the dark vault, wept bitterly, and having no food, in a few days he became very weak. Taking the lamp in his hand, he sat down in a corner, and without knowing what he was doing, began to rub the lamp with his hand. A ring, which he wore on his finger, came into contact with the lamp, and immediately a fairy issued from it, and asked, "What is it you want with me?" He replied, "Open the door and let me out."

The fairy opened the door, and the boy went home taking the lamp with him. Being hungry, he asked for food, but his mother replied: "There is nothing in the house that I can give you." He then went for his lamp, saying, "I will clean it, and then sell it, and with the money buy food." Taking the lamp in his hand he began to rub it, and his ring again touching it, a fairy issued from it and said, "What do you wish for?" The boy said, "Cooked rice, and uncooked rice." The fairy immediately brought him an immense quantity of both kinds of rice.

Sometime after this, certain merchants brought horses for sale, and the boy seeing them wished to buy one. Having no money, he remembered his lamp, and taking it up, pressed his ring against it, and the fairy instantly appeared, and asked him what he wanted. He said, "Bring me a horse," and immediately the fairy presented to him an immense number of horses.

When the boy had become a young man, it so happened that one day the raja's daughter was being carried to the ghat to bathe, and he seeing her palki with the attendants passing, went to his mother and said, "I am going to see the princess." She tried to dissuade him, but he insisted on her giving him permission, so at length she gave him leave. He went secretly, and saw her as she was bathing, and on returning home, said to his mother, "I have seen the princess, and I am in love with her. Go, and inform the raja that your son loves his daughter, and begs her hand in marriage." His mother said, "Do you think the raja will consider us as on an equality with him ?" He would not, however, be gainsaid, but kept urging her daily to carry his message to the raja, until she, being wearied with his importunity, went to the palace, and being admitted to an audience, informed the raja that her son was enamoured of the princess, his daughter, and begged that she might be given to him in marriage. The raja made answer that on her son giving him a large sum of money which he named, and which would have been beyond the means of the raja himself, he would be prepared to give his daughter in marriage to her son. The young man had recourse to his lamp and ring, and the fairy supplied him with a much larger sum of money than the raja had demanded. He took it all, and gave it to the raja, who was astonished beyond measure at the sight of such immense wealth.

After a reasonable time the old mother was sent to the raja to request him to fulfil his promise, but he, being reluctant to see his daughter united to one so much her inferior in station, in hope of being relieved from the obligation to fulfil his promise, demanded that a palace suited to her rank and station in life be prepared for her, after which he would no longer delay the nuptials. The would-be bridegroom applied to his never-failing friends, his lamp and ring, and on the fairy appearing begged him to build a large castle in one night, and to furnish and adorn it as befitted the residence of a raja's daughter. The fairy complied with the request, and the whole city was amazed next morning at the sight of a lordly castle, where the evening before there had not been even a hut. The dewan tried to dissuade the raja, but without effect, and in due time. the marriage was celebrated amid great rejoicings.

On a certain day, some time after the marriage, the raja and his son-in-law went to the forest to hunt. During their absence, the merchant to whom reference has already been made, arrived at the castle gate, bearing in his hand a new lamp which he offered in exchange to the princess for any old lamp she might possess. She thought it a good opportunity to obtain a new lamp in place of her husband's old one, and without knowing what she did, gave the magic lamp to the merchant, and received a new one in return. The merchant rubbed his ring on the magic lamp, and the fairy obeyed the summons, and desired to know what he wanted. He said, "Convey the castle as it stands, with the princess in it, to my own country," and instantly his wish was gratified.

When the raja and his son-in-law returned from the chase, they were surprised and alarmed to find that the palace with its fair occupant had vanished, and had not left a trace behind. The dewan reminded his master that he had tried to dissuade him from rashly giving his daughter in marriage to an unknown person, and had foretold that some calamity was sure to follow.

The raja, being grieved and angry at the loss of his daughter, sent for her husband, and said to him, "I give you thirteen days during which to find my daughter. If you fail, on the morning of the fourteenth I shall surely cause you to be executed." The thirteenth day arrived, and although her husband had sought her everywhere, the princess had not been found.

Her unhappy husband resigned himself to his fate, saying, "1 shall go and rest, to-morrow morning I shall be killed." So he climbed to the top of a high hill, and lay down to sleep upon a rock. At noon he accidentally rubbed his finger ring upon the rock on which he lay, and a fairy issued from it, and awaking him, demanded what he wanted. In reply he said, "I have lost my wife and my palace, if you know where they are, take me to them." The fairy immediately transported him to the gate of his castle in the merchant's country, and then left him to his own devices. Assuming the form of a dog, he entered the palace, and the princess at once recognized him. The merchant had gone out on business, and had taken the lamp with him, suspended by a chain round his neck. After consultation, it was determined that the princess should put poison in the merchant's food that evening.

When he returned, he called for his supper, and the princess set before him the poisoned rice, after eating which he quickly died. The rightful owner repossessed himself of the magic lamp, and an application of the ring brought out the attendant fairy who demanded to know why he had been summoned. "Transport my castle with the princess and myself in it back to the king's country, and place it where it stood before," said the young man, and instantly the castle occupied its former position. So that before the morning of the fourteenth day dawned, not only had the princess been found, but her palace had been restored to its former place.

The raja was delighted at receiving his daughter back again. He divided his kingdom with his son-in-law, giving him one-half, and they ruled the country peacefully and prosperously for many years.

THE STORY OF KARA AND GUJA

THERE were two brothers named Kara and Guja. Guja, who was the elder, did the work at home, and Kara was the ploughman.

One day the two went to the forest to dig edible roots. After they had been thus engaged for some hours, Kara said to Guja, "Look up and see the sun's position in the heavens." Looking up he said, "Oh, brother, one is rising and another is setting." They then said, "The day is not yet past, let us bestir ourselves, and lose no time." So they dug with all their might.

After digging a long time Kara looked up and became aware that it was night. He then exclaimed, "Oh, brother, it is now night, what shall we do? Come, let us seek some place where we can remain until the morning."

After they had wandered awhile in the forest they spied a light in the distance, and on drawing near they found that a tiger had kindled a fire and was warming himself. Going up to the entrance of the cave they called out to the tiger, "Oh, uncle, give us a place to sleep in." He answered, "Come in." So the two went in, and being hungry began to roast and eat the roots they had brought with them. The tiger, hearing them eating, inquired what it was. They replied, "Oh, uncle, we are roasting and eating the roots which we dug up in the forest." He then said, "Oh, my nephews, I will also try how they taste." So they handed him a piece of charcoal, and as he munched it he said, "Oh, my nephews, how is it that I feel it grating between my teeth?" They replied, "It is an old one that you have got, uncle." He then said, "Give me another, and I will try it." So they gave him another piece of charcoal, and after he had crunched it awhile he said, "Oh, my nephews, this is as bad as the other," to which they rejoined, "Oh, uncle, your mouth is old, therefore what is good to us is the reverse to you." The tiger did not wish to try his grinders on another piece of charcoal, so the brothers were left to enjoy their repast alone.

After they had eaten all the roots, Guja said to Kara, "What shall we eat now? Come, let us eat this old tiger's tail." Kara replied, "Do not talk in that way, brother, the tiger will devour us." "Not so, brother," said Guja. "I have a great desire to eat flesh." The old tiger understood their conversation, and being afraid tried to get out of the cave, but the brothers caught hold of him, and wrenched off his tail, which they roasted in the ashes, and then ate.

The tiger after losing his tail summoned a council of all the tigers inhabiting that part of the forest, at which they decided to kill and eat the two brothers. So they went to the cave, but Kara and Guja had fled, and had taken refuge in a palm-tree which grew on the edge of a large deep tank. Not finding them in the cave the tigers, headed by him who had lost his tail, went in quest of them, and coming to the tank saw them reflected in the water, and one after another they dived in, thinking they would be able to seize them, but of course they could not catch a shadow. One of the tigers, when in the act of yawning, looked upward, and seeing them in the tree exclaimed, "There they are. There they are." They then asked the brothers how they had managed to climb up, to which they replied, "We stood on each other's shoulders."

The tigers then said, "Come, let us do the same, and we shall soon reach them." As the tailless tiger was most interested in their capture, they made him stand lowest, and a tiger climbed up and stood on his shoulders, and another on his, and so on; but before they reached the brothers, Kara called out to Guja, "Give me your sharp battle-axe, and I shall ham string the tailless tiger." The tailless tiger, forgetting himself, jumped to one side, and the whole pillar of tigers fell in a heap on the ground. They now began to abuse the old tailless tiger, who, fearing lest they should tear him in pieces, fled into the forest.

After the tigers had left, the two brothers descended from the palmtree, and walked rapidly away as they dreaded that the tigers might yet follow them. Toward evening they came to a village, and entering into the house of an old woman lay down to sleep. The owner of the house observing them said, "Oh, my children, do not sleep to-night, for there is a demon who visits in rotation each house in the village, and each time he comes carries off some one and eats him; it is my turn to receive a visit to-night." They said, "Do not trouble us now, let us sleep, as we are tired." So they slept, but kept their weather eye open.

During the night the old woman came quietly and began to bite their arms, which they had laid aside before retiring to rest. Hearing a sound as if some one were crunching iron between his teeth, the brothers called out, "Old woman, what are you eating?" She replied, "Only a few roasted peas which I brought from the chief's house." About midnight the demon came, and as he was entering the house Kara and Guja shot at him with their bows and arrows, and he fell down dead. Then they cut out his claws and tongue, and placed them in a bag. Afterward they threw out the body of the demon into the garden behind the house.

Now it so happened that the king had promised to give his daughter and half of his kingdom to the man who should slay the demon.

Early in the morning a Dome, who was passing, discovered the body of the demon, and said within himself, "I will take it to the king and claim the reward." So running home he broke all the furniture in his house and beat his old woman, saying, "Get out of this. I am about to bring the King's daughter home as my bride." He then returned quickly, and taking up the body of the demon, carried it to the king, and said, "Oh, sir king, I have slain the demon." The king replied, "Very well, we will inquire into it." So he commanded some of his servants to examine the body, and on doing so they found that the claws had been extracted and the tongue cut out. They reported the condition of the body to the king, who ordered the Dome to state the weapon with which he killed him. The Dome replied, "I hit him with a club on the head." On the head being examined no mark whatever was seen, so in order to arrive at the truth the king ordered all the inhabitants of the village to be brought together to the palace. He then inquired of them as to who killed the demon.

The old woman, in whose house Kara and Guja had passed the night, stepped forward and said, "Oh, sir king, two strangers came to my house yesterday evening, and during the night they slew the demon." The king said, "Where are those two men?" The old woman replied, "There they are, the two walking together."

So the king sent and brought them back, and questioned them as to the slaying of the demon.

They pointed out the arrow-marks on the body, and produced his claws and tongue from their bag. This evidence convinced the king that they, and not the Dome, had slain the demon. Kara and Guja were received with great favour by the king, and received the promised reward.

The king sentenced the Dome to be beaten and driven from the village. After receiving his stripes, the Dome returned home, and gathered the shreds of his property together. He also went in search of his Dome wife and children, but they mocked him, saying, "You went to marry the king's daughter; why do you come again seeking us?"

Thus Kara and Guja gained a kingdom.

THE STORY OF A LIZARD, A TIGER, AND A LAME MAN

O NCE upon a time in a certain jungle a lizard and a tiger were fighting, and a lame man who was tending goats near by saw them. The tiger being beaten by the lizard was ashamed to own it, and coming to the lame man said, "Tell me which of us won." The lame man being in great fear lest the tiger should eat him, said, "You won." On another occasion the lizard was compelled to flee, and took refuge in an anthill. The tiger pursued him, but not being able to get him out, sat down to watch.

The lizard, seeing his opportunity, crept stealthily up to his inveterate enemy, and climbing up his tail, fixed his teeth into his haunch, and held firmly on. The tiger felt the pain of the lizard's bite, but could not reach him to knock him off, so he ran to the lame man, and said, "Release me from this lizard." When he had caused the lizard to let go his grip, the tiger said, "Oh, lame man, which of us won in the encounter?" The poor man in great fear said, "You won."

The same scene was enacted daily for many days. The tiger always came to the lame man and said, "Knock off this lizard," and after he had done so, would say, "Which of us won?" The lame man invariably replied, "You won." This happened so often that the lame man began to feel annoyed at having to tell a lie each day to please the tiger. So one day after an ignominious flight on the part' of the tiger, he being, as usual, requested to give his opinion as to who won, said, "The lizard had the best of it." On hearing this the tiger became angry, and said, "I shall eat you, my fine fellow, because you say the lizard defeated me. Tell me where you sleep." The poor lame man, on hearing the tiger threaten him thus, trembled with fear, and was silent. But the tiger pressed him. He said, "Tell at once, for I shall certainly devour you." The lame man replied, "I sleep in the wall press."

When night fell, the tiger set off to eat the lame man, but after searching in the wall press failed to find him. In the morning the lame man led his goats out to graze, and again met the tiger, who addressed him as follows, "You are a great cheat. I did not find you in the wall press last night." The lame man replied, "How is it you did not find me?

I was sleeping there." "No," said the tiger, "you were not, you have deceived me. Now, tell me truly where you sleep." "I sleep on a rafter," said the lame man. About midnight the tiger went again in search of him to eat him, but did not find him on the rafter, so he returned home. In the morning the lame man, as usual, led his goats out to graze, and again encountered the tiger, who said to him, "How now! Where do you sleep? I could not find you last night." The lame man rejoined, "That is strange, I was there all the same." The tiger said, "You are a consummate liar. Now tell me plainly where you sleep at night, for I shall without doubt eat you." The lame man replied, "I sleep in the fire-place." Again the tiger went at night, but could not find him. Next morning he met the lame man, and said to him, "No more tricks, tell me where you sleep." He, thrown off his guard, said, "In the *gongo.*"[1]

The tiger then withdrew to his den to wait till night came on, and the lame man, cursing his indiscretion, with a heavy heart, drove his goats homeward. Having made his charge safe for the night, he sat down feeling very miserable. He refused the food that was set before him, and continued bewailing his hard lot. In the hope of inducing him to eat, they gave him some *mohwa* wrapped in a *sal* leaf. This also failed to tempt him to eat; but he carried it with him when he crept into the *gongo* to sleep. At night the tiger came and lifting up the *gongo* felt it heavy, and said, "Well, are you inside ?"

He replied, "Yes, I am." So the tiger carried off the *gongo* with the lame man in it. By the time the tiger had gone a considerable distance, the lame man became hungry and said within himself, "I shall have to die in the end, but in the meantime I will appease my hunger." So he opened his small parcel of *mohwa,* and the dry leaf crackled as he did so. The noise frightened the tiger and he said, "What is it you are opening?" The lame man replied, "It is yesterday's lizard." "Hold! hold!" exclaimed the tiger. "Do not let him out yet, let me get clear away first." The lame man said, "Not so, I will not wait, but will let him out at once."

The tiger being terrified at the prospect of again meeting his mortal enemy, the redoubtable lizard, threw down the *gongo* and fled, calling out, "I will not eat you. You have got the lizard with you."

In this way the lame man, by means of the lizard, saved his life.

---

[1] Covering for the head and shoulders, made of leaves pinned together, worn as a protection from the rain by women, while planting rice.

ITALY

THERE is evidence of "a vein of legendary lore" underlying the classic soil of Rome, but for many years neither readers nor writers appeared to be very interested in the subject. When, however, Miss Busk set herself to collect folk-tales and legends from the people, there were great difficulties in the way. Many of the peasants did not like telling her "such childish nonsense." Others were suspicious of her interest in the subject. Many were incapable of putting their stories into shape, and numbers were ignorant of any folk-tales at all.

The tales she collected are very interesting for purposes of comparison and contrast. Ideas of chivalry and heroism are almost entirely absent. There are stories of dragons, but no knightly prowess is recorded. Horrid monsters are rare, and the devil is not often met with. Tales in which animals are prominent actors are infrequent. The four main classes into which these tales fail are moral stories, ghost stories, fairy tales, and gossip tales.

THIRTEENTH

THERE was once a father who had thirteen sons, the youngest of whom was named Thirteenth. The father had hard work to support his children, but made what he could gathering herbs. The mother, to make the children quick, said to them: "The one who comes home first shall have herb soup." Thirteenth always returned the first, and the soup always fell to his share, on which account his brothers hated him and sought to get rid of him.

The king issued a proclamation in the city that he who was bold enough to go and steal the ogre's coverlet should receive a measure of gold.

Thirteenth's brothers went to the king and said: "Majesty, we have a brother, named Thirteenth, who is confident that he can do that and other things, too." The king said: "Bring him to me at once." They brought Thirteenth, who said:

"Majesty, how is it possible to steal the ogre's coverlet? If he sees me he will eat me!"

"No matter, you must go," said the king. "I know that you are bold and this act of bravery you must perform." Thirteenth departed and went to the house of the ogre, who was away. The ogress was in the kitchen. Thirteenth entered quietly and hid himself under the bed. At night the ogre returned. He ate his supper and went to bed, saying as he did so:

"I smell the smell of human flesh;
Where I see it I will swallow it!"

The ogress replied: "Be still; no one has entered here." The ogre began to snore, and Thirteenth pulled the coverlet a little. The ogre awoke and cried: "What is that?"

Thirteenth began to mew like a cat. The ogress said: "Scat! Scat!" and clapped her hands, and then fell asleep again with the ogre. Then Thirteenth gave a hard pull, seized the coverlet, and ran away. The ogre heard him running, recognized him in the dark, and said: "I know you! You are Thirteenth, without doubt!"

After a time the king issued another proclamation, that whoever would steal the ogre's horse and bring it to the king should receive a measure of gold. Thirteenth again presented himself, and asked for a silk ladder and a bag of cakes. With these things he departed, and went at night to the ogre's, climbed up without being heard, and descended to the stable. The horse neighed on seeing him, but he offered it a cake, saying: "Do you see how sweet it is? If you will come with me, my master will give you these always." Then he gave it another, saying: "Let me mount you and see how we go." So he mounted it, kept feeding it with cakes, and brought it to the king's stable.

The king issued another proclamation, that he would give a measure of gold to whoever would bring him the ogre's bolster. Thirteenth said: "Majesty, how is that possible? The bolster is full of little bells, and you must know that the ogre wakens at a breath." "I know nothing about it," said the king. "I wish it at any cost." Thirteenth departed, and went and crept under the ogre's bed. At midnight he stretched out his hand very softly, but the little bells all sounded. "What is that?" said the ogre.

"Nothing," replied the ogress; "perhaps it is the wind that makes them ring." But the ogre, who was suspicious, pretended to sleep, but kept his ears open. Thirteenth stretched out his hand again. Alack! the ogre put out his arm and seized him. "Now you are caught! Just wait; I will make you cry for your first trick, for your second, and for your third."

After this he put Thirteenth in a barrel, and began to feed him on raisins and figs. After a time he said: "Stick out your finger, little Thirteenth, so that I can see whether you are fat." Thirteenth saw there a mouse's tail, and stuck that out. "Ah, how thin you are!" said the ogre; "and besides, you don't smell good! Eat, my son; take the raisins and figs and get fat soon!" After some days the ogre told him again to put out his finger, and Thirteenth stuck out a spindle.

"Eh, wretch! are you still lean? Eat, eat, and get fat soon."

At the end of the month Thirteenth had nothing more to stick out, and was obliged to show his finger. The ogre cried out in joy: "He is fat, he is fat!" The ogress hastened to the spot. "Quick, my ogress, heat the oven three nights and three days, for I am going to invite our relatives, and we will make a fine banquet of Thirteenth."

The ogress heated an oven three days and three nights, and then released
Thirteenth from the barrel, and said to him: "Come here, Thirteenth; we have got
to put the lamb in the oven." But Thirteenth caught her meaning; and when he
approached the oven he said: "Ah, mother ogress, what is that black thing in the
corner of the oven?" The ogress stooped down a little, but saw nothing. "Stoop
down again," said Thirteenth, "so that you can see it." When she stooped down
again, Thirteenth seized her by the feet and threw her into the open oven, and then
closed the oven door. When she was cooked, he took her out carefully, put part
of her on the table, and placed her trunk, with her head and arms, in the bed under
the sheet, and tied a string to the chin and another to the back of her head.

When the ogre arrived with his guests he found the dishes on the table. Then
he went to his wife's bed and asked: "Mother ogress, do you want to dine?"
Thirteenth pulled the string, and the ogress shook her head. "How are you, tired?"

And Thirteenth, who was hidden under the bed, pulled the other string and
made her nod. Now it happened that one of her relatives moved something and
saw that the ogress was dead, and only half of her was there. She cried in a loud
voice: "Treason! treason!" and all hastened to the bed. In the midst of the
confusion Thirteenth escaped from under the bed and ran away to the king with
the bolster and the ogre's most valuable things.

After this, the king said to Thirteenth: "Listen, Thirteenth. To complete your
valiant exploits, I wish you to bring me the ogre himself, in person, alive and well."
"How can I, your Majesty?" said Thirteenth. Then he roused himself, and added:
"I see how, now!" Then he had a very strong chest made, and disguised himself
as a monk, with a long, false beard, and went to the ogre's house, and called out
to him: "Do you know Thirteenth? The wretch! he has killed our superior; but if
I catch him, if I catch him, I will shut him up in this chest!" At these words the ogre
drew near and said: "I, too, would like to help you, against that wretch of an
assassin, for you don't know what he has done to me." And he began to tell the
story. "But what shall we do?" said the pretended monk.

"I do not know Thirteenth. Do you know him?"

"Yes, sir."

"Then tell me, father ogre, how tall is he?"

"As tall as I am."

"If that is so," said Thirteenth, "let us see whether this chest will hold you; if
it will hold you, it will hold him."

"Oh, good!" said the ogre; and got into the chest. Then Thirteenth shut the chest
and said: "Look carefully, father ogre, and see whether there is any hole in the
chest." "There is none."

"Just wait; let us see whether it shuts well, and is heavy to carry."

Meanwhile Thirteenth shut and nailed up the chest, took it on his back, and hastened to the city. When the ogre cried: "Enough, now!" Thirteenth ran all the faster, and laughing, sang this song to taunt the ogre:

> "I am Thirteenth,
> Who carry you on my back;
> I have tricked you and am going to trick you.
> I must deliver you to the king."

When he reached the king, the king had an iron chain attached to the ogre's hands and feet, and made him gnaw bones the rest of his miserable life. The king gave Thirteenth all the riches and treasures he could bestow on him, and always wished him at his side, as a man of the highest valour.

A FEAST DAY

ONCE upon a time there was a husband and wife; the husband was a boatman. One feast day the boatman took it into his head to buy a fowl, which he carried home and said: "See here, wife, to-day is a feast day; I want a good dinner; cook it well, for my friend Tony is coming to dine with us and has said that he would bring a tart."

"Very well," she said, "I will prepare the fowl at once." So she cleaned it, washed it, put it on the fire, and said: "While it is boiling I will go and hear a mass." She shut the kitchen door and left the dog and the cat inside.

Scarcely had she closed the door when the dog went to the hearth and perceived that there was a good odour there and said: "Oh, what a good smell!" He called the cat, also, and said: "Cat, you come here, too; smell what a good odour there is! see if you can push off the cover with your paws." The cat went and scratched and scratched and down went the cover. "Now," said the dog, "see if you can catch it with your claws." Then the cat seized the fowl and dragged it to the middle of the kitchen. The dog said: "Shall we eat half of it?" The cat said: "Let us eat it all." so they ate it all and stuffed themselves like pigs. When they had eaten it they said: "Alas for us! What shall we do when the mistress comes home? She will surely beat us both." So they both ran all over the house, here and there, but could find no place in which to hide. They were going to hide under the bed. "No," they said, "for she will see us." They were going under the sofa; but that would not do, for she would see them there. Finally the cat looked up and saw under the beams a cobweb. He gave a leap and jumped into it. The dog looked at him and said: "Run away! you are mad! you can be seen, for your tail sticks out! come down, come down!" "I cannot, I cannot, for I am stuck fast!" "Wait, I will come and pull you out." He gave a spring to catch him by the tail and pull him down. Instead of that he, too, stuck fast to the cat's tail. He made every effort to loosen himself, but he could not, and there he had to stay.

Meanwhile the mistress does not wait until the priest finishes the mass, but runs quickly home. She runs and opens the door and is going to skim the pot, when she discovers that the fowl is no longer there, and in the middle of the kitchen she sees the bones all gnawed. "Ah, poor me! the cat and the dog have eaten the fowl. Now I will give them both a beating." So she takes a stick and then goes to find them. She looks here, she looks there, but does not find them anywhere. In despair she comes back to the kitchen, but does not find them there. "Where the deuce have they hidden?" Just then she raises her eyes and sees them both stuck fast under the beams. "Ah, are you there? now just wait!" and she climbs on a table and is going to pull them down, when she sticks fast to the dog's tail. She tries to free herself, but cannot.

Her husband knocked at the door. "Here, open!" "I cannot, I am fast." "Loosen yourself, and open the door! Where the deuce are you fastened?" "I cannot, I tell you." "Open! it is noon." "I cannot, for I am fast." "But where are you fast?" "To the dog's tail." "I will give you the dog's tail, you silly woman!" He gave the door two or three kicks, broke it in, went into the kitchen, and saw cat, dog, and mistress all fast. "Ah, you are all fast, are you? just wait, I will loosen you." He went to loosen them, but stuck fast himself. Friend Tony comes and knocks. "Friend? Open! I have the tart here." "I cannot, my friend, I am fast!" "Bad luck to you! You knew I was coming and got fast? Come, loosen yourself and open the door!" He said again: "I cannot come and open, for I am fast." Finally the friend became angry, kicked in the door, went into the kitchen, and saw all those souls stuck fast and laughed heartily. "Just wait, for I will loosen you now." So he gave a great pull, the cat's tail was loosened, the cat fell into the dog's mouth, the dog into his mistress' mouth, the mistress into her husband's, her husband in his friend's, and his friend into the mouth of the blockheads who are listening to me.

GIUFA AND THE MORNING-SINGER

ONE morning, before Giufà[1] was up, he heard a whistle and asked his mother who was passing. She answered that it was the morning-singer. One day Giufà, tired of the noise, went out and killed the man who was blowing the whistle, and came back and told his mother that he had killed the morning-singer. His mother went out and brought the body into the house and threw it into the well,

[1] "Giufà" in Sicilian Folk-lore is the typical booby found in the popular literature all peoples.

which happened to be dry. Then she remembered that she had a lamb, which she killed and also threw in the well.

Meanwhile the family of the murdered man had learned of the murder and had gone to the judge, with their complaint, and all together went to Giufà's house to investigate the matter. The judge said to Giufà: "Where did you put the body?" Giufà, who was silly, replied: "I threw it in the well." Then they tied Giufà to a rope and lowered him into the well. When he reached the bottom he began to feel around and touched wool, and cried out to the son of the murdered man: "Did your father have wool?"

"My father did not have wool."

"This one has wool; he is not your father."

Then he touched the tail: "Did your father have a tail?"

"My father did not have a tail."

"Then it's not your father."

Then he felt four feet and asked: "How many feet did your father have?"

"My father had two feet."

Giufà said: "This one has four feet; he is not your father."

Then he felt the head and said: "Did your father have horns?"

"My father did not have horns."

Giufà replied: "This one has horns; he is not your father." Then the judge said: "Giufà, bring him up either with the horns or with the wool." So they drew up Giufà with the lamb on his shoulder, and when the judge saw that it was a real lamb, they set Giufà at liberty.

CRAB

THERE was once a king who had lost a valuable ring. He looked for it everywhere, but could not find it. So he issued a proclamation that if any astrologer could tell him where it was he would be richly rewarded. A poor peasant by the name of Crab heard of the proclamation. He could neither read nor write, but took it into his head that he wanted to be the astrologer to find the king's ring. So he went and presented himself to the king, to whom he said: "Your Majesty must know that I am an astrologer, although you see me so poorly dressed. I know that you have lost a ring and I will try by study to find out where it is." "Very well," said the king, "and when you have found it, what reward must I give you?" "That is at your discretion, your Majesty." "Go, then, study, and we shall see what kind of an astrologer you turn out to be."

He was conducted to a room, in which he was to be shut up to study. It contained only a bed and a table on which were a large book and writing materials. Crab seated himself at the table and did nothing but turn over the leaves of the book and scribble the paper so that the servants who brought him his food thought him a great man. They were the ones who had stolen the ring, and from the severe glances that the peasant cast at them whenever they entered, they began to fear that they would be found out. They made him endless bows and never opened their mouths without calling him "Mr. Astrologer." Crab, who, although illiterate, was, as a peasant, cunning, all at once imagined that the servants must know about the ring, and this is the way his suspicions were confirmed. He had been shut up in his room turning over his big book and scribbling his paper for a month, when his wife came to visit him. He said to her: "Hide yourself under the bed, and when a servant enters, say: 'That is one'; when another comes, say: 'That is two'; and so on." The woman hid herself. The servants came with the dinner, and hardly had the first one entered when a voice from under the bed said: "That is one." The second one entered; the voice said: "That is two"; and so on. The servants were frightened at hearing that voice, for they did not know where it came from, and held a consultation. One of them said: "We are discovered; if the astrologer denounces us to the king as thieves, we are lost." "Do you know what we must do?" said another. "Let us hear." "We must go to the astrologer and tell him frankly that we stole the ring, and ask him not to betray us, and present him with a purse of money. Are you willing?" "Perfectly."

So they went in harmony to the astrologer, and making him a lower bow than usual, one of them began: "Mr. Astrologer, you have discovered that we stole the ring. We are poor people and if you reveal it to the king, we are undone. So we beg you not to betray us, and accept this purse of money." Crab took the purse and then added: "I will not betray you, but you must do what I tell you, if you wish to save your lives. Take the ring and make that turkey in the court-yard swallow it, and leave the rest to me." The servants were satisfied to do so and departed with a low bow. The next day Crab went to the king and said to him: "Your Majesty must know that after having toiled over a month I have succeeded in discovering where the ring has gone to." "Where is it, then?" asked the king. "A turkey has swallowed it." "A turkey? Very well; let us see."

They went for the turkey, opened it, and found the ring inside. The king, amazed, presented the astrologer with a large purse of money and invited him to a banquet. Among the other dishes there was brought on the table a plate of crabs. Crabs must then have been very rare, because only the king and a few others knew their name.

Turning to the peasant the king said: "You, who are an astrologer, must be able to tell me the name of these things which are in this dish." The poor astrologer was very much puzzled, and, as if speaking to himself, but in such a way that the others heard him, he muttered: "Ah! Crab, Crab, what a plight you are in!" All who did not know that his name was Crab rose and proclaimed him the greatest astrologer in the world.

THE CLEVER PEASANT

THERE was once a king who, while hunting, saw a peasant working in the fields and asked him: "How much do you earn in a day?" "Four *carlini*, your Majesty," answered the peasant. "What do you do with them?" continued the king. The peasant said: "The first I eat; the second I put out to interest; the third I give back, and the fourth I throw away."

The king rode on, but after a time the peasant's answer seemed very curious to him, so he returned and asked him: "Tell me, what do you mean by eating the first *carlino,* putting the second out to interest, giving back the third, and throwing away the fourth?" The peasant answered: "With the first I feed myself; with the second I feed my children, who must care for me when I am old; with the third I feed my father, and so repay him for what he has done for me, and with the fourth I feed my wife, and thus throw it away, because I have no profit from it." "Yes," said the king, "you are right. Promise me, however, that you will not tell anyone this until you have seen my face a hundred times." The peasant promised and the king rode home well pleased.

While sitting at table with his ministers, he said: "I will give you a riddle: A peasant earns four *carlini* a day; the first he eats; the second he puts out at interest; the third he gives back, and the fourth he throws away. What is that?" No one was able to answer it.

One of the ministers remembered finally that the king had spoken the day before with the peasant, and he resolved to find the peasant and obtain from him the answer.

When he saw the peasant he asked him for the answer to the riddle, but the peasant answered: "I cannot tell you, for I promised the king to tell no one until I have seen his face a hundred times." "Oh!" said the minister, "I can show you the king's face," and drew a hundred coins from his purse and gave them to the peasant. On every coin the king's face was to be seen, of course. After the peasant had looked at each coin once, he said: "I have now seen the king's face a hundred times, and can tell you the answer to the riddle," and told him it.

The minister went in great glee to the king and said: "Your Majesty, I have found the answer to the riddle; it is so and so." The king exclaimed: "You can have heard it only from the peasant himself," had the peasant summoned, and took him to task. "Did you not promise me not to tell until you had seen my face a hundred times?"

"But, your Majesty," answered the peasant, "your minister showed me your picture a hundred times."

Then he showed him the bag of money that the minister had given him. The king was so pleased with the clever peasant that he rewarded him, and made him a rich man for the rest of his life.

BUCHETTINO

ONCE upon a time there was a child whose name was Buchettino. One morning his mamma called him and said: "Buchettino, will you do me a favour? Go and sweep the stairs." Buchettino, who was very obedient, did not wait to be told a second time, but went at once to sweep the stairs. All at once he heard a noise, and after looking all around, he found a penny. Then he said to himself: "What shall I do with this penny? I have half a mind to buy some dates . . . but no! for I should have to throw away the stones. I will buy some apples . . . no! I will not, for I should have to throw away the core. I will buy some nuts . . . but no, for I should have to throw away the shells! What shall I buy, then? I will buy—I will buy— enough! I will buy a pennyworth of figs," and went to eat them in a tree. While he was eating, the ogre passed by, and seeing Buchettino eating figs in the tree said:

> "Buchettino,
>   My dear Buchettino,
>   Give me a little fig
>   With your dear little hand,
>   If not I will eat you!"

Buchettino threw him one, but it fell in the dirt. Then the orge repeated:

> "Buchettino,
>   My dear Buchettino,
>   Give me a little fig
>   With your dear little hand,
>   If not I will eat you!"

Then Buchettino threw him another, which also fell in the dirt. The ogre said again:

> "Buchettino,
>   My dear Buchettino,
>   Give me a little fig
>   With your dear little hand,
>   If not I will eat you!"

Poor Buchettino, who did not see the trick, and did not know that the ogre was doing everything to get him into his net and eat him up, what does he do? he leans down and foolishly gives him a fig with his little hand. The ogre, who wanted nothing better, suddenly seized him by the arm and put him in his bag; then he took him on his back and started for home, crying with all his lungs:

> "Wife, my wife,
> Put the kettle on the fire,
> For I have caught Buchettino!
> Wife, my wife,
> Put the kettle on the fire,
> For I have caught Buchettino!"

When the ogre was near his house he put the bag on the ground, and went off to attend to something else. Buchettino, with a knife that he had in his pocket, cut the bag open in a trice, filled it with large stones, and then:

> "My legs, it is no shame
> To run away when there is need."

When the rascal of an ogre returned he picked up the bag, and scarcely had he arrived home when he said to his wife: "Tell me, my wife, have you put the kettle on the fire?" She answered at once: "Yes." "Then," said the ogre, "we will cook Buchettino; come here, help me!" And both taking the bag, they carried it to the hearth and were going to throw poor Buchettino into the kettle, but instead they found only the stones. Imagine how cheated the ogre was. He was so angry that he bit his hands. He could not swallow the trick played on him by Buchettino and swore to find him again and be revenged. So the next day he began to go all about the city and to look into all the hiding places. At last he happened to raise his eyes and saw Buchettino on a roof, ridiculing him and laughing so hard that his mouth extended from ear to ear. The ogre thought he should burst with rage, but he pretended not to see it and in a very sweet tone he said: "O Buchettino; just tell me, how did you manage to climb up there?"

Buchettino answered: "Do you really want to know? Then listen. I put dishes upon dishes, glasses upon glasses, pans upon pans, kettles upon kettles; afterward I climbed up on them and here I am." "Ah! is that so?" said the ogre; "wait a bit!" And quickly he took so many dishes, so many glasses, pans, kettles, and made a great mountain of them; then he began to climb up, to go and catch Buchettino. But when he was on the top—*brututum*—everything fell down; and that rascal of an ogre fell down on the stones and was cheated again.

Then Buchettino, well pleased, ran to his mamma, who put a piece of candy in his little mouth—See whether there is any more!

THE TRANSFORMATION DONKEY

THERE was once a poor chicory-seller; all chicory-sellers are poor, but this was a very poor one, and he had a large family of daughters and two sons. The daughters he left at home with their mother, but the two sons he took with him to gather chicory. While they were out gathering chicory one day, a great bird flew down before them and dropped an egg and then flew away again. The boys picked up the egg and brought it to their father, because there were some figures like strange writing on it which they could not read; but neither could the father read the strange writing, so he took the egg to a farmer. The farmer read the writing, and it said:

"Whoso eats my head, he shall be an emperor.
Whoso eats my heart, he shall never want for money."

"Ho, ho!" said the farmer to himself, "it won't do to tell the fellow this; I must manage to eat both the head and the heart myself." So he said, "The meaning of it is that whoever eats the bird will make a very good dinner; so to-morrow when the bird comes back, as she doubtless will to lay another egg, have a good stick ready and knock her down; then you can make a fire, and bake it between the stones, and I will come and eat it with you if you like."

The poor chicory-seller thought his fortune was made when a farmer offered to dine with him, and the hours seemed long enough till next morning came.

With next morning, however, came the bird again. The chicory-seller was ready with his stick and knocked her down, and the boys made a fire and cooked the bird. But as they were not very apt at the trussing and cooking, the head dropped into the fire, and the youngest boy said: "This will never do to serve up, all burnt as it is," so he ate it. The heart also fell into the fire and got burnt, and the eldest boy said: "This will never do to serve up, all burnt as it is"; so he ate that.

By-and-by the farmer came, and they all sat down on a bank—the farmer quite jovial at the idea of the immense advantage he was going to gain, and the chicory-seller quite elated at the idea of entertaining a farmer.

"Bring forward the roast, boys," said the father; and the boys brought the bird.

"What have you done with the head?" exclaimed the farmer, the moment he saw the bird.

"Oh, it got burnt, and I ate it," said the younger boy.

The farmer ground his teeth and stamped his foot, but he dared not say why he was angry; so he sat silent while the chicory-seller took out his knife and cut the bird in portions.

"Give me the piece with the heart, if I may choose," said the farmer; "I'm very fond of birds' hearts."

"Certainly, any part you like," replied the chicory-seller, nervously turning all the pieces over and over again; "but I can't find any heart. Boys, had the bird no heart?"

"Yes, papa," answered the elder brother, "it had a heart, sure enough; but it tumbled into the fire and got burnt, and so I ate it."

There was no object in disguising his fury any longer, so the farmer exclaimed testily, "Thank you, I'll not have any then; the head and the heart are just the only parts of a bird I care to eat." And so saying he turned on his heel and went away.

"Look, boys, what you've done! You've thrown away the best chance we ever had in our lives!" cried the father in despair. "After the farmer had taken dinner with us he must have asked us to dine with him, and, as one civility always brings another, there is no saying what it might not have led to. However, as you have chosen to throw the chance away, you may go and look out for yourselves. I've done with you." And with a sound cudgelling he drove them away.

The two boys, left to themselves, wandered on till they came to a stable, when they entered the yard and asked to be allowed to do some work or other as a means of subsistence.

"I've nothing for you to do," said the landlord; "but, as it's late, you may sleep on the straw there, on the condition that you go about your business to-morrow first thing."

The boys, glad to get a night's lodging on any condition, went to sleep in the straw. When the elder brother woke in the morning he found a box of sequins under his head.

"How could this have come here?" soliloquized the boy, "unless the host had put it there to see if we were honest? Well, thank God, if we're poor there's no danger of either of us taking what doesn't belong to us." So he took the box to the host, and said: "There's your box of sequins quite safe. You needn't have taken the trouble to test our honesty in that way."

The host was very much surprised, but he thought the best way was to take the money and say nothing but "I'm glad to see you're such good boys." So he gave them breakfast and some provisions for the way.

Next night they found themselves still in the open country and no inn near, and they were obliged to be content to sleep on the bare ground. Next morning when they woke the elder boy again found a box of sequins under his head.

"Only think of that host not being satisfied with trying us once, but to come all this way after us to test our honesty again. However, I suppose we must take it back to him."

So they walked all the way back to the host and said: "Here's your box of sequins back; as we didn't steal it the first time it was not likely we should take it the second time."

The host was more and more astonished but he took the money without saying anything, only he praised the boys for being so good and gave them a hearty meal. And they went their way, taking a new direction.

The next night, the younger brother said: "Do you know I've my doubts about the host having put that box of sequins under your head? How could he have done it out in the open country without our seeing him? To-night I will watch, and if he doesn't come, and in the morning there is another box of sequins, it will be a sign that it is your own."

He did so, and the next morning there was another box of sequins. So they decided it was honestly their own, and they carried it by turns and journeyed on. About noon they came to a great city where the emperor was lately dead, and all the people were in great excitement about choosing another emperor. The population was all divided in factions, each of which had a candidate, and none would let the candidate of the others reign. There was so much fighting and quarrelling in the streets that the brothers got separated, and saw each other no more.

At this time it happened that it was the turn of the younger brother to be carrying the box of sequins. When the sentinels at the gate saw a stranger coming in carrying a box they said, "We must see what this is," and they took him to the minister. When the minister saw his box was full of sequins, he said, "This must be our emperor." And all the people said, "Yes, this is our emperor. Long live our emperor!" And thus the boy became emperor.

But the elder brother had entered unperceived into the town, and went to ask hospitality in a house where was a woman with a beautiful daughter; so they let him stay. That night also there came a box of sequins under his head; so he went out and bought meat and fuel and all manner of provisions, and gave them to the mother, and said, "Because you took me in when I was poor last night, I have bought you all these provisions out of gratitude," and for the beautiful daughter he bought silks and damasks, and ornaments of gold. But the daughter said, "How comes it, tell me, that you, who were a poor footsore wayfarer last night, have now such boundless riches at command?"

And because she was beautiful and spoke kindly to him, he suspected no evil, but told her, saying, "Every morning when I wake now, I find a box of sequins under my head."

"And how comes it," said she, "that you find a box of sequins under your head now, and not formerly?" "I do not know," he answered, "unless it be because one day when I was out with father gathering chicory, a great bird came and dropt an egg with some strange writing on it, which we could not read. But a farmer read it for us; only he would not tell us what it said, but that we should cook the bird and eat it. While we were cooking it the heart fell into the fire and got burnt, and I ate it; and when the farmer heard this he grew very angry. I think, therefore, the writing on the egg said that he who ate the heart of the bird should have many sequins."

After this they spent the day pleasantly together; but the daughter put an emetic in his wine at supper, and so made him bring up the bird's heart, which she kept for herself, and the next morning when he woke there was no box of sequins under his head, When he rose in the morning, also, the beautiful girl and her mother turned him out of the house, and he wandered forth again.

At last, being weary and full of sorrow, he sat down on the ground by the side of a stream, crying. Immediately three fairies appeared to him and asked him why he wept. And when he told them, they said to him: "Weep no more, for instead of the bird's heart we give you this sheepskin jacket, the pockets of which will always be full of sequins. How many soever you may take out they will always remain full." Then they disappeared; but he immediately went back to the house of the beautiful girl, taking her rich and fine presents; but she said to him, "How comes it that you, who had no money left when you went away, have now the means to buy all these fine presents?"

Then he told her of the gift of the three fairies, and they let him sleep in the house again, but the daughter called her maid to her and said: "Make a sheepskin jacket exactly like that in the stranger's room." So she made one, and they put it in his room, and took away the one the fairies had given him, and in the morning they drove him from the house again. Then he went and sat down by the stream and wept again; but the fairies came and asked him why he wept; and he told them, saying, "Because they have driven me away from the house where I stayed, and I have no home to go to, and this jacket has no more sequins in the pockets." Then the fairies looked at the jacket, and they said, "This is not the jacket we gave you; it has been changed by fraud"; so they gave him in place of it a wand, and they said, "With this wand strike the table, and whatever you may desire, be it meat or drink or clothes, or whatsoever you may want, it shall come upon the table." The next day he went back to the house of the woman and her daughter, and sat down without saying anything, but he struck the table with his wand, wishing for a great banquet, and immediately it was covered with the choicest dishes. There was no need to ask him questions this time, for they saw in what his gift consisted, and in the night, when he was asleep, they took his wand away. In the morning they drove him forth out of the house, and he went back to the stream and sat down to cry. Again the fairies appeared to him and comforted him; but they said, "This is the last time we may appear to you. Here is a ring; keep it on your hand; for if you lose this gift there is nothing more we may do for you"; and they went away. But he immediately returned to the house of the woman and her beautiful daughter. They let him in, "Because," they said, "doubtless the fairies have given him some other gift of which we may take profit." And as he sat there he said, "All the other gifts of the fairies have I lost; but this one they have given me now I cannot lose, because it is a ring which fits my finger, and no one can take it from my hand."

"And of what use is your ring?" asked the beautiful daughter.

"Its use is that whatever I wish for while I have it on I obtain directly, whatever it may be."

"Then wish," said she, "that we may be both together on the top of that high mountain, and a sumptuous *merenda* [1] spread out for us."

"To be sure!" he replied, and he repeated her wish. Instantly they found themselves on the top of the high mountain with a plentiful *merenda* before them; but she had a vial of opium with her, and while his head was turned away she poured the opium into his wine. Presently after this he fell into a sound sleep, so sound that there was no fear of waking him. Immediately she took the ring from his finger and put it on her own; then she wished that she might be replaced at home and that he might be left on the top of the mountain. And so it was done.

In the morning when he woke and found himself all alone on the top of the high mountain and his ring gone, he wept bitter tears, and felt too weary to attempt the descent of the steep mountainside. For three days he remained here weary and weeping, and then, becoming faint from hunger, he took some of the herbs that grew on the mountain top for food. As soon as he had eaten these he was turned into a donkey, but as he retained his human intelligence, he said to himself, this herb has its uses, and he filled one of the panniers on his back with it. Then he came down from the mountain, and when he was at the foot of it, being hungry with the long journey, he ate of the grass that grew there, and, behold! he was transformed back into his natural shape; so he filled the other basket with this kind of grass and went his way. Having dressed himself like a street seller, he took the basket of the herb which had the property of changing the eater into a donkey, and stood under the window of the house where he had been so evil entreated, and cried, "Fine salad! fine salad! who will buy my fine salad?"

"What is there so specially good about your salad?" asked the maid, looking out. "My young mistress is particularly fond of salad, so if yours is so very superfine, you had better come up."

He did not wait to be twice told. As soon as he saw the beautiful daughter, he said, "This is fine salad, indeed, the finest of the fine, all fresh gathered, and the first of its kind that ever was sold."

"Very likely it's the first of its kind that ever was sold," said she; "but I don't like to buy things I haven't tried; it may turn out not to be nice."

"Oh, try it, try it freely; don't buy without trying"; and he picked one of the freshest and crispest bunches.

She took one in her hand and bit a few blades, and no sooner had she done so than she too became a donkey. Then he put the panniers on her back and drove her all over the town, constantly cudgelling her till she sank under the blows.

Then one who saw him belabour her thus, said, "This must not be; you must

---

[1] Meal

come and answer before the emperor for thus belabouring the poor brute"; but he refused to go unless he took the donkey with him; so they went to the emperor and said, "Here is one who is belabouring his donkey till she has sunk under his blows, and he refuses to come before the emperor to answer his cruelty unless he bring his donkey with him." And the emperor made answer, "Let him bring the beast with him."

So they brought him and his donkey before the emperor. When he found himself before the emperor he said, "All these must go away; to the emperor alone can I tell why I belabour my donkey." So the emperor commanded all the people to go to a distance while he took him and his donkey apart. As soon as he found himself alone with the emperor he said, "See, it is I, thy brother!" and he embraced him. Then he told him all that had befallen him since they parted. Then said the emperor to the donkey, "Go now with him home, and show him where thou hast laid all the things—the bird's heart, the sheepskin jacket, the wand, and the ring, that he may bring them hither; and if thou deliver them up faithfully I will command that he give thee of that grass to eat which shall give thee back thy natural form."

So they went back to the house and fetched all the things, and the emperor said, "Come thou now and live with me, and give me of thy sequins, and I will share my empire with thee." Thus they reigned together.

But to the donkey they gave of the grass to eat, which restored her natural form, only that her beauty was marred by the cudgelling she had received. And she said, "Had I not been so wilful and malicious I had now been empress."

THE BOOBY

THEY say there was once a widow woman who had a very simple son. Whatever she set him to do he muddled in some way or other.

"What am I to do?" said the poor mother to a neighbour one day. "The boy eats and drinks, and has to be clothed; what am I to do if I am to make no profit of him?"

"You have kept him at home long enough," answered the neighbour. "Try sending him out, now; maybe that will answer better."

The mother took the advice, and the next time she had got a piece of linen spun she called her boy, and said to him:

"If I send you out to sell this piece of linen, do you think you can manage to do it without committing any folly?"

"Yes, mama," answered the booby.

"You always say, 'Yes, mama,' but you do contrive to muddle every thing all the same," replied the mother. "Now, listen attentively to all I say. Walk straight along the road without turning to right or left; don't take less than such and such a price for it. Don't have anything to say to women who chatter; whether you sell it to anyone you meet by the way, or carry it into the market, offer it only to some quiet sort of body whom you may see standing apart, and not gossiping and prating, for such as they will persuade you to take some sort of a price that won't suit me at all."

The booby promised to follow these directions very exactly, and started on his way.

On he walked, turning neither to the right hand nor to the left, thus passing the turnings which led to the villages, to one or other of which he ought to have gone. But his mother had only meant that he was not to turn off the pathway and lose himself.

Presently he met the wife of the syndic of the next town, who was driving out with her maids, but had got out to walk a little stretch of the way, as the day was fine. The syndic's wife was talking cheerfully with her maids, and when one of them caught sight of the simpleton, she said to her mistress:

"Here is the simple son of the poor widow by the brook."

"What are you going to do, my lad?" said the syndic's wife kindly.

"Not going to tell you, because you were chattering and gossiping," replied the booby boorishly, and tried to pass on.

The syndic's wife forgave his boorishness, and added:

"I see your mother has sent you to sell this piece of linen. I will buy it of you, and that will save you walking further; put it in the carriage, and I'll give you so much for it."

Though she had offered him twice as much as his mother had told him to get for it, he would only answer:

"Can't sell it to you, because you were chattering and gossiping."

Nor could they prevail on him to stop a minute longer.

Further along he came to a statue by the roadside. "Here's one who stands apart and doesn't chatter," said the booby to himself. "This is the one to sell the linen to." Then aloud to the statue, "Will you buy my linen, good friend?" Then to himself, "She doesn't speak, so it's all right." Then to the statue, "The price is so-and-so; have the money ready against I come back, as I have to go on and buy some yarn for mother."

On he went and bought the yarn, and then came back to the statue. Some one passing by meanwhile, and seeing the linen lie there had picked it up and walked off with it. Finding it gone, the booby said to himself, "It's all right, she's taken it." Then to the statue, "Where's the money I told you to have ready against I came back?" As the statue remained silent, the booby began to get uneasy. "My mother *will* be finely angry if I go back without the linen or the money," he said to himself. Then to the statue, "If you don't give me the money directly I'll hit you on the head."

The booby was as good as his word; lifting his thick rough walking stick, he gave the statue such a blow that he knocked the head off.

But the statue was hollow, and filled with gold coin.

"That's where you keep your money, is it?" said the booby. "All right, I can pay myself." So he filled his pockets with money and went back to his mother.

"Look, mama! here's the price of the piece of linen."

"All right," said the mother out loud; but to herself she said, "Where can I ever hide all this lot of money? I have got no place to hide it but in this earthen jar, and if he knows how much it is worth, he will be letting out the secret to other people, and I shall be robbed." So she put the money in the earthen jar, and said to the boy:

"They've cheated you in making you think that was coin; it's nothing but a lot of rusty nails; but never mind, you'll know better next time." And she went out to her work.

While she was gone out to her work there came by an old rag-merchant.

"Ho! here, rag-merchant!" said the booby, who had acquired a taste for trading. "What will you give me for this lot of rusty nails!" and he showed him the jar full of gold coin.

The rag-merchant saw that he had to do with an idiot, so he said:

"Well, old nails are not worth very much; but as I'm a good-natured old chap, I'll give you twelve pauls for them," because he knew he must offer enough to seem a prize to the idiot.

"You may have them at that," said the booby.

And the rag-merchant poured the coin out into his sack, and gave the fool the twelve pauls.

"Look, mama, look! I've sold that lot of old rusty worthless nails for twelve pauls. Isn't that a good bargain?"

"Sold them for twelve pauls!" cried the widow, tearing her hair; "why, it was a fortune all in gold coin."

"Can't help it, mama," replied the booby; "you told me they were rusty nails."

Another day she told him to shut the door of the cottage; but as he went to do it he lifted the door off its hinges. His mother called after him in an angry voice, which so frightened him that he ran away, carrying the door on his back.

As he went along, some one to tease him said, 'Where did you steal that door?" which frightened him still more, and he climbed up in a tree with it to hide it.

At night there came a band of robbers under the tree, and counted out all their gains in large bags of money. The booby was so frightened at the sight of so many fierce-looking robbers, that he began to tremble and let go of the door. The door fell with a bang in the midst of the robbers, who, thinking it must be that the police were upon them, decamped, leaving all their money behind.

The booby came down from the tree and carried the money home to his mother, and they became so rich that she was able to appoint a servant to attend to him, and keep him from doing any more mischief.

THE GREEDY DAUGHTER

THERE was a mother who had a daughter so greedy that she did not know what to do with her. Everything in the house she would eat up. When the poor mother came home from work there was nothing left.

But the girl had a godfather-wolf. The wolf had a frying-pan, and the girl's mother was too poor to possess such an article; whenever she wanted to fry anything she sent her daughter to the wolf to borrow his frying-pan, and he always sent a nice omelette in it by way of not sending it empty. But the girl was so greedy and so selfish that she not only always ate the omelette by the way, but when she took the frying-pan back she filled it with all manner of nasty things.

At last the wolf got hurt at this way of going on, and he came to the house to inquire into the matter.

Godfather-wolf met the mother on the step of the door, returning from work.

"How do you like my omelettes?" asked the wolf.

"I am sure they would be good if made by our godfather-wolf," replied the poor woman, "but I never had the honour of tasting them."

"Never tasted them! Why, how many times have you sent to borrow my frying-pan?"

"I am ashamed to say how many times; a great many, certainly."

"And every time I sent you an omelette in it."

"Never one reached me."

"Then that hussy of a girl must have eaten them by the way."

The poor mother, anxious to screen her daughter, burst into all manner of excuses, but the wolf now saw how it all was. To make sure, however, he added: "The omelettes would have been better had the frying-pan not always been full of such nasty things. I did my best always to clean it, but it was not easy."

"Oh, godfather-wolf, you are joking! I always cleaned it, inside and out, as bright as silver, every time before I sent it back!"

The wolf now knew all, and he said no more to the mother; but the next day, when she was out, he came back.

When the girl saw him coming she was so frightened that she ran under the bed to hide herself. But to the wolf it was as easy to go under a bed as anywhere else; so under he went, and he dragged her out and devoured her. And that was the end of the Greedy Daughter.

JAPAN

THE literature of Japan is somewhat meagre when compared with that of many European countries. The folk-tales are pleasingly picturesque and quaint, though there is nothing startlingly new in them. In "Visu" and "Urashima Taro" one sees the Rip Van Winkle of Japan. Compare these also with the Korean story, "The Woodman and the Mountain Fairies." Probably the best story of this type is to be found in gipsy folk-lore under the title "The Red King Witch."

URASHIMA TARO

MANY hundreds of years ago, in a village on the craggy sea-coast of Japan, there dwelt a fisher-lad whose name was Urashima Taro. Of all the fishermen in the village he was the most skilful with his line and net, and he was also the kindest hearted. If one of his comrades had bad luck when his own was good, he always shared his "catch" with him. And he could not bear to see any creature, however lowly, tormented or hurt.

One fine evening, when Urashima was on his way home to his father's little cottage, he came upon a group of mischievous boys teasing an unlucky tortoise. One boy cast pebbles at its shell, another rapped it with a stick, a third tried to poke twigs inside. The sight made Urashima very angry.

"You cruel children," he said, "what evil has the poor thing done? Do you not know that unless you put it back into the sea it will die?"

"What then?" cried the bad boys. "It is only a silly old tortoise. It may die if it pleases. *We* do not care."

"Will you not give your tortoise to me?" asked Urashima.

"No, we will not," returned the bad boys. "It is *ours*. We want it." Now Urashima had in his hand a small stock of money, slung on a string through the hole left for that purpose in the centre of each coin. It was his earnings for an entire week, hard-won with many hours of patient labour.

"Listen to me, boys," said Urashima, "if you will not *give* me your tortoise, perhaps you will *sell* it." And he jingled the string of coins before their eyes. The bad boys hesitated.

"Think," urged Urashima, "what a lot of things you could buy with this money—much better playthings than a poor tortoise."

"There is some truth in what Urashima Taro says," remarked the ringleader. "Let us take the money and give him the tortoise."

So they took Urashima's little store of coin, and ran off, laughing and jumping, and the fisher-lad was left alone with his purchase.

447

"Poor old fellow," said Urashima, stroking the hard, tawny-coloured shell, "I wonder if it is true that you tortoises live for a thousand years. Perhaps you are still young, and may have nine hundred and ninety years of life before you still. Anyhow, I am going to put you back into the sea. And I advise you, as a friend, not to allow yourself to get caught again!"

Then Urashima lifted the tortoise in his arms, went down to the beach, and let it slide softly into the water.

Next day the lad was early astir. He knew that he would have to work extra hard in order to make up for the money he had given the bad boys; all his earnings for a whole week had gone. The sea was as smooth as glass, and reflected the lovely turquoise colour of the cloudless sky. Urashima's slender boat drifted rapidly along, and soon left the craft of the other fishermen far behind.

Presently he heard a soft voice calling him by name.

"Urashima Taro—Urashima!"

Urashima stood up in the boat and shaded his eyes with his hand, but there was no human creature in sight.

"Urashima!" called the voice again.

It came from the sea. Looking down, he saw a tortoise swimming alongside his boat, and he thought it seemed remarkably like the one which he had befriended the day before.

"Honourable Mr. Tortoise," said Urashima, politely, "was it you who called me just now?"

"Yes," replied the tortoise, "do you not remember me? I have come to thank you for your kindness to me yesterday."

"That is very good of you," said Urashima. "Would you care to come into my boat and bask in the sun for a while? I know that you tortoises love to do that."

"Many thanks," responded the tortoise, and Urashima helped it to climb aboard.

Presently his queer passenger began to talk again.

"Have you ever seen the Rin-Gin, the palace of the Dragon-King, Urashima?"

Urashima shook his head. "All we fishermen have heard of that palace, but none of us has ever beheld it."

"If it would interest you to see it," said the tortoise, "I can show you the way thither."

"It would interest me very much," answered Urashima, "but I am only a human being. I could not swim anything like as far as you could."

"*Swim?*" repeated the tortoise. "But why should you *swim?* I can carry you on my back with ease."

"Perhaps I am heavier than you think," hinted the fisher-lad, who was afraid that if he were to say, "You are too small to carry me," he might hurt the feelings of his new friend.

"Not a bit of it," returned the tortoise, clambering over the edge of the boat and slipping down into the bright blue water. "Try and see! Perhaps I am larger than *you* think, honourable Mr. Urashima!"

Urashima looked, and it certainly seemed that the tortoise had grown much bigger since it went back into the sea.

"Come on," urged the tortoise.

"All right!" said Urashima Taro.

He jumped upon the tortoise's back, and away the creature swam, carrying him as easily as if he had been a baby.

"Honourable Mr. Tortoise," said Urashima presently, "I hope you are not going to dive, for if you do, I shall be drowned.

"I *am* going to dive," returned the tortoise, "but you are *not* going to be drowned."

And down, down, down it went, through the clear blue water.

To his astonishment Urashima found that he could breathe quite as well under the sea as above it. Fishes, great and small, of a thousand gorgeous colours and quaint forms, swam over his head as birds fly on dry land, and lovely starry anemones, and delicately fringed seaweeds, grew like flowers on the bed of the sea.

Presently, far off, Urashima saw a great gateway, and beyond that the roofs of some magnificent buildings, all glittering with brilliant green and blue tiles.

"We shall soon be there," remarked the tortoise, swimming faster than ever.

A few moments later the creature halted outside the great gateway, and the porter, who was a large and splendid-looking fish, opened the gate.

"This is the honourable Mr. Urashima Taro, from the land of Japan," explained the tortoise. "He has come to visit the Rin-Gin, the palace of the Dragon-King of the Sea.

"He is very welcome," said the fish.

Urashima now descended from the tortoise's back and the fish, floating slowly before him, led the way into the palace.

No words could possibly describe the beauty of that great palace in the depths of the sea. It was built of green and blue jewels, of coral and beryl, sapphire and pearl. Round it were wide gardens which reminded Urashima of the gardens of his own Japan, for maples and firs and plum and cherry-trees grew there, and wistaria climbed over arches, and little bridges of red lacquer spanned tiny torrents of foaming grey water.

In the eastern part of the garden it was always spring, and the fruit-trees were gay with unfading blossom. To the south was perpetual summer. To the west lay the autumn garden, where the maples were ruddy-golden and the chrysanthe-mums shone like fire. To the north was the realm of winter, and there the fir-trees were white with snow, and the torrents under the little bridges were frozen into long icicles as they fell.

All these marvels and glories took Urashima's breath away. But there remained one far beyond all the rest, and that was the lady Otohimé, the daughter of the Dragon-King of the Sea. When she approached Urashima he fell upon his knees, and bowed his head upon the sand, for never had he dreamt that any being could be so beautiful. Her robes were of green silk shot through with threads of silver and gold, and her long, fine black hair hung like a great mantle upon her shoulders.

"Welcome and greeting, Urashima Taro," said the lady Otohimé.

"Most humbly do I thank your honourable ladyship," stammered Urashima, not daring to raise his head.

"It is *I* who must thank *you*, Urashima Taro," returned the lady Otohimé. "Listen, and you shall learn why. Once a year, as we immortals reckon years, it is the will of my father, the Dragon-King of the Sea, that I should assume the form of some sea-creature, and allow myself to be caught by some mortal's net or snare. If that mortal be merciful, great is his reward. But if he be cruel, his punishment also is great. Urashima Taro, arise. Fear nothing, my friend. I was that tortoise whom you delivered from the hands of the cruel children who would have made me suffer much pain."

So Urashima arose, and he and the lady Otohimé went forth into the garden where it was always spring. And fish-servants brought them rice, and *saké* in cups of pearl, and fish-minstrels made music for them under the blossoming trees. Urashima found favour in the eyes of the lady Otohimé. She sought leave of her father, the Dragon-King of the Sea, to take the fisher-lad for her husband. And so they were married, and even in the Rin-Gin, the sea-palace of many marvels, such rejoicings were never known as the rejoicings at the wedding of Urashima Taro and the beautiful daughter of the Dragon-King.

Urashima was very happy with his royal bride in the depths of the sea, and for a long time he forgot all about his father and mother, and his old home on the craggy coast of Japan. Then, one day, the lady Otohimé noticed that her husband was looking thoughtful and sad.

"What ails you, Urashima Taro?" she asked.

"I have just remembered," said Urashima, "that far away, in the land of the mortals whence I come, I have a father and a mother. They are old. Unless I make haste, perchance I may never see them again. Surely they have wept for me, thinking that I had left them never to return."

"Alas, Urashima," cried the lady Otohimé, "have you ceased to love me? Are you no longer happy in the Rin-Gin?"

"No," said Urashima, sorrowfully, "I have not ceased to love your honourable ladyship. But I cannot be happy until I have beheld my father and my mother again. I am ashamed that I should have forgotten them so long. Let me go to them, even if it be but for one day. Then I will return."

Then the lady Otohimé wept bitter tears. "If you wish to depart," she told him, "I cannot keep you here. Go, then. But take with you this casket, lest I, too, should be forgotten." With these words she placed in Urashima's hands a little box of golden lacquer tied tightly round with a cord and tassels of scarlet silk. "This casket," said the lady Otohimé, "holds something very precious and very rare. Take it with you, my husband, wherever you go. But remember, you must not open it. For if you do, great evil will befall you."

Urashima Taro promised that nothing would ever persuade him to open the golden lacquer box. He bade farewell very sadly to the lady Otohimé, cast a last regretful glance at the gardens of the four seasons, and then went down to the great gateway at which he had arrived, and where he found a tortoise waiting to bear him whence he had come.

The tortoise swam steadily, on and on, till at last the blue peaks of Japan arose upon the horizon. Urashima's heart began to beat faster. He recognized the coastline, the fir-woods and the craggy shore. Soon he would see his old home again, and kneel down before his father and mother, imploring their forgiveness.

He jumped off the tortoise's back in his impatience and waded ashore. Coming toward him was an aged man whom he took for his father. A moment later Urashima realized his mistake. Then he ran in the direction where his father's house had stood.

What a change! The little hut had vanished, and a much larger house, with purple iris-flowers growing between the roof-tiles, occupied its place.

"Surely my family has grown rich in my absence," thought Urashima.

A man came out of the house, and Urashima approached him politely.

"Honourable Sir, can you tell me whether the parents of Urashima Taro the fisherman still live in this house?"

The man stared at him in amazement. "Who may *you* be, Mr. Stranger?" he asked.

"I am Urashima Taro."

The man burst out laughing at this. "You! Why, he has been dead for more than three hundred years, Urashima Taro!"

"Pardon me," said Urashima, "I am he. I have been absent for some time—I do not know exactly how long—perhaps one year, perhaps two—but I have returned because I am anxious to see my aged parents again before they die."

"If you are really Urashima Taro you have arrived three hundred years too late," returned the man. "Why, the house where he lived was pulled down in my great-grandfather's time, and even *then* it was many years since that fisher-lad vanished one fine morning. Either you are joking or you are a ghost."

"I am *not* a ghost," cried Urashima, stamping on the ground. "You know that ghosts have no feet! I am as much alive as you are—I am Urashima Taro!"

"Urashima Taro lived three hundred years ago," retorted the man. "It is all written in the village records, which are kept in the temple. Why do you repeat such a foolish jest?"

Feeling sick with fear and disappointment, Urashima continued his walk along the sea-shore. At every step he saw changes which showed only too plainly that the man had spoken truly, and that not one year, or two, but three centuries had come and gone since he last beheld that place.

"Every one whom I knew and loved in the land of the mortals has long been dead," thought Urashima, sadly; "why should I tarry here? I must go back as quickly as I can to the beautiful land of the immortals, and to my wife, the lady Otohimé.." He walked down to the edge of the sea and gazed anxiously across the waves. The tortoise which had brought him from the Rin-Gin had vanished. How was he to find his way back to the realm of the Dragon-King again?

Urashima sat down on a rock and buried his head in his hands. What could he do? He was alone in a strange, unfriendly world, and his only possession was the golden lacquer casket which he had promised that he would not open. He took it on his knee, and looked wistfully at the scarlet cords which had been knotted by the hands of the lady Otohimé.

"Surely," he said to himself, "if I break my vow, she will forgive me. Surely if I untie these cords, and open the lid, I shall find something that will tell me how to win my way back to her again!"

So Urashima set the casket upon the ground, and untied the scarlet cords, and lifted the lid. The casket was empty! Only there seemed to waft from it a faint purple cloud, which hovered over his head for a moment and then rose into the air and floated away across the sea.

Till that moment Urashima Taro had looked just as he did when he left Japan three hundred years before, a strong, dark-haired, well-built lad of twenty-one. But as he stood watching the purple cloud fading and receding, a great change came over him. His bright eyes grew dim, his black locks turned white, his sturdy limbs became suddenly withered and, bent. Then, with a cry of despair, he fell upon his knees, with his face against the ground.

Next morning some fishermen going down to the sea with their nets found an aged man lying dead beside a casket of golden lacquer. They peeped into the casket, but there was nothing inside.

"Is this the same man who spoke to you yesterday?" one of the fisher men asked the other.

"Oh, no," answered his comrade, "he was a sturdy young fellow, he who tried to make me believe that he was Urashima Taro".

THE MAIDEN WITH THE WOODEN BOWL

THE MAIDEN WITH THE WOODEN BOWL

IN ancient days there lived an old couple with their only child, a girl of remarkable charm and beauty. When the old man fell sick and died his widow became more and more concerned for her daughter's future welfare.

One day she called her child to her, and said: "Little one, your father lies in yonder cemetery, and I, being old and feeble, must needs follow him soon. The thought of leaving you alone in the world troubles me much, for you are beautiful and beauty is a temptation and a snare to men. Not all the purity of a white flower can prevent it from being plucked and dragged down in the mire. My child, your face is all too fair. It must be hidden from the eager eyes of men, lest it cause you to fall from your good and simple life to one of shame."

Having said these words, she placed a lacquered bowl upon the maiden's head, so that it veiled her attractions. "Always wear it, little one," said the mother, "for it will protect you when I am gone."

Shortly after this loving deed had been performed the old woman died, and the maiden was forced to earn her living by working in the rice-fields. It was hard weary work, but the girl kept a brave heart and toiled from dawn to sunset without a murmur. Over and over again her strange appearance created considerable comment, and she was known throughout the land as the "Maiden with the Bowl on her Head." Young men laughed at her and tried to peep under the vessel, and not a few endeavoured to pull off the wooden covering; but it could not be removed, and laughing and jesting, the young men had to be content with a glimpse of the lower part of the fair maiden's face. The poor girl bore this rude treatment with a patient but heavy heart.

One day a rich farmer watched the maiden working in his rice-fields. He was struck by her diligence and the quick and excellent way she performed her tasks. He was pleased with that bent and busy little figure, and did not laugh at the wooden bowl on her head. After observing her for some time, he came to the maiden, and said: "You work well and do not chatter to your companions. I wish you to labour in my rice-fields until the end of the harvest."

When the rice harvest had been gathered and winter had come the wealthy farmer, still more favourably impressed with the maiden, and anxious to do her a service, bade her become an inmate of his house. "My wife is ill," he added, "and I should like you to nurse her for me."

The maiden gratefully accepted this welcome offer. She tended the sick woman with every care. As the farmer and his wife had no daughter they took very kindly to this orphan and regarded her as a child of their own.

At length the farmer's eldest son returned to his old home. He was a wise young man who had studied much in gay Kyoto, and was weary of a merry life of feasting and pleasure.

One day the young man came to his father and said: "Who is this maiden in our house, and why does she wear an ugly black bowl upon her head?"

The farmer told the sad story of the maiden, and as the days went by the son grew more and more fond of her, and resolved he would marry the Maiden with the Bowl on her Head. His friends and relations bade him beware lest she should turn out to be ugly and not beautiful. Many spiteful things were said to her, but the young man loved her the more, and at length asked her to marry him. "No," replied the poor maiden, weeping bitterly, "I cannot marry you, I am but a servant in your father's house," and in spite of all his pleadings she would not change her mind.

That night the poor girl cried herself to sleep, and in a dream her mother came to her, and said: "My dear child, let your good heart be troubled no more. Marry the farmer's son and all will be well again."

The Maiden woke next morning full of joy, and when her lover came to her and asked once more if she would be his bride, she consented.

When all plans had been made for the wedding it was thought high time to remove the maiden's wooden bowl. She herself tried to take it off, but it remained firmly fixed to her head. When some of the relations tried to do so, the bowl uttered strange cries and groans. At length the bridegroom said, "Do not trouble about it. You are just as dear to me with or without the bowl." And he ordered the wedding feast to proceed.

Then the wine cups were brought into the crowded hall and the bride and bridegroom were expected to drink together the "Three times three" in token of their marriage. Just as the maiden put the wine-cup to her lips the bowl on her head broke with a great noise, and from it fell gold and silver and all manner of precious stones, so that the maiden who had once been a beggar, now was rich. The guests were amazed as they looked upon the heap of shining jewels and gold and silver, but they were still more surprised when they chanced to look up and see that the bride was the most beautiful woman in all Japan.

THE JELLY-FISH AND THE MONKEY

RIN-JIN, the King of the Sea, took to wife a young and beautiful Dragon Princess. They had not been married long when the fair Queen fell ill, and all the advice and attention of the great physicians availed nothing.

"Oh," sobbed the Queen, "there is only one thing that will cure me of my illness!"

"What is that?" inquired Rin-Jin.

"If I eat the liver of a live monkey I shall immediately recover. Pray get me a monkey's liver, for I know that nothing else will save my life."

So Rin-Jin called a jelly-fish to his side, and said: "I want you to swim to the land and return with a live monkey on your back, for I wish to use his liver that our Queen may be restored to health again. You are the only creature who can perform this task, for you alone have legs and are able to walk about on shore.

"In order to induce the monkey to come you must tell him of the wonders of the deep and of the rare beauties of my great palace with its floor of pearl and its walls of coral."

The jelly-fish, delighted to think that the health and happiness of his mistress depended upon the success of his enterprise, lost no time in swimming to an island. He had no sooner stepped on shore than he observed a fine-looking monkey playing about in the branches of a pine-tree.

"Hello!" said the jelly-fish, "I don't think much of this island. What a dull and miserable life you must lead here! I come from the Kingdom of the Sea, where Rin-Jin reigns in a palace of great size and beauty. It may be that you would like to see a new country where there is plenty of fruit and where the weather is always fine. If so, get on my back, and I shall have much pleasure in taking you to the Kingdom of the Sea."

"I shall be delighted to accept your invitation," said the monkey, as he got down from the tree and comfortably seated himself on the thick shell the jelly-fish.

"By the way," said the jelly-fish, when he had accomplished about half of the return journey, "I suppose you have brought your liver with you, haven't you?"

"What a personal question!" replied the monkey. "Why do you ask?"

"Our Sea Queen is dangerously ill," said the foolish jelly-fish, "and only the liver of a live monkey will save her life. When we reach the palace a doctor will make use of your liver and my mistress will be restored to health again."

"Dear me!" exclaimed the monkey, "I wish you had mentioned this matter to me before we left the island."

"If I had done so," replied the jelly-fish, "you would most certainly have refused my invitation."

"Believe me, you are quite mistaken, my dear jelly-fish. I have several livers hanging up on a pine-tree, and I would gladly have spared one in order to save the life of your Queen. If you will bring me back to the island again I will get it. It was most unfortunate that I should have forgotten to bring a liver with me."

So the credulous jelly-fish turned round and swam back to the island. Directly the jelly-fish reached the shore the monkey sprang from his back and danced about on the branches of a tree.

"Liver?" said the monkey, chuckling, "did you say *liver?* You silly old jelly-fish, you'll certainly never get mine!"

The jelly-fish at length reached the palace, and told Rin-Jin his dismal tale. The Sea King fell into a great passion. "Beat him to a jelly!" he cried to those about him. "Beat this stupid fellow till he hasn't a bone left in his body!"

So the jelly-fish lost his shell from that unfortunate hour, and all the jelly-fishes that were born in the sea after his death were also without shells, and have remained nothing but jelly to this day.

ROBE OF FEATHERS

IT was spring-time, and along Mio's pine-clad shore there came a sound of birds. The blue sea danced and sparkled in the sunshine, and Hairukoo, a fisherman, sat down to enjoy the scene. As he did so he chanced to see, hanging on a pine-tree, a beautiful robe of pure white feathers.

As Hairukoo was about to take down the robe he saw coming toward him from the sea an extremely lovely maiden, who requested that the fisherman would restore the robe to her.

Hairukoo gazed upon the lady with considerable admiration. Said he: "I found this robe, and I mean to keep it, for it is a marvel to be placed among the treasures of Japan. No, I cannot possibly give it to you."

"Oh," cried the maiden pitifully, "I cannot go soaring into the sky without my robe of feathers, for if you persist in keeping it I can never more return to my celestial home. Oh, good fisherman, I beg of you to restore my robe!"

The fisherman, who must have been a hard-hearted fellow, refused to relent. "The more you plead," said he, "the more determined I am to keep what I have found."

Thus the maiden made answer:

> "Speak not, dear fisherman! speak not that word!
> Ah! know'st thou not that, like the hapless bird
> Whose wings are broke, I seek, but seek in vain,
> Reft of my wings, to soar to heav'n's blue plain?" [1]

After further argument on the subject the fisherman's heart softened a little. "I will restore your robe of feathers," said he, "if you will at once dance before me."

Then the maiden replied: "I will dance it here—the dance that makes the Palace of the Moon turn round, so that even poor transitory man may learn its mysteries. But I cannot dance without my feathers."

"No," said the fisherman suspiciously. "If I give you this robe you will fly away without dancing before me."

This remark made the maiden extremely angry.

"The pledge of mortals may be broken," said she, "but there is no falsehood among the Heavenly Beings."

---

[1] Translated by B.H. Chamberlain.

KOREA

PIGLING AND HER PROUD SISTER

PEAR BLOSSOM had been the name of a little Korean maid who was suddenly left motherless. When her father, Kang Wa, who was a magistrate high in office, married again, he took for his wife a proud widow whose daughter, born to Kang Wa, was named Violet. Mother and daughter hated housework and made Pear Blossom clean the rice, cook the food and attend to the fire in the kitchen. They were hateful in their treatment of Pear Blossom, and, besides never speaking a kind word, called her Pigling, or Little Pig, which made the girl weep often. It did no good to complain to her father, for he was always busy. He smoked his yard-long pipe and played checkers hour by hour, apparently caring more about having his great white coat properly starched and lustred than for his daughter to be happy. His linen had to be beaten with a laundry club until it glistened like hoar frost, and, except his wide-brimmed black horsehair hat, he looked immaculately white when he went out of the house to the Government office.

Poor Pigling had to perform this task of washing, starching, and glossing, in addition to the kitchen work, and the rat-tat-tat of her laundry stick was often heard in the outer room till after midnight, when her heartless stepsister and mother had long been asleep.

There was to be a great festival in the city, and for many days preparations were made in the house to get the father ready in his best robe and hat, and the women in their finery, to go out and see the king and the royal procession.

Poor Pigling wanted very much to have a look at the pageant, but the cruel stepmother, setting before her a huge straw bag of unhulled rice and a big cracked water jar, told her she must husk all the rice, and,drawing water from the well, fill the crock to the brim before she dared to go out on the street.

What a task to hull with her fingers three bushels of rice and fill up a leaky vessel! Pigling wept bitterly. How could it ever be done?

While she was brooding thus and opening the straw bag to begin spreading the rice out on mats, she heard a whir and a rush of wings and down came a flock of pigeons. They first lighted on her head and shoulders, and then hopping to the floor began diligently, with beak and claw, and in a few minutes the rice lay in a heap, clean, white, and glistening, while with their pink toes they pulled away the hulls and put these in a separate pile.

Then, after a great chattering and cooing, the flock was off and away. Pigling was so amazed at this wonderful work of the birds that she scarcely knew how to be thankful enough. But, alas, there was still the cracked crock to be filled. Just as she took hold of the bucket to begin there crawled out of the fire hole a sooty black imp, named Tokgabi.

"Don't cry," he squeaked out. "I'll mend the broken part and fill the big jar for you." Forthwith, he stopped up the crack with clay, and pouring a dozen buckets of water from the well into the crock, it was filled to brimming and the water spilled over on all sides. Then Tokgabi the imp bowed and crawled into the flues again, before the astonished girl could thank her helper.

So Pigling had time to dress in her plain but clean clothes that were snow-white. She went off and saw the royal banners and the king's grand procession of thousands of loyal men.

The next time, the stepmother and her favourite daughter planned a picnic on the mountain. So the refreshments were prepared and Pigling had to work hard in starching the dresses to be worn — jackets, long skirts, belts, sashes, and what not, until she nearly dropped with fatigue. Yet instead of thanking and cheering her, the cruel stepmother told Pigling she must not go out until she hoed all the weeds out of the garden and pulled up all the grass between the stones of the walk.

Again the poor girl's face was wet with tears. She was left at home alone, while the others went off in fine clothes, with plenty to eat and drink, for a day of merrymaking.

While weeping thus, a huge black cow came along and out of its great liquid eyes seemed to beam compassion upon the kitchen slave. Then, in ten mouthfuls, the animal ate up the weeds, and, between its hoof and lips, soon made an end of the grass in the stone pathway.

With her tears dried, Pigling followed this wonderful brute out over the meadows into the woods, where she found the most delicious fruit her eyes ever rested upon. She tasted and enjoyed, feasting to the full, and then returned home.

When the jealous stepsister heard of the astonishing doings of the black cow, she determined to enjoy a feast in the forest also. So on the next gala-day she stayed home and let the kitchen drudge go to see the royal parade. Pigling could not understand why she was excused, even for a few hours, from the pots and kettles, but she was still more surprised by the gift from her stepmother of a rope of cash to spend for dainties. Gratefully thanking the woman, she put on her best clothes and was soon on the main street of the city enjoying the gay sights and looking at the happy people. There were tight-rope dancing, music with drum and flute by bands of strolling players, tricks by conjurers and mountebanks, with mimicking and castanets, posturing by the singing girls and fun of all sorts. Boys peddling honey candy, barley sugar, and sweetmeats were out by the dozen. At the eating-house, Pigling had a good dinner of fried fish, boiled rice with red peppers, turnips, dried persimmons, roasted chestnuts and candied orange, and felt as happy as a queen.

The selfish stepsister had stayed home, not to relieve Pigling of work, but to see the wonderful cow. So, when the black animal appeared and found its friend gone and with nothing to do, it went off into the forest.

The stepsister at once followed in the tracks of the cow but the animal took it into its head to go very fast, and into unpleasant places. Soon the girl found herself in a swamp, wet, miry, and full of brambles. Still hoping for wonderful fruit, she kept on until she was tired out and the cow was no longer to be seen. Then, muddy and bedraggled, she tried to go back, but the thorny bushes tore her clothes, spoiled her hands, and so scratched her face that when at last, nearly dead, she got home, she was in rags and her beauty was gone.

But Pigling, rosy and round, looked so lovely that a young man from the south, of good family and at that time visiting the capital, was struck with her beauty. And as he wanted a wife, he immediately sought to find out where she lived. Then he secured a go-between who visited both families and made all the arrangements for the betrothal and marriage. Grand was the wedding. The groom, Su-wen, was dressed in white and black silk robes, with a rich horsehair cap and head-dress denoting his rank as a Yang-ban, or gentleman. On his breast, crossed by a silver-studded girdle, was a golden square embroidered with flying cranes rising above the waves—the symbols of civil office. He was tall, handsome, richly cultured, and quite famous as a writer of verses, besides being well read in the classics.

Charming, indeed, looked Pear Blossom, as she was now called again, in her robe of brocade, and long undersleeves which extended from her inner dress of snow-white silk. Dainty were her red kid shoes curved upward at the toe. With a baldric of open-worked silver, a high-waisted long skirt, with several linings of her inner silk robes showing prettily at the neck, and the silver bridal ring on her finger, she looked as lovely as a princess.

Besides her bridal dower, her father asked Pear Blossom what she preferred as a special present. When she told him, he laughed heartily. Nevertheless he fulfilled her wishes and to this day, in the boudoir of Pear Bossom, now Mrs. Su-wen, there stands an earthen figure of a black cow moulded and baked from the clay of her home province, while the pigeons like to hover about a pear tree that bursts into bloom every spring-time and sheds on the ground a snowy shower of fragrant petals.

THE GREAT STONE FIRE EATER

AGES ago, there lived a great Fire Spirit inside of a mountain to the southwest of Seoul, the capital of Korea. He was always hungry and his food was anything that would burn. He devoured trees, forests, dry grass, wood, and whatever he could get hold of. When those were not within his reach, he ate stones and rocks. He enjoyed the flames, but threw the hard stuff out of his mouth in the form of lava.

This Fire Monster spent most of his time in a huge volanco some distance away, but in sight of the capital. The city people used to watch the smoke coming out of the crater by day and issuing in red fire, between sunset and sunrise, until all the heavens seemed in flames. Then they said, the Fire Spirit was lighting up his palace. On cloudy nights the inside of the volanco glowed like a furnace. The molten mass inside the crater was reflected on the clouds, so that one could almost see into the monster's belly.

But nothing tasted so good to the Fire Eater as things which men built, such as houses, stables, fences, and general property. An especial titbit, that he longed to swallow, was the royal palace.

Looking out of its crater one day, he saw the king's palace, all silver bright and brand new, rising in the City of Seoul. Thereupon he chuckled, and said to himself, for he was very happy:

"There's a feast for me! I'll just walk out of my mountain home and eat up that dainty morsel. I wonder how the king will like it."

But the Fire Spirit was in no hurry. He felt sure of his meal. So he waited until his friend, the South Wind, was prepared to join him.

"Let me know when you're ready," said the Fire Spirit to the South Wind, "and we'll have a splendid blaze. We'll go up at night and enjoy a lively dance before they can get a drop of water on us. Don't let the rain-clouds know anything about our picnic."

The South Wind promised easily, for she was always glad to have a frolic.

So when the sun went down and it was dark, the Fire Spirit climbed out of his rocky home in the volanco and strode toward Seoul. The South Wind pranced and capered with him until the streets of the capital were so gusty that no one with a wide-brimmed hat dared go outdoors lest, in a lively puff, he might lose his head-gear. As for the men in mourning, who wear straw hats a yardstick wide and as big and deep as washtubs, they locked themselves up at home and played checkers. By the time all the palace guards were asleep the Fire Spirit was ready. He said to the South Wind:

"Blow, blow, your biggest blast, as I begin to touch the roofs of the smaller houses. This will whet my appetite for the palace, and then together we'll eat them all up."

Not till they heard a mighty roar and crackling did the people in Seoul push back their paper windows to find out what was the matter. Oh, what a blaze! It seemed to mount to heaven with red tongues that licked the stars. Those who could see in the direction of the palace supposed the sun had risen, but soon the crash of falling roofs and mighty columns of smoke and flame, with clouds of sparks, told the terrible story. By the time the sun did rise, there was nothing but a level waste of ashes, where the large building had been. Even the smoke had been driven away by the wind.

When the king and his people in the palace enclosure, who had saved their lives by running fast, thought over their loss, they began to plan how to stop the Fire Monster, when he should take it into his head to saunter forth on another walk and gobble up the king's dwelling.

A council of wise men was called to decide upon the question. Many long heads were bowed in hard thought over the matter. All the firemen, stone-cutters, fortune-tellers, dragon-tamers, and skilled people were invited to give their advice about the best way to fight the hungry Fire Demon.

After weeks spent in pondering the problem they all agreed that a dragon from China should be brought over to Korea. If kept in a swamp and fed well, he would surely prevent the Fire Imp from rambling too near Seoul. Besides, the dragon knew how to amuse and persuade the South Wind not to join in the mischief.

So, at tremendous cost and trouble, one of China's biggest dragons, capable of making rain and of spouting tons of water on its enemies, was shipped over and kept in a swamp. It was honoured with a royal decoration, allowed to wear a string of amber beads over its ear, given a horsehair hat, a nobleman's girdle, and fed upon all the turnips it desired to eat. In every way it was treated as the king's favourite.

But it was all in vain. Money and favour were alike wasted. The petted dragon made it rain too often, so that the land was soaked. Then when told not to do this, it grew sulky and neglected its duty. Finally it became fat and lazy and one night fell asleep when it ought to have been on guard, for the winds were out on a dance.

Seeing his jailor thus caught napping, the Fire Imp leaped out of its volcano prison, rode quickly on the South Wind to Seoul and in a few hours had again swallowed the royal palace. There was nothing seen next day except ashes, which the Fire Monster cared no more for than we for nut-shells when the kernels are eaten up.

With big tears in their eyes, the king and his wise men met together again to decide on a new scheme to keep off the Fire Imp. They were ready to drown him, or to see him get eaten up, because he had twice swallowed up the palace. They sent the Chinese dragon home and this time, besides the fortune-tellers and the stone-cutters, the well-diggers were invited also. For many days the wise men studied maps, talked of geography, looked at mountains, valleys, and the volcano, and studied air currents. Finally one man, famous for his deep learning about wood and water, forests and rivers, spoke thus:

"It is evident that the fire has always come from the south-west and up this valley," pointing to a map.

"True, true," shouted all the wise men.

"Well,right in his path let us dig a big pond, a regular artificial lake and very deep, into which the Fire Monster will tumble. This will put him out and he can get no further."

"Agreed, agreed," shouted the wise men in chorus. "Why did we not think of this before?"

All the skilful diggers of wells and ditches were summoned to the capital. With shovel and spade they worked for weeks. Then they let in water from the river until the pond was full.

So everybody in Seoul went to bed thinking that the king's palace was now safe surely.

But the Fire Imp, seeing the dragon gone and his opportunity come, climbed out of his volcano, and moved out for another meal. This time, the South Wind was busy elsewhere and could not go with him. So he went alone, but coming to the pond, tumbled and wet himself so badly that he was chilled and nearly put out when he got to the palace, which was only half burned. So he went home, growling and hungry.

Again the wise men were called and the first thing they did was to thank the boss well-digger, who had made the pond. The king summoned him into his presence to confer rank upon him and his children. He was presented with four rolls of silk, forty pounds of white ginseng, a tiger-skin robe, sixty dried chestnuts, and forty-four strings of copper cash. Loaded with such Korean wealth and honours, the man fell on his hands and knees and thanked His Majesty profusely.

Then they called the master stone-cutter or chief of the guild and asked him if he could chisel out the figure of a beast that could eat flames and be ugly enough to scare away the Fire Imp.

The master had long hoped that he would be invited to rear this bit of sculpture, but hitherto the king and Court had feared it might cost too much.

So the order was given, and out of the heart of the mountains a mighty block of white granite was loosed and brought to Seoul on rollers, pushed, pulled, and hoisted by thousands of labourers. Then, hidden behind canvas, to keep the matter secret, lest the Fire Imp should find it out, the workman toiled. Hammers and chisels clinked, until on a certain day the Great Stone Flame Eater was ready to take his permanent seat in front of the palace gate, as guardian of the royal buildings and treasures.

The Fire Imp laughed when the South Wind told him of what the Koreans in the capital were doing, even though she warned him of the danger of his being eaten up.

"I shall walk out and see for myself anyhow," said the Fire Imp.

One night he crept out quietly and moved toward the city. He was nearly drowned in the pond, but plucking up courage, he went on until he was near the king's dwelling. Hearing the Fire Imp coming, the Great Flame Eater turned his head and licked his chops in anticipation of swallowing the Fire Imp whole, as a toad does a fly.

But one sight of the hideous stony monster was enough for the Fire Imp. There, before him, on a high pedestal was something never before seen in heaven or on earth. It had enormous fire-proof scales like a salamander, with curly hair like asbestos, and its mouth full of big fangs. It was altogether hideous enough to give even a Volcano Spirit a chill.

"Just think of those jaws snapping on me," said the Fire Imp to himself, as he looked at them and the flangs. "I do believe that creature is half alligator and half water-tortoise. I had better go home. No dinner this time!"

So by his freezing glance alone, the Great Flame Eater frightened away the Fire Imp, so that he never came again and the royal palace was not once burned. Today the ugly brute still keeps watch. You have only to look at him to enjoy this story.

MADAGASCAR

The people of Madagascar appear to be allied to the Malayans and Polynesians. They were cruel but possessed great courage. Still retaining some traditions of a Supreme Being, they practised ancestor worship and observed many curious ordeals. Their language was not reduced to written form until the early part of the nineteenth century and consequently there is no ancient literature. They have, however, many fables and folk-tales which give ample proof of intellectual ability and alertness. There are traces of the influence of Arabs, who, as merchants, are known to have visited the island at least a thousand years ago.

THE RICE AND THE SUGAR-CANE

THE Sugar-cane, they say, came to the Rice, to seek friendship with it, and spake thus to it: "I say, O Sir Rice, come, let us be relatives and friends together, and share together the difficult and the bitter, making no difference, for we have one origin, for each is the produce of the ground; besides that alike are the things befalling and the things obtained; equal while living, similar in death. Why, look, our names even are almost alike, there's but a slight difference between *vàry* [rice] and *fàry* [sugarcane]; so let us strike up a firm friendship."

The Rice, however, it is said, answered thus: "Your words are true enough when you relate and particularize our origin, for we certainly are both the produce of the ground, equal while living, and similar in death. But still, here's something which prevents us agreeing, so it's no use, for it's a thing we can't agree about; so let there not be that friendship, and do not you blame us. For it's an exceedingly bad thing to agree without thought; for those who go along with fishermen, they say, stink of fish; those who make friends with vagabonds are themselves vagrants; and those who make friends with workers are workers themselves. And so you see, my good fellow, the reason of our declining friendship with you is *your changing in the end*, and that is why *we* can't join together. For you see that we have not that changing, whatever may befall *us*. You see that we are damped to become rotten, and when we have become so, we are soon put in the ground; but after a little time we are still rice all the same. And when we have become green on the earth again, then we are uprooted and stuck in the ground, where there is much water; yet do we not change, but still remain rice. And after growing again until we are ripe, we are then reaped with the knife; yet do we not change, but still remain rice. And after stopping a little while more, we are then beaten on the stone; yet we do not change but still remain rice. And not only so, but we are buried in the rice pit; we do not change, but still remain rice. And also, we are drawn out thence, and dried in the sun; and when dry we are pounded in the mortar and our skin stripped from us, yet we do not change, but still remain rice. And not only so, but we are put into the cooking pot and covered with water, and heated with a fierce fire; and unless well boiled and thoroughly soft, we are not removed from it. And when removed we are chewed, and when masticated are swallowed. And in all these calamities which overtake and befall us we do not change, but still remain rice. And the land where we are not found is called famine-stricken, and the country where we are not found is called desolate.

"But as for you sugar-canes, on the other hand, you are cut down and chopped up, and stuck about in the ground; and then you do not change at all, but are still sugar-cane. And after you have grown and become tall, you are cut down with the knife; and still you do not change, but are still sugar-cane. And afterward you are chewed into fibres with the teeth and crushed in the mill, but yet that does not change you, for you are still sugar-cane.

"But that is not all, for you are steeped in a great pot; and after a little while you are put into a boiling pot and heated intensely by the fire a long time, and after you thicken, they stop. And upon that you change and take another name, that is, *sugar*.

"And when you have been sent back to the boiler again, then you no longer are a substance in a lump any more, but become steam and distilled drops, and go out along a bamboo or a brass pipe, and emerging thence, you become *rum*, making wise men fools, and are no longer sugar-cane. So that we cannot be friends with you, Sugar-cane," said the Rice.

THE THREE SISTERS AND ITRÌMOBÉ

THERE was once a certain couple who were very rich, and they had three children, all daughters. And of these children of theirs, the youngest, Ifàravàvy was the prettiest.

One day Ifàra had a dream, and told it to her sisters; said she, "I have had a dream, lasses, and I dreamt that the son of the sun came from heaven to take a wife from among us, and it was I whom he took, for you two he left behind."

Then the two sisters were very angry about it, and said, "It is true enough that she is prettier than we are, and if a prince or noble should seek a wife, he would choose her, and not care for us; so let us consider what to do. Come, let us take her out to play, and find out from people which of us they consider the best looking." So they called Ifàra, and said, "Come, Ifàra, let us go and play."

So they went away all dressed in their best, and soon met an old woman. "Granny," said they, "which of us three sisters is the prettiest?"

"Ràmatoà [the eldest] is good looking, Ràivo [the middle one] is good looking, but Ifàra is better looking than either." "Oh, dear," said they, "there's no doubt

Ifàra is prettier than we are." So they took off Ifàra's *làmba* (the outer native dress).

Presently they met an old man. "Grandfather," they said, "who is the prettiest of us three sisters?"

"Ràmatoà is good looking, Raivo is good looking, but Ifàra is better looking than either." "Dear me! although deprived of her *làmba*, she is still prettier than we are." So they stripped her of her underclothing.

Then they met with Itrìmobé (an immense monster, half human and half beast, a man-eating creature, and with a frightfully sharp tail). "Oh, dear, if here isn't Itrìmobé! Who is the prettiest of us three sisters?" But with a snarl he answered just as the old woman and old man had answered.

So the sisters were beside themselves with anger because Ifàra was prettier than they were, and they said, "If we were to kill Ifàra, perhaps father and mother would hear of it and kill us, so let us go and get some of Itrìmobé's vegetables, so that he may eat her."

So the sisters said to her, "Come, Ifàra, let us see who can find the nicest vegetables." "Come along then," she said, "let us take some of those yonder" (meaning those of Itrìmobé). "Shall we get the ripe or the young ones?" said Ifàra. "Get those just sprouting," said they.

Then they went to get them, but the two sisters took the full-grown ones. So when the three showed theirs to each other Ifàra's were the worst. "Oh, dear!" cried she, "why, yours are the full-grown, you've cheated me." "It's yourself, girl, who would take the unripe," said the two; "go along and fetch some full-grown ones."

So Ifàra went off to get them; but while she was gathering them she was caught by Itrìmobé. "I've got you, my lass," said he, "for you are taking my vegetables; I'll eat you, my lass."

Then Ifàra cried, "I am sorry, Itrìmobé, but take me for your wife." "Come along, then," said he (but it was that he might take her home to be fattened, and after that eat her).

The sisters were exceedingly glad at this, and went away to tell their father and mother, saying, "Ifàra stole Itrìmobé's vegetables so he has eaten her." Then the old people wept profusely for sorrow. So Itrìmobé fed up Ifàra at his house, and would not let her go out of doors, but covered her with mats, while he went into the country hunting things to fatten her, so that Ifàra became very fat, and the time approached for Itrìmobé to devour her. But one day, when Itrìmobé happened to have gone abroad hunting, a little mouse wearing plantain fibre cloth jumped by Ifàra's side and said, "Give me a little white rice, Ifàra, and I'll give you advice." "What advice can you give me?" said Ifàra. "Well, then, let Itrìmobé devour you to-morrow." "But what is the advice you can give me?" said Ifàra, "for I'll give you the rice." So she gave some white rice to the little mouse clothed in cloth of

there." And he listened to Rangi's long-drawn sighs, and saw him stretch down his arms lovingly toward his wife Papatua, and he thought that on the horizon they really did touch each other. Now, Papatua grieved because Rangi was not better dressed, so Tané said to his mother, "I will make my father more beautiful and clothe him better." So Tané fetched the Rahuikura, or the sacred red garment, and fastened it round Rangi, so that by day he shone in great splendour. Then Tané went afar where a goblin dwelt who made the stars, and said, "You have some shining things called stars; give me some so that I can deck my father Rangi with them."

The goblin said, "You can have some if you will go and fetch them; but the way is long and difficult." "I wish to go," replied Tané, "for their beauty is so great that it makes my heart throb with delight."

"The places where you will find them," said the goblin, "are beyond the farthest mountain peaks, which are called 'Cracks of the Night' and 'Chinks of the Day.' To get there you must follow the road which you took when you went to sew up the wounds of your father which he got while resting on the jagged mountain tops."

"I will go," said Tané, for he was strong and mighty and feared nothing. When he reached the far-off star lands he was dazzled by the great shining lights, but he gathered up the most beautiful and took them back with him. But the stars did not look well on Rangi's bright robe of day, so Tané gave him a dark mantle for the night, and fastened its folds with myriads of stars both big and little. Then indeed the brilliancy of the stars was wonderful to behold, and Tané was very pleased. And he placed the sun and the moon as eyes for his father, wherewith to gaze upon his beloved wife by day and night. And his mother was delighted with what Tané had done, and she sang sweet songs of her son Tané and the stars. Still she was not quite happy about her husband; and one day she said to Tané, "I fear your father will tumble down and hurt himself; he is not used to being up so high, and my arms no longer enfold him."

"1 will prop him up, mother," said Tané, and he fetched the mighty clouds, and he placed them around and under Rangi, so that he could not fall. Still his mother was not happy, for she said, "He is so far off overhead, Tané; can he not be nearer?" And Tané answered, "I cannot help the heavens being hollow overhead, mother, for it was against that part of him that I kicked him so hard" and he felt for his mother's sadness of heart.

But shouts of applause were given by all the beings of the upper world when they saw all that Tané had accomplished, and they sang:

> "Apart now are Rangi and Papatua.
> Sing the resounding song.
> Sing the resounding song.
> Now is light great and strong.
> Apart are they ever."

And the sorrow-laden voices of Rangi and Papatua chanted:

> "Apart are we ever,
> Apart are we ever!
> But love will we ever!"

But an old witch of the lower world wished much to make mischief between Rangi and Papatua, and she sang in a shrill voice:

> "With dire enchantments, oh, sever them, gods!
> And fill with dislike to each other their days;
> Engulf them in floods, in ocean and sea.
> Let love and regret in each other be hate,
> Nor affection nor love of the past grow again."

But her wicked spells had no power against the strong love of Rangi and Papatua. Then said Rangi sorrowfully to his wife:

"You must stay far away beneath me, O Papatua; but this shall be the sign of my constant love for you: Full oft my tears shall fall on you, and they shall make you yet more beautiful."

And so it is; for are not the rain-drops the tears of heaven which beautify the earth?

Again Rangi spoke, saying:

"Old wife, you must stay where you are, but in the winter, with my cold breath, I shall sigh for you, yet shall my sighs make you still more beautiful." And so it is; for are not the hoar-frost and the snow the wintry sighs of the heavens?

Again Rangi spoke, saying:

"And in the summer, when the fierce heat burns, I shall lament over you, old wife, and my lamentations shall make you fertile and yet more beautiful." And so it is; for these are the dew-drops with which the heavens bless the earth.

And the light of the sun and moon, which are Rangi's eyes, are they not his constant love watching over his dear wife Papatua by day and night?

Then spoke Papatua to her husband Rangi:

"O husband, thy tears, thy sighs, thy lamentations, they indeed shall bless me, and, through the power of thy love, they shall come back to thee, even in soft clouds which shall be ever-faithful messengers of my great love for thee."

And so it is. For ever the rains, the frost, the snow, and the dew fall as blessings on the earth, and the soft clouds rise to the heavens overhead.

Thus, though separated by their children, Rangi, the Heavens, and Papatua, the Earth, are ever united in their love and in their works.

So for ever!

HUIA, OR THE TALE OF THE FISHING-NET

LISTEN, O my braves! Listen unto the word of your chief! In the hours of the night, when the great god Kuo wraps the world in his dark mantle, a vision came to me. And in this vision I saw my tribe greater and more prosperous than any other. And a voice said, 'Go, O Chief, to the far north of the land of Te-ika-a-maui [New Zealand]; there shalt thou find a blessing and a boon for thy people. Go not with followers but alone.' "

For a brief minute after Huia, the great war-chief, ceased speaking, there was silence among his assembled people. Then a great clamour of tongues arose.

"Not alone! Not alone, O our chief!" And one old warrior cried aloud, "I will go with thee." "And I!" "And I!" "And I!" cried others. But Huia upheld his *meré* (club) of greenstone, green and clear as the summer sea, and said in loud, decisive tones: "No, my people. None of you must follow. Alone I must go. I have spoken." Then Huia passed proudly from the midst of the people, and went into his carven *wharé* (dwelling).

When Huia had gone, a withered old hag, the soothsayer of the tribe, muttered, "Ay, alone must it be." But the tumult of the people was great, and they heard her not. The elder warriors consulted, and agreed that Huia must be watched, so that he did not depart unknown to them. They loved their chief, and feared lest ill should befall him. So closely did they watch the movements of Huia that he found it impossible to start alone by day or night. And the weeks went past, and Huia spoke no more of the vision, and of seeking the promised blessing. His tribe thought that he had forgotten about it, but it was not so; his purpose only slumbered in silence until the right time.

There was a rich and quaintly carven meeting-house on the edge of the lake, on the posts of which painted heads, with large protruding tongues and shell-eyes, grinned hideously. Here the people often met in the evening for amusements, or to talk over their war exploits and tell their ancient tales. One night, when they had assembled, they danced the great Haka, or war-dance, to a loud chorus, and the long lines of warriors (tongues protruding, eyes rolling) swayed to and fro as they brandished their spears aloft, and jumped and stamped with uniform and furious gesticulations. And Huia, the chief, danced with more strength and agility than any. When the night was far spent, he went out from amongst the dancers, wrapped himself up in his feather mat, and lay down near the door, and fell asleep. And the Haka still went on. After a while Huia jumped suddenly up, and cried, "The same vision! I must go to seek the blessing! And alone!"

Such was the excitement and noise of the dancers, that they did not heed his words. And Huia stepped out of the door unnoticed, and disappeared into the darkness.

Great was the consternation when Huia was missed. No one knew when or where he had gone. When the day broke they tried to trace his footsteps, but could not. He must have gone over the dry fern-land toward the forest. Then the warriors ordered the two slaves who always guarded and waited on Huia, to find the way he had gone, and they were told when they had done so they were to follow him and protect him from danger, but not to let him see them.

The slaves set out eagerly on their quest, for they loved and admired their master, the great war-chief Huia.

After much searching they found his footsteps on some boggy ground deep in the forest, and they tracked him onward by the trodden ferns, and broken twigs. Having at last come in sight of Huia they followed him at a distance, keeping out of his sight.

Spear in hand, Huia pursued his lonely way through the long hours of day, and at night he often still went on, led by the light of Takiara, the guiding star. After travelling thus for nearly a whole moon, Huia began to feel dispirited. The far north of Te-ika-a-maui and the promised boon seemed still out of his reach. He had no man to whom to speak his thoughts, and the way was dreary, and he had often not enough food to keep up his strength. He had left behind the forest with its birds and berries, and tender palm-shoots, and even the curled fern-fronds began to be scarce. Nothing but sandy wastes, and hillocks covered with long sapless grass, stretched before him. But at last a night came, bright and starlit, when he knew he must have reached the extreme north of the land, for he could hear the waves breaking on the shore. He strode over the sand-hills with renewed spirits, and there at last before him lay the great sea in all its changeful beauty. A fine curving bay stretched from point to point of two low promontories, and long curling lines of foam raced along the sands. He had reached his destination, and he held his head high in pride as he gazed around. But where was the promised blessing? Alas! All was silent, solitary. Not even the screech of wild fowl or the gleam of a white wing in the starlight.

"I must wait," said Huia, with quiet determination. Utterly worn out, he threw himself down in the middle of a large flax-bush, and the circles of high upstanding leaves completely enveloped him, so that he could see nothing but the stars above his head. Here Huia fell into a deep sleep. Some hours later Huia was wakened by the sound of music, softer and sweeter than any he had ever heard. Was he dreaming? He rubbed his eyes, he saw the clustering stars above, and the moon had risen and was high in the sky. The music still went on, and it seemed clearer, nearer than before.

"Is it a vision of the night, or am I indeed awake," mused Huia, and he pinched himself to find out. Still the music continued. Then Huia rose and peeped out from his shelter of leaves. On the water, close to where he lay, and right in the pathway of the moon, he saw numberless tiny canoes filled with very small fair people.

They were singing as they paddled nearer to the shore, and when they had pulled up their canoes, they began to run about and dance on the sands, looking, with their slight fair figures and long yellow hair, like shafts of light playing on the shore. They must be fairies! Huia had often heard of them, and his heart was full of delight at seeing them, for it meant good luck. But he must keep hidden, for they would be frightened away at the sight of a mortal.

Then Huia noticed that two groups of the little folk were drawing something through the water, which gradually unfolded as they neared the shore. It was a net, but Huia had never seen one before. The art of netting was unknown to the people of the land. Now, watching, he knew that these indeed must be the fairies, for as they pulled their burden to the shore, he saw myriads of great and small fishes enclosed, jumping, leaping in the shallow water, their bright scales glittering in the moonlight. Huia was struck with wonder at the novel sight, and he parted the flaxleaves cautiously as he gazed from his hiding-place. He wondered more and more what the strange thing could be which was dragged through the water, and was catching such numbers of fish without hook or line. Why, the fish would feed all his people for days! As the net was dragged up higher and the fish leaped about more frantically, soft peals of laughter arose from the little folk, as they caught at the slippery, gleaming captives and threw them at each other or into their canoes. All at once a pretty young fairy, with a basket on her arm, chased by a lad, ran out from the rest. Her laugh rang on the air like silver bells as she ran up the sands. She sped swiftly over the san-hills, and then, turning, gained the shadow of the flax-bushes, and threw herself, unseen, close beside the very one in which Huia was hidden. What a pretty, fair, bright thing, thought Huia, as he gazed at her golden hair and gleaming eyes, and fair limbs wet with the spray. Surely she was born of the sea-foam and the yellow shore! He dared not move, he dared scarcely breathe, for fear she should see him and be frightened away. He could see her merry face through the leaves, as she lay there watching the scene on the sands. How entrancing was the sight! The whole bay seemed filled with laughter and delight. It was the brightest moonshine everywhere. Sparkling sands, sparkling water, diamond lights dancing on the fairies as they flitted here and there, gathering up the restless, glittering fishes. What varied rainbow colours glinting on the myriad scales! Brilliant incessant motion enchanting the eye, silvery cadences of delight and song enchanting the ear. Beyond was the sea, with its innumerable laughter; above, the white-orbed moon and the myriad trembling stars; and around all, the immensity of the quiet night. Truly the night and all about him was enchanted to Huia. But above all other charms was the charm of that bright presence so near to him. His eyes kept wandering from the scene on the shore to the maiden lying close under his flax-bush. As he gazed on her, the words of the voice in his vision came into his mind: "Thou shalt bring back a blessing and a boon for thy people." What was the meaning of the words? Would he soon know?

Now that night the two slaves had kept some little distance behind their chief, for the way was open and they did not follow quite on his track. Coming suddenly round the far point, they were astonished at the sight on the shore, and walked toward the place where the net with all its freight had been drawn up. At the sight of the slaves coming toward them, the fairies were filled with terror, and ran with shrill screams up the beach. Some of them seized the net, and in their alarm and haste ran right round the flax-bush where Huia and the little fairy maiden were hiding, but saw neither. The slaves followed, and the little folk, getting more and more excited, and finding themselves pursued by mortals, dropped the net and, with wild gesticulations and cries, ran round, in and out of the shadowy masses of the flax-bushes, back to their canoes. At the first sound of alarm, and at the sight of the two slaves, the fairy maiden had risen in order to run away, but, suddenly seeing Huia so close to her, she sank back to the ground, trembling. Again springing up, she made frantic efforts to escape, but she was encircled in the net and entangled in its meshes, and the more she struggled to get out, the more was she held. "Help! Help!" she cried; but her people were already half-way down the beach and heard her not. "The net! The net!" she cried frantically; "I am caught in the net!"

"The net!" echoed Huia. "That then was the name of the strange thing which had taken all the fish without hook or line. Perhaps I have found the boon for my people at last," he thought. And Huia stepped out and lifted the struggling little maiden in his arms into the flax-bush where he had lain.

"Stay with me, maiden, stay; thou art the blessing I need." At the sound of his gentle voice, the fairy maid looked up into the face of the stalwart, dark-browed young chief, and love for him seized her heart, and she lay quiet in his arms.

And the fairy-folk paddled swiftly out of sight, beyond the pathway of the moon, and disappeared in the far distance. And Huia heard no more their music, but only the music of a sweet voice within his flax-bush shelter. And the slaves went away silently over the sand-hills.

So Huia, the great war-chief, took back to his village a young and fair wife, and she taught his people the art of making nets, for she had the implements for netting in her little flax-basket. And the tribe became rich and prosperous, as Huia had seen in his vision, and they were grateful to him for the blessing and boon he had sought for them in the far north.

And if ever the fairy wife of Huia expressed any wish to go back to her people, he would point laughingly to the net in which she had been caught, and which he ever kept hanging on the walls of their *wharé*.

NORSE TALES

I N the Norse mythology frost, fire, and all the other hostile forces of nature are represented as giants while friendly powers, like the sun, are portrayed as gods. The abode of Odin, the chief of the gods, was Valhalla, in Asgard. Here he received the souls of brave warriors who had been slain on the field of battle. These were to assist him in the last terrible conflict with the giants. The gods were friendly to mankind but they were not immortal. Both they and the giants were one day to be destroyed and the unnamed one who is greatest of all would establish a new earth.

The influence of the long dark Northern nights may be seen in the massive grandeur and mysterious nature of the Norse mythology, and the same characteristics on a lower plane are to be observed in the familiar folk-tales represented here. Trolls lurk in the woods, hankering after Christian blood; animals mysteriously assume human qualities; giants emerge strangely from hillsides, turning princes and princesses into stone. These tales aptly express the bizarre element in human life—the fact that you can never be sure what is lurking around the next corner.

SILLY MEN AND CUNNING WIVES

O NCE on a time there were two Goodies, who quarrelled, as women often will; and when they had nothing else to quarrel about, they fell to fighting about their husbands, as to which was the silliest of them. The longer they strove the worse they got, and at last they had almost come to pulling caps about it, for, as every one knows, it is easier to begin than to end, and it is a bad look-out when wit is wanting. At last, one of them said there was nothing she could not get her husband to believe, if she only said it, for he was as easy as a Troll. Then the other said there was nothing so silly that she could not get her husband to do, if she only said it must be done, for he was such a fool, he could not tell *B* from a bull's foot.

"Well! let us put it to the proof, which of us can fool them best, and then we'll see which is the silliest." That was what they said once, and so it was settled.

Now when the first husband, Master Northgrange, came home from the wood, his goody said: "Heaven help us both! what is the matter! you are surely ill, if you are not at death's door?"

"Nothing ails me but want of meat and drink," said the man.

"Now, Heaven be my witness!" screamed out the wife, "it gets worse and worse. You look just like a corpse in face; you must go to bed! Dear! dear! this never can last long!" And so she went on till she got her husband to believe he was

481

hard at death's door, and she put him to bed; and then she made him fold his hands on his breast, and shut his eyes; and so she stretched his limbs, and laid him out, and put him into a coffin; but that he might not be smothered while he lay there, she had some holes made in the sides, so that he could breathe and peep out.

The other goody, she took a pair of carding combs, and began to card wool; but she had no wool on them. In came the man, and saw this tomfoolery. "There's no use," he said, "in a wheel without wool; but carding combs, without wool, is work for a fool."

"Without wool!" said the goody; "I have wool, only you can't see it; it's of the fine sort." So, when she had carded it all, she took her wheel, and fell a-spinning.

"Nay, nay! this is all labour lost!" said the man. "There you sit, wearing out your wheel, as it spins and hums, and all the while you've nothing on it."

"Nothing on it!" said the goody; "the thread is so fine, it takes better eyes than yours to see it, that's all."

So, when her spinning was over, she set up her loom, and put the woof in, and threw the shuttle, and wove cloth. Then she took it out of the loom and pressed it and cut it out, and sewed a new suit of clothes for her husband out of it, and when it was ready, she hung the suit up in the linen closet. As for the man, he could see neither cloth nor clothes; but as he had once for all got it into his head that it was too fine for him to see, he went on saying, "Aye, aye, I understand it all, it is so fine, because it is so fine."

Well! in a day or two his goody said to him, "To-day you must go to a funeral. Farmer Northgrange is dead, and they bury him to-day, and so you had better put on your new clothes."

Yes, very true, he must go to the funeral; and she helped him on with his new suit, for it was so fine, he might tear it asunder if he put it on alone.

So when he came up to the farm, where the funeral was to be, they had all drank hard and long, and you may fancy their grief was not greater when they saw him come in in his new suit. But when the train set off for the churchyard, and the dead man peeped through the breathing holes, he burst out into a loud fit of laughter. "Nay! nay!" he said, "I can't help laughing, though it is my funeral, for if there isn't Olof Southgrange walking to my funeral stark naked!"

When the bearers heard that, they were not slow in taking the lid off the coffin, and the other husband, he in the new suit, asked how it was that he, over whom they had just drank his funeral ale, lay there in his coffin and chatted and laughed, when it would be more seemly if he wept.

"Ah!" said the other; "you know tears never yet dug up any one out of his grave—that's why I laughed myself to life again."

But the end of all their talk was that it came out that their goodies had played them those tricks. So the husbands went home, and did the wisest thing either of them had done for a long time; and if any one wishes to know what it was, he had better go and ask the birch cudgel.

THE TROLLS IN HEDALE WOOD

UP at a place in Vaage, in Gudbrandsdale, there lived once on a time in the days of old a poor couple. They had many children, and two of the sons who were about half grown up had to be always roaming about the country begging. So it was that they were well known with all the highways and by-ways, and they also knew the short cut into Hedale.

It happened once that they wanted to get thither, but at the same time they heard that some falconers had built themselves a hut at Mæla, and so they wished to kill two birds with one stone, and see the birds, and how they are taken, and so they took the cut across Longmoss. But you must know it was far on toward autumn, and so the milkmaids had all gone home from the shielings, and they could neither get shelter nor food. Then they had to keep straight on for Hedale, but the path was a mere track, and when night fell they lost it; and, worse still, they could not find the falconers' hut either, and before they knew where they were, they found themselves in the very depths of the forest. As soon as they saw they could not get on, they began to break boughs, lit a fire, and built themselves a bower of branches, for they had a hand-axe with them; and, after that, they plucked heather and moss and made themselves a bed. So a little while after they had lain down, they heard something which sniffed and snuffed so with its nose; then the boys pricked up their ears and listened sharp to hear whether it were wild beasts or wood trolls, and just then something snuffed up the air louder than ever, and said:

"There's a smell of Christian blood here!" At the same time they heard such a heavy foot-fall that the earth shook under it, and then they knew well enough the trolls must be about.

"Heaven help us! What shall we do?" said the younger boy to his brother.

"Oh! you must stand as you are under the fir, and be ready to take our bags and run away when you see them coming; as for me I will take the hand-axe," said the other.

All at once they saw the trolls coming at them like mad, and they were tall and stout, their heads were just as high as the fir-tops; but it was good thing they had only one eye between them all three, and that they used turn and turn about. They had a hole in their foreheads into which they put it, and turned and twisted it with their hands. The one that went first, he must have it to see his way, and the others went behind and took hold of the first.

"Take up the traps," said the elder of the boys, "but don't run away too far, but see how things go; as they carry their eye so high aloft they'll find it hard to see me when I get behind them."

Yes! the brother ran before and the trolls after him, meanwhile the elder got behind them and chopped the hindmost troll with his axe on the ankle, so that the troll gave an awful shriek, and the foremost troll got so afraid he was all of a shake and dropped the eye. But the boy was not slow to snap it up. It was bigger than two quart pots put together, and so clear and bright, that though it was pitch dark, everything was as clear as day as soon as he looked through it.

When the trolls saw he had taken their eye, and done one of them harm, they began to threaten him with all the evil in the world if he didn't give back the eye at once.

"I don't care a farthing for trolls and threats," said the boy, "now I've got three eyes to myself and you three have got none, and besides two of you have to carry the third."

"If we don't get our eye back this minute, you shall be both turned to stocks and stones," screeched the trolls.

But the boy thought things needn't go so fast; he was not afraid for witchcraft or hard words. If they didn't leave him in peace he'd chop them all three, so that they would have to creep and crawl along the earth like cripples and crabs.

When the trolls heard that, they got still more afraid and began to use soft words. They begged so prettily that he would give them their eye back, and then he should have both gold and silver and all that he wished to ask.

Yes! that seemed all very fine to the lad, but he must have the gold and silver first, and so he said, if one of them would go home and fetch as much gold and silver as would fill his and his brother's bags, and give them two good cross-bows beside, they might have their eye, but he should keep it until they did what he said.

The trolls were very put out, and said none of them could go when he hadn't his eye to see with, but all at once one of them began to bawl out for their goody, for you must know they had a goody between them all three as well as an eye. After a while an answer came from a knoll a long way off to the north. So the trolls said she must come with two steel cross-bows and two buckets full of gold and silver, and then it was not long, you may fancy, before she was there. And when she heard what had happened, she too began to threaten them with witchcraft. But the trolls got so afraid, and begged her beware of the little wasp, for she couldn't be sure he would not take away her eye too. So she threw them the cross-bows and the buckets and the gold and the silver, and strode off to the knoll with the trolls; and since that time no one has ever heard that the trolls have walked in Hedale wood, snuffing after Christian blood.

GOODY 'GAINST-THE-STREAM

ONCE on a time there was a man who had a goody who was so crossgrained that there was no living with her. As for her husband he could not get on with her at all, for whatever he wished she set her face right against it.

So it fell on Sunday in summer that the man and his wife went out into the field to see how the crop looked; and when they came to a field of rye on the other side of the river, the man said—

"Ay! now it is ripe. To-morrow we must set to work and reap it."

"Yes," said the wife, "to-morrow we can set to work and shear it."

"What do you say," said the man; "shall we shear it? Mayn't we just as well reap it?"

"No," said the goody, "it shall be shorn."

"There is nothing so bad as a little knowledge," said the man, "but you must have lost the little wit you had. When did you ever hear of shearing field?"

"I know little, and I care to know little, I dare say," said the goody, "but I know very well that this field shall be shorn and not reaped."

That was what she said, and there was no help for it; it must and should be shorn.

So they walked about and quarrelled and strove till they came to the bridge across the river, just above a deep hole.

"'Tis an old saying," said the man, "that good tools make good work, but it will be a fine swathe that is shorn with a pair of shears. Mayn't we just as well reap the field after all?" he asked.

"No! no! shear, shear," bawled out the goody, who jumped about and clipped like a pair of scissors under her husband's nose. In her shrewishness she took such little heed that she tripped over a beam on the bridge, and down she went *plump* into the stream.

"'Tis hard to wean anyone from bad ways," said the man, "but it were strange if I were not sometimes in the right, I too."

Then he swam out into the hole and caught his wife by the hair of her head, and so got her head above water.

"Shall we reap the field now?" were the first words he said.

"Shear! shear! shear!" screeched the goody.

"I'll teach you to shear," said the man, as he ducked her under the water; but it was no good, they must shear it, she said, as soon as ever she came up again.

"I can't think anything else than that the goody is mad," said the man to himself. "Many are mad and never know it; many have wit and never show it; but all the same, I'll try her once more."

But as soon as ever he ducked her under the water again, she held her hands up out of the water and began to clip with her fingers like a pair of shears. Then the man fell into a great rage and ducked her down both well and long; but while he was about it, the goody's head fell down below the water, and she got so heavy all at once, that he had to let her go.

"No! no!" he said, "you wish to drag me down with you into the hole, but you may lie there by yourself."

So the goody was left in the river.

But after a while the man thought it was ill she should lie there and not get Christian burial, and so he went down the course of the stream and hunted and searched for her, but for all his pains he could not find her. Then he came with all his men and brought his neighbours with him, and they all in a body began to drag the stream and to search for her all along it. But for all their searching they found no goody.

"Oh!" said the man, "I have it. All this is no good, we search in the wrong place. This goody was a sort by herself; there was not such another in the world while she was alive. She was so cross and contrary and I'll be bound it is just the same now she is dead. We had better just go and hunt for her upstream, and drag for her above the force; [1] maybe she has floated up thither."

And so it was. They went upstream and sought for her above the force,[1] and there lay the goody, sure enough! Yes! She was well called GOODY 'GAINST-THE-STREAM.

THE GIANT WHO HAD NO HEART IN HIS BODY

ONCE on a time there was a king who had seven sons, and he loved them so much that he could never bear to be without them all at once, but one must always be with him. Now, when they were grown up, six were to set off to woo, but as for the youngest, his father kept him at home, and the others were to bring back a princess for him to the palace. So the king gave the six the finest clothes you ever set eyes on, so fine that the light gleamed from them a long way off, and each had his horse, which cost many, many hundred dollars, and so they set off. Now, when they had been to many palaces, and seen many princesses, at last they came to a king who had six daughters, such lovely king's daughters they had never seen, and so they fell to wooing them, each one, and, when they had got them for sweethearts, they set off home again, but they quite forgot that they were to bring back with them a sweetheart for Boots, their brother, who stayed at home, for they were over head and ears in love with their own sweethearts.

But when they had gone a good bit on their way, they passed close by a steep

---

[1] Waterfall

hill-side, like a wall, where the giant's house was, and there the giant came out, and set his eyes upon them, and turned them all into stone, princes and princesses and all. Now the king waited and waited for his six sons, but the more he waited, the longer they stayed away; so he fell into great trouble, and said he should never know what it was to be glad again.

"And if I had not you left," he said to Boots, "I would live no longer, so full of sorrow am I for the loss of your brothers."

"Well, but now I've been thinking to ask your leave to set out and find them again; that's what I'm thinking of," said Boots.

"Nay, nay!" said his father; "that leave you shall never get, for then you would stay away too."

But Boots had set his heart upon it; go he would; and he begged and prayed so long that the king was forced to let him go. Now, you must know the king had no other horse to give Boots but an old broken-down jade, for his six other sons and their train had carried off all his horses; but Boots did not care a pin for that, he sprang up on his sorry old steed.

"Farewell, father," said he; "I'll come back, never fear, and like enough I shall bring my six brothers back with me"; and with that he rode off.

So, when he had ridden a while, he came to a Raven, which lay in the road and flapped its wings, and was not able to get out of the way, it was so starved.

"Oh, dear friend," said the Raven, "give me a little food, and I'll help you again at your utmost need."

"I haven't much food," said the Prince, "and I don't see how you'll ever be able to help me much; but still I can spare you a little. I see you want it."

So he gave the Raven some of the food he had brought with him.

Now, when he had gone a bit farther, he came to a brook, and in the brook lay a great Salmon, which had got upon a dry place and dashed itself about, and could not get into the water again.

"Oh, dear friend," said the Salmon to the Prince; "shove me out into the water again, and I'll help you again at your utmost need."

"Well!" said the Prince, "the help you'll give me will not be great, I daresay, but it's a pity you should lie there and choke"; and with that he shot the fish out into the stream again.

After that he went a long, long way, and there met him a Wolf, which was so famished that it lay and crawled along the road on its belly.

"Dear friend, do let me have your horse," said the Wolf; "I'm so hungry the wind whistles through my ribs; I've had nothing to eat these two years."

"No," said Boots, "this will never do; first I came to a Raven, and I was forced to give him my food; and I came to a Salmon, and him I had to help into the water again; and now you will have my horse. It can't be done, that it can't, for then I should have nothing to ride on."

"Nay, dear friend, but you can help me," said Graylegs the wolf; "you can ride upon my back, and I'll help you again in your utmost need."

"Well! the help I shall get from you will not be great, I'll be bound," said the Prince; "but you may take my horse, since you are in such need."

So when the Wolf had eaten the horse, Boots took the bit and put it into the Wolf's jaw, and laid the saddle on his back; and now the Wolf was so strong, after what he had got inside, that he set off with the Prince like nothing. So fast he had never ridden before.

"When we have gone a bit farther," said Graylegs, "I'll show you the Giant's house."

So after a while they came to it.

"See, here is the Giant's house," said the Wolf; "and see, here are your six brothers, whom the Giant has turned into stone; and see, here are their six brides, and away yonder is the door, and in at that door you must go."

"Nay, but I daren't go in," said the Prince; "he'll take my life."

"No! no!" said the Wolf; "when you get in you'll find a Princess, and she'll tell you what to do to make an end of the Giant. Only mind and do as she bids you."

Well! Boots went in, but, truth to say, he was very much afraid. When he came in the Giant was away, but in one of the rooms sat the Princess, just as the Wolf had said, and so lovely a Princess Boots had never yet set eyes on.

"Oh! heaven help you! whence have you come?" said the Princess, as she saw him; "it will surely be your death. No one can make an end of the Giant who lives here, for he has no heart in his body."

"Well! well!" said Boots; "but now that I am here, I may as well try what I can do with him; and I will see if I can't free my brothers, who are standing turned to stone out of doors; and you, too, I will try to save, that I will."

"Well, if you must, you must," said the Princess; "and so let us see if we can't hit on a plan. Just creep under the bed yonder, and mind and listen to what he and I talk about. But, pray, do lie still as a mouse."

So he crept under the bed, and he had scarce got well underneath it before the Giant came.

"Ha!" roared the Giant, "what a smell of Christian blood there is in the house!"

"Yes, I know there is," said the Princess, "for there came a magpie flying with a man's bone, and let it fall down the chimney. I made all the haste I could to get it out, but all one can do, the smell doesn't go off so soon."

So the Giant said no more about it, and when night came they went to bed. After they had lain awhile, the Princess said:

"There is one thing I'd be so glad to ask you about, if I only dared."

"What thing is that?" asked the Giant.

"Only where it is you keep your heart, since you don't carry it about you," said the Princess.

"Ah! that's a thing you've no business to ask about; but if you must know, it lies under the door-sill," said the Giant.

"Ho! ho!" said Boots to himself under the bed, "then we'll soon see if we can't find it."

Next morning the Giant got up cruelly early, and strode off to the wood; but he was hardly out of the house before Boots and the Princess set to work to look under the door-sill for his heart; but the more they dug, and the more they hunted, the more they couldn't find it.

"He has baulked us this time," said the Princess, "but we'll try him once more."

So she picked all the prettiest flowers she could find, and strewed them over the door-sill, which they had laid in its right place again; and when the time came for the Giant to come home again, Boots crept under the bed. Just as he was well under the bed back came the Giant.

Snuff—snuff, went the Giant's nose. "My eyes and limbs, what a smell of Christian blood there is in here," said he.

"I know there is," said the Princess, "for there came a magpie flying with a man's bone in his bill, and let it fall down the chimney. I made as much haste as I could to get it out, but I daresay it's that you smell."

So the Giant held his peace, and said no more about it. A little while after, he asked who it was that had strewed flowers about the door-sill.

"Oh, I, of course," said the Princess.

"And, pray, what's the meaning of all this?" said the Giant.

"Ah!" said the Princess, "I'm so fond of you that I couldn't help strewing them, when I knew that your heart lay under there."

"You don't say so," said the Giant; "but after all it doesn't lie there at all."

So when they went to bed again in the evening, the Princess asked the Giant again where his heart was, for she said she would so like to know.

"Well," said the Giant, "if you must know, it lies away yonder in the cupboard against the wall."

"So, so!" thought Boots and the Princess; "then we'll soon try to find it."

Next morning the Giant was away early, and strode off to the wood, and so soon as he was gone Boots and the Princess were in the cupboard hunting for his heart, but the more they sought for it the less they found it.

"Well," said the Princess, "we'll just try him once more."

So she decked out the cupboard with flowers and garlands, and when the time came for the Giant to come home, Boots crept under the bed again.

Then back came the Giant.

Snuff—snuff! "My eyes and limbs, what a smell of Christian blood there is in here!"

"I know there is," said the Princess; "for a little while since there came a magpie flying with a man's bone in his bill, and let it fall down the chimney. I made all the haste I could to get it out of the house again; but after all my pains, I daresay it's that you smell."

When the Giant heard that, he said no more about it; but a little while after, he saw how the cupboard was all decked about with flowers and garlands; so he asked who it was that had done that. Who could it be but the Princess?

"And, pray, what's the meaning of all this tomfoolery?" asked the Giant.

"Oh, I'm so fond of you I couldn't help doing it when I knew that your heart lay there," said the Princess.

"How can you be so silly as to believe any such thing?" said the Giant. "Oh, yes, how can I help believing it, when you say it?" said the Princess.

"You're a goose," said the Giant; "where my heart is, you will never come."

"Well," said the Princess; "but for all that, 'twould be such a pleasure to know where it really lies."

Then the poor Giant could hold out no longer, but was forced to say:

"Far, far away in a lake lies an island; on that island stands a church; in that church is a well; in that well swims a duck; in that duck there is an egg, and in that egg there lies my heart—you darling!"

In the morning early, while it was still grey dawn, the Giant strode off to the wood.

"Yes! now I must set off too," said Boots; "if I only knew how to find the way." He took a long, long farewell of the Princess, and when he got out of the Giant's door, there stood the Wolf waiting for him. So Boots told him all that had happened inside the house, and said now he wished to ride to the well in the church, if he only knew the way. So the wolf bade him jump on his back, he'd soon find the way; and away they went, till the wind whistled after them, over hedge and field, over hill and dale. After they had travelled many, many days, they came at last to the lake. Then the Prince did not know how to get over it, but the bade him only not be afraid, but stick on, and so he jumped into the lake with the Prince on his back, and swam over to the island. So they came to the church; but the church keys hung high, high up on the top of the tower, and at first the Prince did not know how to get them down.

"You must call on the Raven," said the Wolf.

So the Prince called on the Raven, and in a trice the Raven came, and flew up and fetched the keys, and so the Prince got into the church. But when he came to the well, there lay the duck, and swam about backwards and forwards, just as the Giant had said. So the Prince stood and coaxed it and coaxed it, till it came to him, and he grasped it in his hand; but just as he lifted it up from the water the duck dropped the egg into the well, and then Boots was beside himself to know how to get it out again.

"Well, now you must call on the Salmon to be sure," said the Wolf; and the king's son called on the Salmon, and the Salmon came and fetched up the egg from the bottom of the well.

Then the Wolf told him to squeeze the egg, and as soon as ever he squeezed it the Giant screamed out.

"Squeeze it again," said the Wolf; and when the Prince did so the Giant screamed still more piteously, and begged and prayed so prettily to be spared, saying he would do all that the Prince wished if he would only not squeeze his heart in two.

"Tell him if he will restore to life again your six brothers and their brides, whom he has turned to stone, you will spare his life," said the Wolf. Yes, the Giant was ready to do that, and he turned the six brothers into king's sons again, and their brides into king's daughters.

"Now squeeze the egg in two," said the Wolf. So Boots squeezed the egg to pieces, and the Giant burst at once.

Now, when he had made an end of the Giant, Boots rode back again on the Wolf to the Giant's house, and there stood all his six brothers alive and merry, with their brides. Then Boots went into the hill-side after his bride, and so they all set off home again to their father's house. And you may fancy how glad the old king was when he saw all his seven sons come back, each with his bride—"But the loveliest bride of all is the bride of Boots, after all," said the king, "and he shall sit uppermost at the table, with her by his side."

So he sent out, and called a great wedding-feast, and the mirth was both loud and long and if they have not done feasting, why, they are still at it.

THE HUSBAND WHO WAS TO MIND
THE HOUSE

ONCE on a time there was a man, so surly and cross he never thought his wife did anything right in the house. So, one evening, in haymaking time, he came home, scolding and swearing, and showing his teeth and making a dust.

"Dear love, don't be so angry; there's a good man," said his goody; "to-morrow let's change our work. I'll go out with the mowers and mow, and you shall mind the house at home."

Yes! the husband thought that would do very well. He was quite willing, he said.

So, early next morning, his goody took a scythe over her neck, and went out into the hay-field with the mowers, and began to mow; but the man was to mind the house, and do the work at home.

First of all, he wanted to churn the butter; but when he had churned a while, he got thirsty, and went down to the cellar to tap a barrel of ale. So, just when he had knocked in the bung, and was putting the tap into the cask, he heard overhead the pig come into the kitchen. Then off he ran up the cellar steps, with the tap in his hand, as fast as he could, to look after the pig, lest it should upset the churn; but when he got up, and saw the pig had already knocked the churn over, and stood there, routing and grunting amongst the cream which was running all over the floor, he got so wild with rage that he quite forgot the ale-barrel, and ran at the pig as hard as he could. He caught it, too, just as it ran out of doors, and gave it such a kick, that piggy lay for dead on the spot. Then all at once he remembered he had the tap in his hand; but when he got down to the cellar, every drop of ale had run out of the cask.

Then he went into the dairy and found enough cream left to fill the churn again, and so he began to churn, for butter they must have at dinner. When he had churned a bit, he remembered that their milking cow was still shut up in the byre, and hadn't had a bit to eat or a drop to drink all the morning, though the sun was high. Then all at once he thought 'twas too far to take her down to the meadow, so he'd just get her up on the house-top—for the house, you must know, was thatched with sods, and a fine crop of grass was growing there. Now their house lay close up against a steep down, and he thought if he laid a plank across to the thatch at the back he'd easily get the cow up.

But still he couldn't leave the churn, for there was his little babe crawling about on the floor, and "if I leave it," he thought, "the child is safe to upset it." So he took the churn on his back, and went out with it; but then he thought he'd better first water the cow before he turned her out on the thatch; so he took up a bucket to draw water out of the well; but as he stooped down at the well's brink, all the cream ran out of the churn over his shoulders, and so down into the well.

Now it was near dinner-time, and he hadn't even got the butter yet; so he thought he'd best boil the porridge, and filled the pot with water, and hung it over the fire. When he had done that, he thought the cow might perhaps fall off the thatch and break her legs or her neck. So he got up on the house to tie her up. One end of the rope he made fast to the cow's neck and the other he slipped down the chimney and tied round his own thigh; and he had to make haste, for the water now began to boil in the pot, and he had still to grind the oatmeal.

So he began to grind away; but while he was hard at it, down fell the cow off the house-top after all, and as she fell, she dragged the man up the chimney by the rope. There he stuck fast; and as for the cow, she hung half-way down the wall, swinging between heaven and earth, for she could neither get down nor up.

And now the goody had waited seven lengths and seven breadths for her husband to come and call them home to dinner; but never a call they had. At last she thought she'd waited long enough, and went home. But when she got there and saw the cow hanging in such an ugly place, she ran up and cut the rope in two with her scythe. But as she did this, down came her husband out of the chimney; and so when his old dame came inside the kitchen, there she found him standing on his head in the porridge pot.

THE THREE AUNTS

ONCE on a time there was a poor man who lived in a hut far away in the wood, and got his living by shooting. He had an only daughter who was very pretty, and as she had lost her mother when she was a child, and was now half grown up, she said she would go out into the world and earn her bread.

"Well, lassie!" said her father, "true enough you have learnt nothing here but how to pluck birds and roast them, but still you may as well try to earn your bread."

So the girl went off to seek a place, and when she had gone a little while, she came to a palace. There she stayed and got a place, and the queen liked her so well that all the other maids got envious of her. So they made up their minds to tell the queen how the lassie said she was good to spin a pound of flax in four-and-twenty hours, for you must know the queen was a great housewife, and thought much of good work.

"Have you said this? then you shall do it," said the queen; "but you may have a little longer time if you choose."

Now, the poor lassie dared not say she had never spun in all her life, but she only begged for a room to herself. That she got, and the wheel and the flax were brought up to her. There she sat, sad and weeping, and knew not how to help herself. She pulled the wheel this way and that, and twisted and turned it about, but she made a poor hand of it, for she had never even seen a spinning-wheel in her life.

But all at once, as she sat there, in came an old woman to her.

"What ails you, child?" she said.

"Ah!" said the lassie, with a deep sigh, "it's no good to tell you, for you'll never be able to help me."

"Who knows?" said the old wife. "Maybe I know how to help you after all."

Well, thought the lassie to herself, I may as well tell her, and so she told her how her fellow-servants had given out that she was good to spin a pound of flax in four-and-twenty hours.

"And here am I, wretch that I am, shut up to spin all that heap in a day and a night, when I have never even seen a spinning-wheel in all my born days."

"Well, never mind, child," said the old woman. "If you'll call me Aunt on the happiest day of your life, I'll spin this flax for you, and so you may just go away and lie down to sleep."

Yes, the lassie was willing enough, and off she went and lay down to sleep.

Next morning when she awoke there lay all the flax spun on the table, and that so clean and fine, no one had ever seen such even and pretty yarn. The queen was very glad to get such nice yarn, and she set greater store by the lassie than ever. But the rest were still more envious, and agreed to tell the queen how the lassie had said she was good to weave the yarn she had spun in four-and-twenty hours. So the queen said again, as she had said it she must do it; but if she couldn't quite finish it in four-and twenty hours, she wouldn't be too hard upon her, she might have a little more time. This time, too, the lassie dared not say No, but begged for a room to herself, and then she would try. There she sat again, sobbing and crying, and not knowing which way to turn, when another old woman came in and asked:

"What ails you, child?"

At first the lassie wouldn't say, but at last she told her the whole story of her grief.

"Well, well!" said the old wife, "never mind. If you'll call me Aunt on the happiest day of your life, I'll weave this yarn for you, and so you may just be off, and lie down to sleep."

Yes, the lassie was willing enough; so she went away and lay down to sleep. When she awoke there lay the piece of linen on the table, woven so neat and close, no woof could be better. So the lassie took the piece and ran down to the queen, who was very glad to get such beautiful linen, and set greater store than ever by the lassie. But as for the others, they grew still more bitter against her, and thought of nothing but how to find out something to tell about her. At last they told the queen the lassie had said she was good to make up the piece of linen into shirts in four-and-twenty hours. Well, all happened as before; the lassie dared not say she couldn't sew; so she was shut up again in a room by herself, and there she sat in tears and grief. But then another old wife came, who said she would sew the shirts for her if she would call her Aunt on the happiest day of her life. The lassie was only too glad to do this, and then she did as the old wife told her, and went and lay down to sleep.

Next morning when she woke she found the piece of linen made up into shirts, which lay on the table—and such beautiful work no one had ever set eyes on; and more than that, the shirts were all marked and ready for wear. So, when the queen saw the work, she was so glad at the way in which it was sewn that she clapped her hands and said:

"Such sewing I never had, nor even saw in all my born days"; and after that she was as fond of the lassie as of her own children; and she said to her:

"Now, if you like to have the Prince for your husband, you shall have him; for you will never need to hire work-women. You can sew, and spin, and weave all yourself."

So as the lassie was pretty, and the Prince was glad to have her, the wedding soon came on. But just as the Prince was going to sit down with the bride to the bridal feast in came an ugly old hag with a long nose—I'm sure it was three ells long.

So up got the bride and made a curtsey, and said:

"Good-day, Auntie."

"*That* Auntie to my bride?" said the Prince.

"Yes, she was!"

"Well, then, she'd better sit down with us to the feast," said the Prince; but, to tell you the truth, both he and the rest thought she was a loathsome woman to have next you.

But just then in came another ugly old hag. She had a back so humped and broad she had hard work to get through the door. Up jumped the bride in a trice, and greeted her with "Good-day, Auntie!"

And the Prince asked again if that were his bride's aunt. They both said Yes; so the Prince said, if that were so, she too had better sit down with them to the feast.

But they had scarce taken their seats before another ugly old hag came in, with eyes as large as saucers, and so red and bleared 'twas gruesome to look at her. But up jumped the bride again, with her "Good-day, Auntie," and her, too, the Prince asked to sit down; but I can't say he was very glad, for he thought to himself:

"Heaven shield me from such Aunties as my bride has!" So when he had sat awhile he could not keep his thoughts to himself any longer, but asked:

"But how, in all the world, can my bride, who is such a lovely lassie, have such loathsome, misshapen Aunts?"

"I'll soon tell you how it is," said the first. "I was just as good-looking when I was her age; but the reason why I've got this long nose is, because I was always kept sitting, and poking, and nodding over my spinning, and so my nose got stretched and stretched, until it got as long as you now see it."

"And I," said the second, "ever since I was young, I have sat and scuttled backward and forward over my loom, and that's how my back has got so broad and humped as you now see it."

"And I," said the third, "ever since I was little, I have sat, and stared, and sewn, and sewn and stared, night and day; and that's why my eyes have got so ugly and red, and now there's no help for them."

"So! so!" said the Prince, "'twas lucky I came to know this; for if folk can get so ugly and loathsome by all this, then my bride shall neither spin, nor weave, nor sew all her life long."

GUDBRAND ON THE HILL-SIDE

ONCE on a time there was a man whose name was Gudbrand; he had a farm which lay far, far away upon a hill-side, and so they called him Gudbrand on the Hill-side.

Now, you must know this man and his goodwife lived so happily together, and understood one another so well that all the husband did the wife thought so well done there was nothing like it in the world, and she was always glad whatever he turned his hand to. The farm was their own land, and they had a hundred dollars lying at the bottom of their chest, and two cows tethered up in a stall in their farm-yard. So one day his wife said to Gudbrand:

"Do you know, dear, I think we ought to take one of our cows into town, and sell it; that's what I think; for then we shall have some money in hand, and such well-to-do people as we ought to have ready money like the rest of the world. As for the hundred dollars at the bottom of the chest yonder, we can't make a hole in them, and I'm sure I don't know what we want with more than one cow. Besides, we shall gain a little in another way, for then I shall get off with only looking after one cow, instead of having, as now, to feed and litter and water two."

Well, Gudbrand thought his wife talked right good sense, so he set off at once with the cow on his way to town to sell her; but when he got to the town there was no one who would buy his cow.

"Well! well! never mind," said Gudbrand, "at the worst, I can only go back home again with my cow. I've both stable and tether for her, I should think, and the road is no farther out than in"; and with that he began to toddle home with his cow.

But when he had gone a bit of the way, a man met him who had a horse to sell, so Gudbrand thought 'twas better to have a horse than a cow, so he swopped with the man. A little farther on he met a man walking along and driving a fat pig before him, and he thought it better to have a fat pig than a horse, so he swopped with the man. After that he went a little farther, and a man met him with a goat; so he thought it better to have a goat than a pig, and he swopped with the man that owned the goat. Then he went on a good bit till he met a man who had a sheep, and he swopped with him too, for he thought it always better to have a sheep than a goat. After a while he met a man with a goose, and he swopped away the sheep for the goose; and when he had walked a long, long time, he met a man with a cock, and he swopped with him, for he thought in this wise, "'Tis surely better to have a cock than a goose." Then he went on till the day was far spent, and he began to get very hungry, so he sold the cock for a shilling, and bought food with the money, for, thought Gudbrand on the Hill-side, "'Tis always better to save one's life than to have a cock." After that he went on home till he reached his nearest neighbour's house, where he turned in.

"Well," said the owner of the house, "how did things go with you in town?"

"Rather so so," said Gudbrand, "I can't praise my luck, nor do I blame it either," and with that he told the whole story from first to last.

"Ah!" said his friend, "you'll get nicely called over the coals, that one can see, when you get home to your wife. Heaven help you, I wouldn't stand in your shoes for something."

"Well," said Gudbrand on the Hill-side, "I think things might have gone much worse with me; but now, whether I have done wrong or not, I have so kind a goodwife, she never has a word to say against anything that I do."

"Oh!" answered his neighbour, "I hear what you say, but I don't believe it for all that."

"Shall we lay a bet upon it?" asked Gudbrand on the Hill-side. "I have a hundred dollars at the bottom of my chest at home; will you lay as many against them?"

Yes! the friend was ready to bet; so Gudbrand stayed there till evening, when it began to get dark, and then they went together to his house, and the neighbour was to stand outside the door and listen, while the man went in to see his wife.

"Good evening!" said Gudbrand on the Hill-side.

"Good evening!" said the goodwife. "Oh! is that you? Now God be praised."

Yes! it was he. So the wife asked how things had gone with him in town.

"Oh! only so so," answered Gudbrand; "not much to brag of. When I got to the town there was no one who would buy the cow, so you must know I swopped it away for a horse."

"For a horse," said his wife; "well that is good of you; thanks with all my heart. We are so well to do that we may drive to church, just as well as other people; and if we choose to keep a horse we have a right to get one, I should think. So run out, child, and put up the horse."

"Ah!" said Gudbrand, "but you see I've not got the horse after all; for when I got a bit farther on the road, I swopped it away for a pig."

"Think of that, now!" said the wife; "you did just as I should have done myself; a thousand thanks! Now I can have a bit of bacon in the house to set before people when they come to see me, that I can. What do we want with a horse? People would only say we had got so proud that we couldn't walk to church. Go out, child, and put up the pig in the sty."

"But I've not got the pig either," said Gudbrand; "for when I got a little farther on, I swopped it away for a milch goat."

"Bless us!" cried his wife, "how well you manage everything! Now I think it over, what should I do with a pig? People would only point at us and say, 'Yonder they eat up all they have got.' No! now I have got a goat, and I shall have milk and cheese, and keep the goat too. Run out, child, and put up the goat."

"Nay, but I haven't got the goat either," said Gudbrand, "for a little farther on I swopped it away, and got a fine sheep instead."

"You don't say so!" cried the wife; "why, you do everything to please me, just as if I had been with you; what do we want with a goat? If I had it I should lose half my time in climbing up the hills to get it down. No! if I have a sheep I shall have both wool and clothing, and fresh meat in the house. Run out, child, and put up the sheep."

"But I haven't got the sheep any more than the rest," said Gudbrand; "for when I had gone a bit farther I swopped it away for a goose."

"Thank you! thank you! with all my heart," cried his wife; "what should I do with a sheep? I have no spinning-wheel, nor carding-comb, nor should I care to worry myself with cutting, and shaping, and sewing clothes. We can buy clothes now, as we have always done; and now I shall have roast goose, which I have longed for so often; and, besides, down to stuff my little pillow with. Run out, child, and put up the goose."

"Ah!" said Gudbrand, "but I haven't the goose either, for when I had gone a bit farther I swopped it away for a cock."

"Dear me!" cried his wife, "how you think of everything! just as I should have done myself. A cock! think of that! why, it's as good as an eight-day clock, for every morning the cock crows at four o'clock, and we shall be able to stir our stumps in good time. What should we do with a goose? I don't know how to cook it; and as for my pillow, I can stuff it with cotton grass. Run out, child, and put up the cock."

"But, after all, I haven't got the cock," said Gudbrand; "for when I had gone a bit farther I got as hungry as a hunter, so I was forced to sell the cock for a shilling, for fear I should starve."

"Now, God be praised that you did so!" cried his wife; "whatever you do, you do it always just after my own heart. What should we do with a cock? We are our own masters, I should think, and can lie a-bed in the morning as long as we like. Heaven be thanked that I have got you safe back again; you who do everything so well that I want neither cock nor goose; neither pigs nor kine."

Then Gudbrand opened the door and said: "Well, what do you say now? Have I won the hundred dollars?" And his neighbour was forced to allow that he had.

OSBORN'S PIPE

ONCE upon a time there was a poor tenant farmer who had to give up his farm to his landlord; but if he had lost his farm he had three sons left, and their names were Peter, Paul, and Osborn Boots. They stayed at home and sauntered about, and wouldn't do a stroke of work; *that* they thought was the right thing to do. They thought, too, they were too good for everything, and that nothing was good enough for them.

At last Peter had got to hear that the king would have a keeper to watch his hares; so he said to his father that he would be off thither: the place would just suit him, for he would serve no lower man than the king; that was what he said. The old father thought there might be work for which he was better fitted than that; for he that would keep the king's hares must be light and lissom, and no lazybones, and when the hares began to skip and frisk there would be quite another dance than loitering about from house to house. Well, it was all no good: Peter would go, and must go, so he took his scrip on his back, and toddled away down the hill; and when he had gone far, and farther than far, he came to an old wife, who stood there with her nose stuck fast in a log of wood, and pulled and pulled at it; and as soon as he saw how she stood dragging and pulling to get free he burst into a loud fit of laughter.

"Don't stand there and grin," said the old wife, "but come and help an old cripple; I was to have split asunder a little firewood, and I got my nose fast down here, and so I have stood and tugged and torn and not tasted a morsel of food for hundreds of years." That was what she said.

But for all that Peter laughed more and more. He thought it all fine fun. All he said was, as she had stood so for hundreds of years, she might hold out for hundreds of years still.

When he got to the king's grange, they took him for keeper at once. It was not bad serving there, and he was to have good food and good pay, and maybe the princess into the bargain; but if one of the king's hares got lost, they were to cut three red stripes out of his back and cast him into a pit of snakes.

So long as Peter was in the byre and home-field he kept all the hares in one flock: but as the day wore on, and they got up into the wood, all the hares began to frisk, and skip, and scuttle away up and down the hillocks.

Peter ran after them this way and that, and nearly burst himself with running, so long as he could make out that he had one of them left, and when the last one was gone, he was almost broken-winded. And after that he saw nothing more of them.

When it drew toward evening he sauntered along on his way home, and stood and called and called to them at each fence, but no hares came; and when he got home to the king's grange, there stood the king all ready with his knife, and it happened to Peter even as the king had said.

After a time, Paul was for going to the king's grange to keep the king's hares. The old gaffer said the same thing to him, and even still more; but he must and would set off; there was no help for it, and things went neither better nor worse with him than with Peter.

Now, when a little while had passed, Osborn Boots was all for setting off to keep the king's hares, and he told his mind to the gaffer, who said the same thing to him and even more still. Well it was all no good, however bad it might be; he would go to the king's grange, and serve the king, for no lesser man would he serve, and he would soon keep the hares. They couldn't well be worse than the goat and the calf at home. So Boots threw his scrip on his shoulder, and down the hill he toddled.

So when he had gone far, and farther than far, and had begun to get right down hungry, he too came to the old wife, who stood with her nose fast in the log, who tugged, and tore, and tried to get loose.

"Good-day, grandmother," said Boots. "Are you standing there whetting your nose, poor old cripple that you are?"

"Now, not a soul has called me 'mother' for hundreds of years," said the old wife. "Do come and help me to get free, and give me something to live on; for I haven't had meat in my mouth all that time. See if I don't do you a motherly turn afterward."

So he cleft the log for her, that she might get her nose out of the split, and sat down to eat and drink with her; and as the old wife had a good appetite, you may fancy she got the lion's share of the meal.

When they were done, she gave Boots a pipe, which was in this wise: when he blew into one end of it, anything that he wished away was scattered to the four winds, and when he blew into the other, all things gathered themselves together again; and if the pipe were lost or taken from him, he had only to wish for it, and it came back to him.

"Something like a pipe, this," said Osborn Boots.

When he got to the king's grange, they chose him for keeper on the spot. It was no bad service there, and food and wages he should have, and, if he were man enough to keep the king's hares, he might, perhaps, get the princess too; but if one of them got away, if it were only a leveret, they were to cut three red stripes out of his back. And the king was so sure of this that he went off at once and ground his knife.

It would be a small thing to keep these hares, thought Osborn Boots; for when they set out they were almost as tame as a flock of sheep, and so long as he was in the lane and in the home-field, he had them all easily in a flock and following; but when they got upon the hill by the wood, and it looked toward midday, and the sun began to burn and shine on the slopes and hillsides, all the hares fell to frisking and skipping about, and away over the hills.

"Ho, ho! stop! will you all go? Go, then!" said Boots; and he blew into one end of the pipe, so that they ran off on all sides, and there was not one of them left. But as he went on, and came to an old charcoal pit, he blew into the other end of the pipe; and before he knew where he was the hares were all there, and stood in lines and rows, so that he could take them all in at a glance, just like a troop of soldiers on parade.

"Something like a pipe, this," said Osborn Boots; and with that he laid him down to sleep away under a sunny slope, and the hares frisked and frolicked about till eventide. Then he piped them all together again, and came down to the king's grange with them, like a flock of sheep.

The king and the queen, and the princess too, all stood in the porch, and wondered what sort of fellow this was who so kept the hares that he brought them home again; and the king told and reckoned them on his fingers, and counted them over and over again; but there was not one of them missing—no! not so much as a leveret.

"Something like a lad, this," said the princess.

Next day he went off to the wood, and was to keep the hares again; but as he lay and rested himself on a strawberry brake, they sent the maid after him from the grange that she might find out how it was that he was man enough to keep the king's hares so well.

So he took out the pipe and showed it her, and then he blew into one end and made them fly like the wind over all the hills and dales; and then he blew into the other end, and they all came scampering back to the brake, and all stood in row and rank again.

"What a pretty pipe," said the maid. She would willingly give a hundred dollars for it, if he would sell it, she said.

"Yes! it is something like a pipe," said Osborn Boots; and it was not to be had for money alone; but if she would give him the hundred dollars, and a kiss for each dollar, she should have it, he said.

Well! why not? Of course she would; she would willingly give him two for each dollar, and thanks besides.

So she got the pipe; but when she got as far as the king's grange, the pipe was gone, for Osborn Boots had wished for it back, and so, when it drew toward eventide, home he came with his hares just like any other flock of sheep; and for all the king's counting or telling, there was no help,—not a hair of the hares was missing.

The third day that he kept the hares, they sent the princess on her way to try to get the pipe from him. She made herself as blithe as a lark, and she bade him two hundred dollars if he would sell her the pipe and tell her how she was to behave to bring it safe home with her.

"Yes! yes! it is something like a pipe," said Osborn Boots; and it was not for sale, he said, but all the same, he would do it for her sake, if she would give him two hundred dollars, and a kiss into the bargain for each dollar; then she might have the pipe. If she wished to keep it, she must look sharp after it. That was her look-out.

"This is a very high price for a hare-pipe," thought the princess; and she made mouths at giving him the kisses; "but after all," she said, "it's far away in the wood, no one can see it or hear it—it can't be helped; I must and will have the pipe."

So when Osborn Boots had got all he was to have, she got the pipe, and off she went, and held it fast with her fingers the whole way; but when she came to the grange, and was going to take it out, it slipped through her fingers and was gone!

Next day the queen would go herself and fetch the pipe from him. She made sure she would bring the pipe back with her.

Now she was more stingy about the money, and bade no more than fifty dollars; but she had to raise her price till it came to three hundred. Boots said it was something like a pipe, and it was no price at all; still for her sake it might go, if she would give him three hundred dollars, and a smacking kiss for each dollar into the bargain; then she might have it. And he got the kisses well paid, for on that part of the bargain she was not so squeamish.

So when she had got the pipe, she both bound it fast, and looked after it well; but she was not a hair better off than the others, for when she was going to pull it out at home, the pipe was gone; and at even down came Osborn Boots, driving the king's hares home for all the world like a flock of tame sheep.

"It is all stuff," said the king; "I see I must set off myself, if we are to get this wretched pipe from him; there's no help for it, I can see." And when Osborn Boots had got well into the woods next day with the hares, the king stole after him, and found him lying on the same sunny hillside, where the women had tried their hands on him.

Well! they were good friends and very happy; and Osborn Boots showed him the pipe, and blew first on one end and then on the other, and the king thought it a pretty pipe, and wanted at last to buy it, even though he gave a thousand dollars for it.

"Yes! it is something like a pipe," said Boots, "and it's not to be had for money; but do you see that white horse yonder down there?" and he pointed into the wood.

"See it! of course I see it; it's my own horse Whitey," said the king. No one had need to tell him that.

"Well! if you will give me a thousand dollars, and then go and kiss yon white horse down in the marsh there, behind the big fir-tree, you shall have my pipe."

"Isn't it to be had for any other price?" asked the king.

"No, it is not," said Osborn.

"Well! but I may put my silken pocket-handkerchief between us?" said the king.

Very good; he might have leave to do that. And so he got the pipe, and put it into his purse. And the purse he put into his pocket, and buttoned it up tight; and so off he strode to his home.

But when he reached the grange, and was going to pull out his pipe, he fared no better than the women folk; he hadn't the pipe any more than they, and there came Osborn Boots driving home the flock of hares, and not a hare was missing.

The king was both spiteful and wroth, to think that he had fooled them all round, and cheated him out of the pipe as well; and now he said Boots must lose his life, there was no question of it, and the queen said the same: it was best to put such a rogue out of the way red-handed.

Osborn thought it neither fair nor right, for he had done nothing but what they told him to do; and so he had guarded his back and life as best he might.

So the king said there was no help for it; but if he could lie the great brewing-vat so full of lies that it ran over, then he might keep his life.

That was neither a long nor perilous piece of work: he was quite game to do that, said Osborn Boots. So he began to tell how it had all happened from the very first. He told about the old wife and her nose in the log, and then he went on to say, "Well, I must lie faster if the vat is to be full." So he went on to tell of the pipe and how he got it; and of the maid, how she came to him and wanted to buy it for a hundred dollars, and of all the kisses she had to give besides, away there in the wood. Then he told of the princess how she came and kissed him so sweetly for the pipe when no one could see or hear it all away there in the wood. Then he stopped and said, " I must lie faster if the vat is ever to be full." So he told of the queen, how close she was about the money and how overflowing she was with her smacks.

"You know I must lie hard to get the vat full," said Osborn.

"For my part," said the queen, "I think it's pretty full already."

"No! no! it isn't," said the king.

So he fell to telling how the king came to him, and about the white horse down on the marsh, and how if the king was to have the pipe, he must— "Yes, your majesty, if the vat is ever to be full, I must go on and lie hard," said Osborn Boots.

"Hold! hold, lad! It's full to the brim," roared out the king; "don't you see how it's foaming over?"

So both the king and the queen thought it best he should have the princess to wife and half the kingdom. There was no help for it.

"That was something like a pipe," said Osborn Boots.

PAPUA

THIS delightful group of stories is taken from a collection of folktales by Miss Annie Ker, who lived in a little mission bungalow on the north-east coast of New Guinea in 1910. They were told to her by old women seated round the verandah of the mission-house. There was generally a little incantation or magic verse in each story. This was invariably chanted to an air, which might be called the fairy-tale *motif,* for it appeared very regularly, linked to very diverse words. Sorcerers and witches form a very real factor in Papuan life; gifts are taken to propitiate them; and death is always laid to the charge of witches. The phrasing of the stories gives them an old-world atmosphere and charm that is particularly captivating and beautiful.

HOW THE TURTLE GOT HIS SHELL

LONG ago, our fathers have told us, the Turtle and the Wallaby were friends. Now on a certain day, the Turtle was hungry, and asked his friend to go with him to the beach and from thence to the hornbill's garden, where was much sugar-cane and where bananas also were plentiful. This they did, and fed plentifully on all that was there. The Wallaby trod upon the stalks of the bananas and bowed them to the ground that his friend might eat. Thus did he also to the tall sugar-cane and the orabu, the flowering rush. And they both did eat and their hunger was stayed.

Now while they were eating, the birds were at work in their gardens, tilling the ground. When the work was finished they dug up much taro and returned to the village to cook their food. They peeled the roots and cut them up and placed them in the pots for cooking. Then said Binama the hornbill, "Let one of you go down to the beach and bring sea water that our food may be salted."

But his word bare no fruit, for one by one the birds made excuse, fearing lest an enemy lay in wait. At last the wagtail arose, and ran in the house to make ready to go to the beach. He hung his *kada* (shell breastplate) round his neck, tied waving feathers round his head, and took his spear and went forth. And as he went he leapt from side to side the better to avoid the foe, if foe there were.

In a little he came to Binama's garden and saw the Turtle and Wallaby feeding. Their hearts trembled; nevertheless the Turtle made bold and said to the wagtail, "Thy master has bidden us eat of his bananas that our hunger may be stayed."

Now the wagtail knew in his heart that they lied, but he answered never a word, but filled his bottles with sea water and ran back to the village by another way.

When he reached the village he cried aloud, "Friends, the Turtle and the Wallaby are eating in our master's garden!"

At this word, all arose and ran for their spears, and surrounded the garden. The Wallaby lifted up his head and seeing nought but enemies round about him, tarried not but leaped mightily and escaped. The Turtle could not jump, as he well knew, so he crawled with haste into a yam patch and hid himself under the leaves.

But the birds knew he was still there, and they hunted for him diligently and at last found him and dragged him forth. The Turtle feared greatly, and cried, "Take not vengeance on me, for truly the Wallaby bade me come hither and with his feet he broke the stalks, while I only ate of the fruit." The birds cared little for his words, and tied him to a pole and thus carried him to Binama's house, where they laid him upon a shelf till the morrow.

The next day Binama called his servants together and all went to dig food to make a feast when they should slay the Turtle. None were in the house but the children whom Binama had set to guard the captive. Then the Turtle made his voice soft, and called the children unto him: "Loosen my bonds, O children," quoth he, "that we may play together."

Now the children knew not what was in the Turtle's mind, and they did as he bade them. He crawled down from the shelf, and stretched himself, for he was stiff and sore. Then he said to the children, "Where are your ornaments? Leave the poor ones in the basket, and bring forth only the good ones, that I may see them."

The children ran to the place where Binama kept his ornaments, and brought forth a long necklace of shell money, also two shell armlets and a wooden bowl, and laid them before the Turtle. He forthwith wound the necklace many times round his neck, and put on both the shell armlets. Moreover, the bowl he fastened upon his back. Then he said to the children, "Ye behold me now richly attired. Watch while I run a little and back again and tell me if the sight is a good one or no."

The children watched him crawl a few paces and called to him to return. This the Turtle did and all sat together in the shade of a tree. Then the Turtle crawled once more, and the children laughed to watch his ungainly form decorated with their father's ornaments. Again the Turtle returned to the children, but this time he did not sit with them. For on a sudden he heard voices and knew the men were drawing near. Then he saw them as they came forth, and ran swiftly to the sea. The children cried aloud to their father, "Come, for the Turtle is running away!"

When Binama heard this cry, he and the birds with him threw the sheaves of taro aside and gave chase to the runaway. But the Turtle had already reached the sea, and he hasted to dive. The birds called, "Show thyself now. Lift up thine head." This did the Turtle, and the angry birds cast great stones into the sea, and the left armlet which the Turtle wore was shattered. So he dived, but they called again, "Show thyself. Lift up thine head," and a stone fell upon the right armlet and broke it into small pieces. Again they called, and again the Turtle raised himself in the water, and this time the stones cut in twain the string on which the necklace of shell money was threaded.

And now for the last time came the call, "Show thyself. Lift up thine head." The Turtle once more raised himself and the birds flung after him all the great stones they could find. They fell in scores upon the wooden bowl which had been carried away from Binama's home, but it was not destroyed, nay, nor was it harmed at all. And the Turtle fled far over the sea, nor was he seen again of Binama or his followers. But since that day even until now, so our fathers have told us, all turtles carry upon their back the bowl which in the old days was in the house of Binama.

THE ANT AND THE PHEASANT

IN the old days, so our fathers have told us, the Ant and the Pheasant were friends, and one day they made a plan to go hunting. So they took their pig-net and set out. When they had reached the proper place, they put up their net, and the Pheasant said he would watch while the Ant drove beasts toward it.

It came to pass that after a time the Ant found a pig, and drove it into the net. Now when the Pheasant saw the wild pig rushing upon him he was much afraid, and flew up into a tree. Then was the pig glad, and he made his way out of the net with haste, for there was none to let[1] him. Then came the Pheasant down from the tree, and laid mud upon his wings, and waited for his friend. In a little the Ant came and said, "Where is the pig?"

The Pheasant made answer, "I caught the pig and held him, but he threw me down in the mud. Look now at my wings!"

Now this Pheasant was very deceitful, for he had lied even to his friend.

The Ant did not reproach him. He said, "Come, let us try another place with our net, and thou shalt hunt the game whilst I watch." They did so, and it came to pass that a pig ran into the net and was killed at once by the Ant. By and by the Pheasant came back and said, "Where is our pig?"

Then answered his friend the Ant, "Thou wilt find it over yonder by the tree."

The Pheasant looked by the tree, and there in truth was a pig lying. Then the two friends bound it tightly to a pole, and carried it home upon their shoulders.

---

[1] Hinder.

When they came to the house they cut up the pig, and the Ant said to the Pheasant, "Take the entrails of the pig to the river and wash them." The Pheasant went to do what the Ant bade him, and the Ant stayed alone in the house. Now as he was thus alone, a great hornbill stood in the doorway and said, in a terrible voice, "Ga-a-a-a-a!" Yet did the Ant not fear, but his heart grew hot within him for anger, and he leapt up and killed the hornbill, and hid him in a mat. Then the Pheasant returned, but bearing nought.

"Friend," said the Ant, "where are the entrails of the pig?"

"An eel snatched them from me," answered the Pheasant.

"It matters not," said the Ant gently. "But, I pray thee, come hither, and bring my mat with thee, for I would fain sit upon it."

The Pheasant took up the mat, but straightway saw the dead hornbill, and he cried out, "Friend, why hast thou killed my cousin? Didst thou not know that his kinsfolk are many, and that they will of a surety avenge his death ?"

But the Ant hardened his heart, and said, "I fear not thee nor thy kinsfolk. Go now to them, I pray thee, and tell them what thou hast seen here."

Then went the Pheasant, and told all the birds what the Ant had done. They gathered together in one place and took counsel what they should do. At last they determined to kill the Ant for that he had killed the hornbill.

The Ant climbed into the top of a tree, and each bird which in turn tried to attack him he slew. Then he made for himself a house by gumming leaves together, and he sat therein, and his heart was glad for that he had conquered his enemies.

But while he thus sat quietly inside the leaves, a great raven flew up, and with his sharp beak plucked off the little branch on which hung the Ant's nest. Then he carried the leaves to the shore, and swallowed the Ant, thus making an end of him.

So did he perish, and so was the death of the hornbill avenged.

THE MUD PEOPLE

IN the old days men lived not in houses, but dwelt in caves and holes in the ground, for none knew how they might fashion a shelter which would keep out the rain and sun.

Now it came to pass that two men talking idly together agreed to attempt to build some shelter on the face of the earth where their families might dwell safe from sun and rain, and nevertheless live in the light of day and not in the dark earth as heretofore.

They therefore arose and each went his way, neither did either see the face of other until the work was accomplished. Then came one and said to his fellow, "Come, let us go now and I will show thee the house I have fashioned."

And they went both together until they came to where the man had built his house, and behold, it was a fair sight indeed. For the man had taken of the long grass which is called rei, and had woven it thickly upon a frame of sticks, so that no ray of sun nor drop of rain might pierce the roof or walls of his house. But the other looking upon it saw that it was better than his own, and set about to decry it, that it might be worthless in the eyes of him who had built it.

"This then is thy shelter, brother," quoth he. "It were better for thee and thine to dwell therein than for me and mine. For I should fear greatly lest perchance the sharp rei should enter my eye, and so blind me. Moreover, it must needs be that it will prick thy skin and cause a rash to rise upon it. But come now," he said, turning away, "and I will show thee mine."

So they went together to see the other house. Now it was, in truth, but a sorry place, for its builder had taken handfuls of mud and plastered it over the light sticks he had placed in the ground. And the man who had built his house of rei spake thus, saying, "What wilt thou do, brother, when the rains come?"

"I fear no rain," quoth the other proudly, and bade his family enter the mud house and dwell therein. Then did the other man depart unto his own house, for he was vexed that his words had borne no .fruit. And he sat therein and pondered much what he might do in order that the other might know he had spoken wisely. And as much thought is the mother of deeds, in the morning he set out for the mountain where the great lake spirit dwelt. And there, using his spells, he besought Apogi to send forth his waters and to cause rain to fall upon the earth. Then he went back to his house and sat therein, and waited to see if Apogi would hear his prayer or not.

Not long had he to tarry, for the sun was yet high in the heaven when the rain clouds hid it from the eyes of men, and heavy was the rain which fell, and the man's heart was glad, for he knew that Apogi had done this.

Now it had been but an idle vaunt of the man who dwelt in the house of mud that he feared no rain, for indeed his heart trembled within him as great drops fell and his walls began to crumble. Nevertheless he sat on and did not stir until his wife besought him to seek some place of shelter for their little ones, who were wailing at their mother's knees. Then he rose up, and taking his family with him he left the house, and it was now but a frame of sticks, for the mud lay upon the ground in a pool of water. And the children cried aloud as they followed after their father, who led them to the house which was built of rei.

Now it came to pass that the man who had built his house of *rei* looked forth and saw them as they drew nigh in the rain. And he hardened his heart, and closed the doorway of his house and waited to hear what the man who had trusted in mud would say. And he, having come, beat upon the closed doorway, and cried, "Open to me, brother, and let us in, for the rain is great and my children weep without."

"Nay, brother," answered he from within the house. "How may I dare to do such a thing? Will not the sharp rei enter thine eye and blind thee? Or perchance it will prick the skin of thy children and cause a rash to rise upon it." Thus was the man met with his own words, and had nought wherewith to make answer. Sad was his plight and that of his wife and children as they turned away, and the wife of the man who had built the house of rei, looking on them pitied them, and besought her husband to give them shelter. He therefore, not wishing to displease his wife, opened up the doorway, and bade them enter. The man who had built his house of mud was sad at heart as he sat in shelter, and his head cooled with shame as he thought of his empty boast. When therefore the rain ceased, he set himself with speed to build a house like unto his neighhour's, and from that day even until now is mud contemned and our houses built of rei as it was in the beginning.

THE THREE SISTERS

IN a certain village there lived three sisters, and it fell on a day that they, went a fishing. Now as they went they must needs walk along a narrow path until they reached the river, therefore they went in single file. By and by, the eldest, who walked first, saw a snake lying by the path. He said to her, "I am an hungered. Wilt thou chew a little of the food in thy hand, and give it to me?"

"That will I never do," quoth the girl. "Thou art only a snake. My food is not for thee." And she went her way.

Soon came by the second sister, and the snake seeing ber, said, "Wilt thou chew a little food for me ? I am an hungered."

"Nay, verily," said the second sister. "Thou art but a snake. Let me pass." And she also went her way.

Last of all came the third sister. The snake asked once more, "Wilt thou chew some food for me because I am an hungered?"

"Yea, I will chew some for thee," said she at once, and sat down beside the snake, fearing nought. Then she chewed the taro she held, and made it soft and fed him with it. After a space she said, "Hast thou had enough ?"

"It is enough," he made answer. "I am no longer hungry. Whither goest thou?" he asked.

"I go to the river to fish."

"Then will I tell thee somewhat," quoth he. "When thou hearest a noise in the heavens, fish. But at the second noise climb the hill." Then she bade him farewell and left him, wondering what his words might mean.

Now when she reached the river she saw bought of her sisters, for they had not tarried for her. Then she heard the voice of thunder, of which the snake had spoken. (This is the tale thou askedst of me.) She began therefore to fish, and soon the basket slung at her side was full. Then came the second peal, of which she had been warned. She fled up the side of the mountain, and watched while much rain fell and great trees were swept down by the flood, but she stirred not until the storm was over. Then she came down once more, and set out for home. On the path lay the snake, and he raised his head when he saw her coming.

"Well," he said, "where are thy companions?"

"Alas! where are they?" she made answer. "They must have been swept out to sea when the river rose in flood."

"No doubt," quoth the snake. "Yet if they had fed me when I asked food of them they would be now not dead but living."

Then the girl took from her basket fish which were large, and wrapped them in a green leaf and gave them to the snake. And he held the little brindle in his mouth, and crept away to his home in the bush.

This then is the tale thou askedst of me, and if it seem folly for that snakes do not now hold converse with men, know that this snake of which I have told thee was "bariawa," and spake even as a man. Moreover, there is the snake of Kawakio, which spake twice, and Dubo, the snake which gave fire to the sons of men, but of them will I tell thee on another day.

THE ENCHANTED PILLOW

IN the old days there was a certain village in which three died to avenge a wrong done to a child.

It came to pass that on a day a man from the hills came into the village leading his little son. And when it was night, he went into the potuma, where the men slept, to pass the night, and he took with him the child. Now in the potuma was a man of the village who was fierce and violent in all his ways. When, therefore, he saw the hill-man about to sleep in the potuma, he arose and beat the little child, saying, "What doest thou here, O child? Knowest thou not that this is a house for men ? Begone!"

Now the child's father saw and heard, but he said nothing. And he rose up and took his little son in his arms, and went out of the potuma. Then the fierce man was glad, and he said, "So will I deal with all strangers," and he lay down to sleep.

It came to pass not many days after that all the people of the village were fishing at the river, and none saw the hill-man return and creep into the empty potuma. Now when he entered he had somewhat in his hand, but when he came forth his hands were empty. And he made haste hack to the hills.

At even the men of the village came back, and, after they had eaten, they went into the potuma, and made ready to sleep, for they were weary after fishing. And it befell that the violent man saw before him a headrest carved of wood, and he desired that it should be his. (But he knew not that it was the hill-man who had placed it there.) Therefore, as was his custom, he laid hold of it, saying, "This is now my pillow. If any wish for it let him take it from me if he can." Then he lay down and rested his neck on the wooden pillow, and was soon asleep, for none of the men were willing to wrestle with him as he had said.

Now in the morning the men woke and one by one came forth from the potuma into the village. But the violent man came not forth, and the others marvelled for what cause he tarried so long, such not being his custom. Therefore, after a time, one of them made bold to go once more into the potuma and to draw near to the violent man to waken him. But he was not able to do so, though he shook him and called to him many times. Then, looking upon him, he saw that he was dead, and he called the others, and they saw it and were afraid, for they knew not why he had died so quietly, and they said, "Who hath bewitched him?"

Then he was buried, and his name was no more spoken amongst them for that he was dead. But on the next night, another man, seeing the pillow lying without one to claim it as his, took it for his own, and lay down to sleep. And on the morrow, he also was dead when the other men arose. Therefore they said, "What cometh to the potuma at night that two men have died? Let us set a watch that we may know who is our enemy." And they did even as they had said, and one of them hid in the potuma all that day. Yet saw he nought. But toward evening a little child, who was playing with his friends outside the door, climbed in to see what was in the house. On a sudden the watcher saw the pillow fly into the air and fall with great force on the head of the child. The little lad lay dead upon the ground, and the pillow was standing in its place again ere the man who saw the deed could move. Then he called to the men who were waiting in their houses, and they came and carried the dead child to his mother.

Then they bethought them of the pillow which had caused the death of three people, and they made ready to take vengeance. They brought faggots of wood, and lit a great fire. Then one who was strong and brave went into the potuma and brought out the pillow and cast it into the heart of the fire. The pillow writhed as though it were alive, and it groaned, "A-ge-ge-ge-ge-ge. A-ke-ke-ke-ke-ke!"

until it was burned to ashes. And the ashes flew on the wind over the trees and over the hills to a mountain village, where sat the man from the hills who had thus taken vengeance for the ill done to his little son.

Now, it thou climbest the hills and comest to the village where dwells the hill-man, sleep not in his village, else may thy pillow slay thee as it slew the three who died in the old days.

HOW A MAN FOUND HIS WIFE IN
THE LAND OF THE DEAD

WHEN our dead leave us none knoweth whither they go, nor by much searching hath any man found the way to Ioloa, the land of the dead, save one, and of him will I tell thee.

This man lived in the hills where ariseth the Uruam, the river which flows into the sea between Wamira and Divari. It came to pass that the man's wife died, and he mourned for her many days. But when it was time for the death feast to be made for her, he went forth with his dog to hunt for a cuscus that it might be eaten at the feast. (This tale doth my father tell, and I who have heard it tell it now to thee.)

Now a cuscus sleeps all day, but in the softness of the evening it comes forth to seek its food. Therefore, it was at this time that the man set out to hunt. In a little he had found one, which he killed, and having no one with him who might carry it, he hung it upon a tree and went on. Once more he found one, which also he killed and hung on a tree. Then he saw a third, and the dog ran after it to catch it. But the cuscus ran also, and went down a hole in the earth. Now it went to its home in Ioloa, for it belonged to the Dead.

When the man reached the hole, he found that his dog had also gone down, and he feared lest it might lose its way and come not back to him. Therefore he rolled away the great stone which lay over the hole and looked down. There far below he saw coconuts growing, so he said within himself, "This is a village."

Then he too went down the hole far into the earth. His dog was before him, and he caught him in his arms. Now so it is in Ioloa that all the day the bones of the Dead lie on the ground, but at even each takes his own bones, and lives thus till the dawn. And as the man drew near, it was the time that the bones should live. It so befell that his wife was already walking, and was coming toward him. When she saw him, she said in her heart, "My husband hath died on the earth, and hath come to me." Then she went to him, and with her fingers pinched his arm until the blood showed on his skin. Then said she, "Thou art not dead. Wherefore hast thou come hither?" And when he had told her how it had befallen him to find the hole in the earth, and that he had followed his dog, she said, "Hold thy dog closely

lest he go after the bones of men which lie upon the ground, and come thou with
me while I hide thee, for it may be that the Dead will slay thee if they find thee
here."

Then she took him to her house and bade him lie still nor let the voice of the
dog be heard, for it was now time for the Dead to arise. The man did as she bade
him, and he watched as the Dead laid hold of each his own bones. "This is my
thigh," and "Here is my arm," he heard them say. Now it was night, and the Dead
began to dance, while some of them beat also upon drums. And the man was much
afraid as he watched from the house. But his wife remained with him, and he cared
not for fear nor any other thing while he had her with him once more. "Ah, my
wife," he cried, "how hot was my heart with grief till I found thee!"

But his wife feared for him that the Dead would find him in their land and would
work him some evil; therefore she said, "Thou must not tarry here, for the Dead
if they find thee will certainly fall upon thee. Therefore go now, I pray thee."

Then said the man, "How can I leave thee when I have but now found thee ?"

"Ah, my lord," answered the wife, "of a truth thou must not linger here. Yet
if thou wouldst see me once more go now, and after three nights are past come
again to me, and I will be here."

Then the man, after she had thus spoken, rose up to go. But on the way he stayed
to pick coconuts, and scented herbs, and wild limes, that he might show them to
the people of Uruam. And as he thus did, the Dead saw him and made haste after
him in great numbers, and seized from his hands the coconuts, the scented herbs,
and the wild limes, and he being beset by them could but escape with his life. And
when he had come up to the face of the earth, the Dead closed the hole with a great
stone that no man might lift.

Therefore when the man returned after the three nights were past, he found no
place where he might enter, and he saw his wife no more. Nor since that day have
any found the way to Ioloa. But if the stone had not been placed over the hole we
might even now have seen and talked with our dead after they had left us for their
own land.

WHERE THE COCONUT CAME FROM

THERE was a time, so our fathers have told us, when no coconut grew
throughout the land, and in those evil days men drank water to quench their
thirst, and ate taro upon which no coconut milk had been poured. Yet not knowing
how good is the coconut, they were content that it should be so.

Now in those days there was a certain village, and the men who dwelt there
were for ever fishing. They went forth in the morning, and came back in the

evening with the fish they had caught in long strings. And when the taro was cooked they sat round the pots and ate until none was left for the morrow. But one man, when he went to fish, went always alone, and in the evening he ever returned with a basket full of fish, for they were too many to thread upon grass.

The men of the village wondered that this man should never return without many fish, and also that he always forbade any to follow him, and when he was not with them they talked much of it and took counsel together how they might discover what he did to capture so many fish. And it so chanced that a boy who listened to their talk thought of a plan. "When he sets out to-morrow," said the lad, " I will creep behind him, and will watch from the long grass what he will do."

"Verily, that is well said," cried the men, and all were content that it should be so.

So it came to pass that on the morrow the boy did even as he had said. The man set out along the path, and the boy followed through the grass. And sometimes, in his desire to see what would come to pass, the boy crept too near, and the rustling of his body made the man look round, and even cast a spear into the grass to kill the beast which he thought made the rustling sound. But the lad, seeing the spear coming, moved to one side, and went warily until the man reached the seashore. Then the boy hid behind a corkwood tree, and from thence he saw this strange thing. The man laid down his basket and, putting both hands to his head, he pulled, and the head came off in his two hands.

Then the man laid aside his head beside the basket on the beach, and walked into the sea, until the waters were about his middle. There he stood, and the boy's heart trembled for fear of what might next befall. And it came to pass that the man bowed himself, and a multitude of fishes rushed down the man's throat, which was open to the water, his head being upon the beach. After a short space the man turned and walked slowly to the shore. There he shook out the fish, and feeling for his head he placed it upon his neck and it was a part of him once more. Then he sat down and sorted out the fish he had thus caught, filling his basket with the largest, and throwing away those which were poor.

All this the boy saw from behind the tioba tree, where he lay hidden. And having seen he fled the place, for he feared the man who did such things as these.

Now it came to pass that at supper that night all ate of the fish which had been caught save only the boy. And though many asked him, "Why eatest thou not? Art fasting?" he refused even to touch with his fingers the fish which the man had caught.

After supper, therefore, certain of the men went apart with the boy and inquired of him for what cause he had not eaten the fish that night. Then the boy told them truly all that he had seen that day, and they in their turn were filled with loathing for the food which had been thus caught. They said, therefore, "Let us all go on the morrow and punish the man who hath done us this wrong," and to this all agreed.

Now it came to pass on the morrow that they did even as they had said, and as the man laid his head upon the beach, not one, but many, were watching from their hiding-place. And when he had bowed himself in the water and the watchers had seen the fishes which swam toward him that they might enter his throat, a man rose up and ran to where the head lay, and seizing it, flung it far from him into the bush. Then all waited to see what would happen.

In a little the man, having fish enough, turned and came slowly back to the shore. There he shook out the fish as was his custom, and then he felt for his head with both hands. But lo, it was not there! The watchers saw that he crawled over the pebbles with his two hands outstretched, if haply he might so lay hold of his head. But it was in vain that he sought it, and suddenly he rose, and rushed into the sea again, and there, before their eyes, became a huge fish and dived out of their sight. Then the men, having taken vengeance, went back to the village.

After many days the boy who had first spied upon the man bethought him of the head which had been thrown into the bush. And he went to seek it that he might know what had befallen it. But when he reached the spot where it had been thrown it was no longer there, and in its stead had grown up a slender palm, with spreading leaves. None knew what manner of plant it might be, and when it bore fruit men feared to eat of it lest perchance it might harm them. But at last a woman made bold to eat of the nuts and to anoint herself with the milky juice, and all saw that she was none the worse, but rather the better. Thus did all men come to know of the coconut, and from that time even until now is it our food and drink, and in many other ways doth it serve us. And that thou mayest know that the tale is true, look now upon a coconut from which the husk hath been taken away, and thou shalt see the face of the man whose head became the first coconut.

PERSIA

THE stories of Rustem form part of the great national epic of Persia—
The Shah Nameh, or Book of Kings. The hero is Rustem, and his exploits
remind one of other national heroes—Hercules of the Greeks, Arthur of the Celts,
and Maui of New Zealand, among others. The Persian stories are adorned with
all the glowing imagery of the East, and express its love for bright colours, rich
fabrics, and glittering jewels.

The writer of this great epic was the poet Firdausi, sometimes called the Homer
of Persia. He lived in the eleventh century and for thirty-three years toiled at his
epic. He presented it to the Sultan but received no adequate return and soon had
to leave the court, pursued by the Sultan's hatred. His praise, however, was soon
proclaimed in every city, and, after many years, the Sultan repented that he had
treated the poet so unjustly. He sent him a great sum of money, but the gift came
too late to make amends for Firdausi was being carried to his grave as the present
arrived.

FROM A PERSIAN JEST BOOK

A POOR wrestler, who had passed all his life in forests, resolved to try his
fortune in a great city, and as he drew near it he observed with wonder the
crowds on the road, and thought, "I shall certainly not be able to know myself
among so many people if I have not something about me that the others have not."
So he tied a pumpkin to his right leg and, thus decorated, entered the town.

A young wag, perceiving the simpleton, made friends with him, and induced
him to spend the night at his house. While he was asleep, the joker removed the
pumpkin from his leg and tied it to his own, and then lay down again. In the
morning, when the poor fellow awoke and found the pumpkin on his companion's
leg, he called to him, "Hey! get up, for I am perplexed in my mind. Who am I and
who are you? If I am I myself, why is the pumpkin on your leg? And if you are
yourself, why is the pumpkin not on my leg?"

SOHRAB, THE CHILD OF MANY SMILES

NOW it came to pass one day, when Rustem was hunting in a certain forest,
that he killed a wild ass, and having roasted it and eaten well, he lay down
to sleep. Rakush, as usual, was grazing near by, when a band of seven robbers
passed that way, and seeing the noble animal, determined to take him away with

them. This was no easy task, for the horse fought desperately for freedom, biting off the head of one, and trampling another underfoot before the rest managed to overpower him and lead him away. Now when Rustem awoke, he was sad at heart, for he loved Rakush more than anything in the world; and remembering his loyalty and affection, he said to himself, "He would never have deserted me in my hour of need. Some enemy hath done this; and now will I follow after him and be avenged." So he began to search about for traces of footmarks, and presently found them leading toward a certain city. Thither he took his way, and being known of the king and nobles of that place, he found them all ready to receive him at the gates of the city. But while they greeted him courteously and implored him to enter and feast with them, Rustem, still in a mood of wrath, accused them of stealing Rakush, whose footprints he had traced to the very walls of the city. They, however, denied all knowledge of the theft; and when he began to threaten them with death and destruction the king grew sore afraid and implored him to lay aside his anger, declaring that he would himself punish the offenders the moment they were discovered.

So Rustem agreed to enter the palace in peace, and after sitting at a great banquet hastily prepared in his honour, he was led to a rose-scented couch and soon fell fast asleep. Scarcely had he slept an hour when he was awakened by a slave girl carrying a lamp in her hand. The next moment he was astonished to see before him a most beautiful maiden, "graceful as the lofty cypress tree." "Who art thou?" asked the wondering hero, and she answered: "I am Tamineh, daughter of the king thy host, whom no man save my father has ever yet set eyes upon. But I have heard of thee, my lord, and of the brave deeds thou hast performed, and the glory thou hast won in all the earth. And so I loved thee, lord, and sought about for some pretext to bring thee into this city that I might look upon thee. So I sent spies to watch thy progress, and to bring in Rakush thy steed, as thou layest asleep. For, said I, he will surely follow hard upon his tracks. And now, O Rustem, if thou lovest me in return, do thou ask me in marriage of my father, and Rakush shall be quickly restored to thee." Then Rustem looked upon her and loved her for her beauty and her wisdom; and on the next day, they were married, for the king was exceedingly glad to make alliance with the famous and dreaded Rustem, and all the city rejoiced to hear the news.

Now, when a few days had passed away in feasting and merriment, the neighing of Rakush was heard outside the city gates; and then Rustem was sad, for he knew he must depart to his own country. But he did not wish that men should know that he had taken a wife; for all looked to him to wed a maiden of his own people. So he took a tender farewell of Tamineh, and taking an amulet made of onyx stone from his arm he gave it to her, saying: "If Heaven should grant thee a little daughter in my absence, bind this onyx in her hair; but if a son, place it upon his arm; then shall he be strong of limb as Sahm my grandsire, and graceful of speech as Zal my father."

Then Rustem threw himself upon Rakush, and the good horse quickly bore him out of sight, leaving the weeping Tamineh to mourn his loss in loneliness. And Rustem, when he had returned to his own land, told no man what had happened in his absence.

Now in the course of time a lovely babe was born to Tamineh, a laughing boy, who smiled at the world from the moment he entered it; and so they called him Sohrab, or the child of smiles. Mighty was he like his father, for when he was but a month old, he was as big as a yearling child, and when he grew to nine years he could fight and ride better than any grown man in that land.

Then Tamineh was afraid, for she said, "Surely Rustem will be proud of such a son and will send for him and take him from me." So while he was yet a babe she bound the onyx on his arm, but sent tidings to Rustem that a baby daughter had been born to them. And Rustem was sorrowful, for he had hoped for a brave son; but he sent fine jewels for the child, and bade the mother rear her in tenderness, for meantime he was busy in the battlefield, and could not come to see her.

When Sohrab was about ten years of age he came to his mother one day and said, "See, I am taller and stronger than any one of the boys with whom I play, and yet, when they ask me of my race and my father's name I can answer nothing. Tell me, I pray thee, who is my sire?"

And Tamineh answered, "My son, thy father's name is Rustem, and he is the greatest hero the world has ever seen." Then the boy was glad, and many a brave deed done by his father in old days was told to him. And at length he cried, "Mother, tell me where my father is, that I may go to him and fight by his side."

But Tamineh wept and said, "I have lost my husband, and now shall also lose my only son ? Seek not to find him, I implore thee, for if he knows thou art his child, he will take thee from me and from thy happy home: and then thy mother's heart will break in agony." Yet even the tears of his bereaved mother could not avail to turn Sohrab from his purpose.

Then Tamineh tried to frighten him, telling him of the might and cruelty of Afrasiab, king of the Tartars, and Persia's foe, and warning him that were it once voiced abroad that he was Rustem's son, Afrasiab would never rest till he had got him in his power. But Sohrab answered: "Never again will I hide my father's name—instead, I will march against all these tyrants—the kingdom of stern Afrasiab shall be wrenched from his dominion, and Kai Kaoos shall be hurled from his imperial throne. Then shall Rustem hold his crown and sceptre, and none shall approach my glorious sire in power and majesty."

So he made preparations to depart; first seeking a steed that should be worthy to carry him to the wars. The royal stables were ransacked for the purpose, and one after another the horses were paraded, and Sohrab tested their strength like as did his father before him; and in the same manner each was quickly crushed under the weight of his hand. At length there trotted past him a mighty colt, none other than the foal of Rakush; and Sohrab, leaping on his back, knew that at last he had his soul's desire. And thus mounted, the youth bade his mother farewell, and rode forth to conquer the kingdom of Persia for Rustem his father, whom as yet he had not seen.

Now when Afrasiab, king of the Tartars, heard that Sohrab was preparing an expedition against Kai Kaoos his ancient foe, he rejoiced in his heart; and summoning two of his bravest chieftains he said to them, "See that ye quickly call together an army; for fate has permitted us to settle the affairs of this world. And now let me tell in your ear my purpose; but see that ye divulge it to no man. This Sohrab is the son of Rustem the Mighty, but Rustem knows him not, nor is he aware that he has a son. Let us then strengthen the hands of Sohrab and aid him to fight against the hosts of Persia; for Rustem will surely come to the aid of his country, and if fortune favours our cause the lion will perish before the onset of his fierce young whelp. Then will we turn and rend the forces of Sohrab in the day of their victory, and so will Persia fall a prey into our hands. But should the fates will that Sohrab fall at the hands of Rustem, it will still be well for us; for the mighty one will die with grief when he learns that he has slain his son." So the Tartar warriors made all haste to join the forces of Sohrab, bringing rich gifts and flattering messages from their king; whereat the heart of the youth was glad, and he marched on his way rejoicing.

SOHRAB AND RUSTEM

IN the space midway between the two camps was a little sandy plain; and in this place, within view of the rival hosts, did Rustem take his stand, gazing with gloomy curiosity at Sohrab as he came to meet him. Very young he looked, but tall and straight as some dark cypress tree against the morning sky. And Rustem wondered who he was and whence he came, and pitying him as one fated soon to die at his hand, he beckoned to him to come quite near, and gently said:

> " O thou young man, the air of Heaven is soft,
> And warm and pleasant; but the grave is cold.
> Heaven's air is better than the cold dead grave.
> Behold: I am vast and clad in iron,
> And tried; and I have stood on many a field
> Of blood, and I have fought with many a foe:
> Never was that field lost, or that foe saved.
> O Sohrab, wherefore wilt thou rush on death?

> Be governed: quit the Tartar host, and come
> To Iran and be as my son to me,
> And fight beneath my banner till I die,
> There are no youths in Iran brave as thou."

When Sohrab heard that deep resounding voice, and saw that mighty form planted like some tall rock upon the sand, hope filled his heart, and running forward to embrace his knees, he cried:

"Tell me, I pray thee, by all thou hold'st most dear, art thou not Rustem? Speak! Art thou not he?"

But Rustem's soul was filled with suspicion at these words, and he said within himself, "These Tartar boys are cunning as young foxes; for if I now say 'Rustem stands before thee,' he will neither yield nor run away, but will find some excuse not to fight, and will feign friendship, praising me with flattering words. Then will he go away, and in days to come, perchance in the halls of Afrasiab himself, he will say with boasting lips:

> "'I challenged once, when the two armies camped
> Beside the Oxus, all the Persian lords
> To cope with me in single fight; but they
> Shrank; only Rustem dared: then he and I
> Changed gifts, and went on equal terms away.'

"And so shall shame come upon the princes of Persia and on me." Reflecting thus, he turned to Sohrab and sternly said, "Rise! why dost thou vainly question me of Rustem? I am here, whom thou hast summoned to the fight; therefore, make good thy boast or yield at once. Is it that thou wilt only fight with Rustem? Know, rash boy, that men look upon Rustem's face and straightaway flee. And if to-day he stood before thee here, full well I know that there would be no more talk of fighting for thee. Now yield thee as thou art, or else:

> "Thy bones shall strew this sand, till winds
> Bleach them, or Oxus with his summer floods,
> Oxus in summer wash them all away."

Then Sohrab answered in hot anger: "Think not to frighten me with threats. I am no girl to be made pale by words. Yet thou hast said truly that were Rustem here, there would not be strife between us. But alas! he is far away, and we are here. Begin therefore, and do thy worst."

Then Rustem hurled his spear at the youth, which shivered to pieces against his shield, and then they fought with swords in desperate wise, till the edges were hacked like saws. Casting this weapon aside, Rustem grasped the club which only he could wield, a huge tree-trunk with unlopped branches, and brought it down with all the force of his mighty frame. But Sohrab swerved aside so that it fell thundering to the earth, and once more the champions closed together, fighting so fiercely that their armour was torn in pieces, their weapons bent, and mingled blood and sweat poured upon the ground. Then, as both stood apart for a moment's breathing space, Rustem said to himself, "Never have I seen either man or demon with such activity and strength."

"Come, thou champion," cried Sohrab gaily, "come when thou art ready and let us try the combat with our bows and arrows."

But with these weapons they were both so skilful that neither could get the better of the other. Then they tried wrestling, hand to hand, but though Rustem used such force as might have shaken a mountain, he could not move Sohrab from the ground. Forthwith the young man seized his mace, and struck Rustem such a blow that he reeled backward and nearly fell. And as the youth laughed in his triumph, the champion slowly recovered himself and said, "Night cometh on; let us resume the fight to-morrow."

"Not so!" cried Sohrab tauntingly, "I have given thee enough. I will now let Kai Kaoos feel the edge of my sword." So he rode toward the king's tent, killing all who stood in his way; but Rustem, who had thought to ravage the lines of the Tartar hosts meantime, remembered that his chief duty was to protect the Shah, and returning, prevailed upon Sohrab to call a truce for the night. "To-morrow," said he, "if thou art still for war, thou shall fight again with me alone."

Sohrab was at length weary with the conflict, and so the words of Rustem prevailed, and the two champions retired to their tents.

THE DEATH OF SOHRAB

WHEN all was still in the camps, Kai Kaoos sent for Rustem to question him concerning the strange skill and power of his young adversary. And he was much moved when Rustem frankly said "I have met none like him, for he seems to be made of iron. With sword and arrow and club have I fought him, and yet he is still unhurt. In skill as a warrior he is my superior and Heaven only knows what will be the result of to-morrow's fight."

Sohrab, meantime, had sought the tent of Peran-Wisa, to whom he said with anxious look, "This old man has the strength and appearance of Rustem. God forbid that he should prove my father!" But the Counsellor, whose aged eyes were dim, said: "I have often seen Rustem, and I am persuaded that this champion is not he, though he is very like him."

So Sohrab's mind was at peace.

Yet again when the morning dawned, and the two men faced each other upon the level plain, the heart of Sohrab was strangely full of affection for his opponent and he would willingly have stayed his hand. But Rustem, grimly desirous of avenging his previous lack of success, quickly opened the combat, with a blow from his mighty club delivered with such terrific might, that as Sohrab leaped lightly aside once more, it fell with a force that brought the hero to his knees, with fingers clutching the sand to save himself from complete discomfiture. Now was the moment for Sohrab to draw his sword and pierce the hero, as he knelt dizzy and choked with sand; but he stood by and begged Rustem to make a truce. But while he was speaking, Rustem had risen erect, trembling with rage, his giant form covered with dust, his chest heaving, his lips foaming. He bade Sohrab speak no more but fight.

Then Sohrab, finding all his hopes were in vain, prepared again for the contest. In grim earnest the two men tugged and strained together like lions, while the red blood and sweat flowed down upon the sand. At length young Sohrab with a mighty effort raised the champion in his arms and dashed him backward upon the sandy plain. Then he sat upon the mighty frame and drawing his dagger, prepared to cut off the head of his vanquished foe. But Rustem said: "Dost thou not know that by the custom of this country, when a champion is thrown for the first time his head is not severed from the body, but only after the second fall?"

Then Sohrab was glad in his heart at the excuse, and, sheathing his dagger, he allowed his enemy to rise and both men went in silence to their tents.

When Peran-Wisa heard what had passed, he bewailed the conduct of Sohrab. "Thou hast ensnared the lion and then set him at liberty only to devour thee," said he. But Sohrab replied: "Twice hath he been within my power, and the third time I shall surely slay him, for he is evidently my inferior in skill and strength."

The third morning dawned, and with strength renewed, the heroes faced each other for the last time. Bright sunshine blazed upon the plain, but as the deadly conflict recommenced, the sun was darkened over the spot where they were fighting, and as if in sorrow for the tragic strife, a wind arose and "moaning swept the plain." Yet where the hosts were drawn up on either side it was still broad sunshine; only where those two swayed and grappled was there gloom and darkness.

First Rustem aimed a thrust with his spear which pierced the shield of Sohrab nearly through; but meantime Sohrab with a stroke of his sword, sheared away the blood-red plume from his adversary's helmet. And ever the gloom grew darker, thunder pealed, and lightning cleft the sky; Oxus alone pursued indifferent his wonted course.

Then Rakush, who all this while had stood near his master, gave utterance to a dreadful cry, like the roar of "some pained desert lion"; and all the troops heard it and quaked with fear.

Again Sohrab struck; and this time his blade shivered into pieces on the iron helmet, leaving the hilt only in his hand. Then Rustem raised his giant frame; his fierce eyes glared, and shaking his spear on high, he shouted his dread battle-cry: "Rustem!"

At that word Sohrab staggered aghast and stood bewildered. His covering shield drooped in his nerveless grasp, and ere he could regain the power of resistance the spear of Rustem had found fatal entrance to his side.

> And then the gloom dispersed, and the wind fell,
> And the bright sun broke forth, and melted all the cloud;
> And the two armies saw the pair;
> Saw Rustem standing, safe upon his feet,
> And Sohrab, wounded, on the bloody sand.

Then Rustem bitterly spake:" So thou didst think to slay a Persian lord this day, and that great Rustem would come down to fight with thee! See, thou art slain, and by an unknown man!"

But the youth gasped fiercely out: "Thou art unknown, 'tis true, but 'tis not thou who hast slain me. Rustem hath dealt my death blow, for that name unnerved my arm—that and something in thyself which troubled my heart and made my shield to fall. But hear thou this, thou mighty unknown man:

> "The mighty Rustem shall avenge my death!
> My father, whom 1 seek through all the world,
> He shall avenge my death and punish thee!"

And Rustem unbelieving said:

> "What prate is this of fathers and revenge?
> The mighty Rustem never had a son."

But Sohrab answered with a choking voice, "Ah, yes, he had, and that lost son am I. And one day when this news reaches the home of Rustem, where he sits afar, he will arise and seek vengeance for an only son. Deeply will he grieve, but most I pity her, my mother Tamineh, who, in her distant home, never more will see her Sohrab return from the warriors' camp." Then Rustem pondered these words, for they brought to his mind the scenes of other days, his dark-eyed wife and their pleasant life "in that long distant summer-time." There at his feet lay dying upon the sand a youth, of just the age that his own son might have been, and the sight suffused his eyes with tears: "Oh, Sohrab," he murmured, "thou indeed art such a son as Rustem would have loved. But thy words bear not the mark of truth, for know that Rustem never had a son.

> "One child he had—
> But one—a girl; who with her mother now
> Plies some light female task, nor dreams of us."

Then Sohrab, his strength ebbing fast, raised up his arm and cried, "Behold this onyx, given by Rustem to my mother, that she might bind it on her babe."

Then Rustem looked and saw the onyx stone, on which was cut that bird of wonder which had reared Zal *in* earlier days; and the sight struck with cold horror at his heart. He stood for some moments and then grief found utterance!

"O Boy—thy father!" His voice choked there, and falling down by Sohrab's side he lay awhile as one dead. But ere long Sohrab roused him with loving words, and when the champion realized afresh his awful deed and grasped his sword with intent to slay himself by the side of his son, he prevented him, saying:

> "Come, sit beside me on this sand, and take
> My head betwixt thy hands, and kiss my cheeks,
> And wash them with thy tears, and say, 'My son!'
> Quick! quick! for numbered are my sands of life,
> And swift; for like the lightning to this field
> I came, and like the wind I go away."

Then Rustem clasped him to his heart with many tears; and the opposing hosts looked with awe upon the unwonted sight. And Rakush came close to them with head bowed to the ground and mane sweeping the sand; and big tears of compassion fell from his soft dark eyes. Sohrab stroked the famous horse whose name he knew so well, and pitying his father's overwhelming grief tried to comfort him, saying: "Death comes to all men; why, then, this grief?" He then implored his father to send away the forces without the horrors of a battle and to carry him to his own place, the home of white-haired ZaI, and there to raise over him a tomb of which men might say:

> "Sohrab, the mighty Rustem's son, lies there,
> Whom his great father did in ignorance kill."

But Rustem wept sore, saying: "How shall I live without thee, O my son—if only I might die in thy stead.

> "But now in blood and battles was my youth,
> And full of blood and battles is my age;
> And I shall never end this life of blood."

But Sohrab answered very slowly and solemnly: "Thou shalt have peace in the day when thou shalt sail in a high-masted ship.

> "Returning home over the salt blue sea
> From laying thy dear master in his grave."

And so he died; and the bereaved father covered his face with his horseman's cloak and sat motionless by his side.

PORTUGAL

THE Portuguese language has grown out of a local form of the *Lingua Romana Rustica* and in subsequent years many elements of Arabic, from the Saracen invaders, and of the Frankish and Celtic dialects, from the Burgundian founders of the monarchy, have been ingrafted upon it. The popular tales of the people therefore have many types that are common to other European peoples. The stories of Old Lusitania are more quaint and humorous than the others, being allied more closely to the "beast epics."

THE SEVEN IRON SLIPPERS

THERE lived once together a king and a queen, and a princess who was their daughter. The princess had worn out every evening seven pairs of slippers made of iron; and the king could not make out how that could be, though he was always trying to find out.

The king at last issued a decree, that whosoever should be able to find out how the princess managed to wear out seven slippers made of iron in the short space of time between morning and evening, he would give the princess in marriage if he were a man, and if a woman he would marry her to a prince.

It happened that a soldier was walking along an open country road carrying on his back a sack of oranges, and he saw two men fighting and giving each other great blows. The soldier went up to them and asked them, "Oh, men, why are you giving each other such blows?"

"Why indeed should it be!" they replied, "because our father is dead, and he has left us this cap, and we both wish to possess it."

"Is it possible that for the sake of a cap you should be fighting?" inquired the soldier. The men then said, "The reason is that this cap has a charm, and if anyone puts it on and says, 'Cap, cover me so that no one shall see me!' no one can see us." The soldier upon hearing this said to them, "I'll tell you what I can do for you; you let me remain here with the cap whilst I throw this orange to a great distance, and you run after it, and the one that shall pick it up first shall be the possessor of the cap."

The men agreed to this, and the soldier threw the orange to a great distance, as far as he possibly could, whilst the men both ran to pick it up.

Here the soldier without loss of time put on the cap saying, "Cap, make me invisible." When the men returned with the orange they could see nothing and nobody. The soldier went away with the cap, and further on he met on his road two other men fighting, and he said to them, "Oh, foolish men, why do you give each other such blows?" The men replied, "Indeed, you may well ask why, if it were not that father died and left us this pair of boots, and we, each of us, wish to be the sole possessor of them." The soldier replied, "Is it possible that for the matter of a pair of boots you should be fighting thus?" And they replying said, "It is because these boots are charmed, and when one wishes to go any distance, one has only to say: 'Boots, take me here or there,' wherever one should wish to go, and instantly they convey one to any place?'

The soldier said to them, "I will tell you what to do; I will throw an orange to a great distance, and you give me the boots to keep; you run for the orange, and the first who shall pick it up shall have the pair of boots." He threw the orange to a great distance and both men ran to catch it. Upon this the soldier said, "Cap, make me invisible, boots, take me to the city!" and when the men returned they missed the boots, and the soldier, for he had gone away. He arrived at the capital and heard the decree read which the king had promulgated, and he began to consider what he had better do in this case. "With this cap, and with these boots I can surely find out what the princess does to wear out seven pairs of slippers made of iron in one night." He went and presented himself at the palace. When the king saw him he said, "Do you really know a way of finding out how the princess, my daughter, can wear out seven slippers in one night?" The soldier replied, "I only ask you to let me try .... "

"But you must remember," said the king, "that if at the end of three days you have not found out the mystery, I shall order you to be put to death." The soldier to this replied that he was prepared to take the consequences. The king ordered him to remain in the palace. Every attention was paid to all his wants and wishes, he had his meals with the king at the same table, and slept in the princess's room. But what did the princess do? She took him a beverage to his bedside and gave it to him to drink. This beverage was a sleeping draught which she gave him to make him sleep all night.

Next morning the soldier had not seen the princess do anything, for he had slept very soundly the whole night. When he appeared at breakfast the king asked him, "Well, did you see anything?" "Your majesty must know that I have seen nothing whatever." The king said, "Look well what you are at, for now there only remains two days more to you, or else you die!"

The soldier replied, "I have not the least misgivings."

Night came on and the princess acted as before. Next morning the king asked him again at breakfast, "Well, have you seen anything last night?" The soldier replied, "Your majesty must know that I have seen nothing whatever." "Be careful, then, what you do, only one day more and you die!" The soldier replied, "I have no misgivings." He then began to think it over. "It is very curious that I should sleep all night—it cannot be from anything else but from drinking the beverage which the princess gives me .... Leave me alone, I know what I shall do; when the princess brings me the cup, I shall pretend to drink, but shall throw away the beverage."

The night came and the princess did not fail to bring him the beverage to drink to his bedside. The soldier made a pretence to drink it, but instead threw it away, and feigned sleep though he was awake. In the middle of the night he saw the princess rise up, prepare to go out, and advance toward the door to leave. What did he do then? He put on the cap, drew on the boots, and said, "Cap, make me invisible, boots, take me wherever the princess goes."

The princess entered a carriage, and the soldier followed her into the carriage and accompanied her. He saw the carriage stop at the seashore. The princess then embarked on board a vessel decked with flags. The soldier on seeing this said, "Cap, cover me, that I may be invisible," and embarked with the princess. She reached the land of giants, and when on passing the first sentinel, he challenged her with, "Who's there?" "The Princess of Harmony," she replied. The sentinel rejoined, "Pass with your suite." The princess looked behind her, and not seeing any one following her, she said to herself, "The sentinel cannot be in his sound mind; he said 'pass with your suite'; I do not see any one." She reached the second sentinel, who cried out at the top of his voice, "Who's there ?" "The Princess of Harmony," replied the princess. "Pass with your suite," said the sentinel. The princess was each time more and more astonished. She came to a third sentinel, who challenged her as the others had done, "Who's there?" "The Princess of Harmony." "Pass on with your suite," rejoined the sentinel. The princess as before wondered what the man could mean.

After journeying for a long time the soldier who followed her closely, saw the princess arrive at a beautiful palace, enter in, and go into a hall for dancing where he saw many giants. The princess sat upon a seat by the side of her lover who was a giant. The soldier hid himself under their seat. The band struck up, and she rose to dance with the giant, and when she finished the dance she had her iron slippers all in pieces. She took them off and pushed them under her seat. The soldier immediately took possession of them and put them inside his sack. The princess again sat down to converse with her lover. The band again struck up some dance music and the princess rose to dance.

When she finished this dance another of her slippers had worn out. She took them off and left them under her seat. The soldier put these also into his sack. Finally, she danced seven times, and each time she danced she tore a pair of slippers made of iron. The soldier kept them all in his sack. After the ball the princess sat down to converse with her lover; and what did the soldier do? He turned their chairs over and threw them both on the middle of the floor. They were very much surprised and they searched everywhere and through all the houses and could find no one. The giants then looked out for a book of fates they had, wherein could be seen the course of the winds and other auguries peculiar to their race. They called in a black servant to read in the book and find out what was the matter. The soldier rose up from where he was and said, "Cap, make me invisible." He then gave the negro a slap on the face, the negro fell to the ground, while he took possession of the book and kept it. The time was approaching when the princess must depart and return home, and not being able to stay longer she went away. The soldier followed her and she returned by the same way she came. She went on board and when she reached the city the carriage was already waiting for her. The soldier then said, "Boots, take me to the palace," and he arrived there, took off his clothes, and went to bed. When the princess arrived she found everything in her chamber just as she left it, and even found the soldier fast asleep. In the morning the king said, "Well, soldier, did you see anything remarkable last night?" "Be it known to your majesty that I saw nothing whatever last night," replied the soldier. The king then said, "According to what you say, I do not know if you are aware that you must die to-day." The soldier replied, "If it is so I must have patience, what else can I do!" When the princess heard this she rejoiced much. The king then ordered that everything for the execution should be prepared before the palace windows. When the soldier was proceeding to execution he asked the king to grant him a favour, for the last time and to send for the princess so that she should be present. The king gave the desired permission, and the princess was present, when he said to her, "Is it true to say that the princess went out at midnight?"

"It is not true," replied the princess.

"Is it true to say," again asked the soldier, "that the princess entered a carriage, and afterward went on board a vessel and proceeded to a ball given in the kingdom of the giants?" The princess replied, "It is not true." The soldier yet asked her another question, "Is it true that the princess tore seven pairs of slippers during the seven times she danced?" and then he showed her the slippers. "There is no truth in all this," replied the princess. The soldier at last said to her, "Is it true to say that the princess at the end of the ball fell on the floor from her seat, and the giants had a book brought to them to see what bewitchcry and magic pervaded and had taken possession of the house, and which book is here ?" The princess now said, "It is so." The king was delighted at the discovery and happy ending of this affair, and the soldier came to live in the palace and married the princess.

THE SPIDER

THERE lived once a boy whose father and mother were desirous that he should learn some trade. He had no wish to do so, but, as his parents insisted upon it, he undertook to learn the trade of a shoemaker. But as soon as the father died he desisted from work and gave up making shoes. The mother was very angry with him for this and turned him out of doors. The boy told his mother that he would be sure to return home a rich man some day, and that he meant to marry the first female he met on his way. He took a basket with all his shoemaker's tools and went away. He journeyed many leagues through some forest and overgrown places, and meeting with a large square stone on his way he sat upon it, took out a loaf from his basket, and began to eat. From under the stone a large spider came out, and the boy had hardly seen her when he said to her, "You shall be my wife?"

The spider on hearing this crawled inside the basket, but the boy made a hole in the loaf he carried and put her in it. He walked and he walked, and he sighted at a great distance an old house. He entered it, placed the basket on the floor, and the spider came out of it, and went crawling up the walls until she reached the ceiling, and commenced to make a web.

The boy turned toward her and looking up, said, "That is the way I like to see women, fond of work." The spider made no answer.

The boy then went seeking for work at a neighbouring village. As it happened that in that village there were no shoemakers he was welcomed among them, and they gave him plenty of work to do. As the youth found that he was making a fortune he engaged a servant-maid to attend upon his wife, and brought her to the old house where the spider had remained. He furnished the house and bought a little clay stove and some plates and dishes for the dinner. He then went out and left the servant with the spider. The maid remained much astonished; and wondered still more when the spider told her to open a certain door which led to the fowl-house and kill a chicken, and afterward to open a cupboard where she would find everything necessary for cooking and for the general use of the house. When the youth returned home he found the house swept and a dinner prepared of the best and most delicious viands. Being very pleased, he turned round to the spider and said, "See what a good choice I have made in my wife!" The spider from the ceiling threw down all manner of embroidered stuffs which she had worked for beautifying her house: and after they had lived in this way a whole year, and the youth had already become very rich, and no longer required to work at his trade, for everything he required in the way of clothing and food and everything else necessary for life always made its appearance without his knowing how, he resolved to return to his mother's house as he had promised her he would do at the end of a year. He ordered two horses to be saddled and got ready, and said to his servant, "You shall now act as my wife, because I am going to tell my mother that I am married." The maid was delighted at this and mounted the horse prepared for her and went with the youth. The spider came down from the ceiling and went to the fowl-house where she only found a cock left. She got inside it, and thus went walking behind the two on horseback. On reaching the forest they entered it, and both sat on the same stone, from under which the spider had come out before. They were looking on the ground when they saw the cock and heard it crow:

> " Ki kiri ki,
> Ki kiri kioh!
> Here is the king
> And I am the queen oh!"

At that moment the stone broke open in two parts, and became transformed into a splendid palace. The spider was turned into a beautiful princess, and married the youth, who became king and she a queen. They then sent for the mother; while the servant-maid continued with them as lady-in-waiting.

THE HIND OF THE GOLDEN APPLE

THERE once lived a woman who had a son, and they were so poor that the boy went every day for wood to burn in the pine forest. One day when he was in the forest he saw a hind, which was very small and most beautiful, come toward him with a golden apple hanging from its neck. The pretty hind commenced to speak to the boy to know what he was doing there, and after a while she asked him: "Would you like to come with me to see my lair? If you do I will give you so much money!" The youth then heard a voice say: "Do not accept anything from her!" And he therefore replied to the hind that he did not want anything. The hind again said to him: "Come to my lair, oh youth, and I will give you much money, and I can make you very happy indeed!" The voice again said: "Do not on any account accept anything, but tell her you would like to have the golden apple that hangs from her neck." The youth followed the advice given, and said to the hind, "The only thing I wish to have is the golden apple you possess; I desire nothing else." The hind gave it to him as she said, "Here, take it then!" The boy took it and divided it in two, and instantly four giants came out, who said to him, "What is it you want?"

"Well, I should very much wish to have all this wood taken to my mother's house until she had more than she wanted or knew where to store it."

The youth again opened the apple and the giants appeared as before and asked him, "What can we do for you?"

"I want a palace with a princess in it, and everything requisite?"

The giants at once set to, forming a magnificent palace, and a most comely princess was waiting for him inside; and the youth took possession of it and went to live in it.

There was a man who, seeing the youth's wealth and good fortune, was envious of him, and one day spoke to a witch he knew to ask her to devise some means by which she could take away the apple from the youth. The witch so managed it that she succeeded in taking it away from him; and instantly everything disappeared, and the palace was changed into a beach; and the princess and the youth were seen without a rag of clothes upon them in the midst of the beach. They began to cry and bewail their unfortunate existence. The boy, however, after a while looking about him, said to the princess: "You had better go to your father's house and I will remain here." The princess returned home, and the youth then began to saunter about the beach in an aimless manner, and he met a little old lady, who was the Virgin; but he did not know her. Our Lady asked him, "Where are you going to?"

"I'm only loitering because I do not know what to do." She then said, "Well, listen to me; before many minutes have elapsed you will find a number of cats, who are very sleek and fat, but do not lay hold of any except the one that is covered with sores, and in a dreadful state, and that one you must take with you." The youth walked along and soon saw a quantity of fine-looking cats, but he left them alone; but after a while he saw one very thin and in a wretched condition. He took it up by the neck and went away with it. He walked on further along the beach and he saw a ship and went on board. The man who had stolen the apple, seeing the youth in the ship had him captured and shut up in a tower. The youth took the cat with him to the tower. The man who provided him with food only 'gave him a bean each day, and the boy ate half and gave the other half to the cat; whilst the cat hunted for mice and rats, of which it caught many, laid them down before the youth, ate half of them up, and gave him the other half. One day as the cat was peeping slyly through a chink watching for game, she saw a piece of paper folded. She commenced to mew desperately, calling the youth. He went to see what ailed her, and found a letter there from the king of the rats, asking him what he could do for him, so that the cat in recompense for his services should leave the rats in peace, and not catch any more. The youth sent to say that the only way that the king could serve him would be by trying to get the apple for him which had been stolen from him. The king of the rats formed his subjects into an army, and went to the place where the golden apple was to be found. The man had the apple hanging from his neck. The rats set to work with much prudence and caution, and waited until the man was asleep, and arranged themselves each side of the sleeping man, ready to act. One of the rats then began to tickle the man's nose, and to stop his breath with its tail; and the man awoke, feeling stifled, and he then raised his head. The rats, who were ready to take advantage of the first occasion, on seeing the man raise his head, took off the chain with the apple from his neck, and carried it off in triumph to their king, who himself took it to the youth in the tower. The moment the cat saw the apple coming she began to mew out, loudly calling the youth to come. He came and took possession of it once more in great delight. He opened it, and forthwith the giants came out of it, who said, "What do you want us to do?" And the youth replied, "I want a palace, and my princess back in it." Instantly everything came back as before.

The youth went to the king, and asked his majesty to order the man who had robbed him of his golden apple to be put to death; and he ever after lived happily with the princess.

THE PADRE AND THE NEGRO

ONCE upon a time, a certain Padre had a negro servant, who thought himself very sly and clever at expedients. One morning the Padre told the Negro to cook a chicken for his dinner. The Negro did so, but when he dished it the savoury smell from the roast chicken so whetted his appetite that he cut off a leg and ate it, and then arranged it on the dish so that his master should not detect what was wanting. The Padre, however, soon discovered that there was a leg wanting to the bird, and, turning to his servant, he asked him: "Did you cut a leg off the chicken and eat it?"

"No, sir, I did no such thing; the chicken had only one leg when it was alive."

"Do you think I am such a fool as to believe that?"

"Oh, dear Father, there's a number of other hens in the poultry yard strutting about with only one leg, and the next time I notice one I will call you out to see it."

"Very well, do so."

When the Negro by chance saw a hen standing with one of its legs drawn up under it, he called out to his master, "Oh, dear master, come out and see a hen with only one leg!"

The Padre ran out, and cried out to the bird, "Cho', cho', chuckle!" and the hen instantly putting its leg down, the Padre said to the Negro, "You rascally cheat! do you think I am a donkey?"

"No, indeed, Father, by no means! but when the chicken was on your table, you did not say 'Cho', cho', chuckle!' so it did not find its other leg!"

THE STORY OF A CAT'S TAIL

O NCE, in the old days of romance, a fine handsome cat went to a barber s shop to have his whiskers trimmed. The barber noticed that puss had a long tail, so he said to him: "If you were to have your tail cut and made shorter, you would look far more beautiful than you do now."

"Very well, you may cut a piece off," replied the cat.

The barber did so, and pussy departed well pleased at having been beautified at the expense of losing part of his tail; but half way on his journey home he stopped short, and said to himself: "Why should the barber keep my tail? I will go and ask him for it."

The cat returned to the shop and said to the barber: "Give me back my tail or I'll take one of your razors."

But the barber refused to return him the tail, and so the cat stole one of the razors, as he had said he would, and went out of the shop.

Pussy, bent on a ramble, walked on till he met a fishwife, and perceiving that she had no knife to cut the fish with, said to her:

"Here, my good woman, take this razor, and use it to cut your fish."

He then continued his walk, but he had not gone far when he repented giving the razor to the woman, so he retraced his steps until he met her, and, going up to her, he said: "Return me my razor, or I'll take one of your herrings."

The woman, however, refusing to restore the razor, pussy stole a herring, and went his way.

The cat now saw a poor miller, who was eating dry bread for his dinner, and feeling compassion for the man, he said to him: "My good man, take this fish and have it with your bread." The miller very gratefully took the herring and ate it with his bread. After a while the cat was sorry to have parted with the herring, which would have made a pleasant meal for himself; so he went back to the miller and said: "Give me back my fish, or I'll take a sack of your flour."

The miller had already eaten up the fish, and could not restore it had he wished to do so; therefore the cat took a sack of flour and went off with it.

Pussy next paid a visit to a village school, and finding that the mistress was very poor, and had nothing to give her pupils for supper, he gave her the sack of flour to make some porridge with for herself and children. But pussy soon repented of his generosity, and after a while returned to the mistress, saying: "Give me my sack of flour, or I'll run away with one of your girls."

The mistress could not possibly return what she and the girls had already eaten up; and therefore the cat, as he could not get back his sack of flour, carried off one of the girls.

He took the little maiden to a laundress, and said: "As you are working all alone, take this girl as a helper, and you will get your linen done all the sooner."

Our inconsistent pussy very soon regretted what he had done, and going back to the laundress, said: "I am sorry now I allowed you to have the girl; let me have her again." The laundress very indignantly refused to give up the girl, so pussy stole one of the shirts out of the tub.

He went further on his rambles, and met a shirtless musician, whom he addressed thus: "My good but unfortunate friend, I see you are rather short of clothes, so pray accept this shirt, and go at once and put it on."

But whilst the man went aside to dress himself, the cat stole his violin, and, running up a tree, sat down on one of the branches, and began to play a tune and sing a song, with the following words:

> "'Out of my tail I made a razor;
> With the razor I made a fish;
> Out of the herring I made some flour;
> With the flour I formed a girl;
> Of the girl I cut out a shirt;
> With the shirt I made a violin.
> Fee,— foh,— fum.
> Now I shall go back to school.'"

THE MERRY LITTLE FOX

THERE was once a fox whose godfather and godmother were a crane and a wolf. One day the crane was kind enough to invite the fox to a supper of porridge made of Indian corn flour. The fox accepted the invitation and went to the feast; but the poor thing was unable to get even a taste of the supper, because her hostess put the porridge in a deep vessel with a narrow neck, so that the fox was unable to reach it, whilst the crane very coolly ate it all up before her.

After some time the fox invited the crane to come to supper, and in order to revenge herself for the insult she had received, she cunningly placed the porridge on a perfectly flat stone, off which the crane was hardly able to pick up a morsel, while she this time had the supper all to herself.

But the fox had had such a meal that she felt too heavy to walk, and as she had to make a long journey she asked the wolf to take her on his back, saying that she felt very ill, and so weak that she could not take a single step without assistance. The wolf, believing the fox's words, took her on his back, and carried her all the way; while the artful fox went laughing and singing thus:

"The fox knows how to shift,
    When too full to make tracks;
She's deep enough to get a lift
    On other people's backs."

The wolf, astonished to hear his friend singing like a bird, asked her several times what she was saying; but her only answer was, "Oh, I am so ill, so very ill."

And so they went along till the wolf began to see the trick that was played upon him, and perceiving that there was a well near them, he said to her, "Ah, you have been deceiving me, have you ? telling me you could not walk because you felt so ill and so weak, and yet you can manage to sing so merrily—

"'The fox knows how to shift,
    When too full to make tracks;
She's deep enough to get a lift
    On other people's backs.'

"Very well, you shall soon find yourself deep enough!" and at the same time he threw her off his back and into the well. The fox, however, managed to scramble into one of the buckets that was standing on the edge of the well, ready for anyone who might come for water; her weight of course lowered the bucket into the well, and sent the empty bucket up. She then looked up at the wolf who was watching her and said:

"Oh, my friend, how kind of you to send me down here! Surely this must be heaven. Such lovely sights. Green fields with such dear little lambs skipping about, and not a dog or a shepherd near! If you wish to witness them yourself, you have only to get inside the other bucket, and come down to where I am and be perfectly happy." The wolf, duped again by his wily friend, once more fell into her snares and got inside the empty bucket, which, being now the heavier, went down into the well as the other bucket rose, in which the fox was comfortably seated, enjoying the malicious trick she had played him.

When she saw herself safe at the top of the well, she looked down and said to the poor innocent wolf: "Thank you, that's the second lift you have given me to-day. And now you had better stay where you are so that you may never again be tricked by other foxes as artful as I am."

The fox then went away, leaving the poor wolf to his fate, and continued her journey singing all the way:

"The fox knows how to shift,
    When too full to make tracks;
She's deep enough to get a lift
    On other people's backs."

THE WHITE RABBIT

Here's the white rabbit
That went to the garden
To look for a cabbage
To make herself soup.

W HEN the white rabbit got hack from the garden, she found her door locked on the inside. She knocked and thumped against it, till some one cried from within: "Who is there?" And the rabbit, in great surprise, replied:

"I'm the little white rabbit
Come home from the garden
Where I pulled up a cabbage
To make me some soup."

Then she heard a great gruff voice from within, which said to her:

"I'm the huge jolly goat;
With a spring and a bound
I can cut you in three,
And eat you up in no time."

The poor little white rabbit went away in great haste and fear, and very sad; and presently she met a big bull, and said to him: "Big bull, be my friend.

"I'm the white rabbit
That went to the garden
And brought home a cabbage
To make me some soup;
When I got there I found
The huge jolly goat;
With a spring and a bound
He will cut me in three,
And eat me up in no time."

To this the great bull replied: "I won't go there, and I can't help you, for I am very much afraid of the huge jolly goat."

The rabbit went on further, and she met a powerful dog, and she cried in a piteous voice: "Dear dog, do help me.

"I'm the white rabbit
That went to the garden
And brought home a cabbage
To make me some soup;
When there I reached,
I met the huge jolly goat,
That with a spring and a bound
Will cut me in three,
And eat me up in no time."

The dog replied very civilly: "Oh! I can't go there. I am so afraid!"

She then set off again until she saw a fine cock strutting about, to whom she applied for help in her distress.

> "I'm the white rabbit
> That went to the garden
> And was coming home
> To make some soup;
> When there I reached
> I met the huge jolly goat,
> That with a spring and a bound
> Will cut me in three,
> And eat me up in no time."

"Oh! I won't go there, for I am frightened of the beast!"

The poor little rabbit, in despair of getting any one to go with her and get rid of the goat that had taken possession of her little house, went away very sad indeed, believing she could never get back to her home, when suddenly she came across a busy little ant, who asked her very kindly: "What ails you, little rabbit, that you look so sad ?"

> "I was coming from the garden,
> Where I went for a cabbage
> To make some soup;
> When home I reached
> I met the huge jolly goat,
> That with a spring and a bound
> Will cut me in three,
> And eat me up in no time."

When the good little ant heard her sad tale, she said: "I'll go with you and see what we can do in the matter."

They both went together and knocked at the house door; the great goat said from within:

> "Here no one can enter,
> For here is the great he-goat,
> That with a spring and a bound
> Will fall upon you both
> And cut you in three,
> And eat you up in no time!"
> The little ant replied:
> "I'm the great big ant
> That can make a hole
> In your belly so big
> And take out your inside."

When the little ant had said these terrible words she quietly crept in through the key hole, killed the great goat with her sting; made a hole for the rabbit, who cut up the large cabbage, and put it to boil, and made some soup.

The two friends lived together very happily ever after—the white rabbit and the great big ant.

ROUMANIA

THESE stories form an interesting group. There is a child-like simplicity in them, yet one can see traces of beauty of idea and powerful imagination. The tales illustrate the peasant's interpretation of life and possess a natural charm, which is not found in a more complicated system of civilization.

WHY THE STORK HAS NO TAIL

NOW Floria had once shown kindness to a stork, who afterward turned out to be the king of the storks. In return the stork gave Floria a feather, which when taken up at any time of danger would bring the stork to him and help him. Thus it came to pass that the hero, finding himself in danger, remembered the gift of the stork. He took out the feather from the place where he had hidden it, and waved it. At once the stork appeared and asked Floria what he could do for him. He told him the king had ordered him to bring the water of life and the water of death.[1]

The stork replied that if it could possibly be got he would certainly do it for him. Returning to his palace, the stork, who was the king of the storks, called all the storks together, and asked them whether they had seen or heard or been near the mountains that knock against one another, at the bottom of which are the fountains of the water of life and death.

All the young and strong looked at one another, and not even the oldest one ventured to reply. He asked them again, and then they said they had never heard or seen anything of the waters of life and death. At last there came from the rear a stork, lame on one foot, blind in one eye, and with a shrivelled-up body, and with half of his feathers plucked out. And he said, "May it please your majesty, I have been there where the mountains knock one against the other, and the proofs of it are my blinded eye, and my crooked leg." When the king saw him in the state in which he was, he did not even take any notice of him.

Turning to the other storks, he said: "Is there anyone among you who, for my sake, will run the risk, and go to these mountains and bring the water?" Not one of the young and strong, and not even any of the older ones who were still strong replied. They all kept silence. But the lame stork said to the king, "For your sake, O Master King, I will again put my life in danger and go." The king again did not

---

[1] The water of death means a water which, poured over a body caused all to join together and the wounds to heal. The water of life restored to life the bodies thus healed.

look at him, and turning to the others repeated his question; but when he saw that they all kept silence, he at last turned to the stork and said to him:

"Dost thou really believe, crippled and broken as thou art, that thou wilt be able to carry out my command?"

"I will certainly try," he said.

"Wilt thou put me to shame?" the king again said.

"I hope not; but thou must bind on my wings some meat for my food, and tie the two bottles for the water to my legs."

The other storks, on hearing his words, laughed at what they thought his conceit, but he took no notice of it. The king was very pleased, and did as the stork had asked. He tied on his wings a quantity of fresh meat, which would last him for his journey, and the two bottles were fastened to his legs. He said to him, "A pleasant journey."

The stork, thus prepared for his journey, rose up into the heavens, and away he went straight to the place where the mountains were knocking against one another and prevented anyone approaching the fountains of life and death. It was when the sun had risen as high as a lance that he espied in the distance those huge mountains which, when they knocked against one another, shook the earth and made a noise that struck fear and terror into the hearts of those who were a long distance away.

When the mountains had moved back a little before knocking against one another, the stork wanted to plunge into the depths and get the water. But there came suddenly to him a swallow from the heart of the mountain, and said to him, "Do not go a step further, for thou art surely lost."

"Who art thou who stops me in my way?" asked the stork angrily.

"I am the guardian spirit of these mountains, appointed to save every living creature that has the misfortune to come near them."

"What am I to do then to be safe?"

"Hast thou come to fetch water of life and death?"

"Yes."

"If that be so, then thou must wait till noon, when the mountains rest for half an hour. As soon as thou seest that a short time has passed and they do not move, then rise up as high as possible into the air, and drop down straight to the bottom of the mountains. There standing on the ledge of the stone between the two waters, dip thy bottles into the fountains and wait until they are filled. Then rise as thou hast got down, but beware lest thou touchest the walls of the mountains or even a pebble, or thou art lost."

The stork did as the swallow had told him; he waited till the noontide, and when he saw that the mountains had gone to sleep, he rose up into the air, and, plunging down into the depth, he settled on the ledge of the stone and filled his bottles. Feeling that they had been filled, he rose with them as he had got down, but when he had reached almost the top of the mountains, he touched a pebble. No sooner had he done so, when the two mountains closed furiously upon him; but they did not catch any part of him, except the tail, which remained locked up fast between the two peaks of the mountains.

With a strong movement he tore himself away, happy that he had saved his life and the two bottles with the waters of life and death, not caring for the loss of his tail.

And he returned the way he had come, and reached the palace of the king of the storks in time for the delivery of the bottles. When he reached the palace, all the storks were assembled before the king, waiting to see what would happen to the lame and blind one who had tried to put them to shame. When they saw him coming back, they noticed that he had lost his tail, and they began jeering at him and laughing, for he looked all the more ungainly, from having already been so ugly before.

But the king was overjoyed with the exploit of his faithful messenger; and he turned angrily on the storks and said, "Why are you jeering and mocking? Just look round and see where are your tails. And you have not lost them in so honourable a manner as this my faithful messenger." On hearing this they turned round, and lo! one and all of them had lost their tails.

And this is the reason why they have remained without a tail to this very day.

THE DOG, THE SNAKE, AND THE CURE OF HEADACHE

ONCE upon a time, I do not know how it came about, the dog had a frightful headache, such a headache as he had never had before. It nearly drove him mad, and he ran furiously hither and thither, not knowing what to do to get rid of it. As he was running wildly over a field, he met a snake that was lying there coiled up in the sun.

"What is the matter that you are running about like a madman, brother?" asked the snake.

"Sister, I cannot stop to speak to you. I am clean mad with a splitting headache, and I do not know how to be rid of it."

"I know a remedy," said the snake, "it is excellent for the headache of a dog, but it is of no good to me who am also suffering greatly from a headache."

"Never mind you, what am I to do?"

"You go yonder and eat some of the grass, and you will be cured of the headache."

The dog did as the snake had advised him. He went and ate the grass, and soon felt relieved of his pain.

Now, do you think the dog was grateful? No such luck for the snake. On the contrary, a dog is a dog, and a dog he remains. And why should he be better than many people are? He did as they do, and returned evil for good. Going to the snake, he said, "Now that my headache is gone, I feel much easier; I remember an excellent remedy for the headache of snakes."

"And what might it be?" asked the snake eagerly.

"It is quite simple. When you feel your head aching, go and stretch full length across the high-road and lie still for a while, and the pain is sure to leave you."

"Thank you," said the simpleton of a snake, and she did as the dog had advised her. She stretched herself full length across the high-road and lay still, waiting for the headache to go.

The snake had been lying there for some time, when it so happened that a man came along with a stout cudgel in his hands. To see the snake and to bruise her head was the work of an instant. And the snake had no longer any headache. The cure proved complete. And ever since that time, when a snake has a headache it goes and stretches across the highroad. If its head is crushed, then no other remedy is wanted, but if the snake escapes unhurt, it loses its headache.

WHY THE TORTOISE HAS A ROUND BACK

WHEN God and St. Peter were walking on the earth, one day they made a very long journey, and grew very hungry. Coming to a little hut, they found the woman in, and they asked her for something to eat. "Well," she said, "I have very little flour in the house, but I am going to bake two loaves, and when you come back in half an hour they will be ready and you will be welcome to one." Taking the flour, she kneaded it in the trough and made two loaves, one for herself and one for the travellers. Meanwhile they went to church, but they said before going that they would come back at the end of the service.

The woman covered over the dough, and to her great astonishment, when she lifted the cover, the dough of the loaf for the strangers had risen much higher than the other. Then she put both loaves in the oven. How great was her surprise, on taking out the loaves from the oven, when she found that the one for the travellers had been baked nicely and was a very big loaf, whilst the one for herself was half burned and almost shrivelled to a pancake. When she saw the miracle, her greed overtook her, and she forgot the promise which she had made to the travellers. She said to herself: "Why should I give my best bread to strangers whom I do not know? Let them go elsewhere to richer people than I am."

So she took the pasteboard and put it on the floor, and crouching on it, covered herself over with the trough. She told her little girl to stand in front of the door, and if two old people should come and ask for her, she was to say that her mother had gone away and that she did not know where she was. The travellers, then, of course, would not come in, and she would be able to enjoy the loaf.

After a while God and St. Peter came back from church, and asked the little girl where her mother was, to which the child replied as she had been told. God said, "Where she is, there shall she remain"; and went away. The child came in and tried to lift the trough off the back of her mother, who was lying hidden underneath, but try as hard as she could the trough would not come off. It had grown on to the back of her mother, and the pasteboard had grown underneath on to her. The woman was only able to put out her little head with the glistening, greedy eyes, and her tiny little hands and feet, and the handle of the pasteboard had turned into a waggling tail.

And that is how the tortoise was made, when the old woman became the tortoise always carrying the trough and the pasteboard with her.

THE CUCKOO AND THE HOOPOE

ONCE upon a time there lived in a village a man who was so poor that sometimes days passed and he could not get a crumb of bread. So one day he said to his wife, "What is the good of my stopping here any longer? We are both dying of hunger; I will go away into the wide world and see what luck may bring." So he took up his axe and went along. Before he left, his wife said to him: "Do not go far away, and do not forsake me and the children, for we have no one else to look to for help." So he went away.

Walking alone, he came to a forest. At the edge of the forest he saw a beautiful bush with shining leaves, and all the twigs of equal length. It was so beautiful that the man thought, "I will just cut it up." When he drew near, how great was his astonishment when he saw the bush bending its boughs toward him, and speaking with a human voice, it said, "Do not touch me, do not hurt me, for I will do you much good."

"What good can you do me?" inquired the man.

"Go back to the village and they will appoint you headman. Just go and try."

Amazed as he was on hearing the bush speak, he said to himself, "I shall lose nothing if I go back; I shall see whether the bush is speaking the truth. If not, woe unto it." And so he returned. No sooner had he come near the village, when he saw the people coming out to meet him, and without asking him any questions, they, for reasons of their own, appointed him to be their headman. His poverty was now a thing of the past, and he lived in cheer and comfort. This went on for three years, and then, for the same reasons unknown to him, the people changed their minds, and without saying anything to him one day he was the headman, the next he was so no longer. They had put another man in his stead. So he returned to his want, and again began to feel the pinch of poverty. For a time he went on as best he could, but not being able to stand it any longer, he again took his axe, and going into the forest he went to the bush and said, "Now, I am going to cut you down." The bush again began to speak, and said to the man, "Do not touch me; I will do you much good. You have seen what I have done before. You go now to that and that town and they will appoint you to be judge."

Believing the words of the bush, the man continued his journey, and came to the town of which the bush had spoken to him; and there, as had been foretold, without asking him a single question, the people appointed him mayor over the place. The man now lived in affluence and comfort, forgetting his time of poverty and suffering he had gone through. Here, again, after three years, just as he was appointed without a question, so he was dismissed by the people without a question.

The evil days came back, and he was looking about for a crust of bread, but could not find any for himself and his family. He bethought himself again of the bush, and, taking his axe upon his shoulder, he went away to find it.

The bush said to him: "Don't touch me; much good will I do you, still more than I have done hitherto. You go to such and such a kingdom, and there they will appoint you to be their emperor."

He did as he was bid, and as he came near the town, all the people came out to meet him, and they appointed him to be their emperor. He took his wife and children with him, and there he lived in great state, great power and riches.

The law of that land was that no man could be emperor for more than three years, so that when the three years came round he lost his position and another emperor was appointed in his stead. He had meanwhile amassed great fortune and no longer feared poverty. But his wife was ambitious, and was not satisfied at living in affluence and wealth. Envious of the other emperor, she nagged the man and worried him and sneered at him for being so meek and being satisfied with his lowly state, and made him go to the bush to ask for something more. She wanted him to be even better than any emperor. The poor man, what was he to do? He could not stand the trouble in his house, so again taking his axe upon his shoulder, he came for a fourth time to the bush. When the bush saw him, it said:

"What has brought you hither? You are no longer in want of anything." "Well," he said, "my wife has sent me to you. She says you must make me as great as God, greater than all emperors."

The bush grew angry, and said to him: "O miserable wretch, always dissatisfied! I have made thee headman and judge and emperor, and thou lackest nothing. Thou art not in want of anything. Now, because thou hast become impudent and insolent, for thy impious wishes thou shalt be punished. From the man thou hast been thou shalt henceforth be a bird, restless, without peace, and without quiet, flitting from tree to tree, and from branch to branch, always dissatisfied, without a home, without a family, and thy name shall be Cuckoo. Tell thy wife, who, because she has been urging thee on and driving thee to do this impious thing, that she shall become the Hoopoe; puffing herself up she shall cry whoop, whoop." And so it has remained to this very day.

WHY THE WOODPECKER HAS A LONG BEAK

KNOW that the woodpecker was originally not a bird but an old woman with a very long nose, which she put into everybody's pots and pans, sniffing about, eavesdropping, inquisitive, and curious about everything whether it belonged to her or not, adding a little in her talebearing and taking off a bit from another tale, and so making mischief among her neighbours. When God saw her doings, he took a huge sack and filled it with midges, beetles, ants, and all kinds of insects, and, tying it tightly, gave it to the old woman, and said to her: "Now, take this sack and carry it home, but beware of opening it, for if your curiosity makes you put your nose into it you will find more than you care for, and you will have trouble without end."

"Heaven forbid," replied the old hag, "that I should do such a thing; Im not going against the will of God. I shall be careful."

So she took the sack on her back and started trotting home, but whilst she was carrying it her fingers were already twitching, and she could scarcely restrain herself, so no sooner did she find herself a short distance away than she sat down in a meadow and opened the sack. That was just what the insects wanted, for no sooner did she open it than they started scrambling out and scampered about the field, each one running his own way as fast as its little legs would carry it. Some hid themselves in the earth, others scrambled under the grass, others, again, went up the trees, and all ran away as fast as they could.

When the old woman saw what had happened, she got mightily frightened, and tried to gather the insects to pack them up again, and put them back into the sack.

But the insects did not wait for her. They knew what to do, and a good number escaped into the field. Some she was able to catch, and these she packed into the sack, and tied it up. Then came the Voice of God, who asked her what she had done, and if that was the way she kept her promise.

"Where are the insects, beetles, and midges, which I gave you to carry? From this moment you shall change into a bird and go about picking up all these insects until you get my sack full again, and only then can you become a human being again."

And so she changed into a woodpecker; the long beak is the long nose of the old woman, and she goes about hunting for these midges, beetles, and ants, in the hope of filling up the sack, when she would again resume her human shape. But to this very day she has not completed her task, and has remained the woodpecker.

RUSSIA

THE vast store of Russian folk-tales shows that the Russian has a genuine talent for narrative. The stories are full of dramatic situations, and the language is simple and pleasingly quaint. The English fairy element is absent, but there is boundless freedom of intercourse between mortals and immortals, between man and the animals. The material world and the souls of men are linked together in a magic symbolism which finds expression in the folk-tales or *skazki*.

It is well to note the extreme stupidity of the "devils" of Slavonic folklore. They are less intelligent even than their Teutonic prototypes. One cannot but notice the great part played by the Baba Yaga, the old thunder witch, who lives in a miserable little hut on hen's legs in the forest and who flies through the air at dawn and twilight pursuing a course of cruel destruction. The prophet Elijah (Ilya) is an important and powerful personage in Russian folk-lore. He seems sometimes to take the place of Perun, the god of thunder, among the heathen Slavonians.

FISH IN THE FOREST

IN tilling the ground a labourer found a treasure, and carrying it home, said to his wife, "See! Heaven has sent us a fortune. But where can we conceal it?" She suggested he should bury it under the floor, which he did accordingly. Soon after this the wife went out to fetch water, and the labourer reflected that his wife was a dreadful gossip, and by tomorrow night all the village would know their secret. So he removed the treasure from its hiding-place and buried it in his barn, beneath a heap of corn. When the wife came back from the well, he said to her quite gravely, "To-morrow we shall go to the forest to seek fish; they say there's plenty there at present." "What! fish in the forest?" she exclaimed. "Of course," he rejoined; "and you'll see them there." Very early next morning he got up, and took some fish, which he had concealed in a basket. He went to the grocer's and bought a quantity of sweet cakes. He also caught a hare and killed it. The fish and cakes he disposed of in different parts of the wood, and the hare he hooked on a fishing-line, and then threw it in the river. After breakfast he took his wife with him into the wood, which they had scarcely entered when she found a pike, then a perch, and then a roach, on the ground. With many exclamations of surprise, she gathered up the fish and put them in her basket. Presently they came to a pear-tree, from the branches of which hung sweet cakes. "See!" she cried. "Cakes on a pear-tree!" "Quite natural," replied he; "it has rained cakes, and some have remained on this tree; travellers have picked up the rest." Continuing their way to the village, they passed near a stream.

"Wait a little," said the husband; "I set my line early this morning, and I'll look if anything is caught on it." He then pulled in the line, and behold, there was a hare hooked on to it! "How extraordinary!" cries the good wife; "a hare in the water!" "Why," says he, "don't you know there are hares in the water as well as rats?" "No, indeed, I knew it not." They now returned home, and the wife set about preparing all the nice eatables for supper. In a day or two the labourer found from the talk of his acquaintances that his finding the treasure was no secret in the village, and in less than a week he was summoned to the castle. "Is it true," says the lord, "that you have found a treasure?" "It is not true," was the reply. "But your wife has told me all." "My wife does not know what she says—she is mad, my lord." Hereupon the woman cries, "It is the truth, my lord! he has found a treasure and buried it beneath the floor of our cottage." "When?" "On the eve before the day when we went into the forest to look for fish." "What do you say?" "Yes; it was on the day that it rained cakes; we gathered a basketful of them, and coming home, my husband fished a fine hare out of the river." My lord declared the woman to be an idiot; nevertheless he caused his servants to search under the labourer's cottage floor, but nothing was found there, and so the shrewd fellow secured his treasure.

MARKO THE RICH AND VASILY THE LUCKLESS

NOT in our time, but a long time ago, in a certain realm, lived a very rich merchant, Marko by name, and surnamed the Rich, Cruel and hard was he by nature, greedy of lucre and unmerciful to the poor. Whenever the lowly and the needy came begging beneath his window he sent his servants to drive them away, and let loose his dogs upon them. There was only one thing in the world he loved, and that was his daughter, the thrice-fair Anastasia. To her only he was not hard, and though she was only five years old, he never gainsaid her one of her wishes, and gave her all her heart's desire. And once on a cold frosty day three grey-haired men came under the window and asked for alms. Marko saw them, and ordered the dogs to be let loose. The thrice-fair Anastasia heard of it, and implored her father and said: "My own dear father, for my sake don't drive them away, but let them pass the night in the cattle-stall." The father consented, and bade them let the poor old beggar-men into the cattle-stall for the night. As soon as every one was asleep Anastasia rose up, made her way on tiptoe to the stall, climbed up into the loft, and looked at the beggars. The old beggar-men were crouching together in the middle of the stall, leaning on their crutch-staves with their wrinkled hands, and over their hands flowed their grey beards, and they were talking softly among themselves.

One of the old men, the eldest of the three, looked at the others and said: "What news from the wide world?" The second one immediately replied, "In the village Pogoryeloe, in the house of Ivan the Luckless, a seventh son is born; what shall we call him, and with what inheritance shall we bless him?" And the third old man, after meditating a little, said: "We'll call him Vasily, and we'll enrich him with the riches of Marko the Rich, under Whose roof we are now passing the night.' When they had thus said they prepared to depart, bowed low to the holy icons, and with soft footsteps departed from the stall. Anastasia heard all this, went straight to her father, and told him the words of the old men.

Marko the Rich thought deeply over it. He thought and thought, and he went to the village Pogoryeloe. "I'll find out for certain," thought he, "whether such a babe really has been born there." He went straight to the priest and told him all about it. "Yes," replied the priest, "yesterday we had a babe born here, the son of our poorest serf; I christened him Vasily, and luckless he certainly is; he is the seventh son in the family, and the eldest son of the family is only seven years old; the sons of this poor peasant are wee, wee, little things; there is next to nothing to eat and drink there; and such hunger and want is in the house that there's none in the village who will even stand sponsor." At this news the heart of Marko the Rich began to ache. Marko thought of the unhappy youngster, declared he would be godfather, asked the priest's wife to be godmother, and bade them make ready a rich table; and they brought the little fellow, christened him, and sat down and feasted. At the banquet Marko the Rich spoke friendly words to Ivan the Luckless, and said to him: "Gossip, thou art a poor man, and cannot afford to bring up thy son; give him to me; I will bring him up among well-to-do people, and I will give into thy hand at once for thine own maintenance one thousand roubles." The poor man thought the matter over, and then shook hands upon it. Marko gave gifts to his fellow-sponsor, took the child, wrapped him in fox furs, put him in his carriage, and drove homeward. They had got some ten versts from the village when Marko stopped the horses, took up the child, went to the brink of a great precipice, whirled the child over his head, and pitched it down the precipice, exclaiming: "There you go, and now take possession of my goods if you can!"

Shortly after that some merchants from beyond the sea chanced to be travelling by the self-same road; these merchants brought with them twelve thousand roubles which they owed to Marko the Rich. They passed along by the side of the precipice, and they heard within the precipice the voice of a child. They stopped their horses, went to the precipice, and looked among the snowdrifts of the green meadows, and on a meadow a little child was sitting and playing with flowers. The merchants took up the child, wrapped him round with furs, and went on their way.

They came to the house of Marko the Rich, and told him of their strange discovery. Marko immediately guessed that the matter concerned his own little serf-boy, and he said to the merchants: "I should very much like to look at your foundling; if you will give him to me out and out I'll forgive you your debt to me."

The merchants agreed, gave the child to Marko, and departed. But Marko that same night took the child, put it in a little cask, tarred it all over, and threw it into the sea.

The cask sailed and sailed along and at last it came to a monastery. The monks happened to be on the shore just then; they were spreading out their fishing-nets to dry, and all at once they heard the crying of a child. They guessed that the crying came from the cask, and they immediately seized the cask, broke it open, and there was the babe. They took him to the abbot, and as soon as the abbot heard that the child had been cast upon the shore in a cask he decided that the youngster's name should be Vasily, and that he should be surnamed the Luckless.

And henceforth Vasily lived in the monastery till he was sixteen years old, and he grew up fair of face, soft of heart, and strong in mind. The abbot loved him because he learned his letters so quickly that he was able to read and sing in the church better than all the others, and because he was deft and skilful in affairs. And the abbot made him sacristan.

And it happened that once Marko the Rich was travelling on business, and came to this very monastery. The monks treated him with honour as a rich guest. The abbot commanded the sacristan to run and open the church; the sacristan ran at once, lit the candles, and remained in the choir and read and sang. And Marko the Rich asked the abbot if the young man had dwelt there long, and the abbot told him all about it.

Marko began to think, and it struck him that this could be no other than his serf-boy. And he said to the abbot: "Would that I could lay my hands upon such a smart young fellow as your sacristan! I would place all my treasures beneath his care. I would make him the chief overseer of all my goods, and you know yourselves what goods are mine." The abbot began to make excuses, but Marko promised the monastery a donation of ten thousand roubles. The abbot wavered; he began to consult the brothers, and the brothers said to him: "Why should we stand in Vasily's way? Let Marko the Rich take him and make him his overseer." So they deliberated, and agreed to send away Vasily the Luckless with Marko the Rich.

But Marko sent Vasily home in a ship, and wrote to his wife as follows: "When the bearer of this letter reaches thee, go with him at once to our soap-works, and when thou dost pass the great boiling cauldron, push him in. If thou dost not do this I will punish thee severely, for this youth is my prime enemy and evil-doer."

Vasily duly arrived in port and went on his way, and there met him in the road three poor old men, and they asked him: "Whither art thou going, Vasily the

Luckless?"—"Why, to the house of Marko the Rich. I have a letter for his wife."—
"Show us the letter," said the old men. Vasily took out the letter and gave it them.

The old men breathed on the letter and said: "Go now, and give the letter to the
wife of Marko the Rich—God will not forsake thee."

Vasily came to the house of Marko the Rich and .gave the letter to his wife. The
wife read Marko's letter, and called her daughter, for she could not believe her
own eyes, but in the letter was written as plain as plain could be: "Wife, the next
day after thou dost receive this my letter, marry my daughter, Anastasia, to the
bearer, and do so without delay. If thou dost it not thou shalt answer to me for it."
Anastasia looked at Vasily, and Vasily stared at her. And they dressed Vasily in
rich attire, and the next day they wedded him to Anastasia.

Marko the Rich came home from the sea, and his wife with his daughter and
son-in-law met him on the quay. Marko looked at Vasily, fell into a furious passion
with his wife, and said to her: "How darest thou wed our daughter away without
my consent?" But the wife replied: "I dared not disobey thy strict command!" and
she gave the threatening letter to her husband. Marko read the letter, and saw that
the handwriting was his own if the intention was not, and he thought to himself:
"Good! thrice hast thou escaped ruin at my hands, but now I will send thee where
not even the ravens shall pick thy bones."

Marko lived for a month with his son-in-law and treated him and his daughter
most kindly; from his face nobody could have thought that he nourished evil
thoughts against him in his heart.

One day Marko called Vasily to him and said to him: "Go to the land of Thrice-
nine, in the Empire of Thrice-ten, to Tsar Zmy [1]; twelve years ago he built a palace
on my land. Do thou, therefore, obtain rent from him for all the twelve years, and
get news from him concerning my twelve ships, which have been wrecked about
his kingdom for the last three years, and have left no trace behind them." Vasily
dared not gain say his father-in-law, but prepared for his journey, took leave of
his young wife, took a sack of sweetmeats as provision by the way, and set out.
He went on and on, and whether it was long or short, far or near, matters not, but
at last he heard a voice which said: "Vasily the Luckless, whither art thou going?
Is thy journey far?"—Vasily looked around him on all sides and answered: "Who
called me? Speak!"—" 'Tis I, the old leafless oak, and I ask thee whither art thou
going, and is thy journey far?" —"I am going to Tsar Zmy to collect arrears of rent
for the last twelve years." And again the oak said to him: "If thou arrivest in time,
think of me and say that here the old leafless oak has been standing all these three
hundred years, and is withered and rotten to the very root—how much longer must
he be tormented in this wide world?" Vasily listened attentively, and then went

---

[1] Serpent

farther. He came to a river and sat in the ferry-boat, but the old ferryman looked at him and said: "Is thy journey before thee a long one, Vasily the Luckless?" Vasily told him. "Well," said the ferryman, "if thou art in time, remember me, and say to him I have been ferrying here all these thirty years; how much longer, I should like to know, must I go backward and forward?"—"Good!" said Vasily, "I will say so."

He went on to the straits of the sea, and across the straits a whale-fish was lying stretched out, and a road marked out by posts went across its back, and people passed to and fro there. When Vasily stepped on to the whale, the whale-fish spoke to him with a man's voice and said: "Whither art thou going, Vasily the Luckless, and is thy journey far?" Vasily told it everything, and the whale-fish said again: "If thou art in time, remember me; the poor whale-fish has been lying across this sea these three years, and a road marked out by posts goes across its back, and horse and foot trample into its very ribs, and it has no rest night or day; how much longer, pray, is it to lie here?"—"Good!" said Vasily, "I will say so," and went on farther.

Vasily went on and on, and he came to a broad green meadow. In the meadow stood a gigantic palace; the white marble walls glistened, the roof shone like a rainbow and was covered with mother-of-pearl, and the crystal windows burned like fire in the sun. Vasily entered the palace; he went from room to room, and marvelled at the indescribable wealth of them. He went into the last room of all, and saw a lovely damsel sitting on a bed. When she saw Vasily, she cried: "Is it Vasily the Luckless that has fallen into this accursed place?" Vasily told her everything, and why he had come, and what had befallen him on the way. And the damsel said to Vasily: "Not to take tribute wast thou sent here, but as food for the Serpent, and to thine own destruction." Scarcely had she spoken these words than the whole palace trembled and there was a clanging and a banging in the courtyard. The damsel hid Vasily in a coffer beneath the floor, locked him in, and whispered: "Listen to what I say to the Serpent." And with that she went to meet the Tsar Serpent.

A monstrous serpent rolled into the room, and straightway got on to the bed and said: "I have been flying over the Russian land; I'm very tired, and I want to go to sleep." The lovely damsel flattered him and said: "Everything is known to thee, O Tsar, and without thee I cannot interpret a very hard dream I have dreamed; wilt thou interpret it for me?" "Well, out with it, quick!"—"I dreamt I was going along a road, and an oak-tree cried to me, 'Ask the Tsar how long I am to stand here!'"—"It will stand till some one comes and kicks it with his foot, and then it will be rooted out and fall, and beneath it is a great quantity of gold and silver. Marko the Rich himself has not got as much."—"But then I dreamed that I came to a river, and the ferryman on the ferry-boat said to me: "Shall I ferry here long?"— " 'Tis his own fault. Let him put the first who comes to him on the ferry-boat, and push him with the ferry-boat away from the shore, and he will change places with him, and ferry for evermore."—"And after that I came in my dreams to the sea, and crossed over it on a whale-fish, and it said to me: 'Ask the Tsar how long I am to be here!'"—"He must lie there till he has cast up the twelve ships of Marko the Rich, when he may go into the water, and his body will grow again."

All this the serpent said, and then turned over on its other side and fell a-snoring so loudly that all the crystal windows in the palace rattled. Then the damsel let Vasily out of the coffer, opened the garden gate for him, and showed him the way. Vasily thanked her, and began his return journey.

He came to the straits of the sea where the whale-fish lay, and the whale-fish asked: "Did he say anything about me?"—"Take me over to the other side, and I'll tell thee." When he had crossed over, he said to the whale-fish: "Thou must bring up again the twelve ships of Marko the Rich, which thou swallowed three years ago." The whale-fish cleared its throat and brought up again all the ships quite whole and not a bit hurt, and in its joy leaped about so in the water that Vasily the Luckless, who was standing on the bank, suddenly found himself up to his knees in the sea. He went on farther and came to the ferry. "Hast thou spoken about me to Tsar Serpent?" asked the ferryman. "I have; ferry me over first, and I'll tell thee." And as soon as he had crossed over he said to the ferryman: "Whoever comes to thee after me, seat him in the ferry-boat and shove him from the bank, and he will have to ferry in thy place for ever and ever, but thou wilt be as free as the air." After that, Vasily came to the old leafless oak, kicked it with his foot, and the oak rolled over and the roots sprang out of the ground, and beneath the roots and beneath the stump there was gold and silver and precious stones without number. Vasily looked about him, and lo! up to the very place were sailing the twelve ships of Marko the Rich, the selfsame which the whale fish had brought up; and in the foremost ship, in the very stern, stood the selfsame old men who had met Vasily when he had the letter to Marko the Rich, and saved him from destruction. And the old men said to Vasily: "Dost thou not see, Vasily, how the Lord has blessed thee?" And they got off the ship and went their way. And the sailors put all the gold and silver in the ships, and went home by sea.

Marko the Rich was more furious than ever. He bade them saddle his horse, and hastened off to Tsar Serpent in the land of Thrice-ten; he wanted to arrange matters with Tsar Serpent himself. When he came to the river he got on to the ferry-boat, but the ferryman pushed him away from the shore, and there Marko remained as ferryman ever after, and there he is ferrying still. But Vasily the Luckless lived with his wife and mother-in-law, and was happy and prosperous and kind to the poor, and gave them meat and drink and clothed them, and disposed of all the wealth of Marko the Rich.

VERLIOKA

THERE was once upon a time an old man and an old woman, and they had two orphan grandchildren so lovely, gentle, and good, that the old man and the old woman could not love them enough. The old man once took it into his head to go out into the fields with his grandchildren to look at the peas, and they saw that their peas were growing splendidly. The old man rejoiced at the sight with his grandchildren, and said: "Well now, you won't find peas like that in the whole world! By and by we'll make kisel[1] out of it, and bake us some pea-cakes." And next morning the grandfather sent the eldest grandchild, and said: "Go and drive away the sparrows from the peas!"

The grandchild sat down beside the peas, shook a dry branch, and kept on saying, "Whish! whish! sparrows, ye have pecked at grandfather's peas till you're quite full!" And all at once she heard a rumbling and a roaring in the wood, and Verlioka came, huge of stature, with one eye! a hooked nose, ragged stubbly hair, moustaches half an ell long, swine's bristles on his head, hobbling on one leg, in a wooden boot, leaning on a crutch, grinding all his teeth, and smiling. He went up to the pretty little grandchild, seized her, and dragged her away with him behind the lake. The grandfather waited and waited, but there was no grandchild; and he sent his young grandson after her. Verlioka walked off with him also. The grandfather waited and waited, and said to his wife: "How very late our grandchildren are! I suppose they are running about there and idling their time away, or catching starlings with some lads or other, and meanwhile, the sparrows are stealing our peas! Go along, old woman, and teach them sense!" The old woman rose from the stove, took her stick from the corner, gave the pasties another turn, went away—and never came back. As soon as Verlioka saw her in the field, he cried: "What dost thou want here, old hag? Hast thou come hither to shell peas? Then I'll make thee stand here among the peas for ever and ever!" Then he set to work belabouring her with his crutch, till little by little her very soul oozed out of her, and she lay upon the field more dead than alive.

The grandfather waited in vain for his grandchildren and his old wife, and began to scold at them: "Where on earth have they got to?" said he; "'tis a true saying that a man must expect no good from his ribs." Then the old man himself made his way to the peas, and saw the old woman lying on the ground in such a battered condition that he scarcely knew her, and of his grandchildren there was no trace. The grandfather cried aloud, picked up the old woman, dragged her home by degrees, gradually brought her to with a little cold water, and she opened her eyes at last and told the grandfather who it was that had beaten her so, and dragged

---

[1] A sourish meat-pottage.

her grandchildren away from the field. The grandfather was very wroth with Verlioka, and said: "This is too much of a joke! Wait a bit, friend, we also have arms of our own! Look to thyself, Verlioka, and take care that I don't twist thy moustaches for thee! Thou hast done this thing with thy hand, thou shalt pay for it with thy head!" And as the old grandmother did not hold him back, the grandfather seized his iron crutch and went off to seek Verlioka.

He went on and on till he came to a little pond, and in the pond was swimming a bob-tailed drake. He saw the grandfather and cried: "Tak, tak, tak![2] Live for a hundred years, old grandad! I have been waiting here for thee a long time!"— "Hail to thee also, drake! Why hast thou been awaiting me?"—"Well I know that thou art in quest of thy grand children, and art going to Verlioka to settle accounts with him!"—"And how dost thou come to know of this monster?"—"Tak, tak, tak!" screeched the drake, "I have good cause to know him; 'twas he who docked my tail!"—"Then canst thou show me his dwelling?"—"Tak, tak, tak!" screeched the drake; "here am I but a little tiny bird, but I'll have my tail's worth out of him, I know!"—"Wilt thou go on before and show me the way? I see thou hast a good noddle of thy own, though thou art bob-tailed!" Then the drake came out of the water and climbed up on the bank, waddling from side to side.

They went on and on, and they came upon a little bit of cord lying in the road, and it said, "Hail, little grandad wise-pate!"—"Hail, little cord!"—"Where dost thou dwell, and whither dost thou wander?""I live in such and such a place; I am going to pay off Verlioka; he has beaten my old woman and carried off my two grandchildren, and such splendid grandchildren too!"—"Take me that I may help!" The grand father thought: "I may as well take it; it will do to hang Verlioka with." Then he said to the little cord: "Come along with us, if thou dost know the way." And the little cord wriggled after them just as if it were a little tapering snake.

They went on and on, and they saw lying in the road a little watermill, and it said to them: "Hail, little grandad wise-pate!"—"Hail, little water-mill!"— "Where dost thou dwell, and whither dost thou wander?" —"I live in such and such a place, and I am going to settle accounts with Verlioka. Just fancy! he has beaten my old woman and carried off my grandchildren, and such splendid grandchildren too!"—"Take me with thee that I may help!" And the grandfather thought: "The water-mill may be of use too." Then the water-mill raised itself up, pressed against the ground with its handle, and went along after the grandfather.

Again they went on and on, and in the road lay an acorn, and it said to them in a little squeaky voice: "Hail, grandad long-nose!"—"Hail oakey acorn!"— "Whither art thou striding away like that?"—"I am going to beat Verlioka; dost know him?"—"I should think I did; take me with thee to help!"—"But how canst

---

[2] So, so, so.

thou help?" Then the grandfather thought to himself: "I may as well let him go!" So he said to the acorn: "Roll on behind then!" But that was a strange rolling, for the acorn leaped to its feet and frisked along in front of them all. And they came into a thick forest, a forest most drear and dreadful, and in the forest stood a lonely little hut—oh! so lonely. There was no fire burning in the stove, and there stood there a frumenty-pottage for six. The acorn, who knew what he was about, immediately leaped into the pottage, the little cord stretched itself out on the threshold, the grandfather placed the little water-mill on the bench, the drake sat upon the stove, and the grandfather himself stood in the corner. Suddenly he heard a crashing and a trembling in the wood, and Verlioka came along on one leg, in a wooden boot, leaning on his crutch, and smiling from ear to ear. Verlioka came up to the hut, threw down some firewood on the floor, and began to light the fire in the stove. But the acorn who was sitting in the pottage fell a-singing,

> " Pee, pee, pee!
> To beat Verlioka come we!"

Verlioka flew into a rage and seized the pot by the handle, but the handle broke, and all the pottage was scattered over the floor, and the acorn leaped out of the pot and flipped Verlioka in his one eye so that it was put out entirely. Verlioka fell a-shrieking, fought about the air with his arms, and would have made for the door; but where was the door? He could not see it! Then the little cord wound itself about his legs and he fell on the threshold, and the little water-mill on the top of him off the bench. Then the grandfather rushed out of the corner and pitched into him with his iron crutch, and the drake on the top of the stove screeched with all its might: "Tak, tak, tak! Pitch into him! pitch into him!" Neither his wrath nor his strength was of any good to Verlioka. The grandfather beat him to death with his iron crutch, and after that destroyed his hut and laid bare the dungeon beneath it, and out of the dungeon he drew his grandchildren, and dragged all Verlioka's riches home to his old woman. And so he lived and prospered with his old woman and his grandchildren, and plucked and ate his peas in peace and quietness. So there's skazka[3] for you—and I deserve a cake or two also.

THE LITTLE FEATHER OF FENIST THE BRIGHT FALCON

O NCE upon a time there was an old widower who lived with his three daughters. The elder and the middle one were fond of show and finery, but the youngest only troubled herself about household affairs, although she was of

---

[3] Fairy-tale.

a loveliness which no pen can describe and no tale can tell. One day the old man got ready to go to market in the town, and said: "Now, my dear daughters, say, what shall I buy for you at the fair?"—The eldest daughter said: "Buy me, dear dad, a new dress!" The middle daughter said: "Buy me, dear dad, a silk kerchief!"—But the youngest daughter said: "Buy me, dear dad, a little scarlet flower!"—The old man went to the fair; he bought for his eldest daughter a new dress, for his middle daughter a silk kerchief, but though he searched the whole town through he could not find a little scarlet flower. He was already on his way back when there met him a little old man, whom he knew not, and this little old man was carrying a little scarlet flower. Our old man was delighted, and he asked the stranger: "Sell me thy little scarlet flower, thou dear little old man!"—The old man answered him: "My little scarlet flower is not for sale; 'tis mine by will; it has no price and cannot be priced; but I'll let thee have it as a gift if thou wilt marry thy youngest daughter to my son!"—"And who then is thy son, dear old man?"—"My son is the good and valiant warrior-youth Fenist the bright falcon. By day he dwells in the sky beneath the high clouds, at night he descends to the earth as a lovely youth."—Our old man fell a-thinking; if he did not take the little scarlet flower he would grieve his daughter, and if he did take it there was no knowing what sort of a match he would be making. He thought and thought, and at last he took the little scarlet flower, for it occurred to him that if this Fenist the bright falcon, who was thus to be wedded to his daughter, did not please him, it would be possible to break the match off. But no sooner had the strange old man given him the little scarlet flower than he vanished from before his eyes just as if he had never met him at all.

The old man scratched his head and began to ponder still more earnestly: "I don't like the look of it at all!" he said, and when he got home he gave his elder daughters their things, and his youngest daughter her little scarlet flower, and said to her: "I don't like thy little scarlet flower a bit, my daughter; I don't like it at all!"—"Wherefore so vexed at it, dear father?" quoth she. Then he stooped down and whispered in her ear: "The little scarlet flower of thine is willed away; it has no price, and money could not buy it me—I have married thee beforehand for it to the son of the strange old man whom I met in the way, to Fenist the bright falcon." And he told her everything that the old man had told him of his son.

"Grieve not, dear father!" said the daughter; "judge not of my intended by the sight of thine eyes, for though he come a-flying, we shall love him all the same." And the lovely daughter shut herself up in her little gabled chamber, put her little scarlet flower in water, opened her window, and looked forth into the blue distance. Scarcely had the sun settled down behind the forest when—whence he came who knows?—Fenist the bright falcon darted up in front of her little window. He had feathers like flowers, he lit upon the balustrade, fluttered into the little window, flopped down upon the floor, and turned into a goodly young warrior. The damsel was terrified, she very nearly screamed; but the good youth took her tenderly by the hand, looked tenderly into her eyes, and said: "Fear me not, my destined bride! Every evening until our marriage I will come flying to thee; whenever thou placest in the window the little scarlet flower I'll appear before thee. And here is a little feather out of my little wing, and whatever thou mayest desire, go but out on the balcony and wave this little feather—and immediately it will appear before thee." Then Fenist the bright falcon kissed his bride and fluttered out of the window again. And he found great favour in her eyes, and henceforth she placed the little scarlet flower in the window every evening, and so it was that whenever she placed it there the goodly warrior-youth, Fenist the bright falcon, came down to her. Thus a whole week passed by, and Sunday came round. The elder sisters decked themselves out to go to church, and attired themselves in their new things, and began to laugh at their younger sister. "What art thou going to wear?" said they; "thou hast no new things at all." And she answered: "No, I have nothing, so I'll stay at home." But she bided her time, went out on the balcony, waved her flowery feather in the right direction, and, whence I know not, there appeared before her a crystal carriage and horses and servants in gold galloon, and they brought for her a splendid dress embroidered with precious stones. The lovely damsel sat in the carriage, and went to church. When she entered the church, every one looked at her, and marvelled at her beauty and her priceless splendour.

"Some Tsarevna or other has come to our church, depend upon it!" the good people whispered among themselves. When the service was over, our beauty got into her carriage and rolled home; got into the balcony, waved her flowery feather over her left shoulder, and in an instant the carriage and the servants and the rich garments had disappeared. The sisters came home and saw her sitting beneath the little window as before: "Oh, sister!" cried they, "thou hast no idea what a lovely lady was at Mass this morning; 'twas a thing marvellous to behold, but not to be described by pen or told in tales."

Two more weeks passed by, and two more Sundays, and the lovely damsel threw dust in the eyes of the people as before, and took in her sisters, her father, and all the other orthodox people. But on the last occasion, when she was taking off her finery, she forgot to take out of her hair her diamond pin. The elder sisters came from church, and began to tell her about the lovely Tsarevna, and as their eyes fell upon her hair they cried with one voice: "Ah! little sister, what is that thou hast got?" The lovely damsel cried also, and ran off into her little room beneath the gables. And from that time forth the sisters began to watch the damsel, and to listen of a night at her little room, and discovered and perceived how at dawn Fenist the bright falcon fluttered out of her little window and disappeared behind the dark woods. And the sisters thought evil of their younger sister. And they strewed pieces of broken glass on the window-sill of their sister's little dormer chamber, and stuck sharp knives and needles there, that Fenist the bright falcon when he lit down upon the window might wound himself on the knives. And at night Fenist the bright falcon flew down and beat vainly with his wings, and beat again, but could not get through the little window, but only wounded himself on the knives and cut and tore his wings. And the bright falcon lamented and fluttered upward, and cried to the fair damsel: "Farewell, lovely damsel! farewell, my betrothed! Thou shalt see me no more in thy little dormer chamber! Seek me in the land of Thrice-nine, in the empire of Thrice-ten. The way thither is far, thou must wear out slippers of iron, thou must break to pieces a staff of steel, thou must fret away reins of stone, before thou canst find me, good maiden!" And at the self same hour a heavy sleep fell upon the damsel, and through her sleep she heard these words yet could not awaken. In the morning she awoke, and lo! knives and needles were planted on the window-sill, and blood was trickling from them. All pale and distraught, she wrung her hands and cried: "Lo! my distresses have destroyed my darling beloved!" And the same hour she packed up and started from the house and went to seek her bright-white love, Fenist the shining falcon.

The damsel went on and on through many gloomy forests, she went through many dreary morasses, she went through many barren wildernesses, and at last she came to a certain wretched little hut. She tapped at the window and cried: "Host and hostess, shelter me, a poor damsel, from the dark night!" An old woman came out upon the threshold: "We crave thy pardon, lovely damsel! Whither art thou going, lovey dovey?"—"Alas! granny, I seek my beloved Fenist the bright falcon. Wilt thou not tell me where to find him?"—"Nay, I know not, but pray go to my middle sister, she will show thee the right way; and lest thou shouldst stray from the path, take this little ball; whithersoever it rolls, thither will be thy way!" The lovely damsel passed the night with the old woman, and on the morrow, when she was departing, the old woman gave her a little gift. "Here," said she, "is a silver spinning-board and a golden spindle; thou wilt spin a spindleful of flax and draw out threads of gold. The time will come when my gift will be of service to thee." The damsel thanked her and followed the rolling ball. Whether 'twere a long time or a short matters not, but the ball rolled all the way to another little hut. The damsel knocked at the door and the second old woman opened it. The old woman asked her questions and said to her: "Thou hast still a long way to go, damsel, and it will be no light matter to find thy betrothed. But look now! when thou comest to my elder sister she will be able to tell thee better than I can. But take this gift from me for thy journey—a silver saucer and a golden apple. The time will come when they will be of use to thee." The damsel passed the night in the hut, and then went on farther after the rolling ball; she went through the woods farther and farther, and at every step the woods grew blacker and denser, and the tops of the trees reached to the very sky. The ball rolled right up to the last hut; an old woman came out upon the threshold and invited the lovely damsel to take shelter from the dark night. The damsel told the old woman whither she was going and what she sought. "Thine is a bad business, my child!" said the old woman; "thy Fenist the bright falcon is betrothed to the Tsarevna over sea, and will shortly be married to her. When thou gettest out of the wood on to the shores of the blue sea, sit on a little stone, take out thy silver spinning-board and thy golden spindle and sit down and spin, and the bride of Fenist the bright falcon will come out to thee and will buy thy spindle from thee, but thou must take no money for it, only ask to see the flowery feathers of Fenist the bright falcon!" The damsel went on farther, and the road grew lighter and lighter, and behold! there was the blue sea; free and boundless it lay before her, and there, far, far away above the surface of the sea, bright as a burning fire, gleamed the golden summit of the marble palace halls. "Surely that is the realm of my betrothed which is visible from afar!" thought the lovely damsel, and she sat upon the little stone, took out her silver spinning-board and her golden spindle, and began spinning flax, and drawing golden thread out of it. And all at once she saw, coming to her along the sea-shore, a certain Tsarevna, with her nurses and her guards and her faithful servants, and she came up to her and watched her working , and began to bargain with her for her silver spinning-board and her golden spindle.

"I will give them to thee for nothing, Tsarevna, only let me look on Fenist the bright falcon!"

For a long time the Tsarevna would not consent, but at last she said: "Very well, come and look at him when he is lying down to rest after dinner, and drive the flies away from him!" And she took from the damsel the silver spinning-board and the golden spindle and went to her terem. She made Fenist the bright falcon drunk after dinner with a drink of magic venom, and then admitted the damsel when an unwakable slumber had overpowered him. The damsel sat behind his pillow, and her tears flowed over him in streams. "Awake, arise, Fenist the bright falcon!" said she to her love; "I, thy lovely damsel, have come to thee from afar; I have worn out slippers of iron, I have ground down a staff of steel, I have fretted away reins of stone; everywhere and all times have I been seeking thee, my love." But Fenist the bright falcon slept on, nor knew nor felt that the lovely damsel was weeping and mourning over him. Then the Tsarevna also came in, and bade them lead out the lovely damsel, and awoke Fenist the bright falcon. "I have slept for long," said he to his bride, "and yet it seemed to me as if some one had been here and wept and lamented over me."—"Surely thou hast dreamt it in thy dreams?" said the

Tsarevna; "I myself was sitting here all the time, and suffered not the flies to light on thee."

The next day the damsel again sat by the sea, and held in her hands the silver saucer and rolled the little golden apple about on it.

The Tsarevna came out walking again, went up to her, looked on and said, "Sell me thy toy."—"My toy is not merchandise, but an inheritance; let me but look once more on Fenist the bright falcon, and thou shaft have it as a gift."—"Very well, come again in the evening, and drive the flies away from my bridegroom!" And again she gave Fenist the bright falcon a drink of magic sleeping venom and admitted the lovely damsel to his pillow. And the lovely damsel began to weep over her love, and at last one of the burning tears fell from her eyes upon his cheeks. Then Fenist the bright falcon awoke from his heavy slumbers, and cried, "Alas! who was it who burned me?"—"Oh, darling of my desires!" said the lovely damsel, "I, thy maiden, have come to thee from afar. I have worn out shoes of iron, I have worn down staves of steel, I have gnawed away wafers of stone, and have sought thee everywhere, my beloved! This is the second day that I, thy damsel, have sorrowed over thee, and thou wakedst not from thy slumber, nor made answer to my words!" Then only did Fenist the bright falcon know his beloved again, and was so overjoyed that words cannot tell of it. And the damsel told him all that had happened, how her wicked sisters had envied her, how she had wandered from land to land, and how the Tsarevna had bartered him for toys. Fenist fell in love with her more than ever, kissed her, and bade them set the bells a-ringing without delay, and assemble the boyars and the princes and the men of every degree in the market-place. And he began to ask them, "Tell me, good people, and answer me according to good sense, which bride ought I to take to wife and shorten the sorrow of life: her who sold me, or her who bought me back again?" And the people declared with one voice, "Her who bought thee back again!" And Fenist the bright falcon did so. They crowned him at the altar the same day in wedlock with the lovely damsel. The wedding was joyous and boisterous and magnificent. I also was at this wedding, and drank wine and mead, and the bumpers overflowed, and every one had his fill, and the beard was wet when the mouth was dry.

THE DEVIL AND THE GIPSY

AN old gipsy went to engage himself as servant to a devil; the devil said: "I will give you what you wish to bring me firewood and water regularly, and to put fire under the kettle." "Good!" The devil gave him a pail and said: "Go yonder to the well and draw some water."

Our gipsy went off, got some water into the pail, and drew it up with a hook; but, being old, he couldn't draw it out, and was obliged to pour the water out, in order not to lose the pail in the well. But what was he now to return home with? Well, our gipsy took some stakes out of a fence, and grubbed round about the well, as if he were digging. The devil waited and waited, and as the gipsy didn't appear himself, of course he didn't appear with the water. After awhile he went himself to meet the gipsy, and without thinking inquired: "But why do you loiter so? Why haven't you brought water by this time?" "Well, what? I want to dig out the whole well, and bring it to you!" "But you would have wasted time, if you had purposed anything of the sort; then you wouldn't have brought the pail in time, that the quantity of firewood might not be diminished." And he drew out the water and carried it himself "Eh! if I had but known, I should have brought it long ago."

The devil sent him once to the wood for firewood. The gipsy started off, but rain assailed him in the wood and wetted him through; the old fellow caught cold and couldn't stoop after the sticks. What was he to do? Well, he took and pulled bast; he pulled several heaps, went round the wood, and tied one tree to another with strips of the bast. The devil waited, waited on, and was out of his wits on account of the gipsy. He went himself, and when he saw what was going on: "What are you doing, loiterer?" said he. "What am I doing? I want to bring you wood. I'm tying the whole forest into one bundle, in order not to do useless work." The devil saw that he was having a bad time of it with the gipsy, took up the firewood, and went home.

After settling his affairs at home, he went to an older devil to ask his advice: "I've hired a gipsy, but he's quite a nuisance; *we're* tolerably cute," says he, "but he's still stronger and cuter than we. Unless I kill him—" "Good, when he lies down to sleep, kill him, that he mayn't lead us by the nose any more." The time came to go home; they lay down to sleep; but the gipsy evidently noticed something, for he placed his furcoat on the bench where he usually slept, and crept himself into a corner under the bench. When the time came, the devil thought that the gipsy was now in a dead sleep, took up an iron club, and beat the fur-coat till the sound went on all sides. He then lay down to sleep, thinking: "Oho! it's now amen for the gipsy!" But the gipsy grunted: "Oh!" and made a rustling in the corner. "What ails you?" "Oh, a flea bit me." The devil went again to the older one for advice: "But where to kill him?" said he. "When I smashed him with a club, he only made a rustling and said: 'A flea bit me.'" "Then pay him up now," said the elder devil, "as much as he wants, and pack him off about his business." The gipsy chose a bag with ducats and went off. Then the devil was sorry about the money, and consulted the other one again. "Overtake the gipsy, and say that the one of you that kicks a stone best, so that the sound goes three miles, shall have the money." The devil overtook him: "Stay, gipsy! I've something to say to you."

"What are you after, son of the enemy?" "Oh stay let us kick; the one that kicks loudest against a stone, let his be the money." "Now then, kick away," said the gipsy. The devil kicked once, twice, till it resounded in their ears; but the gipsy meanwhile poured some water on it: "Eh! what's that, you fool?" "When I kick a dry stone, water spurts out." "Ah! when he kicks, tremble! water has spurted out of the stone."

The devil went again for advice. The elder one said: "Let the one who throws the club highest have the money." The gipsy had now got some miles on his way; he looked round; the devil was behind him: "Stop! wait, gipsy!" "What do you want, son of the enemy?" "The one of us that throws the club highest let his be the money." "Well, let us throw now. I've two brothers up yonder in heaven, both smiths, and it will just suit them either for a hammer or for tongs." The devil threw, so that it whizzed, and was scarcely visible. The gipsy took it by the end, scarcely held it up, and shouted: "Hold out your hands there, brothers—hey!" But the devil seized him by the hand: "Ah, stop! don't throw; it would be a pity to lose it."

The elder devil advised him again: "Overtake him once more, and say, 'The one that runs fastest to a certain point, let him have the money.'" The devil overtook him; the gipsy said: "Do you know what? I shan't contend with you any more, for you don't deserve it; but I've a young son, Hare, who's only just three days old; if you overtake him, you shall measure yourself with me." The gipsy had espied a hare in a firwood: "There he is! little Hare! now, then, Hare! Catch him up!" When the hare started he went hither and thither in bounds, only a line of dust rose behind him. "Bah!" said the devil, "he doesn't run straight." "In my family no one ever did run straight. He runs as he pleases."

The elder devil advised him to wrestle; the stronger was to have the money. "Eh!" said the gipsy; "you hear the terms for me to wrestle with you: I have a father; he is so old that for the last seven years I have carried him food into a cave; if you floor him, then you shall wrestle with me." But the gipsy knew of a bear, and led the devil to his cave. "Go," said he, "in there; wake him up, and wrestle with him." The devil went in and said: "Get up, long-beard! let us have a wrestle." Alas! when the bear began to hug him, when he began to claw him, he beat him out, he turned him out, and threw him down on the floor of the cave.

The elder devil advised that the one who whistled best, so that it could be heard for three miles, should have the money. The devil whistled so that it resounded and whizzed again. But the gipsy said: "Do you know what? When I whistle you will go blind and deaf; bind up your eyes and ears." He did so. The gipsy took a mallet for splitting logs, and banged it once and twice against his ears. "Oh, stop! Oh! don't whistle, or you'll kill me! May ill luck smite you with your money! Go where you will never be heard of again!" That's all.

SPAIN

THE Spanish peasant, though in a large measure untaught, is intelligent, imaginative, and superstitious. The greater part of the people have found some of their chief pleasures in folk-lore. Though many of the peasants cannot read or write, they learn with ease large numbers of plays, for they possess wonderful memories. Neither in speech nor manner is there in Spain that gulf between the educated and uneducated classes which existed in England during the nineteenth century. The legendary stories are weird and tragic, while the fairy tales have, more or less, the same elements as are to be found in other European types.

THE FOX AND THE GOOSE

A FOX and a goose were very great friends. The goose, which, as you know, is a very honest and industrious bird, said to the fox:

"Friend fox, I have a little bit of property here, and if you like to join with me, we will cultivate it between us."

"That would greatly please me," answered the fox.

"Then it will be necessary to till it together when the season arrives," said the goose.

"Very well," replied the fox.

A little afterward, when they met, the goose said:

"It is time to sow the seed."

"That is your business," said the fox; "I have nothing to do with that."

Some months passed, when the goose said to the fox:

"Friend, the grass is choking the wheat; it is necessary to weed the field."

"Very well," answered the fox, "you see to that; it is not my business."

A short time passed by, when the goose said to the fox:

"Friend, the wheat is ripe and must be reaped."

"All right," replied the fox, "you attend to that; it is not my business."

Then the goose, for all its good nature, began to be distrustful, and told its friend the greyhound what had passed.

The greyhound, who was very shrewd, saw at once that the fox was going to play off one of its tricks upon the goose's good nature, and said to it:

"Reap the wheat; put it in the barn, and hide me in a sheaf of corn, without leaving more than one eye uncovered, so that I may see all that may happen."

563

The goose did as the greyhound had said; and after a time the fox arrived, and when it saw the barn filled with splendid wheat already thrashed, it was very delighted, and, dancing about, sang:

> "Lio, lio,
> The straw and the wheat are mine!
> Lio, lio,
> The straw and the wheat are mine!"

As it said this, it approached the sheaf in which the greyhound was concealed, and on seeing the eye among the straw, said:

"Ah, there's a grape!"

"But it is not ripe," replied the greyhound, and it leaped out of its hiding-place, and killed the fox.

THE KNAVISH LITTLE BIRD

A CERTAIN little bird went to a tailor and ordered him to make it a little woollen coat. The tailor took his measure, and agreed to have it ready for him in three days. Then he went to a hatter and ordered a little hat, and the hatter promised as the tailor had done; finally, the little bird went to a shoemaker, and the shoemaker took his measure, and like the others told him they should be ready on the third day. When the appointed time arrived, the bird went to the tailor, who had the little woollen coat ready, and said to him:

"Put it upon my little bill, and I will pay you."

And the tailor did so, but instead of paying him, the little rogue flew away. And the same trick was played with the hatter, and with the shoemaker.

Then the little bird dressed itself in the new things and went to the king's garden and placed itself upon a tree before the banqueting room. Whilst the king was dining, it sang:

> "In my little woollen coat I am as fine
> As the king in his mantle of scarlet."

And it sang and re-sang its song so many times, that his Majesty got angry and ordered it to be caught and cooked, and brought before him. This was done; and after it had been plucked of its feathers and cooked, it was so small that the king swallowed it whole, in a single mouthful.

When the little bird found itself in the king's inside, which seemed to it to be a cavern darker than midnight, it began to kick about right and left with all its might. Then the king began to complain, and to say that his food had not agreed with him, but had made him ill. The doctors came and ordered the king to take a draught, and this made the little bird so uncomfortable that he flew out of the king's mouth like a flash of lightning.

In the first place, the bird now dived into a fountain; and then it went to a carpenter's shop and rubbed itself all over with glue. Afterward it went to the other birds, and told them what had happened to it, and begged each of them to give it a feather, and each of them did so, and as it was covered with glue, the feathers all stuck to it; and each feather being of a different colour, the little bird at last became more beautiful than it had been before, with plumage as many-coloured as the rainbow.

Then it went and fluttered about the tree that was before the king's balcony, singing lustily:

> "To whom has happened what has chanced to me?
> Into the king to enter, and from the king come free."

The king said:

"Catch that little rascal of a bird!"

But the little bird was now forewarned, so it flew like the wind, and did not stop until it perched upon the nose of the man in the moon!

THE SINGING SACK

THERE was once a mother who had an only daughter whom she loved very dearly; and because the girl was very good she had given her a pretty coral necklace. One day the child went to fill her pitcher with water at a fountain near the cottage. When she reached the fountain, she took off her coral necklace and put it down, so that it should not fall into the water as she filled her pitcher. A very hideous old beggar-man with a sack was seated at the fountain, and he gave the child such a terrible look that she was afraid, and scarcely stayed to fill her pitcher before she ran away, quite forgetting the necklace in her fright.

When she reached home the girl remembered her necklace, and ran back to the fountain to seek it; but when she arrived the old beggar, who was still seated there, seized her and thrust her into his sack. He then went on his way begging alms from door to door, saying that he carried a wonderful thing with him, *a sack that could sing*. The folks wished to hear it, so the old rogue cried out with a voice of thunder:

> "Sing, sack, sing;
> Or your neck I will wring!"

The poor girl, half dead with fear, had no help but to sing, which she weepingly did, as follows:

"I went to the well for water—
    The well near by my home,
And I lost my coral necklace,
    That came from far off Rome.
Alas! my darling mother,
How troubled you will be!

"I went to the well to seek it—
    But could not find it there;
I have lost my coral necklace;
    My necklace rich and rare!
Alas! my darling mother,
How saddened you will be!

"'Oh, I could not find my necklace—
    My mother's gift to me!
Oh, I could not find my necklace—
    And I lost my liberty!
Alas! my darling mother,
How wretched you will be!"

The poor child sang this so well, that the people were very glad to listen to her; and everywhere much money was given to the old man to hear the sack sing.

Going thus from house to house, at last he arrived at the home of the girl's mother, who at once recognized her daughter's voice, and therefore said to the beggar:

"Father, the weather is very bad; the wind increases and the rain falls; shelter yourself here to-night, and I will give you some supper."

The old rascal was very willing; and the girl's mother gave him so much to eat and drink that he became stupid, and after his supper went to sleep, and slept as sound as a top. Then the mother drew her little darling out of the sack, where she was nearly frozen, and gave her many kisses and a good warm supper, and put her to bed. She then put a dog and a cat into the sack.

The following morning the old beggar thanked her, and went away. On arriving at the next house, he said his usual say of:

"Sing, sack, sing,
    Or your neck I will wring!"

when the dog answered,

"Old rogue, bow-wow;"

and the cat added,

"Old thief, mieau-mieau."

In a rage, the beggar, thinking it was the girl who said this, opened the sack to punish her, when the dog and cat sprang out furiously; and the cat jumped at his face and clawed out his eyes, whilst the dog bit a piece out of his nose.

THE SERPENT WOMAN

THERE lived in the twelfth century a certain Don Juan de Amarillo, who dwelt not far from Cordova. Although not very young himself, he had a handsome young wife, whom he adored. He introduced her to all his friends; but though she made a great sensation by her beauty, wherever she appeared, yet, in some way or other, she contrived to make enemies and no friends among either sex.

No one knew where she came from, nor what her name was before she was married. All that was certain was that Don Juan had been absent from home for many years, that he had never been heard of by either friend or foe in all that time, and that he had returned as suddenly as he had departed, but bringing with him a wife.

There were many stories afloat of her origin and character. Some said that she was a strolling player, whom Don Juan had rescued from ill-treatment and persuaded to marry him for his name and position. Others said that she was a witch, and had bewitched the old Don Juan by means of love-philtres and noxious herbs.

These stories were none of them true. But people repeated them to each other, and were quite satisfied in believing them, Meanwhile, Doña Pepa went about and enjoyed herself, unconscious of the tales that were told of her, but not unconscious of the terror she inspired. She was quite aware that people shunned her, and avoided her whenever they could. She was a wonderfully handsome woman, with regular features, dark eyes, and a head like that of a beautiful statue. Her figure was singularly flexible and lithe. But in spite of her beauty, people looked askance at her, and felt, without being able to say why, that there was something wrong about her. She had some curious tricks of manner which were startling. When she was pleased, she would raise her head so that it seemed really to lengthen two or three inches, and she would sway her body to and fro with delight. Whereas, if anything displeased her, or she disliked anyone, her head seemed to flatten out, and the touch of her hand was like a bite. She delighted in hearing and repeating all the ill-natured stories that she could about her neighbours, and, in short, seemed as spiteful as a woman could possibly be.

To all outward appearances, she and Don Juan got on excellently well together. But the servants of the household told a different tale. They said that at home they wrangled from morning till night, and that sometimes Don Juan was positively afraid of his wife, especially when her head flattened, for then she looked, and really was, dangerous. People said that they also had seen a look of alarm creep over the old man's face, even in company, when she showed any signs of anger.

Things went on like this for many years, but still Don Juan and his wife seemed to live in peace and harmony. To be sure, the servants, who had been in the family for years, left one after another; and when questioned as to their leaving, answered that the señora was a witch, and that the angel Gabriel himself could not live with her. How their master managed, they could not imagine, unless she had bewitched him.

Then it was rumoured about that a favourite nephew of Don Juan was coming from Aragon to pay him a visit, and to be formally acknowledged as his heir. As he and his wife had no children he wished to leave his wealth to this nephew, the son of an only sister who was dead; and in course of time the friends and neighbours of Don Juan were invited to meet the stranger.

He was a frank, open-faced, and open-hearted young man, about twenty-seven years old, who at once won the hearts of all who saw him. He was not at all jubilant or overweening at the honours thrust upon him as his uncle's heir, but spoke quite ingeniously of his former poverty and the disadvantages as well as the pleasures of his boyhood, to his aunt's intense disgust,

Doña Pepa could not bear to *hear* of poor relations, much less to let the world know the Don Juan de Amarillo had any such belongings. And she gave young Don Luis such a look of mingled scorn, hatred, and disgust as made him shudder, and kept his tongue quiet for the rest of the evening. The guests tried in vain to draw him into conversation; he had received such a rebuff in Doña Pepa's glance that he became utterly silenced and wondered what sort of woman she could be. He had seen what the guests had not observed (for nobody else had at that moment noticed her), that her head had flattened, and that her eyes had grown long and narrow; that she had moistened her lips (which were white with rage) with a hissing sound, and that *her tongue was forked.* He had heard queer stories about his aunt, but had hitherto never paid much attention to them. Now everything he had ever heard in his life came back to his memory, and it was with the utmost effort that he forced himself to sit through the evening, and tried to appear interested in all that went on.

The more Don Luis was known, the more popular he became. Every one liked him. His uncle worshipped him, and could hardly bear him out of his sight; for he reminded him of his dearly loved lost sister, and of his own past youth, before he became entangled in the world's wickedness and folly.

Even Doña Pepa could not withstand the freshness and charm of her innocent young nephew, and although she was continually angry with him for his careful avoidance of her, she could not retaliate upon him as she had often retaliated on others—for as time went on she had learned to *love* him.

He lived in constant fear of her, and tried to keep out of her way by every courteous means in his power. But she would not let him escape from her. She dogged his footsteps everywhere. If he went out for a walk, she was sure to come and meet him, and he felt certain that he was watched—not for his good, but with a jealous eye.

One evening he went to see a friend who was having a sort of reception, and stayed out rather later than usual. When he got to his uncle's house he lit his little taper and proceeded to his room. As he did so, he stumbled over what he supposed to be a coil of rope. To his horror the rope unwound itself, and proved to be a large black snake, which glided upstairs before him, and disappeared under his uncle's door. The thought instantly flashed across his mind that his uncle was in danger of his life; and without hesitation he pounded and knocked and shouted at the door for at least five minutes. They seemed to him five hours. But his uncle was old and sleepy, and it took him some time to wake up. However, at last he came to the door and demanded crossly what his nephew meant by disturbing his rest at that time of night.

"I saw a large black snake creep under this door, my dear uncle, and I was afraid that you might suffer from it before I could help you," replied his nephew.

"Nonsense!" said Don Juan, turning pale, "there is no serpent here"; and he tried to shut the door again. But Don Luis was determined to search the room. Doña Pepa was apparently asleep.

The room was carefully searched, but nothing could be found. His uncle was very angry; but as Don Luis was leaving the room, crestfallen at his failure, and wondering whether he was losing his mind, Doña Pepa opened her eyes and gave him one of her evil glances; her head flattened, and her eyes grew long and narrow. He left the room with an undefined sensation of terror; he could not sleep, and when he dozed for a few minutes, his dreams were of snakes and of loathsome reptiles.

The next morning he found only his aunt when he went down. His uncle had gone out, Doña Pepa said. Don Luis had taken such an aversion to her that he could hardly bring himself to speak to her, and she took intense delight in plying him with questions, which he felt himself obliged to answer as became a Spanish gentleman.

But at last he could bear it no longer. Doña Pepa was giving very evident signs of rage, and he was hastily beating a retreat, when she strode across the room, seized him by the arm, and said: "You shall not treat me with such disdain; you shall learn to fear me if you cannot learn to love me."

At the same moment that her hand touched his wrist, he felt a sharp sensation as if something had stung him. He threw her hand off and hurried out, thinking for the time no more about his pain. But in the course of the day his arm began to swell rapidly and to throb painfully, until at last the hand and fingers were swollen to such a degree that he could neither close them nor hold anything with them. He then became rather alarmed, and decided to go to a hermit who lived not far off, and who was renowned for his skill in the treatment of poisons, as well as for his piety.

After examining the arm the old man said, "It is a serpent's bite."

"No, it is not," interrupted Don Luis. "My aunt grasped my arm, in a frenzy of rage, and this is the result."

"Worse still," answered the hermit; "a serpent woman's bite is sometimes deadly." [1]

"Can you do nothing for me?" cried Don Luis, in despair. "I hate her, and I have been persecuted by her for weeks."

"Yes, and you will be persecuted by her still more. She will take refuge in your room instead of on the landing. Put these leaves upon your arm, and keep wetting them when they become dry, and your arm will probably get better. As to conquering her, that will be a more difficult matter. If you can keep awake you will get the better of her. But if you sleep *one minute* you will be at her mercy."

"What shall I do to her? I would do anything short of murdering her," said Don Luis excitedly.

"Take your sword, when you find her a little way from the door, and hack off a piece of the snake, and see the effect. Then come to me again."

With this advice Don Luis was obliged to be content. His arm was so much soothed by the hermit's treatment, that he determined to try the rest of his advice.

That night, when he went to his room, he undressed and was just getting into bed when he espied the snake coiled in a huge mass at the foot of it. Without a sound he drew his sword, gave a stroke at the snake and cut off a piece of the tail. The snake reared its head and showed its fangs, preparing apparently for a spring; but Don Luis gave another blow, and another piece of the tail came off. With a hiss the snake uncoiled, dragged itself to the door, disappeared down the stairs, and crept under Don Juan's door.

The next morning Doña Pepa did not appear. His uncle said that she had a habit of sleep-walking, and had run something sharp into her foot.

"I can guess what ails her," thought Don Luis to himself, as he condoled with his uncle, who seemed really troubled.

Don Luis had carefully preserved in a drawer the pieces of the tail which he had cut off; and on looking at them the next morning had found that they were the toes and instep of a human foot.

---

[1] The superstition still exists in Spain that an evil woman is obliged for a certain number of years to become a snake every night; those with whom she is angry are bitten, and their cure is more difficult than when the bite is that of a serpent.

For some days he neither saw nor heard anything more of his aunt in any shape. But at last she reappeared and greeted him most cordially.

He noticed, however, that she halted decidedly in her gait, and reported everything to the hermit.

"Have no pity for her, my son," replied the hermit, "for she intends your destruction. If you have any mercy upon her, she will have none for you. The next time strike about a foot from the head, where she cannot hide her disfigurement."

A few evenings after this conversation with the hermit, he found the snake awaiting him in the courtyard, and as usual it went upstairs before him, and coiled itself on a chest in the farthest corner of the room. All the doors in the house seemed to be constructed for harbouring and helping snakes, for they were scooped away underneath for two inches.

Don Luis drew his sword and struck as nearly a foot from the head as he could. The snake made a bound to the door and disappeared, the head first and the body following and joining it outside, and it then disappeared under his uncle's door.

The next day Doña Pepa disappeared from human ken for a month. "She had a dreadful abscess on her finger," his uncle said, "which had kept her awake for many nights, and she must lie by for a time and have it lanced."

"I can guess what ails her," thought Don Luis, and went to his friend the hermit to report matters.

On the way he met an old servant who had been in his grandfather's family, and had lived with Don Juan after his marriage, but had been amongst the first to leave. The old servant stopped him and said:

"I have been anxious for a long time about my master and you. Is he well? and what is going on there? I did not like to call at the house, a I left of my own accord. But I had to leave, for I could not bear to live with that horrid snake in the house, Doña Pepa."

"What do you mean by 'snake in the house,' Jorge?" asked Don Luis. "Did you ever *see* a snake in that house?"

"Indeed I have," replied the old servant indignantly. "She followed me all over the house, until I nearly lost my wits. If I went into the kitchen, it was there; in my room, it was there; and at last I went away because when I spoke to my master about it, he grew so angry that I saw he thought I was lying. Have *you* never seen the snake yourself, señor? for every one else who lived there has."

"Yes, I have seen the same thing myself, if you press me so hard," answered Don Luis; "but what can I do more than I have? In snake form, I have cut off one foot and one hand. What can I do more short of murder?"

"One thing more," said old Jorge earnestly, "one thing more, and that is to watch until she is out. Go to the chest in the master's room, under the left-hand window, and open it. You will find a queer skin, striped like a serpent's, folded up in the right-hand corner. Burn that, and will find that the snake will not torment you any more."

"Are you sure?" inquired Don Luis, earnestly.

"Quite sure," answered Jorge, as earnestly.

Then they parted.

But the more Don Luis thought over the advice of the old servant, the less inclined he felt to act upon it. It seemed a treacherous thing to do, to go into his uncle's room, steal a serpent's skin out of his chest, and burn it without knowing what might be the consequences of such a deed. So he resolved to go to his friend the hermit, and ask him what he thought. When he had told his story, the old man sat a long while musing and silent. At last he said: "I can quite understand your scruples, and sympathize with you in your feeling for your uncle. But I am afraid that there is no other way of destroying an influence so pernicious as that of Doña Pepa; for you are not the only one whom she has either utterly depraved or injured in some way. And such people are better out of the world than in it, as the mischief they do is incomparably greater than the pleasure they give by their beauty. However, for a month at least, she cannot do you much harm. She is too much injured to show herself until she can hide her misfortune. But if she begins her torments again, I should be inclined to tell the whole case to your uncle, and then say to him what you intend to do."

Upon this advice Don Luis acted. For a month Doña Pepa kept her room, and he saw no more of the snake. After that time, however, she reappeared, and he watched to see how she concealed her wounded hand. It was all covered with a silk handkerchief, and he asked after it with apparent zeal. Doña Pepa coloured deeply, but answered with much dignity; she looked thin and pale, and her face was worn with pain. Don Luis's kind heart ached when he saw how he had hurt her. His uncle took great pains to tell every one that poor Doña Pepa had had to have her hand amputated for a wound which had mortified, and which had threatened her life. Very few people believed the story, for somehow or other Don Luis's adventures with the serpent had got wind and everyone suspected that Doña Pepa's sufferings were the first punishment for her many deeds of sorcery.

But after a short interval the same troubles began again. Don Luis found the serpent rolled up anywhere and everywhere; in the courtyard, on the stairs, in his room, in every nook and corner, in his boots, under his rug, over his clothes, until he began to think that he was going mad and saw snakes *everywhere*. One morning, however, he awoke and found the snake on his bed, winding itself around his body. He gave it several hard blows, and wounded it in various places, till it glided quietly out of the room. He then at last decided that the time had come to tell his uncle the whole story. When he saw him in the dining-hall, he asked him how Doña Pepa was.

The old man looked very much disturbed, and said hesitatingly:

"I have not seen her this morning. But I suppose she is well."

"Have not seen her this morning!" repeated Don Luis, feiging surprise. "Is she not at home?"

"Well, yes, she is at home," replied his uncle, more embarrassed than ever. "But sometimes she is not well enough to see me."

"Oh," said Don Luis significantly; and the matter dropped for the time.

Later in the day, however, Don Luis contrived to find his uncle alone, and then he told him all that he had heard. At first Don Juan was very angry, but as his nephew proceeded and he heard the long list of annoyances and torments to which he had been subjected under his roof, he became very pale and silent.

There was a long pause after Don Luis had finished, and then his uncle said:

"Well, I can say nothing—nor can I help you in any way. This much I *can* tell you, that I sympathize most deeply with you—for—for that snake has been the bane of my life."

"Then," said Don Luis earnestly, "you will not blame me if I punish the snake the next time as it deserves."

"No, I should not blame you, if you can do it," sighed old Don Juan, little dreaming that his nephew already possessed the secret of killing her. And the conversation ended.

For his uncle's sake Don Luis bore with patience the annoying attentions of the snake as long as he could; but after a month more of torment he watched his opportunity when Don Juan and Doña Pepa were out, and went into his uncle's room. There he found the chest under the left window, just as old Jorge had said. On one side was a queer striped skin, which he immediately recognized as the snake's. He was preparing to light a fire and burn it, when he heard his uncle and Doña Pepa returning. He had only time to close the chest, slip away to his room, and hide the skin, before they entered their room.

As soon as he heard them descend into the hall, he prepared and lit a fire, and took out the skin, rolling it up in his hand to make it smaller, when he heard fearful shrieks below. He rushed out to learn the cause, and was told by one of the servants that Doña Pepa had had fearful cramps, as though her body had been folded up. Then Don Luis knew that what he had heard was true; and, without giving himself time to think, he threw the skin upon the fire. In a moment it was in a blaze, and crisped and curled into nothing.

Having watched it burn to the end, he went down to his uncle. Don Juan was walking up and down the room, wringing his hands. Doña Pepa was stretched out upon a couch, looking very white and ill. The family physician was sitting beside her, holding her hand and feeling her pulse.

"What has happened?" asked Don Luis. "Is Doña Pepa ill?"

"She is dead," replied the physician solemnly; "and I cannot discover what was the matter nor what can have killed her. She was in excellent health, as far as I could make out, an hour ago, when I was called in to see her for convulsions; and now, with no bad symptoms at all, she has suddenly died. I cannot understand the cause at all."

Don Luis thought to himself that he perhaps could throw a good deal of light upon the subject. But he held his tongue.

When Doña Pepa was laid out for burial, the old nun who had prepared her for her last resting-place, confessed that she had seen the figure of a large snake distinctly traced upon the entire length of her body.

Don Luis and Don Juan lived very happily together for years after the death of Doña Pepa. His uncle seemed like a boy again, so light-hearted and gay was he. When his friends came to see him, he would say: "I have not been so happy for many a long year."

And Don Juan's friends thought it strange, but Don Luis did not. The hermit and one or two others only knew the secret of the Serpent Woman.

SWITZERLAND

THE story of the famous archer is most commonly associated with the Swiss patriot William Tell, but there are similar stories of an earlier date from the records of other races. Saxo Grammaticus, the celebrated Danish scholar of the twelfth century, wrote a chronicle of the early kings of Denmark. He tells the story of one Palnatoki, who boasted that he was so skilled an archer that he could hit the smallest apple placed a long way off upon a wand. Harold the king heard of this and ordered that Palnatoki's own son should stand some distance away while an apple should be placed on the lad's head. Palnatoki's task was to strike off the apple without wounding the child. Taking three arrows from the quiver he struck the mark with the first that he fitted to the string. When asked by the king why he had taken more than one arrow, he replied, "That I might avenge myself on thee if I had injured my son."

From the Vilkina Saga of Norway in about the thirteenth century comes the story of Egill, Völundr's younger brother. Egill was the fairest of men and one thing he had before all others—he shot better with the bow than any other man. King Nidung took to him well and Egill was with him a long time. Wishing to test his skill, Nidung ordered that Egill's son, a child of three years, should be placed with an apple on his head. Egill was then ordered to shoot one arrow so that the apple only was to be split. Taking three arrows, he stroked the feathers smooth, fitted one to his bow, and took aim. The arrow pierced the apple and then fell to the ground. King Nidung asked Egill why he took three arrows when only one was to be used. To this Egill replied, "Lord, I will not lie to you; had I stricken the lad with that one arrow, then I had meant these two for you."

In Percy's *Reliques* occurs the ballad of Adam Bell, Clym of the Clough, and William of Cloudesly. These were three noted outlaws whose skill in archery made them famous in the North of England. William of Cloudesly, at a distance of 120 yards, shot the apple from his son's head and by this feat saved the lives of the three outlaws.

HOW THE ALPINE HORN CAME
TO THE HERDSMAN

AT sunset the deep and powerful notes of the Alpine horn float adown the mountains in solemn melody as some lone shepherd sounds his good-night call. And thereby comes my story.

In olden times there lived a daring young huntsman, who was loved by all the mountain fairies. Often would they whisper dream-tales to him, and guard his steps o'er perilous paths. But so fond did he grow of the huntsman's life that the mountain gnomes (who, unlike the fairies, protected the wild mountain creatures from the needless greed of hunters) took steps to curb his power. One day he sought shelter from a mountain storm in a herdsman's deserted hut; the floor was wet and cold, so he climbed into the loft and fell asleep.

When he awoke he looked down into the room below, and was surprised to see three strange little figures standing round a fire that had been lit. These he knew to be gnomes, to whom he thought his presence was unknown. Very busy were these little people, and at last they dragged to the door a great horn and blew upon it. Its strange sweet melody echoed and re-echoed among the hills, and at its sound herds of lowing cows came from all the steeps. Then the gnomes called the huntsman from his hiding-place, and bade him drink from one of three crystal bowls. He chose that which looked like milk and drained it to the bottom. "You are a wise man," said they, "for the red and yellow liquid would have secured you lesser gifts, but in choosing the milk this magic horn becomes yours. Only once in many hundred years is this offered to man. Learn therefore to make other horns like it, that other herdsmen may call their flocks o'er the mountain slopes. They will grow prosperous, and have less time to slay the harmless chamois. Wild creatures may come at sound of the horn, but if you would live long and happily harm not one of these beautiful creatures." All the gnomes as they vanished called in chorus: "Remember! Remember! Remember!"

FENETTE THE ALPINE SHEPHERDESS

THE brave young huntsman (to whom the mountain gnomes had given the Alpine horn) loved the fair young shepherdess Fenette. She was very poor, but a happy soul, and often did she beg her lover to give up the wild life of a huntsman and become a herdsman. This he at last consented to do, and during the winter nights he made another Alpine horn for Fenette, that she might call her cattle therewith and speak to him also across the valleys.

Happy was their life, till one evening at sunset he saw a young chamois coming toward him. Forgetting the gnomes' parting words, "Harm not one of these. Remember!" he seized his bow, and sent an arrow straight to the heart of the beautiful wild creature.

Then through his Alpine horn he called good-night to Fenette across the hills. No answer save that of the echoes came to his anxious ear, though he called many a time. For Fenette at sunset, standing on the edge of a deep crevice, had raised her own horn to sound her good-night call, when at the very instant she disappeared, and an arrow, the same with which the herdsman had shot the chamois, fell upon the ice.

Long he sought for Fenette, but in vain. The grief-stricken herdsmen carried on the work Fenette had loved. He lived alone on one of the highest pastures of the Alps. In winter he searched for lost travellers, and sounded :his horn to guide many to his mountain hut.

One evening, when the last sunset shadows fell across the cold mountain lakes, the sorrowful, wandering herdsman left his hut. Nevermore did the solemn melody of his horn float adown the mountains, nor was he ever seen again.

WILLIAM TELL

WILLIAM TELL was the most famous crossbowman of Switzerland. He lived in a little mountain cottage and loved the freedom and peace of the life there. He spent many days hunting the deer; often too he went fishing on the storm-swept lake of Uri and none could surpass his skill in managing a boat.

Now one day there was a fair in the little market town of Altdorf. Thither went William with his little son. But the Austrians had conquered the Swiss, and the tyrant Gessler was ordering all who entered Altdorf to pay homage to the Duke of Austria's cap, which was set up on a pole in the market square. William Tell hated this sign of bondage, and, though threatened with death, he refused to bend his knee in submission to those who had destroyed the liberty of the Swiss people.

Gessler then seized William's son and ordered the soldiers to bind him to the trunk of a linden tree some distance away and place an apple on his head. Then, turning to the lad's father, he said, "All praise is given you for your skill as a crossbowman. I have a mind to test you. You must shoot an arrow so as to split the apple on your son's head. If you can do this, your life will be spared; if not, or if you injure the child, your life will be forfeited."

William saw the crafty smile on Gessler's lips and thrust *two* arrows into his girdle. With an anxious heart, yet steady hand, he fitted one arrow to his bow string. Slowly he took aim, then swiftly sped the arrow through the air, and, splitting the apple in half, it buried itself in the tree beyond, leaving the child untouched.

Gessler's anger knew no bounds, yet must he grant William his life. Noting the other arrow in William's belt, however, he asked why it had been placed there. With fearless words William replied: "Had I hurt my child, this arrow would have entered your heart."

TIBET

T HE literature of Tibet consists chiefly of translations from the Sanskrit, and the oral tales bear an obvious resemblance to those of India. The people are considered intelligent, but have little initiative, and their isolated position, as well as their dislike of interference from strangers, makes it difficult to obtain a good *raconteur*.

THE STORY OF THE HOME-BRED BOY

1. How He Found the Turquoise

T HERE was once an old woman living in Tibet whose husband had died and left her alone with her only son.

As the Boy grew up, his Mother grew more and more fond of him, and disliked parting from him even for a moment. She was afraid that if he left her house and began wandering about by himself some accident might happen to him, and she would be left desolate in her old age. So the older he grew the more careful she became, until at last she saw that it was impossible to restrain the Boy any longer, and it would be necessary for him to go out into the world to seek his fortune, just as other young men of his age had to do. So when he had reached the age of fifteen she waited till the fifteenth day of the sixth month, which is a very auspicious date, and calling the Boy to her, she presented him with a new suit of clothes, a horse, a dog, a gun, and a sword; and she told him that he was now at liberty to leave his home and to go out into the world to seek his fortune.

The Boy was greatly delighted at receiving these gifts and with the prospect of meeting with some adventures, so after saying farewell to his Mother, he mounted his horse, and with the dog trotting at his heels he started away down the road. All day he rode quietly along by himself without meeting with any adventures, and toward evening he reached a high plateau near the top of a range of mountains. As he was crossing the plateau a fox jumped up in front of him and ran off toward the mountains. The dog, on seeing the fox, started to chase it; while the young Man, thinking he was to have some fun at last, galloped after the dog as fast as he could.

After running for some distance the fox suddenly disappeared into his earth, and the Boy, riding up, dismounted at the mouth of the hole, and began to scheme how he was to catch the fox when he came out. So he took off his cloak and fastened it to the saddle with his sword and his gun, and then placed his horse a little to one side of the fox's earth, whilst his dog stood ready at the other side; and he himself took off his hat and put it over the mouth of the hole, and taking a large stone in his hand, he crouched down ready to slay the fox when it came out.

After sitting waiting for some time the fox all of a sudden darted out of its earth, and ran off toward the hills, with the Boy's hat sticking over its head. It came so suddenly that he had no time to hit it with his stone, or to interrupt its flight. The dog, on seeing the fox go off, at once started in full pursuit; and the horse, excited by the dog's cries, galloped off after the pair, and in a few moments all three were lost to sight in the gathering darkness.

The poor Boy found himself in a moment bereft of all his possessions—his horse, his dog, his gun, his sword, his hat, and even his outer robe, which he had strapped on his saddle, had all disappeared. After running after his horse for some distance he gave it up in despair, and lay down to pass the night as best he could under a big poplar tree.

He woke toward dawn, and, looking up into the branches of the tree, he saw a large Raven's nest, on which an old Raven was sitting hatching her eggs, whilst Father Raven perched on a branch near by. When day broke the two Ravens began talking to one another.

"Good morning, Father Raven," said the old bird on the nest, "who is this sleeping under our tree?"

"That," replied Father Raven, "is a foolish home-bred Boy who has no experience of the world. In trying to catch a fox last night he lost his horse, his gun, his sword, his dog, and even his clothes, and now he has not the least idea where to find them."

"Yes, so I see," replied Mother Raven, "but it is clear, nevertheless, that all he has to do is to go toward the villages which lie toward the east from here—there he will meet with good fortune."

On hearing this the Boy at once started off toward the east, and proceeding for some little distance, he met an old Beggar Man, to whom he related the whole of his story, and asked him if by any chance he had seen the missing property. The old Man, seeing before him only a poor Boy, without even a hat or a cloak, did not believe a word of this story, so he only laughed at him and mocked him; and finally, when the Boy grew angry, gave him a sound beating, and left him to go on his way, disconsolate.

Wandering on a little further, he came to a big house where a wedding feast was being celebrated. Coming timidly up to the door of the house, he peeped in at the guests, and presently one of the servants happening to pass by, he related his sad story. But just then the Bridegroom caught sight of him, and called out in a rough voice:

"Who are you who come crying here at my wedding feast? We want no woe-begone faces here to-day to bring us bad luck. Go away, you ill-omened creature."

So the poor Boy slunk away sadly, and after wandering about till night fall he reached another large house further toward the east. After the reception he had received from the wedding party he was afraid to go in or to knock at the door, so creeping into the backyard he dug himself a nest in the rubbish heap and crouched down in this for warmth, all hidden except his head. Thus he spent the night comfortably enough.

Early next morning the pigs belonging to the place began to poke about the yard and the rubbish heap, and several of them, as they passed, rooted at his head with their snouts to see if he was anything good to eat.

He could not stand this very long, so finally, screwing up his courage, he went to the back door of the house, and asked one of the servants to lend him a knife, saying that he wanted it to cut up the dry meat which formed his breakfast. The servant lent him a knife, and as soon as he had got it he enticed one of the pigs away to a quiet corner, where he killed it and cut off its head; and taking with him some strips of its flesh, he returned to his nest in the rubbish, and hid himself there again, together with the pig's head, waiting to see what would turn up.

Toward noon the Lady of the house came out into the yard, and as she was moving about superintending the various farming operations, it happened that a large and valuable turquoise fell out of her head-dress without her noticing it. When, after a few minutes, she went back into the house, leaving the turquoise lying in the middle of the yard, the Boy thought that this would be a good opportunity of getting the turquoise for himself, but he was afraid to leave his nest for fear of being noticed; so picking up a piece of rag from amongst the rubbish he threw it over the turquoise, concealing it from sight.

Shortly after, one of the maid-servants came out of the house, and seeing a piece of rag lying in the middle of the yard, she picked it up, and the turquoise with it, and thrust them both into a crevice in the wall.

Just then a great uproar arose from the house, where the Lady had discovered the loss of her turquoise. The whole household was summoned, and set to work to search for the missing jewel.

For some time great bustle prevailed, every one searching hither and thither, and ransacking every hole and corner; but no one thought of examining the piece of dirty rag thrust carelessly into a crevice of the farmyard wall.

Finding that all their efforts were of no avail, the Lady of the house sent off in hot haste to summon all the most famous diviners, magicians, and lamas of the neighbourhood, and these, when they arrived, began practising all kinds of spells and casting auguries in the hope of discovering what had become of the turquoise; but all in vain, and when nightfall arrived, they were no better off than they were before.

Toward evening they packed up their various magical instruments and spells, and went away very down-hearted; and as soon as they were gone the Boy emerged from his hiding-place, and going boldly to the house, he said that he was a famous magician and could find the turquoise for them; and he asked that on the following morning all the diviners and lamas should again be summoned, as well as the inhabitants of all the neighbouring houses. The Lady of the house was at first inclined to ridicule the idea of this disreputable-looking beggar being able to accomplish what none of these famous sorcerers could do; but thinking it worth while to give the Boy a chance, she decided to do what he suggested, and meanwhile ordered her servants to let him have a good supper, of which he stood badly in need.

Next morning, about ten o'clock, a large crowd of people assembled in the courtyard of the house. In addition to the magicians and lamas of the day before, a great many of the neighhours had obeyed the summons, and amongst them were the people who had treated the poor Boy so badly during their wedding feast, and the Beggar who had reviled and beaten him. As soon as they were all seated in rows ready to see what was going to happen the Boy, holding the pig's head under his arm, presented himself before them all, and addressed them as follows:

"Now," said he, "I hope in a few minutes to be able to discover the missing turquoise, for I am possessed of magic qualities of unusual power. In my search I shall be assisted by this enchanted pig's head which I hold under my arm. Owing to the spell I have cast upon it, it is able at once to detect a thief or a dishonest person, and also to discover stolen property."

So saying he took the pig's head in both hands, and holding its snout toward the company, he went round from person to person, halting for a moment in front of each. Presently he arrived in front of the Bridegroom, who had been so rude to him some days before, and the pig's head at once became violently agitated, and kept poking itself towards this man.

"Ah!" said the Boy, "here is evidently a dishonest man; it is no good our proceeding any further in our search until he has been beaten and turned out of here."

The other people at once seized upon the wretched man, and after giving him a severe thrashing, they turned him out of the place. Next to him was sitting the Beggar who had so insulted the Boy, and who had disbelieved his story. Here, again, the pig's head became violently agitated, and the Beggar, too, was well beaten and turned out. Having got rid of these two persons, the Boy now began to walk round the yard, the pig's snout apparently sniffing carefully at every part of the wall in the farm buildings. Presently, coming to the crevice into which the rag had been thrust by the servant-maid, he moved the pig's head violently to and fro.

"Ah!' cried he, "the missing turquoise must be somewhere near here."

On hearing this every one began to search about in that neighbourhood, and in a few minutes the turquoise was found inside the rag thrust into the crevice of the wall.

The Mistress of the house on recovering her turquoise was greatly elated. She took the Boy into the house, and having presented him with a new suit of clothes, and given him all he wanted to eat and drink, she handed him a large sum of money, and he went on his way in a far better plight than when he first arrived there.

2. How He Dislodged the Spider

After leaving the house where he had found the turquoise, the home bred Boy wandered along until, toward nightfall, he arrived at the same poplar-tree where he had previously stayed the night, and, lying down under its branches, he fell fast asleep, and did not wake up until toward morning.

As day was dawning the two Ravens overhead began talking to one another as before, and the boy overheard their conversation.

"Good morning, Father Raven," said the hen bird on the nest. "What kept you so late last night?"

"Well," replied Father Raven, "the fact is, I was visiting a farmhouse down yonder, where the mistress of the house, as it happens, is very ill. She is suffering from a severe pain in her left ear, which drives her almost distracted, and no one about the place knows what it is nor how to cure it. They have consulted all of the most famous doctors and lamas in the neighbourhood without, however, affording her any relief at all. Indeed, no one knows what is the cause of the disease except myself. I have ascertained that the pain in her ear is due to the fact that some days ago a large Spider effected an entrance during her sleep, and that the Spider and her young ones have now taken up their abode inside the Lady's head. It is impossible to dislodge them except by a stratagem. As you are aware, Spiders are in the habit of sleeping all through the winter months, and only wake up and emerge from their retreat in the spring. If it were possible to make the Spiders believe that the spring had arrived, they would come out of the ear at once; otherwise they will remain there all through the winter."

"Indeed," replied Mother Raven, "that is very interesting; but how would it be possible to make the Spider believe that spring had come?"

"There is a very simple stratagem, which I have often seen employed," replied Father Raven, "which is as follows: a piece of green cloth must first be spread upon a table and well sprinkled with water, and the Lady must bend her ear over this so that the Spiders can see it. It will appear to them to be a green field, wet with the spring rains, and they will imagine it is time to come out; and then, if they still display any reluctance to emerge, it is only necessary to beat a drum to simulate thunder. Thunderstorms, as you know, only occur in the spring, and the Spiders on hearing this noise will feel convinced that spring has really come, and will emerge without any further hesitation. The moment they come out on the table they must be wrapped up in the cloth with the greatest expedition and carried away and killed, for if this is not done, they will always be ready at the slightest alarm to climb back into the ear by the threads which they have left suspended behind them."

Mother Raven thanked Father Raven for his information and she then said:

"But you yourself are not looking at all well this morning, what is the matter with you?"

"Well," said he, "I am sorry to say I over-ate myself yesterday. The people of the house kept praying to the gods, and were all day long occupied in making offerings of rice and flour. Most of these offerings were thrown out into the garden, and I was able to eat as much as I wanted. In fact, I ate a great deal too much, and I fear that I am going to die. If I do, you must faithfully promise to remain in mourning for me, in accordance with Tibetan custom, for three years, three months and three days."

Mother Raven, on hearing this, was greatly affected, and solemnly vowed to carry out the wishes of her husband, and poor old Father Raven, getting into the nest, shortly after breathed his last.

As soon as he was dead Mother Raven remarked to herself that she had a great deal too much to do in looking after her family and household duties to think for a moment of following so absurd a custom as mourning for a dead bird for any period at all. So she pushed old Father Raven's body out of the nest with her bill and let it fall to the ground below, while she herself flew off to find food for the young ravens, which had just been hatched out.

Meanwhile the Boy, who had listened attentively to the colloquy of the Ravens overhead, went straight off to hunt for the house where the Lady was suffering from pains in her ear, and he decided in his own mind to make this another opportunity for displaying his magical powers.

He soon arrived at the house in question, and found the whole family in great grief, and the poor mistress of the house suffering torments with the pain in her ear. Going to the house, he asked what was the matter, and on hearing the cause of their sorrow he at once announced that he was possessed of very wonderful magic powers, and was prepared to effect a cure. The people of the house, who had seen him on the previous day, when he had found the turquoise, were inclined to believe him, and asked him what they should do to procure relief for their mistress.

"All that is necessary," replied he, "is a square piece of green cloth, some clean water in a jug and a couple of drums."

When these things had been made ready he spread the piece of green cloth on the table and sprinkled some water over it, and he then told the Lady of the house to lean across the table so that her painful ear should come above the patch of green cloth. No sooner had she done so than the Spiders inside, seeing the green expanse with water still lying upon it, thought that the spring had come and began moving about, and the old Mother Spider at once let herself down by a thread to see if it was really spring.

The people of the house were greatly astonished at seeing the Spider emerge, but the Boy ordered them not to touch her; and having satisfied herself that there was really water on the cloth, she climbed again up her thread, and went back into the Lady's ear to impart the good news to her family. The Boy now ordered the drums to be beaten, and on hearing this sound the whole of the Spider family, thinking that the noise was thunder, and that spring had undoubtedly arrived, hastily emerged from the Lady's ear and let themselves down, one after another, on to the green cloth. As soon as they were all, to the number of seven, arrived upon the table, the Boy snatched up the piece of cloth and, wrapping up the spiders inside it, he carried them all outside and destroyed them.

The Lady of the house was now completely cured and overwhelmed the Boy with gifts and compliments, and he left the house carrying with him a large sum of gold, in addition to that which he had received the day before. He now bent his steps toward his Mother's house, and as he was going along the road to his home he suddenly came face to face with the old Beggar who had previously insulted him, and whom he had had beaten and turned out when he was looking for the turquoise. The old man, who was of a very jealous and vindictive temper, was very much incensed against the Boy, and had determined to avenge himself upon him. As the Boy came down the road the old Beggar suddenly emerged from behind a clump of bushes, holding a sword in his right hand and a fly in the hollow of his left fist.

"Now," said he, "I believe you to be an impostor. You have twice made pretence to magical powers, which in reality you do not possess, and I am about to put you to a final test. If you can tell me what I hold in my left hand I shall let you go free; but if you fail to do so, I shall immediately kill you with this sword."

The poor Boy was greatly alarmed at hearing these words, and having no weapon himself he was completely at the old man's mercy. So at a loss to know what to say, he replied:

"Well, then, you can kill me if you like, for I am as much in your power as though I were a fly which you hold in your left hand and which you can crush at your pleasure."

The old man was so much astonished at hearing this reply, which he looked upon as a proof of the Boy's supernatural powers, that he forthwith became one of his most ardent admirers, and as he had seen where the Boy's horse, dog, and other belongings had disappeared to on the occasion when they had all followed the fox, he was able to lead the boy to a distant valley, where he found his horse and dog together. Here having recovered his sword and his gun, his clothing and other possessions, he mounted upon his horse and, followed by his dog, he returned to his Mother's house a very much richer Boy than when he had left it.

THE FROG AND THE CROW

A CROW once caught a fine fat Frog, and taking him in her bill she flew with him to the roof of a neighbouring house in order to devour him at her leisure. As she alighted on the roof of the house the Frog gave an audible chuckle.

"What are you laughing at, Brother Frog!" said the Crow.

"Oh, nothing, Sister Crow," said the Frog; "never mind me. I was just thinking to myself that, as it fortunately happens, my Father lives close by here, on this very roof, and as he is exceedingly fierce, and strong, he will certainly avenge my death if anyone injures me."

The Crow did not quite like this, and thinking it as well to be on the safe side, she hopped off to another corner of the roof near to where a gutter led away the rain water by means of a small hole in the parapet and a wooden spout. She paused here for a moment and was just about to begin to swallow the Frog, when the Frog gave another chuckle.

"What are you laughing at this time, Brother Frog!" asked the Crow.

"Oh, it's only a small matter, Sister Crow, hardly worth mentioning," replied the Frog, "but it just occurred to me that my Uncle, who is even a stronger and fiercer man than my Father, lives in this very gutter, and that if anybody was to do me an injury here they would have a very small chance of escaping from his clutches."

The Crow was somewhat alarmed at hearing this, and she thought that, on the whole, it would be safer to leave the roof altogether; so again picking up the Frog in her bill, she flew off to the ground below, and alighted near the edge of a well. Here she placed the Frog upon the ground and was just about to eat him when the Frog said:

"Oh, Sister Crow, I notice your bill seems rather blunt. Before you begin to eat me don't you think it would be a good thing to sharpen it a little? You can strop it very nicely on that flat stone over there."

The Crow, thinking this was a good idea, took two or three hops toward the stone, and began sharpening her bill. As soon as she had turned her back the Frog gave one desperate jump, and dived into the well.

As soon as the Crow had made her bill nice and sharp she returned from the stone, and looked ,about for the Frog. Not finding him where she had left him she hopped to the edge of the well and peeped over, craning her head from side to side. Presently she spied the Frog in the water, and called out to him:

"Oh, Brother Frog, I was afraid you were lost. My bill is quite nice and sharp now, so come along up and be eaten."

"I am so sorry, Sister Crow," replied the Frog, "but the fact is, I cannot get up the sides of this well. The best thing would be for you to come down here to eat me."

And so saying he dived to the bottom of the well.

THE KYANG,[1] THE FOX, THE WOLF, AND THE HARE

ONE day a hungry Wolf was roaming about in search of something to eat in the upper part of a Tibetan valley far beyond the level of cultivation, when he came across a young Kyang about a year old. The Wolf at once proceeded to stalk the Kyang, thinking that he would make an excellent meal off him, and just as he was about to seize upon him the Kyang, noticing his approach, addressed him as follows:

"Oh, Uncle Wolf," said he, "it is no good your eating me now; this is the spring time and after the hard winter I am still very thin. If you will wait for a few months until next autumn you will find that I shall be twice as fat as I am now and will make you a much better feast."

"Very well," said the Wolf, "I will wait until then, on condition that you meet me on this very spot in six months' time."

And so saying, he galloped off in search of some other prey.

When autumn came the Wolf started off one morning to meet the Kyang at the appointed place, and as he was going across the hills he came across a Fox.

"Good morning, Brother Wolf," said the Fox. "Where are you going to?"

"Oh!" replied the Wolf, "I am going into the valley to meet a young Kyang by appointment, as I have arranged to catch him and eat him this very day."

"That is very pleasant for you, Brother Wolf," answered the Fox; "but as a Kyang is such a large animal you will scarcely be able to eat him all by yourself. I hope you will allow me to come too and share in the spoil."

"Certainly, Brother Fox," replied the Wolf. "I shall be very glad of your company."

And so saying, the two went on together. After proceeding a short distance they came across a Hare.

"Good morning, Brother Wolf and Brother Fox," said the Hare; "where are you two going this fine morning?"

---

[1] A kyang is the wild ass of Tibet.

"Good morning, Brother Hare," replied the wolf; "I am just going off to yonder valley to keep an appointment with a fat Kyang, whom I have arranged to kill and eat this very day, and Brother Fox is coming with me to share in the spoil."

"Oh! really, Brother Wolf," said the Hare, "I wish you would allow me to come too. A Kyang is such a large animal that you can scarcely eat him all yourselves, and I am sure you will allow a small creature like me to have a little bit of the spoil."

"Certainly, Brother Hare," replied the Wolf. "We shall be glad if you will accompany us."

And so the three animals went along together toward the appointed spot. When they got near the place they saw the young Kyang waiting for them. During the summer months he had eaten a quantity of grass and had now become fat and sleek, and was about twice as big as he had been in the spring. When the Wolf caught sight of him he was much pleased and began to lick his chops in anticipation.

"Well, Brother Kyang," said he, "here I'am according to agreement, ready to kill and eat you, and I am glad to see you look so plump and well. And here are Brother Fox and Brother Hare who have come along with me to have a bit too."

And so saying the Wolf crouched down ready to spring upon the Kyang and kill him.

"Oh, Brother Wolf," called out the Hare at this moment, "just wait one moment, for I have a suggestion to make to you. Don't you think it would be a pity to kill this fine young Kyang in the ordinary way by seizing his throat, for if you do so a great deal of his blood will be wasted? I would suggest to you, instead, that it would be a very much better plan if you would strangle him, as in that case no blood would be lost, and we should derive the full benefit from his carcase."

The Wolf thought this was a good idea and he said to the Hare:

"Very well, Brother Hare, I think that is an excellent idea of yours, but how is it to be done?"

"Oh! easily enough," answered the Hare. "There is a shepherd's encampment over there where we can borrow a rope, and then all we have to do is to make a slip-knot in the rope, put it over the Kyang's neck, and pull as hard as we can."

So they agreed that this should be done, and the Fox went off to the encampment near by and borrowed a rope from the shepherd, which he carried back to where the three other animals were standing.

"Now," said the Hare, "leave it all to me; I will show you exactly how it is to be done." So he took the rope and made a large slip-knot at one end and two smaller slip-knots at the other end.

"Now," said he, "this is the way we must proceed: we will put this large slip-knot over the Kyang's neck, and as he is such a large heavy animal the only way to strangle him will be for us three to pull together at the other end of the rope. So you, Brother Wolf, and you, Brother Fox, can put your heads through these smaller loops, and I will seize the loose end of the rope with my teeth, and when I give the signal we will all pull together."

The other two thought this was a very good plan, and so they threw the slip-knot over the Kyang's neck, and the Wolf and the Fox put their heads through the smaller loops. When they were all ready the Hare took up his position at the end of the rope and caught hold of it with his teeth.

Now, said he, "are you all ready?"

"Yes, quite ready," replied the Wolf and the Fox.

"Well, then, pull," said the Hare.

So they began to pull as hard as they could. When the Kyang felt the pull on the rope he walked forward a few paces, much to the surprise of the Wolf and the Fox, who found themselves being dragged along the ground.

"Pull, can't you!" shrieked the Wolf, as the rope began to tighten round his neck.

"Pull yourself!" shrieked the Fox, who was now beginning to feel very uncomfortable.

"Pull, all of you," called out the Hare, and so saying he let go of the end of the rope and the Kyang galloped off dragging the Wolf and the Fox after him. In a few minutes they were both strangled, and the Kyang, shaking off the rope from his neck, proceeded to graze quietly on his usual pastures, and the Hare scampered off home, feeling that he had done a good day's work.

THE STORY OF THE STONE LION

ONCE upon a time there were two brothers whose father was dead, and who lived alone with their mother in a big house in a well-cultivated valley.

Now the elder of these brothers was a smart, clever man, but was of a very selfish, cold-hearted disposition; and the younger brother was simple and kind, but rather dull. The consequence was that after the death of their father the elder brother conducted most of the business of the family himself, and entirely supported his brother and his mother; whilst the younger brother, although quite willing to do his best, was not clever enough to be of any assistance in the household.

After a time the elder brother decided in his mind that he could no longer endure this state of affairs, so he one day called his young brother aside, and told him plainly that he would no longer continue to support such a lout, and that it would be better for him to go out into the world and seek his own fortune alone. The poor boy was much grieved on hearing this decision from his brother; but he was quite unable to protest or dispute, so, having packed up his few belongings, he went to say goodbye to his mother, and told her what had occurred. The good woman was very angry when she heard the news, and she said to her son:

"Very well, if your hard-hearted brother insists on turning you out of the house, I will accompany you. I cannot consent to remain any longer with such an unnatural and cruel son."

So next day the mother and her younger son left the house and set off together to seek some means of livelihood on their own account. After travelling for some little distance they reached an empty hut situated at the foot of a large hill, not far from a populous town; and finding that the place was apparently deserted and that the owner, whoever he was, had left nothing to show that he proposed to return, they took possession of the hut, and slept during the night.

Next morning early the boy, taking an axe with him, went out on to the hillside and began chopping wood. By evening he had chopped a fine big bundle of wood, and taking it down into the town he sold it in the market for a good sum of money. Greatly elated at the success of his labours he returned to his mother in the hut, and showing her the money he had earned, he told her that she need no longer have any anxiety regarding the future, for he would now be able to support her without any difficulty.

Next morning, shouldering his axe, he started off again, and as before, began to chop wood. He had done a good morning's work, and was walking a little further up the hill in order to search for some better timber, when, in a sheltered part of the hill-side he suddenly found himself face to face with a life-sized Lion carved out of the stone.

"Now," thought he to himself, on seeing the Lion, "this, no doubt, is the guardian deity of this mountain, and to him must be due my good fortune in so easily obtaining a means of livelihood. I will certainly make him some offering to-morrow."

So that evening, after selling his wood, he purchased two candles in the town, and on the following day he went straight to where the stone Lion stood, and lighting the candles, he placed one upon each side of the image, and prostrating himself humbly upon the ground before it, he prayed for renewed good fortune. Suddenly, to his surprise and alarm, the Lion opened its mouth, and asked him what he was doing there.

The young man replied that having been driven from his home by his proud and hard-hearted brother, he was now engaged in earning his livelihood by chopping wood upon that hill; and that, thinking that the Lion must be the guardian deity of the mountain, he had considered it right to make him some sort of an offering, and to request his continued patronage and assistance.

"Very good," replied the Lion in a guttural tone of voice, "come again at this time to-morrow, and bring with you a large bucket, and I will furnish you at once with what wealth you require."

The boy thanked the Lion for his kindness, and carrying his load of firewood down to the village he sold it for a good price, and with the proceeds he purchased himself a large wooden bucket.

Next morning he went up onto the hilt again, carrying his bucket, and arriving near the stone Lion, he again prostrated himself upon the ground and announced his presence.

"Very good," replied the Lion, "you must now act as follows: hold the bucket under my mouth, and I will vomit gold into it. But as soon as the bucket is nearly full you must tell me, as on no account must a single morsel of gold fall to the ground."

The young man proceeded to do as the Lion had instructed him. He held the bucket below the Lion's mouth, and the Lion forthwith began to vomit into it a stream of gold pieces. When the bucket was nearly full the young man informed the Lion of the fact, and forthwith the stream of gold came to an end; and the youth, having thanked the Lion most heartily for his munificent gift, carried off his bucket of gold in triumph to his mother. The poor woman was at first quite frightened at seeing so much wealth, but her son having explained to her how he had come by it, she became greatly excited, and pleased.

Next day the widow and her son set about placing themselves in more comfortable circumstances. They purchased a large farm-house in the neighbourhood, and a large stock of cattle and sheep, and settled down in their new abode, and henceforward they began to live in a very comfortable and prosperous manner.

The news of the changed condition of life of his mother and younger brother soon reached the ears of the eldest son, and overcome with curiosity as to how this result had been brought about, he decided to call upon them, and to ascertain the cause of their prosperity. So, accompanied by his wife, and carrying with him a very small piece of cloth as a present, he set out to pay them a visit. When he reached the house his younger brother was away engaged upon his farm business, but the mother received her elder son and his wife very kindly and made them as comfortable as she could.

In the evening, when the younger brother returned, he greeted his brother heartily, and being of a most kind-hearted and forgiving disposition, he related to him fully the manner in which he had come by his wealth, and strongly recommended his brother to act in a similar way.

The elder brother and his wife, as they returned home together that evening, talked the matter over between them, and decided that so good an opportunity of making money so easily was not to be lost. So next day the husband proceeded to the town, and after a prolonged search purchased the largest bucket which was to be had in the whole place. Carrying this with him, and bringing also a couple of candles, he proceeded to the hillside, and following the directions he had received from his brother, he soon found himself face to face with the stone Lion. He at once lighted his candles and placed them one on each side of the Lion, while he prostrated himself upon the ground, and prayed to the Lion for good fortune.

"Who are you?" said the Lion in a gruff voice; "and what do you want?"

"I," replied the eider brother, "am the brother of the young man who was here the other day, and to whom you gave so much gold; and, following his advice, I have now come to ask you for a similar benefit for myself."

"Very well," said the Lion, "place your bucket under my mouth and I will vomit gold into it; but as soon as the bucket is nearly full you must inform me of the fact, as on no account must a single piece of gold fall to the ground. If this should happen, you will meet with misfortune."

So the elder brother, trembling with eagerness, held his bucket as directed, and forthwith a stream of gold pieces began to pour from the Lion's mouth into the bucket. The covetous fellow shook the bucket slightly from time to time in order to make the gold lie well together and so to obtain a larger quantity; and, overcome by greed, he could not bring himself to inform the Lion that the bucket was nearly full until it brimmed over and a piece of gold, slipping off the heap, fell to the ground. As it touched the ground the stream of gold suddenly ceased, and the Lion, in a hoarse voice, said:

"The largest piece of gold of all has stuck in my throat. Put your hand into my mouth and pull it out."

The elder brother, on hearing this, immediately thrust his hand into the Lion's mouth, hoping to secure a large lump of gold; and no sooner had he done so than the Lion, closing his jaws, held him fast. It was in vain that he struggled and wrenched his arm to and fro, endeavouring to release it; the stone jaws of the Lion gripped him so tight that he was totally unable to effect his escape, and the Lion, deaf to all prayers and entreaties, had relapsed apparently into an insensible figure of stone. And worst of all, when he glanced at his bucket of gold he saw, to his horror, that instead of gold it held nothing but stones and earth.

Toward evening the elder brother's wife grew anxious concerning her husband's absence, and knowing the direction in which he had gone, she set forth to the hillside to seek him. After hunting for some time she suddenly came across him, and asked him what he was doing and why he did not come home.

"Oh, wife," said be, "a horrible thing has happened to me. I put my hand into the Lion's mouth in order to extract a lump of gold which was stuck in his throat, when all of a sudden he closed his jaws, and gripped my arm, and now I am unable to effect my escape."

The poor woman, on hearing this, wept and wailed, but all her entreaties to the Lion proved of no avail, and she went off to her home, and soon returned carrying her husband some food. Every day, for many days after, she returned to her husband, bringing him such provisions as he required to keep him alive; but as she had now no one to work for her, and was obliged to support her husband and her child entirely by her own exertions, she became gradually poorer and poorer, and was soon obliged to sell her household goods to procure the necessary food. Some months passed away and the poor woman, falling ill, was at length reduced to such complete destitution that she had not even a morsel of bread to bring to her husband, and one morning she came weeping up the hill, and addressed him as follows:

"I have sold everything in the house, and have now no money to buy food. There is not a scrap left to eat anywhere, and now nothing remains but for us to starve to death."

On hearing this the Lion was so tickled that he could not refrain from laughing.

"Ha, ha!" said he, and opened his great jaws. As quickly as he could, and before the Lion had time to close his mouth again, the man withdrew his arm, and, finding himself free, he at once hastened down the hill with his wife. Then, taking their child with them, they proceeded straight to the house of the younger brother, and having related to him the whole of their story, begged some relief from their misery. The young man reproached his brother for his greedy conduct in trying to obtain an extra supply of gold from the Lion in spite of his warning; but being of a very forgiving nature, he consented at last to supply his brother with a sum of money sufficient for him to take a small farm in the neighbourhood. Here the proud brother and his wife settled down in very humble circumstances, whilst the younger son lived for many years very happily with his mother and prospered exceedingly in all he undertook.

TURKEY

THE folk-tales of Turkey are generally of three types. There are those which deal with religious and semi-religious legends connected with the prophet Mohammed and his family and with the holy men of Islam. The second class includes mythical stories of the magical exploits of David and Solomon. This Solomon is the Chaldean King of Gods, the wise Ea, one of whose names is Sallimann. He is supposed to preside over the whole race of genii. Lastly, there are wild romances concerning Djins, or Genii, who are an intermediate race between gods and men. They are supposed to have been created 2900 years before Adam, but they sinned and were cast out by Allah for refusing to worship Adam as made of clay. In this connexion should be noted the power of the Afrit in the *Arabian Nights' Entertainments*.

YOUTH WITHOUT AGE AND LIFE WITHOUT DEATH

ONCE upon a time there was a great Emperor and an Empress; both were young and beautiful, and as they would fain have been blessed with offspring they went to all the wise men and all the wise women and bade them read the stars to see if they would have children or not; but all in vain. At last the Emperor heard that in a certain village, hard by, dwelt a wiser old man than all the rest; so he sent and commanded him to appear at court. But the wise old man sent the messengers back with the answer that those who needed him must come to him. So the Emperor and the Empress set out, with their lords and their ladies, and their servants and their soldiers, and came to the house of the wise old man. And when the old man saw them coming from afar he went out to meet them.

"Welcome," cried he; "but I tell thee, oh Emperor! that the wish of thy heart will only work thee woe."

"I came not hither to take counsel of thee," replied the Emperor; "but to know if thou hast herbs by eating whereof we may get us children."

"Such herbs have I," replied the old man; "but ye will have but one child, and him ye will not be able to keep, though he be never so nice and charming"

So when the Emperor and the Empress had gotten the wondrous herbs, they returned joyfully back to their palace, and a few days afterward the Empress became a mother. At his birth the child screamed so loudly that all the enchantments of the magicians could not make him silent. Then the Emperor began to promise him everything in the wide world, but even this would not quiet him.

"Be silent, my heart's darling," said he, "and I will give thee all the kingdoms east of the sun and west of the moon! Be silent, my son, and I will give thee a consort more lovely than the Fairy Queen herself." Then at last, when he perceived that the child still kept on screaming, he said: "Silence, my son, and I will give thee Youth without Age, and Life without Death!"

Then the child ceased to cry and all the courtiers beat the drums and blew the trumpets, and there was great joy in the whole realm for many days.

The older the child grew the more pensive and melancholy he became. He went to school, and to the wise men, and there was no learning and wisdom that he did not make his own, so that the Emperor, his father, died and came to life again for sheer joy. And the whole realm was proud that it was going to have so wise and goodly an Emperor, and all men looked up to him as to a second Solomon. But one day, when the child had already completed his fifteenth year, and the Emperor and all his lords and great men were at table diverting themselves, the fair young prince arose and said: "Father, the time has now come when thou must give me what thou didst promise me at my birth!"

At these words the Emperor was sorely troubled. "Nay, but, my son," said he, "how can I give thee a thing which the world has never heard of? If I did promise it to thee, it was but to make thee quiet."

"Then, oh my father, if thou canst not give it to me, I must needs go forth into the world, and seek until I find that fair thing for which I was born."

Then the Emperor and his nobles all fell down on their knees, and besought him not to leave the empire. "For," said the nobles, "thy father is now growing old, and we would place thee on the throne, and give thee to wife the most beautiful Empress under the sun." But they were unable to turn him from his purpose, for he was as steadfast as a rock, so at last his father gave him leave to go forth into the wide world to find what he sought.

Then Boy Beautiful went into his father's stables, where were the most beautiful chargers in the whole empire, that he might choose one from among them; but no sooner had he laid his hand on one of them than it fell to the ground trembling, and so it was with all the other stately chargers. At last, just as he was about to leave the stable in despair, he cast his eye over it once more, and there in one corner he beheld a poor knacker, all weak, spavined, and covered with boils and sores. Up to it he went, and laid his hand upon its tail, and then the horse turned its head and said to him: "What are thy commands, my master? God be praised who hath had mercy upon me and sent a warrior to lay his hand over me!"

Then the horse shook itself and became straight in the legs again, and Boy Beautiful asked him what he should do next.

"In order that thou mayest attain thy heart's desire," said the horse, "ask thy father for the sword and lance, the bow, quiver, and armour which he himself wore when he was a youth; but thou must comb and curry me with thine own hand six weeks, and give me barley to eat cooked in milk."

So the Emperor called the steward of his household, and ordered him to open all the coffers and wardrobes that his son might choose what he would, and Boy Beautiful, after searching for three days and three nights, found at last at the bottom of an old armoury, the arms and armour which his father had worn as a youth, but very rusty were these ancient weapons. But he set to work with his own hands to polish them up and rub off the rust, and at the end of six weeks they shone like mirrors. He also cherished the steed as he had been told. Grievous was the labour, but it came to an end at last.

When the good steed heard that Boy Beautiful had cleansed and polished his armour, he shook himself once more, and all his boils and sores fell off from him. There he now stood a stout horse, and strong, and with four large wings growing out of his body. Then said Boy Beautiful: "We go hence in three days!"—"Long life to thee, my master!" replied the steed; "I will go wherever thou dost command."

When the third day came the Emperor and all his court were full of grief. Boy Beautiful, attired as became a hero, with his sword in his hand, bounded on to his horse, took leave of the Emperor and the Empress, of all the great nobles and all the little nobles, of all the warriors and all the courtiers. With tears in their eyes, they besought him not to depart on this quest; but he, giving spurs to his horse, departed like a whirlwind, and after him went sumpter horses with money and provisions, and some hundreds of chosen warriors whom the Emperor had ordered to accompany him on his journey.

But when he had reached a wilderness on the confines of his father's realm, Boy Beautiful took leave of the warriors, and sent them back to his father, taking of the provisions only so much as his good steed could carry. Then he pursued his way toward sunrise, and went on and on for three days and three nights till he came to an immense plain covered with the bones of many dead men. Here they stopped to rest, and the horse said to him: "Know, my master, that we are now in the domains of the witch Gheonoea, who is so evil a being that none can set a foot on her domains and live. Once she was a woman like other women, but the curse of her parents, whom she would never obey, fell like a withering blast upon her, and she became what she now is. At this moment she is with her children in the forest, but she will come speedily to seek and destroy thee. Great and terrible is she, yet fear not, but make ready thy bows and arrows, thy sword and lance, that thou mayst make use of them when the time comes."

Then they rested, and while one slept the other watched.

When the day dawned they prepared to traverse the forest; Boy Beautiful bridled and saddled his horse, drew the reins tighter than at other times, and set out. At that moment they heard a terrible racket.

Then the horse said: "Beware, my master, Gheonoea is approaching." The trees of the forest fell to this side and to that as the witch drew nigh like the tempest, but Boy Beautiful struck off one of her feet with an arrow from his bow, and he was about to shoot a second time when she cried: "Stay thy hand, Boy Beautiful, for I'll do thee no harm!" And seeing he did not believe her, she gave him a promise written in her blood.

"Look well to thy horse, Boy Beautiful," said she, "for he is a greater magician than I. But for him I should have roasted thee, but now thou must dine at my table. Know too that no mortal hath yet succeeded in reaching this spot, though some have got as far as the plain where thou didst see all the bones."

Then Gheonoea hospitably entertained Boy Beautiful as men entertain travellers, but now and then, as they conversed together, Gheonoea groaned with pain, but as soon as Boy Beautiful threw her her foot which he had shot off, she put it in its place and immediately it grew fast on to her leg again. Then, in her joy, Gheonoea feasted him for three days and begged him to take for his consort one of her three daughters, who were divinely beautiful, but he would not. Then he asked her concerning his quest. "With such valour and such a good steed as thine," she answered, "thou must needs succeed."

So after the three days were over they went on their way again. Boy Beautiful went on and on, and the way was very long, but when they had passed the boundaries of Gheonoea they came to a beauteous meadowland, but on one side the grass was fresh and bright and full of flowers, and on the other side it was burnt to cinders. Then Boy Beautiful asked the horse the meaning of the singed grass, and this is what the horse replied: "We are now in the territory of Scorpia, the sister of Gheonoea. Yet so evil minded are these two sisters that they cannot live together in one place. The curse of their parents has blasted them, and they have become witches as thou dost see; their hatred of each other is great, and each of them is ever striving to wrest a bit of land from the dominions of the other. And when Scorpia is angry she vomits forth fire and flame, and so when she comes to her sister's boundaries the grass of the border withers up before her. She is even more dreadful than her sister, and has, besides, three heads; but be of good cheer, my master, and to-morrow morning be ready to meet her."

At dawn, next day, they were preparing to depart when they heard a roaring and a crashing noise, the like of which man has never heard since the world began.

"Be ready, my master, for now Scorpia is approaching," cried the faithful steed.

And indeed Scorpia it was. With jaws reaching from earth to heaven, and spitting forth fire as she approached, Scorpia drew near, and the noise of her coming was like the roar of a whirlwind. But the good steed rose into the air like a dart, and Boy Beautiful shot an arrow which struck off one of the witch's three heads. He was about to lay another arrow on his bow, when Scorpia begged him to forgive her and she would do him no harm, and by way of assurance she gave him a promise written in her blood.

Then she feasted him as her sister had done before, and he gave her back her severed head, which she stuck in its place again, and then, after three days, Boy Beautiful and his faithful steed took to the road again.

When they had crossed Scorpia's borders they went on and on without stopping till they came to a vast meadow covered with nothing but flowers, where Spring reigned eternally. Every flower was wondrously beautiful and full of a fragrance that comforted the soul, and a light zephyr ran continually over the flowery billows. Here then they sat them down to rest, and the good steed said:

"Hitherto, oh my master! we have prospered, but now a great danger awaits us, which if by the help of the Lord God we overcome, then shall we be heroes indeed. Not far from here stands the palace of Youth without Age, and Life without Death, but it is surrounded by a high and deep forest, and in this forest are all the savage monsters of the wide world.

"Day and night they guard it, and if a man can count the grains of sand on the sea-shore, then also can he count the number of these monsters. We cannot fight them, they would tear us to pieces before we were halfway through the forest, so we must try if we can leap clean over it without touching it."

So they rested them two days to gather strength, and then the steed drew a long breath and said to Boy Beautiful: "Draw my saddle-girths as tightly as thou art able, and when thou hast mounted me, hold on fast with all thy might to my mane, and press thy feet on my neck instead of on my flanks, that thou mayest not hinder me."

Boy Beautiful arose and did as his steed told him, and the next moment they were close up to the forest.

"Now is the time, my master," cried the good steed. "The wild monsters are now being fed, and are gathered together in one place. Now let us spring over!"

"I am with thee, and the Lord have mercy upon us both," replied Boy Beautiful.

Then up in the air they flew, and before them lay the palace, and so gloriously bright was it that a man could sooner took into the face of the midday sun than upon the glory of the Palace of Youth without Age, and Life without Death. Right over the forest they flew, and just as they were about to descend at the foot of the palace-staircase, the steed with the tip of his hind leg touched lightly, oh, ever so lightly! a twig on the topmost summit of the tallest tree of the forest. Instantly the whole forest was alive and alert, and the monsters began to howl so awfully that, brave as he was, the hair of Boy Beautiful stood up on his head. Hastily they descended, but had not the mistress of the palace been outside there in order to feed her kittens (for so she called the monsters), Boy Beautiful and his faithful steed would have been torn to pieces. But the mistress of the monsters, for pure joy at the sight of a human being, held the monsters back, and sent them back to their places. Fair, tail, and of goodly stature was the Fairy of the Palace, and Boy Beautiful felt his heart die away within him as he beheld her. But she was full of compassion at the sight of him, and said: "Welcome, Boy Beautiful! What dost thou seek?"

"We seek Youth without Age, and Life without Death," he replied.

Then he dismounted from his steed and entered the palace, and there he met two other fair dames of equal beauty; these were the elder sisters of the Fairy of the Palace. They regaled Boy Beautiful with a banquet served on gold plate, and the good steed had leave to graze where he would, and the Fairy made him known to all her Monsters, that so he might wander through the woods in peace. Then the fair dames begged Boy Beautiful to abide with them always, and Boy Beautiful did not want to be asked twice, for to stay with the Fairy of the Palace was his darling desire.

Then he told them his story, and of all the dangers he had passed through to get there, and so the Fairy of the Palace became his bride, and she gave him leave to roam at will throughout her domains. "Nevertheless," said she, "there is one valley thou must not enter or it will work thee woe, and the name of that valley is the Vale of Complaint."

There then Boy Beautiful abode, and he took no count of time, for though many days passed away, he was yet as young and strong as when he first came there. He went through leagues of forest without once feeling weary. He rejoiced in the golden palace, and lived in peace and tranquillity with his bride and her sisters. Oftentimes too he went a-hunting.

One day he was pursuing a hare, and shot an arrow after it, and then another, but neither of them hit the hare. Never before had Boy Beautiful missed his prey, and his heart was vexed within him. He pursued the hare still more hotly, and sent another arrow after her. This time he did bring her down, but in his haste the unhappy man had not perceived that in following the hare he had passed through the Vale of Complaint! He took up the hare and returned homeward, but while he was still on the way a strange yearning after his father and his mother came over him. He durst not tell his bride of it, but she and her sisters immediately guessed the cause of his heaviness.

"Wretched man!" they cried, "thou hast passed through the Vale of Complaint!"

"I have done so, darling, without meaning it," he replied; "but now I am perishing with longing for my father and mother. Yet need I desert thee for that? I have now been many days with thee, and am as hale and well as ever. Suffer me then to go and see my parents but once, and then will I return to thee to part no more."

"Forsake us not, oh beloved!" cried his bride and her sisters. "Hundreds of years have passed away since thy parents were alive; and thou also, if thou dost leave us, wilt never return more. Abide with us, or, an evil omen tells us, thou wilt perish!"

But the supplications of the three ladies and his faithful steed likewise could not prevail against the gnawing longing to see his parents which consumed him.

At last the horse said to him: "If thou wilt not listen to me, my master, then 'tis thine own fault alone if evil befall thee. Yet I will promise to bring thee back on one condition."

"I consent whatever it may be," said Boy Beautiful; "speak, and I will listen gratefully."

"I will bring thee back to thy father's palace, but if thou dismount but for a moment, I shall return without thee."

"Be it so," replied Boy Beautiful.

So they made them ready for their journey, and Boy Beautiful embraced his bride and departed, but the ladies stood there looking after him, and their eyes were filled with tears.

And now Boy Beautiful and his faithful steed came to the place where the domains of Scorpia had been, but the forests had become fields of corn, and cities stood thickly on what had once been desolate places. Boy Beautiful asked all whom he met concerning Scorpia and her habitations, but they only answered that these were but idle fables which their grandfathers had heard from their great-grandfathers.

"But how is that possible?" replied Boy Beautiful. "'Twas but the other day that I passed by—" and he told them all he knew. Then they laughed at him as at one who raves or talks in his sleep; but he rode away wrathfully without noticing that his beard and the hair of his head had grown white.

When he came to the domain of Gheonoea he put the same questions and received the same answers. He could not understand how the whole region could have utterly changed in a few days, and again he rode away, full of anger, with a white beard that now reached down to his girdle and with legs that began to tremble beneath him.

At length he came to the empire of his father. Here there were new men and new buildings, and the old ones had so altered that he scarce knew them.

So he came to the palace where he had first seen the light of day. As he dismounted the horse kissed his hand and said: "Fare thee well, my master! I return from whence I came. But if thou also wouldst return, mount again and we'll be off instantly."

"Nay," he replied, "fare thee well, I also will return soon."

Then the horse flew away like a dart.

But when Boy Beautiful beheld the palace all in ruins and overgrown with evil weeds, he sighed deeply, and with tears in his eyes he sought to recall the glories of that fallen palace. Round about the place he went, not once nor twice: he searched in every room, in every corner for some vestige of the past; he searched the stable in which he had found his steed, and then he went down into the cellar, the entrance to which was choked up by fallen rubbish.

Here and there and everywhere he searched about, and now his long white beard reached below his knee, and his eyelids were so heavy that he had to raise them on high with his hands, and he found he could scarce totter along. All he found there was a huge old coffer which he opened, but inside it there was nothing. Yet he lifted up the cover, and then a voice spoke to him out of the depths of the coffer and said:

"Welcome, for hadst thou kept me waiting much longer, I also would have perished."

Then his Death, who was already shrivelled up like a withered leaf at the bottom of the coffer, rose up and laid his hand upon him, and Boy Beautiful instantly fell dead to the ground and crumbled into dust. But had he remained away but a little time longer, his Death would have died, and he himself would have been living now. And so I mount my nag and utter an "Our Father" ere I go.

THE SERPENT-PERI AND THE MAGIC MIRROR

THERE was once upon a time a poor wood-cutter who had an only son. One day this poor man fell sick and said to his son: "If I should die follow thou my handicraft, and go every day into the wood. Thou mayest cut down whatever trees thou dost find there, but at the edge of the wood is a cypress-tree, that thou must leave standing." Two days afterward the man died and was buried.

But the son went into the wood and cut down the trees, only the cypress-tree he left alone. One day the youth stood close to this tree and thought to himself: "What can be the matter with this tree, seeing that I am not allowed to lay a hand upon it?"

So he looked at it, and considered it curiously, till at last he took his axe and went with evil intent toward the tree. But he had scarcely lifted his foot when the cypress-tree drew away from him. The wood-cutter mounted his ass and pursued the tree but could not overtake it, and in the meantime eventide came upon them. Then he dismounted from his ass and tied it to a tree, but he himself climbed to the top of the tree to await the dawn.

Next morning, when the sky grew red, he descended from the tree, and there at the foot of it lay only the bones of his ass. "Never mind, I'll go on foot," said the wood-cutter, and he continued his pursuit of the cypress, the tree going on before and he following after. All that day he pursued but could not come up with it. The third day also he shouldered his axe and pursued the tree, when he suddenly came upon an elephant and a serpent fighting with each other. Believe the truth or not as you will, but the truth is this, that the serpent was swallowing the elephant; but the elephant's great tusk stuck in the serpent's throat, and both beasts, seeing the youth staring at them, begged him to help them.

What didn't the elephant promise him if only he would slay the serpent! "Nay, but all I would have thee do," said the serpent, "is to break his tusk off; the work is lighter, and the reward will be greater."

At these words the youth seized his axe and chopped the elephant's tusk right off. The serpent then swallowed the elephant, thanked the youth, and promised to keep his word and give him his reward.

While they were on the road the serpent stopped at a spring and said to the youth: "Wait while I bathe in this water, and whatever may happen, fear not!" With that the serpent plunged into the water, and immediately there arose such a terrific storm, such a tempest, such a hurricane, with lightning-flash upon lightning-flash, and thunder-bolt upon thunder-bolt, that the Day of Judgment could not well be worse. Presently the serpent came out of the bath, and then all was quiet again.

They went a long way, and they went a little way, they took coffee, they smoked their chibooks, they gathered violets on the road, till at last they drew near to a house, and then the serpent said: "In a short time we shall arrive at my mother's house. When she opens the door, say thou art my kinsman, and she will invite thee into the house. She will offer thee coffee but do not drink it; she will offer thee meat but do not eat it; but there's a little bit of a mirror hanging up in the corner of the door, ask my mother for that!"

So they came to the house, and no sooner had the Peri knocked at the door than his mother came and opened it. "Come, my brother!" said the serpent to the youth behind him.—"Who is thy brother?" asked his mother.—"He who hath saved my life," replied her son, and with that he told her the whole story. So they went into the house, and the woman brought the youth coffee and a chibook, but he would not take them. "My journey is a hasty one," said he; "I cannot remain very long."

"Rest awhile at least," said the woman, "we cannot let our guests depart without anything."

"Nothing do I want, but if thou wilt give me that bit of mirror in the corner of the door I will take it," said the youth. The woman did not want to give it, but the youth insisted that perhaps his life might depend upon that very piece of mirror, so at last she gave it to him, though very unwillingly.

So the youth went on his way with the bit of mirror, and as he looked into it he turned over in his mind what use he should make of it. As he was still turning it over and looking at it, suddenly there stood before him a negro efrit, one of whose lips touched the heavens, and the other lip the earth. The poor youth was so frightened, that if the negro had not said: "What are thy commands, my Sultan?" he would have run away for ever and ever. As it was, it was as much as he could do to ask for something to eat, and immediately there stood before him a rich and rare banquet, the like of which he had never seen at his father's, the wood-cutter's.

Then the youth felt very curious about the mirror, and looked into it again, and immediately the black efrit stood before him again and said: "What dost thou command, my Sultan?"

Nothing would occur to his mind at first, but at last his lips murmured the word "Palace," and immediately there stood before him a palace so beautiful that the Padishah himself could not have a finer one. "Open!" cried the youth, and immediately the gates of the palace flew open before him.

The youth rejoiced greatly in his bit of mirror, and his one thought was what he should ask it to get him next. The beautiful Sultana-damsel, the Padishah's daughter, occurred to his mind, and the next moment his eye sought his mirror, and he desired from the big-lipped negro efrit a palace in which the world-renowned daughter of the Padishah should be sitting beside him, and he had scarce time to look around him when he found himself sitting in the palace, with the Sultan's daughter by his side. Then they kissed and embraced each other, and lived a whole world of joy.

Meanwhile the Sultan learnt that his daughter had disappeared from her own palace. He searched for her the whole realm through, he sent heralds in every direction, but in vain were all his labours, the girl could not be discovered. At last an old woman came to the Padishah and told him to make a large casket, line it well with zinc, put her inside it, and cast it into the sea. She would find the daughter of the Sultan, she said, for if she was not here, she must be beyond the sea. So they made ready the great casket, put the old woman inside it, put food for nine days beside her, and cast it into the sea. The casket was tossed from wave to wave, till at last it came to that city where the Sultan's daughter dwelt with the youth.

Now the fishermen were just then on the shore, and saw the huge casket floating in the sea. They drew it ashore with ropes and hooks, and when they opened it an old woman crept out of it. They asked her how she had got inside it.

"Oh, that my enemy might lose the sight of his little eye that is so dear to him!" lamented the old woman; "I have not deserved this of him!" and with that she fell a-weeping and wailing till the men believed every word she said. "Where is the Bey of your city?" cried she; "perhaps he will have compassion upon me and receive me into his house," she said to the men. Then they showed her the palace, and exhorted her to go thither, as perhaps she might get an alms.

So the old woman went to the palace, and when she knocked at the door, the Sultan's daughter came down to see who it was. The old woman immediately recognized the damsel, and begged her (for the damsel knew not the old woman) to take her into her service. "My lord comes home to-night, I will ask him," replied the damsel; "meanwhile rest in this corner!" And the damsel's lord allowed her to receive the old woman into the house, and the next day she waited upon them.

There the old woman was for one day, and for two days, for a week, for two weeks, and there was no cook to cook the food, and no servant to keep the place clean, and yet every day there was a costly banquet and everything was as clean as clean could be. Then the old woman went to the damsel and asked her whether she did not feel dull at being alone all day. "If I were allowed to help thee pass the time away," added she, "perhaps it might be better."—"I must first ask my lord," replied the damsel. The youth did not mind the old woman helping his wife to pass away the time, and so she went up to the rooms of the damsel and stayed with her for days together.

One day the old woman asked the damsel whence came all the rare meats, and who did the service of the house. But the damsel knew not of the piece of mirror, so that she could tell the old woman nothing. "Find out from thy lord," said the old woman, and scarcely had the youth come home, scarce had he had time to eat, than she wheedled him so that he showed her the mirror.

That was all the old woman wanted. A couple of days she let go by, but on the third and the fourth days she bade the damsel beg her lord for the piece of mirror so that she might amuse herself therewith, and make the time pass more easily. And indeed she had only to ask her lord for it, for he, not suspecting her falseness, gave it to her. And in the meantime the old woman was not asleep. She knew where the damsel had put the mirror, stole it, and when she looked into it the negro efrit appeared. "What is thy command?" inquired he of the old woman. "Take me with this damsel to her father's palace," was her first command. Her second command made of the youth's palace a heap of ashes, so that when the young wood-cutter returned home he found nought but the cat meowing among the ashes. There was also a small piece of meat there; the Sultan's daughter had thrown it down for the cat.

The youth took up the fragment of meat and set out to seek his consort. Find her he would, though he roamed the whole world over. He went on and on, he searched and searched till he came to the city where his wife lived. He went up to the palace, and there he begged the cook to take him into the kitchen as a servant out of pure compassion. In a couple of days he had learnt from his fellow-servants in the kitchen, that the Sultan's daughter had returned home.

One day the cook fell sick and there was no heart in him to attend to the cooking. The youth, seeing this, bade him rest, and said he would cook the food in his stead. The cook agreed, and told him what to cook, and how to season it. So the youth set to work, roasting and stewing, and when he sent up the dishes, he also sent up the scrap of food that he had found on the ashes, and put it on the damsel's plate. Scarcely had the damsel cast eyes on this little scrap than she knew within herself that her lord was near her. So she called the cook and asked whom he had with him in the kitchen. At first he denied that he had anyone, but at last he confessed that he had taken a poor lad in to assist him.

Then the damsel went to her father and said to him that there was a young lad in the kitchen who prepared coffee so well that she should like some coffee from his hands. So the lad was ordered up, and from thenceforth he prepared the coffee and took it to the Sultan's daughter.

So they came together again, and she told her lord how the matter had gone. Then they took counsel how they should await their turn and get the mirror back again.

Scarcely had the youth gone in to the damsel than the old woman appeared. Although she had not seen him for long, she recognized him, and, looking into the mirror, caused the poor boy to be sent back again to the ashes of his old palace. There he found the cat still squatting. When she felt hungry she caught mice, and such ravages did she make upon them that at last the Padishah of the mice had scarce a soldier left.

Very wroth was the poor Padishah, but he durst not tackle the cat. One day, however, he observed the youth, went up to him, and begged his assistance in his dire distress, for if he waited till the morrow his whole realm would be ruined.

"I'll help thee," said the youth, "though, indeed, I have enough troubles of my own to carry already."

"What is thy trouble?" asked the Padishah of the mice. The youth told him about the history of the piece of looking-glass, and how it had been stolen from him, and into whose hands it had fallen.

"Then I can help thee," cried the Padishah, whereupon he called together all the mice in the world. And he asked which of them had access to this palace, and which knew of such-and-such an old woman, and the piece of looking-glass. At these words a lame mouse hobbled forth, kissed the ground at the feet of the Padishah, and said that it was his wont to steal food from the old woman's box. He had seen through the keyhole how she took out a little bit of looking-glass every evening and hid it under a cushion.

Then the Padishah commanded him to go and steal this bit of mirror. The